Prose Works

OTHER THAN
SCIENCE AND HEALTH

Prose Works

OTHER THAN
SCIENCE AND HEALTH
WITH KEY TO THE SCRIPTURES

by MARY BAKER EDDY

Discoverer and Founder of Christian Science
and Author of Science and Health
with Key to the Scriptures

Marcas Registradas

Published by The First Church of Christ, Scientist, in Boston, Massachusetts, U.S.A.

The facsimile of the signature of Mary Baker Eddy
and the design of the Cross and Crown seal are
trademarks of The Christian Science Board of Directors,
registered in the United States and other countries.

ISBN: **0-87952-077-9** Blue Cloth, side-indexed
ISBN: **0-87952-078-7** Brown Leather, side-indexed
ISBN: **0-87952-079-5** Burgundy Bonded Leather, side-indexed
ISBN: **0-87952-080-9** Black Leather, side-indexed

Printed in the United States of America

Miscellaneous Writings

Miscellaneous
Writings

Miscellaneous Writings 1883-1896

by MARY BAKER EDDY

Discoverer and Founder of Christian Science
and Author of Science and Health
with Key to the Scriptures

Marcas Registradas

Published by The First Church of Christ, Scientist, in Boston, Massachusetts, U.S.A.

To
LOYAL CHRISTIAN SCIENTISTS
in this and every land

*I lovingly dedicate these practical teachings
indispensable to the culture and achievements which
constitute the success of a student
and demonstrate the ethics
of Christian Science*

MARY BAKER EDDY

PRAY thee, take care, that tak'st my book in hand,
To read it well; that is, to understand.
BEN JONSON: *Epigram* I

WHEN I would know thee . . . my thought looks
Upon thy well made choice of friends and books;
Then do I love thee, and behold thy ends
In making thy friends books, and thy books friends.
BEN JONSON: *Epigram* 86

———

IF worlds were formed by matter,
    And mankind from the dust;
Till time shall end more timely,
    There's nothing here to trust.

Thenceforth to evolution's
    Geology, we say, —
Nothing have we gained therefrom,
    And nothing have to pray:

My world has sprung from Spirit,
    In everlasting day;
Whereof, I've more to glory,
    Wherefor, have much to pay.
MARY BAKER EDDY

Preface

A CERTAIN apothegm of a Talmudical philosopher 1
suits my sense of doing good. It reads thus: "The
noblest charity is to prevent a man from accepting 3
charity; and the best alms are to show and to enable a
man to dispense with alms."

In the early history of Christian Science, among my 6
thousands of students few were wealthy. Now, Christian
Scientists are not indigent; and their comfortable fortunes
are acquired by healing mankind morally, physically, 9
spiritually. The easel of time presents pictures — once
fragmentary and faint — now rejuvenated by the touch
of God's right hand. Where joy, sorrow, hope, disap- 12
pointment, sigh, and smile commingled, now hope sits
dove-like.

To preserve a long course of years still and uniform, 15
amid the uniform darkness of storm and cloud and
tempest, requires strength from above, — deep draughts
from the fount of divine Love. Truly may it be said: 18
There is an old age of the heart, and a youth that never
grows old; a Love that is a boy, and a Psyche who is
ever a girl. The fleeting freshness of youth, however, 21
is not the evergreen of Soul; the coloring glory of

ix

1 perpetual bloom; the spiritual glow and grandeur of
a consecrated life wherein dwelleth peace, sacred and
3 sincere in trial or in triumph.

The opportunity has at length offered itself for me to
comply with an oft-repeated request; namely, to collect
6 my miscellaneous writings published in *The Christian
Science Journal,* since April, 1883, and republish them
in book form, — accessible as reference, and reliable as
9 old landmarks. Owing to the manifold demands on my
time in the early pioneer days, most of these articles
were originally written in haste, without due preparation.
12 To those heretofore in print, a few articles are herein
appended. To some articles are affixed data, where these
are most requisite, to serve as mile-stones measuring the
15 distance, — or the difference between then and now, —
in the opinions of men and the progress of our Cause.

My signature has been slightly changed from my
18 Christian name, Mary Morse Baker. Timidity in early
years caused me, as an author, to assume various *noms
de plume.* After my first marriage, to Colonel Glover
21 of Charleston, South Carolina, I dropped the name of
Morse to retain my maiden name, — thinking that otherwise the name would be too long.
24 In 1894, I received from the Daughters of the American
Revolution a certificate of membership made out to Mary
Baker Eddy, and thereafter adopted that form of signa-
27 ture, except in connection with my published works.

The first edition of Science and Health having been 1
copyrighted at the date of its issue, 1875, in my name
of Glover, caused me to retain the initial "G" on my 3
subsequent books.

These pages, although a reproduction of what has
been written, are still in advance of their time; and are 6
richly rewarded by what they have hitherto achieved for
the race. While no offering can liquidate one's debt of
gratitude to God, the fervent heart and willing hand are 9
not unknown to nor unrewarded by Him.

May this volume be to the reader a graphic guide-
book, pointing the path, dating the unseen, and enabling 12
him to walk the untrodden in the hitherto unexplored
fields of Science. At each recurring holiday the Christian
Scientist will find herein a "canny" crumb; and thus 15
may time's pastimes become footsteps to joys eternal.

Realism will at length be found to surpass imagination,
and to suit and savor all literature. The shuttlecock of 18
religious intolerance will fall to the ground, if there be
no battledores to fling it back and forth. It is reason for
rejoicing that the *vox populi* is inclined to grant us peace, 21
together with pardon for the preliminary battles that
purchased it.

With tender tread, thought sometimes walks in memory, 24
through the dim corridors of years, on to old battle-
grounds, there sadly to survey the fields of the slain and
the enemy's losses. In compiling this work, I have tried 27

1 to remove the pioneer signs and ensigns of war, and to
retain at this date the privileged armaments of peace.

3   With armor on, I continue the march, command and
countermand; meantime interluding with loving thought
this afterpiece of battle. Supported, cheered, I take my
6 pen and pruning-hook, to "learn war no more," and with
strong wing to lift my readers above the smoke of conflict
into light and liberty.

MARY BAKER EDDY

<small>CONCORD, N. H.</small>
January, 1897

Contents

Contents

Contents

Contents

CHAPTER IX
The Fruit of Spirit

Contents

Contents

Miscellaneous Writings

CHAPTER I

Introductory

PROSPECTUS

THE ancient Greek looked longingly for the Olympiad. The Chaldee watched the appearing of a 3 star; to him, no higher destiny dawned on the dome of being than that foreshadowed by signs in the heavens. The meek Nazarene, the scoffed of all scoffers, 6 said, "Ye can discern the face of the sky; but can ye not discern the signs of the times?" — for he forefelt and foresaw the ordeal of a perfect Christianity, hated 9 by sinners.

To kindle all minds with a gleam of gratitude, the new idea that comes welling up from infinite Truth needs 12 to be understood. The seer of this age should be a sage.

Humility is the stepping-stone to a higher recognition 15 of Deity. The mounting sense gathers fresh forms and strange fire from the ashes of dissolving self, and drops the world. Meekness heightens immortal attributes 18 only by removing the dust that dims them. Goodness reveals another scene and another self seemingly rolled up in shades, but brought to light by the evolutions of 21

1

1 advancing thought, whereby we discern the power of
Truth and Love to heal the sick.

3   Pride is ignorance; those assume most who have the
least wisdom or experience; and they steal from their
neighbor, because they have so little of their own.

6   The signs of these times portend a long and strong
determination of mankind to cleave to the world, the
flesh, and evil, causing great obscuration of Spirit.

9 When we remember that God is just, and admit the
total depravity of mortals, *alias* mortal mind, — and that
this Adam legacy must first be seen, and then must be

12 subdued and recompensed by justice, the eternal attribute of Truth, — the outlook demands labor, and the
laborers seem few. To-day we behold but the first

15 faint view of a more spiritual Christianity, that embraces
a deeper and broader philosophy and a more rational and
divine healing. The time approaches when divine Life,

18 Truth, and Love will be found alone the remedy for sin,
sickness, and death; when God, man's saving Principle,
and Christ, the spiritual idea of God, will be revealed.

21   Man's probation after death is the necessity of his
immortality; for good dies not and evil is self-destructive, therefore evil must be mortal and self-destroyed.

24 If man should not progress after death, but should remain in error, he would be inevitably self-annihilated.
Those upon whom "the second death hath no power"

27 are those who progress here and hereafter out of evil,
their mortal element, and into good that is immortal;
thus laying off the material beliefs that war against

30 Spirit, and putting on the spiritual elements in divine
Science.

   While we entertain decided views as to the best method

for elevating the race physically, morally, and spiritu- 1
ally, and shall express these views as duty demands, we
shall claim no especial gift from our divine origin, no 3
supernatural power. If we regard good as more natural
than evil, and spiritual understanding — the true knowledge of God — as imparting the only power to heal the 6
sick and the sinner, we shall demonstrate in our lives the
power of Truth and Love.

The lessons we learn in divine Science are applica- 9
ble to all the needs of man. Jesus taught them for this
very purpose; and his demonstration hath taught us
that "through his stripes" — his life-experience — and 12
divine Science, brought to the understanding through
Christ, the Spirit-revelator, is man healed and saved.
No opinions of mortals nor human hypotheses enter this 15
line of thought or action. Drugs, inert matter, never are
needed to aid spiritual power. Hygiene, manipulation,
and mesmerism are not Mind's medicine. The Prin- 18
ciple of all cure is God, unerring and immortal Mind.
We have learned that the erring or mortal thought holds
in itself all sin, sickness, and death, and imparts these 21
states to the body; while the supreme and perfect Mind,
as seen in the truth of being, antidotes and destroys these
material elements of sin and death. 24

Because God is supreme and omnipotent, *materia
medica,* hygiene, and animal magnetism are impotent;
and their only supposed efficacy is in apparently delud- 27
ing reason, denying revelation, and dethroning Deity.
The tendency of mental healing is to uplift mankind; but
this method perverted, is "Satan let loose." Hence the 30
deep demand for the Science of psychology to meet sin,
and uncover it; thus to annihilate hallucination.

1 Thought imbued with purity, Truth, and Love, instructed in the Science of metaphysical healing, is the
3 most potent and desirable remedial agent on the earth.
At this period there is a marked tendency of mortal
mind to plant mental healing on the basis of hypnotism,
6 calling this method "mental science." All *Science* is
Christian Science; the Science of the Mind that is God,
and of the universe as His idea, and their relation to each
9 other. Its only power to heal is its power to do good,
not evil.

A TIMELY ISSUE

12 At this date, 1883, a newspaper edited and published
by the Christian Scientists has become a necessity. Many
questions important to be disposed of come to the Col-
15 lege and to the practising students, yet but little time
has been devoted to their answer. Further enlightenment is necessary for the age, and a periodical de-
18 voted to this work seems alone adequate to meet the
requirement. Much interest is awakened and expressed
on the subject of metaphysical healing, but in many
21 minds it is confounded with isms, and even infidelity, so
that its religious specialty and the vastness of its worth
are not understood.

24 It is often said, "You must have a very strong will-
power to heal," or, "It must require a great deal of faith
to make your demonstrations." When it is answered
27 that there is no will-power required, and that something
more than faith is necessary, we meet with an expression
of incredulity. It is not alone the mission of Christian
30 Science to heal the sick, but to destroy sin in mortal

thought. This work well done will elevate and purify 1
the race. It cannot fail to do this if we devote our best
energies to the work. 3

Science reveals man as spiritual, harmonious, and eternal. This should be understood. Our College should
be crowded with students who are willing to consecrate 6
themselves to this Christian work. Mothers should be
able to produce perfect health and perfect morals in their
children — and ministers, to heal the sick — by study- 9
ing this scientific method of practising Christianity.
Many say, "I should like to study, but have not sufficient faith that I have the power to heal." The healing 12
power is Truth and Love, and these do not fail in the
greatest emergencies.

Materia medica says, "I can do no more. I have 15
done all that can be done. There is nothing to build
upon. There is no longer any reason for hope." Then
metaphysics comes in, armed with the power of Spirit, 18
not matter, takes up the case hopefully and builds on
the stone that the builders have rejected, and is successful. 21

Metaphysical therapeutics can seem a miracle and a
mystery to those only who do not understand the grand
reality that Mind controls the body. They acknowledge 24
an erring or mortal mind, but believe it to be brain matter. That man is the idea of infinite Mind, always perfect
in God, in Truth, Life, and Love, is something not easily 27
accepted, weighed down as is mortal thought with material beliefs. That which never existed, can seem solid
substance to this thought. It is much easier for people 30
to believe that the body affects the mind, than that the
mind affects the body.

1 We hear from the pulpits that sickness is sent as a
discipline to bring man nearer to God, — even though
3 sickness often leaves mortals but little time free from
complaints and fretfulness, and Jesus cast out disease as
evil.

6 The most of our Christian Science practitioners have
plenty to do, and many more are needed for the advancement of the age. At present the majority of the
9 acute cases are given to the M. D.'s, and only those
cases that are pronounced incurable are passed over to
the Scientist. The healing of such cases should cer-
12 tainly prove to all minds the power of metaphysics over
physics; and it surely does, to many thinkers, as the
rapid growth of the work shows. At no distant day,
15 Christian healing will rank far in advance of allopathy
and homœopathy; for Truth must ultimately succeed
where error fails.

18 Mind governs all. That we exist in God, perfect,
there is no doubt, for the conceptions of Life, Truth, and
Love must be perfect; and with that basic truth we con-
21 quer sickness, sin, and death. Frequently it requires
time to overcome the patient's faith in drugs and material hygiene; but when once convinced of the uselessness
24 of such material methods, the gain is rapid.

It is a noticeable fact, that in families where laws
of health are strictly enforced, great caution is observed
27 in regard to diet, and the conversation chiefly confined
to the ailments of the body, there is the most sickness.
Take a large family of children where the mother has
30 all that she can attend to in keeping them clothed and
fed, and health is generally the rule; whereas, in small
families of one or two children, sickness is by no means

the exception. These children must not be allowed to 1
eat certain food, nor to breathe the cold air, because
there is danger in it; when they perspire, they must be 3
loaded down with coverings until their bodies become
dry, — and the mother of one child is often busier than
the mother of eight. 6

Great charity and humility is necessary in this work
of healing. The loving patience of Jesus, we must
strive to emulate. "Thou shalt love thy neighbor as 9
thyself" has daily to be exemplified; and, although
skepticism and incredulity prevail in places where
one would least expect it, it harms not; for if serving 12
Christ, Truth, of what can mortal opinion avail? Cast
not your pearls before swine; but if you cannot bring
peace to all, you can to many, if faithful laborers in His 15
vineyard.

Looking over the newspapers of the day, one naturally
reflects that it is dangerous to live, so loaded with disease 18
seems the very air. These descriptions carry fears to
many minds, to be depicted in some future time upon
the body. A periodical of our own will counteract to 21
some extent this public nuisance; for through our paper,
at the price at which we shall issue it, we shall be able
to reach many homes with healing, purifying thought. 24
A great work already has been done, and a greater work
yet remains to be done. Oftentimes we are denied the
results of our labors because people do not understand 27
the nature and power of metaphysics, and they think
that health and strength would have returned naturally without any assistance. This is not so much from 30
a lack of justice, as it is that the *mens populi* is not sufficiently enlightened on this great subject. More thought

1 is given to material illusions than to spiritual facts. If
we can aid in abating suffering and diminishing sin,
3 we shall have accomplished much; but if we can bring
to the general thought this great fact that drugs do not,
cannot, produce health and harmony, since "in Him
6 [Mind] we live, and move, and have our being," we shall
have done more.

LOVE YOUR ENEMIES

9 Who is thine enemy that thou shouldst love him? Is
it a creature or a thing outside thine own creation?
Can you see an enemy, except you first formulate this
12 enemy and then look upon the object of your own conception? What is it that harms you? Can height, or
depth, or any other creature separate you from the
15 Love that is omnipresent good, — that blesses infinitely
one and all?
Simply count your enemy to be that which defiles,
18 defaces, and dethrones the Christ-image that you should
reflect. Whatever purifies, sanctifies, and consecrates
human life, is not an enemy, however much we suffer in
21 the process. Shakespeare writes: "Sweet are the uses
of adversity." Jesus said: "Blessed are ye, when men
shall revile you, and persecute you, and shall say all
24 manner of evil against you *falsely,* for my sake; . . . .
for so persecuted they the prophets which were before
you."
27 The Hebrew law with its "Thou shalt not," its demand and sentence, can only be fulfilled through the
gospel's benediction. Then, "Blessed are ye," inso-

much as the consciousness of good, grace, and peace, 1
comes through affliction rightly understood, as sanctified
by the purification it brings to the flesh, — to pride, self- 3
ignorance, self-will, self-love, self-justification. Sweet,
indeed, are these uses of His rod! Well is it that the
Shepherd of Israel passes all His flock under His rod 6
into His fold; thereby numbering them, and giving them
refuge at last from the elements of earth.

"Love thine enemies" is identical with "Thou hast 9
no enemies." Wherein is this conclusion relative to
those who have hated thee without a cause? Simply, in
that those unfortunate individuals are virtually thy best 12
friends. Primarily and ultimately, they are doing thee
good far beyond the present sense which thou canst entertain of good. 15

Whom we call friends seem to sweeten life's cup and
to fill it with the nectar of the gods. We lift this cup
to our lips; but it slips from our grasp, to fall in frag- 18
ments before our eyes. Perchance, having tasted its
tempting wine, we become intoxicated; become lethar-
gic, dreamy objects of self-satisfaction; else, the con- 21
tents of this cup of selfish human enjoyment having lost
its flavor, we voluntarily set it aside as tasteless and
unworthy of human aims. 24

And wherefore our failure longer to relish this fleeting sense, with its delicious forms of friendship,
wherewith mortals become educated to gratification in 27
personal pleasure and trained in treacherous peace?
Because it is the great and only danger in the path
that winds upward. A false sense of what consti- 30
tutes happiness is more disastrous to human progress
than all that an enemy or enmity can obtrude upon

1 the mind or engraft upon its purposes and achievements
wherewith to obstruct life's joys and enhance its sor-
3 rows.

We have no enemies. Whatever envy, hatred, revenge
— the most remorseless motives that govern mortal mind
6 — whatever these try to do, shall "work together for good
to them that love God."

Why?

9 Because He has called His own, armed them, equipped
them, and furnished them defenses impregnable. Their
God will not let them be lost; and if they fall they shall
12 rise again, stronger than before the stumble. The good
cannot lose their God, their help in times of trouble.
If they mistake the divine command, they will recover
15 it, countermand their order, retrace their steps, and
reinstate His orders, more assured to press on safely.
The best lesson of their lives is gained by crossing
18 swords with temptation, with fear and the besetments
of evil; insomuch as they thereby have tried their
strength and proven it; insomuch as they have found
21 their strength made perfect in weakness, and their fear
is self-immolated.

This destruction is a moral chemicalization, wherein
24 old things pass away and all things become new. The
worldly or material tendencies of human affections and
pursuits are thus annihilated; and this is the advent of
27 spiritualization. Heaven comes down to earth, and
mortals learn at last the lesson, "I have no enemies."

Even in belief you have but one (that, not in reality),
30 and this one enemy is yourself — your erroneous belief
that you have enemies; that evil is real; that aught but
good exists in Science. Soon or late, your enemy will

wake from his delusion to suffer for his evil intent; to 1
find that, though thwarted, its punishment is tenfold.

Love is the fulfilling of the law: it is grace, mercy, 3
and justice. I used to think it sufficiently just to abide
by our State statutes; that if a man should aim a ball at
my heart, and I by firing first could kill him and save 6
my own life, that this was right. I thought, also, that
if I taught indigent students gratuitously, afterwards
assisting them pecuniarily, and did not cease teach- 9
ing the wayward ones at close of the class term, but
followed them with precept upon precept; that if my
instructions had healed them and shown them the sure way 12
of salvation, — I had done my whole duty to students.

Love metes not out human justice, but divine mercy.
If one's life were attacked, and one could save it only 15
in accordance with common law, by taking another's,
would one sooner give up his own? We must love our
enemies in all the manifestations wherein and whereby 18
we love our friends; must even try not to expose their
faults, but to do them good whenever opportunity
occurs. To mete out human justice to those who per- 21
secute and despitefully use one, is not leaving all retribu-
tion to God and returning blessing for cursing. If special
opportunity for doing good to one's enemies occur not, 24
one can include them in his general effort to benefit the
race. Because I can do much general good to such as
hate me, I do it with earnest, special care — since they 27
permit me no other way, though with tears have I striven
for it. When smitten on one cheek, I have turned the
other: I have but two to present. 30

I would enjoy taking by the hand all who love me not,
and saying to them, "*I* love *you*, and would not know-

1 ingly harm you." *Because* I thus feel, I say to others:
Hate no one; for hatred is a plague-spot that spreads
3 its virus and kills at last. If indulged, it masters us;
brings suffering upon suffering to its possessor, throughout time and beyond the grave. If you have been badly
6 wronged, forgive and forget: God will recompense this
wrong, and punish, more severely than you could, him
who has striven to injure you. Never return evil for evil;
9 and, above all, do not fancy that you have been wronged
when you have not been.

The present is ours; the future, big with events.
12 Every man and woman should be to-day a law to himself, herself, — a law of loyalty to Jesus' Sermon on the
Mount. The means for sinning unseen and unpunished
15 have so increased that, unless one be watchful and steadfast in Love, one's temptations to sin are increased a
hundredfold. Mortal mind at this period mutely works
18 in the interest of both good and evil in a manner least
understood; hence the need of watching, and the danger
of yielding to temptation from causes that at former
21 periods in human history were not existent. The action
and effects of this so-called human mind in its silent arguments, are yet to be uncovered and summarily dealt with
24 by divine justice.

In Christian Science, the law of Love rejoices the heart;
and Love is Life and Truth. Whatever manifests aught
27 else in its effects upon mankind, demonstrably is not Love.
We should measure our love for God by our love for man;
and our sense of Science will be measured by our obedience
30 to God, — fulfilling the law of Love, doing good to all;
imparting, so far as we reflect them, Truth, Life, and Love
to all within the radius of our atmosphere of thought.

The only justice of which I feel at present capable, 1
is mercy and charity toward every one, — just so far as
one and all permit me to exercise these sentiments toward 3
them, — taking special care to mind my own business.

The falsehood, ingratitude, misjudgment, and sharp
return of evil for good — yea, the real wrongs (if wrong 6
can be real) which I have long endured at the hands of
others — have most happily wrought out for me the law
of loving mine enemies. This law I now urge upon the 9
solemn consideration of all Christian Scientists. Jesus
said, "If ye love them which love you, what thank have
ye? for sinners also love those that love them." 12

CHRISTIAN THEISM

Scholastic theology elaborates the proposition that
evil is a factor of good, and that to believe in the reality 15
of evil is essential to a rounded sense of the existence of
good.

This frail hypothesis is founded upon the basis of mate- 18
rial and mortal evidence — only upon what the shifting
mortal senses confirm and frail human reason accepts.
The Science of Soul reverses this proposition, overturns 21
the testimony of the five erring senses, and reveals in
clearer divinity the existence of good only; that is, of
God and His idea. 24

This postulate of divine Science only needs to be conceded, to afford opportunity for proof of its correctness
and the clearer discernment of good. 27

Seek the Anglo-Saxon term for God, and you will
find it to be good; then define good as God, and you
will find that good is omnipotence, has all power; it fills 30

1 all space, being omnipresent; hence, there is neither place
nor power left for evil. Divest your thought, then, of
3 the mortal and material view which contradicts the ever-
presence and all-power of good; take in only the immortal facts which include these, and where will you see or
6 feel evil, or find its existence necessary either to the origin
or ultimate of good?

It is urged that, from his original state of perfec-
9 tion, man has fallen into the imperfection that requires
evil through which to develop good. Were we to
admit this vague proposition, the Science of man could
12 never be learned; for in order to learn Science, we
begin with the correct statement, with harmony and
its Principle; and if man has lost his Principle and
15 its harmony, from evidences before him he is incapable of knowing the facts of existence and its concomitants: therefore to him evil is as real and eternal
18 as good, God! This awful deception is evil's umpire
and empire, that good, God, understood, forcibly
destroys.

21 What appears to mortals from their standpoint to be
the necessity for evil, is proven by the law of opposites
to be without necessity. Good is the primitive Princi-
24 ple of man; and evil, good's opposite, has no Principle,
and is not, and cannot be, the derivative of good.
Thus evil is neither a primitive nor a derivative, but
27 is suppositional; in other words, a lie that is incapable
of proof — therefore, wholly problematical.

The Science of Truth annihilates error, deprives evil
30 of all power, and thereby destroys all error, sin, sickness,
disease, and death. But the sinner is not sheltered from
suffering from sin: he makes a great reality of evil, iden-

tifies himself with it, fancies he finds pleasure in it, and 1
will reap what he sows; hence the sinner must endure
the effects of his delusion until he awakes from it. 3

THE NEW BIRTH

St. Paul speaks of the new birth as "waiting for the
adoption, to wit, the redemption of our body." The 6
great Nazarene Prophet said, "Blessed are the pure in
heart: for they shall see God." Nothing aside from the
spiritualization — yea, the highest Christianization — of 9
thought and desire, can give the true perception of God
and divine Science, that results in health, happiness, and
holiness. 12

The new birth is not the work of a moment. It begins
with moments, and goes on with years; moments of surrender to God, of childlike trust and joyful adoption 15
of good; moments of self-abnegation, self-consecration,
heaven-born hope, and spiritual love.

Time may commence, but it cannot complete, the 18
new birth: eternity does this; for progress is the law
of infinity. Only through the sore travail of mortal mind
shall soul as sense be satisfied, and man awake in His 21
likeness. What a faith-lighted thought is this! that
mortals can lay off the "old man," until man is found
to be the image of the infinite good that we name God, 24
and the fulness of the stature of man in Christ appears.

In mortal and material man, goodness seems in em-
bryo. By suffering for sin, and the gradual fading out 27
of the mortal and material sense of man, thought is developed into an infant Christianity; and, feeding at first
on the milk of the Word, it drinks in the sweet revealings 30

1 of a new and more spiritual Life and Love. These nourish
the hungry hope, satisfy more the cravings for immor-
3 tality, and so comfort, cheer, and bless one, that he saith:
In mine infancy, this is enough of heaven to come down
to earth.

6   But, as one grows into the manhood or womanhood
of Christianity, one finds so much lacking, and so very
much requisite to become wholly Christlike, that one
9 saith: The Principle of Christianity is infinite: it is
indeed God; and this infinite Principle hath infinite
claims on man, and these claims are divine, not human;
12 and man's ability to meet them is from God; for, being
His likeness and image, man must reflect the full
dominion of Spirit — even its supremacy over sin, sick-
15 ness, and death.

Here, then, is the awakening from the dream of life
in matter, to the great fact that *God is the only Life;*
18 that, therefore, we must entertain a higher sense of both
God and man. We must learn that God is infinitely
more than a person, or finite form, can contain; that
21 God is a divine *Whole,* and *All,* an all-pervading intelligence and Love, a divine, infinite Principle; and
that Christianity is a divine Science. This newly
24 awakened consciousness is wholly spiritual; it emanates
from Soul instead of body, and is the new birth begun
in Christian Science.

27   Now, dear reader, pause for a moment with me, earnestly to contemplate this new-born spiritual altitude; for
this statement demands demonstration.

30   Here you stand face to face with the laws of infinite
Spirit, and behold for the first time the irresistible conflict between the flesh and Spirit. You stand before the

awful detonations of Sinai. You hear and record the 1
thunderings of the spiritual law of Life, as opposed to
the material law of death; the spiritual law of Love, as 3
opposed to the material sense of love; the law of omnipotent harmony and good, as opposed to any supposititious law of sin, sickness, or death. And, before the 6
flames have died away on this mount of revelation, like
the patriarch of old, you take off your shoes — lay aside
your material appendages, human opinions and doc- 9
trines, give up your more material religion with its rites
and ceremonies, put off your *materia medica* and hygiene
as worse than useless — to sit at the feet of Jesus. Then, 12
you meekly bow before the Christ, the spiritual idea
that our great Master gave of the power of God to heal
and to save. Then it is that you behold for the first 15
time the divine Principle that redeems man from under
the curse of materialism, — sin, disease, and death.
This spiritual birth opens to the enraptured understand- 18
ing a much higher and holier conception of the supremacy
of Spirit, and of man as His likeness, whereby man reflects
the divine power to heal the sick. 21

A material or human birth is the appearing of a mortal, not the immortal man. This birth is more or less
prolonged and painful, according to the timely or un- 24
timely circumstances, the normal or abnormal material
conditions attending it.

With the spiritual birth, man's primitive, sinless, 27
spiritual existence dawns on human thought, — through
the travail of mortal mind, hope deferred, the perishing
pleasure and accumulating pains of sense, — by which 30
one loses himself as matter, and gains a truer sense of
Spirit and spiritual man.

1 The purification or baptismals that come from Spirit,
develop, step by step, the original likeness of perfect man,
3 and efface the mark of the beast. "Whom the Lord
loveth He chasteneth, and scourgeth every son whom
He receiveth;" therefore rejoice in tribulation, and wel-
6 come these spiritual signs of the new birth under the law
and gospel of Christ, Truth.

The prominent laws which forward birth in the divine
9 order of Science, are these: "Thou shalt have no other
gods before me;" "Love thy neighbor as thyself."
These commands of infinite wisdom, translated into
12 the new tongue, their spiritual meaning, signify: Thou
shalt love Spirit only, not its opposite, in every God-
quality, even in substance; thou shalt recognize thy-
15 self as God's spiritual child only, and the true man
and true woman, the all-harmonious "male and female,"
as of spiritual origin, God's reflection, — thus as chil-
18 dren of one common Parent, — wherein and whereby
Father, Mother, and child are the divine Principle and
divine idea, even the divine "Us" — one in good, and
21 good in One.

With this recognition man could never separate himself from good, God; and he would necessarily entertain
24 habitual love for his fellow-man. Only by admitting
evil as a reality, and entering into a state of evil
thoughts, can we in belief separate one man's interests
27 from those of the whole human family, or thus attempt
to separate Life from God. This is the mistake that
causes much that must be repented of and overcome.
30 Not to know what is blessing you, but to believe that
aught that God sends is unjust, — or that those whom
He commissions bring to you at His demand that which

is unjust, — is wrong and cruel. Envy, evil thinking, 1
evil speaking, covetousness, lust, hatred, malice, are
always wrong, and will break the rule of Christian 3
Science and prevent its demonstration; but the rod of
God, and the obedience demanded of His servants in
carrying out what He teaches them, — these are never 6
unmerciful, never unwise.

The task of healing the sick is far lighter than that
of so teaching the divine Principle and rules of Chris- 9
tian Science as to lift the affections and motives of men
to adopt them and bring them out in human lives. He
who has named the name of Christ, who has virtually 12
accepted the divine claims of Truth and Love in divine
Science, is daily departing from evil; and all the wicked
endeavors of suppositional demons can never change the 15
current of that life from steadfastly flowing on to God,
its divine source.

But, taking the livery of heaven wherewith to cover 18
iniquity, is the most fearful sin that mortals can commit.
I should have more faith in an honest drugging-doctor,
one who abides by his statements and works upon as 21
high a basis as he understands, healing me, than I could
or would have in a smooth-tongued hypocrite or mental
malpractitioner.   24

Between the centripetal and centrifugal mental forces
of material and spiritual gravitations, we go into or we
go out of materialism or sin, and choose our course and 27
its results. Which, then, shall be our choice, — the sinful, material, and perishable, or the spiritual, joy-giving,
and eternal?   30

The spiritual sense of Life and its grand pursuits is
of itself a bliss, health-giving and joy-inspiring. This

1 sense of Life illumes our pathway with the radiance of
divine Love; heals man spontaneously, morally and
3 physically, — exhaling the aroma of Jesus' own words,
"Come unto me, all ye that labor and are heavy laden,
and I will give you rest."

CHAPTER II

One Cause and Effect

CHRISTIAN SCIENCE begins with the First Com- 1
mandment of the Hebrew Decalogue, "Thou
shalt have no other gods before me." It goes on in 3
perfect unity with Christ's Sermon on the Mount, and
in that age culminates in the Revelation of St. John,
who, while on earth and in the flesh, like ourselves, 6
beheld "a new heaven and a new earth," — the spiritual
universe, whereof Christian Science now bears testimony.

Our Master said, "The works that I do shall ye do 9
also;" and, "The kingdom of God is within you." This
makes practical all his words and works. As the ages
advance in spirituality, Christian Science will be seen 12
to depart from the trend of other Christian denominations in no wise except by increase of spirituality.

My first plank in the platform of Christian Science 15
is as follows: "There is no life, truth, intelligence, nor
substance in matter. All is infinite Mind and its infinite
manifestation, for God is All-in-all. Spirit is immortal 18
Truth; matter is mortal error. Spirit is the real and
eternal; matter is the unreal and temporal. Spirit is
God, and man is His image and likeness. Therefore man 21
is not material; he is spiritual." [1]

[1] The order of this sentence has been conformed to the text of
the 1908 edition of Science and Health. **24**

21

1 I am strictly a theist — believe in one God, one Christ
or Messiah.

3 Science is neither a law of matter nor of man. It is
the unerring manifesto of Mind, the law of God, its
divine Principle. Who dare say that matter or
6 mortals can evolve Science? Whence, then, is it, if not
from the divine source, and what, but the contempo-
rary of Christianity, so far in advance of human knowl-
9 edge that mortals must work for the discovery of even a
portion of it? Christian Science translates Mind, God,
to mortals. It is the infinite calculus defining the line,
12 plane, space, and fourth dimension of Spirit. It absolutely refutes the amalgamation, transmigration, absorption, or annihilation of individuality. It shows the
15 impossibility of transmitting human ills, or evil, from one
individual to another; that all true thoughts revolve
in God's orbits: they come from God and return to
18 Him, — and untruths belong not to His creation, therefore these are null and void. It hath no peer, no com-
petitor, for it dwelleth in Him besides whom "there is
21 none other."

That Christian Science is Christian, those who have
demonstrated it, according to the rules of its divine
24 Principle, — together with the sick, the lame, the deaf, and
the blind, healed by it, — have proven to a waiting world.
He who has not tested it, is incompetent to condemn it;
27 and he who is a willing sinner, cannot demonstrate it.

A falling apple suggested to Newton more than the
simple fact cognized by the senses, to which it seemed
30 to fall by reason of its own ponderosity; but the primal
cause, or Mind-force, invisible to material sense, lay
concealed in the treasure-troves of Science. True,

Newton named it gravitation, having learned so much; 1
but Science, demanding more, pushes the question:
Whence or what is the power back of gravitation, — the 3
intelligence that manifests power?   Is pantheism true?
Does mind "sleep in the mineral, or dream in the
animal, and wake in man"?   Christianity answers this 6
question.   The prophets, Jesus, and the apostles, demonstrated a divine intelligence that subordinates so-called
material laws;   and disease, death, winds, and waves, 9
obey this intelligence.   Was it Mind or matter that spake
in creation, "and it was done"?   The answer is self-
evident, and the command remains, "Thou shalt have 12
no other gods before me."

It is plain that the Me spoken of in the First Commandment, must be Mind;   for matter is not the Chris- 15
tian's God, and is not intelligent.   Matter cannot even
talk;   and the serpent, Satan, the first talker in its behalf,
lied.   Reason and revelation declare that God is both 18
noumenon and phenomena, — the first and only cause.
The universe, including man, is not a result of atomic
action, material force or energy;   it is not organized dust. 21
God, Spirit, Mind, are terms synonymous for the one
God, whose reflection is creation, and man is His image
and likeness.   Few there are who comprehend what Chris- 24
tian Science means by the word *reflection*.   God is seen
only in that which reflects good, Life, Truth, Love —
yea, which manifests all His attributes and power, even 27
as the human likeness thrown upon the mirror repeats
precisely the looks and actions of the object in front of it.
All must be Mind and Mind's ideas;   since, according to 30
natural science, God, Spirit, could not change its species
and evolve matter.

1 These facts enjoin the First Commandment; and knowledge of them makes man spiritually minded. St.
3 Paul writes: "For to be carnally minded is death; but to be spiritually minded is life and peace." This knowledge came to me in an hour of great need; and I give it
6 to you as death-bed testimony to the daystar that dawned on the night of material sense. This knowledge is practical, for it wrought my immediate recovery from
9 an injury caused by an accident, and pronounced fatal by the physicians. On the third day thereafter, I called for my Bible, and opened it at Matthew ix. 2. As I
12 read, the healing Truth dawned upon my sense; and the result was that I rose, dressed myself, and ever after was in better health than I had before enjoyed. That
15 short experience included a glimpse of the great fact that I have since tried to make plain to others, namely, Life in and of Spirit; this Life being the sole reality of
18 existence. I learned that mortal thought evolves a subjective state which it names matter, thereby shutting out the true sense of Spirit. *Per contra,* Mind and man
21 are immortal; and knowledge gained from mortal sense is illusion, error, the opposite of Truth; therefore it cannot be true. A knowledge of both good and evil
24 (when good is God, and God is All) is impossible. Speaking of the origin of evil, the Master said: "When he speaketh a lie, he speaketh of his own: for he is a liar,
27 and the father of it." God warned man not to believe the talking serpent, or rather the allegory describing it. The Nazarene Prophet declared that his followers
30 should handle serpents; that is, put down all subtle falsities or illusions, and thus destroy any supposed effect arising from false claims exercising their supposed power

on the mind and body of man, against his holiness and 1
health.

That there is but one God or Life, one cause and 3
one effect, is the *multum in parvo* of Christian Science;
and to my understanding it is the heart of Christianity,
the religion that Jesus taught and demonstrated. In 6
divine Science it is found that matter is a phase of
error, and that neither one really exists, since God is
Truth, and All-in-all. Christ's Sermon on the Mount, 9
in its direct application to human needs, confirms this
conclusion.

Science, understood, translates matter into Mind, 12
rejects all other theories of causation, restores the spiritual and original meaning of the Scriptures, and explains the teachings and life of our Lord. It is religion's 15
"new tongue," with "signs following," spoken of by
St. Mark. It gives God's infinite meaning to mankind,
healing the sick, casting out evil, and raising the spirit- 18
ually dead. Christianity is Christlike only as it reiterates the word, repeats the works, and manifests the
spirit of Christ.   21

Jesus' only medicine was omnipotent and omniscient
Mind. As *omni* is from the Latin word meaning *all*,
this medicine is all-power; and omniscience means as 24
well, all-science. The sick are more deplorably situated
than the sinful, if the sick cannot trust God for help and
the sinful can. If God created drugs good, they cannot be 27
harmful; if He could create them otherwise, then they
are bad and unfit for man; and if He created drugs for
healing the sick, why did not Jesus employ them and 30
recommend them for that purpose?

No human hypotheses, whether in philosophy, medi-

1 cine, or religion, can survive the wreck of time; but whatever is of God, hath life abiding in it, and ulti-
3 mately will be known as self-evident truth, as demonstrable as mathematics. Each successive period of progress is a period more humane and spiritual. The only logical
6 conclusion is that all is Mind and its manifestation, from the rolling of worlds, in the most subtle ether, to a potato-patch.

9 The agriculturist ponders the history of a seed, and believes that his crops come from the seedling and the loam; even while the Scripture declares He made "every
12 plant of the field before it was in the earth." The Scientist asks, Whence came the first seed, and what made the soil? Was it molecules, or material atoms? Whence
15 came the infinitesimals, — from infinite Mind, or from matter? If from matter, how did matter originate? Was it self-existent? Matter is not intelligent, and thus able
18 to evolve or create itself: it is the very opposite of Spirit, intelligent, self-creative, and infinite Mind. The belief of mind in matter is pantheism. Natural history shows
21 that neither a genus nor a species produces its opposite. God is All, in all. What can be more than All? Nothing: and this is just what I call matter, *nothing*. Spirit,
24 God, has no antecedent; and God's consequent is the spiritual cosmos. The phrase, "express image," in the common version of Hebrews i. 3, is, in the Greek Tes-
27 tament, *character*.

The Scriptures name God as good, and the Saxon term for God is also good. From this premise comes
30 the logical conclusion that God is naturally and divinely infinite good. How, then, can this conclusion change, or be changed, to mean that good is evil, or the creator

of evil? What can there be besides infinity? Nothing! 1
Therefore the Science of good calls evil *nothing*. In
divine Science the terms God and good, as Spirit, are 3
synonymous. That God, good, creates evil, or aught
that can result in evil, — or that Spirit creates its opposite, named matter, — are conclusions that destroy their 6
premise and prove themselves invalid. Here is where
Christian Science sticks to its text, and other systems
of religion abandon their own logic. Here also is found 9
the pith of the basal statement, the cardinal point in
Christian Science, that matter and evil (including all
inharmony, sin, disease, death) are *unreal*. Mortals 12
accept natural science, wherein no species ever produces its opposite. Then why not accept divine Science on this ground? since the Scriptures maintain 15
this fact by parable and proof, asking, "Do men
gather grapes of thorns, or figs of thistles?" "Doth a
fountain send forth at the same place sweet water and 18
bitter?"

According to reason and revelation, evil and matter
are negation: for evil signifies the absence of good, God, 21
though God is ever present; and matter claims something besides God, when God is really *All*. Creation,
evolution, or manifestation, — being in and of Spirit, 24
Mind, and all that really is, — must be spiritual and
mental. This is Science, and is susceptible of proof.

But, say you, is a stone spiritual?   27

To erring material sense, No! but to unerring spiritual
sense, it is a small manifestation of Mind, a type of spiritual substance, "the substance of things hoped for." 30
Mortals can know a stone as substance, only by first admitting that it is substantial. Take away the mortal sense

1 of substance, and the stone itself would disappear, only
to reappear in the spiritual sense thereof. Matter can
3 neither see, hear, feel, taste, nor smell; having no sensation of its own. Perception by the five personal senses
is mental, and dependent on the beliefs that mortals
6 entertain. Destroy the belief that you can walk, and
volition ceases; for muscles cannot move without mind.
Matter takes no cognizance of matter. In dreams, things
9 are only what mortal mind makes them; and the phenomena of mortal life are as dreams; and this so-called
life is a dream soon told. In proportion as mortals turn
12 from this mortal and material dream, to the true sense
of reality, everlasting Life will be found to be the only
Life. That death does not destroy the beliefs of the flesh,
15 our Master proved to his doubting disciple, Thomas. Also,
he demonstrated that divine Science alone can overbear
materiality and mortality; and this great truth was shown
18 by his ascension after death, whereby he arose above
the illusion of matter.

The First Commandment, "Thou shalt have no other
21 gods before me," suggests the inquiry, What meaneth
this Me, — Spirit, or matter? It certainly does not
signify a graven idol, and must mean Spirit. Then
24 the commandment means, Thou shalt recognize no
intelligence nor life in matter; and find neither pleasure
nor pain therein. The Master's practical knowledge
27 of this grand verity, together with his divine Love,
healed the sick and raised the dead. He literally
annulled the claims of physique and of physical law,
30 by the superiority of the higher law; hence his declaration, "These signs shall follow them that believe; . . .
if they drink any deadly thing, it shall not hurt them;

they shall lay hands on the sick, and they shall re- 1
cover."

Do you believe his words? I do, and that his prom- 3
ise is perpetual. Had it been applicable only to his
immediate disciples, the pronoun would be *you*, not *them*.
The purpose of his life-work touches universal human- 6
ity. At another time he prayed, not for the twelve
only, but "for them also which shall believe on me through
their word." 9

The Christ-healing was practised even before the Christian era; "the Word was with God, and the Word was
God." There is, however, no analogy between Christian 12
Science and spiritualism, or between it and any speculative theory.

In 1867, I taught the first student in Christian Science. 15
Since that date I have known of but fourteen deaths
in the ranks of my about five thousand students. The
census since 1875 (the date of the first publication of 18
my work, "Science and Health with Key to the Scriptures") shows that longevity has *increased*. Daily letters
inform me that a perusal of my volume is healing the 21
writers of chronic and acute diseases that had defied medical skill.

Surely the people of the Occident know that esoteric 24
magic and Oriental barbarisms will neither flavor Christianity nor advance health and length of days.

Miracles are no infraction of God's laws; on the 27
contrary, they fulfil His laws; for they are the signs following Christianity, whereby matter is proven powerless and subordinate to Mind. Christians, like students 30
in mathematics, should be working up to those higher
rules of Life which Jesus taught and proved. Do we

1 really understand the divine Principle of Christianity
before we prove it, in at least some feeble demonstra-
3 tion thereof, according to Jesus' example in healing the
sick? Should we adopt the "simple addition" in Christian Science and doubt its higher rules, or despair of
6 ultimately reaching them, even though failing at first to
demonstrate all the possibilities of Christianity?

St. John spiritually discerned and revealed the sum
9 total of transcendentalism. He saw the real earth and
heaven. They were spiritual, not material; and they
were without pain, sin, or death. Death was not the
12 door to this heaven. The gates thereof he declared were
inlaid with pearl, — likening them to the priceless understanding of man's real existence, to be recognized here
15 and now.

The great Way-shower illustrated Life unconfined, uncontaminated, untrammelled, by matter. He proved the
18 superiority of Mind over the flesh, opened the door to
the captive, and enabled man to demonstrate the law of
Life, which St. Paul declares "hath made me free from
21 the law of sin and death."

The stale saying that Christian Science "is neither
Christian nor science!" is to-day the fossil of wisdom-
24 less wit, weakness, and superstition. "The fool hath
said in his heart, There is no God."

Take courage, dear reader, for any seeming mysti-
27 cism surrounding realism is explained in the Scripture,
"There went up a mist from the earth [matter];" and
the mist of materialism will vanish as we approach spirit-
30 uality, the realm of reality; cleanse our lives in Christ's
righteousness; bathe in the baptism of Spirit, and awake
in His likeness.

CHAPTER III

Questions and Answers

What do you consider to be mental malpractice? 1

MENTAL malpractice is a bland denial of Truth, and is the antipode of Christian Science. To 3 mentally argue in a manner that can disastrously affect the happiness of a fellow-being — harm him morally, physically, or spiritually — breaks the Golden 6 Rule and subverts the scientific laws of being. This, therefore, is not the use but the abuse of mental treatment, and is mental malpractice. It is needless to 9 say that such a subversion of right is not scientific. Its claim to power is in proportion to the faith in evil, and consequently to the lack of faith in good. Such false 12 faith finds no place in, and receives no aid from, the Principle or the rules of Christian Science; for it denies the grand verity of this Science, namely, that God, good, 15 has *all* power.

This leaves the individual no alternative but to relinquish his faith in evil, or to argue against his own 18 convictions of good and so destroy his power to be or to do good, because he has no faith in the *omnipotence* of God, good. He parts with his understanding of good, 21 in order to retain his faith in evil and so succeed with his

31

1 wrong argument, — if indeed he desires success in this
broad road to destruction.

3 *How shall we demean ourselves towards the students
of disloyal students? And what about that clergyman's
remarks on "Christ and Christmas"?*

6 From this question, I infer that some of my students
seem not to know in what manner they should act towards
the students of false teachers, or such as have strayed
9 from the rules and divine Principle of Christian Science.
The query is abnormal, when "precept upon precept;
line upon line" are to be found in the Scriptures, and in
12 my books, on this very subject.

In Mark, ninth chapter, commencing at the thirty-
third verse, you will find my views on this subject; love
15 alone is admissible towards friend and foe. My sympathies extend to the above-named class of students more
than to many others. If I had the time to talk with all
18 students of Christian Science, and correspond with them,
I would gladly do my best towards helping those unfortunate seekers after Truth whose teacher is straying
21 from the straight and narrow path. But I have not moments enough in which to give to my own flock all the
time and attention that they need, — and charity must
24 begin at home.

Distinct denominational and social organizations and
societies are at present necessary for the individual,
27 and for our Cause. But all people can and should be
just, merciful; they should never envy, elbow, slander,
hate, or try to injure, but always should try to bless their
30 fellow-mortals.

To the query in regard to some clergyman's com-

ments on my illustrated poem, I will say: It is the righteous 1
prayer that avails with God. Whatever is wrong will
receive its own reward. The high priests of old caused 3
the crucifixion of even the great Master; and thereby
they lost, and he won, heaven. I love all ministers and
ministries of Christ, Truth. 6

All clergymen may not understand the illustrations
in "Christ and Christmas;" or that these refer not to
personality, but present the type and shadow of Truth's 9
appearing in the womanhood as well as in the manhood
of God, our divine Father and Mother.

Must I have faith in Christian Science in order to be 12
healed by it?

This is a question that is being asked every day. It
has not proved impossible to heal those who, when they 15
began treatment, had no faith whatever in the Science,
— other than to place themselves under my care, and
follow the directions given. Patients naturally gain con- 18
fidence in Christian Science as they recognize the help
they derive therefrom.

What are the advantages of your system of healing, over 21
the ordinary methods of healing disease?

Healing by Christian Science has the following advantages: — 24

First: It does away with all material medicines, and
recognizes the fact that, as mortal mind is the cause of
all "the ills that flesh is heir to," the antidote for sickness, 27
as well as for sin, may and must be found in mortal mind's
opposite, — the divine Mind.

Second: It is more effectual than drugs; curing where 30

1 these fail, and leaving none of the harmful "after effects" of these in the system; thus proving that metaphysics
3 is above physics.

Third: One who has been healed by Christian Science is not only healed of the disease, but is improved
6 morally. The body is governed by mind; and mortal mind must be improved, before the body is renewed and harmonious, — since the physique is simply thought
9 made manifest.

Is spiritualism or mesmerism included in Christian Science?

12 They are wholly apart from it. Christian Science is based on divine Principle; whereas spiritualism, so far as I understand it, is a mere speculative opinion and
15 human belief. If the departed were to communicate with us, we should see them as they were before death, and have them with us; after death, they can no more
18 come to those they have left, than we, in our present state of existence, can go to the departed or the adult can return to his boyhood. We may pass on to their state
21 of existence, but they cannot return to ours. Man is *im*-mortal, and there is not a moment when he ceases to exist. All that are called "communications from spirits,"
24 lie within the realm of mortal thought on this present plane of existence, and are the antipodes of Christian Science; the immortal and mortal are as direct opposites as light
27 and darkness.

Who is the Founder of mental healing?

The author of "Science and Health with Key to the
30 Scriptures," who discovered the Science of healing em-

bodied in her works. Years of practical proof, through 1
homœopathy, revealed to her the fact that Mind, instead of matter, is the Principle of pathology; and 3
subsequently her recovery, through the supremacy of
Mind over matter, from a severe casualty pronounced
by the physicians incurable, sealed that proof with the 6
signet of Christian Science. In 1883, a million of people acknowledge and attest the blessings of this mental
system of treating disease. Perhaps the following 9
words of her husband, the late Dr. Asa G. Eddy,
afford the most concise, yet complete, summary of the
matter: — 12

"Mrs. Eddy's works are the outgrowths of her life.
I never knew so unselfish an individual."

Will the book Science and Health, that you offer for sale 15
at three dollars, teach its readers to heal the sick, — or is
one obliged to become a student under your personal in-
struction? And if one is obliged to study under you, of 18
what benefit is your book?

Why do we read the Bible, and then go to church to
hear it expounded? Only because both are important. 21
Why do we read moral science, and then study it at
college?
You are benefited by reading Science and Health, but 24
it is greatly to your advantage to be taught its Science
by the author of that work, who explains it in detail.

What is immortal Mind? 27

In reply, we refer you to "Science and Health with
Key to the Scriptures," [1] Vol. I. page 14: "That which

---

1 is erring, sinful, sick, and dying, termed material or
mortal man, is neither God's man nor Mind; but to be
3 understood, we shall classify evil and error as mortal
mind, in contradistinction to good and Truth, or the
Mind which is immortal."

6   *Do animals and beasts have a mind?*

Beasts, as well as men, express Mind as their origin;
but they manifest less of Mind. The first and only
9 cause is the eternal Mind, which is God, and there is
but one God. The ferocious mind seen in the beast is
mortal mind, which is harmful and proceeds not from
12 God; for His beast is the lion that lieth down with
the lamb. Appetites, passions, anger, revenge, subtlety,
are the animal qualities of sinning mortals; and the
15 beasts that have these propensities express the lower
qualities of the so-called animal man; in other words,
the nature and quality of mortal mind, — not immortal
18 Mind.

*What is the distinction between mortal mind and im-
mortal Mind?*

21   Mortal mind includes all evil, disease, and death;
also, all beliefs relative to the so-called material laws,
and all material objects, and the law of sin and death.
24   The Scripture says, "The carnal mind [in other words,
mortal mind] is enmity against God; for it is not subject to the law of God, neither indeed can be." Mortal
27 mind is an illusion; as much in our waking moments
as in the dreams of sleep. The belief that intelligence,
Truth, and Love, are in matter and separate from God,
30 is an error; for there is no intelligent evil, and no power

besides God, good. God would not be omnipotent if 1
there were in reality another mind creating or governing
man or the universe. 3

Immortal Mind is God; and this Mind is made
manifest in all thoughts and desires that draw mankind toward purity, health, holiness, and the spiritual 6
facts of being.

Jesus recognized this relation so clearly that he said,
"I and my Father are one." In proportion as we oppose 9
the belief in material sense, in sickness, sin, and death,
and recognize ourselves under the control of God,
spiritual and immortal Mind, shall we go on to leave the 12
animal for the spiritual, and learn the meaning of those
words of Jesus, "Go ye into all the world . . . heal the
sick." 15

Can your Science cure intemperance?

Christian Science lays the axe at the root of the tree.
Its antidote for all ills is God, the perfect Mind, which 18
corrects mortal thought, whence cometh all evil. God
can and does destroy the thought that leads to moral
or physical death. Intemperance, impurity, sin of every 21
sort, is destroyed by Truth. The appetite for alcohol
yields to Science as directly and surely as do sickness
and sin. 24

Does Mrs. Eddy take patients?

She now does not. Her time is wholly devoted to instruction, leaving to her students the work of healing; 27
which, at this hour, is in reality the least difficult of the
labor that Christian Science demands.

1 *Why do you charge for teaching Christian Science, when
all the good we can do must be done freely?*

3 When teaching imparts the ability to gain and maintain health, to heal and elevate man in every line of
life, — as this teaching certainly does, — is it un-
6 reasonable to expect in return something to support
one's self and a Cause? If so, our whole system
of education, secular and religious, is at fault, and the
9 instructors and philanthropists in our land should expect no compensation. "If we have sown unto you
spiritual things, is it a great thing if we shall reap your
12 carnal things?"

*How happened you to establish a college to instruct in
metaphysics, when other institutions find little interest in
15 such a dry and abstract subject?*

Metaphysics, as taught by me at the Massachusetts
Metaphysical College, is far from dry and abstract. It
18 is a Science that has the animus of Truth. Its practical
application to benefit the race, heal the sick, enlighten
and reform the sinner, makes divine metaphysics need-
21 ful, indispensable. Teaching metaphysics at other colleges means, mainly, elaborating a man-made theory,
or some speculative view too vapory and hypothetical
24 for questions of practical import.

*Is it necessary to study your Science in order to be healed
by it and keep well?*

27 It is not necessary to make each patient a student
in order to cure his present disease, if this is what
you mean. Were it so, the Science would be of less

practical value. Many who apply for help are not 1
prepared to take a course of instruction in Christian
Science. 3

To avoid being *subject* to disease, would require the
understanding of how you are healed. In 1885, this
knowledge can be obtained in its genuineness at the 6
Massachusetts Metaphysical College. There are abroad
at this early date some grossly incorrect and false
teachers of what they term Christian Science; of such 9
beware. They have risen up in a day to make this claim;
whereas the Founder of genuine Christian Science has
been all her years in giving it birth. 12

Can you take care of yourself?

God giveth to every one this *puissance;* and I have
faith in His promise, "Lo, I am with you alway" — 15
all the way. Unlike the M. D.'s, Christian Scientists
are not afraid to take their own medicine, for this
medicine is divine Mind; and from this saving, ex- 18
haustless source they intend to fill the human mind with
enough of the leaven of Truth to leaven the whole lump.
There may be exceptional cases, where one Christian 21
Scientist who has more to meet than others needs support
at times; then, it is right to bear "one another's burdens,
and so fulfil the law of Christ." 24

*In what way is a Christian Scientist an instrument by
which God reaches others to heal them, and what most
obstructs the way?* 27

A Christian, or a Christian Scientist, assumes no more
when claiming to work with God in healing the sick,
than in converting the sinner. Divine help is as neces- 30

1 sary in the one case as in the other. The scientific Principle of healing demands such cooperation; but this
3 unison and its power would be arrested if one were to
mix material methods with the spiritual, — were to mingle hygienic rules, drugs, and prayers in the same pro-
6 cess, — and thus serve "other gods." Truth is as
effectual in destroying sickness as in the destruction
of sin.

9   It is often asked, "If Christian Science is the same
method of healing that Jesus and the apostles used,
why do not its students perform as instantaneous cures
12 as did those in the first century of the Christian era?"

In some instances the students of Christian Science
equal the ancient prophets as healers. All true healing
15 is governed by, and demonstrated on, the same Principle as theirs; namely, the action of the divine Spirit,
through the power of Truth to destroy error, discord
18 of whatever sort. The reason that the same results follow not in every case, is that the student does not in
every case possess sufficiently the Christ-spirit and its
21 power to cast out the disease. The Founder of Christian Science teaches her students that they must possess
the spirit of Truth and Love, must gain the power
24 over sin in themselves, or they cannot be instantaneous
healers.

In this Christian warfare the student or practitioner
27 has to master those elements of evil too common to other
minds. If it is hate that is holding the purpose to kill
his patient by mental means, it requires more divine
30 understanding to conquer this sin than to nullify either
the disease itself or the ignorance by which one unintentionally harms himself or another. An element of

brute-force that only the cruel and evil can send forth, is 1
given vent in the diabolical practice of one who, having
learned the power of liberated thought to do good, per- 3
verts it, and uses it to accomplish an evil purpose. This
mental malpractice would disgrace Mind-healing, were it
not that God overrules it, and causes "the wrath of man" 6
to praise Him. It deprives those who practise it of the
power to heal, and destroys their own possibility of
progressing. 9

The honest student of Christian Science is purged
through Christ, Truth, and thus is ready for victory in
the ennobling strife. The good fight must be fought by 12
those who keep the faith and finish their course. Mental
purgation must go on: it promotes spiritual growth,
scales the mountain of human endeavor, and gains the 15
summit in Science that otherwise could not be reached,
— where the struggle with sin is forever done.

Can all classes of disease be healed by your method?   18

We answer, Yes. Mind is the architect that builds
its own idea, and produces all harmony that appears.
There is no other healer in the case. If mortal mind, 21
through the action of fear, manifests inflammation and a
belief of chronic or acute disease, by removing the cause
in that so-called mind the effect or disease will disappear 24
and health will be restored; for health, *alias* harmony,
is the normal manifestation of man in Science. The
divine Principle which governs the universe, including 27
man, if demonstrated, is sufficient for all emergencies.
But the practitioner may not always prove equal to
bringing out the result of the Principle that he knows to 30
be true.

1   *After the change called death takes place, do we meet
those gone before? — or does life continue in thought only
3 as in a dream?*

Man is not annihilated, nor does he lose his identity,
by passing through the belief called death. After the
6 momentary belief of dying passes from mortal mind, this
mind is still in a conscious state of existence; and the individual has but passed through a moment of extreme
9 mortal fear, to awaken with thoughts, and being, as
material as before. Science and Health clearly states
that spiritualization of thought is not attained by the death
12 of the body, but by a conscious union with God. When
we shall have passed the ordeal called death, or destroyed
this last enemy, and shall have come upon the same plane
15 of conscious existence with those gone before, then we
shall be able to communicate with and to recognize them.

If, before the change whereby we meet the dear de-
18 parted, our life-work proves to have been well done, we
shall not have to repeat it; but our joys and means of advancing will be proportionately increased.

21   The difference between a belief of material existence
and the spiritual fact of Life is, that the former is a dream
and unreal, while the latter is real and eternal. Only
24 as we understand God, and learn that good, not evil,
lives and is immortal, that immortality exists only in
spiritual perfection, shall we drop our false sense of Life
27 in sin or sense material, and recognize a better state of
existence.

Can I be treated without being present during treatment?

30   Mind is not confined to limits; and nothing but our
own false admissions prevent us from demonstrating this

great fact. Christian Science, recognizing the capabili- 1
ties of Mind to act of itself, and independent of matter,
enables one to heal cases without even having seen the 3
individual, — or simply after having been made acquainted with the mental condition of the patient.

Do all who at present claim to be teaching Christian 6
Science, teach it correctly?

By no means: Christian Science is not sufficiently understood for that. The student of this Science who under- 9
stands it best, is the one least likely to pour into other
minds a trifling sense of it as being adequate to make safe
and successful practitioners. The simple sense one gains 12
of this Science through careful, unbiased, contemplative
reading of my books, is far more advantageous to the
sick and to the learner than is or can be the spurious 15
teaching of those who are spiritually unqualified. The
sad fact at this early writing is, that the letter is gained
sooner than the spirit of Christian Science: time is re- 18
quired thoroughly to qualify students for the great ordeal
of this century.

If one student tries to undermine another, such sinister 21
rivalry does a vast amount of injury to the Cause. To
fill one's pocket at the expense of his conscience, or to
build on the downfall of others, incapacitates one to 24
practise or teach Christian Science. The occasional temporary success of such an one is owing, in part, to the impossibility for those unacquainted with the mighty Truth 27
of *Christian* Science to recognize, as such, the barefaced
errors that are taught — and the damaging effects these
leave on the practice of the learner, on the Cause, and 30
on the health of the community.

1 Honest students speak the truth "according to the pattern showed to thee in the mount," and live it: these 3 are not working for emoluments, and may profitably teach people, who are ready to investigate this subject, the rudiments of Christian Science.

6 *Can Christian Science cure acute cases where there is necessity for immediate relief, as in membranous croup?*

The remedial power of Christian Science is positive, 9 and its application direct. It cannot fail to heal in every case of disease, when conducted by one who understands this Science sufficiently to demonstrate its 12 highest possibilities.

If I have the toothache, and nothing stops it until I have the tooth extracted, and then the pain ceases, has 15 the mind, or extracting, or both, caused the pain to cease?

What you thought was pain in the bone or nerve, could 18 only have been a belief of pain in matter; for matter has no sensation. It was a state of mortal thought made manifest in the flesh. You call this body matter, when 21 awake, or when asleep in a dream. That matter can report pain, or that mind is *in* matter, reporting sensations, is but a dream at all times. You believed that if 24 the tooth were extracted, the pain would cease: this demand of mortal thought once met, your belief assumed a new form, and said, There is no more pain. When 27 your belief in pain ceases, the pain stops; for matter has no intelligence of its own. By applying this mental remedy or antidote directly to your belief, you scien-

tifically prove the fact that Mind is supreme. This is not 1
done by will-power, for that is not Science but mesmerism.
The full understanding that God is Mind, and that mat- 3
ter is but a belief, enables you to control pain. Christian Science, by means of its Principle of metaphysical
healing, is able to do more than to heal a toothache; 6
although its power to allay fear, prevent inflammation,
and destroy the necessity for ether — thereby avoiding
the fatal results that frequently follow the use of that 9
drug — render this Science invaluable in the practice
of dentistry.

Can an atheist or a profane man be cured by metaphysics, 12
or Christian Science?

The moral status of the man demands the remedy of
Truth more in this than in most cases; therefore, under 15
the deific law that supply invariably meets demand, this
Science is effectual in treating moral ailments. Sin is
not the master of divine Science, but *vice versa;* and 18
when Science in a single instance decides the conflict,
the patient is better both morally and physically.

If God made all that was made, and it was good, where 21
did evil originate?

It never originated or existed as an entity. It is but a
false belief; even the belief that God is not what the 24
Scriptures imply Him to be, All-in-all, but that there
is an opposite intelligence or mind termed evil. This
error of belief is idolatry, having "other gods before me." 27
In John i. 3 we read, "All things were made by Him;
and without Him was not anything made that was made."

1 The admission of the reality of evil perpetuates the belief
or faith in evil. The Scriptures declare, "To whom ye
3 yield yourselves servants to obey, his servants ye are."
The leading self-evident proposition of Christian Science
is: good being real, evil, good's opposite, is unreal. This
6 truism needs only to be tested scientifically to be found
true, and adapted to destroy the appearance of evil to an
extent beyond the power of any doctrine previously
9 entertained.

Do you teach that you are equal with God?

A reader of my writings would not present this ques-
12 tion. There are no such indications in the premises or
conclusions of Christian Science, and such a misconception of Truth is not scientific. Man is not equal with
15 his Maker; that which is formed is not cause, but effect,
and has no power underived from its creator. It is possible, and it is man's duty, so to throw the weight of his
18 thoughts and acts on the side of Truth, that he be ever
found in the scale *with* his creator; not weighing
equally with Him, but comprehending at every point, in
21 divine Science, the full significance of what the apostle
meant by the declaration, "The Spirit itself beareth witness with our spirit, that we are the children of God: and
24 if children, then heirs; heirs of God, and joint-heirs with
Christ." In Science, man represents his divine Principle, — the Life and Love that are God, — even as the
27 idea of sound, in tones, represents harmony; but thought
has not yet wholly attained unto the Science of being,
wherein man is perfect even as the Father, his divine
30 Principle, is perfect.

How can I believe that there is no such thing as matter, 1
when I weigh over two hundred pounds and carry about
this weight daily? 3

By learning that matter is but manifest mortal mind.
You entertain an adipose belief of yourself as substance;
whereas, substance means more than matter: it is the 6
glory and permanence of Spirit: it is that which is
hoped for but unseen, that which the material senses
cannot take in. Have you never been so preoccupied in 9
thought when moving your body, that you did this without consciousness of its weight? If never in your waking
hours, you have been in your night-dreams; and these 12
tend to elucidate your day-dream, or the mythical nature
of matter, and the possibilities of mind when let loose
from its own beliefs. In sleep, a sense of the body ac- 15
companies thought with less impediment than when
awake, which is the truer sense of being. In Science,
body is the servant of Mind, not its master: Mind is 18
supreme. Science reverses the evidence of material
sense with the spiritual sense that God, Spirit, is the only
substance; and that man, His image and likeness, is 21
spiritual, not material. This great Truth does not destroy but substantiates man's identity, — together with
his immortality and preexistence, or his spiritual co- 24
existence with his Maker. That which has a beginning
must have an ending.

What should one conclude as to Professor Carpenter's 27
exhibitions of mesmerism?

That largely depends upon what one accepts as either
useful or true. I have no knowledge of mesmerism, 30

1 practically or theoretically, save as I measure its demonstrations as a false belief, and avoid all that works ill. If
3 mesmerism has the power attributed to it by the gentleman referred to, it should neither be taught nor practised, but should be conscientiously condemned. One thing
6 is quite apparent; namely, that its so-called power is despotic, and Mr. Carpenter deserves praise for his public exposure of it. If such be its power, I am opposed to it,
9 as to every form of error, — whether of ignorance or fanaticism, prompted by money-making or malice. It is enough for me to know that animal magnetism is neither
12 of God nor Science.

It is alleged that at one of his recent lectures in Boston Mr. Carpenter made a man drunk on water, and
15 then informed his audience that he could produce the effect of alcohol, or of any drug, on the human system, through the action of mind alone. This honest declara-
18 tion as to the animus of animal magnetism and the possible purpose to which it can be devoted, has, we trust, been made in season to open the eyes of the people to the
21 hidden nature of some tragic events and sudden deaths at this period.

Was ever a person made insane by studying meta-
24 *physics?*

Such an occurrence would be impossible, for the proper study of Mind-healing would cure the insane.
27 That persons have gone away from the Massachusetts Metaphysical College "made insane by Mrs. Eddy's teachings," like a hundred other stories, is a baseless
30 fabrication offered solely to injure her or her school. The enemy is trying to make capital out of the follow-

ing case. A young lady entered the College class who, 1
I quickly saw, had a tendency to monomania, and requested her to withdraw before its close. We are cred- 3
ibly informed that, before entering the College, this
young lady had manifested some mental unsoundness,
and have no doubt she could have been restored by 6
Christian Science treatment. Her friends employed a
homœopathist, who had the skill and honor to state, as his
opinion given to her friends, that "Mrs. Eddy's teach- 9
ings had not produced insanity." This is the only case
that could be distorted into the claim of insanity ever
having occurred in a class of Mrs. Eddy's; while ac- 12
knowledged and notable cases of insanity have been
cured in her class.

If all that is mortal is a dream or error, is not 15
our capacity for formulating a dream, real; is it not
God-made; and if God-made, can it be wrong, sinful, or
an error? 18

The spirit of Truth leads into all truth, and enables
man to discern between the real and the unreal. Entertaining the common belief in the opposite of goodness, 21
and that evil is as real as good, opposes the leadings of
the divine Spirit that are helping man Godward: it prevents a recognition of the nothingness of the dream, or 24
belief, that Mind is in matter, intelligence in non-intelligence, sin, and death. This belief presupposes not
only a power opposed to God, and that God is not All- 27
in-all, as the Scriptures imply Him to be, but that the
capacity to err proceeds from God.

That God is Truth, the Scriptures aver; that Truth 30
never created error, or such a capacity, is self-evident;

1 that God made all that was made, is again Scriptural;
therefore your answer is, that error is an illusion of
3 mortals; that God is not its author, and it cannot be
real.

Does "Science and Health with Key to the Scriptures"
6 *explain the entire method of metaphysical healing, or is*
there a secret back of what is contained in that book, as
some say?

9 "Science and Health with Key to the Scriptures"
is a complete textbook of Christian Science; and its
metaphysical method of healing is as lucid in presenta-
12 tion as can be possible, under the necessity to express
the metaphysical in physical terms.   There is absolutely
no additional secret outside of its teachings, or that gives
15 one the power to heal; but it is essential that the student
gain the spiritual understanding of the contents of this
book, in order to heal.

18 *Do you believe in change of heart?*

We do believe, and understand — which is more —
that there must be a change from human affections, de-
21 sires, and aims, to the divine standard, "Be ye therefore
perfect;" also, that there must be a change from the belief that the heart is matter and sustains life, to the
24 understanding that God is our Life, that we exist in
Mind, live thereby, and have being.   This change of
heart would deliver man from heart-disease, and ad-
27 vance Christianity a hundredfold.   The human affections
need to be changed from self to benevolence and love
for God and man; changed to having but *one* God and
30 loving Him supremely, and helping our brother man.

This change of heart is essential to Christianity, and 1
will have its effect physically as well as spiritually,
healing disease. Burnt offerings and drugs, God does 3
not require.

*Is a belief of nervousness, accompanied by great mental
depression, mesmerism?* 6

All mesmerism is of one of three kinds; namely, the
ignorant, the fraudulent, or the malicious workings of
error or mortal mind. We have not the particulars of 9
the case to which you may refer, and for this reason cannot answer your question professionally.

How can I govern a child metaphysically? Doesn't the 12
use of the rod teach him life in matter?

The use of the rod is virtually a declaration to the
child's mind that sensation belongs to matter. Motives 15
govern acts, and Mind governs man. If you make clear
to the child's thought the right motives for action, and
cause him to love them, they will lead him aright: if you 18
educate him to love God, good, and obey the Golden
Rule, he will love and obey you without your having to
resort to corporeal punishment. 21

> "When from the lips of Truth one mighty breath
>   Shall, like a whirlwind, scatter in its breeze
>   The whole dark pile of human mockeries; 24
>   Then shall the reign of Mind commence on earth,
>   And starting fresh, as from a second birth,
>   Man in the sunshine of the world's new spring, 27
>   Shall walk transparent like some holy thing."

Are both prayer and drugs necessary to heal?

The apostle James said, "Ye ask, and receive not, 30
because ye ask amiss, that ye may consume it upon your

1 lusts." This text may refer to such as seek the material
to aid the spiritual, and take drugs to support God's
3 power to heal them. It is difficult to say how much
one can do for himself, whose faith is divided between catnip and Christ; but not so difficult to know
6 that if he were to serve one master, he could do vastly
more. Whosoever understands the power of Spirit, has
no doubt of God's power, — even the might of Truth, —
9 to heal, through divine Science, beyond all human means
and methods.

What do you think of marriage?

12 That it is often convenient, sometimes pleasant, and
occasionally a love affair. Marriage is susceptible of
many definitions. It sometimes presents the most
15 wretched condition of human existence. To be normal,
it must be a union of the affections that tends to lift
mortals higher.

18 *If this life is a dream not dispelled, but only changed,
by death, — if one gets tired of it, why not commit
suicide?*

21 Man's existence is a problem to be wrought in divine
Science. What progress would a student of science
make, if, when tired of mathematics or failing to dem-
24 onstrate one rule readily, he should attempt to work
out a rule farther on and more difficult — and this,
because the first rule was not easily demonstrated? In
27 that case he would be obliged to turn back and work
out the previous example, before solving the advanced
problem. Mortals have the sum of being to work out,
30 and up, to its spiritual standpoint. They must work

out of this dream or false claim of sensation and life 1
in matter, and up to the spiritual realities of existence,
before this false claim can be wholly dispelled. Com- 3
mitting suicide to dodge the question is not working
it out. The error of supposed life and intelligence in
matter, is dissolved only as we master error with Truth. 6
Not through sin or suicide, but by *overcoming* temptation and sin, shall we escape the weariness and wickedness of mortal existence, and gain heaven, the harmony 9
of being.

Do you sometimes find it advisable to use medicine to
assist in producing a cure, when it is difficult to start the 12
patient's recovery?

You only weaken your power to heal through Mind,
by any compromise with matter; which is virtually ac- 15
knowledging that under difficulties the former is not equal
to the latter. He that resorts to physics, seeks what is
below instead of above the standard of metaphysics; 18
showing his ignorance of the meaning of the term and
of Christian Science.

If Christian Science is the same as Jesus taught, why is 21
it not more simple, so that all can readily understand it?

The teachings of Jesus were simple; and yet he found
it difficult to make the rulers understand, because of 24
their great lack of spirituality. Christian Science is
simple, and readily understood by the children; only
the thought educated away from it finds it abstract or 27
difficult to perceive. Its seeming abstraction is the
mystery of godliness; and godliness is simple to the
godly; but to the unspiritual, the ungodly, it is dark 30

1 and difficult. The carnal mind cannot discern spiritual things.

3 *Has Mrs. Eddy lost her power to heal?*

Has the sun forgotten to shine, and the planets to revolve around it? Who is it that discovered, dem-
6 onstrated, and teaches Christian Science? That one, whoever it be, does understand something of what cannot be lost. Thousands in the field of metaphysical
9 healing, whose lives are worthy testimonials, are her students, and they bear witness to this fact. Instead of losing her power to heal, she is demonstrating the
12 power of Christian Science over all obstacles that envy and malice would fling in her path. The reading of her book, "Science and Health with Key to the Scriptures,"
15 is curing hundreds at this very time; and the sick, unasked, are testifying thereto.

Must I study your Science in order to keep well all my
18 *life? I was healed of a chronic trouble after one month's treatment by one of your students.*

When once you are healed by Science, there is no rea-
21 son why you should be liable to a return of the disease that you were healed of. But not to be subject again to any disease whatsoever, would require an understanding
24 of the Science by which you were healed.

Because none of your students have been able to perform as great miracles in healing as Jesus and his disciples did,
27 *does it not suggest the possibility that they do not heal on the same basis?*

You would not ask the pupil in simple equations to
30 solve a problem involving logarithms; and then, because

he failed to get the right answer, condemn the pupil 1
and the science of numbers. The simplest problem
in Christian Science is healing the sick, and the least 3
understanding and demonstration thereof prove all its
possibilities. The ability to demonstrate to the extent
that Jesus did, will come when the student possesses as 6
much of the divine Spirit as he shared, and utilizes its
power to overcome sin.

Opposite to good, is the universal claim of evil that 9
seeks the proportions of good. There may be those
who, having learned the power of the unspoken thought,
use it to harm rather than to heal, and who are using 12
that power against Christian Scientists. This giant sin
is the sin against the Holy Ghost spoken of in Matt.
xii. 31, 32. 15

*Is Christian Science based on the facts of both Spirit
and matter?*

Christian Science is based on the facts of Spirit and 18
its forms and representations, but these facts are the
direct antipodes of the so-called facts of matter; and
the eternal verities of Spirit assert themselves over their 21
opposite, or matter, in the final destruction of all that
is unlike Spirit.

Man knows that he can have one God only, when 24
he regards God as the only Mind, Life, and substance.
If God is Spirit, as the Scriptures declare, and All-in-
all, matter is mythology, and its laws are mortal 27
beliefs.

If Mind is in matter and beneath a skull bone, it is
in something unlike Him; hence it is either a godless and 30
material Mind, or it is God in matter, — which are theo-

1 ries of agnosticism and pantheism, the very antipodes
of Christian Science.

3 *What is organic life?*

   Life is inorganic, infinite Spirit; if Life, or Spirit,
were organic, disorganization would destroy Spirit and
6 annihilate man.

   If Mind is not substance, form, and tangibility, God
is substanceless; for the substance of Spirit is divine
9 Mind. Life is God, the only creator, and Life is immortal Mind, not matter.

   Every indication of matter's constituting life is mortal,
12 the direct opposite of immortal Life, and infringes the
rights of Spirit. Then, to conclude that Spirit constitutes or ever has constituted laws to that effect, is a mor-
15 tal error, a human conception opposed to the divine
government. Mind and matter mingling in perpetual
warfare is a kingdom divided against itself, that shall be
18 brought to desolation. The final destruction of this
false belief in matter will appear at the full revelation
of Spirit, — one God, and the brotherhood of man.
21 Organic life is an error of statement that Truth destroys.
The Science of Life needs only to be understood; its demonstration proves the correctness of my statements, and
24 brings blessings infinite.

   *Why did God command, "Be fruitful, and multiply,
and replenish the earth," if all minds (men) have existed
27 from the beginning, and have had successive stages of
existence to the present time?*

   Your question implies that Spirit, which first spirit-
30 ually created the universe, including man, created man

over again materially; and, by the aid of mankind, all 1
was later made which *He had made.* If the first record
is true, what evidence have you — apart from the evi- 3
dence of that which you admit cannot discern spiritual
things — of any other creation? The creative "Us"
made all, and Mind was the creator. Man originated 6
not from dust, materially, but from Spirit, spiritually.
This work had been done; the true creation was finished,
and its spiritual Science is alluded to in the first chapter 9
of Genesis.

Jesus said of error, "That thou doest, do quickly."
By the law of opposites, after the truth of man had been 12
demonstrated, the postulate of error must appear. That
this addendum was untrue, is seen when Truth, God,
denounced it, and said: "I will greatly multiply thy 15
sorrow." "In the day that thou eatest thereof thou shalt
surely die." The opposite error said, "I am true," and
declared, "God doth know . . . that your eyes shall be 18
opened, and ye shall be as gods," creators. This was false;
and the Lord God never said it. This history of a falsity
must be told in the name of Truth, or it would have no 21
seeming. The Science of creation is the universe with man
created spiritually. The false sense and error of creation
is the sense of man and the universe created materially.   24

*Why does the record make man a creation of the sixth
and last day, if he was coexistent with God?*

In its genesis, the Science of creation is stated in mathe- 27
matical order, beginning with the lowest form and ascending the scale of being up to man. But all that really is,
always was and forever is; for it existed in and of the Mind 30
that is God, wherein man is foremost.

1 *If one has died of consumption, and he has no remem-*
brance of that disease or dream, does that disease have any
3 *more power over him?*

Waking from a dream, one learns its *unreality;* then
it has no power over one. Waking from the dream of
6 death, proves to him who thought he died that it was a
dream, and that he did not die; then he learns that consumption did not kill him. When the belief in the power
9 of disease is destroyed, disease cannot return.

How does Mrs. Eddy know that she has read and studied
correctly, if one must deny the evidences of the senses?
12 *She had to use her eyes to read.*

Jesus said, "Having eyes, see ye not?" I read the inspired page through a higher than mortal sense. As
15 matter, the eye cannot see; and as mortal mind, it is a
belief that sees. I may read the Scriptures through a
belief of eyesight; but I must spiritually understand
18 them to interpret their Science.

Does the theology of Christian Science aid its heal-
ing?

21 Without its theology there is no mental science, no
order that proceeds from God. All Science is divine,
not human, in origin and demonstration. If God does
24 not govern the action of man, it is inharmonious: if He
does govern it, the action is Science. Take away the
theology of mental healing and you take away its science,
27 leaving it a human "mind-cure," nothing more nor less,
— even one human mind governing another; by which,
if you agree that God is Mind, you admit that there is

more than one government and God. Having no true 1
sense of the healing theology of Mind, you can neither
understand nor demonstrate its Science, and will prac- 3
tise your belief of it in the name of Truth. This is the
mortal "mind-cure" that produces the effect of mesmerism. It is using the power of human will, instead 6
of the divine power understood, as in Christian Science;
and without this Science there had better be no "mind-
cure," — in which the last state of patients is worse than 9
the first.

Is it wrong to pray for the recovery of the sick?

Not if we pray Scripturally, with the understanding 12
that God *has* given all things to those who love **Him**;
but pleading with infinite Love to love us, or to restore
health and harmony, and then to admit that it has been 15
lost under His government, is the prayer of doubt and
mortal belief that is unavailing in divine Science.

Is not all argument mind over mind? 18

The Scriptures refer to God as saying, "Come now, and
let us reason together." There is but one right Mind, and
that one should and does govern man. Any copartnership 21
with that Mind is impossible; and the only benefit in
speaking often one to another, arises from the success that
one individual has with another in leading his thoughts 24
away from the human mind or body, and guiding them
with Truth. That individual is the best healer who asserts himself the least, and thus becomes a transparency 27
for the divine Mind, who is the only physician; the divine
Mind is the scientific healer.

1 *How can you believe there is no sin, and that God does not recognize any, when He sent His Son to save from*
3 *sin, and the Bible is addressed to sinners? How can you believe there is no sickness, when Jesus came healing the sick?*

6 To regard sin, disease, and death with less deference, and only as the woeful unrealities of being, is the only way to destroy them; Christian Science is proving this by
9 healing cases of disease and sin after all other means have failed. The Nazarene Prophet could make the unreality of both apparent in a moment.

12 *Does it not limit the power of Mind to deny the possibility of communion with departed friends — dead only in belief?*

15 Does it limit the power of Mind to say that addition is not subtraction in mathematics? The Science of Mind reveals the impossibility of two individual sleepers, in
18 different phases of thought, communicating, even if touching each other corporeally; or for one who sleeps to communicate with another who is awake. Mind's possi-
21 bilities are not lessened by being confined and conformed to the Science of being.

If mortal mind and body are myths, what is the con-
24 *nection between them and real identity, and why are there as many identities as mortal bodies?*

Evil in the beginning claimed the power, wisdom, and
27 utility of good; and every creation or idea of Spirit has its counterfeit in some matter belief. Every material belief hints the existence of spiritual reality; and if mortals
30 are instructed in spiritual things, it will be seen that ma-

terial belief, in all its manifestations, reversed, will be 1
found the type and representative of verities priceless,
eternal, and just at hand. 3

The education of the future will be instruction, in spiritual Science, against the material symbolic counterfeit
sciences. All the knowledge and vain strivings of mortal 6
mind, that lead to death, — even when aping the wisdom
and magnitude of immortal Mind, — will be swallowed
up by the reality and omnipotence of Truth over error, 9
and of Life over death.

"Dear Mrs. Eddy: — In the October *Journal* I read
the following: 'But the real man, who was created in the 12
image of God, does not commit sin.' *What then does sin?*
What commits theft? Or who does murder? For instance,
the man is held responsible for the crime; for I went once 15
to a place where a man was said to be 'hanged for murder' — and certainly I saw him, or his effigy, dangling
at the end of a rope. This 'man' was held responsible 18
for the 'sin.'"

What sins?

According to the Word, man is the image and likeness 21
of God. Does God's essential likeness sin, or dangle at
the end of a rope? If not, what does? A culprit, a sinner,
— anything but a man! Then, what is a sinner? A 24
mortal; but man is *immortal.*

Again: mortals are the embodiments (or bodies, if
you please) of error, not of Truth; of sickness, sin, and 27
death. Naming these His embodiment, can neither make
them so nor overthrow the logic that man is God's likeness. Mortals seem very material; man in the likeness 30

1 of Spirit is spiritual. Holding the *right* idea of man in my
mind, I can improve my own, and other people's individ-
3 uality, health, and morals; whereas, the opposite image
of man, a sinner, kept constantly in mind, can no more
improve health or morals, than holding in thought the
6 form of a boa-constrictor can aid an artist in painting a
landscape.

Man is seen only in the true likeness of his Maker.
9 Believing a lie veils the truth from our vision; even as
in mathematics, in summing up positive and negative
quantities, the negative quantity offsets an equal positive
12 quantity, making the aggregate positive, or true quantity,
by that much, less available.

Why do Christian Scientists hold that their theology is
15 *essential to heal the sick, when the mind-cure claims to heal*
without it?

The theology of Christian Science is Truth; opposed
18 to which is the error of sickness, sin, and death, that
Truth destroys.

A "mind-cure" is a matter-cure. An adherent to this
21 method honestly acknowledges this fact in her work
entitled "Mind-cure on a Material Basis." In that
work the author grapples with Christian Science, attempts
24 to solve its divine Principle by the rule of human mind,
fails, and ends in a parody on this Science which is amusing to astute readers, — especially when she tells them
27 that she is practising this Science.

The theology of Christian Science is based on the action
of the divine Mind over the human mind and body;
30 whereas, "mind-cure" rests on the notion that the human
mind can cure its own disease, or that which it causes,

and the *sickness of matter,* — which is infidel in the one 1
case, and anomalous in the other. It was said of old by
Truth-traducers, that Jesus healed through Beelzebub; 3
but the claim that one erring mind cures another one was
at first gotten up to hinder his benign influence and to hide
his divine power. 6

Our Master understood that Life, Truth, Love are the
triune Principle of all pure theology; also, that this divine
trinity is one infinite remedy for the opposite triad, sick- 9
ness, sin, and death.

If there is no sin, why did Jesus come to save sinners?

If there is no reality in sickness, why does a Chris- 12
tian Scientist go to the bedside and address himself to
the healing of disease, on the basis of its unreality?
Jesus came to seek and to save such as believe in the 15
reality of the unreal; to save them from *this false belief;*
that they might lay hold of eternal Life, the great reality
that concerns man, and understand the final fact, — that 18
God is omnipotent and omnipresent; yea, "that the Lord
He is God; there is none else beside Him," as the Scriptures declare. 21

If Christ was God, why did Jesus cry out, "My God,
why hast Thou forsaken me?"

Even as the struggling heart, reaching toward a higher 24
goal, appeals to its hope and faith, Why failest thou
me? Jesus as the son of man was human: Christ as
the Son of God was divine. This divinity was reaching 27
humanity through the crucifixion of the human, — that
momentous demonstration of God, in which Spirit proved
its supremacy over matter. Jesus assumed for mortals the 30

1 weakness of flesh, that Spirit might be found "All-in-all."
Hence, the human cry which voiced that struggle;
3 thence, the way he made for mortals' escape. Our
Master bore the cross to show his power over death;
then relinquished his earth-task of teaching and dem-
6 onstrating the nothingness of sickness, sin, and death,
and rose to his native estate, man's indestructible eternal
life in God.

9 *What can prospective students of the College take for*
preliminary studies? Do you regard the study of litera-
ture and languages as objectionable?

12 Persons contemplating a course at the Massachusetts
Metaphysical College, can prepare for it through no
books except the Bible, and "Science and Health with
15 Key to the Scriptures." Man-made theories are narrow, else extravagant, and are always materialistic.
The ethics which guide thought spiritually must bene-
18 fit every one; for the only philosophy and religion that
afford instruction are those which deal with facts and
resist speculative opinions and fables.
21 Works on science are profitable; for science is not
human. It is spiritual, and not material. Literature
and languages, to a limited extent, are aids to a student
24 of the Bible and of Christian Science.

Is it possible to know why we are put into this condition
of mortality?

27 It is quite as possible to know wherefore man is thus
conditioned, as to be certain that he *is* in a state of
mortality. The only evidence of the existence of a mor-
30 tal man, or of a material state and universe, is gathered

from the five personal senses. This delusive evidence, 1
Science has dethroned by repeated proofs of its falsity.

We have no more proof of human discord, — sin, 3
sickness, disease, or death, — than we have that the
earth's surface is flat, and her motions imaginary. If
man's *ipse dixit* as to the stellar system is correct, this 6
is because Science is true, and the evidence of the senses
is false. Then why not submit to the affirmations of
Science concerning the greater subject of human weal 9
and woe? Every question between Truth and error,
Science must and will decide. Left to the decision of
Science, your query concerns a negative which the posi- 12
tive Truth destroys; for God's universe and man are
immortal. We must not consider the false side of existence in order to gain the true solution of Life and its 15
great realities.

Have you changed your instructions as to the right way
of treating disease?   18

I have not; and this important fact must be, and already is, apprehended by those who understand my instructions on this question. Christian Science demands 21
both law and gospel, in order to demonstrate healing,
and I have taught them both in its demonstration, and
with signs following. They are a unit in restoring the 24
equipoise of mind and body, and balancing man's account with his Maker. The sequence proves that strict
adherence to one is inadequate to compensate for the 27
absence of the other, since both constitute the divine law
of healing.

The Jewish religion demands that "whoso sheddeth 30
man's blood, by man shall his blood be shed." But this

1 law is not infallible in wisdom; and obedience thereto
may be found faulty, since false testimony or mistaken
3 evidence may cause the innocent to suffer for the guilty.
Hence the gospel that fulfils the law in righteousness,
the genius whereof is displayed in the surprising wisdom
6 of these words of the New Testament: "Whatsoever
a man soweth, that shall he also reap." No possible
injustice lurks in this mandate, and no human mis-
9 judgment can pervert it; for the offender alone suffers,
and always according to divine decree. This sacred,
solid precept is verified in all directions in Mind-
12 healing, and is supported in the Scripture by parallel
proof.

The law and gospel of Truth and Love teach, through
15 divine Science, that sin is identical with suffering, and
that suffering is the lighter affliction. To reach the summit of Science, whence to discern God's perfect ways
18 and means, the material sense must be controlled by
the higher spiritual sense, and Truth be enthroned,
while "we look not at the things which are seen, but at
21 the things which are not seen."

Cynical critics misjudge my meaning as to the scientific treatment of the sick. Disease that is superin-
24 duced by sin is not healed like the more physical
ailment. The beginner in sin-healing must know this, or
he never can reach the Science of Mind-healing, and
27 so "overcome evil with good." Error in premise is met
with error in practice; yea, it is "the blind leading the
blind." Ignorance of the cause of disease can neither
30 remove that cause nor its effect.

I endeavor to accommodate my instructions to the
present capability of the learner, and to support the

liberated thought until its altitude reaches beyond the 1
mere alphabet of Mind-healing. Above physical wants,
lie the higher claims of the law and gospel of healing. 3
First is the law, which saith: —

"Thou shalt not commit adultery;" in other words,
thou shalt not adulterate Life, Truth, or Love, — men- 6
tally, morally, or physically. "Thou shalt not steal;"
that is, thou shalt not rob man of money, which is but
trash, compared with his rights of mind and character. 9
"Thou shalt not kill;" that is, thou shalt not strike at the
eternal sense of Life with a malicious aim, but shalt
know that by doing thus thine own sense of Life shall be 12
forfeited. "Thou shalt not bear false witness;" that is,
thou shalt not utter a lie, either mentally or audibly, nor
cause it to be thought. Obedience to these command- 15
ments is indispensable to health, happiness, and length
of days.

The gospel of healing demonstrates the law of Love. 18
Justice uncovers sin of every sort; and mercy demands
that if you see the danger menacing others, you shall,
Deo volente, inform them thereof. Only thus is the right 21
practice of Mind-healing achieved, and the wrong practice discerned, disarmed, and destroyed.

Do you believe in translation?   24

If your question refers to language, whereby one expresses the sense of words in one language by equivalent words in another, I do. If you refer to the removal 27
of a person to heaven, without his subjection to death,
I modify my affirmative answer. I believe in this
removal being possible after all the footsteps requisite 30
have been taken up to the very throne, up to the

1 spiritual sense and fact of divine substance, intelligence,
Life, and Love. This translation is not the work of mo-
3 ments; it requires both time and eternity. It means more
than mere disappearance to the human sense; it must
include also man's changed appearance and diviner form
6 visible to those beholding him here.

*The Rev. —— said in a sermon: A true Christian
would protest against metaphysical healing being called*
9 *Christian Science. He also maintained that pain and
disease are not illusions but realities; and that it is not
Christian to believe they are illusions. Is this so?*

12   It is unchristian to believe that pain and sickness are
anything *but* illusions. My proof of this is, that the
penalty for believing in their reality is the very pain and
15 disease. Jesus cast out a devil, and the dumb spake;
hence it is right to know that the works of Satan are the
illusion and error which Truth casts out.

18   Does the gentleman above mentioned know the
meaning of divine metaphysics, or of metaphysical
theology?

21   According to Webster, metaphysics is defined thus:
"The science of the conceptions and relations which are
necessary to thought and knowledge; science of the
24 mind." Worcester defines it as "the philosophy of mind,
as distinguished from that of matter; a science of which
the object is to explain the principles and causes of
27 all things existing." Brande calls metaphysics "the
science which regards the ultimate grounds of being, as
distinguished from its phenomenal modifications." "A
30 speculative science, which soars beyond the bounds of
experience," is a further definition.

Divine metaphysics is that which treats of the exist- 1
ence of God, His essence, relations, and attributes. A
sneer at metaphysics is a scoff at Deity; at His goodness, 3
mercy, and might.

Christian Science is the unfolding of true metaphysics;
that is, of Mind, or God, and His attributes. Science rests 6
on Principle and demonstration. The Principle of Christian Science is divine. Its rule is, that man shall utilize
the divine power. 9

In Genesis i. 26, we read: "Let us make man in
our image, after our likeness: and let them have
dominion over the fish of the sea, and over the fowl of 12
the air."

I was once called to visit a sick man to whom the
regular physicians had given three doses of Croton 15
oil, and then had left him to die. Upon my arrival I
found him barely alive, and in terrible agony. In one
hour he was well, and the next day he attended to his 18
business. I removed the stoppage, healed him of enteritis, and neutralized the bad effects of the poisonous oil. His physicians had failed even to move his 21
bowels, — though the wonder was, with the means
used in their effort to accomplish this result, that
they had not quite killed him. According to their 24
diagnosis, the exciting cause of the inflammation and
stoppage was — eating smoked herring. The man is
living yet; and I will send his address to any one 27
who may wish to apply to him for information about
his case.

Now comes the question: Had that sick man dominion 30
over the fish in his stomach?

His want of control over "the fish of the sea" must

1 have been an illusion, or else the Scriptures misstate
man's power. That the Bible is true I believe, not
3 only, but I *demonstrated* its truth when I exercised
my power over the fish, cast out the sick man's illusion, and healed him. Thus it was shown that the
6 healing action of Mind upon the body has its only explanation in divine metaphysics. As a man "thinketh
in his heart, so is he." When the mortal thought, or be-
9 lief, was removed, the man was well.

*What did Jesus mean when he said to the dying thief,
"To-day shalt thou be with me in paradise"?*

12　Paradisaical rest from physical agony would come to
the criminal, if the dream of dying should startle him
from the dream of suffering. The paradise of Spirit
15 would come to Jesus, in a spiritual sense of Life and
power. Christ Jesus lived and reappeared. He was too
good to die; for goodness is immortal. The thief was
18 not equal to the demands of the hour; but sin was destroying itself, and had already begun to die, — as
the poor thief's prayer for help indicated. The dy-
21 ing malefactor and our Lord were inevitably separated through Mind. The thief's body, as matter,
must dissolve into its native nothingness; whereas the
24 body of the holy Spirit of Jesus was eternal. That
day the thief would be with Jesus only in a finite
and material sense of relief; while our Lord would
27 soon be rising to the supremacy of Spirit, working
out, even in the silent tomb, those wonderful demonstrations of divine power, in which none could equal his
30 glory.

Is it right for me to treat others, when I am not entirely 1
well myself?

The late John B. Gough is said to have suffered from 3
an appetite for alcoholic drink until his death; yet he
saved many a drunkard from this fatal appetite. Paul
had a thorn in the flesh: one writer thinks that he was 6
troubled with rheumatism, and another that he had sore
eyes; but this is certain, that he healed others who were
sick. It is unquestionably right to do right; and heal- 9
ing the sick is a very right thing to do.

Does Christian Science set aside the law of transmission,
prenatal desires, and good or bad influences on the unborn 12
child?

Science never averts law, but supports it. All actual
causation must interpret omnipotence, the all-knowing 15
Mind. Law brings out Truth, not error; unfolds divine
Principle, — but neither human hypothesis nor matter.
Errors are based on a mortal or material formation; they 18
are suppositional modes, not the factors of divine presence
and power.

Whatever is humanly conceived is a departure from 21
divine law; hence its mythical origin and certain end.
According to the Scriptures, — St. Paul declares astutely,
"For of Him, and through Him, and to Him, are all 24
things," — man is incapable of originating: nothing can
be formed apart from God, good, the all-knowing Mind.
What seems to be of human origin is the counterfeit 27
of the divine, — even human concepts, mortal shadows
flitting across the dial of time.

Whatever is real is right and eternal; hence the im- 30
mutable and just law of Science, that God is good only,

1 and can transmit to man and the universe nothing evil,
or unlike Himself. For the innocent babe to be born a
3 lifelong sufferer because of his parents' mistakes or sins,
were sore injustice. Science sets aside man as a creator,
and unfolds the eternal harmonies of the only living and
6 true origin, God.

According to the beliefs of the flesh, both good and
bad traits of the parents are transmitted to their help-
9 less offspring, and God is supposed to impart to man
this fatal power. It is cause for rejoicing that this belief
is as false as it is remorseless. The immutable Word
12 saith, through the prophet Ezekiel, "What mean ye, that
ye use this proverb concerning the land of Israel, saying,
The fathers have eaten sour grapes, and the children's
15 teeth are set on edge? As I live, saith the Lord God,
ye shall not have occasion any more to use this proverb
in Israel."

18 *Are material things real when they are harmonious, and
do they disappear only to the natural sense? Does this
Scripture, "Your heavenly Father knoweth that ye have
21 need of all these things," imply that Spirit takes note of
matter?*

The Science of Mind, as well as the material uni-
24 verse, shows that nothing which is material is in
perpetual harmony. Matter is manifest mortal mind,
and it exists only to material sense. Real sensation
27 is not material; it is, and must be, mental: and Mind
is not mortal, it is immortal. Being is God, infinite
Spirit; therefore it cannot cognize aught material, or
30 outside of infinity.

The Scriptural passage quoted affords no evidence of

the reality of matter, or that God is conscious of it. 1
The so-called material body is said to suffer, but this
supposition is proven erroneous when Mind casts out 3
the suffering. The Scripture saith, "Whom the Lord
loveth He chasteneth;" and again, "He doth not
afflict willingly." Interpreted materially, these pas- 6
sages conflict; they mingle the testimony of immortal Science with mortal sense; but once discern their
spiritual meaning, and it separates the false sense from 9
the true, and establishes the reality of what is spiritual,
and the unreality of materiality.

Law is never material: it is always mental and moral, 12
and a commandment to the wise. The foolish disobey
moral law, and are punished. Human wisdom therefore
can get no farther than to say, He knoweth that we have 15
need of experience. Belief fulfils the conditions of a belief, and these conditions destroy the belief. Hence the
verdict of experience: We have need of *these* things; we 18
have need to know that the so-called pleasures and pains
of matter — yea, that all subjective states of false sensation — are *unreal.* 21

"And Jesus said unto them, Verily I say unto you,
That ye which have followed me, in the regeneration when
the Son of man shall sit in the throne of his glory, 24
ye also shall sit upon twelve thrones, judging the
twelve tribes of Israel." (Matt. xix. 28.) *What is meant*
by regeneration? 27

It is the appearing of divine law to human understanding; the spiritualization that comes from spiritual
sense in contradistinction to the testimony of the so- 30
called material senses. The phenomena of Spirit in

1 Christian Science, and the divine correspondence of
noumenon and phenomenon understood, are here signi-
3 fied. This new-born sense subdues not only the false
sense of generation, but the human will, and the unnatural enmity of mortal man toward God. It quickly
6 imparts a new apprehension of the true basis of being,
and the spiritual foundation for the affections which enthrone the Son of man in the glory of his Father; and
9 judges, through the stern mandate of Science, all human
systems of etiology and teleology.

If God does not recognize matter, how did Jesus, who was
12 *"the way, the truth, and the life," cognize it?*

Christ Jesus' sense of matter was the opposite of that
which mortals entertain: his nativity was a spiritual and
15 immortal sense of the ideal world. His earthly mission
was to translate substance into its original meaning,
Mind. He walked upon the waves; he turned the water
18 into wine; he healed the sick and the sinner; he raised
the dead, and rolled away the stone from the door of his
own tomb. His demonstration of Spirit virtually van-
21 quished matter and its supposed laws. Walking the
wave, he proved the fallacy of the theory that matter is
substance; healing through Mind, he removed any sup-
24 position that matter is intelligent, or can recognize or
express pain and pleasure. His triumph over the grave
was an everlasting victory for Life; it demonstrated the
27 lifelessness of matter, and the power and permanence
of Spirit. He met and conquered the resistance of the
world.
30   If you will admit, with me, that matter is neither
substance, intelligence, nor Life, you may have all that

is left of it; and you will have touched the hem of the 1
garment of Jesus' idea of matter. Christ was "the way;"
since Life and Truth were the way that gave us, through 3
a human person, a spiritual revelation of man's possible
earthly development.

Why do you insist that there is but one Soul, and that 6
Soul is not in the body?

First: I urge this fundamental fact and grand verity
of Christian Science, because it includes a rule that must 9
be understood, or it is impossible to demonstrate the Science. Soul is a synonym of Spirit, and God is Spirit.
There is but one God, and the infinite is not within the 12
finite; hence Soul is one, and is God; and God is not in
matter or the mortal body.

Second: Because Soul is a term for Deity, and this 15
term should seldom be employed except where the word
God can be used and make complete sense. The word
Soul may sometimes be used metaphorically; but if this 18
term is warped to signify human quality, a substitution
of *sense* for *soul* clears the meaning, and assists one to
understand Christian Science. Mary's exclamation, 21
"My *soul* doth magnify the Lord," is rendered in Science, "My *spiritual sense* doth magnify the Lord;"
for the name of Deity used in that place does not bring 24
out the meaning of the passage. It was evidently an
illuminated sense through which she discovered the
spiritual origin of man. "The soul that sinneth, it shall 27
die," means, that mortal man (*alias* material sense) that
sinneth, shall die; and the commonly accepted view is
that *soul* is deathless. Soul is the divine Mind, — for 30
Soul cannot be formed or brought forth by human

1 thought, — and must proceed from God; hence it must
be sinless, and destitute of self-created or derived capacity
3 to sin.

Third: Jesus said, "If a man keep my saying, he
shall never see death." This statement of our Master
6 is true, and remains to be demonstrated; for it is the
ultimatum of Christian Science; but this immortal saying
can never be tested or proven true upon a false premise,
9 such as the mortal belief that soul is in body, and life
and intelligence are in matter. That doctrine is not
theism, but pantheism. According to human belief the
12 bodies of mortals are mortal, but they contain immortal
souls! hence these bodies must die for these souls to
escape and be immortal. The theory that death must
15 occur, to set a human soul free from its environments,
is rendered void by Jesus' divine declaration, who spake
as never man spake, — and no man can rationally reject
18 his authority on this subject and accept it on other topics
less important.

Now, exchange the term *soul* for *sense* whenever this
21 word means the so-called soul in the body, and you will
find the right meaning indicated. The misnamed human
soul is material sense, which sinneth and shall die; for
24 it is an error or false sense of mentality in matter, and
matter has no sense. You will admit that Soul is the
Life of man. Now if Soul sinned, it would die; for "the
27 wages of sin is death." The Scripture saith, "When
Christ, who is our life, shall appear, then shall ye also
appear with him in glory." The Science of Soul, Spirit,
30 involves this appearing, and is essential to the fulfilment
of this glorious prophecy of the master Metaphysician,
who overcame the last enemy, death.

Did the salvation of the eunuch depend merely on his 1
believing that Jesus Christ was the Son of God?

It did; but this believing was more than faith in the 3
fact that Jesus was the Messiah. Here the verb *believe*
took its original meaning, namely, to be *firm*, — yea, to
understand those great truths asserted of the Messiah: 6
it meant to discern and consent to that infinite demand
made upon the eunuch in those few words of the apostle.
Philip's requirement was, that he should not only ac- 9
knowledge the incarnation, — God made manifest through
man, — but even the eternal unity of man and God, as
the divine Principle and spiritual idea; which is the in- 12
dissoluble bond of union, the power and presence, in
divine Science, of Life, Truth, and Love, to support their
ideal man. This is the Father's great Love that He 15
hath bestowed upon us, and it holds man in endless
Life and one eternal round of harmonious being. It
guides him by Truth that knows no error, and with 18
supersensual, impartial, and unquenchable Love. To
believe is to *be firm*. In adopting all this vast idea of
Christ Jesus, the eunuch was to *know* in whom he be- 21
lieved. To *believe* thus was to enter the spiritual sanctuary
of Truth, and there learn, in divine Science, somewhat
of the All-Father-Mother God. It was to understand 24
God and man: it was sternly to rebuke the mortal
belief that man has fallen away from his first estate; that
man, made in God's own likeness, and reflecting Truth, 27
could fall into mortal error; or, that man is the father
of man. It was to enter unshod the Holy of Holies, where
the miracle of grace appears, and where the miracles of 30
Jesus had their birth, — healing the sick, casting out
evils, and resurrecting the human *sense* to the belief

1 that Life, God, is not buried in matter. This is the spiritual dawn of the Messiah, and the overture of the
3 angels. This is when God is made manifest in the
flesh, and thus it destroys all sense of sin, sickness, and
death, — when the brightness of His glory encompasseth
6 all being.

*Can Christian Science Mind-healing be taught to those
who are absent?*

9   The Science of Mind-healing can no more be taught
thus, than can science in any other direction. I know
not how to teach either Euclid or the Science of Mind
12 silently; and never dreamed that either of these partook
of the nature of occultism, magic, alchemy, or necromancy. These "ways that are vain" are the inventions
15 of animal magnetism, which would deceive, if possible,
the very elect. We will charitably hope, however, that
some people employ the *et cetera* of ignorance and self-
18 conceit unconsciously, in their witless ventilation of false
statements and claims. Misguiding the public mind and
taking its money in exchange for this abuse, has become
21 too common: we will hope it is the froth of error passing
off; and that Christian Science will some time appear all
the clearer for the purification of the public thought con-
24 cerning it.

Has man fallen from a state of perfection?

If God is the Principle of man (and He is), man is the
27 idea of God; and this idea cannot fail to express the exact nature of its Principle, — any more than goodness,
to present the quality of good. Human hypotheses are
30 always human vagaries, formulated views antagonistic

to the divine order and the nature of Deity. All these 1
mortal beliefs will be purged and dissolved in the crucible of Truth, and the places once knowing them will 3
know them no more forever, having been swept clean
by the winds of history. The grand verities of Science
will sift the chaff from the wheat, until it is clear to hu- 6
man comprehension that man was, and is, God's perfect
likeness, that reflects all whereby we can know God. In
Him we live, move, and have being. Man's origin and 9
existence being in Him, man is the ultimatum of perfection, and by no means the medium of imperfection.
Immortal man is the eternal idea of Truth, that cannot 12
lapse into a mortal belief or error concerning himself
and his origin: he cannot get out of the focal distance of
infinity. If God is upright and eternal, man as His like- 15
ness is erect in goodness and perpetual in Life, Truth,
and Love. If the great cause is perfect, its effect is perfect also; and cause and effect in Science are immutable 18
and immortal. A mortal who is sinning, sick, and dying,
is not immortal man; and never was, and never can be,
God's image and likeness, the true ideal of immortal 21
man's divine Principle. The spiritual man is that perfect and unfallen likeness, coexistent and coeternal with
God. "As in Adam all die, even so in Christ shall all be 24
made alive."

*What course should Christian Scientists take in regard
to aiding persons brought before the courts for violation of* 27
medical statutes?

Beware of joining any medical league which in any
way obligates you to assist — because they chance to be 30
under arrest — vendors of patent pills, mesmerists,

1 occultists, sellers of impure literature, and authors of
spurious works on mental healing. By rendering error
3 such a service, you lose much more than can be gained
by mere unity on the single issue of opposition to unjust
medical laws.

6   A league which obligates its members to give money
and influence in support and defense of medical charlatans in general, and possibly to aid individual rights
9 in a wrong direction — which Christian Science eschews
— should be avoided. Anybody and everybody, who
will fight the medical faculty, can join this league. It is
12 better to be friendly with cultured and conscientious
medical men, who leave Christian Science to rise or fall
on its own merit or demerit, than to affiliate with a wrong
15 class of people.

Unconstitutional and unjust coercive legislation and
laws, infringing individual rights, must be "of few days,
18 and full of trouble." The *vox populi,* through the providence of God, promotes and impels all true reform; and,
at the best time, will redress wrongs and rectify injus-
21 tice. Tyranny can thrive but feebly under our Government. God reigns, and will "turn and overturn" until
right is found supreme.

24   In a certain sense, we should commiserate the lot of
regular doctors, who, in successive generations for centuries, have planted and sown and reaped in the fields
27 of what they deem pathology, hygiene, and therapeutics,
but are now elbowed by a new school of practitioners,
outdoing the healing of the old. The old will not patronize
30 the new school, at least not until it shall come to understand the medical system of the new.

Christian Science Mind-healing rests demonstrably on

the broad and sure foundation of Science; and this is 1
not the basis of *materia medica,* as some of the most skilful and scholarly physicians openly admit. 3

To prevent all unpleasant and unchristian action — as
we drift, by right of God's dear love, into more spiritual
lines of life — let each society of practitioners, the matter- 6
physicians and the metaphysicians, agree to disagree, and
then patiently wait on God to decide, as surely He will,
which is the true system of medicine. 9

Do we not see in the commonly accepted teachings of the
day, the Christ-idea mingled with the teachings of John
the Baptist? or, rather, Are not the last eighteen centuries 12
but the footsteps of Truth being baptized of John, and com-
ing up straightway out of the ceremonial (or ritualistic)
waters to receive the benediction of an honored Father, and 15
afterwards to go up into the wilderness, in order to over-
come mortal sense, before it shall go forth into all the cities
and towns of Judea, or see many of the people from beyond 18
Jordan? Now, if all this be a fair or correct view of this
question, why does not John hear this voice, or see the
dove, — or has not Truth yet reached the shore? 21

Every individual character, like the individual John
the Baptist, at some date must cry in the desert of
earthly joy; and his voice be heard divinely and 24
humanly. In the desolation of human understanding,
divine Love hears and answers the human call for help;
and the voice of Truth utters the divine verities of being 27
which deliver mortals out of the depths of ignorance
and vice. This *is* the Father's benediction. It gives
lessons to human life, guides the understanding, peoples 30

the mind with spiritual ideas, reconstructs the Judean religion, and reveals God and man as the Principle and idea of all good.

Understanding this fact in Christian Science, brings the peace symbolized by a dove; and this peace floweth as a river into a shoreless eternity. He who knew the foretelling Truth, beheld the forthcoming Truth, as it came up out of the baptism of Spirit, to enlighten and redeem mortals. Such Christians as John cognize the symbols of God, reach the sure foundations of time, stand upon the shore of eternity, and grasp and gather — in all glory — what eye hath not seen.

Is there infinite progression with man after the destruction of mortal mind?

Man is the offspring and idea of the Supreme Being, whose law is perfect and infinite. In obedience to this law, man is forever unfolding the endless beatitudes of Being; for he is the image and likeness of infinite Life, Truth, and Love.

Infinite progression is concrete being, which finite mortals see and comprehend only as abstract glory. As mortal mind, or the material sense of life, is put off, the spiritual sense and Science of being is brought to light.

Mortal mind is a myth; the one Mind is immortal. A mythical or mortal sense of existence is consumed as a moth, in the treacherous glare of its own flame — the errors which devour it. Immortal Mind is God, immortal good; in whom the Scripture saith "we live, and move, and have our being." This Mind, then, is not subject to growth, change, or diminution, but is the divine

intelligence, or Principle, of all real being; holding 1
man forever in the rhythmic round of unfolding bliss,
as a living witness to and perpetual idea of inexhaustible 3
good.

In your book, Science and Health,[1] *page* 181, *you
say:* *"Every sin is the author of itself, and every* 6
invalid the cause of his own sufferings." *On page*
182 *you say:* *"Sickness is a growth of illusion, springing from a seed of thought, — either your own thought* 9
or another's." *Will you please explain this seeming
contradiction?*

No person can accept another's belief, except it be 12
with the consent of his own belief. If the error which
knocks at the door of your own thought originated in
another's mind, you are a free moral agent to reject or 15
to accept this error; hence, you are the arbiter of your
own fate, and sin is the author of sin. In the words
of our Master, you are "a liar, and the father of it 18
[the lie]."

Why did Jesus call himself "the Son of man"?

In the life of our Lord, meekness was as conspicuous 21
as might. In John xvii. he declared his sonship with
God: "These words spake Jesus, and lifted up his
eyes to heaven, and said, Father, the hour is come; 24
glorify Thy Son, that Thy Son also may glorify Thee."
The hour had come for the avowal of this great truth,
and for the proof of his eternal Life and sonship. Jesus' 27

---

[1] Quoted from the sixteenth edition.

1 wisdom ofttimes was shown by his forbearing to speak, as well as by speaking, the whole truth. Haply he waited 3 for a preparation of the human heart to receive startling announcements. This wisdom, which characterized his sayings, did not prophesy his death, and thereby 6 hasten or permit it.

The disciples and prophets thrust disputed points on minds unprepared for them. This cost them their lives, 9 and the world's temporary esteem; but the prophecies were fulfilled, and their motives were rewarded by growth and more spiritual understanding, which dawns 12 by degrees on mortals. The spiritual Christ was infallible; Jesus, as material manhood, was not Christ. The "man of sorrows" knew that the man of joys, his spiritual 15 self, or Christ, was the Son of God; and that the mortal mind, not the immortal Mind, suffered. The human manifestation of the Son of God was called the Son of 18 man, or Mary's son.

Please explain Paul's meaning in the text, "For to me to live is Christ, and to die is gain."

21   The Science of Life, overshadowing Paul's sense of life in matter, so far extinguished the latter as forever to quench his love for it. The discipline of the flesh is 24 designed to turn one, like a weary traveller, to the home of Love. To lose error thus, is to live in Christ, Truth. A true sense of the falsity of material joys and sorrows, 27 pleasures and pains, takes them away, and teaches Life's lessons aright. The transition from our lower sense of Life to a new and higher sense thereof, even though it be 30 through the door named death, yields a clearer and nearer sense of Life to those who have utilized the present,

and are ripe for the harvest-home. To the battle- 1
worn and weary Christian hero, Life eternal brings
blessings. 3

*Is a Christian Scientist ever sick, and has he who is
sick been regenerated?*

The Christian Scientist learns spiritually all that he 6
knows of Life, and demonstrates what he understands.
God is recognized as the divine Principle of his being,
and of every thought and act leading to good. His pur- 9
pose must be right, though his power is temporarily limited. Perfection, the goal of existence, is not won in a
moment; and regeneration leading thereto is gradual, 12
for it culminates in the fulfilment of this divine rule in
Science: "Be ye therefore perfect, even as your Father
which is in heaven is perfect." 15

The last degree of regeneration rises into the rest of
perpetual, spiritual, individual existence. The first
feeble flutterings of mortals Christward are infantile 18
and more or less imperfect. The new-born Christian
Scientist must mature, and work out his own salvation.
Spirit and flesh antagonize. Temptation, that mist of 21
mortal mind which seems to be matter and the environment of mortals, suggests pleasure and pain in matter;
and, so long as this temptation lasts, the warfare is not 24
ended and the mortal is not regenerated. The pleasures — more than the pains — of sense, retard regeneration; for pain compels human consciousness to escape 27
from sense into the immortality and harmony of Soul.
Disease in error, more than ease in it, tends to destroy
error: the sick often are thereby led to Christ, Truth, 30
and to learn their way out of both sickness and sin.

1 The material and physical are imperfect. The individual and spiritual are perfect; these have no fleshly
3 nature. This final degree of regeneration is saving, and the Christian will, must, attain it; but it doth not yet appear. Until this be attained, the Christian Scientist
6 must continue to strive with sickness, sin, and death — though in lessening degrees — and manifest growth at every experience.

9 *Is it correct to say of material objects, that they are nothing and exist only in imagination?*

Nothing and *something* are words which need correct
12 definition. They either mean formations of indefinite and vague human opinions, or scientific classifications of the unreal and the real. My sense of the beauty of
15 the universe is, that beauty typifies holiness, and is something to be desired. Earth is more spiritually beautiful to my gaze now than when it was more earthly to the
18 eyes of Eve. The pleasant sensations of human belief, of form and color, must be spiritualized, until we gain the glorified sense of substance as in the new heaven and
21 earth, the harmony of body and Mind.

Even the human conception of beauty, grandeur, and utility is something that defies a sneer. It is more than
24 imagination. It is next to divine beauty and the grandeur of Spirit. It lives with our earth-life, and is the subjective state of high thoughts. The atmos-
27 phere of mortal mind constitutes our mortal environment. What mortals hear, see, feel, taste, smell, constitutes their present earth and heaven: but we must
30 grow out of even this pleasing thraldom, and find wings to reach the glory of supersensible Life; then we shall

soar above, as the bird in the clear ether of the blue tem- 1
poral sky.

To take all earth's beauty into one gulp of vacuity 3
and label beauty nothing, is ignorantly to caricature
God's creation, which is unjust to human sense and
to the divine realism. In our immature sense of spirit- 6
ual things, let us say of the beauties of the sensuous
universe: "I love your promise; and shall know, some
time, the spiritual reality and substance of form, light, 9
and color, of what I now through you discern dimly; and
knowing this, I shall be satisfied. Matter is a frail conception of mortal mind; and mortal mind is a poorer 12
representative of the beauty, grandeur, and glory of the
immortal Mind."

Please inform us, through your Journal, if you sent 15
*Mrs. —— to ——. She said that you sent her there to look
after the students; and also, that no one there was working
in Science, — which is certainly a mistake.* 18

I never commission any one to teach students of mine.
After class teaching, he does best in the investigation of
Christian Science who is most reliant on himself and 21
God. My students are taught the divine Principle and
rules of the Science of Mind-healing. What they need
thereafter is to study thoroughly the Scriptures and 24
"Science and Health with Key to the Scriptures." To
watch and pray, to be honest, earnest, loving, and truthful, is indispensable to the demonstration of the truth 27
they have been taught.

If they are haunted by obsequious helpers, who, un-
called for, imagine they can help anybody and steady 30
God's altar — this interference prolongs the struggle

1 and tends to blight the fruits of my students. A faithful student may even sometimes feel the need of
3 physical help, and occasionally receive it from others;
but the less this is required, the better it is for that
student.

6 *Please give us, through your Journal, the name of
the author of that genuine critique in the September
number, "What Quibus Thinks."*

9 I am pleased to inform this inquirer, that the author
of the article in question is a Boston gentleman whose
thought is appreciated by many liberals. Patience, ob-
12 servation, intellectual culture, reading, writing, extensive travel, and twenty years in the pulpit, have equipped
him as a critic who knows whereof he speaks. His allu-
15 sion to Christian Science in the following paragraph,
glows in the shadow of darkling criticism like a midnight sun. Its manly honesty follows like a benediction
18 after prayer, and closes the task of talking to deaf ears
and dull debaters.

"We have always insisted that this Science is natural,
21 spiritually natural; that Jesus was the highest type of
real nature; that Christian healing is supernatural, or
extra-natural, only to those who do not enter into its
24 sublimity or understand its modes — as imported ice
was miraculous to the equatorial African, who had never
seen water freeze."

27 *Is it right for a Scientist to treat with a doctor?*

This depends upon what kind of a doctor it is. Mind-
healing, and healing with drugs, are opposite modes of
30 medicine. As a rule, drop one of these doctors when you

employ the other. The Scripture saith, "No man can 1
serve two masters;" and, "Every kingdom divided
against itself is brought to desolation." 3

*If Scientists are called upon to care for a member of
the family, or a friend in sickness, who is employing a
regular physician, would it be right to treat this patient 6
at all; and ought the patient to follow the doctor's
directions?*

When patients are under material medical treatment, 9
it is advisable in most cases that Scientists do not treat
them, or interfere with *materia medica*. If the patient
is in peril, and you save him or alleviate his sufferings, 12
although the medical attendant and friends have no
faith in your method, it is humane, and not unchristian,
to do him all the good you can; but your good will gen- 15
erally "be evil spoken of." The hazard of casting "pearls
before swine" caused our Master to refuse help to some
who sought his aid; and he left this precaution for 18
others.

*If mortal man is unreal, how can he be saved, and why
does he need to be saved? I ask for information, not for 21
controversy, for I am a seeker after Truth.*

You will find the proper answer to this question in
my published works. Man is immortal. Mortal man 24
is a false concept that is not spared or prolonged by being
saved from itself, from whatever is false. This salvation means: saved from error, or error overcome. Im- 27
mortal man, in God's likeness, is safe in divine Science.
Mortal man is saved on this divine Principle, if he will
only avail himself of the efficacy of Truth, and recog- 30

1 nize his Saviour. He must know that God is omnipotent; hence, that sin is impotent. He must know that
3 the power of sin is the pleasure in sin. Take away this
pleasure, and you remove all reality from its power. Jesus
demonstrated sin and death to be powerless. This
6 practical Truth saves from sin, and will save all who
understand it.

Is it wrong for a wife to have a husband treated for
9 *sin, when she knows he is sinning, or for drinking and
smoking?*

It is always right to act rightly; but sometimes, under
12 circumstances exceptional, it is inexpedient to attack
evil. This rule is forever golden: "As ye would that
men should do to you, do ye even so to them." Do you
15 desire to be freed from sin? Then help others to be free;
but in your measures, obey the Scriptures, "Be ye wise
as serpents." Break the yoke of bondage in every wise
18 way. First, be sure that your means for doing good
are equal to your motives; then judge them by their
fruits.

21 *If not ordained, shall the pastor of the Church of
Christ, Scientist, administer the communion, — and
shall members of a church not organized receive the*
24 *communion?*

Our great Master administered to his disciples the
Passover, or last supper, without this prerogative being
27 conferred by a visible organization and ordained priesthood. His spiritually prepared breakfast, after his
resurrection, and after his disciples had left their nets
30 to follow him, is the spiritual communion which Chris-

tian Scientists celebrate in commemoration of the Christ. 1
This ordinance is significant as a type of the true worship,
and it should be observed at present in our churches. 3

It is not indispensable to organize materially Christ's
church. It is not absolutely necessary to ordain pastors and to dedicate churches; but if this be done, 6
let it be in concession to the period, and not as a perpetual or indispensable ceremonial of the church. If
our church is organized, it is to meet the demand, 9
"Suffer it to be so now." The real Christian compact
is love for one another. This bond is wholly spiritual
and inviolate. 12

It is imperative, at all times and under every circumstance, to perpetuate no ceremonials except as
types of these mental conditions, — remembrance and 15
love; a real affection for Jesus' character and example.
Be it remembered, that all types employed in the service of Christian Science should represent the most spir- 18
itual forms of thought and worship that can be made
visible.

Should not the teacher of Christian Science have our 21
textbook, "Science and Health with Key to the Scriptures,"
in his schoolroom and teach from it?

I never dreamed, until informed thereof, that a loyal 24
student did not take his textbook with him into the class-
room, ask questions from it, answer them according to
it, and, as occasion required, read from the book as au- 27
thority for what he taught. I supposed that students
had followed my example, and that of other teachers,
sufficiently to do this, and also to require their pupils to 30
study the lessons before recitations.

1 To omit these important points is anomalous, considering the necessity for understanding Science, and
3 the present liability of deviating from Christian Science.
Centuries will intervene before the statement of the inexhaustible topics of that book become sufficiently under-
6 stood to be absolutely demonstrated. The teacher of
Christian Science needs continually to study this textbook.
His work is to replenish thought, and to spiritualize human
9 life, from this open fount of Truth and Love.

He who sees most clearly and enlightens other minds
most readily, keeps his own lamp trimmed and burning.
12 He will take the textbook of Christian Science into his
class, repeat the questions in the chapter on Recapitulation, and his students will answer them from the same
15 source. Throughout his entire explanations, the teacher
should strictly adhere to the questions and answers contained in that chapter of "Science and Health with Key
18 to the Scriptures." It is important to point out the
lesson to the class, and to require the students thoroughly to study it before the recitations; for this spirit-
21 ualizes their thoughts. When closing his class, the
teacher should require each member to own a copy of
the above-named book and to continue the study of this
24 textbook.

The opinions of men cannot be substituted for God's
revelation. It must not be forgotten that in times past,
27 arrogant ignorance and pride, in attempting to steady
the ark of Truth, have dimmed the power and glory of
the Scriptures, to which this Christian Science textbook
30 is the Key.

That teacher does most for his students who most
divests himself of pride and self, spiritualizes his own

thought, and by reason thereof is able to empty his stu- 1
dents' minds, that they may be filled with Truth.

Beloved students, *so* teach that posterity shall call 3
you blessed, and the heart of history shall be made
glad!

Can fear or sin bring back old beliefs of disease that have 6
been healed by Christian Science?

The Scriptures plainly declare the allness and oneness
of God to be the premises of Truth, and that God is 9
good: in Him dwelleth no evil. Christian Science authorizes the logical conclusion drawn from the Scriptures,
that there is in reality none besides the eternal, infinite 12
God, good. Evil is temporal: it is the illusion of time
and mortality.

This being true, sin has no power; and fear, its coeval, 15
is without divine authority. Science sanctions only what
is supported by the unerring Principle of being. Sin can
do nothing: all cause and effect are in God. Fear is a 18
belief of sensation in matter: this belief is neither maintained by Science nor supported by facts, and exists only
as fable. Your answer is, that neither fear nor sin can 21
bring on disease or bring back disease, since there is in
reality no disease.

Bear in mind, however, that human consciousness does 24
not test sin and the fact of its nothingness, by believing
that sin is pardoned without repentance and reformation. Sin punishes itself, because it cannot go unpun- 27
ished either here or hereafter. Nothing is more fatal than
to indulge a sinning sense or consciousness for even one
moment. Knowing this, obey Christ's Sermon on the 30
Mount, even if you suffer for it in the first instance, —

1 are misjudged and maligned; in the second, you will reign with him.

3   I never knew a person who knowingly indulged evil, to be grateful; to understand me, or himself. He must first see himself and the hallucination of sin; then he 6 must repent, and love good in order to understand God. The sinner and the sin are the twain that are one flesh, — but which God hath not joined together.

CHAPTER IV

Addresses

CHRISTIAN SCIENCE IN TREMONT TEMPLE   1

FROM the platform of the Monday lectureship in
Tremont Temple, on Monday, March 16, 1885, as 3
will be seen by what follows, Reverend Mary Baker G.
Eddy was presented to Mr. Cook's audience, and allowed
ten minutes in which to reply to his public letter con- 6
demning her doctrines; which reply was taken in full by
a shorthand reporter who was present, and is transcribed
below.   9

Mrs. Eddy responding, said: —

As the time so kindly allotted me is insufficient for
even a synopsis of Christian Science, I shall confine my- 12
self to questions and answers.

Am I a spiritualist?

I am not, and never was. I understand the impossi- 15
bility of intercommunion between the so-called dead and
living. There have always attended my life phenomena
of an uncommon order, which spiritualists have mis- 18
called mediumship; but I clearly understand that no
human agencies were employed, — that the divine Mind
reveals itself to humanity through spiritual law. And 21
to such as are "waiting for the adoption, to wit, the redemption of our body," Christian Science reveals the in-

95

1 finitude of divinity and the way of man's salvation from
sickness and death, as wrought out by Jesus, who robbed
3 the grave of victory and death of its sting. I understand
that God is an ever-present help in all times of trouble, —
have found Him so; and would have no other gods, no
6 remedies in drugs, no material medicine.

Do I believe in a personal God?

I believe in God as the Supreme Being. I know not
9 what the person of omnipotence and omnipresence is,
or what the infinite includes; therefore, I worship that
of which I can conceive, first, as a loving Father and
12 Mother; then, as thought ascends the scale of being to
diviner consciousness, God becomes to me, as to the
apostle who declared it, "God is Love," — divine Prin-
15 ciple, — which I worship; and "after the manner of my
fathers, so worship I God."

Do I believe in the atonement of Christ?

18 I do; and this atonement becomes more to me since
it includes man's redemption from sickness as well as
from sin. I reverence and adore Christ as never before.

21 It brings to my sense, and to the sense of all who entertain this understanding of the Science of God, a *whole*
salvation.

24 How is the healing done in Christian Science?

This answer includes too much to give you any conclusive idea in a brief explanation. I can name some
27 means by which it is not done.

It is not one mind acting upon another mind; it is
not the transference of human images of thought to
30 other minds; it is not supported by the evidence before
the personal senses, — Science contradicts this evidence;
it is not of the flesh, but of the Spirit. It is Christ come

to destroy the power of the flesh; it is Truth over error; 1
that understood, gives man ability to rise above the evidence of the senses, take hold of the eternal energies of 3
Truth, and destroy mortal discord with immortal harmony, — the grand verities of being. It is not one mortal
thought transmitted to another's thought from the human 6
mind that holds within itself all evil.

Our Master said of one of his students, "He is a devil,"
and repudiated the idea of casting out devils through 9
Beelzebub. Erring human mind is by no means a desirable or efficacious healer. Such suppositional healing
I deprecate. It is in no way allied to divine power. All 12
human control is animal magnetism, more despicable
than all other methods of treating disease.

Christian Science is not a remedy of faith alone, but 15
combines faith with understanding, through which we
may touch the hem of His garment; and know that omnipotence has all power. "I am the Lord, and there is 18
none else, there is no God beside me."

Is there a personal man?

The Scriptures inform us that man was made in the 21
image and likeness of God. I commend the Icelandic
translation: "He created man in the image and likeness
of Mind, in the image and likeness of Mind created 24
He him." To my sense, we have not seen all of man;
he is more than personal sense can cognize, who is the
image and likeness of the infinite. I have not seen a 27
perfect man in mind or body, — and such must be the
personality of him who is the true likeness: the lost
image is not this personality, and corporeal man is this 30
lost image; hence, it doth not appear what is the real
personality of man. The only cause for making this

1 question of personality a point, or of any importance, is
that man's perfect model should be held in mind, whereby
3 to improve his present condition; that his contemplation
regarding himself should turn away from inharmony, sickness, and sin, to that which is the image of his Maker.

6   SCIENCE AND THE SENSES

Substance of my Address at the National Convention in Chicago,
June 13, 1888

9   The National Christian Scientist Association has
brought us together to minister and to be ministered
unto; mutually to aid one another in finding ways and
12 means for helping the whole human family; to quicken
and extend the interest already felt in a higher mode of
medicine; to watch with eager joy the individual growth
15 of Christian Scientists, and the progress of our common
Cause in Chicago, — the miracle of the Occident. We
come to strengthen and perpetuate our organizations
18 and institutions; and to find strength in union, — strength
to build up, through God's right hand, that pure and
undefiled religion whose Science demonstrates God and
21 the perfectibility of man. This purpose is immense,
and it must begin with individual growth, a "consummation devoutly to be wished." The lives of all re-
24 formers attest the authenticity of their mission, and call
the world to acknowledge its divine Principle. Truly
is it written: —

27   "Thou must be true thyself, if thou the truth would'st teach;
       Thy heart must overflow, if thou another's heart would'st
       reach."

Science is absolute and final. It is revolutionary in 1
its very nature; for it upsets all that is not upright.
It annuls false evidence, and saith to the five material 3
senses, "Having eyes ye see not, and ears ye hear not;
neither can you understand." To weave one thread of
Science through the looms of time, is a miracle in itself. 6
The risk is stupendous. It cost Galileo, what? This
awful price: the temporary loss of his self-respect. His
fear overcame his loyalty; the courage of his convictions 9
fell before it. Fear is the weapon in the hands of
tyrants.

Men and women of the nineteenth century, are you 12
called to voice a higher order of Science? Then obey
this call. Go, if you must, to the dungeon or the scaffold, but take not back the words of Truth. How many 15
are there ready to suffer for a righteous cause, to stand
a long siege, take the front rank, face the foe, and be
in the battle every day? 18

In no other one thing seemed Jesus of Nazareth more
divine than in his faith in the immortality of his words.
He said, "Heaven and earth shall pass away, but my 21
words shall not pass away;" and they have not. The
winds of time sweep clean the centuries, but they can
never bear into oblivion his words. They still live, and 24
to-morrow speak louder than to-day. They are to-day
as the voice of one crying in the wilderness, "Make
straight God's paths; make way for health, holiness, 27
universal harmony, and come up hither." The grandeur of the word, the power of Truth, is again casting
out evils and healing the sick; and it is whispered, "This 30
is Science."

Jesus taught by the wayside, in humble homes. He

1 spake of Truth and Love to artless listeners and dull
disciples. His immortal words were articulated in a
3 decaying language, and then left to the providence of
God. Christian Science was to interpret them; and
woman, "last at the cross," was to awaken the dull senses,
6 intoxicated with pleasure or pain, to the infinite meaning of those words.

Past, present, future, will show the word and might of
9 Truth — healing the sick and reclaiming the sinner —
so long as there remains a claim of error for Truth to
deny or to destroy. Love's labors are not lost. The
12 five personal senses, that grasp neither the meaning nor
the magnitude of self-abnegation, may lose sight thereof;
but Science voices unselfish love, unfolds infinite good,
15 leads on irresistible forces, and will finally show the fruits
of Love. Human reason is inaccurate; and the scope
of the senses is inadequate to grasp the word of Truth,
18 and teach the eternal.

Science speaks when the senses are silent, and then
the evermore of Truth is triumphant. The spiritual mon-
21 itor understood is coincidence of the divine with the
human, the acme of Christian Science. Pure humanity,
friendship, home, the interchange of love, bring to earth
24 a foretaste of heaven. They unite terrestrial and celestial joys, and crown them with blessings infinite.

The Christian Scientist loves man more because he
27 loves God most. He understands this Principle, — Love.
Who is sufficient for these things? Who remembers that
patience, forgiveness, abiding faith, and affection, are
30 the symptoms by which our Father indicates the different stages of man's recovery from sin and his entrance into Science? Who knows how the feeble lips

are made eloquent, how hearts are inspired, how heal- 1
ing becomes spontaneous, and how the divine Mind is
understood and demonstrated? He alone knows these 3
wonders who is departing from the thraldom of the
senses and accepting spiritual truth, — that which blesses
its adoption by the refinement of joy and the dismissal of 6
sorrow.

Christian Science and the senses are at war. It is a
revolutionary struggle. We already have had two in 9
this nation; and they began and ended in a contest for
the true idea, for human liberty and rights. Now cometh
a third struggle; for the freedom of health, holiness, and 12
the attainment of heaven.

The scientific sense of being which establishes harmony, enters into no compromise with finiteness and 15
feebleness. It undermines the foundations of mortality,
of physical law, breaks their chains, and sets the captive
free, opening the doors for them that are bound. 18

He who turns to the body for evidence, bases his conclusions on mortality, on imperfection; but Science saith
to man, "God hath all-power." 21

The Science of omnipotence demonstrates but one
power, and this power is good, not evil; not matter,
but Mind. This virtually destroys matter and evil, in- 24
cluding sin and disease.

If God is All, and God is good, it follows that all
must be good; and no other power, law, or intelligence 27
can exist. On this proof rest premise and conclusion in
Science, and the facts that disprove the evidence of the
senses. 30

God is individual Mind. This one Mind and His
individuality comprise the elements of all forms and

1 individualities, and prophesy the nature and stature of Christ, the ideal man.

3 A corporeal God, as often defined by lexicographers and scholastic theologians, is only an infinite finite being, an unlimited man, — a theory to me inconceivable. If 6 the unlimited and immortal Mind could originate in a limited body, Mind would be chained to finity, and the infinite forever finite.

9 In this limited and lower sense God is not personal. His infinity precludes the possibility of corporeal personality. His being is individual, but not physical.

12 God is like Himself and like nothing else. He is universal and primitive. His character admits of no degrees of comparison. God is not part, but the whole. In His 15 individuality I recognize the loving, divine Father-Mother God. Infinite personality must be incorporeal.

God's ways are not ours. His pity is expressed in 18 modes above the human. His chastisements are the manifestations of Love. The sympathy of His eternal Mind is fully expressed in divine Science, which blots 21 out all our iniquities and heals all our diseases. Human pity often brings pain.

Science supports harmony, denies suffering, and de-24 stroys it with the divinity of Truth. Whatever seems material, seems thus only to the material senses, and is but the subjective state of mortal and material thought.

27 Science has inaugurated the irrepressible conflict between sense and Soul. Mortal thought wars with this sense as one that beateth the air, but Science outmasters 30 it, and ends the warfare. This proves daily that "one on God's side is a majority."

Science defines *omnipresence* as universality, that which

precludes the presence of evil. This verity annuls the tes- 1
timony of the senses, which say that sin is an evil power,
and substance is perishable. Intelligent Spirit, Soul, is 3
substance, far more impregnable and solid than matter; for
one is temporal, while the other is eternal, the ultimate
and predicate of being.   6

Mortality, materiality, and destructive forces, such as
sin, disease, and death, mortals virtually name *substance;*
but these are the substance of things *not* hoped for. For 9
lack of knowing what substance is, the senses say vaguely:
"The substance of life is sorrow and mortality; for who
knoweth the substance of good?" In Science, form and 12
individuality are never lost, thoughts are outlined, individualized ideas, which dwell forever in the divine Mind
as tangible, true substance, because eternally conscious. 15
Unlike mortal mind, which must be ever in bondage,
the eternal Mind is free, unlimited, and knows not the
temporal.   18

Neither does the temporal know the eternal. Mortal
man, as mind or matter, is neither the pattern nor Maker
of immortal man. Any inference of the divine derived 21
from the human, either as mind or body, hides the actual
power, presence, and individuality of God.

Jesus' personality in the flesh, so far as material sense 24
could discern it, was like that of other men; but Science
exchanges this human concept of Jesus for the divine
ideal, his spiritual individuality that reflected the Im- 27
manuel, or "God with us." This God was not outlined.
He was too mighty for that. He was eternal Life, infinite
Truth and Love. The individuality is embraced in Mind, 30
therefore is forever with the Father. Hence the Scripture, "I am a God at hand, saith the Lord." Even while

1 his personality was on earth and in anguish, his individual
being, the Christ, was at rest in the eternal harmony.
3 His unseen individuality, so superior to that which was
seen, was not subject to the temptations of the flesh, to
laws material, to death, or the grave.   Formed and gov-
6 erned by God, this individuality was safe in the substance
of Soul, the substance of Spirit, — yea, the substance of
God, the one inclusive good.

9   In Science all being is individual; for individuality is
endless in the calculus of forms and numbers.   Herein
sin is miraculous and supernatural; for it is not in the
12 nature of God, and good is forever good.   According to Christian Science, perfection is normal, — not
miraculous.   Clothed, and in its right Mind, man's
15 individuality is sinless, deathless, harmonious, eternal.
His materiality, clad in a false mentality, wages feeble
fight with his individuality, — his physical senses with
18 his spiritual senses.   The latter move in God's grooves
of Science: the former revolve in their own orbits, and
must stand the friction of false selfhood until self-
21 destroyed.

In obedience to the divine nature, man's individuality
reflects the divine law and order of being.   How shall
24 we reach our true selves?   Through Love.   The Principle of Christian Science is Love, and its idea represents
Love.   This divine Principle and idea are demonstrated,
27 in healing, to be God and the real man.

Who wants to be mortal, or would not gain the true
ideal of Life and recover his own individuality?   I will
30 love, if another hates.   I will gain a balance on the side of
good, my true being.   This alone gives me the forces of
God wherewith to overcome all error.   On this rests the

implicit faith engendered by Christian Science, which 1
appeals intelligently to the facts of man's spirituality, individuality, to disdain the fears and destroy the discords 3
of this material personality.

On our Master's individual demonstrations over sin,
sickness, and death, rested the anathema of priesthood 6
and the senses; yet this demonstration is the foundation
of Christian Science. His physical sufferings, which
came from the testimony of the senses, were over when 9
he resumed his individual spiritual being, after showing
us the way to escape from the material body.

Science would have no conflict with Life or common 12
sense, if this sense were consistently sensible. Man's real
life or existence is in harmony with Life and its glorious
phenomena. It upholds being, and destroys the too 15
common sense of its opposites — death, disease, and sin.
Christian Science is an everlasting victor, and vanquish-
ment is unknown to the omnipresent Truth. I must ever 18
follow this line of light and battle.

Christian Science is my only ideal; and the individual
and his ideal can never be severed. If either is misunder- 21
stood or maligned, it eclipses the other with the shadow
cast by this error.

Truth destroys error. Nothing appears to the physi- 24
cal senses but their own subjective state of thought. The
senses join issue with error, and pity what has no right
either to be pitied or to exist, and what does not exist in 27
Science. Destroy the thought of sin, sickness, death, and
you destroy their existence. "Whatsoever a man soweth,
that shall he also reap." 30

Because God is Mind, and this Mind is good, all
is good and all is Mind. God is the sum total of the

1 universe. Then what and where are sin, sickness, and
death?
3   Christian Science and Christian Scientists will, *must*,
have a history; and if I could write the history in poor
parody on Tennyson's grand verse, it would read
6 thus: —

> Traitors to right of them,
> M. D.'s to left of them,
> 9   Priestcraft in front of them,
>   Volleyed and thundered!
>   Into the jaws of hate,
> 12   Out through the door of Love,
>   On to the blest above,
>   Marched the one hundred.

15 EXTRACT FROM MY FIRST ADDRESS IN THE MOTHER
CHURCH, MAY 26, 1895

Friends and Brethren: — Your Sunday Lesson, com-
18 posed of Scripture and its correlative in "Science and
Health with Key to the Scriptures," has fed you. In addition, I can only bring crumbs fallen from this table of
21 Truth, and gather up the fragments.

It has long been a question of earnest import, How
shall mankind worship the most adorable, but most
24 unadored, — and where shall begin that praise that shall
never end? Beneath, above, beyond, methinks I hear
the soft, sweet sigh of angels answering, "So live, that
27 your lives attest your sincerity and resound His praise."

Music is the harmony of being; but the music of Soul
affords the only strains that thrill the chords of feeling
30 and awaken the heart's harpstrings. Moved by mind,
your many-throated organ, in imitative tones of many

instruments, praises Him; but even the sweetness and 1
beauty in and of this temple that praise Him, are earth's
accents, and must not be mistaken for the oracles of God. 3
Art must not prevail over Science. Christianity is not
superfluous. Its redemptive power is seen in sore trials,
self-denials, and crucifixions of the flesh. But these come 6
to the rescue of mortals, to admonish them, and plant
the feet steadfastly in Christ. As we rise above the seeming mists of sense, we behold more clearly that all the 9
heart's homage belongs to God.

More love is the great need of mankind. A pure affection, concentric, forgetting self, forgiving wrongs and 12
forestalling them, should swell the lyre of human love.

Three cardinal points must be gained before poor
humanity is regenerated and Christian Science is dem- 15
onstrated: (1) A proper sense of sin; (2) repentance;
(3) the understanding of good. Evil is a negation: it
never started with time, and it cannot keep pace with 18
eternity. Mortals' false senses pass through three states
and stages of human consciousness before yielding error.
The deluded sense must first be shown its falsity through 21
a knowledge of evil as evil, so-called. Without a sense
of one's oft-repeated violations of divine law, the individual may become morally blind, and this deplorable 24
mental state is moral idiocy. The lack of seeing one's
deformed mentality, and of *repentance* therefor, deep,
never to be repented of, is retarding, and in certain mor- 27
bid instances stopping, the growth of Christian Scientists.
Without a knowledge of his sins, and repentance so severe
that it destroys them, no person is or can be a Christian 30
Scientist.

Mankind thinks either too much or too little of sin.

1 The sensitive, sorrowing saint thinks too much of it: the
sordid sinner, or the so-called Christian asleep, thinks too
3 little of sin.

To allow sin of any sort is anomalous in Christian
Scientists, claiming, as they do, that good is infinite, All.
6 Our Master, in his definition of Satan as a liar from the
beginning, attested the absolute powerlessness — yea,
nothingness — of evil: since a lie, being without founda-
9 tion in fact, is merely a falsity; spiritually, literally, it
is nothing.

Not to know that a false claim is false, is to be in danger
12 of believing it; hence the utility of knowing evil aright,
then reducing its claim to its proper denominator, —
nobody and nothing. Sin should be conceived of only
15 as a delusion. This true conception would remove mortals'
ignorance and its consequences, and advance the second
stage of human consciousness, repentance. The first
18 state, namely, the knowledge of one's self, the proper
knowledge of evil and its subtle workings wherein evil
seems as real as good, is indispensable; since that which
21 is truly conceived of, we can handle; but the misconception of what we need to know of evil, — or the conception of it at all as something real, — costs much. Sin
24 needs only to be known for what it is not; then we are
its master, not servant. Remember, and act on, Jesus'
definition of sin as a *lie*. This cognomen makes it less
27 dangerous; for most of us would not be seen believing
in, or adhering to, that which we know to be untrue.
What would be thought of a Christian Scientist who be-
30 lieved in the use of drugs, while declaring that they have
no intrinsic quality and that there is no matter? What
should be thought of an individual believing in that

which is untrue, and at the same time declaring the unity 1
of Truth, and its allness? Beware of those who misrepresent facts; or tacitly assent where they should dis- 3
sent; or who take me as authority for what I disapprove,
or mayhap never have thought of, and try to reverse, in-
vert, or controvert, Truth; for this is a sure pretext of 6
moral defilement.

Examine yourselves, and see what, and how much, sin
claims of you; and how much of this claim you admit 9
as valid, or comply with. The knowledge of evil that
brings on repentance is the most hopeful stage of mortal
mentality. Even a mild mistake must be seen as a mis- 12
take, in order to be corrected; how much more, then,
should one's sins be seen and repented of, before they
can be reduced to their native nothingness!   15

Ignorance is only blest by reason of its nothingness;
for seeing the need of somethingness in its stead, blesses
mortals. Ignorance was the first condition of sin in the 18
allegory of Adam and Eve in the garden of Eden. Their
mental state is not desirable, neither is a knowledge of
sin and its consequences, repentance, *per se;* but, ad- 21
mitting the existence of both, mortals must hasten through
the second to the third stage, — the knowledge of good;
for without this the valuable sequence of knowledge 24
would be lacking, — even the power to escape from the
false claims of sin. To understand good, one must discern
the nothingness of evil, and consecrate one's life anew. 27

Beloved brethren, Christ, Truth, saith unto you, "Be
not afraid!" — fear not sin, lest thereby it master you;
but only *fear to sin.* Watch and pray for self-knowledge; 30
since then, and thus, cometh repentance, — and your
superiority to a delusion is won.

1 Repentance is better than sacrifice. The costly balm of Araby, poured on our Master's feet, had not the value 3 of a single *tear*.

Beloved children, the world has need of you, — and more as children than as men and women: it needs your 6 innocence, unselfishness, faithful affection, uncontaminated lives. You need also to watch, and pray that you preserve these virtues unstained, and lose them not through 9 contact with the world. What grander ambition is there than to maintain in yourselves what Jesus loved, and to know that your example, more than words, makes morals 12 for mankind!

ADDRESS BEFORE THE ALUMNI OF THE MASSACHUSETTS
METAPHYSICAL COLLEGE, 1895

15 *My Beloved Students:* — Weeks have passed into months, and months into years, since last we met; but time and space, when encompassed by divine presence, 18 do not separate us. Our hearts have kept time together, and our hands have wrought steadfastly at the same object-lesson, while leagues have lain between us.

21 We may well unite in thanksgiving for the continued progress and unprecedented prosperity of our Cause. It is already obvious that the world's acceptance and the 24 momentum of Christian Science, increase rapidly as years glide on.

As Christian Scientists, you have dared the perilous de-27 fense of Truth, and have succeeded. You have learned how fleeting is that which men call great; and how permanent that which God calls good.

You have proven that the greatest piety is scarcely 1
sufficient to demonstrate what you have adopted and
taught; that your work, well done, would dignify angels. 3

Faithfully, as meekly, you have toiled all night; and
at break of day caught much. At times, your net has
been so full that it broke: human pride, creeping into 6
its meshes, extended it beyond safe expansion; then,
losing hold of divine Love, you lost your fishes, and possibly blamed others more than yourself. But those whom 9
God makes "fishers of men" will not pull for the shore;
like Peter, they launch into the depths, cast their nets
on the right side, compensate loss, and gain a higher sense 12
of the true idea. Nothing is lost that God gives: had He
filled the net, it would not have broken.

Leaving the seed of Truth to its own vitality, it propa- 15
gates: the tares cannot hinder it. Our Master said,
"Heaven and earth shall pass away, but my words shall
not pass away;" and Jesus' faith in Truth must not ex- 18
ceed that of Christian Scientists who prove its power to
be immortal.

The Christianity that is merely of sects, the pulpit, and 21
fashionable society, is brief; but the Word of God abideth.
Plato was a pagan; but no greater difference existed between his doctrines and those of Jesus, than to-day exists 24
between the Catholic and Protestant sects. I love the
orthodox church; and, in time, that church will love
Christian Science. Let me specially call the attention of 27
this Association to the following false beliefs inclining
mortal mind more deviously: —

The belief in anti-Christ: that somebody in the flesh 30
is the son of God, or is another Christ, or is a spiritually
adopted child, or is an incarnated babe, is the evil one—

1 in other words, the one evil — disporting itself with the subtleties of sin!

3   Even honest thinkers, not knowing whence they come, may deem these delusions verities, before they know it, or really look the illusions in the face.   The ages are bur-
6 dened with material modes. Hypnotism, microbes, X-rays, and ex-common sense, occupy time and thought; and error, given new opportunities, will improve them.   The
9 most just man can neither defend the innocent nor detect the guilty, unless he knows *how* to be just; and this knowl-edge demands our time and attention.

12   The mental stages of crime, which seem to belong to the latter days, are strictly classified in metaphysics as some of the many features and forms of what is properly
15 denominated, in extreme cases, moral idiocy.   I visited in his cell the assassin of President Garfield, and found him in the mental state called moral idiocy.   He had no
18 sense of his crime; but regarded his act as one of simple justice, and himself as the victim.   My few words touched him; he sank back in his chair, limp and pale; his flip-
21 pancy had fled. The jailer thanked me, and said, "Other visitors have brought to him bouquets, but you have brought what will do him good."

24   This mental disease at first shows itself in extreme sensitiveness; then, in a loss of self-knowledge and of self-condemnation, — a shocking inability to see one's
27 own faults, but an exaggerating sense of other people's. Unless this mental condition be overcome, it ends in a total loss of moral, intellectual, and spiritual discernment,
30 and is characterized in this Scripture: "The fool hath said in his heart, There is no God." This state of mind is the exemplification of total depravity, and the result

of sensuous mind in matter. Mind that is God is not in 1
matter; and God's presence gives spiritual light, wherein
is no darkness. 3

If, as is indisputably true, "God is Spirit," and Spirit
is our Father and Mother, and that which it includes is
all that is real and eternal, when evil seems to predomi- 6
nate and divine light to be obscured, free moral agency
is lost; and the Revelator's vision, that "no man might
buy or sell, save he that had the mark, or the name of the 9
beast, or the number of his name," is imminent.

Whoever is mentally manipulating human mind, and
is not gaining a higher sense of Truth by it, is losing in 12
the scale of moral and spiritual being, and may be carried to the depths of perdition by his own consent. He
who refuses to be influenced by any but the divine Mind, 15
commits his way to God, and rises superior to suggestions from an evil source. Christian Science shows that
there is a way of escape from the latter-day ultimatum 18
of evil, through scientific truth; so that all are without
excuse.

Already I clearly recognize that mental malpractice, 21
if persisted in, will end in insanity, dementia, or moral
idiocy. Thank God! this evil can be resisted by true
Christianity. Divine Love is our hope, strength, and 24
shield. We have nothing to fear when Love is at the
helm of thought, but everything to enjoy on earth and
in heaven. 27

The systematized centres of Christian Science are life-
giving fountains of truth. Our churches, *The Christian
Science Journal,* and the *Christian Science Quarterly,* 30
are prolific sources of spiritual power whose intellectual,
moral, and spiritual animus is felt throughout the land.

1 Our Publishing Society, and our Sunday Lessons, are
of inestimable value to all seekers after Truth. The Com-
3 mittee on Sunday School Lessons cannot give too much
time and attention to their task, and should spare no
research in the preparation of the *Quarterly* as an educa-
6 tional branch.

The teachers of Christian Science need to watch incessantly the trend of their own thoughts; watch that these
9 be not secretly robbed, and themselves misguided, and
so made to misteach others. Teachers must conform
strictly to the rules of divine Science announced in the
12 Bible and their textbook, "Science and Health with Key
to the Scriptures." They must themselves practise, and
teach others to practise, the Hebrew Decalogue, the Ser-
15 mon on the Mount, and the understanding and enuncia-
tion of these according to Christ.

They must always have on armor, and resist the foe
18 within and without. They cannot arm too thoroughly
against original sin, appearing in its myriad forms: passion, appetites, hatred, revenge, and all the *et cetera* of
21 evil. Christian Scientists cannot watch too sedulously,
or bar their doors too closely, or pray to God too fervently, for deliverance from the claims of evil. Thus
24 doing, Scientists will silence evil suggestions, uncover
their methods, and stop their hidden influence upon the
lives of mortals. Rest assured that God in His wisdom
27 will test all mankind on all questions; and then, if found
faithful, He will deliver us from temptation and show us
the powerlessness of evil, — even its utter nothingness.
30 The teacher in Christian Science who does not specially instruct his pupils how to guard against evil and
its silent modes, and to be able, through Christ, the liv-

ing Truth, to protect themselves therefrom, is commit- 1
ting an offense against God and humanity. With Science
and Health for their textbook, I am astounded at the 3
apathy of some students on the subject of sin and mental
malpractice, and their culpable ignorance of the workings of these — and even the teacher's own deficiency in 6
this department. I can account for this state of mind in
the teacher only as the result of sin; otherwise, his own
guilt as a mental malpractitioner, and fear of being found 9
out.

The helpless ignorance of the community on this subject is pitiable, and plain to be seen. May God enable 12
my students to take up the cross as I have done, and meet
the pressing need of a proper preparation of heart to practise, teach, and live Christian Science! Your means of 15
protection and defense from sin are, constant watchfulness and prayer that you enter not into temptation and
are delivered from every claim of evil, till you intelligently 18
know and demonstrate, in Science, that evil has neither
prestige, power, nor existence, since God, good, is All-
in-all. 21

The increasing necessity for relying on God to defend us against the subtler forms of evil, turns us more
unreservedly to Him for help, and thus becomes a means 24
of grace. If one lives rightly, every effort to hurt one
will only help that one; for God will give the ability to
overcome whatever tends to impede progress. Know 27
this: that you cannot overcome the baneful effects of
sin on yourself, if you in any way indulge in sin; for,
sooner or later, you will fall the victim of your own as 30
well as of others' sins. Using mental power in the right
direction only, doing to others as you would have them

1 do to you, will overcome evil with good, and destroy
your own sensitiveness to the power of evil.

3 The God of all grace be with you, and save you from
"spiritual wickedness in high places."

PLEASANT VIEW, CONCORD, N. H.,
6 June 3, 1895

ADDRESS BEFORE THE CHRISTIAN SCIENTIST ASSOCIA-
TION OF THE MASSACHUSETTS METAPHYSICAL COL-
9 LEGE, IN 1893

SUBJECT: *Obedience*

My Beloved Students: — This question, ever nearest
12 to my heart, is to-day uppermost: Are we filling the
measures of life's music aright, emphasizing its grand
strains, swelling the harmony of being with tones whence
15 come glad echoes? As *crescendo* and *diminuendo* accent
music, so the varied strains of human chords express
life's loss or gain, — loss of the pleasures and pains and
18 pride of life: gain of its sweet concord, the courage of
honest convictions, and final obedience to spiritual law.
The ultimate of scientific research and attainment in
21 divine Science is not an argument: it is not merely saying, but doing, the Word — demonstrating Truth — even
as the fruits of watchfulness, prayer, struggles, tears, and
24 triumph.

Obeying the divine Principle which you profess to understand and love, demonstrates Truth. Never absent
27 from your post, never off guard, never ill-humored, never
unready to work for God, — is obedience; being "faithful over a few things." If in one instance obedience be
30 lacking, you lose the scientific rule and its reward: namely,

to be made "ruler over many things." A progressive 1
life is the reality of Life that unfolds its immortal Principle. 3

The student of Christian Science must first separate the
tares from the wheat; discern between the thought,
motive, and act superinduced by the wrong motive or 6
the true — the God-given intent and volition — arrest
the former, and obey the latter. This will place him on
the safe side of practice. We always know where to look 9
for the real Scientist, and always find him there. I agree
with Rev. Dr. Talmage, that "there are wit, humor, and
enduring vivacity among God's people." 12

Obedience is the offspring of Love; and Love is the
Principle of unity, the basis of all right thinking and
acting; it fulfils the law. We see eye to eye and know as we 15
are known, reciprocate kindness and work wisely, in
proportion as we love.

It is difficult for me to carry out a divine commission 18
while participating in the movements, or *modus operandi,*
of other folks. To point out every step to a student and
then watch that each step be taken, consumes time, — 21
and experiments ofttimes are costly. According to my
calendar, God's time and mortals' differ. The neophyte is inclined to be too fast or too slow: he works 24
somewhat in the dark; and, sometimes out of season,
he would replenish his lamp at the midnight hour and
borrow oil of the more provident watcher. God is the 27
fountain of light, and He illumines one's way when one
is obedient. The disobedient make their moves before
God makes His, or make them too late to follow Him. 30
Be sure that God *directs* your way; then, hasten to follow
under every circumstance.

1 Human will must be subjugated. We cannot obey
both God, good, and evil, — in other words, the ma-
3 terial senses, false suggestions, self-will, selfish motives,
and human policy. We shall have no faith in evil
when faith finds a resting-place and scientific under-
6 standing guides man. Honesty in every condition,
under every circumstance, is the indispensable rule of
obedience. To obey the principle of mathematics ninety-
9 nine times in one hundred and then allow one numeral
to make incorrect your entire problem, is neither Science
nor obedience.

12 However keenly the human affections yearn to forgive a mistake, and pass a friend over it smoothly, one's
sympathy can neither atone for error, advance individual
15 growth, nor change this immutable decree of Love: "Keep
My commandments." The guerdon of meritorious
faith or trustworthiness rests on being willing to work
18 alone with God and for Him, — willing to suffer patiently
for error until all error is destroyed and His rod and His
staff comfort you.

21 Self-ignorance, self-will, self-righteousness, lust, covetousness, envy, revenge, are foes to grace, peace, and
progress; they must be met manfully and overcome,
24 or they will uproot all happiness. Be of good cheer;
the warfare with one's self is grand; it gives one plenty
of employment, and the divine Principle worketh with
27 you, — and obedience crowns persistent effort with
everlasting victory. Every attempt of evil to harm good
is futile, and ends in the fiery punishment of the
30 evil-doer.

Jesus said, "Not that which goeth into the mouth
defileth a man; but that which cometh out of the mouth,

this defileth a man." If malicious suggestions whisper 1
evil through the mind's tympanum, this were no apology
for acting evilly. We are responsible for our thoughts and 3
acts; and instead of aiding other people's devices by
obeying them, — and then whining over misfortune, —
rise and overthrow both. If a criminal coax the unwary 6
man to commit a crime, our laws punish the dupe as accessory to the fact. Each individual is responsible for
himself. 9

Evil is impotent to turn the righteous man from his
uprightness. The nature of the individual, more stubborn than the circumstance, will always be found argu- 12
ing for itself, — its habits, tastes, and indulgences. This
material nature strives to tip the beam against the spiritual nature; for the flesh strives against Spirit, — against 15
whatever or whoever opposes evil, — and weighs mightily
in the scale against man's high destiny. This conclusion
is not an argument either for pessimism or for optimism, 18
but is a plea for free moral agency, — full exemption
from all necessity to obey a power that should be and is
found powerless in Christian Science. 21

Insubordination to the law of Love even in the least,
or strict obedience thereto, tests and discriminates between the real and the unreal Scientist. Justice, a 24
prominent statute in the divine law, demands of all
trespassers upon the sparse individual rights which one
justly reserves to one's self, — Would you consent that 27
others should tear up your landmarks, manipulate your
students, nullify or reverse your rules, countermand
your orders, steal your possessions, and escape the 30
penalty therefor? No! "Therefore all things whatsoever ye would that men should do to you, do ye even

1 so to them." The professors of Christian Science must take off their shoes at our altars; they must unclasp
3 the material sense of things at the very threshold of Christian Science: they must obey implicitly each and every injunction of the divine Principle of life's long
6 problem, or repeat their work in tears. In the words of St. Paul, "Know ye not, that to whom ye yield yourselves servants to obey, his servants ye are to whom ye
9 obey; whether of sin unto death, or of *obedience* unto righteousness?"

Beloved students, loyal laborers are ye that have wrought
12 valiantly, and achieved great guerdons in the vineyard of our Lord; but a mighty victory is yet to be won, a great freedom for the race; and Christian success is
15 under arms, — with armor on, not laid down. Let us rejoice, however, that the clarion call of peace will at length be heard above the din of battle, and come more
18 sweetly to our ear than sound of vintage bells to villagers on the Rhine.

I recommend that this Association hereafter meet tri-
21 ennially: many of its members reside a long distance from Massachusetts, and they are members of The Mother Church who would love to be with you on Sunday, and
24 once in three years is perhaps as often as they can afford to be away from their own fields of labor.

COMMUNION ADDRESS, JANUARY, 1896

27 *Friends and Brethren:* — The Biblical record of the great Nazarene, whose character we to-day commemorate, is scanty; but what is given, puts to flight every doubt as
30 to the immortality of his words and works. Though

written in a decaying language, his words can never pass 1
away: they are inscribed upon the hearts of men: they
are engraved upon eternity's tablets. 3

Undoubtedly our Master partook of the Jews' feast
of the Passover, and drank from their festal wine-cup.
This, however, is not the cup to which I call your at- 6
tention, — even the cup of martyrdom: wherein Spirit
and matter, good and evil, seem to grapple, and the
human struggles against the divine, up to a point of 9
discovery; namely, the impotence of evil, and the omnipotence of good, as divinely attested. Anciently, the
blood of martyrs was believed to be the seed of the Church. 12
Stalled theocracy would make this fatal doctrine just
and sovereign, even a divine decree, a law of Love! That
the innocent shall suffer for the guilty, is inhuman. The 15
prophet declared, "Thou shalt put away the guilt of
innocent blood from Israel." This is plain: that whatever belittles, befogs, or belies the nature and essence of 18
Deity, is not divine. Who, then, shall father or favor
this sentence passed upon innocence? thereby giving the
signet of God to the arrest, trial, and crucifixion of His 21
beloved Son, the righteous Nazarene, — christened by
John the Baptist, "the Lamb of God."

Oh! shameless insult to divine royalty, that drew 24
from the great Master this answer to the questions of the
rabbinical rabble: "If I tell you, ye will not believe; and
if I also ask you, ye will not answer me, nor let me go." 27

Infinitely greater than human pity, is divine Love, —
that cannot be unmerciful. Human tribunals, if just,
borrow their sense of justice from the divine Principle 30
thereof, which punishes the guilty, not the innocent. The
Teacher of both law and gospel construed the substitution

1 of a good man to suffer for evil-doers — a *crime!* When
foretelling his own crucifixion, he said, "Woe unto the
3 world because of offenses! for it must needs be that
offenses come; but woe to that man by whom the offense
cometh!"
6 Would Jesus thus have spoken of what was indispensable for the salvation of a world of sinners, or of the
individual instrument in this holy (?) alliance for accom-
9 plishing such a monstrous work? or have said of him
whom God foreordained and predestined to fulfil a divine
decree, "It were better for him that a millstone were
12 hanged about his neck, and that he were drowned in the
depth of the sea"?

The divine order is the acme of mercy: it is neither
15 questionable nor assailable: it is not evil producing good,
nor good ultimating in evil. Such an inference were
impious. Holy Writ denounces him that declares, "Let
18 us do evil, that good may come! whose damnation is
just."

Good is not educed from its opposite: and Love divine
21 spurned, lessens not the hater's hatred nor the criminal's
crime; nor reconciles justice to injustice; nor substitutes
the suffering of the Godlike for the suffering due to sin.
24 Neither spiritual bankruptcy nor a religious chancery can
win high heaven, or the "Well done, good and faithful
servant, . . . enter thou into the joy of thy Lord."
27 Divine Love knows no hate; for hate, or the hater, is
nothing: God never made it, and He made all that was
made. The hater's pleasures are unreal; his sufferings,
30 self-imposed; his existence is a parody, and he ends —
with suicide.

The murder of the just Nazarite was incited by the

same spirit that in our time massacres our missionaries, 1
butchers the helpless Armenians, slaughters innocents.
Evil was, and is, the illusion of breaking the First Com- 3
mandment, "Thou shalt have no other gods before me:"
it is either idolizing something and somebody, or hating
them: it is the spirit of idolatry, envy, jealousy, covet- 6
ousness, superstition, lust, hypocrisy, *witchcraft*.

That man can break the forever-law of infinite Love,
was, and is, the serpent's biggest lie! and ultimates in 9
a religion of pagan priests bloated with crime; a religion
that demands human victims to be sacrificed to human
passions and human gods, or tortured to appease the 12
anger of a so-called god or a miscalled man or woman!
The Assyrian Merodach, or the god of sin, was the "lucky
god;" and the Babylonian Yawa, or Jehovah, was the 15
Jewish tribal deity. The *Christian's* God is neither, and
is too pure to behold iniquity.

Divine Science has rolled away the stone from the sepul- 18
chre of our Lord; and there has risen to the awakened
thought the majestic atonement of divine Love. The
at-one-ment with Christ has appeared — not through 21
vicarious suffering, whereby the just obtain a pardon for
the unjust, — but through the eternal law of justice;
wherein sinners suffer for their own sins, repent, forsake 24
sin, love God, and keep His commandments, thence to
receive the reward of righteousness: salvation from sin,
not through the *death* of a man, but through a divine *Life*, 27
which is our Redeemer.

Holy Writ declares that God is Love, is Spirit; hence
it follows that those who worship Him, must worship 30
Him spiritually, — far apart from physical sensation
such as attends eating and drinking corporeally. It is

1 plain that aught unspiritual, intervening between God
and man, would tend to disturb the divine order, and
3 countermand the Scripture that those who worship the
Father must worship Him in spirit. It is also plain,
that we should not seek and cannot find God in mat-
6 ter, or through material methods; neither do we love
and obey Him by means of matter, or the flesh, — which
warreth against Spirit, and will not be reconciled
9 thereto.

We turn, with sickened sense, from a pagan Jew's
or Moslem's misconception of Deity, for peace; and find
12 rest in the spiritual ideal, or Christ. For "who is so
great a God as our God!" unchangeable, all-wise, all-
just, all-merciful; the ever-loving, ever-living Life, Truth,
15 Love: comforting such as mourn, opening the prison
doors to the captive, marking the unwinged bird, pitying
with more than a father's pity; healing the sick, cleansing
18 the leper, raising the dead, saving sinners. As we think
thereon, man's true sense is filled with peace, and power;
and we say, It is well that Christian Science has taken
21 expressive silence wherein to muse His praise, to kiss the
feet of Jesus, adore the white Christ, and stretch out our
arms to God.

24   The last act of the tragedy on Calvary rent the veil
of matter, and unveiled Love's great legacy to mortals:
Love forgiving its enemies. This grand act crowned
27 and still crowns Christianity: it manumits mortals; it
translates love; it gives to suffering, inspiration; to
patience, experience; to experience, hope; to hope, faith;
30 to faith, understanding; and to understanding, Love triumphant!

In proportion to a man's spiritual progress, he will

Communion Address

indeed drink of our Master's cup, and be baptized with 1
his baptism! be purified as by fire, — the fires of suffering;
then hath he part in Love's atonement, for "whom the 3
Lord loveth He chasteneth." Then shall he also reign
with him: he shall rise to know that there is no sin,
that there is no suffering; since all that is *real* is *right*. 6
This knowledge enables him to overcome the world, the
flesh, and all evil, to have dominion over his own sinful
sense and self. Then shall he drink anew Christ's cup, 9
in the kingdom of God — the reign of righteousness —
within him; he shall sit down at the Father's right hand:
sit down; not stand waiting and weary; but rest on the 12
bosom of God; rest, in the understanding of divine Love
that passeth all understanding; rest, in that which "to
know aright is Life eternal," and whom, not having seen, 15
we love.

Then shall he press on to Life's long lesson, the eternal
lore of Love; and learn forever the infinite meanings of 18
these short sentences: "God is Love;" and, All that is
real is divine, for God is All-in-all.

MESSAGE TO THE ANNUAL MEETING OF THE MOTHER 21
CHURCH, BOSTON, 1896

Beloved Brethren, Children, and Grandchildren: —
Apart from the common walks of mankind, revolving 24
oft the hitherto untouched problems of being, and
oftener, perhaps, the controversies which baffle it,
Mother, thought-tired, turns to-day to you; turns to 27
her dear church, to tell the towers thereof the remarkable
achievements that have been ours within the past few
years: the rapid transit from halls to churches, from un- 30

1 settled questions to permanence, from danger to escape,
from fragmentary discourses to one eternal sermon; yea,
3 from darkness to daylight, in physics and metaphysics.

Truly, I half wish for society again; for once, at least,
to hear the soft music of our Sabbath chimes saluting the
6 ear in tones that leap for joy, with love for God and
man.

Who hath not learned that when alone he has his
9 own thoughts to guard, and when struggling with mankind his temper, and in society his tongue? We also
have gained higher heights; have learned that trials lift
12 us to that dignity of Soul which sustains us, and finally
conquers them; and that the ordeal refines while it
chastens.

15   Perhaps our church is not yet quite sensible of what
we owe to the strength, meekness, honesty, and obedience of the Christian Science Board of Directors; to
18 the able editors of *The Christian Science Journal,* and
to our efficient Publishing Society.

No reproof is so potent as the silent lesson of a good
21 example. Works, more than words, should characterize
Christian Scientists. Most people condemn evil-doing,
evil-speaking; yet nothing circulates so rapidly: even gold
24 is less current. Christian Scientists have a strong race to
run, and foes in ambush; but bear in mind that, in the
long race, honesty always defeats dishonesty.

27   God hath indeed smiled on my church, — this
daughter of Zion: she sitteth in high places; and to de-
ride her is to incur the penalty of which the Hebrew
30 bard spake after this manner: "He that sitteth in the
heavens shall laugh: the Lord shall have them in
derision."

Hitherto, I have observed that in proportion as this 1
church has smiled on His "little ones," He has blessed
her. Throughout my entire connection with The Mother 3
Church, I have seen, that in the ratio of her love for
others, hath His love been bestowed upon her; watering
her waste places, and enlarging her borders.   6

One thing I have greatly desired, and again earnestly
request, namely, that Christian Scientists, here and
elsewhere, pray daily for themselves; not verbally, nor 9
on bended knee, but mentally, meekly, and importunately. When a hungry heart petitions the divine Father-
Mother God for bread, it is not given a stone, — but 12
more grace, obedience, and love. If this heart, humble
and trustful, faithfully asks divine Love to feed it with the
bread of heaven, health, holiness, it will be conformed to 15
a fitness to receive the answer to its desire; then will flow
into it the "river of His pleasure," the tributary of divine
Love, and great growth in Christian Science will follow, — 18
even that joy which finds one's own in another's good.

To love, and to be loved, one must do good to others.
The inevitable condition whereby to become blessed, is to 21
bless others: but here, you must so know yourself, under
God's direction, that you will do His will even though
your pearls be downtrodden. Ofttimes the rod is His 24
means of grace; then it must be ours, — we cannot avoid
wielding it if we reflect Him.

Wise sayings and garrulous talk may fall to the ground, 27
rather than on the ear or heart of the hearer; but a tender
sentiment felt, or a kind word spoken, at the right moment,
is never wasted. Mortal mind presents phases of charac- 30
ter which need close attention and examination. The
human heart, like a feather bed, needs often to be *stirred,*

1 sometimes roughly, and given a variety of *turns,* else it
grows hard and uncomfortable whereon to repose.

3   The lessons of this so-called life in matter are too vast
and varied to learn or to teach briefly; and especially
within the limits of a letter. Therefore I close here,
6 with the apostle's injunction: "Finally, brethren, whatsoever things are true, whatsoever things are honest,
whatsoever things are just, whatsoever things are pure,
9 whatsoever things are lovely, whatsoever things are of
good report; if there be any virtue, and if there be any
praise, think on these things. Those things, which ye
12 have both learned, and received, and heard, and seen in
me, do: and the God of peace shall be with you."

With love, Mother,
MARY BAKER G. EDDY

CHAPTER V

Letters

1

M Y BELOVED BRETHREN: — If a member of the church
is inclined to be uncharitable, or to condemn his 3
brother without cause, let him put his finger to his lips,
and forgive others as he would *be* forgiven. One's first
lesson is to learn one's self; having done this, one will 6
naturally, through grace from God, forgive his brother and
love his enemies. To avenge an imaginary or an actual
wrong, is suicidal. The law of our God and the rule of 9
our church is to tell thy brother his fault and thereby help
him. If this rule fails in effect, then take the next Scriptural step: drop this member's name from the church, and 12
thereafter "let the dead bury their dead," — let silence
prevail over his remains.

If a man is jealous, envious, or revengeful, he will seek 15
occasion to balloon an atom of another man's indis-
cretion, inflate it, and send it into the atmosphere of mortal
mind — for other green eyes to gaze on: he will always 18
find somebody in his way, and try to push him aside;
will see somebody's faults to magnify under the lens that
he never turns on himself. 21

What have been your Leader's precepts and example!
Were they to save the sinner, and to spare his exposure

1 so long as a hope remained of thereby benefiting him?
Has her life exemplified long-suffering, meekness, charity,
3 purity?

She readily leaves the answer to those who know
her.

6   Do we yet understand how much better it is to be
wronged, than to commit wrong? What do we find in
the Bible, and in the Christian Science textbook, on this
9 subject? Does not the latter instruct you that looking
continually for a fault in somebody else, talking about it,
thinking it over, and how to meet it, — "rolling sin as a
12 sweet morsel under your tongue," — has the same power
to make you a sinner that acting thus regarding disease
has to make a man sick? Note the Scripture on this
15 subject: "Vengeance is mine; I will repay, saith the
Lord."

The Christian Science Board of Directors has borne
18 the burden in the heat of the day, and it ought not to
be expected that they could have accomplished, without
one single mistake, such Herculean tasks as they have
21 accomplished. He who judges others should know well
whereof he speaks. Where the motive to do right exists,
and the majority of one's acts are right, we should avoid
24 referring to past mistakes. The greatest sin that one can
commit against himself is to wrong one of God's "little
ones."

27   Know ye not that he who exercises the largest charity,
and waits on God, renews his strength, and is exalted?
Love is not puffed up; and the meek and loving, God
30 anoints and appoints to lead the line of mankind's tri-
umphal march out of the wilderness, out of darkness
into light.

Whoever challenges the errors of others and cherishes 1
his own, can neither help himself nor others; he will be
called a moral nuisance, a fungus, a microbe, a mouse 3
gnawing at the vitals of humanity. The darkness in
one's self must first be cast out, in order rightly to discern
darkness or to reflect light. 6

If the man of more than average avoirdupois kneels on
a stool in church, let the leaner sort console this brother's
necessity by doing likewise. Christian Scientists preserve 9
unity, and so shadow forth the substance of our sublime
faith, and the evidence of its being built upon the rock of
divine oneness, — one faith, one God, one baptism. 12

If our Board of Directors is prepared to itemize a report
of the first financial year since the erection of the edifice of
The First Church of Christ, Scientist, let it do so; other- 15
wise, I recommend that you waive the church By-law
relating to finances this year of your firstfruits. This
Board did not act under that By-law; it was not in ex- 18
istence all of the year. It is but just to consider the great
struggles with perplexities and difficulties which the
Directors encountered in Anno Domini 1894, and which 21
they have overcome. May God give unto us all that loving sense of gratitude which delights in the opportunity to
cancel accounts. I, for one, would be pleased to have the 24
Christian Science Board of Directors itemize a bill of this
church's gifts to Mother; and then to have them let her
state the value thereof, if, indeed, it could be estimated. 27

After this financial year, when you call on the members
of the Christian Science Board of Directors to itemize or
audit their accounts, these will be found already itemized, 30
and last year's records immortalized, with perils past and
victories won.

1 A motion was made, and a vote passed, at your last
meeting, on a subject the substance whereof you had al-
3 ready accepted as a By-law. But, I shall take this as a
favorable omen, a fair token that heavy lids are opening,
even wider than before, to the light of Love — and By-laws.
6   Affectionately yours,
                              MARY BAKER EDDY

                    TO ——, ON PRAYER

9   MASSACHUSETTS METAPHYSICAL COLLEGE,
                       571 COLUMBUS AVENUE,
                       BOSTON, March 21, 1885

12 *Dear Sir:* — In your communication to *Zion's Herald,*
March 18, under the heading, "Prayer and Healing; sup-
plemental," you state that you would "like to hear from
15 Dr. Cullis; and, by the way, from Mrs. Eddy, also."
    Because of the great demand upon my time, consisting
in part of dictating answers through my secretary, or an-
18 swering personally manifold letters and inquiries from all
quarters, — having charge of a church, editing a magazine, teaching Christian Science, receiving calls, etc., — I
21 find it inconvenient to accept your invitation to answer
you through the medium of a newspaper; but, for information as to what I believe and teach, would refer you to
24 the Holy Scriptures, to my various publications, and to my
Christian students.
    It was with a thrill of pleasure that I read in your arti-
27 cle these words: "If we have in any way misrepresented
either Dr. Cullis or Mrs. Eddy, we are sorry." Even the
desire to be just is a vital spark of Christianity. And those
30 words inspire me with the hope that you wish to be just.

If this is so, you will not delay corrections of the statement 1
you make at the close of your article, when referring to
me, "the pantheistic and prayerless Mrs. Eddy, of Boston." 3

It would be difficult to build a sentence of so few words
conveying ideas more opposite to the fact.

In refutation of your statement that I am a pantheist, 6
I request you to read my sermons and publications.

As to being "prayerless," I call your attention and
deep consideration to the following Scripture, that voices 9
my impressions of prayer: —

"When thou prayest, thou shalt not be as the hypocrites
are: for they love to pray standing in the synagogues and 12
in the corners of the streets, that they may be seen of men.
. . . But thou, when thou prayest, enter into thy closet,
and when thou hast shut thy door, pray to thy Father 15
which is in secret; and thy Father which seeth in secret
shall reward thee openly."

I hope I am not wrong in literally following the dictum 18
of Jesus; and, were it not because of my desire to set
you right on this question, I should feel a delicacy in making the following statement: — 21

Three times a day, I retire to seek the divine blessing
on the sick and sorrowing, with my face toward the Jerusalem of Love and Truth, in silent prayer to the Father 24
which "seeth in secret," and with childlike confidence that
He will reward "openly." In the midst of depressing care
and labor I turn constantly to divine Love for guidance, 27
and find rest. It affords me great joy to be able to attest to
the truth of Jesus' words. Love makes all burdens light,
it giveth a peace that passeth understanding, and with 30
"signs following." As to the peace, it is unutterable; as
to "signs," behold the sick who are healed, the sorrowful

1 who are made hopeful, and the sinful and ignorant who have become "wise unto salvation"!

3   And now, dear sir, as you have expressed contrition for an act which you have immediately repeated, you are placed in this dilemma: To reiterate such words of 6 apology as characterize justice and Christianity.

Very truly,

MARY BAKER G. EDDY

9 TO THE NATIONAL CHRISTIAN SCIENTIST ASSOCIATION

Beloved Students: — Meet together and meet *en masse,* in 1888, at the annual session of the National Christian 12 Scientist Association. Be "of one mind," "in one place," and God will pour you out a blessing such as you never before received. He who dwelleth in eternal light is 15 bigger than the shadow, and will guard and guide His own.

Let no consideration bend or outweigh your purpose 18 to be in Chicago on June 13. Firm in your allegiance to the reign of universal harmony, go to its rescue. In God's hour, the powers of earth and hell are proven powerless. 21 The reeling ranks of *materia medica,* with poisons, nostrums, and knives, are impotent when at war with the omnipotent! Like Elisha, look up, and behold: "They 24 that be with us, are more than they that be with them."

Error is only fermenting, and its heat hissing at the "still, small voice" of Truth; but it can neither silence 27 nor disarm God's voice. Spiritual wickedness is standing in high places; but, blind to its own fate, it will tumble into the bottomless.

Christians, and all *true* Scientists, marching under what- 1
soever ensign, come into the ranks! Again I repeat, person is not in the question of Christian Science. Principle, 3
instead of person, is next to our hearts, on our lips, and
in our lives. Our watchwords are Truth and Love; and
if we abide in these, they will abound in us, and we shall 6
be one in heart, — one in motive, purpose, pursuit. Abiding in Love, not one of you can be separated from me; and
the sweet sense of journeying on together, doing unto 9
others as ye would they should do unto you, conquers all
opposition, surmounts all obstacles, and secures success.
If you falter, or fail to fulfil this Golden Rule, though you 12
should build to the heavens, you would build on sand.

Is it a cross to give one week's time and expense to the
jubilee of Spirit? Then take this cross, and the crown 15
with it. Sending forth currents of Truth, God's methods
and means of healing, and so spreading the gospel of
Love, is in itself an eternity of joy that outweighs an 18
hour. Add one more noble offering to the unity of good,
and so cement the bonds of Love.

With love,   21

MARY BAKER EDDY

TO THE COLLEGE ASSOCIATION

Letter read at the meeting of the Massachusetts Metaphysical 24
College Association, June 3, 1891

TO THE MEMBERS OF THE CHRISTIAN SCIENTISTS' ASSOCIATION OF
THE MASSACHUSETTS METAPHYSICAL COLLEGE   27

My Beloved Students: — You may be looking to see me
in my accustomed place with you, but this you must no

1 longer expect. When I retired from the field of labor,
it was a departure, socially, publicly, and finally, from
3 the routine of such material modes as society and our
societies demand. Rumors are rumors, — nothing more.
I am still with you on the field of battle, taking forward
6 marches, broader and higher views, and with the hope
that you will follow.

The eternal and infinite, already brought to your
9 earnest consideration, so grow upon my vision that I
cannot feel justified in turning aside for one hour from
contemplation of them and of the faith unfeigned.
12 When the verities of being seem to you as to me, — as
they must some time, — you will understand the necessity for my seclusion, and its fulfilment of divine order.
15 "Wherefore come out from among them, and be ye separate, saith the Lord."

All our thoughts should be given to the absolute
18 demonstration of Christian Science. You can well
afford to give me up, since you have in my last revised edition of Science and Health your teacher and
21 guide.

I recommend that the June session of this honorable
body shall close your meetings for the summer; also, that
24 hereafter you hold three sessions annually, convening
once in four months; oftener is not requisite, and the
members coming from a distance will be accommodated
27 by this arrangement.

Yours affectionately,
MARY B. G. EDDY

TO THE NATIONAL CHRISTIAN SCIENTIST ASSOCIATION 1

My Dear Students and Friends: — Accept my thanks
for your card of invitation, your badge, and order of exer- 3
cise, all of which are complete.

When I gave you a meagre reception in Boston at the
close of the first convention of the National Christian 6
Scientist Association, it was simply to give you the privilege, poor as it was, of speaking a few words aside to your
teacher. I remember my regret, when, having asked in 9
general assembly if you had any questions to propose, I
received no reply. Since then you have doubtless realized
that such opportunity might have been improved; but 12
that time has passed.

I greatly rejoice over the growth of my students within
the last few years. It was kind of you to part so gently 15
with the protecting wings of the mother-bird, and to spread
your own so bravely. Now, dear ones, if you take my
advice again, you will do — what? 18

Even this: Disorganize the National Christian Scientist Association! and each one return to his place of
labor, to work out individually and alone, for himself and 21
for others, the sublime ends of human life.

To accomplish this, you must give much time to self-
examination and correction; you must control appetite, 24
passion, pride, envy, evil-speaking, resentment, and each
one of the innumerable errors that worketh or maketh
a lie. Then you can give to the world the benefit of all 27
this, and heal and teach with increased confidence. My
students can *now* organize their students into associations, form churches, and hold these organizations of their 30

1 own, — until, in turn, their students will sustain themselves and work for others.

3 The time it takes yearly to prepare for this national convention is worse than wasted, if it causes thought to wander in the wilderness or ways of the world. The detail of conforming to society, in any way, costs you what it would to give time and attention to hygiene in your ministry and healing.

9 For students to work together is not always to coöperate, but sometimes to coelbow! Each student should seek alone the guidance of our common Father — even the divine Principle which he claims to demonstrate, — and especially should he prove his faith by works, ethically, physically, and spiritually. Remember that the first and last lesson of Christian Science is love, perfect love, and love made perfect through the cross.

I once thought that in unity was human strength; but have grown to know that human strength is weakness, — that unity is divine might, giving to human power, peace.

My counsel is applicable to the state of general growth in the members of the National Christian Scientist Association, but it is not so adapted to the members of students' organizations. And wherefore? Because the growth of these at first is more gradual; but whenever they are equal to the march triumphant, God will give to all His soldiers of the cross the proper command, and under the banner of His love, and with the "still, small voice" for the music of our march, we all shall take step and march on in spiritual organization.

30   Your loving teacher,

                            MARY BAKER G. EDDY

CONCORD, N. H., May 23, 1890

N. B. I recommend this honorable body to adjourn, 1
if it does not disorganize, to three years from this date;
or, if it does disorganize, to meet again in three years. 3
Then bring your tithes into the storehouse, and God will
pour you out a blessing such as you even yet have not
received. 6

M. B. G. E.

TO THE FIRST CHURCH OF CHRIST, SCIENTIST,
BOSTON 9

*(For the weapons of our warfare are not carnal, but mighty
through God to the pulling down of strong holds;) casting down
imaginations, and every high thing that exalteth itself against the 12
knowledge of God, and bringing into captivity every thought to the
obedience of Christ. — 2 COR. x. 4, 5.*

In April, 1883, I started the *Journal* of Christian 15
Science, with a portion of the above Scripture for its
motto.

On December 10, 1889, I gave a lot of land — in 18
Boston, situated near the beautiful Back Bay Park, now
valued at $20,000 and rising in value — for the purpose
of having erected thereon a church edifice to be called The 21
Church of Christ, Scientist.

I had this desirable site transferred in a circuitous,
novel way, at the wisdom whereof a few persons have 24
since scrupled; but to my spiritual perception, like all
true wisdom, this transaction will in future be regarded
as greatly wise, and it will be found that this act was in 27
advance of the erring mind's apprehension.

As with all former efforts in the interest of Christian
Science, I took care that the provisions for the land and 30

1 building were such as error could not control. I knew
that to God's gift, foundation and superstructure, no one
3 could hold a wholly material title. The land, and the
church standing on it, must be conveyed through a type
representing the true nature of the gift; a type morally
6 and spiritually inalienable, but materially questionable
— even after the manner that all spiritual good comes
to Christian Scientists, to the end of taxing their faith
9 in God, and their adherence to the superiority of the
claims of Spirit over matter or merely legal titles.

No one could buy, sell, or mortgage my gift as I had
12 it conveyed. Thus the case rested, and I supposed the
trustee-deed was legal; but this was God's business, not
mine. Our church was prospered by the right hand of
15 His righteousness, and contributions to the Building Fund
generously poured into the treasury. Unity prevailed, —
till mortal man sought to know who owned God's temple,
18 and adopted and urged only the material side of this
question.

The lot of land which I donated I redeemed from under
21 mortgage. The foundation on which our church was to
be built had to be rescued from the grasp of legal power,
and now it must be put back into the arms of Love, if we
24 would not be found fighting against God.

The diviner claim and means for upbuilding the Church
of Christ were prospered. Our title to God's acres will
27 be safe and sound — when we can "read our title clear"
to heavenly mansions. Built on the rock, our church
will stand the storms of ages: though the material super-
30 structure should crumble into dust, the fittest would survive, — the spiritual idea would live, a perpetual type of
the divine Principle it reflects.

The First Church of Christ, Scientist, our prayer in 1
stone, will be the prophecy fulfilled, the monument up-
reared, of Christian Science. It will speak to you of the 3
Mother, and of your hearts' offering to her through whom
was revealed to you God's all-power, all-presence, and
all-science. This building begun, will go up, and no one 6
can suffer from it, for no one can resist the power that
is behind it; and against this church temple "the gates
of hell" cannot prevail. 9

All loyal Christian Scientists hail with joy this proposed type of universal Love; not so, however, with
error, which hates the bonds and methods of Truth, and 12
shudders at the freedom, might, and majesty of Spirit,
— even the annihilating law of Love.

I vindicate both the law of God and the laws of our 15
land. I believe, — yea, I understand, — that with the
spirit of Christ actuating all the parties concerned about
the legal quibble, it can easily be corrected to the satis- 18
faction of all. Let this be speedily done. Do not, I im-
plore you, stain the early history of Christian Science by
the impulses of human will and pride; but let the divine 21
will and the nobility of human meekness rule this business transaction, in obedience to the law of Love and the
laws of our land. 24

As the ambassador of Christ's teachings, I admonish
you: Delay not longer to commence building our church
in Boston; or else return every dollar that you yourselves 27
declare you have had no legal authority for obtaining, to
the several contributors, — and let them, not you, say
what shall be done with their money. 30

Of our first church in Boston, O recording angel!
write: God is in the midst of her: how beautiful are her

1 feet! how beautiful are her garments! how hath He enlarged her borders! how hath He made her wildernesses
3 to bud and blossom as the rose!

With love,
MARY BAKER EDDY

6 TO DONORS OF BOAT, FROM TORONTO, CANADA

Written on receipt of a beautiful boat presented by Christian
Scientists in Toronto, for the little pond at Pleasant View. The
9 boat displays, among other beautiful decorations, a number of
masonic symbols.

Beloved Students and Friends: — Accept my thanks
12 for the beautiful boat and presentation poem. Each day
since they arrived I have said, Let me write to the donors,
— and what?
15 My first impression was to indite a poem; my second,
a psalm; my third, a letter. Why the letter alone? Because your dear hearts expressed in their lovely gift such
18 varying types of true affection, shaded as autumn leaves
with bright hues of the spiritual, that my Muse lost her
lightsome lyre, and imagery of thought gave place to
21 chords of feeling too deep for words.

A boat song seemed more Olympian than the psalm in
spiritual strains of the Hebrew bard. So I send my
24 answer in a commonplace letter. Poor return, is it
not?

The symbols of freemasonry depicted on the boat
27 wakened memory, touched tender fibres of thought, and
I longed to say to the masonic brothers: If as a woman
I may not unite with you in freemasonry, nor you with
30 me in Christian Science, yet as friends we can feel the

touch of heart to heart and hand to hand, on the broad 1
basis and sure foundation of true friendship's "level"
and the "square" of moral sentiments.   3

My dear students may have explained to the kind participants in beautifying this boat our spiritual points,
above the plane of matter. If so, I may hope that a 6
closer link hath bound us. Across lakes, into a kingdom,
I reach out my hand to clasp yours, with this silent benediction: May the kingdom of heaven come in each of 9
your hearts!

With love,

MARY BAKER EDDY 12

ADDRESS, — LAYING THE CORNER-STONE

Beloved Students: — On the 21st day of May, A. D.
1894, with quiet, imposing ceremony, is laid the corner- 15
stone of "The First Church of Christ, Scientist," in
Boston.

It gives me great pleasure to say that you, principally 18
the Normal class graduates of my College, well known
physicians, teachers, editors, and pastors of churches,
by contributions of one thousand dollars each, husband 21
and wife reckoned as one, have, within about three
months, donated the munificent sum of forty-two thousand dollars toward building The Mother Church. A 24
quiet call from me for this extra contribution, in aid of
our Church Building Fund, found you all "with one
accord in one place." Each donation came promptly; 27
sometimes at much self-sacrifice, but always accompanied
with a touching letter breathing the donor's privileged joy.

1 The granite for this church was taken from the quarries in New Hampshire, my native State. The money 3 for building "Mother's Room," situated in the second story of the tower on the northeast corner of this building, and the name thereof, came from the dear children 6 of Christian Scientists; a little band called Busy Bees, organized by Miss Maurine R. Campbell.

On this memorable day there are laid away a copy of 9 this address, the subscription list on which appear your several names in your own handwriting, your textbook, "Science and Health with Key to the Scriptures," and 12 other works written by the same author, your teacher, the Discoverer and Founder of Christian Science; * without pomp or pride, laid away as a sacred secret in the 15 heart of a rock, there to typify the prophecy, "And a man shall be as an hiding place from the wind, and a covert from the tempest; . . . as the shadow of a great rock in 18 a weary land:" henceforth to whisper our Master's promise, "Upon this rock I will build my church; and the gates of hell shall not prevail against it."

21 To-day, be this hope in each of our hearts, — precious in God's sight as shall be the assembling of His people in this temple, sweet as the rest that remaineth for the 24 righteous, and fresh as a summer morn, — that, from earth's pillows of stone, our visible lives are rising to God. As in the history of a seed, so may our earthly 27 sowing bear fruit that exudes the inspiration of the wine poured into the cup of Christ.

To-day I pray that divine Love, the life-giving Principle 30 of Christianity, shall speedily wake the long night of materialism, and the universal dawn shall break upon the spire of this temple. The Church, more than any

* A copy of the Bible was included among the books placed in the corner-stone.

other institution, at present is the cement of society, and 1
it should be the bulwark of civil and religious liberty.
But the time cometh when the religious element, or Church 3
of Christ, shall exist alone in the affections, and need no
organization to express it. Till then, this form of godliness seems as requisite to manifest its spirit, as individ- 6
uality to express Soul and substance.

Does a single bosom burn for fame and power? Then
when that person shall possess these, let him ask him- 9
self, and answer to his name in this corner-stone of our
temple: Am I greater for them? And if he thinks that
he is, then is he less than man to whom God gave "do- 12
minion over all the earth," less than the meek who "inherit the earth." Even vanity forbids man to be vain;
and pride is a hooded hawk which flies in darkness. Over 15
a wounded sense of its own error, let not mortal thought
resuscitate too soon.

In our rock-bound friendship, delicate as dear, our 18
names may melt into one, and common dust, and their
modest sign be nothingness. Be this as it may, the visible
unity of spirit remains, to quicken even dust into sweet 21
memorial such as Isaiah prophesied: "The wolf also shall
dwell with the lamb, and the leopard shall lie down with
the kid; and the calf and the young lion and the fatling 24
together; and a little child shall lead them."

When the *hearts* of Christian Scientists are woven together as are their names in the web of history, earth will 27
float majestically heaven's heraldry, and echo the song
of angels: "Glory to God in the highest, and on earth
peace, good will toward men." 30

To The Church of Christ, Scientist, in Boston, and to
the dear children that my heart folds within it, let me

1 say, 'Tis sweet to remember thee, and God's Zion, with
healing on her wings. May her walls be vocal with sal-
3 vation; and her gates with praise!

TO THE FIRST CHURCH OF CHRIST, SCIENTIST, BOSTON

6   *My Beloved Students:* — I cannot conscientiously lend
my counsel to direct your action on receiving or dismiss-
ing candidates. To do this, I should need to be with
9 you. I cannot accept hearsay, and would need to know
the circumstances and facts regarding both sides of the
subject, to form a proper judgment. This is not my
12 present province; hence I have hitherto declined to be
consulted on these subjects, and still maintain this
position.
15   These are matters of grave import; and you cannot
be indifferent to this, but will give them immediate attention, and be governed therein by the spirit and the
18 letter of this Scripture: "Whatsoever ye would that men
should do unto you, do ye even so to them."
   I cannot be the conscience for this church; but if I
21 were, I would gather every reformed mortal that desired
to come, into its fold, and counsel and help him to walk
in the footsteps of His flock. I feel sure that as Chris-
24 tian Scientists you will act, relative to this matter, up to
your highest understanding of justice and mercy.

Affectionately yours,

27   MARY BAKER EDDY
   Feb. 12, 1895

THE FIRST MEMBERS OF THE FIRST CHURCH OF CHRIST, 1
SCIENTIST, BOSTON, MASSACHUSETTS

My Beloved Students: — Another year has rolled on, 3
another annual meeting has convened, another space of
time has been given us, and has another duty been done
and another victory won for time and eternity? Do you 6
meet in unity, preferring one another, and demonstrating
the divine Principle of Christian Science? Have you
improved past hours, and ladened them with records 9
worthy to be borne heavenward? Have you learned
that sin is inadmissible, and indicates a small mind?
Do you manifest love for those that hate you and de- 12
spitefully use you?

The man of integrity is one who makes it his constant
rule to follow the road of duty, according as Truth and 15
the voice of his conscience point it out to him. He is not
guided merely by affections which may some time give
the color of virtue to a loose and unstable character. 18

The upright man is guided by a fixed Principle, which
destines him to do nothing but what is honorable, and to
abhor whatever is base or unworthy; hence we find him 21
ever the same, — at all times the trusty friend, the affectionate relative, the conscientious man of business, the
pious worker, the public-spirited citizen. 24

He assumes no borrowed appearance. He seeks no
mask to cover him, for he acts no studied part; but he
is indeed what he appears to be, — full of truth, candor, 27
and humanity. In all his pursuits, he knows no path
but the fair, open, and direct one, and would much rather
fail of success than attain it by reproachable means. He 30

1 never shows us a smiling countenance while he meditates
evil against us in his heart. We shall never find one part
3 of his character at variance with another.

Lovingly yours,
MARY BAKER EDDY

6   Sept. 30, 1895

EXTRACT FROM A LETTER

The Rules and By-laws in the Manual of The First
9 Church of Christ, Scientist, Boston, originated not in
solemn conclave as in ancient Sanhedrim. They were
not arbitrary opinions nor dictatorial demands, such as
12 one person might impose on another. They were impelled by a power not one's own, were written at different dates, and as the occasion required. They sprang
15 from necessity, the logic of events, — from the immediate demand for them as a help that must be supplied to
maintain the dignity and defense of our Cause; hence
18 their simple, scientific basis, and detail so requisite to
demonstrate genuine Christian Science, and which will
do for the race what absolute doctrines destined for future
21 generations might not accomplish.

TO THE MOTHER CHURCH

Beloved Brethren: — Until recently, I was not aware
24 that the contribution box was presented at your Friday
evening meetings. I specially desire that you collect no
moneyed contributions from the people present on these
27 occasions.

Let the invitation to this sweet converse be in the words
of the prophet Isaiah: "Ho, every one that thirsteth,

come ye to the waters, and he that hath no money; come 1
ye, buy, and eat; yea, come, buy wine and milk without
money and without price." 3
Invite all cordially and freely to this banquet of Christian Science, this feast and flow of Soul. Ask them to
bring what they possess of love and light to help leaven 6
your loaf and replenish your scanty store. Then, after
presenting the various offerings, and one after another
has opened his lips to discourse and distribute what God 9
has given him of experience, hope, faith, and understanding, gather up the fragments, and count the baskets
full of accessions to your love, and see that nothing has 12
been lost.

With love,

MARY BAKER EDDY 15

TO FIRST CHURCH OF CHRIST, SCIENTIST, IN
OCONTO

My Beloved Brethren: — Lips nor pen can ever ex- 18
press the joy you give me in parting so promptly with
your beloved pastor, Rev. Mr. Norcross, to send him to
aid me. It is a refreshing demonstration of Christianity, 21
brotherly love, and all the rich graces of the Spirit. May
this sacrifice bring to your beloved church a vision of the
new church, that cometh down from heaven, whose altar 24
is a loving heart, whose communion is fellowship with
saints and angels. This example of yours is a light that
cannot be hid. 27
Guided by the pillar and the cloud, this little church
that built the first temple for Christian Science worship
shall abide steadfastly in the faith of Jesus' words: "Fear 30

1 not, little flock; for it is your Father's good pleasure to
give you the kingdom." May He soon give you a pastor;
3 already you have the great Shepherd of Israel watching over you. Give my forever-love to your dear church.

Yours in bonds of Christ,

6   MARY BAKER G. EDDY

Boston, Mass., 1889

TO FIRST CHURCH OF CHRIST, SCIENTIST, IN
9   SCRANTON

Beloved Brethren: — Space is no separator of hearts.
Spiritually, I am with all who are with Truth, and whose
12 hearts to-day are repeating their joy that God dwelleth
in the congregation of the faithful, and loveth the gates
of Zion.

15   The outlook is cheering. We have already seen the
salvation of many people by means of Christian Science.
Chapels and churches are dotting the entire land. Con-
18 venient houses and halls can now be obtained wherein, as
whereout, Christian Scientists may worship the Father
"in spirit and in truth," as taught by our great Master.

21   "If God be for us, who can be against us?" If He
be with us, the wayside is a sanctuary, and the desert a
resting-place peopled with living witnesses of the fact
24 that "God is Love."

God is universal; confined to no spot, defined by no
dogma, appropriated by no sect. Not more to one than
27 to all, is God demonstrable as divine Life, Truth, and
Love; and His people are they that reflect Him — that
reflect Love. Again, this infinite Principle, with its uni-
30 versal manifestation, is all that really is or can be;
hence God is our Shepherd. He guards, guides, feeds,

and folds the sheep of His pasture; and their ears are 1
attuned to His call. In the words of the loving disciple,
"My sheep hear my voice, . . . and they follow me; 3
. . . neither shall any man pluck them out of my
hand."

God is a consuming fire. He separates the dross from 6
the gold, purifies the human character, through the
furnace of affliction. Those who bear fruit He purgeth,
that they may bear more fruit. Through the sacred law, 9
He speaketh to the unfruitful in tones of Sinai: and, in
the gospel, He saith of the barren fig-tree, "Cut it down;
why cumbereth it the ground?"   12

God is our Father and our Mother, our Minister and
the great Physician: He is man's only real relative on
earth and in heaven. David sang, "Whom have I in 15
heaven but thee? and there is none upon earth that I
desire beside thee."

Brother, sister, beloved in the Lord, knowest thou 18
thyself, and art thou acquainted with God? If not, I
pray thee as a Christian Scientist, delay not to make Him
thy first acquaintance.   21

Glorious things are spoken of you in His Word. Ye
are a chosen people, whose God is — what? Even *All*.
May mercy and truth go before you: may the lamp of 24
your life continually be full of oil, and you be wedded
to the spiritual idea, Christ; then will you heal, and
teach, and preach, on the ascending scale of everlasting 27
Life and Love.

Affectionately yours in Christ,

MARY BAKER EDDY 30

1   TO FIRST CHURCH OF CHRIST, SCIENTIST,
IN DENVER

3   *Beloved Pastor and Brethren:* — "As in water face
answereth to face," and in love continents clasp hands, so
the oneness of God includes also His presence with those
6   whose hearts unite in the purposes of goodness. Of this
we may be sure: that thoughts winged with peace and
love breathe a silent benediction over all the earth, co-
9   operate with the divine power, and brood unconsciously
o'er the work of His hand.

I, as a corporeal person, am not in your midst: I, as a
12   dictator, arbiter, or ruler, am not present; but I, as a
mother whose heart pulsates with every throb of theirs
for the welfare of her children, am present, and rejoice
15   with them that rejoice.

May meekness, mercy, and love dwell forever in the
hearts of those who worship in this tabernacle: then
18   will they receive the heritage that God has prepared for
His people, — made ready for the pure in affection, the
meek in spirit, the worshipper in truth, the follower of
21   good.

Thus founded upon the rock of Christ, when storm
and tempest beat against this sure foundation, you,
24   safely sheltered in the strong tower of hope, faith, and
Love, are God's nestlings; and He will hide you in His
feathers till the storm has passed. Into His haven of
27   Soul there enters no element of earth to cast out angels,
to silence the right intuition which guides you safely
home.

30   Exercise more faith in God and His spiritual means

and methods, than in man and his material ways and 1
means, of establishing the Cause of Christian Science.
If right yourself, God will confirm His inheritance. "Be 3
not weary in well doing." Truth is restful, and Love is
triumphant.

When God went forth before His people, they were 6
fed with manna: they marched through the wilderness:
they passed through the Red Sea, untouched by the billows. At His command, the rock became a fountain; 9
and the land of promise, green isles of refreshment. In
the words of the Psalmist, when "the Lord gave the word:
great was the company of those that published it."   12

God is good to Israel, — washed in the waters of
Meribah, cleansed of the flesh, — good to His Israel
encompassed not with pride, hatred, self-will, and self- 15
justification; wherein violence covereth men as a garment, and as captives are they enchained.

Christian Scientists bring forth the fruits of Spirit, 18
not flesh; and God giveth this "new name" to no man
who honors Him not by positive proof of trustworthiness.
May you be able to say, "I have not cleansed my heart 21
in vain."

Sir Edwin Arnold, to whom I presented a copy of
my first edition of "Science and Health with Key to the 24
Scriptures," writes: —

> Peace on earth and Good-will!
> Souls that are gentle and still   27
> Hear the first music of this
> Far-off, infinite, Bliss!

So may the God of peace be and abide with this church. 30

Affectionately yours,

MARY BAKER EDDY

1   TO FIRST CHURCH OF CHRIST, SCIENTIST,
IN LAWRENCE

3   *Beloved Brethren:* — The spreading branches of The
Church of Christ, Scientist, are fast reaching out their
broad shelter to the entire world. Your faith has not
6 been without works, — and God's love for His flock is
manifest in His care. He will dig about this little church,
prune its encumbering branches, water it with the dews
9 of heaven, enrich its roots, and enlarge its borders with
divine Love. God only waits for man's worthiness to
enhance the means and measure of His grace. You
12 have already proof of the prosperity of His Zion. You
sit beneath your own vine and fig-tree as the growth
of spirituality — even that vine whereof our Father is
15 husbandman.

It is the purpose of divine Love to resurrect the understanding, and the kingdom of God, the reign of har-
18 mony already within us. Through the word that is
spoken unto you, are you made free. Abide in His word,
and it shall abide in you; and the healing Christ will
21 again be made manifest in the flesh — understood and
glorified.

Honor thy Father and Mother, God. Continue in
24 His love. Bring forth fruit — "signs following" — that
your prayers be not hindered. Pray without ceasing.
Watch diligently; never desert the post of spiritual ob-
27 servation and self-examination. Strive for self-abnegation, justice, meekness, mercy, purity, love. Let your
light reflect Light. Have no ambition, affection, nor
30 aim apart from holiness. Forget not for a moment, that

God is All-in-all — therefore, that in reality there is but 1
one cause and effect.

The pride of circumstance or power is the prince of 3
this world that has nothing in Christ. All power and
happiness are spiritual, and proceed from goodness.
Sacrifice self to bless one another, even as God has 6
blessed you. Forget self in laboring for mankind; then
will you woo the weary wanderer to your door, win the
pilgrim and stranger to your church, and find access to 9
the heart of humanity. While pressing meekly on, be
faithful, be valiant in the Christian's warfare, and peace
will crown your joy.   12

Lovingly yours,
MARY BAKER EDDY

TO CORRESPONDENTS   15

Beloved Students: — Because Mother has not the time
even to read all of her interesting correspondence, and
less wherein to answer it (however much she desires 18
thus to do), she hereby requests: First, that you, her
students' students, who write such excellent letters to
her, will hereafter, as a general rule, send them to the 21
editors of *The Christian Science Journal* for publication,
and thereby give to us all the pleasure of hearing from you.

If my own students cannot spare time to write to God, 24
— when they address me I shall be apt to forward their
letters to Him as our common Parent, and by way of
The Christian Science Journal; thus fulfilling their moral 27
obligation to furnish some reading-matter for our denominational organ. Methinks, were they to contemplate the
universal charge wherewith divine Love has entrusted us, 30

1 in behalf of a suffering race, they would contribute oftener
to the pages of this swift vehicle of scientific thought;
3 for it reaches a vast number of earnest readers, and seekers after Truth.   With love,

MARY BAKER EDDY

6   TO STUDENTS

Beloved Christian Scientists: — Please send in your
contributions as usual to our *Journal.* All is well at head-
9 quarters, and when the mist shall melt away you will see
clearly the signs of Truth and the heaven of Love within
your hearts. Let the reign of peace and harmony be
12 supreme and forever yours.

I proposed to merge the adjourned meeting in the one
held at Chicago, because I saw no advantage, but great
15 disadvantage, in one student's opinions or *modus operandi* becoming the basis for others: read "Retrospection"
on this subject. Science is absolute, and best under-
18 stood through the study of my works and the daily Christian demonstration thereof. It is their *materiality* that
clogs the progress of students, and "this kind goeth not
21 forth but by prayer and fasting." It is materialism through
which the animal magnetizer preys, and in turn becomes
a prey. Spirituality is the basis of all true thought and
24 volition. Assembling themselves together, and listening
to each other amicably, or contentiously, is no aid to
students in acquiring solid Christian Science. Experi-
27 ence and, above all, *obedience,* are the aids and tests of
growth and understanding in this direction.

With love,

30   MARY B. G. EDDY

TO A STUDENT   1

My Dear Student: — It is a great thing to be found worthy to suffer for Christ, Truth. Paul said, "If we 3 suffer, we shall also reign with him." Reign then, my beloved in the Lord. He that marketh the sparrow's fall will direct thy way.   6

I have written, or caused my secretary to write, to Mr. and Mrs. Stewart, of Toronto, Canada (you will find their card in *The C. S. Journal*), that you or your lawyer will 9 ask them all questions important for your case, and requested that they furnish all information possible. They will be glad to help you. Every true Christian Scientist 12 will feel "as bound with you," but as free in Truth and Love, safe under the shadow of His wing.

Yes, my student, my Father is your Father; and He 15 helps us most when help is most needed, for He is the ever-present help.

I am glad that you are in good cheer. I enclose you 18 the name of Mr. E. A. Kimball, C. S. D., of Chicago, — 5020 Woodlawn Ave., — for items relative to Mrs. Stebbin's case.   21

"Commit thy way unto the Lord; trust also in Him; and He shall bring it to pass. And He shall bring forth thy righteousness as the light, and thy judgment as the 24 noonday." This I know, for God is for us.

Write me when you need me. Error has no power but to destroy itself. It *cannot harm you;* it cannot stop 27 the eternal currents of Truth.

Ever with love,

MARY B. G. EDDY   30

1   TO A STUDENT

My Beloved Student: — In reply to your letter I will
3 say: God's ways are not as our ways; but higher far
than the heavens above the earth is His wisdom above
ours. When I requested you to be ordained, I little
6 thought of the changes about to be made. When I insisted on your speaking without notes, I little knew that
so soon another change in your pulpit would be demanded.
9 But now, after His messenger has obeyed the message
of divine Love, comes the interpretation thereof. But you
see we both had first to obey, and to do this through faith,
12 not sight.

The meaning of it all, as now shown, is this: when
you were bidden to be ordained, it was in reward for your
15 faithful service, thus to honor it. The second command,
to drop the use of notes, was to rebuke a lack of faith in
divine help, and to test your humility and obedience in
18 bearing this cross.

All God's servants are minute men and women. As
of old, I stand with sandals on and staff in hand, wait-
21 ing for the watchword and the revelation of what, how,
whither. Let us be faithful and obedient, and God will
do the rest.

24   In the April number of *The Christian Science Journal*
you will find the forthcoming completion (as I now think)
of the divine directions sent out to the churches. It is
27 satisfactory to note, however, that the order therein given
corresponds to the example of our Master. Jesus was
not ordained as our churches ordain ministers. We
30 have no record that he used notes when preaching. He

spake in their synagogues, reading the Scriptures and 1
expounding them; and God has given to this age "Science
and Health with Key to the Scriptures," to elucidate 3
His Word.

You may read this letter to your church, and then
send it to Rev. Mr. Norcross, and he will understand. 6
May the God of all grace give you peace.

With love,

MARY BAKER EDDY   9

EXTRACT FROM A CHRISTMAS LETTER

Beloved Students: — My heart has many rooms: one
of these is sacred to the memory of my students. Into 12
this upper chamber, where all things are pure and of
good report, — into this sanctuary of love, — I often
retreat, sit silently, and ponder. In this chamber is 15
memory's wardrobe, where I deposit certain recollections and rare grand collections once in each year. This
is my Christmas storehouse. Its goods commemorate, 18
— not so much the Bethlehem babe, as the man of God,
the risen Christ, and the adult Jesus. Here I deposit
the gifts that my dear students offer at the shrine of 21
Christian Science, and to their lone Leader. Here I talk
once a year, — and this is a bit of what I said in 1890:
"O glorious Truth! O Mother Love! how has the sense 24
of Thy children grown to behold *Thee!* and how have
many weary wings sprung upward! and how has our
Model, Christ, been unveiled to us, and to the age!" 27

I look at the rich devices in embroidery, silver, gold,
and jewels, — all gifts of Christian Scientists from all
parts of our nation, and some from abroad, — then al- 30

1 most marvel at the power and permanence of affection
under the *régime* of Christian Science! Never did grati-
3 tude and love unite more honestly in uttering the word
thanks, than ours at this season. But a mother's love
behind words has no language; it may give no material
6 token, but lives steadily on, through time and circumstance, as part and paramount portion of her being.

Thus may our lives flow on in the same sweet rhythm
9 of head and heart, till they meet and mingle in bliss supernal. There is a special joy in knowing that one is gaining
constantly in the knowledge of Truth and divine Love.
12 Your progress, the past year, has been marked. It satisfies my present hope. Of this we rest assured, that every
trial of our faith in God makes us stronger and firmer in
15 understanding and obedience.

Lovingly yours,

MARY BAKER G. EDDY

CHAPTER VI

Sermons

A CHRISTMAS SERMON

Delivered in Chickering Hall, Boston, Mass., on the
Sunday before Christmas, 1888

Subject: *The Corporeal and Incorporeal Saviour*

Text: *For unto us a child is born, unto us a son is given: and the
government shall be upon his shoulder: and his name shall be called
Wonderful, Counsellor, The mighty God, The everlasting Father, The
Prince of Peace.* — Isaiah ix. 6.

TO the senses, Jesus was the son of man: in Science,
man is the son of God. The material senses could
not cognize the Christ, or Son of God: it was Jesus'
approximation to this state of being that made him the
Christ-Jesus, the Godlike, the anointed.

The prophet whose words we have chosen for our
text, prophesied the appearing of this dual nature, as
both human and divinely endowed, the personal and the
impersonal Jesus.

The only record of our Master as a public benefactor,
or personal Saviour, opens when he was thirty years of
age; owing in part, perhaps, to the Jewish law that none
should teach or preach in public under that age. Also,
it is natural to conclude that at this juncture he was
specially endowed with the Holy Spirit; for he was given
the new name, Messiah, or Jesus Christ, — the God-

1 anointed; even as, at times of special enlightenment,
Jacob was called Israel; and Saul, Paul.

3   The third event of this eventful period, — a period of
such wonderful spiritual import to mankind! — was the
advent of a higher Christianity.

6   From this dazzling, God-crowned summit, the Nazarene stepped suddenly before the people and their schools
of philosophy; Gnostic, Epicurean, and Stoic. He must
9 stem these rising angry elements, and walk serenely over
their fretted, foaming billows.

Here the cross became the emblem of Jesus' history;
12 while the central point of his Messianic mission was peace,
good will, love, teaching, and healing.

Clad with divine might, he was ready to stem the tide
15 of Judaism, and prove his power, derived from Spirit, to
be supreme; lay himself as a lamb upon the altar of
materialism, and therefrom rise to his nativity in Spirit.

18   The corporeal Jesus bore our infirmities, and through
his stripes we are healed. He was the Way-shower, and
suffered in the flesh, showing mortals how to escape from
21 the sins of the flesh.

There was no incorporeal Jesus of Nazareth. The
spiritual man, or Christ, was after the similitude of the
24 Father, without corporeality or finite mind.

Materiality, worldliness, human pride, or self-will, by
demoralizing his motives and Christlikeness, would have
27 dethroned his power as the Christ.

To carry out his holy purpose, he must be oblivious of
human self.

30   Of the lineage of David, like him he went forth, simple
as the shepherd boy, to disarm the Goliath. Panoplied
in the strength of an exalted hope, faith, and understand-

ing, he sought to conquer the three-in-one of error: the world, the flesh, and the devil.

Three years he went about doing good. He had for thirty years been preparing to heal and teach divinely; but his three-years mission was a marvel of glory: its chaplet, a grave to mortal sense dishonored — from which sprang a sublime and everlasting victory!

He who dated time, the Christian era, and spanned eternity, was the meekest man on earth. He healed and taught by the wayside, in humble homes: to arrant hypocrite and to dull disciples he explained the Word of God, which has since ripened into interpretation through Science.

His words were articulated in the language of a declining race, and committed to the providence of God. In no one thing seemed he less human and more divine than in his unfaltering faith in the immortality of Truth. Referring to this, he said, "Heaven and earth shall pass away, but my words shall not pass away!" and they have not: they still live; and are the basis of divine liberty, the medium of Mind, the hope of the race.

Only three years a personal Saviour! yet the foundations he laid are as eternal as Truth, the chief cornerstone.

After his brief brave struggle, and the crucifixion of the corporeal man, the incorporeal Saviour — the Christ or spiritual idea which leadeth into all Truth — must needs come in Christian Science, demonstrating the spiritual healing of body and mind.

This idea or divine essence was, and is, forever about the Father's business; heralding the Principle of health, holiness, and immortality.

1 Its divine Principle interprets the incorporeal idea, or Son of God; hence the incorporeal and corporeal are
3 distinguished thus: the former is the spiritual idea that represents divine good, and the latter is the human presentation of goodness in man. The Science of Chris-
6 tianity, that has appeared in the ripeness of time, reveals the incorporeal Christ; and this will continue to be seen more clearly until it be acknowledged, under-
9 stood, — and the Saviour, which is Truth, be comprehended.

To the vision of the Wisemen, this spiritual idea of the
12 Principle of man or the universe, appeared as a star. At first, the babe Jesus seemed small to mortals; but from the mount of revelation, the prophet beheld it from the
15 beginning as the Redeemer, who would present a wonderful manifestation of Truth and Love.

In our text Isaiah foretold, "His name shall be called
18 Wonderful, Counsellor, The mighty God, The everlasting Father, The Prince of Peace."

As the Wisemen grew in the understanding of Christ,
21 the spiritual idea, it grew in favor with them. Thus it will continue, as it shall become understood, until man be found in the actual likeness of his Maker. Their
24 highest human concept of the man Jesus, that portrayed him as the only Son of God, the only begotten of the Father, full of grace and Truth, will become so magnified
27 to human sense, by means of the lens of Science, as to reveal man collectively, as individually, to be the son of God.

30 The limited view of God's ideas arose from the testimony of the senses. Science affords the evidence that God is the Father of man, of all that is real and eternal. This spir-

itual idea that the personal Jesus demonstrated, casting 1
out evils and healing, more than eighteen centuries ago,
disappeared by degrees; both because of the ascension 3
of Jesus, in which it was seen that he had grown beyond
the human sense of him, and because of the corruption of
the Church. 6

The last appearing of Truth will be a wholly spiritual
idea of God and of man, without the fetters of the flesh, or
corporeality. This infinite idea of infinity will be, is, as 9
eternal as its divine Principle. The daystar of this appearing
is the light of Christian Science — the Science which
rends the veil of the flesh from top to bottom. The light 12
of this revelation leaves nothing that is material; neither
darkness, doubt, disease, nor death. The material corporeality
disappears; and individual spirituality, perfect 15
and eternal, appears — never to disappear.

The truth uttered and lived by Jesus, who passed on
and left to mortals the rich legacy of what he said and 18
did, makes his followers the heirs to his example; but
they can neither appreciate nor appropriate his treasures
of Truth and Love, until lifted to these by their own 21
growth and experiences. His goodness and grace purchased
the means of mortals' redemption from sin; but,
they never paid the price of sin. This cost, none but the 24
sinner can pay; and accordingly as this account is settled
with divine Love, is the sinner ready to avail himself of
the rich blessings flowing from the teaching, example, 27
and suffering of our Master.

The secret stores of wisdom must be discovered, their
treasures reproduced and given to the world, before man 30
can truthfully conclude that he has been found in the
order, mode, and virgin origin of man according to divine

1 Science, which alone demonstrates the divine Principle
and spiritual idea of being.

3   The monument whose finger points upward, commemorates the earthly life of a martyr; but this is not all of
the philanthropist, hero, and Christian. The Truth he
6 has taught and spoken lives, and moves in our midst a
divine afflatus. Thus it is that the ideal Christ — or
impersonal infancy, manhood, and womanhood of Truth
9 and Love — is still with us.

    And what of *this* child? — "For unto us a child *is*
born, unto us a son *is* given: and the government shall
12 be upon his shoulder."

    This child, or spiritual idea, has evolved a more ready
ear for the overture of angels and the scientific under-
15 standing of Truth and Love. When Christ, the incorporeal idea of God, was nameless, and a Mary knew not
how to declare its spiritual origin, the idea of man was
18 not understood. The Judæan religion even required the
Virgin-mother to go to the temple and be purified, for
having given birth to the corporeal child Jesus, whose
21 origin was more spiritual than the senses could interpret. Like the leaven that a certain woman hid in three
measures of meal, the Science of God and the spiritual
24 idea, named in this century Christian Science, is leavening the lump of human thought, until the whole shall
be leavened and all materialism disappear. This action
27 of the divine energy, even if not acknowledged, has
come to be seen as diffusing richest blessings. This
spiritual idea, or Christ, entered into the minutiæ of the
30 life of the personal Jesus. It made him an honest man,
a good carpenter, and a good man, before it could make
him the glorified.

The material questions at this age on the reappearing 1
of the infantile thought of God's man, are after the manner of a mother in the flesh, though their answers per- 3
tain to the spiritual idea, as in Christian Science: —

Is he deformed?
He is wholly symmetrical; the one altogether lovely. 6

Is the babe a son, or daughter?
Both son and daughter: even the compound idea of
all that resembles God. 9

How much does he weigh?
His substance outweighs the material world.

How old is he? 12
Of his days there is no beginning and no ending.

What is his name?
Christ Science. 15

Who are his parents, brothers, and sisters?
His Father and Mother are divine Life, Truth, and
Love; and they who do the will of his Father are his 18
brethren.

Is he heir to an estate?
"The government shall be upon his shoulder!" He 21
has dominion over the whole earth; and in admiration
of his origin, he exclaims, "I thank Thee, O Father, Lord
of heaven and earth, that Thou hast hid these things 24
from the wise and prudent, and hast revealed them unto
babes!"

Is he wonderful? 27
His works thus prove him. He giveth power, peace,
and holiness; he exalteth the lowly; he giveth liberty

1 to the captive, health to the sick, salvation from sin to
the sinner — and overcometh the world!

3   Go, and tell what things ye shall see and hear: how
the blind, spiritually and physically, receive sight; how
the lame, those halting between two opinions or hob-
6 bling on crutches, walk; how the physical and moral
lepers are cleansed; how the deaf — those who, having
ears, hear not, and are afflicted with "tympanum on the
9 brain" — hear; how the dead, those buried in dogmas
and physical ailments, are raised; that to the poor —
the lowly in Christ, not the man-made rabbi — the
12 gospel is preached. Note this: only such as are pure
in spirit, emptied of vainglory and vain knowledge, receive Truth.

15   Here ends the colloquy; and a voice from heaven seems
to say, "Come and see."

The nineteenth-century prophets repeat, "Unto us a
18 son is given."

The shepherds shout, "We behold the appearing of
the star!" — and the pure in heart clap their hands.

21   EDITOR'S EXTRACTS FROM SERMON

TEXT: *Ye do err, not knowing the Scriptures, nor the power of
God.* — MATT. xxii. 29.

24   *The Christian Science Journal* reported as follows: —
The announcement that the Rev. Mary B. G. Eddy
would speak before the Scientist denomination on the
27 afternoon of October 26, drew a large audience. Hawthorne Hall was densely packed, and many had to go
away unable to obtain seats. The distinguished speaker
30 began by saying: —

Within Bible pages she had found all the divine Science 1
she preaches; noticing, all along the way of her researches
therein, that whenever her thoughts had wandered into 3
the bypaths of ancient philosophies or pagan literatures,
her spiritual insight had been darkened thereby, till
she was God-driven back to the inspired pages. Early 6
training, through the misinterpretation of the Word,
had been the underlying cause of the long years of invalidism she endured before Truth dawned upon her 9
understanding, through right interpretation. With the
understanding of Scripture-meanings, had come physical
rejuvenation. The uplifting of spirit was the upbuild- 12
ing of the body.

She affirmed that the Scriptures cannot properly be
interpreted in a literal way. The truths they teach must 15
be spiritually discerned, before their message can be
borne fully to our minds and hearts. That there is a
dual meaning to every Biblical passage, the most eminent 18
divines of the world have concluded; and to get at the
highest, or metaphysical, it is necessary rightly to read
what the inspired writers left for our spiritual instruction. 21
The literal rendering of the Scriptures makes them nothing valuable, but often is the foundation of unbelief and
hopelessness. The metaphysical rendering is health and 24
peace and hope for all. The literal or material reading is
the reading of the carnal mind, which is enmity toward
God, Spirit. 27

Taking several Bible passages, Mrs. Eddy showed how
beautiful and inspiring are the thoughts when rightly
understood. "Let the dead bury their dead; follow 30
thou me," was one of the passages explained metaphysically. In their fullest meaning, those words are salvation

1 from the belief of death, the last enemy to be overthrown;
for by following Christ truly, resurrection and life im-
3 mortal are brought to us. If we follow him, to us there
can be no dead. Those who know not this, may still
believe in death and weep over the graves of their beloved;
6 but with him is Life eternal, which never changes to
death. The eating of bread and drinking of wine at the
Lord's supper, merely symbolize the spiritual refresh-
9 ment of God's children having rightly read His Word,
whose entrance into their understanding is healthful life.
This is the reality behind the symbol.

12   So, also, she spoke of the hades, or hell of Scripture,
saying, that we make our own heavens and our own hells,
by right and wise, or wrong and foolish, conceptions of
15 God and our fellow-men. Jesus interpreted all spiritually: "I have bread to eat that ye know not of," he
said. The bread he ate, which was refreshment of divine
18 strength, we also may all partake of.

The material record of the Bible, she said, is no more
important to our well-being than the history of Europe
21 and America; but the spiritual application bears upon
our eternal life. The method of Jesus was purely metaphysical; and no other method is Christian Science. In
24 the passage recording Jesus' proceedings with the blind
man (Mark viii.) he is said to have spat upon the dust.
Spitting was the Hebrew method of expressing the utmost
27 contempt. So Jesus is recorded as having expressed
contempt for the belief of material eyes as having any
power to see. Having eyes, ye see not; and ears, ye hear
30 not, he had just told them. The putting on of hands
mentioned, she explained as the putting forth of power.
"Hand," in Bible usage, often means spiritual power.

"His hand is not shortened that it cannot save," can 1
never be wrested from its true meaning to signify human
hands. Jesus' first effort to realize Truth was not wholly 3
successful; but he rose to the occasion with the second
attempt, and the blind saw clearly. To suppose that
Jesus did actually anoint the blind man's eyes with his 6
spittle, is as absurd as to think, according to the report
of some, that Christian Scientists sit in back-to-back
seances with their patients, for the divine power to filter 9
from vertebræ to vertebræ. When one comes to the age
with spiritual translations of God's messages, expressed
in literal or physical terms, our right action is not to con- 12
demn and deny, but to "try the spirits" and see what
manner they are of. This does not mean communing
with spirits supposed to have departed from the earth, 15
but the seeking out of the basis upon which are accomplished the works by which the new teacher would prove
his right to be heard. By these signs are the true disciples 18
of the Master known: the sick are healed; to the poor
the gospel is preached.

EXTRACT FROM A SERMON DELIVERED IN BOSTON, 21
JANUARY 18, 1885

TEXT: *The kingdom of heaven is like unto leaven, which a woman
took, and hid in three measures of meal, till the whole was leavened.* — 24
MATT. xiii. 33.

Few people at present know aught of the Science of
mental healing; and so many are obtruding upon the 27
public attention their ignorance or false knowledge in
the name of Science, that it behooves all clad in the shining mail to keep bright their invincible armor; to keep 30

1 their demonstrations modest, and their claims and lives
steadfast in Truth.

3   Dispensing the Word charitably, but separating the
tares from the wheat, let us declare the positive and
the negative of metaphysical Science; what it is, and
6 what it is not. Intrepid, self-oblivious Protestants in
a higher sense than ever before, let us meet and defeat
the claims of sense and sin, regardless of the bans or
9 clans pouring in their fire upon us; and white-winged
charity, brooding over all, shall cover with her feathers
the veriest sinner.

12   Divine and unerring Mind measures man, until the
three measures be accomplished, and he arrives at
fulness of stature; for "the Lord God omnipotent
15 reigneth."

Science is divine: it is neither of human origin nor of
human direction. That which is termed "natural science,"
18 the evidences whereof are taken in by the five personal
senses, presents but a finite, feeble sense of the infinite
law of God; which law is written on the heart, received
21 through the affections, spiritually understood, and demonstrated in our lives.

This law of God is the Science of mental healing,
24 spiritually discerned, understood, and obeyed.

Mental Science, and the five personal senses, are at
war; and peace can only be declared on the side of im-
27 mutable right, — the health, holiness, and immortality
of man. To gain this scientific result, the first and fundamental rule of Science must be understood and adhered
30 to; namely, the oft-repeated declaration in Scripture
that God is good; hence, good is omnipotent and
omnipresent.

Ancient and modern philosophy, human reason, or 1
man's theorems, misstate mental Science, its Principle
and practice. The most enlightened sense herein sees 3
nothing but a law of matter.

Who has ever learned of the schools that there is but
one Mind, and that this is God, who healeth all our sick- 6
ness and sins?

Who has ever learned from the schools, pagan philosophy, or scholastic theology, that Science is the law of 9
Mind and not of matter, and that this law has no relation
to, or recognition of, matter?

Mind is its own great cause and effect. Mind is God, 12
omnipotent and omnipresent. What, then, of an opposite so-called science, which says that man is both matter
and mind, that Mind is in matter? Can the infinite 15
be within the finite? And must not man have preexisted
in the All and Only? Does an evil mind exist without
space to occupy, power to act, or vanity to pretend that 18
it is man?

If God is Mind and fills all space, is everywhere, matter
is nowhere and sin is obsolete. If Mind, God, is all-power 21
and all-presence, man is not met by another power
and presence, that — obstructing his intelligence —
pains, fetters, and befools him. The perfection of man 24
is intact; whence, then, is something besides Him that
is not the counterpart but the counterfeit of man's creator?
Surely not from God, for He made man in His own 27
likeness. Whence, then, is the atom or molecule called
matter? Have attraction and cohesion formed it?
But are these forces laws of matter, or laws of 30
Mind?

For matter to be matter, it must have been self-created.

1 Mind has no more power to evolve or to create matter than has good to produce evil. Matter is a misstatement
3 of Mind; it is a lie, claiming to talk and disclaim against Truth; idolatry, having other gods; evil, having presence and power over omnipotence!
6 Let us have a clearing up of abstractions. Let us come into the presence of Him who removeth all iniquities, and healeth all our diseases. Let us attach our sense
9 of Science to what touches the religious sentiment within man. Let us open our affections to the Principle that moves all in harmony, — from the falling of a sparrow
12 to the rolling of a world. Above Arcturus and his sons, broader than the solar system and higher than the atmosphere of our planet, is the Science of mental
15 healing.

What is the kingdom of heaven? The abode of Spirit, the realm of the real. No matter is there, no night is
18 there — nothing that maketh or worketh a lie. Is this kingdom afar off? No: it is ever-present here. The first to declare against this kingdom is matter. Shall
21 that be called heresy which pleads for Spirit — the All of God, and His omnipresence?

The kingdom of heaven is the reign of divine Science:
24 it is a mental state. Jesus said it is within you, and taught us to pray, "Thy kingdom come;" but he did not teach us to pray for death whereby to gain heaven.
27 We do not look into darkness for light. Death can never usher in the dawn of Science that reveals the spiritual facts of man's Life here and now.
30 The leaven which a woman took and hid in three measures of meal, is Divine Science; the Comforter; the Holy Ghost that leadeth into all Truth; the "still,

small voice" that breathes His presence and power, cast- 1
ing out error and healing the sick. And woman, the
spiritual idea, takes of the things of God and showeth 3
them unto the creature, until the whole sense of being
is leavened with Spirit. The three measures of meal
may well be likened to the false sense of life, substance, 6
and intelligence, which says, I am sustained by bread,
matter, instead of Mind. The spiritual leaven of divine
Science changes this false sense, giving better views of 9
Life; saying, Man's Life is God; and when this shall
appear, it shall be "the substance of things hoped for."

The measure of Life shall increase by every spiritual 12
touch, even as the leaven expands the loaf. Man shall
keep the feast of Life, not with the old leaven of the
scribes and Pharisees, neither with "the leaven of malice 15
and wickedness; but the unleavened bread of sincerity
and truth."

Thus it can be seen that the Science of mental healing 18
must be understood. There are false Christs that would
"deceive, if it were possible, the very elect," by institut-
ing matter and its methods in place of God, Mind. Their 21
supposition is, that there are other minds than His; that
one mind controls another; that one belief takes the
place of another. But this ism of to-day has nothing 24
to do with the Science of mental healing which acquaints
us with God and reveals the one perfect Mind and His
laws.   27

The attempt to mix matter and Mind, to work by
means of both animal magnetism and divine power, is
literally saying, Have we not in thy name cast out devils, 30
and done many wonderful works?

But remember God in all thy ways, and thou shalt

1 find the truth that breaks the dream of sense, letting the
harmony of Science that declares *Him,* come in with
3 healing, and peace, and perfect love.

SUNDAY SERVICES ON JULY FOURTH

EXTEMPORE REMARKS

6   The great theme so deeply and solemnly expounded
by the preacher, has been exemplified in all ages, but
chiefly in the great crises of nations or of the human race.
9 It is then that supreme devotion to Principle has especially been called for and manifested. It is then that we
learn a little more of the nothingness of evil, and more
12 of the divine energies of good, and strive valiantly for the
liberty of the sons of God.

The day we celebrate reminds us of the heroes and
15 heroines who counted not their own lives dear to them,
when they sought the New England shores, not as the
flying nor as conquerors, but, steadfast in faith and love,
18 to build upon the rock of Christ, the true idea of God —
the supremacy of Spirit and the nothingness of matter.
When first the Pilgrims planted their feet on Plymouth
21 Rock, frozen ritual and creed should forever have melted
away in the fire of love which came down from heaven.
The Pilgrims came to establish a nation in true freedom,
24 in the rights of conscience.

But what of ourselves, and our times and obligations?
Are we duly aware of our own great opportunities and
27 responsibilities? Are we prepared to meet and improve
them, to act up to the acme of divine energy wherewith
we are armored?

Never was there a more solemn and imperious call 1
than God makes to us all, right here, for fervent devotion and an absolute consecration to the greatest and 3
holiest of all causes. The hour is come. The great
battle of Armageddon is upon us. The powers of evil
are leagued together in secret conspiracy against the 6
Lord and against His Christ, as expressed and operative in Christian Science. Large numbers, in desperate
malice, are engaged day and night in organizing action 9
against us. Their feeling and purpose are deadly, and
they have sworn enmity against the lives of our standard-
bearers.   12

What will you do about it? Will you be equally in
earnest for the truth? Will you doff your lavender-kid
zeal, and become real and consecrated warriors? Will 15
you give yourselves wholly and irrevocably to the great
work of establishing the truth, the gospel, and the Science
which are necessary to the salvation of the world from 18
error, sin, disease, and death? Answer at once and practically, and answer aright!

EASTER SERVICES   21

The editor of *The Christian Science Journal* said that
at three o'clock, the hour for the church service proper,
the pastor, Rev. Mary Baker G. Eddy, accompanied 24
by Rev. D. A. Easton, who was announced to preach
the sermon, came on the platform. The pastor introduced Mr. Easton as follows: —   27

Friends: — The homesick traveller in foreign lands
greets with joy a familiar face. I am constantly homesick for heaven. In my long journeyings I have met 30

1 one who comes from the place of my own sojourning
for many years, — the Congregational Church. He is
3 a graduate of Bowdoin College and of Andover Theological School. He has left his old church, as I did,
from a yearning of the heart; because he was not sat-
6 isfied with a manlike God, but wanted to become a Godlike man. He found that the new wine could not be
put into old bottles without bursting them, and he came
9 to us.

Mr. Easton then delivered an interesting discourse
from the text, "If ye then be risen with Christ, seek
12 those things which are above, where Christ sitteth on the
right hand of God" (Col. iii. 1), which he prefaced by
saying: —
15   "I think it was about a year ago that I strayed into
this hall, a stranger, and wondered what sort of people
you were, and of what you were worshippers. If any
18 one had said to me that to-day I should stand before
you to preach a sermon on Christian Science, I should
have replied, 'Much learning' — or something else —
21 'hath made thee mad.' If I had not found Christian
Science a new gospel, I should not be standing before you:
if I had not found it truth, I could not have stood up
24 again *to* preach, here or elsewhere."

At the conclusion of the sermon, the pastor again came
forward, and added the following: —
27   My friends, I wished to be excused from speaking
to-day, but will yield to circumstances. In the flesh, we
are as a partition wall between the old and the new;
30 between the old religion in which we have been educated,
and the new, living, impersonal Christ-thought that has
been given to the world to-day.

The old churches are saying, "He is not here;" and, 1 "Who shall roll away the stone?"

The stone has been rolled away by human suffer- 3 ing. The first rightful desire in the hour of loss, when believing we have lost sight of Truth, is to know where He is laid. This appeal resolves itself into these 6 questions: —

Is our consciousness in matter or in God? Have we any other consciousness than that of good? If we have, 9 He is saying to us to-day, "Adam, where art thou?" We are wrong if our consciousness is in sin, sickness, and death. This is the old consciousness. 12

In the new religion the teaching is, "He is not here; Truth is not in matter; he is risen; Truth has become more to us, — more true, more spiritual." 15

Can we say this to-day? Have we left the conscious- ness of sickness and sin for that of health and holiness? 18

What is it that seems a stone between us and the resurrection morning?

It is the belief of mind in matter. We can only come 21 into the spiritual resurrection by quitting the old con- sciousness of Soul in sense.

These flowers are floral apostles. God does all this 24 through His followers; and He made every flower in Mind before it sprang from the earth: yet we look into matter and the earth to give us these smiles of God! 27

We must lay aside material consciousness, and then we can perceive Truth, and say with Mary, "Rabboni!" — Master! 30

In 1866, when God revealed to me this risen Christ, this Life that knows no death, that saith, "Because he

1 lives, I live," I awoke from the dream of Spirit in the
flesh so far as to take the side of Spirit, and strive to cease
3 my warfare.

When, through this consciousness, I was delivered from
the dark shadow and portal of death, my friends were
6 frightened at beholding me restored to health.

A dear old lady asked me, "How is it that you are
restored to us? Has Christ come again on earth?"
9   "Christ never left," I replied; "Christ is Truth, and
Truth is always here, — the impersonal Saviour."

Then another person, more material, met me, and I
12 said, in the words of my Master, "Touch me not."   I
shuddered at her material approach; then my heart went
out to God, and I found the open door from this sepulchre
15 of matter.

I *love* the Easter service: it speaks to me of Life, and
not of death.

18   Let us do our work; then we shall have part in his
resurrection.

BIBLE LESSONS

21   *But as many as received him, to them gave he power to become the*
sons of God, even to them that believe on his name: which were born,
not of blood, nor of the will of the flesh, nor of the will of man, but of
24 *God.* — JOHN i. 12, 13.

Here, the apostle assures us that man has power to
become the son of God.   In the Hebrew text, the word
27 "son" is defined variously; a month is called the son
of a year.   This term, as applied to man, is used in both
a material and a spiritual sense.   The Scriptures speak
30 of Jesus as the Son of God and the Son of man; but

Jesus said to call no man father; "for one is your Father," 1
even God.

Is man's spiritual sonship a personal gift to man, or 3
is it the reality of his being, in divine Science? Man's
knowledge of this grand verity gives him power to demonstrate his divine Principle, which in turn is requisite 6
in order to understand his sonship, or unity with God,
good. A personal requirement of blind obedience to
the law of being, would tend to obscure the order of 9
Science, unless that requirement should express the claims
of the divine Principle. Infinite Principle and infinite
Spirit must be one. What avail, then, to quarrel over 12
what is the person of Spirit, — if we recognize infinitude
as personality, — for who can tell what is the form of
infinity? When we understand man's true birthright, that 15
he is "born, not . . . of the will of the flesh, nor of the
will of man, but of God," we shall understand that man
is the offspring of Spirit, and not of the flesh; recognize 18
him through spiritual, and not material laws; and regard
him as spiritual, and not material. His sonship, referred
to in the text, is his spiritual relation to Deity: it is not, 21
then, a personal gift, but is the order of divine Science.
The apostle urges upon our acceptance this great fact:
"But as many as received him, to them gave he power 24
to become the sons of God." Mortals will lose their sense
of mortality — disease, sickness, sin, and death — in
the proportion that they gain the sense of man's spirit- 27
ual preexistence as God's child; as the offspring of
good, and not of God's opposite, — evil, or a fallen
man. 30

John the Baptist had a clear discernment of divine
Science: being born not of the human will or flesh, he

1 antedated his own existence, began spiritually instead
of materially to reckon himself logically; hence the im-
3 possibility of putting him to death, only in belief, through
violent means or material methods.

"As many as received him;" that is, as many as per-
6 ceive man's actual existence in and of his divine Principle, receive the Truth of existence; and these have no
other God, no other Mind; no other origin; therefore, in
9 time they lose their false sense of existence, and find
their adoption with the Father; to wit, the redemption
of the body. Through divine Science man gains the
12 power to become the son of God, to recognize his perfect
and eternal estate.

"Which were born, not of blood, nor of the will of
15 the flesh." This passage refers to man's primal, spiritual existence, created neither from dust nor carnal desire. "Nor of the will of man." Born of no doctrine,
18 no human faith, but beholding the truth of being; even
the understanding that man was never lost in Adam,
since he is and ever was the image and likeness of God,
21 good. But no mortal hath seen the spiritual man, more
than he hath seen the Father. The apostle indicates
no personal plan of a personal Jehovah, partial and finite;
24 but the possibility of all finding their place in God's great
love, the eternal heritage of the Elohim, His sons and
daughters. The text is a metaphysical statement of exist-
27 ence as Principle and idea, wherein man and his Maker
are inseparable and eternal.

When the Word is made flesh, — that is, rendered
30 practical, — this eternal Truth will be understood; and
sickness, sin, and death will yield to it, even as they did
more than eighteen centuries ago. The lusts of the flesh

and the pride of life will then be quenched in the divine 1
Science of being; in the ever-present good, omnipotent
Love, and eternal Life, that know no death. In the great 3
forever, the verities of being exist, and must be acknowledged and demonstrated. Man must love his neighbor
as himself, and the power of Truth must be seen and 6
felt in health, happiness, and holiness: then it will be
found that Mind is All-in-all, and there is no matter to
cope with.   9

Man is free born: he is neither the slave of sense, nor a
silly ambler to the so-called pleasures and pains of self-
conscious matter. Man is God's image and likeness; 12
whatever is possible to God, is possible to man *as God's
reflection.* Through the transparency of Science we learn
this, and receive it: learn that man can fulfil the Scrip- 15
tures in every instance; that if he open his mouth it shall
be filled — not by reason of the schools, or learning, but
by the natural ability, that reflection already has bestowed 18
on him, to give utterance to Truth.

"Who hath believed our report?" Who understands
these sayings? He to whom the arm of the Lord is re- 21
vealed; to whom divine Science unfolds omnipotence,
that equips man with divine power while it shames human
pride. Asserting a selfhood apart from God, is a denial 24
of man's spiritual sonship; for it claims another father.
As many as do receive a knowledge of God through
Science, will have power to reflect His power, in proof of 27
man's "dominion over all the earth." He is bravely
brave who dares at this date refute the evidence of material
sense with the facts of Science, and will arrive at the true 30
status of man because of it. The material senses would
make man, that the Scriptures declare reflects his Maker,

1 the very opposite of that Maker, by claiming that God is
Spirit, while man is matter; that God is good, but man is
3 evil; that Deity is deathless, but man dies. Science and
sense conflict, from the revolving of worlds to the death
of a sparrow.

6 The Word will be made flesh and dwell among mortals,
only when man reflects God in body as well as in mind.
The child born of a woman has the formation of his
9 parents; the man born of Spirit is spiritual, not material.
Paul refers to this when speaking of presenting our bodies
holy and acceptable, which is our reasonable service;
12 and this brings to remembrance the Hebrew strain,
"Who healeth all thy diseases."

If man should say of the power to be perfect which he
15 possesses, "I am the power," he would trespass upon
divine Science, yield to material sense, and lose his power;
even as when saying, "I have the power to sin and be
18 sick," and persisting in believing that he is sick and a
sinner. If he says, "I am of God, therefore good," yet
persists in evil, he has denied the power of Truth, and
21 must suffer for this error until he learns that all power is
good because it is of God, and so destroys his self-deceived sense of power in evil. The Science of being gives
24 back the lost likeness and power of God as the seal of
man's adoption. Oh, for that light and love ineffable,
which casteth out all fear, all sin, sickness, and death;
27 that seeketh not her own, but another's good; that saith
Abba, Father, and *is* born of God!

John came baptizing with water. He employed a type
30 of physical cleanliness to foreshadow metaphysical purity,
even mortal mind purged of the animal and human, and
submerged in the humane and divine, giving back the

lost sense of man in unity with, and reflecting, his Maker. 1
None but the pure in heart shall see God, — shall be able
to discern fully and demonstrate fairly the divine Principle 3
of Christian Science. The will of God, or power of Spirit,
is made manifest as Truth, and through righteousness, —
not as or through matter, — and it strips matter of all 6
claims, abilities or disabilities, pains or pleasures. Self-
renunciation of all that constitutes a so-called material
man, and the acknowledgment and achievement of his 9
spiritual identity as the child of God, is Science that
opens the very flood-gates of heaven; whence good
flows into every avenue of being, cleansing mortals of 12
all uncleanness, destroying all suffering, and demonstrating the true image and likeness. There is no other
way under heaven whereby we can be saved, and man 15
be clothed with might, majesty, and immortality.

"As many as received him," — as accept the truth
of being, — "to them gave he power to become the sons 18
of God." The spiritualization of our sense of man opens
the gates of paradise that the so-called material senses
would close, and reveals man infinitely blessed, upright, 21
pure, and free; having no need of statistics by which to
learn his origin and age, or to measure his manhood, or to
know how much of a man he ever has been: for, "as 24
many as received him, to them gave he power to become
the sons of God."

And so it is written, The first man Adam was made a living soul; 27
the last Adam was made a quickening spirit. — I COR. xv. 45.

When reasoning on this subject of man with the Corin-
thian brethren, the apostle first spake from their stand- 30
point of thought; namely, that creation is material:

1 he was not at this point giving the history of the spiritual
man who originates in God, Love, who created man
3 in His own image and likeness. In the creation of Adam
from dust, — in which Soul is supposed to enter the
embryo-man after his birth, — we see the material self-
6 constituted belief of the Jews as referred to by St. Paul.
Their material belief has fallen far below man's original
standard, the spiritual man made in the image and like-
9 ness of God; for this erring belief even separates its
conception of man from God, and ultimates in the opposite of *im*mortal man, namely, in a sick and sinning
12 mortal.

We learn in the Scriptures, as in divine Science, that
God made all; that He is the universal Father and Mother
15 of man; that God is divine Love: therefore divine Love
is the divine Principle of the divine idea named man;
in other words, the spiritual Principle of spiritual man.
18 Now let us not lose this Science of man, but gain it clearly;
then we shall see that man cannot be separated from
his perfect Principle, God, inasmuch as an idea cannot
21 be torn apart from its fundamental basis. This scientific knowledge affords self-evident proof of immortality;
proof, also, that the Principle of man cannot produce a
24 less perfect man than it produced in the beginning. A
material sense of existence is not the scientific fact of
being; whereas, the spiritual sense of God and His uni-
27 verse is the immortal and true sense of being.

As the apostle proceeds in this line of thought, he
undoubtedly refers to the last Adam represented by the
30 Messias, whose demonstration of God restored to mortals
the lost sense of man's perfection, even the sense of the
real man in God's likeness, who restored this sense by

the spiritual regeneration of both mind and body, — 1
casting out evils, *healing the sick,* and raising the dead.
The man Jesus demonstrated over sin, sickness, disease, 3
and death. The great Metaphysician wrought, over and
above every sense of matter, into the proper sense of the
possibilities of Spirit. He established health and har- 6
mony, the perfection of mind and body, as the reality of
man; while discord, as seen in disease and death, was to
him the opposite of man, hence the unreality; even as in 9
Science a chord is manifestly the reality of music, and
discord the unreality. This rule of harmony must be accepted as true relative to man. 12

The translators of the older Scriptures presuppose a
material man to be the first man, solely because their
transcribing thoughts were not lifted to the inspired sense 15
of the spiritual man, as set forth in original Holy Writ.
Had both writers and translators in that age fully comprehended the later teachings and demonstrations of 18
our human and divine Master, the Old Testament might
have been as spiritual as the New.

The origin, substance, and life of man are one, and 21
that one is God, — Life, Truth, Love. The self-existent,
perfect, and eternal are God; and man is their reflection
and glory. Did the substance of God, Spirit, become a 24
clod, in order to create a sick, sinning, dying man? The
primal facts of being are eternal; they are never extinguished in a night of discord. 27

That man must be evil before he can be good; dying,
before deathless; material, before spiritual; sick and a
sinner in order to be healed and saved, is but the declara- 30
tion of the material senses transcribed by pagan religionists, by wicked mortals such as crucified our Master, —

1 whose teachings opposed the doctrines of Christ that
demonstrated the opposite, Truth.

3   Man is as perfect now, and henceforth, and forever,
as when the stars first sang together, and creation joined
in the grand chorus of harmonious being. It is the trans-
6 lator, not the original Word, who presents as being first
that which appears second, material, and mortal; and
as last, that which is primal, spiritual, and eternal. Be-
9 cause of human misstatement and misconception of God
and man, of the divine Principle and idea of being, there
seems to be a war between the flesh and Spirit, a contest
12 between Truth and error; but the apostle says, "There
is therefore now no condemnation to them which are in
Christ Jesus, who walk not after the flesh, but after the
15 Spirit."

On our subject, St. Paul first reasons upon the basis
of what is seen, the effects of Truth on the material senses;
18 thence, up to the unseen, the testimony of spiritual sense;
and right there he leaves the subject.

Just there, in the intermediate line of thought, is where
21 the present writer found it, when she discovered Christian
Science.   And she has *not* left it, but continues the explanation of the power of Spirit up to its infinite meaning,
24 its allness.   The recognition of this power came to her
through a spiritual sense of the real, and of the unreal
or mortal sense of things; not that there is, or can
27 be, an actual change in the realities of being, but
that we can discern more of them.   At the moment
of her discovery, she knew that the last Adam, namely,
30 the true likeness of God, was the first, the only man.
This knowledge did become to her "a quickening
spirit;" for she beheld the meaning of those words

of our Master, "The last shall be first, and the first 1
last."

When, as little children, we are receptive, become 3
willing to accept the divine Principle and rule of being,
as unfolded in divine Science, the interpretation therein
will be found to be the Comforter that leadeth into all 6
truth.

The meek Nazarene's steadfast and true knowledge of
preexistence, of the nature and the inseparability of God 9
and man, — made him mighty. Spiritual insight of
Truth and Love antidotes and destroys the errors of flesh,
and brings to light the true reflection: man as God's 12
image, or "the first man," for Christ plainly declared,
through Jesus, "Before Abraham was, I am."

The supposition that Soul, or Mind, is breathed into 15
matter, is a pantheistic doctrine that presents a false
sense of existence, and the quickening spirit takes it
away: revealing, in place thereof, the power and per- 18
fection of a released sense of Life in God and Life *as*
God. The Scriptures declare Life to be the infinite I
AM, — not a dweller in matter. For man to know Life 21
as it is, namely God, the eternal good, gives him not
merely a sense of existence, but an accompanying consciousness of spiritual power that subordinates matter 24
and destroys sin, disease, and death. This, Jesus demonstrated; insomuch that St. Matthew wrote, "The people
were astonished at his doctrine: for he taught them 27
as one having authority, and not as the scribes." This
spiritual power, healing sin and sickness, was not confined to the first century; it extends to all time, inhabits 30
eternity, and demonstrates Life without beginning or
end.

1   Atomic action is Mind, not matter. It is neither the
energy of matter, the result of organization, nor the out-
3 come of life infused into matter: it is infinite Spirit, Truth,
Life, defiant of error or matter. Divine Science demonstrates Mind as dispelling a false sense and giving the
6 true sense of itself, God, and the universe; wherein the
mortal evolves not the immortal, nor does the material
ultimate in the spiritual; wherein man is coexistent with
9 Mind, and is the recognized reflection of infinite Life and
Love.

And he was casting out a devil, and it was dumb. And it came to
12 *pass, when the devil was gone out, the dumb spake.* — LUKE xi. 14.

The meaning of the term "devil" needs yet to be
learned. Its definition as an individual is too limited
15 and contradictory. When the Scripture is understood,
the spiritual signification of its terms will be understood,
and will contradict the interpretations that the senses
18 give them; and these terms will be found to include the
inspired meaning.

It could not have been a person that our great Master
21 cast out of another person; therefore the devil herein
referred to was an impersonal evil, or whatever worketh
ill. In this case it was the evil of dumbness, an error of
24 material sense, cast out by the spiritual truth of being;
namely, that speech belongs to Mind instead of matter,
and the wrong power, or the lost sense, must yield to the
27 right sense, and exist in Mind.

In the Hebrew, "devil" is denominated Abaddon; in
the Greek, Apollyon, serpent, liar, the god of this world,
30 etc. The apostle Paul refers to this personality of evil
as "the god of this world;" and then defines this god

as "dishonesty, craftiness, handling the word of God 1
deceitfully." The Hebrew embodies the term "devil"
in another term, serpent, — which the senses are supposed 3
to take in, — and then defines this serpent as "more
subtle than all the beasts of the field." Subsequently,
the ancients changed the meaning of the term, to their 6
sense, and then the serpent became a symbol of wisdom.

The Scripture in John, sixth chapter and seventieth
verse, refers to a wicked man as the devil: "Have not 9
I chosen you twelve, and one of you is a devil?" According to the Scripture, if devil is an individuality, there is
more than one devil. In Mark, ninth chapter and thirty- 12
eighth verse, it reads: "Master, we saw one casting out
devils in thy name." Here is an assertion indicating
the existence of more than one devil; and by omitting the 15
first letter, the name of his satanic majesty is found
to be evils, apparent wrong traits, that Christ, Truth,
casts out. By no possible interpretation can this passage 18
mean several individuals cast out of another individual
no bigger than themselves. The term, being here employed in its plural number, destroys all consistent sup- 21
position of the existence of one personal devil. Again,
our text refers to the devil as dumb; but the original
devil was a great talker, and was supposed to have out- 24
talked even Truth, and carried the question with Eve.
Also, the original texts define him as an "accuser," a
"calumniator," which would be impossible if he were 27
speechless. These two opposite characters ascribed to
him could only be possible as evil beliefs, as different
phases of sin or disease made manifest.   30

Let us obey St. Paul's injunction to reject fables, and
accept the Scriptures in their broader, more spiritual

1 and practical sense. When we speak of a good man, we
do not mean that man is God because the Hebrew term
3 for Deity was "good," and *vice versa;* so, when referring
to a liar, we mean not that he is a personal devil, because
the original text defines devil as a "liar."
6   It is of infinite importance to man's spiritual progress,
and to his demonstration of Truth in casting out error,
— sickness, sin, disease, and death, in all their forms, —
9 that the terms and nature of Deity and devil be understood.

*He that believeth on me, the works that I do shall he do also; and
greater works than these shall he do; because I go unto my Father. —*
12 JOHN xiv. 12.

Such are the words of him who spake divinely, well
knowing the omnipotence of Truth. The Hebrew bard
15 saith, "His name shall endure forever: His name shall
be continued as long as the sun." Luminous with the
light of divine Science, his words reveal the great Principle
18 of a full salvation. Neither can we question the practi-
cability of the divine Word, who have learned its adaptability to human needs, and man's ability to prove the
21 truth of prophecy.

The fulfilment of the grand verities of Christian healing
belongs to every period; as the above Scripture plainly
24 declares, and as primitive Christianity confirms. Also,
the last chapter of Mark is emphatic on this subject;
making healing a condition of salvation, that extends to
27 all ages and throughout all Christendom. Nothing can
be more conclusive than this: "And these signs shall
follow them that believe; . . . they shall lay hands on
30 the sick, and they shall recover." This declaration of
our Master settles the question; else we are entertaining

the startling inquiries, Are the Scriptures inspired? Are 1
they true? Did Jesus mean what he said?

If this be the cavil, we reply in the affirmative that the 3
Scripture is true; that Jesus did mean all, and even more
than he said or deemed it safe to say at that time. His
words are unmistakable, for they form propositions of 6
self-evident demonstrable truth. Doctrines that deny
the substance and practicality of all Christ's teachings
cannot be evangelical; and evangelical religion can be 9
established on no other claim than the authenticity of
the Gospels, which support unequivocally the proof that
Christian Science, as defined and practised by Jesus, 12
heals the sick, casts out error, and will destroy death.

Referring to The Church of Christ, Scientist, in Boston,
of which I am pastor, a certain clergyman charitably 15
expressed it, "the so-called Christian Scientists."

I am thankful even for his allusion to truth; it being
a modification of silence on this subject, and also of what 18
had been said when critics attacked me for supplying the
word Science to Christianity, — a word which the people
are now adopting. 21

The next step for ecclesiasticism to take, is to admit
that all Christians are properly called Scientists who
follow the commands of our Lord and His Christ, Truth; 24
and that no one is following his full command without
this enlarged sense of the spirit and power of Christianity.
"He that believeth on me, the works that I do shall he do," 27
is a radical and unmistakable declaration of the right and
power of Christianity to heal; for this is Christlike,
and includes the understanding of man's capabilities and 30
spiritual power. The condition insisted upon is, first,
"belief;" the Hebrew of which implies understanding.

1 How many to-day believe that the power of God equals
even the power of a drug to heal the sick! Divine Science
3 reveals the Principle of this power, and the rule whereby
sin, sickness, disease, and death are destroyed; and God
is this Principle. Let us, then, seek this Science; that we
6 may know Him better, and love Him more.

Though a man were begirt with the Urim and Thummim of priestly office, yet should deny the validity or
9 permanence of Christ's command to heal in all ages,
this denial would dishonor that office and misinterpret
evangelical religion. Divine Science is not an interpo-
12 lation of the Scriptures, but is redolent with love, health,
and holiness, for the whole human race. It only needs
the prism of this Science to divide the rays of Truth, and
15 bring out the entire hues of Deity, which scholastic theology has hidden. The lens of Science magnifies the divine
power to human sight; and we then see the supremacy
18 of Spirit and the nothingness of matter.

The context of the foregoing Scriptural text explains
Jesus' words, "because I go unto my Father." "Because"
21 in following him, you understand God and *how* to turn
from matter to Spirit for healing; *how* to leave self, the
sense material, for the sense spiritual; *how* to accept
24 God's power and guidance, and become imbued with
divine Love that casts out all fear. Then are you baptized in the Truth that destroys all error, and you receive
27 the sense of Life that knows no death, and you *know* that
God is the only Life.

To reach the consummate naturalness of the Life that
30 is God, good, we must comply with the first condition
set forth in the text, namely, believe; in other words,
understand God sufficiently to exclude all faith in any

other remedy than Christ, the Truth that antidotes all 1
error. Thence will follow the absorption of all action,
motive, and mind, into the rules and divine Principle of 3
metaphysical healing.

Whosoever learns the letter of Christian Science but
possesses not its spirit, is unable to demonstrate this 6
Science; or whosoever hath the spirit without the letter,
is held back by reason of the lack of understanding. Both
the spirit and the letter are requisite; and having these, 9
every one can prove, in some degree, the validity of those
words of the great Master, "For the Son of man is come
to save that which was lost."   12

It has been said that the New Testament does not au-
thorize us to expect the ministry of healing at this period.
We ask what is the authority for such a conclusion, 15
the premises whereof are not to be found in the Scriptures.
The Master's divine logic, as seen in our text, contradicts
this inference, — these are his words: "He that believeth 18
on me, the works that I do shall he do also." That perfect syllogism of Jesus has but one correct premise and
conclusion, and it cannot fall to the ground beneath the 21
stroke of unskilled swordsmen. He who never unsheathed
his blade to try the edge of truth in Christian Science, is
unequal to the conflict, and unfit to judge in the case; 24
the shepherd's sling would slay this Goliath. I once believed that the practice and teachings of Jesus relative to
healing the sick, were spiritual abstractions, impractical 27
and impossible to us; but deed, not creed, and practice
more than theory, have given me a higher sense of
Christianity.   30

The "I" will go to the Father when meekness, purity,
and love, informed by divine Science, the Comforter,

1 lead to the one God: then the ego is found not in
matter but in Mind, for there is but one God, one
3 Mind; and man will then claim no mind apart from God.
Idolatry, the supposition of the existence of many minds
and more than one God, has repeated itself in all manner
6 of subtleties through the entire centuries, saying as in
the beginning, "Believe in me, and I will make you as
gods;" that is, I will give you a separate mind from God
9 (good), named evil; and this so-called mind shall open
your eyes and make you know evil, and thus become
material, sensual, evil. But bear in mind that a serpent
12 said that; therefore that saying came not from Mind,
good, or Truth. God was not the author of it; hence the
words of our Master: "He is a liar, and the father of it;"
15 also, the character of the votaries to "other gods" which
sprung from it.

The sweet, sacred sense and permanence of man's
18 unity with his Maker, in Science, illumines our present
existence with the ever-presence and power of God, good.
It opens wide the portals of salvation from sin, sickness,
21 and death. When the Life that is God, good, shall appear, "we shall be like Him;" we shall do the works of
Christ, and, in the words of David, "the stone which the
24 builders refused is become the head stone of the corner,"
because the "I" does go unto the Father, the ego does
arise to spiritual recognition of being, and is exalted, —
27 not through death, but Life, God understood.

Believe on the Lord Jesus Christ, and thou shalt be saved. — Acts
xvi. 31.

30   The Scriptures require more than a simple admission
and feeble acceptance of the truths they present; they

require a living faith, that so incorporates their lessons 1
into our lives that these truths become the motive-power
of every act.   3

Our chosen text is one more frequently used than
many others, perhaps, to exhort people to turn from sin
and to strive after holiness; but we fear the full import 6
of this text is not yet recognized. It means a *full* salvation, — man saved from sin, sickness, and death; for,
unless this be so, no man can be wholly fitted for heaven 9
in the way which Jesus marked out and bade his followers
pursue.

In order to comprehend the meaning of the text, let 12
us see what it is to believe. It means more than an opinion
entertained concerning Jesus as a man, as the Son of God,
or as God; such an action of mind would be of no more 15
help to save from sin, than would a belief in any historical
event or person. But it does mean so to understand the
beauty of holiness, the character and divinity which Jesus 18
presented in his power to heal and to save, that it will
compel us to pattern after both; in other words, to "let
this Mind be in you, which was also in Christ Jesus." 21
(Phil. ii. 5.)

Mortal man believes in, but does not understand life
in, Christ. He believes there is another power or intelli- 24
gence that rules over a kingdom of its own, that is both
good and evil; yea, that is divided against itself, and therefore cannot stand. This belief breaks the First Command- 27
ment of God.

Let man abjure a theory that is in opposition to God,
recognize God as omnipotent, having all-power; and, 30
placing his trust in this grand Truth, and working from
no other Principle, he can neither be sick nor forever a

1 sinner. When wholly governed by the one perfect Mind, man has no sinful thoughts and will have no desire 3 to sin.

To arrive at this point of unity of Spirit, God, one must commence by turning away from material gods; denying 6 material so-called laws and material sensation, — or mind in matter, in its varied forms of pleasure and pain. This must be done with the understanding that matter has no 9 sense; thus it is that consciousness silences the mortal claim to life, substance, or mind in matter, with the words of Jesus: "When he speaketh a lie, he speaketh of his 12 own." (John viii. 44.)

When tempted to sin, we should know that evil proceedeth not from God, good, but is a false belief of the 15 personal senses; and if we deny the claims of these senses and recognize man as governed by God, Spirit, not by material laws, the temptation will disappear.

18   On this Principle, disease also is treated and healed. We know that man's body, as matter, has no power to govern itself; and a belief of disease is as much the prod- 21 uct of mortal thought as sin is. All suffering is the fruit of the tree of the knowledge of *both* good and evil; of adherence to the "doubleminded" senses, to some belief, 24 fear, theory, or bad deed, based on physical material law, so-called as opposed to good, — all of which is corrected alone by Science, divine Principle, and its spiritual laws. 27 Suffering is the supposition of another intelligence than God; a belief in self-existent evil, opposed to good; and in whatever seems to punish man for doing good, — 30 by saying he has overworked, suffered from inclement weather, or violated a law of matter in doing good, therefore he must suffer for it.

God does not reward benevolence and love with pen- 1
alties; and because of this, we have the right to deny the
supposed power of matter to do it, and to allege that only 3
mortal, erring mind can claim to do thus, and dignify the
result with the name of law: thence comes man's ability
to annul his own erring mental law, and to hold himself 6
amenable only to moral and spiritual law, — God's government. By so doing, male and female come into their
rightful heritage, "into the glorious liberty of the children 9
of God."

Therefore I take pleasure in infirmities, in reproaches, in neces-
sities, in persecutions, in distresses for Christ's sake. — 2 COR. 12
xii. 10.

The miracles recorded in the Scriptures illustrate the
life of Jesus as nothing else can; but they cost him the 15
hatred of the rabbis. The rulers sought the life of Jesus;
they would extinguish whatever denied and defied their
superstition. We learn somewhat of the qualities of the 18
divine Mind through the human Jesus. The power of
his transcendent goodness is manifest in the control it
gave him over the qualities opposed to Spirit which mor- 21
tals name matter.

The Principle of these marvellous works is divine; but
the actor was human. This divine Principle is discerned 24
in Christian Science, as we advance in the spiritual understanding that all substance, Life, and intelligence are
God. The so-called miracles contained in Holy Writ are 27
neither supernatural nor preternatural; for God is good,
and goodness is more natural than evil. The marvellous
healing-power of goodness is the outflowing life of Chris- 30
tianity, and it characterized and dated the Christian era.

1   It was the consummate naturalness of Truth in the
mind of Jesus, that made his healing easy and instan-
3 taneous. Jesus regarded good as the normal state of man,
and evil as the abnormal; holiness, life, and health as
the better representatives of God than sin, disease, and
6 death. The master Metaphysician understood omnipotence to be All-power: because Spirit was to him All-
in-all, matter was palpably an error of premise and
9 conclusion, while God was the only substance, Life,
and intelligence of man.

The apostle Paul insists on the rare rule in Christian
12 Science that we have chosen for a text; a rule that is susceptible of proof, and is applicable to every stage and
state of human existence. The divine Science of this rule
15 is quite as remote from the general comprehension of mankind as are the so-called miracles of our Master, and for
the sole reason that it is their basis. The foundational
18 facts of Christian Science are gathered from the supremacy
of spiritual law and its antagonism to every supposed material law. Christians to-day should be able to say, with
21 the sweet sincerity of the apostle, "I take pleasure in
infirmities," — I enjoy the touch of weakness, pain, and
all suffering of the flesh, *because* it compels me to seek the
24 remedy for it, and to find happiness, apart from the personal senses. The holy calm of Paul's well-tried hope
met no obstacle or circumstances paramount to the tri-
27 umph of a reasonable faith in the omnipotence of good,
involved in its divine Principle, God: the so-called pains
and pleasures of matter were alike unreal to Jesus; for he
30 regarded matter as only a vagary of mortal belief, and subdued it with this understanding.

The abstract statement that all is Mind, supports the

entire wisdom of the text; and this statement receives 1
the mortal scoff only because it meets the immortal demands of Truth.   The Science of Paul's declaration re- 3
solves the element misnamed matter into its original sin,
or human will; that will which would oppose bringing the
qualities of Spirit into subjection to Spirit.   Sin brought 6
death; and death is an element of matter, or material
falsity, never of Spirit.

When Jesus reproduced his body after its burial, he 9
revealed the myth or material falsity of evil; its powerlessness to destroy good, and the omnipotence of the
Mind that knows this: he also showed forth the error 12
and nothingness of supposed life in matter, and the great
somethingness of the good we possess, which is of Spirit,
and immortal.   15

Understanding this, Paul took pleasure in infirmities,
for it enabled him to triumph over them, — he declared
that "the law of the Spirit of life in Christ Jesus hath 18
made me free from the law of sin and death;" he took
pleasure in "reproaches" and "persecutions," because
they were so many proofs that he had wrought the prob- 21
lem of being beyond the common apprehension of sinners;
he took pleasure in "necessities," for they tested and developed latent power.   24

We protect our dwellings more securely after a robbery,
and our jewels have been stolen; so, after losing those
jewels of character, — temperance, virtue, and truth, — 27
the young man is awakened to bar his door against further
robberies.

Go to the bedside of pain, and there you can demon- 30
strate the triumph of good that has pleasure in infirmities;
because it illustrates through the flesh the divine power

1 of Spirit, and reaches the basis of all supposed miracles;
whereby the sweet harmonies of Christian Science are
3 found to correct the discords of sense, and to lift man's
being into the sunlight of Soul.

"The chamber where the good man meets his fate
6   Is privileged beyond the walks of common life,
            Quite on the verge of heaven."

CHAPTER VII

Pond and Purpose

BELOVED STUDENTS:— In thanking you for your 1
gift of the pretty pond contributed to Pleasant View,
in Concord, New Hampshire, I make no distinction be- 3
tween my students and your students; for here, thine
becomes mine through gratitude and affection.

From my tower window, as I look on this smile of 6
Christian Science, this gift from my students and their
students, it will always mirror their love, loyalty, and
good works. Solomon saith, "As in water face answereth 9
to face, so the heart of man to man."

The waters that run among the valleys, and that
you have coaxed in their course to call on me, have 12
served the imagination for centuries. Theology religiously
bathes in water, medicine applies it physically, hydrology
handles it with so-called science, and metaphysics appro- 15
priates it topically as type and shadow. Metaphysically,
baptism serves to rebuke the senses and illustrate Christian
Science. 18

First: The baptism of repentance is indeed a stricken
state of human consciousness, wherein mortals gain
severe views of themselves; a state of mind which rends 21
the veil that hides mental deformity. Tears flood the eyes,

1 agony struggles, pride rebels, and a mortal seems a
monster, a dark, impenetrable cloud of error; and falling
3 on the bended knee of prayer, humble before God, he
cries, "Save, or I perish." Thus Truth, searching the
heart, neutralizes and destroys error.

6 This mental period is sometimes chronic, but oftener
acute. It is attended throughout with doubt, hope, sorrow,
joy, defeat, and triumph. When the good fight is fought,
9 error yields up its weapons and kisses the feet of Love,
while white-winged peace sings to the heart a song of
angels.

12 *Second:* The baptism of the Holy Ghost is the spirit
of Truth cleansing from all sin; giving mortals new
motives, new purposes, new affections, all pointing up-
15 ward. This mental condition settles into strength, freedom, deep-toned faith in God; and a marked loss of faith
in evil, in human wisdom, human policy, ways, and means.
18 It develops individual capacity, increases the intellectual
activities, and so quickens moral sensibility that the
great demands of spiritual sense are recognized, and they
21 rebuke the material senses, holding sway over human
consciousness.

By purifying human thought, this state of mind per-
24 meates with increased harmony all the minutiæ of human
affairs. It brings with it wonderful foresight, wisdom,
and power; it unselfs the mortal purpose, gives steadi-
27 ness to resolve, and success to endeavor. Through the
accession of spirituality, God, the divine Principle of
Christian Science, literally governs the aims, ambition,
30 and acts of the Scientist. The divine ruling gives pru-
dence and energy; it banishes forever all envy, rivalry,
evil thinking, evil speaking and acting; and mortal

mind, thus purged, obtains peace and power outside of 1
itself.

This practical Christian Science is the divine Mind, 3
the incorporeal Truth and Love, shining through the mists
of materiality and melting away the shadows called sin,
disease, and death. 6

In mortal experience, the fire of repentance first separates the dross from the gold, and reformation brings
the light which dispels darkness. Thus the operation 9
of the spirit of Truth and Love on the human thought,
in the words of St. John, "shall take of mine and show it
unto you." 12

Third: The baptism of Spirit, or final immersion of
human consciousness in the infinite ocean of Love, is the
last scene in corporeal sense. This omnipotent act drops 15
the curtain on material man and mortality. After this,
man's identity or consciousness reflects only Spirit, good,
whose visible being is invisible to the physical senses: eye 18
hath not seen it, inasmuch as it is the disembodied individual Spirit-substance and consciousness termed in
Christian metaphysics the ideal man — forever permeated 21
with eternal life, holiness, heaven. This order of Science
is the chain of ages, which maintain their obvious correspondence, and unites all periods in the divine design. 24
Mortal man's repentance and absolute abandonment of
sin finally dissolves all supposed material life or physical
sensation, and the corporeal or mortal man disappears 27
forever. The encumbering mortal molecules, called man,
vanish as a dream; but man born of the great Forever,
lives on, God-crowned and blest. 30

Mortals who on the shores of time learn Christian
Science, and live what they learn, take rapid transit to

1 heaven, — the hinge on which have turned all revolutions, natural, civil, or religious, the former being servant
3 to the latter, — from flux to permanence, from foul to pure, from torpid to serene, from extremes to intermediate. Above the waves of Jordan, dashing against the receding
6 shore, is heard the Father and Mother's welcome, saying forever to the baptized of Spirit: "This is my beloved Son." What but divine Science can interpret man's
9 eternal existence, God's allness, and the scientific indestructibility of the universe?

The advancing stages of Christian Science are gained
12 through growth, not accretion; idleness is the foe of progress. And scientific growth manifests no weakness, no emasculation, no illusive vision, no dreamy absentness,
15 no insubordination to the laws that be, no loss nor lack of what constitutes true manhood.

Growth is governed by intelligence; by the active,
18 all-wise, law-creating, law-disciplining, law-abiding Principle, God. The real Christian Scientist is constantly accentuating harmony in word and deed, mentally and
21 orally, perpetually repeating this diapason of heaven: "Good is my God, and my God is good. Love is my God, and my God is Love."

24 Beloved students, you have entered the path. Press patiently on; God is good, and good is the reward of all who diligently seek God. Your growth will be rapid, if
27 you love good supremely, and understand and obey the Way-shower, who, going before you, has scaled the steep ascent of Christian Science, stands upon the mount of
30 holiness, the dwelling-place of our God, and bathes in the baptismal font of eternal Love.

As you journey, and betimes sigh for rest "beside the

still waters," ponder this lesson of love. Learn its pur- 1
pose; and in hope and faith, where heart meets heart
reciprocally blest, drink with me the living waters of the 3
spirit of my life-purpose,— to impress humanity with
the genuine recognition of practical, operative Christian
Science. 6

CHAPTER VIII

Precept upon Precept

1   "THY WILL BE DONE"

THIS is the law of Truth to error, "Thou shalt surely
3   die." This law is a divine energy. Mortals cannot
prevent the fulfilment of this law; it covers all sin and
its effects. God is All, and by virtue of this nature and
6 allness He is cognizant only of good. Like a legislative
bill that governs millions of mortals whom the legislators
know not, the universal law of God has no knowledge
9 of evil, and enters unconsciously the human heart and
governs it.

    Mortals have only to submit to the law of God, come
12 into sympathy with it, and to let His will be done. This
unbroken motion of the law of divine Love gives, to the
weary and heavy-laden, rest. But who is willing to do
15 His will or to let it be done? Mortals obey their own
wills, and so disobey the divine order.

    All states and stages of human error are met and
18 mastered by divine Truth's negativing error in the way
of God's appointing. Those "whom the Lord loveth He
chasteneth." His rod brings to view His love, and inter-
21 prets to mortals the gospel of healing. David said, "Before I was afflicted I went astray: but now have I
kept Thy word." He who knows the end from the be-

ginning, attaches to sin due penalties as its antidotes and 1
remedies.

Who art thou, vain mortal, that usurpest the preroga- 3
tive of divine wisdom, and wouldst teach God not to punish sin? that wouldst shut the mouth of His prophets,
and cry, "Peace, peace; when there is no peace," — yea, 6
that healest the wounds of my people slightly?

The Principle of divine Science being Love, the divine
rule of this Principle demonstrates Love, and proves that 9
human belief fulfils the law of belief, and dies of its own
physics. Metaphysics also demonstrates this Principle of
cure when sin is self-destroyed. Short-sighted physics 12
admits the so-called pains of matter that destroy its more
dangerous pleasures.

Insomnia compels mortals to learn that neither obliv- 15
ion nor dreams can recuperate the life of man, whose
Life is God, for God neither slumbers nor sleeps. The
loss of gustatory enjoyment and the ills of indigestion 18
tend to rebuke appetite and destroy the peace of a false
sense. False pleasure will be, is, chastened; it has no
right to be at peace. To suffer for having "other gods 21
before me," is divinely wise. Evil passions die in their
own flames, but are punished before extinguished. Peace
has no foothold on the false basis that evil should be 24
concealed and that life and happiness should still attend
it. Joy is self-sustained; goodness and blessedness are
one: suffering is self-inflicted, and good is the master of 27
evil.

To this scientific logic and the logic of events, egotism
and false charity say, " 'Not so, Lord;' it is wise to 30
cover iniquity and punish it not, then shall mortals have
peace." Divine Love, as unconscious as incapable of

1 error, pursues the evil that hideth itself, strips off its
disguises, and — behold the result: evil, uncovered, is
3 self-destroyed.

Christian Science never healed a patient without proving with mathematical certainty that error, when found
6 out, is two-thirds destroyed, and the remaining third
kills itself. Do men whine over a nest of serpents, and
post around it placards warning people not to stir up
9 these reptiles because they have stings? Christ said,
"They shall take up serpents;" and, "Be ye therefore
wise as serpents and harmless as doves." The wisdom
12 of a serpent is to hide itself. The wisdom of God, as
revealed in Christian Science, brings the serpent out of
its hole, handles it, and takes away its sting. Good deeds
15 are harmless. He who has faith in woman's special adaptability to lead on Christian Science, will not be shocked
when she puts her foot on the head of the serpent, as it
18 biteth at the heel.

Intemperance begets a belief of disordered brains,
membranes, stomach, and nerves; and this belief serves
21 to uncover and kill this lurking serpent, intemperance,
that hides itself under the false pretense of human need,
innocent enjoyment, and a medical prescription. The
24 belief in venereal diseases tears the black mask from the
shameless brow of licentiousness, torments its victim, and
thus may save him from his destroyer.

27   Charity has the courage of conviction; it may suffer
long, but has neither the cowardice nor the foolhardiness
to cover iniquity. Charity is Love; and Love opens
30 the eyes of the blind, rebukes error, and casts it out.
Charity never flees before error, lest it should suffer
from an encounter. Love your enemies, or you will not

lose them; and if you love them, you will help to reform 1
them.

Christ points the way of salvation. His mode is not 3
cowardly, uncharitable, nor unwise, but it teaches mortals to handle serpents and cast out evil. Our own vision
must be clear to open the eyes of others, else the blind 6
will lead the blind and both shall fall. The sickly charity
that supplies criminals with bouquets has been dealt
with summarily by the good judgment of people in 9
the old Bay State. Inhuman medical bills, class legislation, and Salem witchcraft, are not indigenous to her
soil. 12

"Out of the depths have I delivered thee." The
drowning man just rescued from the merciless wave is
unconscious of suffering. Why, then, do you break his 15
peace and cause him to suffer in coming to life? Because
you wish to save him from death. Then, if a criminal
is at peace, is he not to be pitied and brought back to 18
life? Or, are you afraid to do this lest he suffer, trample
on your pearls of thought, and turn on you and rend you?
Cowardice is selfishness. When one protects himself at 21
his neighbor's cost, let him remember, "Whosoever will
save his life shall lose it." He risks nothing who obeys
the law of God, and shall find the Life that cannot be 24
lost.

Our Master said, "Ye shall drink indeed of my cup."
Jesus stormed sin in its citadels and kept peace with 27
God. He drank this cup giving thanks, and he said to
his followers, "Drink ye all of it," — drink it all, and let
all drink of it. He lived the spirit of his prayer, — "Thy 30
kingdom come." Shall we repeat our Lord's Prayer
when the heart denies it, refuses to bear the cross and

1 to fulfil the conditions of our petition?   Human policy
is a fool that saith in his heart, "No God" — a caressing
3 Judas that betrays you, and commits suicide.   This godless policy never knows what happiness is, and how it is
obtained.

6   Jesus did his work, and left his glorious career for our
example.   On the shore of Gennesaret he tersely reminded his students of their worldly policy.   They had
9 suffered, and seen their error.   This experience caused
them to remember the reiterated warning of their Master and cast their nets on the right side.   When they
12 were fit to be blest, they received the blessing.   The
ultimatum of their human sense of ways and means
ought to silence ours.   One step away from the direct
15 line of divine Science cost them — what?   A speedy return under the reign of difficulties, darkness, and unrequited toil.

18   The currents of human nature rush in against the right
course;   health, happiness, and life flow not into one of
their channels.   The law of Love saith, "Not my will,
21 but Thine, be done," and Christian Science proves that
human will is lost in the divine;   and Love, the white
Christ, is the remunerator.

24   If, consciously or unconsciously, one is at work in a
wrong direction, who will step forward and open his
eyes to see this error?   He who *is* a Christian Scientist,
27 who has cast the beam out of his own eye, speaks plainly
to the offender and tries to show his errors to him before
letting another know it.

30   Pitying friends took down from the cross the fainting
form of Jesus, and buried it out of their sight.   His disciples, who had not yet drunk of his cup, lost sight of

him; they could not behold his immortal being in the 1
form of Godlikeness.

All that I have written, taught, or lived, that is good, 3
flowed through cross-bearing, self-forgetfulness, and my
faith in the right. Suffering or Science, or both, in the
proportion that their instructions are assimilated, will 6
point the way, shorten the process, and consummate the
joys of acquiescence in the methods of divine Love. The
Scripture saith, "He that covereth his sins shall not pros- 9
per." No risk is so stupendous as to neglect opportunities which God giveth, and not to forewarn and forearm
our fellow-mortals against the evil which, if seen, can 12
be destroyed.

May my friends and my enemies so profit by these
waymarks, that what has chastened and illumined 15
another's way may perfect their own lives by gentle
benedictions. In every age, the pioneer reformer must
pass through a baptism of fire. But the faithful adher- 18
ents of Truth have gone on rejoicing. Christian Science
gives a fearless wing and firm foundation. These are
its inspiring tones from the lips of our Master, "My 21
sheep hear my voice, and I know them, and they follow
me: and I give unto them eternal life; and they shall
never perish, neither shall any man pluck them out of 24
my hand." He is but "an hireling" who fleeth when he
seeth the wolf coming.

Loyal Christian Scientists, be of good cheer: the night 27
is far spent, the day dawns; God's universal kingdom
will appear, Love will reign in every heart, and *His* will
be done on earth as in heaven.   30

1   "PUT UP THY SWORD"

   While Jesus' life was full of Love, and a demonstra-
3 tion of Love, it appeared hate to the carnal mind, or
   mortal thought, of his time. He said, "Think not that
   I am come to send peace on earth: I came not to send
6 peace, but a sword. For I am come to set a man at
   variance against his father, and the daughter against her
   mother, and the daughter-in-law against her mother-in-
9 law. And a man's foes shall be they of his own household."
   This action of Jesus was stimulated by the same Love
12 that closed — to the senses — that wondrous life, and
   that summed up its demonstration in the command,
   "Put up thy sword." The very conflict his Truth brought,
15 in accomplishing its purpose of Love, meant, all
   the way through, "Put up thy sword;" but the sword
   must have been drawn before it could be returned into
18 the scabbard.
   My students need to search the Scriptures and "Science
   and Health with Key to the Scriptures," to understand
21 the personal Jesus' labor in the flesh for their salvation:
   they need to do this even to understand my works, their
   motives, aims, and tendency.
24   The attitude of mortal mind in being healed morally,
   is the same as its attitude physically. The Christian
   Scientist cannot heal the sick, and take error along with
27 Truth, either in the recognition or approbation of it.
   This would prevent the possibility of destroying the
   tares: they must be separated from the wheat before
30 they can be burned, and Jesus foretold the harvest hour

and the final destruction of error through this very pro- 1
cess, — the sifting and the fire. The tendency of mortal
mind is to go from one extreme to another: Truth comes 3
into the intermediate space, saying, "I wound to heal;
I punish to reform; I do it all in love; my peace I leave
with thee: not as the world giveth, give I unto thee. 6
Arise, let us go hence; let us depart from the material
sense of God's ways and means, and gain a spiritual
understanding of them."   9

But let us not seek to climb up some other way, as we
shall do if we take the end for the beginning or start
from wrong motives. Christian Science demands order 12
and truth. To abide by these we must first understand
the Principle and object of our work, and be clear that
it is Love, peace, and good will toward men. Then we 15
shall demonstrate the Principle in the way of His appointment, and not according to the infantile conception of our way; as when a child in sleep walks on the 18
summit of the roof of the house because he is a som-
nambulist, and thinks he is where he is not, and would
fall immediately if he knew where he was and what he 21
was doing.

My students are at the beginning of their demonstration; they have a long warfare with error in themselves 24
and in others to finish, and they must at this stage use
the sword of Spirit.

They cannot in the beginning take the attitude, nor 27
adopt the words, that Jesus used at the *end* of his
demonstration.

If you would follow in his footsteps, you must not try 30
to gather the harvest while the corn is in the blade, nor
yet when it is in the ear; a wise spiritual discernment

1 must be used in your application of his words and inference from his acts, to guide your own state of combat
3 with error. There *remaineth,* it is true, a Sabbath rest
for the people of God; but we must first have done our
work, and entered into our rest, as the Scriptures give
6 example.

SCIENTIFIC THEISM

In the May number of our *Journal,* there appeared a
9 review of, and some extracts from, "Scientific Theism,"
by Phare Pleigh.

Now, Phare Pleigh evidently means more than "hands
12 off." A live lexicographer, given to the Anglo-Saxon
tongue, might add to the above definition the "laying
on of hands," as well. Whatever his *nom de plume*
15 means, an acquaintance with the author justifies one
in the conclusion that he is a power in criticism, a
big protest against injustice; but, the best may be
18 mistaken.

One of these extracts is the story of the Cheshire Cat,
which "vanished quite slowly, beginning with the end
21 of the tail, and ending with the grin, which remained
some time after the rest of it had gone." Was this a witty
or a happy hit at idealism, to illustrate the author's fol-
24 lowing point? —

"When philosophy becomes fairy-land, in which neither
laws of nature nor the laws of reason hold good, the
27 attempt of phenomenism to conceive the universe as a
phenomenon without a noumenon may succeed, but not
before; for it is an attempt to conceive a grin without
30 a cat."

True idealism is a divine Science, which combines in 1
logical sequence, nature, reason, and revelation. An
effect without a cause is inconceivable; neither philoso- 3
phy nor reason attempts to find one; but all should conceive and understand that Spirit cannot become less than
Spirit; hence that the universe of God is spiritual, — even 6
the ideal world whose cause is the self-created Principle,
with which its ideal or phenomenon must correspond in
quality and quantity. 9

The fallacy of an unscientific statement is this: that
matter and Spirit are one and eternal; or, that the phenomenon of Spirit is the antipode of Spirit, namely, mat- 12
ter. Nature declares, throughout the mineral, vegetable,
and animal kingdoms, that the specific nature of all things
is unchanged, and that nature is constituted of and by 15
Spirit.

Sensuous and material realistic views presuppose that
nature is matter, and that Deity is a finite person con- 18
taining infinite Mind; and that these opposites, in suppositional unity and personality, produce matter, — a
third quality unlike God. Again, that matter is both 21
cause and effect, but that the effect is antagonistic to its
cause; that death is at war with Life, evil with good, —
and man a rebel against his Maker. This is neither 24
Science nor theism. According to Holy Writ, it is a
kingdom divided against itself, that shall be brought
to desolation. 27

The nature of God must change in order to become
matter, or to become both finite and infinite; and matter
must *dis*appear, for Spirit to appear. To the material 30
sense, everything is matter; but spiritualize human
thought, and our convictions change: for spiritual sense

1 takes in new views, in which nature becomes Spirit; and Spirit is God, and God is good. Science unfolds the fact 3 that Deity was forever Mind, Spirit; that matter never produced Mind, and *vice versa*.

The visible universe declares the invisible only by re- 6 version, as error declares Truth. The testimony of material sense in relation to existence is false; for matter can neither see, hear, nor feel, and mortal mind must change 9 all its conceptions of life, substance, and intelligence, before it can reach the immortality of Mind and its ideas. It is erroneous to accept the evidence of the material 12 senses whence to reason out God, when it is conceded that the five personal senses can take no cognizance of Spirit or of its phenomena. False realistic views sap the 15 Science of Principle and idea; they make Deity unreal and inconceivable, either as mind or matter; but Truth comes to the rescue of reason and immortality, and un- 18 folds the real nature of God and the universe to the spiritual sense, which beareth witness of things spiritual, and not material.

21 To begin with, the notion of Spirit as cause and end, with matter as its effect, is more ridiculous than the "grin without a cat;" for a grin expresses the nature of a cat, 24 and this nature may linger in memory: but matter does not express the nature of Spirit, and matter's graven grins are neither eliminated nor retained by Spirit. What 27 can illustrate Dr. ——'s views better than Pat's echo, when he said "How do you do?" and echo answered, "Pretty well, I thank you!"

30 Dr. —— says: "The recognition of teleology in nature is necessarily the recognition of purely spiritual personality in God."

According to lexicography, teleology is the science of 1
the final cause of things; and divine Science (and all
Science is divine) neither reveals God in matter, cause 3
in effect, nor teaches that nature and her laws are the
material universe, or that the personality of infinite Spirit
is finite or material. Jesus said, "Ye do err, not know- 6
ing the Scriptures, nor the power of God." Now, what
saith the Scripture? "God is a Spirit: and they that
worship Him must worship Him in spirit and in 9
truth."

MENTAL PRACTICE

It is admitted that mortals think wickedly and act 12
wickedly: it is beginning to be seen by thinkers, that
mortals think also after a sickly fashion. In common
parlance, one person feels sick, another feels wicked. A 15
third person knows that if he would remove this feeling
in either case, in the one he must change his patient's
consciousness of dis-ease and suffering to a consciousness 18
of ease and loss of suffering; while in the other he must
change the patient's sense of sinning at ease to a sense of
discomfort in sin and peace in goodness. 21

This is Christian Science: that mortal mind makes
sick, and immortal Mind makes well; that mortal mind
makes sinners, while immortal Mind makes saints; that 24
a state of health is but a state of consciousness made manifest on the body, and *vice versa;* that while one person
feels wickedly and acts wickedly, another knows that if 27
he can change this evil sense and consciousness to a good
sense, or conscious goodness, the fruits of goodness will
follow, and he has reformed the sinner. 30

1   Now, demonstrate this rule, which obtains in every
line of mental healing, and you will find that a good rule
3 works one way, and a false rule the opposite way.

Let us suppose that there is a sick person whom another would heal mentally. The healer begins by mental
6 argument. He mentally says, "You are well, and you
know it;" and he supports this silent mental force by
audible explanation, attestation, and precedent. His
9 mental and oral arguments aim to refute the sick man's
thoughts, words, and actions, in certain directions, and
turn them into channels of Truth. He persists in this
12 course until the patient's mind yields, and the harmonious
thought has the full control over this mind on the point
at issue. The end is attained, and the patient says and
15 feels, "I am well, and I know it."

This mental practitioner has changed his patient's
consciousness from sickness to health. The patient's
18 mental state is now the diametrical opposite of what it
was when the mental practitioner undertook to transform
it, and he is improved morally and physically.
21   That this mental method has power and bears fruit,
is patent both to the conscientious Christian Scientist and
the observer. Both should understand with equal clear-
24 ness, that if this mental process and power be reversed,
and people believe that a man is sick and knows it, and
speak of him as being sick, put it into the minds of others
27 that he is sick, publish it in the newspapers that he is
failing, and persist in this action of mind over mind, it
follows that he will believe that he is sick, — and Jesus
30 said it would be according to the woman's belief; but if
with the certainty of Science he knows that an error of
belief has not the power of Truth, and cannot, does

not, produce the slightest effect, it has no power over 1
him. Thus a mental malpractitioner may lose his
power to harm by a false mental argument; for it 3
gives one opportunity to handle the error, and when
mastering it one gains in the rules of metaphysics, and
thereby learns more of its divine Principle. Error pro- 6
duces physical sufferings, and these sufferings show
the fundamental Principle of Christian Science; namely,
that error and sickness are one, and Truth is their 9
remedy.

The evil-doer can do little at removing the effect of sin
on himself, unless he believes that sin has produced the 12
effect and knows he is a sinner; or, knowing that he is a
sinner, if he denies it, the good effect is lost. Either of
these states of mind will stultify the power to heal men- 15
tally. This accounts for many helpless mental practitioners and mysterious diseases.

Again: If error is the cause of disease, Truth being 18
the cure, denial of this fact in one instance and
acknowledgment of it in another saps one's understanding of the Science of Mind-healing. Such denial 21
dethrones demonstration, baffles the student of Mind-
healing, and divorces his work from Science. Such denial also contradicts the doctrine that we must mentally 24
struggle against both evil and disease, and is like saying
that five times ten are fifty while ten times five are not
fifty; as if the multiplication of the same two numbers 27
would not yield the same product whichever might serve
as the multiplicand.

Who would tell another of a crime that he himself is 30
committing, or call public attention to that crime? The
belief in evil and in the process of evil, holds the issues

1 of death to the evil-doer. It takes away a man's proper
sense of good, and gives him a false sense of both evil
3 and good. It inflames envy, passion, evil-speaking, and
strife. It reverses Christian Science in all things. It
causes the victim to believe that he is advancing while
6 injuring himself and others. This state of false consciousness in many cases causes the victim great physical suffering; and conviction of his wrong state of feeling reforms
9 him, and so heals him: or, failing of conviction and reform, he becomes morally paralyzed — in other words,
a moral idiot.

12   In this state of misled consciousness, one is ready to
listen complacently to audible falsehoods that once he
would have resisted and loathed; and this, because the
15 false seems true. The malicious mental argument and
its action on the mind of the perpetrator, is fatal, morally
and physically. From the effects of mental malpractice
18 the subject scarcely awakes in time, and must suffer its
full penalty after death. This sin against divine Science
is cancelled only through human agony: the measure it
21 has meted must be remeasured to it.

The crimes committed under this new *régime* of mind-
power, when brought to light, will make stout hearts quail.
24 Its mystery protects it now, for it is not yet known. Error
is more abstract than Truth. Even the healing Principle,
whose power seems inexplicable, is not so obscure; for
27 this is the power of God, and good should seem more
natural than evil.

I shall not forget the cost of investigating, for this age,
30 the methods and power of error. While the ways, means,
and potency of Truth had flowed into my consciousness
as easily as dawns the morning light and shadows flee,

the metaphysical mystery of error — its hidden paths, 1
purpose, and fruits — at first defied me. I was saying all the time, "Come not thou into the secret" — 3
but at length took up the research according to God's
command.

Streams which purify, necessarily have pure fountains; 6
while impure streams flow from corrupt sources. Here,
divine light, logic, and revelation coincide.

Science proves, beyond cavil, that the tree is known 9
by its fruit; that mind reaches its own ideal, and cannot
be separated from it. I respect that moral sense which
is sufficiently strong to discern what it believes, and to say, 12
if it must, "I discredit Mind with having the power to
heal." This individual disbelieves in Mind-healing, and
is consistent. But, alas! for the mistake of believing in 15
mental healing, claiming full faith in the divine Principle,
and saying, "I am a Christian Scientist," while doing
unto others what we would resist to the hilt if done unto 18
ourselves.

May divine Love so permeate the affections of all those
who have named the name of Christ in its fullest sense, 21
that no counteracting influence can hinder their growth
or taint their examples.

TAKING OFFENSE   24

There is immense wisdom in the old proverb, "He
that is slow to anger is better than the mighty." Hannah
More said, "If I wished to punish my enemy, I should 27
make him hate somebody."

To punish ourselves for others' faults, is superlative
folly. The mental arrow shot from another's bow is 30

1 practically harmless, unless our own thought barbs it.
It is our pride that makes another's criticism rankle, our
3 self-will that makes another's deed offensive, our egotism
that feels hurt by another's self-assertion. Well may we
feel wounded by our own faults; but we can hardly afford
6 to be miserable for the faults of others.

A courtier told Constantine that a mob had broken
the head of his statue with stones. The emperor lifted
9 his hands to his head, saying: "It is very surprising, but
I don't feel hurt in the least."

We should remember that the world is wide; that there
12 are a thousand million different human wills, opinions,
ambitions, tastes, and loves; that each person has a different history, constitution, culture, character, from all the
15 rest; that human life is the work, the play, the ceaseless
action and reaction upon each other of these different
atoms. Then, we should go forth into life with the smallest
18 expectations, but with the largest patience; with a keen
relish for and appreciation of everything beautiful, great,
and good, but with a temper so genial that the friction
21 of the world shall not wear upon our sensibilities; with
an equanimity so settled that no passing breath nor
accidental disturbance shall agitate or ruffle it; with a
24 charity broad enough to cover the whole world's evil, and
sweet enough to neutralize what is bitter in it, — determined not to be offended when no wrong is meant, nor
27 even when it is, unless the offense be against God.

Nothing short of our own errors should offend us. He
who can wilfully attempt to injure another, is an object
30 of pity rather than of resentment; while it is a question
in my mind, whether there is enough of a flatterer, a fool,
or a liar, *to* offend a whole-souled woman.

HINTS TO THE CLERGY

At the residence of Mr. Rawson, of Arlington, Massachusetts, a happy concourse of friends had gathered to celebrate the eighty-second birthday of his mother — a friend of mine, and a Christian Scientist.

Among the guests, were an orthodox clergyman, his wife and child.

In the course of the evening, conversation drifted to the seventh modern wonder, Christian Science; whereupon the mother, Mrs. Rawson, who had drunk at its fount, firmly bore testimony to the power of Christ, Truth, to heal the sick.

Soon after this conversation, the clergyman's son was taken violently ill. Then was the clergyman's opportunity to demand a proof of what the Christian Scientist had declared; and he said to this venerable Christian: —

"If you heal my son, when seeing, I may be led to believe."

Mrs. Rawson then rose from her seat, and sat down beside the sofa whereon lay the lad with burning brow, moaning in pain.

Looking away from all material aid, to the spiritual source and ever-present help, silently, through the divine power, she healed him.

The deep flush faded from the face, a cool perspiration spread over it, and he slept.

In about one hour he awoke, and was hungry.

The parents said: —

"Wait until we get home, and you shall have some gruel."

1   But Mrs. Rawson said: —
"Give the child what he relishes, and doubt not that
3 the Father of all will care for him."

Thus, the unbiased youth and the aged Christian
carried the case on the side of God; and, after eating
6 several ice-creams, the clergyman's son returned home
— *well.*

PERFIDY AND SLANDER

9   What has an individual gained by losing his own self-
respect? or what has he lost when, retaining his own,
he loses the homage of fools, or the pretentious praise of
12 hypocrites, false to themselves as to others?

Shakespeare, the immortal lexicographer of mortals,
writes: —

15   To thine own self be true,
         And it must follow, as the night the day,
         Thou canst not then be false to any man.

18   When Aristotle was asked what a person could gain
by uttering a falsehood, he replied, "Not to be credited
when he shall tell the truth."

21   The character of a liar and hypocrite is so contempti-
ble, that even of those who have lost their honor it might
be expected that from the violation of truth they should
24 be restrained by their pride.

Perfidy of an inferior quality, such as manages to evade
the law, and which dignified natures cannot stoop to
27 notice, except legally, disgraces human nature more than
do most vices.

Slander is a midnight robber; the red-tongued assas-
30 sin of radical worth; the conservative swindler, who

sells himself in a traffic by which he can gain nothing. 1
It can retire for forgiveness to no fraternity where its
crime may stand in the place of a virtue; but must at 3
length be given up to the hisses of the multitude, without friend and without apologist.

Law has found it necessary to offer to the innocent, 6
security from slanderers — those pests of society — when
their crime comes within its jurisdiction. Thus, to evade
the penalty of law, and yet with malice aforethought to 9
extend their evil intent, is the nice distinction by which
they endeavor to get their weighty stuff into the hands
of gossip! Some uncharitable one may give it a forward 12
move, and, ere that one himself become aware, find
himself responsible for kind (?) endeavors.

Would that my pen or pity could raise these weak, 15
pitifully poor objects from their choice of self-degrada-
tion to the nobler purposes and wider aims of a life made
honest: a life in which the fresh flowers of feeling blos- 18
som, and, like the camomile, the more trampled upon,
the sweeter the odor they send forth to benefit mankind;
a life wherein calm, self-respected thoughts abide in 21
tabernacles of their own, dwelling upon a holy hill, speaking the truth in the heart; a life wherein the mind can
rest in green pastures, beside the still waters, on isles 24
of sweet refreshment. The sublime summary of an
honest life satisfies the mind craving a higher good, and
bathes it in the cool waters of peace on earth; till it 27
grows into the full stature of wisdom, reckoning its
own by the amount of happiness it has bestowed upon
others. 30

Not to avenge one's self upon one's enemies, is the
command of almighty wisdom; and we take this to be

1 a safer guide than the promptings of human nature. To know that a deception dark as it is base has been 3 practised upon thee, — by those deemed at least indebted friends whose welfare thou hast promoted, — and yet not to avenge thyself, is to do good to thyself; is to take 6 a new standpoint whence to look upward; is to be calm amid excitement, just amid lawlessness, and pure amid corruption.

9 To be a great man or woman, to have a name whose odor fills the world with its fragrance, is to bear with patience the buffetings of envy or malice — even while 12 seeking to raise those barren natures to a capacity for a higher life. We should look with pitying eye on the momentary success of all villainies, on mad ambition 15 and low revenge. This will bring us also to look on a kind, true, and just person, faithful to conscience and honest beyond reproach, as the only suitable fabric out 18 of which to weave an existence fit for earth and heaven.

CONTAGION

21 Whatever man sees, feels, or in any way takes cognizance of, must be caught through mind; inasmuch as perception, sensation, and consciousness belong to 24 mind and not to matter. Floating with the popular current of mortal thought without questioning the reliability of its conclusions, we do what others do, 27 believe what others believe, and say what others say. Common consent is contagious, and it makes disease catching.

30 People believe in infectious and contagious diseases,

and that any one is liable to have them under certain 1
predisposing or exciting causes. This mental state prepares one to have any disease whenever there appear the 3
circumstances which he believes produce it. If he believed
as sincerely that health is catching when exposed to contact with healthy people, he would catch their state of 6
feeling quite as surely and with better effect than he does
the sick man's.

If only the people would believe that good is more 9
contagious than evil, since God is omnipresence, how
much more certain would be the doctor's success, and
the clergyman's conversion of sinners. And if only the 12
pulpit would encourage faith in God in this direction,
and faith in Mind over all other influences governing
the receptivity of the body, theology would teach man 15
as David taught: "Because thou hast made the Lord,
which is my refuge, even the most High thy habitation;
there shall no evil befall thee, neither shall any plague 18
come nigh thy dwelling."

The confidence of mankind in contagious disease would
thus become beautifully less; and in the same propor- 21
tion would faith in the power of God to heal and to save
mankind increase, until the whole human race would
become healthier, holier, happier, and longer lived. A 24
calm, Christian state of mind is a better preventive of
contagion than a drug, or than any other possible sana-
tive method; and the "perfect Love" that "casteth out 27
fear" is a sure defense.

1 IMPROVE YOUR TIME

Success in life depends upon persistent effort, upon
3 the improvement of moments more than upon any other
one thing. A great amount of time is consumed in talking
nothing, doing nothing, and indecision as to what one
6 should do. If one would be successful in the future, let
him make the most of the present.

Three ways of wasting time, one of which is con-
9 temptible, are gossiping mischief, making lingering calls,
and mere motion when at work, thinking of nothing or
planning for some amusement, — travel of limb more
12 than mind. Rushing around smartly is no proof of accomplishing much.

All successful individuals have become such by hard
15 work; by improving moments before they pass into hours,
and hours that other people may occupy in the pursuit
of pleasure. They spend no time in sheer idleness, in
18 talking when they have nothing to say, in building air-
castles or floating off on the wings of sense: all of which
drop human life into the ditch of nonsense, and worse
21 than waste its years.

> "Let us, then, be up and doing,
> With a heart for any fate;
24 Still achieving, still pursuing,
> Learn to labor and to wait."

THANKSGIVING DINNER

27 It was a beautiful group! needing but canvas and the
touch of an artist to render it pathetic, tender, gorgeous.

Age, on whose hoary head the almond-blossom formed a 1
crown of glory; middle age, in smiles and the full fruition
of happiness; infancy, exuberant with joy, — ranged side 3
by side.   The sober-suited grandmother, rich in experience, had seen sunshine and shadow fall upon ninety-
six years.   Four generations sat at that dinner-table. 6
The rich viands made busy many appetites; but, what
of the poor!   Willingly — though I take no stock in
spirit-rappings — would I have had the table give a 9
spiritual groan for the unfeasted ones.

Under the skilful carving of the generous host, the
mammoth turkey grew beautifully less.   His was the 12
glory to vie with guests in the dexterous use of knife and
fork, until delicious pie, pudding, and fruit caused unconditional surrender.   15

And the baby!   Why, he made a big hole, with two
incisors, in a big pippin, and bit the finger presump-
tuously poked into the little mouth to arrest the peel! 18
Then he was caught walking! one, two, three steps, —
and papa knew that he could walk, but grandpa was
taken napping.   Now! baby has tumbled, soft as thistle- 21
down, on the floor; and instead of a real set-to at crying,
a look of cheer and a toy from mamma bring the soft
little palms patting together, and pucker the rosebud 24
mouth into saying, "Oh, pretty!"   That was a scientific
baby; and his first sitting-at-table on Thanksgiving Day
— yes, and his little rainbowy life — brought sunshine 27
to every heart.   How many homes echo such tones of
heartfelt joy on Thanksgiving Day!   But, alas! for the
desolate home; for the tear-filled eyes looking longingly 30
at the portal through which the loved one comes not, or
gazing silently on the vacant seat at fireside and board —

1 God comfort them all! we inwardly prayed — but the memory was too much; and, turning from it, in a bumper
3 of pudding-sauce we drank to peace, and plenty, and happy households.

CHRISTIAN SCIENCE

6 This age is reaching out towards the perfect Principle of things; is pushing towards perfection in art, invention, and manufacture. Why, then, should religion be
9 stereotyped, and we not obtain a more perfect and practical Christianity? It will never do to be behind the times in things most essential, which proceed from the
12 standard of right that regulates human destiny. Human skill but foreshadows what is next to appear as its divine origin. Proportionately as we part with material systems
15 and theories, personal doctrines and dogmas, meekly to ascend the hill of Science, shall we reach the maximum of perfection in all things.
18 Spirit is omnipotent; hence a more spiritual Christianity will be one having more power, having perfected in Science that most important of all arts, — healing.
21 Metaphysical healing, or Christian Science, is a demand of the times. Every man and every woman would desire and demand it, if he and she knew its infinite
24 value and firm basis. The unerring and fixed Principle of all healing is God; and this Principle should be sought from the love of good, from the most spiritual
27 and unselfish motives. Then will it be understood to be of God, and not of man; and this will prevent mankind from striking out promiscuously, teaching and practising

in the *name* of Science without knowing its fundamental 1
Principle.

It is important to know that a malpractice of the best 3
system will result in the worst form of medicine. Moreover, the feverish, disgusting pride of those who call
themselves metaphysicians or Scientists, — but are such 6
in name only, — fanned by the breath of mental malpractice, is the death's-head at the feast of Truth; the
monkey in harlequin jacket that will retard the onward 9
march of life-giving Science, if not understood and withstood, and so strangled in its attempts.

The standard of metaphysical healing is traduced by 12
thinking to put into the old garment of drugging the new
cloth of metaphysics; or by trying to twist the fatal
magnetic force of mortal mind, termed hypnotism, into 15
a more fashionable cut and naming that "mind-cure,"
or — which is still worse in the eyes of Truth — terming
it metaphysics! Substituting good words for a good life, 18
fair-seeming for straightforward character, mental malpractice for the practice of true medicine, is a poor shift
for the weak and worldly who think the standard of 21
Christian Science too high for them.

What think you of a scientist in mathematics who finds
fault with the exactness of the rule because unwilling to 24
work hard enough to practise it? The perfection of the
rule of Christian Science is what constitutes its utility:
having a true standard, if some fall short, others will 27
approach it; and these are they only who adhere to that
standard.

Matter must be understood as a false belief or product 30
of mortal mind: whence we learn that sensation is not
in matter, but in this so-called mind; that we see and

1 feel disease only by reason of our belief in it: then shall
matter remain no longer to blind us to Spirit, and clog
3 the wheels of progress. We spread our wings in vain when
we attempt to mount above error by speculative views
of Truth.

6   Love is the Principle of divine Science; and Love is
not learned of the material senses, nor gained by a culpable attempt to seem what we have not lifted ourselves
9 to *be,* namely, a Christian. In love for man, we gain a
true sense of Love as God; and in no other way can we
reach this spiritual sense, and rise — and still rise — to
12 things most essential and divine. What hinders man's
progress is his vain conceit, the Phariseeism of the times,
also his effort to steal from others and avoid hard work;
15 errors which can never find a place in Science. Empiri-
cal knowledge is worse than useless: it never has advanced
man a single step in the scale of being.

18   That one should have ventured on such unfamiliar
ground, and, self-forgetful, should have gone on to establish this mighty system of metaphysical healing, called
21 Christian Science, against such odds, — even the entire
current of mortality, — is matter of grave wonderment to
profound thinkers. That, in addition to this, she has made
24 some progress, has seen far into the spiritual facts of being which constitute physical and mental perfection, in
the midst of an age so sunken in sin and sensuality, seems
27 to them still more inconceivable.

In this new departure of metaphysics, God is regarded
more as absolute, supreme; and Christ is clad with a
30 richer illumination as our Saviour from sickness, sin,
and death. God's fatherliness as Life, Truth, and Love,
makes His sovereignty glorious.

By this system, too, man has a changed recognition 1
of his relation to God. He is no longer obliged to sin,
be sick, and die to reach heaven, but is required and em- 3
powered to conquer sin, sickness, and death; thus, as
image and likeness, to reflect Him who destroys death
and hell. By this reflection, man becomes the partaker 6
of that Mind whence sprang the universe.

In Christian Science, progress is demonstration, not
doctrine. This Science is ameliorative and regenerative, 9
delivering mankind from all error through the light and
love of Truth. It gives to the race loftier desires and new
possibilities. It lays the axe at the root of the tree of 12
knowledge, to cut down all that bringeth not forth good
fruit; "and blessed is he, whosoever shall not be offended
in me." It touches mind to more spiritual issues, sys- 15
tematizes action, gives a keener sense of Truth and a
stronger desire for it.

Hungering and thirsting after a better life, we shall 18
have it, and become Christian Scientists; learn God
aright, and know something of the ideal man, the real
man, harmonious and eternal. This movement of thought 21
must push on the ages: it must start the wheels of reason
aright, educate the affections to higher resources, and
leave Christianity unbiased by the superstitions of a 24
senior period.

INJUSTICE

Who that has tried to follow the divine precept, "All 27
things whatsoever ye would that men should do unto
you, do ye even so to them," has not suffered from the

1 situation? — has not found that human passions in their
reaction have misjudged motives?

3   Throughout our experience since undertaking the
labor of uplifting the race, we have been made the re-
pository of little else than the troubles, indiscretions,
6 and errors of others; until thought has shrunk from
contact with family difficulties, and become weary with
study to counsel wisely whenever giving advice on per-
9 sonal topics.

To the child complaining of his parents we have said,
"Love and honor thy parents, and yield obedience to
12 them in all that is right; but you have the rights of conscience, as we all have, and must follow God in all your
ways."

15   When yielding to constant solicitations of husband or
wife to give, to one or the other, advice concerning difficulties and the best way to overcome them, we have done
18 this to the best of our ability, — and always with the purpose to restore harmony and prevent dishonor. In such
cases we have said, "Take no counsel of a mortal, even
21 though it be your best friend; but be guided by God
alone;" meaning by this, Be not estranged from each
other by anything that is said to you, but seek in divine
24 Love the remedy for all human discord.

Yet, notwithstanding one's good intentions, in some
way or at some step in one's efforts to help another, as
27 a general rule, one will be blamed for all that is not right:
but this must not deter us from doing our duty, whatever
else may appear, and at whatever cost.

REFORMERS 1

The olden opinion that hell is fire and brimstone, has yielded somewhat to the metaphysical fact that suffering 3 is a thing of mortal mind instead of body: so, in place of material flames and odor, mental anguish is generally accepted as the penalty for sin. This changed belief 6 has wrought a change in the actions of men. Not a few individuals serve God (or try to) from fear; but remove that fear, and the worst of human passions belch forth 9 their latent fires. Some people never repent until earth gives them such a cup of gall that conscience strikes home; then they are brought to realize how impossible it is to 12 sin and not suffer. All the different phases of error in human nature the reformer must encounter and help to eradicate. 15

This period is not essentially one of conscience: few feel and live now as when this nation began, and our forefathers' prayers blended with the murmuring winds 18 of their forest home. This is a period of doubt, inquiry, speculation, selfishness; of divided interests, marvellous good, and mysterious evil. But sin can only work out 21 its own destruction; and reform does and must push on the growth of mankind.

Honor to faithful merit is delayed, and always has 24 been; but it is sure to follow. The very streets through which Garrison was dragged were draped in honor of the dead hero who did the hard work, the immortal work, 27 of loosing the fetters of one form of human slavery. I remember, when a girl, and he visited my father, how a childish fear clustered round his coming. I had heard 30

1 the awful story that "he helped 'niggers' kill the white folks!" Even the loving children are sometimes made 3 to believe a lie, and to hate reformers. It is pleasant, now, to contrast with that childhood's wrong the reverence of my riper years for all who dare to be true, honest to 6 their convictions, and strong of purpose.

The reformer has no time to give in defense of his own life's incentive, since no sacrifice is too great for the 9 silent endurance of his love. What has not unselfed love achieved for the race? All that ever was accomplished, and more than history has yet recorded. The reformer 12 works on unmentioned, save when he is abused or his work is utilized in the interest of somebody. He may labor for the establishment of a cause which is fraught 15 with infinite blessings, — health, virtue, and heaven; but what of all that? Who should care for everybody? It is enough, say they, to care for a few. Yet the good 18 done, and the love that foresees more to do, stimulate philanthropy and are an ever-present reward. Let one's life answer well these questions, and it already hath a 21 benediction:

Have you renounced self? Are you faithful? Do you love?

24 MRS. EDDY SICK

The frequent public allegement that I am "sick, unable to speak a loud word," or that I died of palsy, and am 27 dead, — is but another evidence of the falsehoods kept constantly before the public.

While I accord these evil-mongers due credit for their

desire, let me say to you, dear reader: Call at the 1
Massachusetts Metaphysical College, in 1889, and judge
for yourself whether I can talk — and laugh too! I 3
never was in better health. I have had but four
days' vacation for the past year, and am about to commence a large class in Christian Science. Lecturing, 6
writing, preaching, teaching, etc., give fair proof that
my shadow is not growing less; and substance is taking
larger proportions. 9

"I'VE GOT COLD"

Out upon the sidewalk one winter morning, I observed
a carriage draw up before a stately mansion; a portly 12
gentleman alight, and take from his carriage the ominous
hand-trunk.

"Ah!" thought I, "somebody has to take it; and what 15
may the potion be?"

Just then a tiny, sweet face appeared in the vestibule,
and red nose, suffused eyes, cough, and tired look, told 18
the story; but, looking up quaintly, the poor child said, —

"I've got cold, doctor."

Her apparent pride at sharing in a popular influenza 21
was comical. However, her dividend, when compared
with that of the household stockholders, was new; and
doubtless their familiarity with what the stock paid, made 24
them more serious over it.

What if that sweet child, so bravely confessing that
she had something that she ought not to have, and which 27
mamma thought must be gotten rid of, had been taught
the value of saying even more bravely, and believing
it, — 30

1 "I have *not* got cold."

Why, the doctor's squills and bills would have been
3 avoided; and through the cold air the little one would
have been bounding with sparkling eyes, and ruby cheeks
painted and fattened by metaphysical hygiene.

6 Parents and doctors must not take the sweet freshness
out of the children's lives by that flippant caution, "You
will get cold."

9 Predicting danger does not dignify life, whereas fore-
casting liberty and joy does; for these are strong pro-
moters of health and happiness. All education should
12 contribute to moral and physical strength and freedom.
If a cold could get into the body without the assent of
mind, nature would take it out as gently, or let it remain
15 as harmlessly, as it takes the frost out of the ground or
puts it into the ice-cream to the satisfaction of all.

The sapling bends to the breeze, while the sturdy oak,
18 with form and inclination fixed, breasts the tornado. It
is easier to incline the early thought rightly, than the
biased mind. Children not mistaught, naturally love
21 God; for they are pure-minded, affectionate, and generally brave. Passions, appetites, pride, selfishness, have
slight sway over the fresh, unbiased thought.

24 Teach the children early self-government, and teach
them nothing that is wrong. If they see their father with
a cigarette in his mouth — suggest to them that the habit
27 of smoking is not nice, and that nothing but a loathsome
worm *naturally* chews tobacco. Likewise soberly inform
them that "Battle-Axe Plug" takes off men's heads; or,
30 leaving these on, that it takes from their bodies a sweet
something which belongs to nature, — namely, pure
odors.

From a religious point of view, the faith of both youth 1
and adult should centre as steadfastly in God to benefit
the body, as to benefit the mind. Body and mind are 3
correlated in man's salvation; for man will no more
enter heaven sick than as a sinner, and Christ's Christianity casts out sickness as well as sin of every sort. 6

Test, if you will, metaphysical healing on two patients:
one having morals to be healed, the other having a physical ailment. Use as your medicine the great alterative, 9
Truth: give to the immoralist a mental dose that says,
"You have no pleasure in sin," and witness the effects.

Either he will hate you, and try to make others do like- 12
wise, so taking a dose of error big enough apparently to
neutralize your Truth, else he will doubtingly await the
result; during which interim, by constant combat and 15
direful struggles, you get the victory and Truth heals him
of the moral malady.

On the other hand, to the bedridden sufferer admin- 18
ister this alterative Truth: "God never made you sick:
there is no necessity for pain; and Truth destroys the
error that insists on the necessity of any man's bondage 21
to sin and sickness. 'Ye shall know the truth, and the
truth shall make you free.'"

Then, like blind Bartimeus, the doubting heart looks 24
up through faith, and your patient rejoices in the gospel
of health.

Thus, you see, it is easier to heal the physical than the 27
moral ailment. When divine Truth and Love heal, of
sin, the sinner who is at ease in sin, how much more should
these heal, of sickness, the sick who are dis-eased, dis- 30
comforted, and who long for relief!

1   "PRAYER AND HEALING"

The article of Professor T——, having the above cap-
3 tion, published in *Zion's Herald*, December third, came
not to my notice until January ninth. In it the Professor
offered me, as President of the Metaphysical College in
6 Boston, or one of my students, the liberal sum of one
thousand dollars if either would reset certain dislocations
without the use of hands, and two thousand dollars if
9 either would give sight to one born blind.

Will the gentleman accept my thanks due to his generosity; for, if I should accept his bid on Christianity, he
12 would lose his money.

Why?

Because I performed more difficult tasks fifteen years
15 ago. At present, I am in another department of Christian
work, "where there shall no signs be given them," for
they shall be instructed in the Principle of Christian
18 Science that furnishes its own proof.

But, to reward his liberality, I offer him three thousand dollars if he will heal one single case of opium-eating
21 where the patient is very low and taking morphine powder
in its most concentrated form, at the rate of one ounce in
two weeks, — having taken it twenty years; and he is to
24 cure that habit in three days, leaving the patient well. I
cured precisely such a case in 1869.

Also, Mr. C. M. H——, of Boston, formerly partner
27 of George T. Brown, pharmacist, No. 5 Beacon St., will
tell you that he was my student in December, 1884; and
that before leaving the class he took a patient thoroughly
30 addicted to the use of opium — if she went without it

twenty-four hours she would have delirium — and in 1
forty-eight hours cured her perfectly of this habit,
with no bad results, but with decided improvement in 3
health.

I have not yet made surgery one of the mental branches
taught in my college; although students treat sprains, 6
contusions, etc., successfully. In the case of sprain of the
wrist-joint, where the regular doctor had put on splints
and bandages to remain six weeks, a student of mine 9
removed these appliances the same day and effected the
cure in less than one week. Reference, Mrs. M. A. F——,
107 Eutaw Street, East Boston. 12

I agree with the Professor, that every system of medicine claims more than it practises. If the system is Science,
it includes of necessity the Principle, which the learner 15
can demonstrate only in proportion as he understands it.
Boasting is unbecoming a mortal's poor performances.
My Christian students are proverbially modest: their 18
works alone should declare them, since my system of medicine is not generally understood. There are charlatans
in "mind-cure," who practise on the basis of matter, or 21
human will, not Mind.

The Professor alludes to Paul's advice to Timothy.
Did he refer to that questionable counsel, "Take a little 24
wine for thy stomach's sake"? Even doctors disagree
on that prescription: some of the medical faculty will
tell you that alcoholic drinks cause the coats of the stomach 27
to thicken and the organ to contract; will prevent the
secretions of the gastric juice, and induce ulceration,
bleeding, vomiting, death. 30

Again, the Professor quotes, in justification of material
methods, and as veritable: "He took a bone from the

1 side of Adam, closed up the wound thereof, and builded
up the woman." (Gen. ii. 21.)

3 Here we have the Professor on the platform of Christian
Science! even a "surgical operation" that he says was
performed by divine power, — Mind alone constructing
6 the human system, before surgical instruments were
invented, and closing the incisions of the flesh.

He further states that God cannot save the soul without
9 compliance to ordained conditions. But, we ask, have
those conditions named in Genesis been perpetuated in
the multiplication of mankind? And, are the conditions
12 of salvation mental, or physical; are they bodily penance
and torture, or repentance and reform, which are the
action of mind?

15 He asks, "Has the law been abrogated that demands
the employment of visible agencies for specific ends?"

Will he accept my reply as derived from the life and
18 teachings of Jesus? — who annulled the so-called laws of
matter by the higher law of Spirit, causing him to walk
the wave, turn the water into wine, make the blind to see,
21 the deaf to hear, the lame to walk, and the dead to be
raised without matter-agencies. And he did this for man's
example; not to teach himself, but others, the way of
24 healing and salvation. He said, "And other sheep I have,
which are not of this fold."

The teachings and demonstration of Jesus were for
27 all peoples and for all time; not for a privileged class or
a restricted period, but for as many as should believe in
him.

30 Are the discoverers of quinine, cocaine, etc., especially the children of our Lord because of their medical
discoveries?

We have no record showing that our Master ever used, 1
or recommended others to use, drugs; but we have his
words, and the prophet's, as follows: "Take no thought, 3
saying, What shall we eat? or, What shall we drink?"
"And Asa . . . sought not to the Lord, but to the physicians. And Asa slept with his fathers." 6

VERITAS ODIUM PARIT

The combined efforts of the materialistic portion of
the pulpit and press in 1885, to retard by misrepresen- 9
tation the stately goings of Christian Science, are giving
it new impetus and energy; calling forth the *vox populi*
and directing more critical observation to its uplifting 12
influence upon the health, morals, and spirituality of
mankind.

Their movements indicate fear and weakness, a physi- 15
cal and spiritual need that Christian Science should remove with glorious results. The conclusion cannot now
be pushed, that women have no rights that man is bound 18
to respect. This is woman's hour, in all the good tendencies, charities, and reforms of to-day. It is difficult
to say which may be most mischievous to the human 21
heart, the praise or the dispraise of men.

I have loved the Church and followed it, thinking that
it was following Christ; but, if the pulpit allows the people 24
to go no further in the direction of Christlikeness, and
rejects apostolic Christianity, seeking to stereotype infinite
Truth, it is a thing to be thankful for that one can walk 27
alone the straight and narrow way; that, in the words of
Wendell Phillips, "one with God is a majority."

1   It is the pulpit and press, clerical robes and the pro-
hibiting of free speech, that cradles and covers the sins of
3 the world, — all unmitigated systems of crime; and it
requires the enlightenment of these worthies, through
civil and religious reform, to blot out all inhuman codes.
6 It was the Southern pulpit and press that influenced the
people to wrench from man both human and divine rights,
in order to subserve the interests of wealth, religious caste,
9 civil and political power.   And the pulpit had to be
purged of that sin by human gore, — when the love of
Christ would have washed it divinely away in Christian
12 Science!

The cry of the colored slave has scarcely been heard
and hushed, when from another direction there comes
15 another sharp cry of oppression.   Another form of inhu-
manity lifts its hydra head to forge anew the old fetters;
to shackle conscience, stop free speech, slander, vilify;
18 to invite its prey, then turn and refuse the victim a solitary
vindication in this most unprecedented warfare.

A conflict more terrible than the battle of Gettysburg
21 awaits the crouching wrong that refused to yield its
prey the peace of a desert, when a voice was heard
crying in the wilderness, — the spiritual famine of 1866,
24 — "Prepare ye the way of the Lord, make His paths
straight."

Shall religious intolerance, arrayed against the rights
27 of man, again deluge the earth in blood?   The question
at issue with mankind is: Shall we have a spiritual Christianity and a spiritual healing, or a materialistic religion
30 and a *materia medica?*

The advancing faith and hope of Christianity, the
earnest seeking after practical truth that shall cast out

error and heal the sick, wisely demand for man his God- 1
given heritage, both human and divine rights; namely,
that his honest convictions and *proofs* of advancing truth 3
be allowed due consideration, and treated not as pearls
trampled upon.

Those familiar with my history are more tolerant; those 6
who know me, know that I found health in just what I
teach. I have professed Christianity a half-century; and
now I calmly challenge the world, upon fair investigation, 9
to furnish a single instance of departure in one of my
works from the highest possible ethics.

The charges against my views are false, but natural, 12
since those bringing them do not understand my statement of the Science I introduce, and are unwilling to be
taught it, even gratuitously. If they did understand it, they 15
could demonstrate this Science by healing the sick; hence
the injustice of their interpretations.

To many, the healing force developed by Christian 18
Science seems a mystery, because they do not understand
that Spirit controls body. They acknowledge the existence of mortal mind, but believe it to reside in matter 21
of the brain; but that man is the idea of infinite Mind,
is not so easily accepted. That which is temporary
seems, to the common estimate, solid and substantial. 24
It is much easier for people to believe that the body
affects mind, than that the body is an expression of
mind, and reflects harmony or discord according to 27
thought.

Everything that God created, He pronounced good.
He never made sickness. Hence *that* is only an evil belief 30
of mortal mind, which must be met, in every instance,
with a denial by Truth.

1   This is the "new tongue," the language of them that "lay hands on the sick, and they shall recover," whose
3 spiritual interpretation they refuse to hear. For instance: the literal meaning of the passage "lay hands on the sick" would be manipulation; its moral meaning, found in the
6 "new tongue," is spiritual power, — as, in another Scripture, "I will triumph in the works of Thy hands."

FALSEHOOD

9   The Greeks showed a just estimate of the person they called slanderer, when they made the word synonymous with devil. If the simple falsehoods uttered about me
12 were compounded, the mixture would be labelled thus: "Religionists' mistaken views of Mrs. Eddy's book, 'Science and Health with Key to the Scriptures,' and the
15 malice aforethought of sinners."

That I take opium; that I am an infidel, a mesmerist, a medium, a "pantheist;" or that my hourly life is prayer-
18 less, or not in strict obedience to the Mosaic Decalogue, — is not more true than that I am dead, as is oft reported. The St. Louis Democrat is alleged to have reported my
21 demise, and to have said that I died of poison, and bequeathed my property to Susan Anthony.

The opium falsehood has only this to it: Many years
24 ago my regular physician prescribed morphine, which I took, when he could do no more for me. Afterwards, the glorious revelations of Christian Science saved me
27 from that necessity and made me well, since which time I have not taken drugs, with the following exception: When the mental malpractice of poisoning people was

first undertaken by a mesmerist, to test that malprac- 1
tice I experimented by taking some large doses of morphine, to see if Christian Science could not obviate its 3
effect; and I say with tearful thanks, "The drug had
no effect upon me whatever." The hour has struck,
— "If they drink any deadly thing, it shall not hurt 6
them."

The false report that I have appropriated other people's
manuscripts in my works, has been met and answered 9
legally. Both in private and public life, and especially
through my teachings, it is well known that I am not a
spiritualist, a pantheist, or prayerless. The most devout 12
members of evangelical churches will say this, as well as
my intimate acquaintances. None are permitted to remain in my College building whose morals are not un- 15
questionable. I have neither purchased nor ordered a
drug since my residence in Boston; and to my knowledge,
not one has been sent to my house, unless it was something 18
to remove stains or vermin.

The report that I was dead arose no doubt from the
combined efforts of some malignant students, expelled 21
from my College for immorality, to kill me: of their mental
design to do this I have proof, but no fear. My heavenly
Father will never leave me comfortless, in the amplitude 24
of His love; coming nearer in my need, more tenderly to
save and bless.

LOVE   27

What a word! I am in awe before it. Over what
worlds on worlds it hath range and is sovereign! the un-

1 derived, the incomparable, the infinite All of good, the
alone God, is Love.

3 By what strange perversity is the best become the most
abused, — either as a quality or as an entity? Mortals
misrepresent and miscall affection; they make it what
6 it is not, and doubt what it is. The so-called affection
pursuing its victim is a butcher fattening the lamb to
slay it. What the lower propensities express, should be
9 repressed by the sentiments. No word is more misconstrued; no sentiment less understood. The divine
significance of Love is distorted into human qualities,
12 which in their human abandon become jealousy and
hate.

Love is not something put upon a shelf, to be taken
15 down on rare occasions with sugar-tongs and laid on a
rose-leaf. I make strong demands on love, call for active
witnesses to prove it, and noble sacrifices and grand
18 achievements as its results. Unless these appear, I cast
aside the word as a sham and counterfeit, having no ring
of the true metal. Love cannot be a mere abstraction, or
21 goodness without activity and power. As a human quality,
the glorious significance of affection is more than words:
it is the tender, unselfish deed done in secret; the silent,
24 ceaseless prayer; the self-forgetful heart that overflows;
the veiled form stealing on an errand of mercy, out of a
side door; the little feet tripping along the sidewalk; the
27 gentle hand opening the door that turns toward want and
woe, sickness and sorrow, and thus lighting the dark
places of earth.

ADDRESS ON THE FOURTH OF JULY AT PLEASANT VIEW, 1
    CONCORD, N. H., BEFORE 2,500 MEMBERS OF THE
    MOTHER CHURCH, 1897   3

My beloved brethren, who have come all the way from
the Pacific to the Atlantic shore, from the Palmetto to the
Pine Tree State, I greet you; my hand may not touch 6
yours to-day, but my heart will with tenderness untalkable.

His Honor, Mayor Woodworth, has welcomed you to
Concord most graciously, voicing the friendship of this 9
city and of my native State — loyal to the heart's core to
religion, home, friends, and country.

To-day we commemorate not only our nation's civil 12
and religious freedom, but a greater even, the liberty of
the sons of God, the inalienable rights and radiant reality
of Christianity, whereof our Master said: "The works 15
that I do shall he do;" and, "The kingdom of God cometh
not with observation" (with knowledge obtained from
the senses), but "the kingdom of God is within you," — 18
within the present possibilities of mankind.

Think of this inheritance! Heaven right here, where
angels are as men, clothed more lightly, and men as angels 21
who, burdened for an hour, spring into liberty, and the
good they would do, that they do, and the evil they would
not do, that they do not.   24

From the falling leaves of old-time faiths men learn a
parable of the period, that all error, physical, moral, or
religious, will fall before Truth demonstrated, even as 27
dry leaves fall to enrich the soil for fruitage.

Sin, sickness, and disease flee before the evangel of
Truth as the mountain mists before the sun. Truth is 30

1 the tonic for the sick, and this medicine of Mind is not
necessarily infinitesimal but infinite. Herein the mental
3 medicine of divine metaphysics and the medical systems
of allopathy and homœopathy differ. Mental medicine gains no potency by attenuation, and its largest
6 dose is never dangerous, but the more the better in every
case.

Christian Science classifies thought thus: Right thoughts
9 are reality and power; wrong thoughts are unreality and
powerless, possessing the nature of dreams. Good thoughts
are potent; evil thoughts are impotent, and they should
12 appear thus. Continuing this category, we learn that
sick thoughts are unreality and weakness; while healthy
thoughts are reality and strength. My proof of these
15 novel propositions is demonstration, whereby any man
can satisfy himself of their verity.

Christian Science is not only the acme of Science
18 but the crown of Christianity. It is universal. It appeals to man as man; to the whole and not to a portion; to man physically, as well as spiritually, and to all
21 mankind.

It has one God. It demonstrates the divine Principle,
rules and practice of the great healer and master of meta-
24 physics, Jesus of Nazareth. It spiritualizes religion and
restores its lost element, namely, healing the sick. It
consecrates and inspires the teacher and preacher; it
27 equips the doctor with safe and sure medicine; it encourages and empowers the business man and secures
the success of honesty. It is the dear children's toy and
30 strong tower; the wise man's spiritual dictionary; the
poor man's money; yea, it is the pearl priceless whereof
our Master said, if a man findeth, he goeth and selleth

all that he hath and buyeth it. Buyeth it! Note the 1
scope of that saying, even that Christianity is not merely
a gift, as St. Paul avers, but is bought with a price, a great 3
price; and what man knoweth as did our Master its
value, and the price that he paid for it?

Friends, I am not enough the new woman of the period 6
for outdoor speaking, and the incidental platform is not
broad enough for me, but the speakers that will now address you — one a congressman — may improve our 9
platforms; and make amends for the nothingness of
matter with the allness of Mind.

WELL DOINGE IS THE FRUITE OF DOINGE WELL   12
HERRICK

This period is big with events. Fraught with history,
it repeats the past and portends much for the future.   15

The Scriptural metaphors, — of the woman in travail,
the great red dragon that stood ready to devour the child
as soon as it was born, and the husbandmen that said, 18
"This is the heir: come, let us kill him, that the inheritance may be ours," — are type and shadow of this
hour.   21

A mother's love touches the heart of God, and should
it not appeal to human sympathy? Can a mother tell
her child one tithe of the agonies that gave that child 24
birth? Can that child conceive of the anguish, until she
herself is become a mother?

Do the children of this period dream of the spiritual 27
Mother's sore travail, through the long night, that has
opened their eyes to the light of Christian Science? Cherish

1 these new-born children that filial obedience to which the
Decalogue points with promise of prosperity? Should not
3 the loving warning, the far-seeing wisdom, the gentle entreaty, the stern rebuke have been heeded, in return for
all that love which brooded tireless over their tender
6 years? for all that love that hath fed them with Truth, —
even the bread that cometh down from heaven, — as the
mother-bird tendeth her young in the rock-ribbed nest of
9 the raven's callow brood!

And what of the hope of that parent whose children
rise up against her; when brother slays brother, and
12 the strength of union grows weak with wickedness?
The victim of mad ambition that saith, "This is
the heir: come, let us kill him, that the inheritance
15 may be ours," goes on to learn that he must at last
kill this evil in "self" in order to gain the kingdom
of God.

18   Envy, the great red dragon of this hour, would obscure
the light of Science, take away a third part of the stars
from the spiritual heavens, and cast them to the earth.
21 This is not Science. *Per contra,* it is the mortal mind
sense — mental healing on a material basis — hurling
its so-called healing at random, filling with hate its
24 deluded victims, or resting in silly peace upon the
laurels of headlong human will. "What shall, therefore,
the Lord of the vineyard do? He will come and de-
27 stroy the husbandmen, and will give the vineyard unto
others."

LITTLE GODS   1

It is sometimes said, cynically, that Christian Scientists set themselves on pedestals, as so many petty deities; 3
but there is no fairness or propriety in the aspersion.

Man is not equal to his Maker. That which is formed
is not cause, but effect; and has no underived power. 6
But it is possible, and dutiful, to throw the weight of
thought and action on the side of right, and to be thus
lifted up.   9

Man should be found not claiming equality with, but
growing into, that altitude of Mind which was in Christ
Jesus. He should comprehend, in divine Science, a 12
recognition of what the apostle meant when he said:
"The Spirit itself beareth witness with our spirit, that
we are the children of God: and if children, then heirs; 15
heirs of God, and joint-heirs with Christ."

ADVANTAGE OF MIND–HEALING

It is sometimes asked, What are the advantages of your 18
system of healing?

I claim for healing by Christian Science the following
advantages: —   21

First: It does away with material medicine, and recognizes the fact that the antidote for sickness, as well
as for sin, may be found in God, the divine Mind.   24

Second: It is more effectual than drugs, and cures
where they fail, because it is this divine antidote, and
metaphysics is above physics.   27

1   *Third:* Persons who have been healed by Christian
Science are not only cured of their belief in disease, but
3 they are at the same time improved morally. The body
is governed by Mind, and mortal mind must be corrected
in order to make the body harmonious.

6   A CARD

While gratefully acknowledging the public confidence
manifested in daily letters that protest against receiving
9 instruction in the Massachusetts Metaphysical College
from any other than Mrs. Eddy, I feel, deeply, that of
necessity this imposes on me the severe task of remain-
12 ing at present a public servant: also, that this must prevent my classes from forming as frequently as was announced in the October number of the *Journal,* and
15 necessitates receiving but a select number of students.
To meet the old impediment, lack of time, that has occasioned the irregular intervals between my class terms,
18 I shall continue to send to each applicant a notice from
one to two weeks previous to the opening term.
                                MARY BAKER G. EDDY

21   SPIRIT AND LAW

We are accustomed to think and to speak of gravitation as a law of matter; while every quality of matter,
24 in and of itself, is inert, inanimate, and non-intelligent.
The assertion that matter is a law, or a lawgiver, is
anomalous. Wherever law is, Mind is; and the notion

that Mind can be in matter is rank infidelity, which either 1
excludes God from the universe, or includes Him in every
mode and form of evil. Pantheism presupposes that 3
God sleeps in the mineral, dreams in the animal, and
wakes in a wicked man.

The distinction between that which is and that which 6
is not law, must be made by Mind and as Mind. Law is
either a moral or an immoral force. The law of God is
the law of Spirit, a moral and spiritual force of immor- 9
tal and divine Mind. The so-called law of matter is an
immoral force of erring mortal mind, *alias* the minds of
mortals. This so-called force, or law, at work in nature 12
as a power, prohibition, or license, is cruel and merciless.
It punishes the innocent, and repays our best deeds
with sacrifice and suffering. It is a code whose modes 15
trifle with joy, and lead to immediate or ultimate death.
It fosters suspicion where confidence is due, fear where
courage is requisite, reliance where there should be 18
avoidance, a belief in safety where there is most
danger. Our Master called it "a murderer from the
beginning." 21

Electricity, governed by this so-called law, sparkles
on the cloud, and strikes down the hoary saint. Floods
swallow up homes and households; and childhood, age, 24
and manhood go down in the death-dealing wave. Earthquakes engulf cities, churches, schools, and mortals.
Cyclones kill and destroy, desolating the green earth. 27
This pitiless power smites with disease the good Samari-
tan ministering to his neighbor's need. Even the chamber
where the good man surrenders to death is not exempt 30
from this law. Smoothing the pillow of pain may infect
you with smallpox, according to this lawless law which

1 dooms man to die for loving his neighbor as himself, —
when Christ has said that love is the fulfilling of the
3 law.

Our great Ensample, Jesus of Nazareth, met and abolished this unrelenting false claim of matter with the
6 righteous scorn and power of Spirit. When, through
Mind, he restored sight to the blind, he figuratively and
literally spat upon matter; and, anointing the wounded
9 spirit with the great truth that God is All, he demonstrated the healing power and supremacy of the law of
Life and Love.

12 In the spiritual Genesis of creation, all law was vested
in the Lawgiver, who was a law to Himself. In divine
Science, God is One and All; and, governing Himself,
15 He governs the universe. This is the law of creation:
"My defense is of God, which saveth the upright in
heart." And that infinite Mind governs all things. On
18 this infinite Principle of freedom, God named Himself, I AM. Error, or Adam, might give names to itself,
and call Mind by the name of matter, but error could
21 neither name nor demonstrate Spirit. The name, I
AM, indicated no personality that could be paralleled
with it; but it did declare a mighty individuality,
24 even the everlasting Father, as infinite consciousness,
ever-presence, omnipotence; as all law, Life, Truth, and
Love.

27 God's interpretation of Himself furnishes man with
the only suitable or true idea of Him; and the divine
definition of Deity differs essentially from the human.
30 It interprets the law of Spirit, not of matter. It explains
the eternal dynamics of being, and shows that nature
and man are as harmonious to-day as in the beginning,

when "all things were made by Him; and without Him 1
was not any thing made."

Whatever appears to be law, but partakes not of the 3
nature of God, is not law, but is what Jesus declared
it, "a liar, and the father of it." God is the law of Life,
not of death; of health, not of sickness; of good, not 6
of evil. It is this infinitude and oneness of good that
silences the supposition that evil is a claimant or a claim.
The consciousness of good has no consciousness or knowl- 9
edge of evil; and evil is not a quality to be known or
eliminated by good: while iniquity, too evil to conceive
of good as being unlike itself, declares that God knows 12
iniquity!

When the Lawgiver was the only law of creation, freedom reigned, and was the heritage of man; but this 15
freedom was the moral power of good, not of evil: it
was divine Science, in which God is supreme, and the
only law of being. In this eternal harmony of Science, 18
man is not fallen: he is governed in the same rhythm
that the Scripture describes, when "the morning stars
sang together, and all the sons of God shouted for joy." 21

TRUTH-HEALING

The spiritual elevator of the human race, physically,
morally, and Christianly, is the truism that Truth dem- 24
onstrates good, and is natural; while error, or evil,
is really non-existent, and must have produced its own
illusion, — for it belongs not to nature nor to God. Truth 27
is the power of God which heals the sick and the sinner,
and is applicable to all the needs of man. It is the uni-

1 versal, intelligent Christ-idea illustrated by the life of
Jesus, through whose "stripes we are healed." By con-
3 flicts, defeats, and triumphs, Christian Science has been
reduced to the understanding of mortals, and found able
to heal them.

6   Pagan mysticism, Grecian philosophy, or Jewish religion, never entered into the line of Jesus' thought or
action. His faith partook not of drugs, matter, nor of
9 the travesties of mortal mind. The divine Mind was
his only instrumentality and potency, in religion or medicine. The Principle of his cure was God, in the laws
12 of Spirit, not of matter; and these laws annulled all other
laws.

    Jesus knew that erring mortal thought holds only in
15 itself the supposition of evil, and that sin, sickness, and
death are its subjective states; also, that pure Mind is
the truth of being that subjugates and destroys any sup-
18 positional or elementary opposite to Him who is All.

    Truth is supreme and omnipotent. Then, whatever
else seemeth to be intelligence or power is false, delud-
21 ing reason and denying revelation, and seeking to dethrone
Deity. The truth of Mind-healing uplifts mankind, by
acknowledging pure Mind as absolute and entire, and
24 that evil is naught, although it seems to be.

    Pure Mind gives out an atmosphere that heals and
saves. Words are not always the auxiliaries of Truth.
27 The spirit, and not the letter, performs the vital functions of Truth and Love. Mind, imbued with this Science
of healing, is a law unto itself, needing neither license
30 nor prohibition; but lawless mind, with unseen motives,
and silent mental methods whereby it may injure the
race, is the highest attenuation of evil.

Again: evil, as *mind,* is doomed, already sentenced, 1
punished; for suffering is commensurate with evil, and
lasts as long as the evil. As *mind,* evil finds no escape 3
from itself; and the sin and suffering it occasions can
only be removed by reformation.

According to divine law, sin and suffering are not 6
cancelled by repentance or pardon. Christian Science
not only elucidates but demonstrates this verity of being; namely, that mortals suffer from the wrong they 9
commit, whether intentionally or ignorantly; that every
effect and amplification of wrong will revert to the wrong-
doer, until he pays his full debt to divine law, and the 12
measure he has meted is measured to him again, full,
pressed down, and running over. Surely "the way of
the transgressor is hard." 15

In this law of justice, the atonement of Christ loses
no efficacy. Justice is the handmaid of mercy, and showeth mercy by punishing sin. Jesus said, "I came not to 18
destroy the law," — the divine requirements typified in
the law of Moses, — "but to fulfil it" in righteousness,
by Truth's destroying error. No greater type of divine 21
Love can be presented than effecting so glorious a purpose.
This spirit of sacrifice always has saved, and still saves
mankind; but by mankind I mean mortals, or a kind 24
of men after man's own making. Man as God's idea
is already saved with an everlasting salvation. It is impossible to be a Christian Scientist without apprehend- 27
ing the moral law so clearly that, for conscience' sake,
one will either abandon his claim to even a knowledge
of this Science, or else make the claim valid. All Science 30
is divine. Then, to be Science, it must produce physical
and moral harmony.

1 Dear readers, our *Journal* is designed to bring health
and happiness to all households wherein it is permitted
3 to enter, and to confer increased power to be good and
to do good. If you wish to brighten so pure a purpose,
you will aid our prospect of fulfilling it by your kind
6 patronage of *The Christian Science Journal,* now entering upon its fifth volume, clad in Truth-healing's new
and costly spring dress.

9   HEART TO HEART

When the heart speaks, however simple the words,
its language is always acceptable to those who have
12 hearts.

I just want to say, I thank you, my dear students, who
are at work conscientiously and assiduously, for the good
15 you are doing. I am grateful to you for giving to the
sick relief from pain; for giving joy to the suffering and
hope to the disconsolate; for lifting the fallen and strength-
18 ening the weak, and encouraging the heart grown faint
with hope deferred. We are made glad by the divine
Love which looseth the chains of sickness and sin, open-
21 ing the prison doors to such as are bound; and we should
be more grateful than words can express, even through
this white-winged messenger, our *Journal.*
24 With all the homage beneath the skies, yet were our
burdens heavy but for the Christ-love that makes them
light and renders the yoke easy. Having his word, you
27 have little need of words of approval and encouragement
from me. Perhaps it is even selfish in me sometimes to
relieve my heart of its secrets, because I take so much

pleasure in thus doing; but if my motives are sinister, 1
they will harm myself only, and I shall have the unselfish joy of knowing that the wrong motives are not yours, 3
to react on yourselves.

These two words in Scripture suggest the sweetest
similes to be found in any language — *rock* and *feathers:* 6
"Upon this rock I will build my church;" "He shall
cover thee with His feathers." How blessed it is to
think of you as "beneath the shadow of a great rock in 9
a weary land," safe in His strength, building on His
foundation, and covered from the devourer by divine
protection and affection. Always bear in mind that His 12
presence, power, and peace meet all human needs and
reflect all bliss.

THINGS TO BE THOUGHT OF   15

The need of their teacher's counsel, felt by students,
especially by those at a distance, working assiduously for
our common Cause, — and their constant petitions for 18
the same, should be met in the most effectual way.

To be responsible for supplying this want, and poise
the wavering balance on the right side, is impracticable 21
without a full knowledge of the environments. The
educational system of Christian Science lacks the aid
and protection of State laws. The Science is hampered 24
by immature demonstrations, by the infancy of its discovery, by incorrect teaching; and especially by unprincipled claimants, whose mad ambition drives them to 27
appropriate my ideas and discovery, without credit, appreciation, or a single original conception, while they

1 quote from other authors and give them credit for every
random thought in line with mine.

3 My noble students, who are loyal to Christ, Truth, and
human obligations, will not be disheartened in the midst
of this seething sea of sin. They build for time and eter-
6 nity. The others stumble over misdeeds, and their own
unsubstantiality, without the groundwork of right, till,
like camera shadows thrown upon the mists of time, they
9 melt into darkness.

Unity is the essential nature of Christian Science. Its
Principle is One, and to demonstrate the divine One,
12 demands oneness of thought and action.

Many students enter the Normal class of my College
whom I have not fitted for it by the Primary course.
15 They are taught their first lessons by my students; hence
the aptness to assimilate pure and abstract Science is
somewhat untested.

18 "As the twig is bent, the tree's inclined." As mortal
mind is directed, it acts for a season. Some students
leave my instructions before they are quite free from
21 the bias of their first impressions, whether those be correct or incorrect. Such students are more or less subject
to the future mental influence of their former teacher.
24 Their knowledge of Mind-healing may be right theoretically, but the moral and spiritual status of thought
must be right also. The tone of the teacher's mind must
27 be pure, grand, true, to aid the mental development of
the student; for the tint of the instructor's mind must
take its hue from the divine Mind. A single mistake in
30 metaphysics, or in ethics, is more fatal than a mistake in
physics.

If a teacher of Christian Science unwittingly or inten-

tionally offers his own thought, and gives me as authority 1
for it; if he diverges from Science and knows it not, or,
knowing it, makes the venture from vanity, in order to 3
be thought original, or wiser than somebody else, — this
divergence widens. He grows dark, and cannot regain,
at will, an upright understanding. This error in the 6
teacher also predisposes his students to make mistakes
and lose their way. Diverse opinions in Science are
stultifying. All must have *one* Principle and the same 9
rule; and all *who follow the Principle and rule* have but
one opinion of it.

Whosoever understands a single rule in Science, and 12
demonstrates its Principle according to rule, is master
of the situation. Nobody can gainsay this. The egotistical theorist or shallow moralist may presume to 15
make innovations upon simple proof; but his mistake
is visited upon himself and his students, whose minds
are, must be, disturbed by this discord, which extends 18
along the whole line of reciprocal thought. An error
in premise can never bring forth the real fruits of Truth.
After thoroughly explaining spiritual Truth and its ethics 21
to a student, I am not morally responsible for the misstatements or misconduct of this student. My teachings
are uniform. Those who abide by them do well. If 24
others, who receive the same instruction, do ill, the fault
is not in the culture but the soil.

I am constantly called to settle questions and disaf- 27
fections toward Christian Science growing out of the
departures from Science of self-satisfied, unprincipled
students. If impatient of the loving rebuke, the stu- 30
dent must stop at the foot of the grand ascent, and there
remain until suffering compels the downfall of his self-

1 conceit. Then that student must struggle up, with bleeding footprints, to the God-crowned summit of unselfish
3 and pure aims and affections.

To be two-sided, when these sides are moral opposites, is neither politic nor scientific; and to abridge a
6 single human right or privilege is an error. Whoever
does this may represent me as doing it; but he mistakes
me, and the subjective state of his own mind for mine.
9   The true leader of a true cause is the unacknowledged
servant of mankind. Stationary in the background, this
individual is doing the work that nobody else can or will
12 do. An erratic career is like the comet's course, dashing through space, headlong and alone. A clear-headed
and honest Christian Scientist will demonstrate the Prin-
15 ciple of Christian Science, and hold justice and mercy as
inseparable from the unity of God.

UNCHRISTIAN RUMOR

18   The assertion that I have said hard things about my
loyal students in Chicago, New York, or any other place,
is utterly false and groundless. I speak of them as I feel,
21 and I cannot find it in my heart not to love them. They
are essentially dear to me, who are toiling and achieving
success in unison with my own endeavors and prayers.
24 If I correct mistakes which may be made in teaching or
lecturing on Christian Science, this is in accordance with
my students' desires, and thus we mutually aid each other,
27 and obey the Golden Rule.

The spirit of lies is abroad. Because Truth has spoken
aloud, error, running to and fro in the earth, is scream-

ing, to make itself heard above Truth's voice. The 1
audible and inaudible wail of evil never harms Scientists,
steadfast in their consciousness of the nothingness of 3
wrong and the supremacy of right.

Our worst enemies are the best friends to our growth.
Charity students, for whom I have sacrificed the most 6
time, — those whose chief aim is to injure me, — have
caused me to exercise most patience. When they report
me as "*hating* those whom I do not love," let them re- 9
member that there never was a time when I saw an opportunity really to help them and failed to improve it;
and this, too, when I knew they were secretly striving 12
to injure me.

VAINGLORY

Comparisons are odorous. — SHAKESPEARE 15

Through all human history, the vital outcomes of
Truth have suffered temporary shame and loss from
individual conceit, cowardice, or dishonesty. The bird 18
whose right wing flutters to soar, while the left beats its
way downward, falls to the earth. Both wings must be
plumed for rarefied atmospheres and upward flight. 21

Mankind must gravitate from sense to Soul, and human
affairs should be governed by Spirit, intelligent good.
The antipode of Spirit, which we name *matter,* or *non-* 24
intelligent evil, is no real aid to being. The predisposing
and exciting cause of all defeat and victory under the
sun, rests on this scientific basis: that action, in obedi- 27
ence to God, spiritualizes man's motives and methods,
and crowns them with success; while disobedience to

1 this divine Principle materializes human modes and consciousness, and defeats them.

3   Two personal queries give point to human action: Who
shall be greatest? and, Who shall be best? Earthly
glory is vain; but not vain enough to attempt pointing
6 the way to heaven, the harmony of being. The imaginary
victories of rivalry and hypocrisy are defeats. The Holy
One saith, "O that thou hadst hearkened to My com-
9 mandments! then had thy peace been as a river." He
is unfit for Truth, and the demonstration of divine power,
who departs from Mind to matter, and from Truth to
12 error, in pursuit of better means for healing the sick and
casting out error.

The Christian Scientist keeps straight to the course.
15 His whole inquiry and demonstration lie in the line of
Truth; hence he suffers no shipwreck in a starless night
on the shoals of vainglory. His medicine is Mind —
18 the omnipotent and ever-present good. His "help is
from the Lord," who heals body and mind, head and
heart; changing the affections, enlightening the mis-
21 guided senses, and curing alike the sin and the mortal
sinner. God's preparations for the sick are potions of
His own qualities. His therapeutics are antidotes for
24 the ailments of mortal mind and body. Then let us not
adulterate His preparations for the sick with material
means.

27   From lack of moral strength empires fall. Right alone
is irresistible, permanent, eternal. Remember that human pride forfeits spiritual power, and either vacillating
30 good or self-assertive error dies of its own elements.
Through patience we must possess the sense of Truth;
and Truth is used to waiting. "Commit thy way unto

the Lord; trust also in Him; and He shall bring it to 1
pass."

By using falsehood to regain his liberty, Galileo vir- 3
tually lost it. He cannot escape from barriers who commits his moral sense to a dungeon. Hear the Master
on this subject: "No man can serve two masters: for 6
either he will hate the one, and love the other; or else he
will hold to the one, and despise the other. Ye cannot
serve God and mammon." 9

Lives there a man who can better define ethics, better
elucidate the Principle of being, than he who "spake as
never man spake," and whose precepts and example have 12
a perpetual freshness in relation to human events?

Who is it that understands, unmistakably, a fraction
of the actual Science of Mind-healing? 15

It is he who has fairly proven his knowledge on a Christian, mental, scientific basis; who has made his choice
between matter and Mind, and proven the divine Mind 18
to be the only physician. These are self-evident propositions: That man can only be Christianized through Mind;
that without Mind the body is without action; that Science 21
is a law of divine Mind. The conclusion follows that the
correct Mind-healing is the proper means of Christianity,
and is Science. 24

Christian Science may be sold in the shambles. Many
are bidding for it, — but are not willing to pay the price.
Error is vending itself on trust, well knowing the will- 27
ingness of mortals to buy error at par value. The Revelator beheld the opening of this silent mental seal, and
heard the great Red Dragon *whispering* that "no man 30
might buy or sell, save he that had the mark, or the name
of the beast, or the number of his name."

1   We are in the Valley of Decision. Then, let us take
the side of him who "overthrew the tables of the money-
3 changers, and the seats of them that sold doves," — of
such as barter integrity and peace for money and fame.
What artist would question the skill of the masters in
6 sculpture, music, or painting? Shall we depart from the
example of the Master in Christian Science, Jesus of
Nazareth, — than whom mankind hath no higher ideal?
9 He who demonstrated his power over sin, disease, and
death, is the master Metaphysician.

To seek or employ other means than those the Master
12 used in demonstrating Life scientifically, is to lose the
priceless knowledge of his Principle and practice. He
said, "Seek ye first the kingdom of God, and His right-
15 eousness; and all these things shall be added unto you."
Gain a pure Christianity; for that is requisite for healing the sick. Then you will need no other aid, and will
18 have full faith in his prophecy, "And there shall be one
fold, and one shepherd;" but, the Word must abide in
us, if we would obtain that promise. We cannot depart
21 from his holy example, — we cannot leave Christ for the
schools which crucify him, and yet follow him in healing. Fidelity to his precepts and practice is the only pass-
24 port to his power; and the pathway of goodness and
greatness runs through the modes and methods of God.
"He that glorieth, let him glory in the Lord."

27   COMPOUNDS

Homœopathy is the last link in material medicine.
The next step is Mind-medicine. Among the foremost

virtues of homœopathy is the exclusion of compounds 1
from its pharmacy, and the attenuation of a drug up to
the point of its disappearance as matter and its manifesta- 3
tion in effect as a thought, instead of a thing.

Students of Christian Science (and many who are not
students) understand enough of this to keep out of their 6
heads the notion that compounded metaphysics (so-called)
is, or can be, Christian Science, — that rests on oneness;
one cause and one effect. 9

They should take our magazine, work for it, write for
it, and read it. They should eschew all magazines and
books which are less than the best. 12

"Choose you this day whom ye will serve." Cleanse
your mind of the cobwebs which spurious "compounds"
engender. Before considering a subject that is unworthy 15
of thought, take in this axiomatic truism: "Trust her
not, she's fooling thee;" and Longfellow is right.

CLOSE OF THE MASSACHUSETTS METAPHYSICAL 18
COLLEGE

Much is said at this date, 1889, about Mrs. Eddy's
Massachusetts Metaphysical College being the only 21
chartered College of Metaphysics. To make this plain,
the Publishing Committee of the Christian Scientist
Association has published in the *Boston Traveler* the 24
following: —

"To benefit the community, and more strongly mark
the difference between true and false teachers of mental 27
healing, the following history and statistics are officially
submitted: —

1   "Rev. Mary Baker G. Eddy obtained a college charter
in January, 1881, with all the rights and privileges per-
3 taining thereunto (*including the right to grant degrees*)
under Act of 1874, Chapter 375, Section 4.

"This Act was *repealed* from and after January 31,
6 1882. Mrs. Eddy's grant for a college, for metaphysical
purposes *only*, is the first on record in history, and no
charters were granted for similar colleges, except hers,
9 from January, 1881, till the repealing of said Act in
January, 1882.

"The substance of this Act is at present incorporated
12 in Public Statutes, Chapter 115, Section 2, with the following important restrictions: In accordance with Statutes
of 1883, Chapter 268, any officer, agent, or servant of any
15 corporation or association, who confers, or authorizes
to be conferred, any diploma or degree, shall be punished by a fine not less than five hundred dollars and
18 not more than one thousand dollars.

"All the mind-healing colleges (except Rev. Mrs.
Eddy's) have simply an incorporated grant, which may
21 be called a charter, such as any stock company may obtain for any secular purposes; but these so-called charters bestow no rights to *confer degrees*. Hence to name
24 these institutions, under such charters, *colleges*, is a fraudulent claim. There is but one legally chartered college
of metaphysics, with powers to confer diplomas and de-
27 grees, and that is the Massachusetts Metaphysical College,
of which Rev. Mrs. Eddy is founder and president."

I have endeavored to act toward all students of Chris-
30 tian Science with the intuition and impulse of love. If
certain natures have not profited by my rebukes, —

some time, as Christian Scientists, they will know the value of these rebukes. I am thankful that the neophyte will be benefited by experience, although it will cost him much, and in proportion to its worth.

I close my College in order to work in other directions, where I now seem to be most needed, and where none other can do the work. I withdraw from an overwhelming prosperity. My students have never expressed so grateful a sense of my labors with them as now, and never have been so capable of relieving my tasks as at present.

God bless my enemies, as well as the better part of mankind, and gather all my students, in the bonds of love and perfectness, into one grand family of Christ's followers.

Loyal Christian Scientists should go on in their present line of labor for a good and holy cause. Their institutes have not yet accomplished all the good they are capable of accomplishing; therefore they should continue, as at present, to send out students from these sources of education, to promote the growing interest in Christian Science Mind-healing.

There are one hundred and sixty applications lying on the desk before me, for the Primary class in the Massachusetts Metaphysical College, and I cannot do my best work for a class which contains that number. When these were taught, another and a larger number would be in waiting for the same class instruction; and if I should teach that Primary class, the other three classes — one Primary and two Normal — would be delayed. The work is more than one person can well accomplish, and the imperative call is for my exclusive teaching.

1   From the scant history of Jesus and of his disciples,
we have no Biblical authority for a public institution.
3 This point, however, had not impressed me when I opened
my College. I desire to revise my book "Science and
Health with Key to the Scriptures," and in order to do
6 this I must stop teaching at present. The work that
needs to be done, and which God calls me to outside
of College work, if left undone might hinder the progress
9 of our Cause more than my teaching would advance it:
therefore I leave all for Christ.

Deeply regretting the disappointment this will occa-
12 sion, and with grateful acknowledgments to the public
for its liberal patronage, I close my College.

MARY BAKER G. EDDY

15   MALICIOUS REPORTS

Truth is fallen in the street, and equity cannot enter. — ISAIAH lix. 14.

When the press is gagged, liberty is besieged; but
18 when the press assumes the liberty to lie, it discounts
clemency, mocks morality, outrages humanity, breaks
common law, gives impulse to violence, envy, and hate,
21 and prolongs the reign of inordinate, unprincipled clans.
At this period, 1888, those quill-drivers whose consciences
are in their pockets hold high carnival. When news-
24 dealers shout for class legislation, and decapitated reputa-
tions, headless trunks, and quivering hearts are held up
before the rabble in exchange for money, place, and
27 power, the *vox populi* is suffocated, individual rights
are trodden under foot, and the car of the modern In-
quisition rolls along the streets besmeared with blood.

Would not our Master say to the chief actors in scenes 1
like these, "Ye fools and blind!" Oh, tardy human
justice! would you take away even woman's trembling, 3
clinging faith in divine power? Who can roll away the
stone from the door of this sepulchre? Who — but God's
avenging angel! 6

In times like these it were well to lift the veil on the
sackcloth of home, where weepeth the faithful, stricken
mother, and the bruised father bendeth his aching head; 9
where the bereft wife or husband, silent and alone, looks
in dull despair at the vacant seat, and the motherless
little ones, wondering, huddle together, and repeat with 12
quivering lips words of strange import. May the great
Shepherd that "tempers the wind to the shorn lamb,"
and binds up the wounds of bleeding hearts, just comfort, 15
encourage, and bless all who mourn.

Father, we thank Thee that Thy light and Thy love
reach earth, open the prison to them that are bound, con- 18
sole the innocent, and throw wide the gates of heaven.

LOYAL CHRISTIAN SCIENTISTS

Pen can never portray the satisfaction that you afforded 21
me at the grand meeting in Chicago of the National Christian Scientist Association in 1888. Your public and
private expressions of love and loyalty were very touch- 24
ing. They moved me to speechless thanks.

Chicago is the wonder of the western hemisphere. The
Palmer House, where we stopped, is magnificent and 27
orderly. The servants are well-mannered, and the fare
is appetizing. The floral offerings sent to my apartments

1 were superb, especially the large book of rare flowers, and the crescent with a star.

3 The reception in the spacious rooms of the Palmer House, like all else, was purely Western in its cordiality and largeness. I did not hold interviews with all with 6 whom I desired to, solely because so many people and circumstances demanded my attention that my personality was not big enough to fill the order; but rest as-9 sured my heart's desire met the demand.

My students, our delegates, about one thousand Christian Scientists, active, earnest, and loyal, formed a goodly 12 assemblage for the third convention of our National Association, — an assemblage found waiting and watching for the full coming of our Lord and Christ.

15 In Christian Science the midnight hour will always be the bridal hour, until "no night is there." The wise will have their lamps aglow, and light will illumine the 18 darkness.

Out of the gloom comes the glory of our Lord, and His divine Love is found in affliction. When a false 21 sense suffers, the true sense comes out, and the bridegroom appears. We are then wedded to a purer, higher affection and ideal.

24 I pray that all my students shall have their lamps trimmed and burning at the noon of night, that not one of them be found borrowing oil, and seeking light from 27 matter instead of Spirit, or at work erroneously, thus shutting out spiritual light. Such an error and loss will be quickly learned when the door is shut. Error giveth 30 no light, and it closes the door on itself.

In the dark hours, wise Christian Scientists stand firmer than ever in their allegiance to God. Wisdom

is wedded to their love, and their hearts are not 1
troubled.

Falsehood is on the wings of the winds, but Truth 3
will soar above it.   Truth is speaking louder, clearer,
and more imperatively than ever.   Error is walking to
and fro in the earth, trying to be heard above Truth, 6
but its voice dies out in the distance.   Whosoever proclaims Truth loudest, becomes the mark for error's shafts.
The archers aim at Truth's mouthpiece; but a heart 9
loyal to God is patient and strong.   Justice waits, and
is used to waiting; and right wins the everlasting
victory. 12

The stake and scaffold have never silenced the messages of the Most High.   Then can the present mode of
attempting this — namely, by slanderous falsehoods, and 15
a secret mind-method, through which to effect the purposes of envy and malice — silence Truth?   Never.   They
but open the eyes to the truth of Benjamin Franklin's 18
report before the French Commissioners on Mesmerism:
"It is one more fact to be recorded in the history of the
errors of the human mind." 21

"The Lord reigneth; let the earth rejoice."

No evidence before the material senses can close my
eyes to the scientific proof that God, good, is supreme. 24
Though clouds are round about Him, the divine justice
and judgment are enthroned.   Love is especially near
in times of hate, and never so near as when one can be 27
just amid lawlessness, and render good for evil.

I thunder His law to the sinner, and sharply lighten
on the cloud of the intoxicated senses.   I cannot help 30
loathing the phenomena of drunkenness produced by
animality.   I rebuke it wherever I see it.   The vision

1 of the Revelator is before me. The wines of fornication, envy, and hatred are the distilled spirits of evil,
3 and are the signs of these times; but I am not dismayed,
and my peace returns unto me.

Error will hate more as it realizes more the presence
6 of its tormentor. I shall fulfil my mission, fight the good
fight, and keep the faith.

There is great joy in this consciousness, that through-
9 out my labors, and in my history as connected with the
Cause of Christian Science, it can be proven that I have
never given occasion for a single censure, when my mo-
12 tives and acts are understood and seen as my Father
seeth them. I once wondered at the Scriptural declaration that Job sinned not in all he said, even when he cursed
15 the hour of his birth; but I have learned that a curse on
sin is always a blessing to the human race.

Those only who are tried in the furnace reflect the
18 image of their Father. You, my beloved students, who
are absent from me, and have shared less of my labors
than many others, seem stronger to resist temptation
21 than some of those who have had line upon line and
precept upon precept. This may be a serviceable hint,
since necessities and God's providence are foreshadowed.
24 I have felt for some time that perpetual instruction of
my students might substitute my own for their growth,
and so dwarf their experience. If they must learn by
27 the things they suffer, the sooner this lesson is gained
the better.

For two years I have been gradually withdrawing from
30 active membership in the Christian Scientist Association.
This has developed higher energies on the part of true
followers, and led to some startling departures on the

other hand. "Offenses will come: but woe unto him, 1
through whom they come."

Why does not the certainty of individual punishment 3
for sin prevent the wrong action? It is the love of God,
and not the fear of evil, that is the incentive in Science.
I rejoice with those who rejoice, and am too apt to weep 6
with those who weep, but over and above it all are eternal sunshine and joy unspeakable.

THE MARCH PRIMARY CLASS   9

To the Primary Class of the Massachusetts Metaphysical
    College, 571 Columbus Avenue, that Assembled Feb. 25,
    1889, with an Attendance of Sixty-five Students   12

My students, three picture-stories from the Bible present themselves to my thought; three of those pictures
from which we learn without study. The first is that of 15
Joshua and his band before the walls of Jericho. They
went seven times around these walls, the seven times
corresponding to the seven days of creation: the six days 18
are to find out the nothingness of matter; the seventh
is the day of rest, when it is found that evil is naught
and good is all.   21

The second picture is of the disciples met together in
an upper chamber; and they were of one mind. Mark,
that in the case of Joshua and his band they had all to 24
shout *together* in order that the walls might fall; and the
disciples, too, were of one mind.

We, to-day, in this class-room, are enough to con- 27
vert the world if we are of one Mind; for then the whole
world will feel the influence of this Mind; as when the

1 earth was without form, and Mind spake and form
appeared.

3   The third picture-lesson is from Revelation, where, at
the opening of the seals, one of the angels presented himself with balances to weigh the thoughts and actions of
6 men; not angels with wings, but messengers of pure and
holy thoughts that say, See thou hurt not the holy things
of Truth.

9   You have come to be weighed; and yet, I would not
weigh you, nor have you weighed. How is this? Because God does all, and there is nothing in the opposite
12 scale.   There are not two, — Mind *and* matter.   We
must get rid of that notion. As we commonly think, we
imagine all is well if we cast something into the scale of
15 Mind, but we must realize that Mind is not put into the
scales with matter; then only are we working on one side
and in Science.

18   The students of this Primary class, dismissed the fifth
of March, at close of the lecture on the fourth presented
their teacher with an elegant album costing fifty dollars,
21 and containing beautiful hand-painted flowers on each
page, with their autographs. The presentation was made
in a brief address by Mr. D. A. Easton, who in appro-
24 priate language and metaphor expressed his fellow-stu-
dents' thanks to their teacher.

On the morning of the fifth, I met the class to answer
27 some questions before their dismissal, and allude briefly
to a topic of great import to the student of Christian
Science, — the rocks and sirens in their course, on and
30 by which so many wrecks are made. The doors of animal
magnetism open wide for the entrance of error, sometimes just at the moment when you are ready to enter on

the fruition of your labors, and with laudable ambition are about to chant hymns of victory for triumphs.

The doors that this animal element flings open are those of rivalry, jealousy, envy, revenge. It is the self-asserting mortal will-power that you must guard against. But I find also another mental condition of yours that fills me with joy. I learned long ago that the world could neither deprive me of something nor give me anything, and I have now one ambition and one joy. But if one cherishes ambition unwisely, one will be chastened for it.

Admiral Coligny, in the time of the French Huguenots, was converted to Protestantism through a stray copy of the Scriptures that fell into his hands. He replied to his wife, who urged him to come out and confess his faith, "It is wise to count the cost of becoming a true Christian." She answered him, "It is wiser to count the cost of *not* becoming a true Christian." So, whatever we meet that is hard in the Christian warfare we must count as nothing, and must think instead, of our poverty and help-lessness without this understanding, and count ourselves always as debtors to Christ, Truth.

Among the gifts of my students, this of yours is one of the most beautiful and the most costly, because you have signed your names. I felt the weight of this yes-terday, but it came to me more clearly this morning when I realized what a responsibility you assume when sub-scribing to Christian Science. But, whatever may come to you, remember the words of Solomon, "Though hand join in hand, the wicked shall not go unpunished: but the seed of the righteous shall be delivered."

You will need, in future, *practice* more than theory.

1 You are going out to demonstrate a living faith, a true
sense of the infinite good, a sense that does not limit God,
3 but brings to human view an enlarged sense of Deity.
Remember, it is personality, and the sense of personality
in God or in man, that limits man.

6   OBTRUSIVE MENTAL HEALING

The question will present itself: Shall people be treated
mentally without their knowledge or consent? The
9 direct rule for practice of Christian Science is the Golden
Rule, "As ye would that men should do to you, do ye."
Who of us would have our houses broken open or our
12 locks picked? and much less would we have our minds
tampered with.
Our Master said, "When ye enter a house, salute it."
15 Prolonging the metaphysical tone of his command, I say,
When you enter mentally the personal precincts of human
thought, you should know that the person with whom
18 you hold communion desires it.   There are solitary ex-
ceptions to most given rules: the following is an exception
to the above rule of mental practice.
21   If the friends of a patient desire you to treat him without his knowing it, and they believe in the efficacy of
Mind-healing, it is sometimes wise to do so, and the end
24 justifies the means; for he is restored through Christian
Science when other means have failed.   One other occasion which may call for aid unsought, is a case from
27 accident, when there is no time for ceremony and no other
aid is near.
The abuse which I call attention to, is promiscuous

and unannounced mental practice where there is no neces- 1
sity for it, or the motive is mercenary, or one can to advantage speak the truth audibly; then the case is not 3
exceptional. As a rule, one has no more right to enter
the mind of a person, stir, upset, and adjust his thoughts
without his knowledge or consent, than one has to enter 6
a house, unlock the desk, displace the furniture, and suit
one's self in the arrangement and management of another
man's property. 9

It would be right to break into a burning building and
rouse the slumbering inmates, but wrong to burst open
doors and break through windows if no emergency de- 12
manded this. Any exception to the old wholesome rule,
"Mind your own business," is rare. For a student of
mine to treat another student without his knowledge, is 15
a breach of good manners and morals; it is nothing less
than a mistaken kindness, a culpable ignorance, or a
conscious trespass on the rights of mortals. 18

I insist on the etiquette of Christian Science, as well
as its morals and Christianity. The Scriptural rule of
this Science may momentarily be forgotten; but this is 21
seldom the case with loyal students, or done without
incriminating the person who did it.

Each student should, must, work out his own problem 24
of being; conscious, meanwhile, that God worketh with
him, and that he needs no personal aid. It is the genius
of Christian Science to demonstrate good, not evil, — 27
harmony, not discord; for Science is the mandate of
Truth which destroys all error.

Whoever is honestly laboring to learn the principle of 30
music and practise it, seldom calls on his teacher or musician to practise for him. The only personal help re-

1 quired in this Science is for each one to do his own work
well, and never try to hinder others from doing theirs
3 thus.

Christian Science, more than any other system of
religion, morals, or medicine, is subject to abuses. Its
6 infinite nature and uses occasion this. Even the human-
itarian at work in this field of limitless power and good
may possess a zeal without knowledge, and thus mistake
9 the sphere of his present usefulness.

Students who strictly adhere to the right, and make the
Bible and Science and Health a study, are in no danger
12 of mistaking their way.

This question is often proposed, How shall I treat
malicious animal magnetism? The hour has passed for
15 this evil to be treated personally, but it should have been
so dealt with at the outset. Christian Scientists should
have gone personally to the malpractitioner and told
18 him his fault, and vindicated divine Truth and Love
against human error and hate. This growing sin must
now be dealt with as evil, and not as an evil-doer or per-
21 sonality. It must also be remembered that neither an evil
claim nor an evil person is *real,* hence is neither to be
feared nor honored.

24 Evil is not something to fear and flee before, or that
becomes more real when it is grappled with. Evil let
alone grows more real, aggressive, and enlarges its claims;
27 but, met with Science, it can and will be mastered by
Science.

I deprecate personal animosities and quarrels. But if
30 one is intrusted with the rules of church government, to
fulfil that trust those rules must be carried out; thus it
is with all moral obligations. I am opposed to all personal

attacks, and in favor of combating evil only, rather than 1
person.

An edition of one thousand pamphlets I ordered to 3
be laid away and not one of them circulated, because I
had been personal in condemnation. Afterwards, by a
blunder of the gentleman who fills orders for my books, 6
some of these pamphlets were mistaken for the corrected
edition, and sold.

Love is the fulfilling of the law. Human life is too 9
short for foibles or failures. *The Christian Science Journal* will hold high the banner of Truth and Love, and be
impartial and impersonal in its tenor and tenets. 12

WEDLOCK

It was about the year 1875 that Science and Health
first crossed swords with free-love, and the latter fell *hors* 15
de combat; but the whole warfare of sensuality was not
then ended. Science and Health, the book that cast the
first stone, is still at work, deep down in human conscious- 18
ness, laying the axe at the root of error.

We have taken the precaution to write briefly on marriage, showing its relation to Christian Science. In the 21
present or future, some extra throe of error may conjure
up a new-style conjugality, which, *ad libitum,* severs the
marriage covenant, puts virtue in the shambles, and 24
coolly notifies the public of broken vows. Springing
up from the ashes of free-love, this nondescript phœnix,
in the face and eyes of common law, common sense, and 27
common honesty, may appear in the *rôle* of a superfine
conjugality; but, having no Truth, it will have no past,
present, or future. 30

1   The above prophecy, written years ago, has already been fulfilled.   It is seen in Christian Science that the
3 gospel of marriage is not without the law, and the solemn vow of fidelity, "until death do us part;" this verity in human economy can neither be obscured nor throttled.
6 Until time matures human growth, marriage and progeny will continue unprohibited in Christian Science. We look to future generations for ability to comply with absolute
9 Science, when marriage shall be found to be man's oneness with God, — the unity of eternal Love.   At present, more spiritual conception and education of children will
12 serve to illustrate the superiority of spiritual power over sensuous, and usher in the dawn of God's creation, wherein they neither marry nor are given in marriage,
15 but are as the angels.   To abolish marriage at this period, and maintain morality and generation, would put ingenuity to ludicrous shifts; yet this is possible in *Science*,
18 although it is to-day problematic.

It should be understood that Spirit, God, is the only

The time cometh, and now is, for spiritual and eternal existence to be recognized and understood in Science.
21 All is Mind.   Human procreation, birth, life, and death are subjective states of the human erring mind; they are the phenomena of mortality, nothingness, that illus-
24 trate mortal mind and body as *one,* and neither real nor eternal.

It should be understood that Spirit, God, is the only
27 creator: we should recognize this verity of being, and shut out all sense of other claims.   Until this absolute Science of being is seen, understood, and demonstrated
30 in the offspring of divine Mind, and man is perfect even as the Father is perfect, human speculation will go on, and stop at length at the spiritual ultimate: creation

understood as the most exalted divine conception. The offspring of an improved generation, however, will go out before the forever fact that man is eternal and has no human origin. Hence the Scripture: "It is He that hath made us, and not we ourselves;" and the Master's demand, "Call no man your father upon the earth: for one is your Father, which is in heaven."

To an ill-attuned ear, discord is harmony; so personal sense, discerning not the legitimate affection of Soul, may place love on a false basis and thereby lose it. Science corrects this error with the truth of Love, and restores lost Eden. Soul is the infinite source of bliss: only high and holy joy can satisfy immortal cravings. The good in human affections should preponderate over the evil, and the spiritual over the animal, — until progress lifts mortals to discern the Science of mental formation and find the highway of holiness.

In the order of wisdom, the higher nature of man governs the lower. This lays the foundations of human affection in line with progress, giving them strength and permanence.

When asked by a wife or a husband important questions concerning their happiness, the substance of my reply is: God will guide you. Be faithful over home relations; they lead to higher joys: obey the Golden Rule for human life, and it will spare you much bitterness. It is pleasanter to do right than wrong; it makes one ruler over one's self and hallows home, — which is woman's world. Please your husband, and he will be apt to please you; preserve affection on both sides.

Great mischief comes from attempts to steady other people's altars, venturing on valor without discretion,

1 which is virtually meddlesomeness. Even your sincere
and courageous convictions regarding what is best for
3 others may be mistaken; you must be demonstratively
right yourself, and work out the greatest good to the
greatest number, before you are sure of being a fit coun-
6 sellor. Positive and imperative thoughts should be dropped
into the balances of God and weighed by spiritual Love,
and not be found wanting, before being put into action.
9 A rash conclusion that regards only one side of a question, is weak and wicked; this error works out the results
of error. If the premise of mortal existence is wrong,
12 any conclusion drawn therefrom is not absolutely right.
Wisdom in human action begins with what is nearest
right under the circumstances, and thence achieves the
15 absolute.

Is marriage nearer right than celibacy?

Human knowledge inculcates that it is, while Science
18 indicates that it *is not*. But to force the consciousness
of scientific being before it is understood is impossible,
and believing otherwise would prevent scientific demon-
21 stration. To reckon the universal cost and gain, as well
as thine own, is right in every state and stage of being.
The selfish *rôle* of a martyr is the shift of a dishonest
24 mind, nothing short of self-seeking; and real suffering
would stop the farce.

The cause of temperance receives a strong impulse
27 from the cause of Christian Science: temperance and
truth are allies, and their cause prospers in proportion
to the spirit of Love that nerves the struggle. People
30 will differ in their opinions as to means to promote the
ends of temperance; that is, abstinence from intoxicat-
ing beverages. Whatever intoxicates a man, stultifies

and causes him to degenerate physically and morally. 1
Strong drink is unquestionably an evil, and evil cannot
be used temperately: its slightest use is abuse; hence 3
the only temperance is total abstinence. Drunkenness
is sensuality let loose, in whatever form it is made
manifest.   6

What is evil? It is suppositional absence of good.
From a human standpoint of good, mortals must first
choose between evils, and of two evils choose the less; 9
and at present the application of scientific rules to human life seems to rest on this basis.

All partnerships are formed on agreements to certain 12
compacts: each party voluntarily surrenders independent action to act as a whole and per agreement. This
fact should be duly considered when by the marriage 15
contract two are made one, and, according to the divine
precept, "they twain shall be one flesh." Oneness in
spirit is Science, compatible with home and heaven. 18
Neither divine justice nor human equity has *divorced*
two minds in one.

Rights that are bargained away must not be retaken 21
by the contractors, except by mutual consent. Human
nature has bestowed on a wife the right to become a
mother; but if the wife esteems not this privilege, by 24
mutual consent, exalted and increased affections, she
may win a higher. Science touches the conjugal question on the basis of a bill of rights. Can the bill of con- 27
jugal rights be fairly stated by a magistrate, or by a
minister? Mutual interests and affections are the spirit
of these rights, and they should be consulted, augmented, 30
and allowed to rise to the spiritual altitude whence they
can choose only good.

1   A third person is not a party to the compact of two
hearts. Let other people's marriage relations *alone:* two
3 persons only, should be found within their precincts.
The nuptial vow is never annulled so long as the animus
of the contract is preserved intact. Science lifts humanity
6 higher in the scale of harmony, and must ultimately break
all bonds that hinder progress.

JUDGE NOT

9   Mistaken views ought to be dissolving views, since
whatever is false should disappear. To suppose that human love, guided by the divine Principle, which is Love,
12 is partial, unmerciful, or unjust, indicates misapprehension of the divine Principle and its workings in the human
heart.
15   A person wrote to me, naming the time of the occurrence, "I felt the influence of your thought on my mind,
and it produced a wonderful illumination, peace, and
18 understanding;" but, I had not thought of the writer
at that time. I knew that this person was doing well,
and my affections involuntarily flow out towards all.
21   When will the world cease to judge of causes from a
personal sense of things, conjectural and misapprehen-
sive! When thought dwells in God, — and it should not,
24 to our consciousness, dwell elsewhere, — one must benefit those who hold a place in one's memory, whether it
be friend or foe, and each share the benefit of that radia-
27 tion. This individual blessedness and blessing comes
not so much from individual as from universal love: it
emits light because it reflects; and all who are receptive
30 share this equally.

Mistaken or transient views are human: they are not 1
governed by the Principle of divine Science: but the
notion that a mind governed by Principle can be forced 3
into personal channels, affinities, self-interests, or obligations, is a grave mistake; it dims the true sense of God's
reflection, and darkens the understanding that demon- 6
strates above personal motives, unworthy aims and
ambitions.

Too much and too little is attached to me as authority 9
for other people's thoughts and actions. A tacit acquiescence with others' views is often construed as direct
orders, — or at least it so appears in results. I desire 12
the equal growth and prosperity of all Christian Scientists, and the world in general; each and every one has
equal opportunity to be benefited by my thoughts and 15
writings. If any are not partakers thereof, this is not
my fault, and is far from my desire; the possible per-
version of Christian Science is the irony of fate, if the 18
spirit thereof be lacking. I would part with a blessing
myself to bestow it upon others, but could not deprive
them of it. False views, however engendered, relative 21
to the true and unswerving course of a Christian Scientist,
will at length dissolve into thin air. The dew of heaven
will fall gently on the hearts and lives of all who are found 24
worthy to suffer for righteousness, — and have taught
the truth which is energizing, refreshing, and consecrat-
ing mankind. 27

To station justice and gratitude as sentinels along the
lines of thought, would aid the solution of this problem,
and counteract the influence of envious minds or the mis- 30
guided individual who keeps not watch over his emotions
and conclusions.

NEW COMMANDMENT

The divinity of St. John's Gospel brings to view over-whelming tides of revelation, and its spirit is baptismal; he chronicles this teaching, "A new commandment I give unto you, That ye love one another."

Jesus, who so loved the world that he gave his life (in the flesh) for it, saw that Love had a new commandment even for him. What was it?

It must have been a rare revelation of infinite Love, a new tone on the scale ascending, such as eternity is ever sounding. Could I impart to the student the higher sense I entertain of Love, it would partly illustrate the divine energy that brings to human weakness might and majesty. Divine Love eventually causes mortals to turn away from the open sepulchres of sin, and look no more into them as realities. It calls loudly on them to bury the dead out of sight; to forgive and forget whatever is unlike the risen, immortal Love; and to shut out all opposite sense. Christ enjoins it upon man to help those who know not what he is doing in their behalf, and therefore curse him; enjoins taking them by the hand and leading them, if *possible,* to Christ, by loving words and deeds. Charity thus serves as admonition and instruction, and works out the purposes of Love.

Christian Science, full of grace and truth, is accomplishing great good, both seen and unseen; but have mortals, with the penetration of Soul, searched the secret chambers of sense? I never knew a student who fully understood my instructions on this point of handling evil, — as to just how this should be done, — and carried

out my ideal. It is safe not to teach prematurely the 1
infant thought in Christian Science — just breathing new
Life and Love — all the claims and modes of evil; there- 3
fore it is best to leave the righteous unfolding of error
(as a general rule) alone, and to the special care of the
unerring modes of divine wisdom. This uncovering and 6
punishing of sin must, will come, at some date, to the
rescue of humanity. The teacher of divine metaphysics
should impart to his students the general knowledge that 9
he has gained from instruction, observation, and mental
practice.

Experience weighs in the scales of God the sense and 12
power of Truth against the opposite claims of error.
If spiritual sense is not dominant in a student, he will
not understand all your instructions; and if evil domi- 15
nates his character, he will pervert the rules of Christian
Science, and the last error will be worse than the first —
inasmuch as wilful transgression brings greater torment 18
than ignorance.

A CRUCE SALUS

The sum total of Love reflected is exemplified, and 21
includes the whole duty of man: Truth perverted, in
belief, becomes the creator of the claim of error. To
affirm mentally and audibly that God is All and there is 24
no sickness and no sin, makes mortals either saints or
sinners.

Truth talked and not lived, rolls on the human heart 27
a stone; consigns sensibility to the charnel-house of sensuality, ease, self-love, self-justification, there to moulder
and rot. 30

1   The noblest work of God is man in the image of his
Maker; the last infirmity of evil is so-called man, swayed
3 by the maëlstrom of human passions, elbowing the concepts of his own creating, making place for himself and
displacing his fellows.

6   A real Christian Scientist is a marvel, a miracle in the
universe of mortal mind. With selfless love, he inscribes
on the heart of humanity and transcribes on the page
9 of reality the living, palpable presence — the might and
majesty! — of goodness. He lives for all mankind, and
honors his creator.

12 The *vice versa* of this man is sometimes called a
man, but he is a small animal: a hived bee, with sting
ready for each kind touch, he makes honey out of
15 the flowers of human hearts and hides it in his cell of
ingratitude.

O friendly hand! keep back thy offerings from asps
18 and apes, from wolves in sheep's clothing and all raven-
ing beasts. Love such specimens of mortality just enough
to reform and transform them, — if it be possible, —
21 and then, look out for their stings, and jaws, and claws;
but thank God and take courage, — that you desire to
help even such as these.

24   COMPARISON TO ENGLISH BARMAIDS

Since my residence in Concord, N. H., I have read
the daily paper, and had become an admirer of Edgar
27 L. Wakeman's terse, graphic, and poetic style in his
"Wanderings," richly flavored with the true ideas of
humanity and equality. In an issue of January 17, how-

ever, were certain references to American women which 1
deserve and elicit brief comment.

Mr. Wakeman writes from London, that a noted Eng- 3
lish leader, whom he quotes without naming, avers that
the "cursed barmaid system" in England is evolved by
the same power which in America leads women "along 6
a gamut of isms and ists, from female suffrage, past a
score of reforms, to Christian Science." This anonymous talker further declares, that the central cause of 9
this "same original evil" is "a female passion for some
manner of notoriety."

Is Mr. Wakeman *awake,* and caught napping? While 12
praising the Scotchman's national pride and affection,
has our American correspondent lost these sentiments
from his own breast? Has he forgotten how to honor 15
his native land and defend the dignity of her daughters
with his ready pen and pathos?

The flaunting and floundering statements of the great 18
unknown for whose ability and popularity Mr. Wakeman
strongly vouches, should not only be queried, but flatly
contradicted, as both untrue and uncivil. English senti- 21
ment is not wholly represented by one man. Nor is the
world ignorant of the fact that high and pure ethical
tones do resound from Albion's shores. The most ad- 24
vanced ideas are inscribed on tablets of such an organization as the Victoria Institute, or Philosophical Society
of Great Britain, an institution which names itself after 27
her who is unquestionably the best queen on earth; who
for a half century has with such dignity, clemency, and
virtue worn the English crown and borne the English 30
sceptre.

Now, I am a Christian Scientist, — the Founder of

1 this system of religion, — widely known; and, by special
invitation, have allowed myself to be elected an associate
3 life-member of the Victoria Institute, which numbers
among its constituents and managers — not barmaids,
but bishops — profound philosophers, brilliant scholars.

6 Was it ignorance of American society and history,
together with unfamiliarity with the work and career
of American women, which led the unknown author
9 cited by Mr. Wakeman to overflow in shallow sarcasm,
and place the barmaids of English alehouses and rail-
ways in the same category with noble women who min-
12 ister in the sick-room, give their time and strength to
binding up the wounds of the broken-hearted, and live
on the plan of heaven?

15 This writer classes Christian Science with theosophy
and spiritualism; whereas, they are by no means identical — nor even similar. Christian Science, antagonis-
18 tic to intemperance, as to all immorality, is by no means
associated therewith. Do manly Britons patronize tap-
rooms and lazar-houses, and thus note or foster a fem-
21 inine ambition which, in this unknown gentleman's
language, "poises and poses, higgles and wriggles" itself into publicity? Why fall into such patronage, unless
24 from their affinity for the worst forms of vice?

And the barmaids! Do they enter this line of occupation from a desire for notoriety and a wish to promote
27 female suffrage? or are they incited thereto by their
own poverty and the bad appetites of men? What manner of man *is* this unknown individual who utters bar-
30 maid and Christian Scientist in the same breath? If he
but knew whereof he speaks, *his* shame would not lose
its blush!

Taking into account the short time that has elapsed 1
since the discovery of Christian Science, one readily sees
that this Science has distanced all other religious and 3
pathological systems for physical and moral reformation. In the direction of temperance it has achieved far
more than has been accomplished by legally coercive 6
measures, — and because this Science bases its work on
ethical conditions and mentally destroys the appetite for
alcoholic drinks. 9

Smart journalism is allowable, nay, it is commend-
able; but the public cannot swallow reports of American
affairs from a surly censor ventilating his lofty scorn of 12
the sects, or societies, of a nation that perhaps he has
never visited.

A CHRISTIAN SCIENCE STATUTE 15

I hereby state, in unmistakable language, the following statute in the *morale* of Christian Science: —

A man or woman, having voluntarily entered into 18
wedlock, and accepted the claims of the marriage covenant, is held in Christian Science as morally bound to
fulfil all the claims growing out of this contract, unless 21
such claims are relinquished by mutual consent of both
parties, or this contract is legally dissolved. If the man
is dominant over the animal, he will count the conse- 24
quences of his own conduct; will consider the effects,
on himself and his progeny, of selfishness, unmercifulness, tyranny, or lust. 27

Trust Truth, not error; and Truth will give you all
that belongs to the rights of freedom. The Hebrew bard

1 wrote, "Trust in the Lord with all thine heart; and lean
not unto thine own understanding." Nothing is gained
3 by wrong-doing. St. Paul's words take in the situation:
"Not . . . (as we be slanderously reported, and as some
affirm that we say,) Let us do evil, that good may come?
6 whose damnation is just."

When causing others to go astray, we also are wan-
derers. "With what measure ye mete, it shall be meas-
9 ured to you again." Ask yourself: Under the same
circumstances, in the same spiritual ignorance and power
of passion, would I be strengthened by having my best
12 friend break troth with me? These words of St. Matthew
have special application to Christian Scientists; namely,
"It is not good to marry."

15 To build on selfishness is to build on sand. When
Jesus received the material rite of water baptism, he did
not say that it was God's command; but implied that
18 the period demanded it. Trials purify mortals and deliver
them from themselves, — all the claims of sensuality.
Abide by the *morale* of absolute Christian Science, —
21 self-abnegation and purity; then Truth delivers you from
the seeming power of error, and faith vested in righteousness triumphs!

24   ADVICE TO STUDENTS

The true consciousness is the true health. One says,
"I find relief from pain in unconscious sleep." I say,
27 You mistake; through unconsciousness one no more
gains freedom from pain than immunity from evil. When
unconscious of a mistake, one thinks he is not mistaken;
30 but this false consciousness does not change the fact, or

its results; suffering and mistakes recur until one is awake 1
to their cause and character. To know the what, when,
and how of error, destroys error. The error that is seen 3
aright as error, has received its death-blow; but never
until then.

Let us look through the lens of Christian Science, 6
not of "self," at the following mistake, which demands
our present attention. I have no time for detailed report
of this matter, but simply answer the following question 9
sent to me; glad, indeed, that this query has finally come
with the courage of conviction to the minds of many
students. 12

"Is it right to copy your works and read them for our
public services?"

The good which the material senses see not is the only 15
absolute good; the evil which these senses see not is the
only absolute evil.

If I enter Mr. Smith's store and take from it his gar- 18
ments that are on sale, array myself in them, and put
myself and them on exhibition, can I make this right
by saying, These garments are Mr. Smith's; he manu- 21
factured them and owns them, but you must pay me,
not him, for this exhibit?

The spectators may ask, Did he give you permission 24
to do this, did he sell them or loan them to you? No.
Then have you asked yourself this question on the subject, namely, What right have I to do this? True, it 27
saves your purchasing these garments, and gives to the
public new patterns which are useful to them; but does
this silence your conscience? or, because you have con- 30
fessed that they are the property of a noted firm, and
you wished to handle them, does it justify you in appro-

1 priating them, and so avoiding the cost of hiring or
purchasing?

3   Copying my published works *verbatim*, compiling them
in connection with the Scriptures, taking this copy into
the pulpit, announcing the author's name, then reading
6 it publicly as your own compilation, is — what?

We answer, It is a mistake; in common parlance, it
is an *ignorant* wrong.

9   If you should print and publish your copy of my works,
you would be liable to arrest for infringement of copyright, which the law defines and punishes as theft. Read-
12 ing in the pulpit from copies of my publications gives
you the clergyman's salary and spares you the printer's
bill, but does it spare you our Master's condemnation?
15 You literally publish my works through the pulpit, instead
of the press, and thus evade the law, *but not the gospel*.
When I consent to this act, you will then be justified
18 in it.

Your manuscript copy is liable, in some way, to be
printed as your original writings, thus incurring the pen-
21 alty of the law, and increasing the record of theft in the
United States Circuit Court.

To The Church of Christ, Scientist, in Boston, which I
24 had organized and of which I had for many years been
pastor, I gave permission to cite, in the *Christian Science
Quarterly*, from my work Science and Health, passages
27 giving the spiritual meaning of Bible texts; but this was
a special privilege, and the author's gift.

Christian Science demonstrates that the patient who
30 pays whatever he is able to pay for being healed, is more
apt to recover than he who withholds a slight equivalent for health. Healing morally and physically are one.

Then, is compiling and delivering that sermon for which 1
you pay nothing, and which you deliver without the
author's consent, and receive pay therefor, the *precedent* 3
for preaching Christian Science, — and are you doing
to the author of the above-named book as you would
have others do unto you?   6

Those authors and editors of pamphlets and periodicals whose substance is made up of my publications, are
morally responsible for what the law construes as crime. 9
There are startling instances of the above-named law-
breaking and gospel-opposing system of authorship, which
characterize the writings of a few professed Christian 12
Scientists. My Christian students who have read copies
of my works in the pulpit require only a word to be wise;
too sincere and morally statuesque are they to be long 15
led into temptation; but I must not leave persistent
plagiarists without this word of warning in public, since
my private counsel they disregard.   18

To the question of my true-hearted students, "Is it
right to copy your works and read them for our public
services?" I answer: It is not right to copy my book 21
and read it publicly *without my consent*. My reasons are
as follows: —

First: This method is an unseen form of injustice 24
standing in a holy place.

Second: It breaks the Golden Rule, — a divine rule
for human conduct.   27

Third: All error tends to harden the heart, blind
the eyes, stop the ears of understanding, and inflate
self; counter to the commands of our hillside Priest, to 30
whom Isaiah alluded thus: "I have trodden the winepress alone; and of the people there was none with me."

1   Behind the scenes lurks an evil which you can prevent: it is a purpose to kill the reformation begun and increas-
3 ing through the instructions of "Science and Health with Key to the Scriptures;" it encourages infringement of my copyright, and seeks again to "cast lots for his vesture,"
6 — while the perverter preserves in his own consciousness and teaching the name without the Spirit, the skeleton without the heart, the form without the comeliness, the
9 sense without the Science, of Christ's healing. My students are expected to know the teaching of Christian Science sufficiently to discriminate between error and Truth,
12 thus sparing their teacher a task and themselves the temptation to be misled.

   Much good has been accomplished through Christian
15 Science Sunday services. If Christian Scientists occasionally mistake in interpreting revealed Truth, of two evils the less would be *not* to leave the Word unspoken and
18 untaught. I allowed, till this permission was *withdrawn,* students working faithfully for Christ's cause on earth, the privilege of copying and reading my works for Sunday
21 service; *provided,* they each and all destroyed the copies at once after said service. When I should so elect and give suitable notice, they were to desist from further copy-
24 ing of my writings as aforesaid.

   This injunction did not curtail the benefit which the student derived from making his copy, nor detract from
27 the good that his hearers received from his reading thereof; but it was intended to forestall the possible evil of putting the divine teachings contained in "Science and Health
30 with Key to the Scriptures" into human hands, to subvert or to liquidate.

   I recommend that students stay within their own fields

of labor, to work for the race; they are lights that can- 1
not be hid, and need only to shine from their home sum-
mits to be sought and found as healers physical and 3
moral.

The kindly shepherd has his own fold and tends his
own flock.   Christian students should have their own 6
institutes and, *unmolested,* be governed by divine Love
alone in teaching and guiding their students.   When
wisdom garrisons these strongholds of Christian Science, 9
peace and joy, the fruits of Spirit, will rest upon us all.
We are brethren in the fullest sense of that word; therefore no queries should arise as to "who shall be great- 12
est."   Let us serve instead of rule, knock instead of
push at the door of human hearts, and allow to each
and every one the same rights and privileges that we 15
claim for ourselves.   If ever I wear out from serving
students, it shall be in the effort to help them to obey
the Ten Commandments and imbibe the spirit of Christ's 18
Beatitudes.

NOTICE

Editor of Christian Science Journal: — You will oblige 21
me by giving place in your *Journal* to the following notice.
The idea and purpose of a Liberty Bell is pleasing, and
can be made profitable to the heart of our country.   I feel 24
assured that many Christian Scientists will respond to this
letter by contributions.

MARY BAKER EDDY   27

COLUMBIAN LIBERTY BELL COMMITTEE,
1505 PENNA. AVE., WASHINGTON, D. C.

To the Daughters of the American Revolution: —

It has been determined to create a Columbian Liberty Bell, to be placed by the lovers of liberty and peace in the most appropriate place in the coming World's Exposition at Chicago. After the close of the Exhibition this bell will pass from place to place throughout the world as a missionary of freedom, coming first to the capital of the nation under the care of our society.

Then it will go to Bunker Hill or Liberty Island, to the battle-field of New Orleans (1812), to San Francisco, to the place where any great patriotic celebration is being held, until 1900, when it will be sent to the next World's Exhibition, which takes place at Paris, France. There it will continue until that Exhibition closes.

When not in use in other places, it will return to Washington under the care of the Daughters of the American Revolution. Washington will be its home, and from there it will journey from place to place, fulfilling its mission throughout the world.

The following is the proposed use of the bell: It shall ring at sunrise and sunset; at nine o'clock in the morning on the anniversaries of the days on which great events have occurred marking the world's progress toward liberty; at twelve o'clock on the birthdays of the "creators of liberty;" and at four o'clock it will toll on the anniversaries of their death. (It will always ring at nine o'clock on October 11th, in recognition of the organization on that day of the Daughters of the American Revolution.) . . . The responsibility of its production, and the direction of its use, have been placed in the hands of a

committee of women representing each State and Ter- 1
ritory, one representative from each Republic in the
world, and a representative from the patriotic societies, 3
— Daughters and Sons of the American Revolution,
the Lyceum League of America, the Society of German Patriots, the Human Freedom League, and kindred 6
organizations.

The National Board of Management has placed upon
me the responsibility of representing the National Society 9
of the Daughters of the American Revolution upon the
General Committee, and this circular is sent to every
member of the society, asking for her personal coopera- 12
tion in making the undertaking successful. In creating
the bell it is particularly desired that the largest number
of persons possible shall have a part in it. For this reason 15
small contributions from many persons are to be asked
for, rather than large contributions from a few. They
are to be of two kinds: — 18

First: Material that can be made a part of the bell;
articles of historic interest will be particularly appreciated — gold, silver, bronze, copper, and nickel can be 21
fused.

Second: Of money with which to pay for the bell.
Each member of the society is asked to contribute one 24
cent to be fused into the bell, and twenty-five cents to
pay for it. She is also asked to collect two dollars from
others, in pennies, if possible, and send with the amount 27
the name of each contributor. In order that the bell
shall be cast April 30th, the anniversary of the inauguration of George Washington as the first President of 30
the United States, we ask every one receiving this circular *to act at once.*

1   In forwarding material to be melted into the bell, please
send fullest historical description.   This will be entered
3 carefully in a book which will accompany the bell wherever
it goes.

. . . As the motto has not yet been decided upon, any
6 ideas on that subject will be gratefully received; we will
also welcome suggestions of events to be celebrated and
names to be commemorated.

9   Very cordially yours,
                                    MARY DESHA,
                        ex-Vice-President General, D. A. R.

12 Contributions should be sent to the Liberty National
Bank, corner Liberty and West Streets, New York, and
a duplicate letter written, as a notification of the same,
15 to Miss Mary Desha, 1505 Penna. Ave., Washington,
D. C., or to Miss Minnie F. Mickley, Mickleys, Pa.

We would add, as being of interest, that Mrs. Eddy is
18 a member of the above organization, having been made
such by the special request of the late Mrs. Harrison,
wife of the ex-President, who was at that time the Presi-
21 dent thereof. — ED.

ANGELS

When angels visit us, we do not hear the rustle of wings,
24 nor feel the feathery touch of the breast of a dove; but
we know their presence by the love they create in our
hearts.   Oh, may you feel *this* touch, — it is not the
27 clasping of hands, nor a loved person present; it is more
than this: it is a spiritual idea that lights your path!
The Psalmist saith: "He shall give His angels charge

over thee." God gives you His spiritual ideas, and in 1
turn, they give you daily supplies. Never ask for to-
morrow: it is enough that divine Love is an ever-present 3
help; and if you wait, never doubting, you will have
all you need every moment. What a glorious inheritance
is given to us through the understanding of omnipresent 6
Love! More we cannot ask: more we do not want:
more we cannot have. This sweet assurance is the
"Peace, be still" to all human fears, to suffering of every 9
sort.

DEIFICATION OF PERSONALITY

Notwithstanding the rapid sale already of two editions 12
of "Christ and Christmas," and many orders on hand, I
have thought best to stop its publication.

In this revolutionary religious period, the increasing 15
inquiry of mankind as to Christianity and its unity —
and above all, God's love opening the eyes of the blind
— is fast fitting all minds for the proper reception of 18
Christian Science healing.

But I must stand on this absolute basis of Christian
Science; namely, Cast not pearls before the unprepared 21
thought. Idolatry is an easily-besetting sin of all peoples.
The apostle saith, "Little children, keep yourselves from
idols." 24

The illustrations were not intended for a golden calf,
at which the sick may look and be healed. Christian
Scientists should beware of unseen snares, and adhere 27
to the divine Principle and rules for demonstration.
They must guard against the deification of finite personality. Every human thought must turn instinctively to 30

1 the divine Mind as its sole centre and intelligence. Until
this be done, man will never be found harmonious and
3 immortal.

Whosoever looks to me personally for his health or
holiness, mistakes. He that by reason of human love or
6 hatred or any other cause clings to my material personality, greatly errs, stops his own progress, and loses
the path to health, happiness, and heaven. The Scrip-
9 tures and Christian Science reveal "the way," and personal revelators will take their proper place in history,
but will not be deified.

12 Advanced scientific students are ready for "Christ
and Christmas;" but those are a minority of its readers,
and even they know its practicality only by healing
15 the sick on its divine Principle. In the words of the
prophet, "Hear, O Israel: The Lord our God is one
Lord."

18 Friends, strangers, and Christian Scientists, I thank
you, each and all, for your liberal patronage and scholarly,
artistic, and scientific notices of my book. This little
21 messenger has done its work, fulfilled its mission, retired
with honor (and mayhap taught me more than it has
others), only to reappear in due season. The knowledge
24 that I have gleaned from its fruitage is, that intensely
contemplating personality impedes spiritual growth; even
as holding in mind the consciousness of disease prevents
27 the recovery of the sick.

Christian Science is taught through its divine Principle, which is invisible to corporeal sense. A material
30 human likeness is the antipode of man in the image and
likeness of God. Hence, a finite person is not the model
for a metaphysician. I earnestly advise all Christian
33 Scientists to remove from their observation or study

the personal sense of any one, and not to dwell in thought 1
upon their own or others' corporeality, either as good or
evil.   3

According to Christian Science, material personality is
an error in premise, and must result in erroneous conclusions. All will agree with me that material portraiture 6
often fails to express even mortal man, and this declares
its unfitness for fable or fact to build upon.

The face of Jesus has uniformly been so unnaturally 9
delineated that it has turned many from the true contemplation of his character. He advances most in divine
Science who meditates most on infinite spiritual sub- 12
stance and intelligence. Experience proves this true.
Pondering on the finite personality of Jesus, the son of
man, is not the channel through which we reach the 15
Christ, or Son of God, the true idea of man's divine
Principle.

I warn students against falling into the error of anti- 18
Christ. The consciousness of corporeality, and whatever is connected therewith, must be outgrown. Corporeal
falsities include all obstacles to health, holiness, and 21
heaven. Man's individual life is infinitely above a
bodily form of existence, and the human concept an-
tagonizes the divine. "Science and Health with Key 24
to the Scriptures," on page 229, third and fourth paragraphs, elucidates this topic.[1]

My Christmas poem and its illustrations are not a text- 27
book. Scientists sometimes take things too intensely.
Let them soberly adhere to the Bible and Science and
Health, which contain all and much more than they 30
have yet learned. We should prohibit ourselves the

[1] See the revised edition of 1890, or page 334, lines 10–30 in current editions.

1 childish pleasure of studying Truth through the senses,
for this is neither the intent of my works nor possible
3 in Science.

Even the teachings of Jesus would be misused by substituting personality for the Christ, or the impersonal
6 form of Truth, amplified in this age by the discovery of
Christian Science. To impersonalize scientifically the
material sense of existence — rather than cling to per-
9 sonality — is the lesson of to-day.

A CARD

My answer to manifold letters relative to the return
12 of members that have gone out of The First Church of
Christ, Scientist, in Boston, is this: While my affections plead for all and every one, and my desire is that
15 all shall be redeemed, I am not unmindful that the Scriptures enjoin, "Let all things be done decently and in
order."
18   To continue one's connection with this church, or to
regain it, one must comply with the church rules. All
who desire its fellowship, and to become members of it,
21 must send in their petitions to this effect to the Clerk
of the church; and upon a meeting being called, the
First Members will determine the action of the church
24 on this subject.

OVERFLOWING THOUGHTS

In this receding year of religious jubilee, 1894, I as
27 an individual would cordially invite all persons who
have left our fold, together with those who never have

been in it, — all who love God and keep His command- 1
ments, — to come and unite with The Mother Church in
Boston. The true Christian Scientists will be welcomed, 3
greeted as brethren endeavoring to walk with us hand
in hand, as we journey to the celestial city.

Also, I would extend a tender invitation to Christian 6
Scientists' students, those who are ready for the table of
our Lord: so, should we follow Christ's teachings; so,
bury the dead past; so, loving one another, go forth to 9
the full vintage-time, exemplifying what we profess. But
some of the older members are not quite ready to take
this advanced step in the full spirit of that charity which 12
thinketh no evil; and if it be not taken thus, it is impractical, unfruitful, Soul-less.

My deepest desires and daily labors go to prove that 15
I love my enemies and would help all to gain the abiding
consciousness of health, happiness, and heaven.

I hate no one; and love others more than they can 18
love me. As I now understand Christian Science, I would
as soon harm myself as another; since by breaking
Christ's command, "Thou shalt love thy neighbor as 21
thyself," I should lose my hope of heaven.

The works I have written on Christian Science contain absolute Truth, and my necessity was to tell it; 24
therefore I did this even as a surgeon who wounds
to heal. I was a scribe under orders; and who can
refrain from transcribing what God indites, and ought 27
not that one to take the cup, drink all of it, and give
thanks?

Being often reported as saying what never escaped 30
from my lips, when rehearsing facts concerning others
who were reporting false charges, I have been sorry that

1 I spoke at all, and wished I were wise enough to guard
against that temptation. Oh, may the love that is talked,
3 be *felt!* and so *lived,* that when weighed in the scale of
God we be not found wanting. Love is consistent, uniform, sympathetic, self-sacrificing, unutterably kind; even
6 that which lays all upon the altar, and, speechless and
alone, bears all burdens, suffers all inflictions, endures
all piercing for the sake of others, and for the kingdom
9 of heaven's sake.

A GREAT MAN AND HIS SAYING

Hon. Charles Carrol Bonney, President of the World's
12 Congress Auxiliary, in his remarks before that body,
said, "No more striking manifestation of the interposi-
tion of divine Providence in human affairs has come in
15 recent years, than that shown in the raising up of the
body of people known as Christian Scientists, who are
called to declare the real harmony between religion and
18 Science, and to restore the waning faith of many in the
verities of the sacred Scriptures."

In honest utterance of veritable history, and his own
21 spiritual discernment, this man must have risen above
worldly schemes, human theorems or hypotheses, to
conclusions which reason too supine or misemployed
24 cannot fasten upon. He spake inspired; he touched a
tone of Truth that will continue to reverberate and renew
its emphasis throughout the entire centuries, into the vast
27 forever.

WORDS OF COMMENDATION   1

Editor of The Christian Science Journal: — Permit me
to say that your editorial in the August number is *par* 3
excellence.

It is a digest of good manners, morals, methods, and
means. It points to the scientific spiritual molecule, 6
pearl, and pinnacle, that everybody needs. May the
Christlikeness it reflects rest on the dear readers, and
throw the light of penetration on the page; even as the 9
dawn, kindling its glories in the east, lightens earth's
landscape.

I thank the contributors to *The Christian Science* 12
Journal for their jewels of thought, so adapted to the
hour, and without ill-humor or hyperbolic tumor. I
was impressed by the articles entitled "The New Pas- 15
tor," by Rev. Lanson P. Norcross, "The Lamp," by
Walter Church, "The Temptation," a poem by J. J.
Rome, etc. 18

The field waves its white ensign, the reapers are strong,
the rich sheaves are ripe, the storehouse is ready: pray
ye therefore the God of harvest to send forth more 21
laborers of the excellent sort, and garner the supplies
for a world.

CHURCH AND SCHOOL   24

Humbly, and, as I believe, divinely directed, I hereby
ordain the Bible, and "Science and Health with Key
to the Scriptures," to be hereafter the only pastor of 27

1 The Church of Christ, Scientist, throughout our land
and in other lands.

3   From this date the Sunday services of our denomination shall be conducted by Readers in lieu of pastors.
Each church, or society formed for Sunday worship,
6 shall elect two Readers: a male, and a female. One of
these individuals shall open the meeting by reading the
hymns, and chapter (or portion of the chapter) in the
9 Bible, lead in silent prayer, and repeat in concert with
the congregation the Lord's Prayer. Also, this First
Reader shall give out any notices from the pulpit, shall
12 read the Scriptures indicated in the Sunday School Lesson of the *Christian Science Quarterly,* and shall pronounce the benediction.

15   The First Reader shall read from my book, "Science
and Health with Key to the Scriptures," alternately in
response to the congregation, the spiritual interpreta-
18 tion of the Lord's Prayer; also, shall read all the selections from Science and Health referred to in the Sunday
Lessons.

21   The Reader of the Scriptures shall name, at each
reading, the book, chapter, and verses. The Reader of
"Science and Health with Key to the Scriptures" shall
24 commence by announcing the full title of this book, with
the name of its author, and add to this announcement,
"the Christian Science textbook." It is unnecessary to
27 repeat the title or page. This form shall also be observed
at the Communion service; the selections from both the
Bible and the Christian Science textbook shall be taken
30 from the *Quarterly,* as heretofore, and this Lesson shall
be such as is adapted to that service. On the first Sunday
of each month, except Communion Sunday, a sermon

shall be preached to the children, from selections taken 1
from the Scriptures and Science and Health, especially
adapted to the occasion, and read after the manner of 3
the Sunday service. The children's service shall be
held on the Sunday following Communion Day.

No copies from my books are allowed to be written, 6
and read from manuscripts, either in private or in public assemblies, except by their author.

Christian Scientists, all over the world, who are let- 9
terly fit and specially spiritually fitted for teachers, can
teach annually three classes only. They shall teach
from the Christian Science textbook. Each class shall 12
consist of not over thirty-three students, carefully selected,
and only of such as have promising proclivities toward
Christian Science. The teacher shall hold himself mor- 15
ally obligated to look after the welfare of his students,
not only through class term, but after it; and to watch
well that they prove sound in sentiment, health, and 18
practical Christian Science.

Teaching Christian Science shall be no question of
money, but of morals and of uplifting the race. Teachers 21
shall form associations for this purpose; and for the
first few years, convene as often as once in three months.
Teachers shall not silently mentally address the thought, 24
to handle it, nor allow their students to do thus, except
the individual needing it asks for mental treatment.
They shall steadily and patiently strive to educate their 27
students in conformity to the unerring wisdom and law
of God, and shall enjoin upon them habitually to study
His revealed Word, the Scriptures, and "Science and 30
Health with Key to the Scriptures."

They shall teach their students how to defend them-

1 selves against mental malpractice, but never to return
evil for evil; never to attack the malpractitioner, but
3 to know the truth that makes free, — and so to be a law
not unto others, but themselves.

CLASS, PULPIT, STUDENTS' STUDENTS

6   When will you take a class in Christian Science or
speak to your church in Boston? is often asked.

I shall speak to my dear church at Boston very seldom.
9 The Mother Church must be self-sustained by God.
The date of a class in Christian Science should depend
on the fitness of things, the tide which flows heavenward,
12 the hour best for the student. Until minds become less
worldly-minded, and depart farther from the primitives
of the race, and have profited up to their present capac-
15 ity from the written word, they are not ready for the
word spoken at this date.

My juniors can tell others what they know, and turn
18 them slowly toward the haven. Imperative, accumulative, sweet demands rest on my retirement from life's
bustle. What, then, of continual recapitulation of tired
21 aphorisms and disappointed ethics; of patching breaches
widened the next hour; of pounding wisdom and love
into sounding brass; of warming marble and quench-
24 ing volcanoes! Before entering the Massachusetts Metaphysical College, had my students achieved the point
whence they could have derived most benefit from their
27 pupilage, to-day there would be on earth paragons of
Christianity, patterns of humility, wisdom, and might
for the world.

To the students whom I have not seen that ask, "May 1
I call you mother?" my heart replies, *Yes,* if you are
doing God's work. When born of Truth and Love, we 3
are all of one kindred.

The hour has struck for Christian Scientists to do their
own work; to appreciate the signs of the times; to dem- 6
onstrate self-knowledge and self-government; and to
demonstrate, as this period demands, over all sin, disease,
and death. The dear ones whom I would have great 9
pleasure in instructing, know that the door to my teaching
was shut when my College closed.

Again, it is not absolutely requisite for some people 12
to be taught in a class, for they can learn by spiritual
growth and by the study of what is written. Scarcely a
moiety, compared with the whole of the Scriptures and 15
the Christian Science textbook, is yet assimilated spiritually by the most faithful seekers; yet this assimilation is
indispensable to the progress of every Christian Scientist. 18
These considerations prompt my answers to the above
questions. Human desire is inadequate to adjust the
balance on subjects of such earnest import. These 21
words of our Master explain this hour: "What I do
thou knowest not now; but thou shalt know hereafter."

My sympathies are deeply enlisted for the students 24
of students; having already seen in many instances their
talents, culture, and singleness of purpose to uplift the
race. Such students should not pay the penalty for 27
other people's faults; and divine Love will open the
way for them. My soul abhors injustice, and loves
mercy. St. John writes: "Whom God hath sent speaketh 30
the words of God: for God giveth not the Spirit by measure unto him."

1   MY STUDENTS AND THY STUDENTS

Mine and thine are obsolete terms in absolute Christian
3 Science, wherein and whereby the universal brotherhood
of man is stated and demands to be demonstrated. I have
a large affection, not alone for my students, but for thy
6 students, — for students of the second generation. I cannot but love some of those devoted students better than
some of mine who are less lovable or Christly. This
9 natural affection for goodness must go on *ad libitum* unto
the third and fourth and final generation of those who
love God and keep His commandments. Hence the
12 following is an amendment of the paragraph on page 47 [1]
of "Retrospection and Introspection": —

Any student, having received instructions in a Primary
15 class from me, or from a loyal student of Christian Science,
and afterwards studied thoroughly "Science and Health
with Key to the Scriptures," can enter upon the gospel
18 work of teaching Christian Science, and so fulfil the command of Christ. Before entering this sacred field of labor,
the student must have studied faithfully the latest edi-
21 tions of my works, and be a good Bible scholar and a
devout, consecrated Christian.

These are the indispensable demands on all those who
24 become teachers.

UNSEEN SIN

Two points of danger beset mankind; namely, making
27 sin seem either too large or too little: if too large, we

[1] See edition of 1909.

are in the darkness of all the ages, wherein the true sense 1
of the unity of good and the unreality of evil is lost.

If good is God, even as God is good, then good and 3
evil can neither be coeval nor coequal, for God is All-in-
all. This closes the argument of aught besides Him, aught
else than good.   6

If the sense of sin is too little, mortals are in danger
of not seeing their own belief in sin, but of seeing too
keenly their neighbor's. Then they are beset with 9
egotism and hypocrisy. Here Christian Scientists must
be most watchful. Their habit of mental and audible
protest against the reality of sin, tends to make sin less 12
or more to them than to other people. They must either
be overcoming sin in themselves, or they must not lose
sight of sin; else they are self-deceived sinners of the 15
worst sort.

A WORD TO THE WISE

Will all the dear Christian Scientists accept my tender 18
greetings for the forthcoming holidays, and grant me
this request, — let the present season pass without one
gift to me.   21

Our church edifice must be built in 1894. Take thither
thy saintly offerings, and lay them in the outstretched
hand of God. The object to be won affords ample oppor- 24
tunity for the grandest achievement to which Christian
Scientists can direct attention, and feel themselves alone
among the stars.   27

No doubt must intervene between the promise and
event; faith and resolve are friends to Truth; seize them,

1 trust the divine Providence, push upward our prayer in
stone, — and God will give the benediction.

3 <center>CHRISTMAS</center>

This interesting day, crowned with the history of
Truth's idea, — its earthly advent and nativity, — is
6 especially dear to the heart of Christian Scientists; to
whom Christ's appearing in a fuller sense is so precious,
and fraught with divine benedictions for mankind.

9 The star that looked lovingly down on the manger of
our Lord, lends its resplendent light to this hour: the
light of Truth, to cheer, guide, and bless man as he
12 reaches forth for the infant idea of divine perfection
dawning upon human imperfection, — that calms man's
fears, bears his burdens, beckons him on to Truth and
15 Love and the sweet immunity these bring from sin, sickness, and death.

This polar star, fixed in the heavens of divine Science,
18 shall be the sign of his appearing who "healeth all our
diseases;" it hath traversed night, wading through
darkness and gloom, on to glory. It doth meet the
21 antagonism of error; addressing to dull ears and undis-
ciplined beliefs words of Truth and Life.

The star of Bethlehem is the star of Boston, high in
24 the zenith of Truth's domain, that looketh down on the
long night of human beliefs, to pierce the darkness and
melt into dawn.

27 The star of Bethlehem is the light of all ages; is the
light of Love, to-day christening religion undefiled, divine
Science; giving to it a new name, and the white stone in
30 token of purity and permanence.

The wise men follow this guiding star; the watchful 1
shepherd chants his welcome over the cradle of a great
truth, and saith, "Unto us a child is born," whose birth 3
is less of a miracle than eighteen centuries ago; and "his
name shall be called Wonderful, Counsellor, The mighty
God, The everlasting Father, The Prince of Peace." 6

My heart is filled with joy, that each receding year sees
the steady gain of Truth's idea in Christian Science; that
each recurring year witnesses the balance adjusted more 9
on the side of God, the supremacy of Spirit; as shown
by the triumphs of Truth over error, of health over sickness, of Life over death, and of Soul over sense. 12

"The hour cometh, and now is, when the true worshippers shall worship the Father in spirit and in truth."
"For the law of the Spirit of life in Christ Jesus hath made 15
me free from the law of sin and death." "Fear not, little
flock; for it is your Father's good pleasure to give you
the kingdom." 18

> Press on, press on! ye sons of light,
> Untiring in your holy fight,
> Still treading each temptation down, 21
> And battling for a brighter crown.

CARD

In reply to all invitations from Chicago to share the 24
hospitality of their beautiful homes at any time during
the great wonder of the world, the World's Fair, I say,
Do not expect me. I have no desire to see or to hear 27
what is to be offered upon this approaching occasion.

I have a world of wisdom and Love to contemplate,
that concerns me, and you, infinitely beyond all earthly 30

1 expositions or exhibitions. In return for your kindness,
I earnestly invite you to its contemplation with me, and
3 to preparation to behold it.

MESSAGE TO THE MOTHER CHURCH

Beloved Brethren: — People coming from a distance
6 expecting to hear me speak in The Mother Church,
are frequently disappointed. To avoid this, I may hereafter notify the Directors when I shall be present to
9 address this congregation, and the Clerk of the church
can inform correspondents. Your dual and impersonal
pastor, the Bible, and "Science and Health with Key to
12 the Scriptures," is with you; and the Life these give, the
Truth they illustrate, the Love they demonstrate, is
the great Shepherd that feedeth my flock, and leadeth
15 them "beside the still waters." By any personal presence, or word of mine, your thought must not be diverted
or diverged, your senses satisfied, or self be justified.

18   Therefore, beloved, my often-coming is unnecessary;
for, though I be present or absent, it is God that feedeth the hungry heart, that giveth grace for grace, that
21 healeth the sick and cleanseth the sinner. For this
consummation He hath given you Christian Science,
and my past poor labors and love. He hath shown you
24 the amplitude of His mercy, the justice of His judgment,
the omnipotence of His love; and this, to compensate
your zealous affection for seeking good, and for labor-
27 ing in its widening grooves from the infinitesimal to the
infinite.

CHAPTER IX

The Fruit of Spirit

AN ALLEGORY

PICTURE to yourself "a city set upon a hill," a celestial city above all clouds, in serene azure and unfathomable glory: having no temple therein, for God is the temple thereof; nor need of the sun, neither of the moon, for God doth lighten it. Then from this sacred summit behold a Stranger wending his way downward, to where a few laborers in a valley at the foot of the mountain are working and watching for his coming.

The descent and ascent are beset with peril, privation, temptation, toil, suffering. Venomous serpents hide among the rocks, beasts of prey prowl in the path, wolves in sheep's clothing are ready to devour; but the Stranger meets and masters their secret and open attacks with serene confidence.

The Stranger eventually stands in the valley at the foot of the mountain. He saith unto the patient toilers therein: "What do ye here? Would ye ascend the mountain, — climbing its rough cliffs, hushing the hissing serpents, taming the beasts of prey, — and bathe in its streams, rest in its cool grottos, and drink from its living fountains? The way winds and widens in the valley; up the hill it is straight and narrow, and few there be that find it."

1

3

6

9

12

15

18

21

24

1 His converse with the watchers and workers in the valley closes, and he makes his way into the streets of a 3 city made with hands.

Pausing at the threshold of a palatial dwelling, he knocks and waits. The door is shut. He hears the 6 sounds of festivity and mirth; youth, manhood, and age gayly tread the gorgeously tapestried parlors, dancing-halls, and banquet-rooms. But a little while, and the 9 music is dull, the wine is unsipped, the footfalls abate, the laughter ceases. Then from the window of this dwelling a face looks out, anxiously surveying him who waiteth 12 at the door.

Within this mortal mansion are adulterers, fornicators, idolaters; drunkenness, witchcraft, variance, envy, emu-15 lation, hatred, wrath, murder. Appetites and passions have so dimmed their sight that he alone who looks from that dwelling, through the clearer pane of his own heart 18 tired of sin, can see the Stranger.

Startled beyond measure at beholding him, this mortal inmate withdraws; but growing more and more troubled, 21 he seeks to leave the odious company and the cruel walls, and to find the Stranger. Stealing cautiously away from his comrades, he departs; then turns back, — he is afraid 24 to go on and to meet the Stranger. So he returns to the house, only to find the lights all wasted and the music fled. Finding no happiness within, he rushes again 27 into the lonely streets, seeking peace but finding none. Naked, hungry, athirst, this time he struggles on, and at length reaches the pleasant path of the valley at the 30 foot of the mountain, whence he may hopefully look for the reappearance of the Stranger, and receive his heavenly guidance.

The Stranger enters a massive carved stone mansion, 1
and saith unto the dwellers therein, "Blessed are the
poor in spirit: for theirs is the kingdom of heaven." But 3
they understand not his saying.

These are believers of different sects, and of no sect;
some, so-called Christian Scientists in sheep's clothing; 6
and all "drunken without wine." They have small conceptions of spiritual riches, few cravings for the immortal,
but are puffed up with the applause of the world: they 9
have plenty of pelf, and fear not to fall upon the Stranger,
seize his pearls, throw them away, and afterwards try to
kill him. 12

Somewhat disheartened, he patiently seeks another
dwelling, — only to find its inmates asleep at noontide!
Robust forms, with manly brow nodding on cushioned 15
chairs, their feet resting on footstools, or, flat on their
backs, lie stretched on the floor, dreaming away the
hours. Balancing on one foot, with eyes half open, 18
the porter starts up in blank amazement and looks at
the Stranger, calls out, rubs his eyes, — amazed beyond
measure that anybody is animated with a purpose, and 21
seen working for it!

They in this house are those that "provoke Him in
the wilderness, and grieve Him in the desert." Away 24
from this charnel-house of the so-called living, the Stranger
turns quickly, and wipes off the dust from his feet as a
testimony against sensualism in its myriad forms. As 27
he departs, he sees robbers finding ready ingress to that
dwelling of sleepers in the midst of murderous hordes,
without watchers and the doors unbarred! 30

Next he enters a place of worship, and saith unto them,
"Go ye into all the world; preach the gospel, heal the

1 sick, cast out devils, raise the dead; for the Scripture
saith the law of the Spirit of life in Christ Jesus hath
3 made you free from the law of sin and death." And *they
cast him out.*

Once more he seeks the dwelling-place of mortals and
6 knocks loudly. The door is burst open, and sufferers
shriek for help: that house is on fire! The flames caught
in the dwelling of luxury, where the blind saw them not,
9 but the flesh at length did feel them; thence they spread
to the house of slumberers who heeded them not, until
they became unmanageable; fed by the fat of hypocrisy
12 and vainglory, they consumed the next dwelling; then
crept unseen into the synagogue, licking up the blood
of martyrs and wrapping their altars in ruins. "God is a
15 consuming fire."

Thus are all mortals, under every hue of circumstances,
driven out of their houses of clay and, homeless wan-
18 derers in a beleaguered city, forced to seek the Father's
house, if they would be led to the valley and up the
mount.

21   Seeing the wisdom of withdrawing from those who
persistently rejected him, the Stranger returned to the
valley; first, to meet with joy his own, to wash their
24 feet, and take them up the mountain. Well might this
heavenly messenger exclaim, "O Jerusalem, Jerusalem,
thou that killest the prophets, and stonest them which
27 are sent unto thee, . . . Behold, your house is left unto
you desolate."

Discerning in his path the penitent one who had groped
30 his way from the dwelling of luxury, the Stranger saith
unto him, "Wherefore comest thou hither?"

He answered, "The sight of thee unveiled my sins, and

turned my misnamed joys to sorrow. When I went back
into the house to take something out of it, my misery
increased; so I came hither, hoping that I might follow
thee whithersoever thou goest."

And the Stranger saith unto him, "Wilt thou climb
the mountain, and take nothing of thine own with thee?"

He answered, "I will."

"Then," saith the Stranger, "thou hast chosen the
good part; follow me."

Many there were who had entered the valley to speculate in worldly policy, religion, politics, finance, and to
search for wealth and fame. These had heavy baggage
of their own, and insisted upon taking all of it with them,
which must greatly hinder their ascent.

The journey commences. The encumbered travellers
halt and disagree. They stoutly belay those who, having less baggage, ascend faster than themselves, and
betimes burden them with their own. Despairing of
gaining the summit, loaded as they are, they conclude to
stop and lay down a few of the heavy weights, — but
only to take them up again, more than ever determined
not to part with their baggage.

All this time the Stranger is pointing the way, showing them their folly, rebuking their pride, consoling their
afflictions, and helping them on, saying, "He that loseth
his life for my sake, shall find it."

Obstinately holding themselves back, and sore-footed,
they fall behind and lose sight of their guide; when,
stumbling and grumbling, and fighting each other, they
plunge headlong over the jagged rocks.

Then he who has no baggage goes back and kindly
binds up their wounds, wipes away the blood stains, and

1 would help them on; but suddenly the Stranger shouts, "Let them alone; they must learn from the things they 3 suffer. Make thine own way; and if thou strayest, listen for the mountain-horn, and it will call thee back to the path that goeth upward."

6   Dear reader, dost thou suspect that the valley is humility, that the mountain is heaven-crowned Christianity, and the Stranger the ever-present Christ, the spiritual 9 idea which from the summit of bliss surveys the vale of the flesh, to burst the bubbles of earth with a breath of heaven, and acquaint sensual mortals with the mystery 12 of godliness, — unchanging, unquenchable Love? Hast not thou heard this Christ knock at the door of thine own heart, and closed it against Truth, to "eat and drink 15 with the drunken"? Hast thou been driven by suffering to the foot of the mount, but earth-bound, burdened by pride, sin, and self, hast thou turned back, stumbled, 18 and wandered away? Or hast thou tarried in the habitation of the senses, pleased and stupefied, until wakened through the baptism of fire?

21   He alone ascends the hill of Christian Science who follows the Way-shower, the spiritual presence and idea of God. Whatever obstructs the way, — causing to 24 stumble, fall, or faint, those mortals who are striving to enter the path, — divine Love will remove; and uplift the fallen and strengthen the weak. Therefore, give 27 up thy earth-weights; and observe the apostle's admonition, "Forgetting those things which are behind, and reaching forth unto those which are before." Then, 30 loving God supremely and thy neighbor as thyself, thou wilt safely bear thy cross up to the throne of everlasting glory.

VOICES OF SPRING   1

Mine is an obstinate *penchant* for nature in all her
moods and forms, a satisfaction with whatever is hers. 3
And what shall this be named, a weakness, or a —
virtue?

In spring, nature like a thrifty housewife sets the earth 6
in order; and between taking up the white carpets and
putting down the green ones, her various apartments are
dismally dirty.   9

Spring is my sweetheart, whose voices are sad or glad,
even as the heart may be; restoring in memory the sweet
rhythm of unforgotten harmonies, or touching tenderly 12
its tearful tones.

Spring passes over mountain and meadow, waking up
the world; weaving the wavy grass, nursing the timid 15
spray, stirring the soft breeze; rippling all nature in
ceaseless flow, with "breath all odor and cheek all bloom."
Whatever else droops, spring is gay: her little feet trip 18
lightly on, turning up the daisies, paddling the water-
cresses, rocking the oriole's cradle; challenging the sed-
entary shadows to activity, and the streams to race for the 21
sea. Her dainty fingers put the fur cap on pussy-willow,
paint in pink the petals of arbutus, and sweep in soft
strains her Orphean lyre. "The voice of the turtle is 24
heard in our land." The snow-bird that tarried through
the storm, now chirps to the breeze; the cuckoo sounds
her invisible lute, calling the feathered tribe back to their 27
summer homes. Old robin, though stricken to the heart
with winter's snow, prophesies of fair earth and sunny
skies. The brooklet sings melting murmurs to merry 30

1 meadows; the leaves clap their hands, and the winds make melody through dark pine groves.

3   What is the anthem of human life?

Has love ceased to moan over the new-made grave, and, looking upward, does it patiently pray for the per-
6 petual springtide wherein no arrow wounds the dove? Human hope and faith should join in nature's grand harmony, and, if on minor key, make music in the heart.
9 And man, more friendly, should call his race as gently to the springtide of Christ's dear love. St. Paul wrote, "Rejoice in the Lord always." And why not, since man's
12 possibilities are infinite, bliss is eternal, and the consciousness thereof is here and now?

The alders bend over the streams to shake out their
15 tresses in the water-mirrors; let mortals bow before the creator, and, looking through Love's transparency, behold man in God's own image and likeness, arranging in the
18 beauty of holiness each budding thought. It is good to talk with our past hours, and learn what report they bear, and how they might have reported more spirit-
21 ual growth. With each returning year, higher joys, holier aims, a purer peace and diviner energy, should freshen the fragrance of being. Nature's first and last
24 lessons teach man to be kind, and even pride should sanction what our natures need. Popularity, — what is it? A mere mendicant that boasts and begs, and God
27 denies charity.

When gentle violet lifts its blue eye to heaven, and crown imperial unveils its regal splendor to the sun;
30 when the modest grass, inhabiting the whole earth, stoops meekly before the blast; when the patient corn waits on the elements to put forth its slender blade, construct

the stalk, instruct the ear, and crown the full corn in the 1
ear, — then, are mortals looking up, waiting on God,
and committing their way unto Him who tosses earth's 3
mass of wonders into their hands? When downtrodden
like the grass, did it make them humble, loving, obedient, full of good odor, and cause them to wait patiently 6
on God for man's rich heritage, — "dominion over all
the earth"? Thus abiding in Truth, the warmth and
sunlight of prayer and praise and understanding will 9
ripen the fruits of Spirit, and goodness will have its springtide of freedom and greatness.

When the white-winged dove feeds her callow brood, 12
nestles them under her wings, and, in tones tremulous
with tenderness, calls them to her breast, do mortals
remember *their* cradle hymns, and thank God for those 15
redemptive words from a mother's lips which taught
them the Lord's Prayer?

O gentle presence, peace and joy and power;   18
O Life divine, that owns each waiting hour;
Thou Love that guards the nestling's faltering flight!
Keep Thou my child on upward wing to-night.   21

Midst the falling leaves of old-time faiths, above the
frozen crust of creed and dogma, the divine Mind-force,
filling all space and having all power, upheaves the earth. 24
In sacred solitude divine Science evolved nature as thought,
and thought as things. This supreme potential Principle
reigns in the realm of the real, and is "God with us," 27
the I AM.

As mortals awake from their dream of material sensation, this adorable, all-inclusive God, and all earth's 30
hieroglyphics of Love, are understood; and infinite Mind

1 is seen kindling the stars, rolling the worlds, reflecting all space and Life, — but not life in matter. Wisely
3 governing, informing the universe, this Mind is Truth, — not laws of matter. Infinitely just, merciful, and wise, this Mind is Love, — but not fallible love.

6 Spring is here! and doors that closed on Christian Science in "the long winter of our discontent," are open flung. Its seedtime has come to enrich earth and en-
9 robe man in righteousness; may its sober-suited autumn follow with hues of heaven, ripened sheaves, and harvest songs.

12   "WHERE ART THOU?"

In the allegory of Genesis, third chapter and ninth verse, two mortals, walking in the cool of the day midst
15 the stately palms, many-hued blossoms, perfume-laden breezes, and crystal streams of the Orient, pondered the things of man and God.

18 A sense of evil is supposed to have spoken, been listened to, and afterwards to have formed an evil sense that blinded the eyes of reason, masked with deformity the
21 glories of revelation, and shamed the face of mortals.

What was this sense? Error versus Truth: first, a supposition; second, a false belief; third, suffering;
24 fourth, death.

Is man the supposer, false believer, sufferer?

Not man, but a mortal — the antipode of immortal
27 man. Supposing, false believing, suffering are not faculties of Mind, but are qualities of error.

The supposition is, that God and His idea are not all-
30 power; that there is something besides Him; that this

something is intelligent matter; that sin — yea, self- 1
hood — is apart from God, where pleasure and pain,
good and evil, life and death, commingle, and are for- 3
ever at strife; even that every ray of Truth, of infinity,
omnipotence, omnipresence, goodness, could be absorbed
in error! God cannot be obscured, and this renders error 6
a palpable falsity, yea, nothingness; on the basis that
black is not a color because it absorbs all the rays of
light. 9

The "Alpha and Omega" of Christian Science voices
this question: Where do we hold intelligence to be? Is
it in both evil and good, in matter as well as Spirit? 12
If so, we are literally and practically denying that God,
good, is supreme, *all* power and presence, and are turning away from the only living and true God, to "lords 15
many and gods many."

Where art thou, O mortal! who turnest away from
the divine source of being, — calling on matter to work 18
out the problem of Mind, to aid in understanding and
securing the sweet harmonies of Spirit that relate to the
universe, including man? 21

Paul asked: "What communion hath light with darkness? And what concord hath Christ with Belial?" The
worshippers of Baal worshipped the sun. They believed 24
that something besides God had authority and power,
could heal and bless; that God wrought through matter
— by means of that which does not reflect Him in a single 27
quality or quantity! — the grand realities of Mind, thus
to exemplify the power of Truth and Love.

The ancient Chaldee hung his destiny out upon the 30
heavens; but ancient or modern Christians, instructed in
divine Science, know that the prophet better understood

1 Him who said: "He doeth according to His will in the
army of heaven, and among the inhabitants of the earth;
3 and none can stay His hand, or say unto Him, What doest
Thou?"

Astrology is well in its place, but this place is second-
6 ary.   Necromancy has no foundation, — in fact, no
intelligence; and the belief that it has, deceives itself.
Whatever simulates power and Truth in matter, does this
9 as a lie declaring itself, that mortals' faith in matter may
have the effect of power; but when the whole fabrication
is found to be a lie, away goes all its supposed power and
12 prestige.

Why do Christian Scientists treat disease *as* disease,
since there is no disease?
15   This is done only as one gives the lie to a lie; because
it is a lie, without one word of Truth in it.   You must
find error to be *nothing:* then, and *only* then, do you
18 handle it in Science.   The diabolism of suppositional
evil at work in the name of good, is a lie of the highest
degree of nothingness: just reduce this falsity to its proper
21 denomination, and you have done with it.

How shall we treat a negation, or error — by means
of matter, or Mind?   Is matter Truth?   No!   Then it
24 cannot antidote error.

Can belief destroy belief?   No: understanding is required to do this.   By the substitution of Truth demon-
27 strated, Science remedies the ills of material beliefs.

Because I have uncovered evil, and dis-covered for
you divine Science, which saith, "Be not overcome of
30 evil, but overcome evil with good," and you have not
loved sufficiently to understand this Golden Rule and
demonstrate the might of perfect Love that casteth out

all fear, shall you turn away from this divine Principle 1
to graven images? Remember the Scripture: —

"But and if that evil servant shall say in his heart, 3
My lord delayeth his coming;

"And shall begin to smite his fellow-servants, and to
eat and drink with the drunken; 6

"The lord of that servant shall come in a day when
he looketh not for him, and in an hour that he is not
aware of, 9

"And shall cut him asunder, and appoint him his portion with the hypocrites."

One mercilessly assails me for opposing the subtle lie, 12
others charge upon me with full-fledged invective for, as
they say, having too much charity; but neither moves
me from the path made luminous by divine Love. 15

In my public works I lay bare the ability, in belief, of
evil to break the Decalogue, — to murder, steal, commit
adultery, and so on. Those who deny my wisdom or 18
right to expose error, are either willing participants in
wrong, afraid of its supposed power, or ignorant of it.

The notion that one is covering iniquity by asserting 21
its nothingness, is a fault of zealots, who, like Peter,
sleep when the Watcher bids them watch, and when the
hour of trial comes would cut off somebody's ears. Such 24
people say, "Would you have me get out of a burning
house, or stay in it?"

I would have you already out, and *know* that you are 27
out; also, to remember the Scripture concerning those
who do evil that good may come, — "whose damnation
is just;" and that whoso departeth from divine Science, 30
seeking power or good aside from God, has done himself
harm.

1 Mind is supreme: Love is the master of hate; Truth, the victor over a lie. Hath not Science voiced this les-
3 son to you, — that evil is powerless, that a lie is never true? It is your province to wrestle with error, to handle the serpent and bruise its head; but you cannot, as a
6 Christian Scientist, resort to stones and clubs, — yea, to matter, — to kill the serpent of a material mind.

Do you love that which represents God most, His high-
9 est idea as seen to-day? No!

Then you would hate Jesus if you saw him personally, and knew your right obligations towards him. He would
12 insist on the rule and demonstration of divine Science: even that you first cast out your own dislike and hatred of God's idea, — the beam in your own eye that hinders
15 your seeing clearly how to cast the mote of evil out of other eyes. You cannot demonstrate the Principle of Christian Science and not love its idea: we gather not
18 grapes of thorns, nor figs of thistles.

Where art thou?

DIVINE SCIENCE

21 What is it but another name for Christian Science, the cognomen of all true religion, the quintessence of Christianity, that heals disease and sin and destroys
24 death! Part and parcel of Truth and Love, wherever one ray of its effulgence looks in upon the heart, behold a better man, woman, or child.

27 Science is the fiat of divine intelligence, which, hoary with eternity, touches time only to take away its frailty. That it rests on everlasting foundations, the sequence
30 proves.

Have I discovered and founded at this period Chris- 1
tian Science, that which reveals the truth of Love, — is
the question. 3

And how can you be certain of so momentous an
affirmative? By proving its effect on yourself to be —
divine. 6

What is the Principle and rule of Christian Science?

Infinite query! Wonder in heaven and on earth, —
who shall say? The immaculate Son of the Blessed 9
has spoken of them as the Golden Rule and its Principle,
God who is Love. Listen, and *he* illustrates the rule:
"Jesus called a little child unto him, and set him in the 12
midst of them, and said, . . . Whosoever . . . shall
humble himself as this little child, the same is greatest
in the kingdom of heaven." 15

Harmony is heaven. Science brings out harmony;
but this harmony is not understood unless it produces a
growing affection for all good, and consequent disaffec- 18
tion for all evil, hypocrisy, evil-speaking, lust, envy, hate.
Where these exist, Christian Science has no sure foothold: they obscure its divine element, and thus seem 21
to extinguish it. Even the life of Jesus was belittled
and belied by personalities possessing these defacing de-
formities. Only the devout Marys, and such as lived 24
according to his precepts, understood the concrete character of him who taught — by the wayside, in humble
homes, to itching ears and to dull disciples — the words 27
of Life.

The ineffable Life and light which he reflected through
divine Science is again reproduced in the character which 30
sensualism, as heretofore, would hide or besmear. Sin
of any sort tends to hide from an individual this grand

1 verity in Science, that the appearing of good in an individual involves the disappearing of evil. He who first
3 brings to humanity some great good, must have gained
its height beforehand, to be able to lift others toward
it. I first proved to myself, not by "words," — these
6 afford no proof, — but by demonstration of Christian
Science, that its Principle is divine. All must go and do
likewise.

9   Faith illumined by works; the spiritual understanding
which cannot choose but to labor and love; hope holding steadfastly to good in the midst of seething evil;
12 charity that suffereth long and is kind, but cancels not
sin until it be destroyed, — these afford the only rule I
have found which demonstrates Christian Science.

15   And remember, a pure faith in humanity will subject
one to deception; the uses of good, to abuses from evil;
and calm strength will enrage evil. But the very heavens
18 shall laugh at them, and move majestically to your defense when the armies of earth press hard upon you.

<blockquote>
"Thou must be true thyself,
    If thou the truth wouldst teach;
Thy soul must overflow, if thou
    Another's soul wouldst reach;
It needs the overflow of heart,
    To give the lips full speech.
</blockquote>

<blockquote>
"Think truly, and thy thoughts
    Shall the world's famine feed;
Speak truly, and each word of thine
    Shall be a fruitful seed;
Live truly, and thy life shall be
    A great and noble creed."
</blockquote>

FIDELITY

If people would confine their talk to subjects that are profitable, that which St. John informs us took place once in heaven, would happen very frequently on earth, — silence for the space of half an hour.

Experience is victor, never the vanquished; and out of defeat comes the secret of victory. That to-morrow starts from to-day and is one day beyond it, robes the future with hope's rainbow hues.

In the battle of life, good is made more industrious and persistent because of the supposed activity of evil. The elbowing of the crowd plants our feet more firmly. In the mental collisions of mortals and the strain of intellectual wrestlings, moral tension is tested, and, if it yields not, grows stronger. The past admonishes us: with finger grim and cold it points to every mortal mistake; or smiling saith, "Thou hast been faithful over a few things."

Art thou a child, and hast added one furrow to the brow of care? Art thou a husband, and hast pierced the heart venturing its all of happiness to thy keeping? Art thou a wife, and hast bowed the o'erburdened head of thy husband? Hast thou a friend, and forgettest to be grateful? Remember, that for all this thou alone canst and must atone. Carelessly or remorselessly thou mayest have sent along the ocean of events a wave that will some time flood thy memory, surge dolefully at the door of conscience, and pour forth the unavailing tear.

Change and the grave may part us; the wisdom that might have blessed the past may come too late. One

1 backward step, one relinquishment of right in an evil
hour, one faithless tarrying, has torn the laurel from many
3 a brow and repose from many a heart. Good is never
the reward of evil, and *vice versa.*

There is no excellence without labor; and the time to
6 work, is *now.* Only by persistent, unremitting, straightforward toil; by turning neither to the right nor to the
left, seeking no other pursuit or pleasure than that which
9 cometh from God, can you win and wear the crown of the
faithful.

That law-school is not at fault which sends forth a
12 barrister who never brings out a brief. Why? Because
he followed agriculture instead of litigation, forsook
Blackstone for gray stone, dug into soils instead of delv-
15 ing into suits, raised potatoes instead of pleas, and drew
up logs instead of leases. He has not been faithful over
a few things.

18   Is a musician made by his teacher? He makes himself a musician by practising what he was taught. The
conscientious are successful. They follow faithfully;
21 through evil or through good report, they work on to the
achievement of good; by patience, they inherit the promise. Be active, and, however slow, thy success is sure:
24 toil is triumph; and — thou hast been faithful over a few
things.

The lives of great men and women are miracles of pa-
27 tience and perseverance. Every luminary in the constel-
lation of human greatness, like the stars, comes out in
the darkness to shine with the reflected light of God.

30   Material philosophy, human ethics, scholastic theology,
and physics have not sufficiently enlightened mankind.
Human wrong, sickness, sin, and death still appear in

mortal belief, and they never bring out the right action 1
of mind or body. When will the whole human race have
one God, — an undivided affection that leaves the unreal 3
material basis of things, for the spiritual foundation and
superstructure that is real, right, and eternal?

First purify thought, then put thought into words, 6
and words into deeds; and after much slipping and
clambering, you will go up the scale of Science to the
second rule, and be made ruler over many things. Fidelity 9
finds its reward and its strength in exalted purpose. Seeking is not sufficient whereby to arrive at the results of
Science: you must strive; and the glory of the strife 12
comes of honesty and humility.

Do human hopes deceive? is joy a trembler? Then,
weary pilgrim, unloose the latchet of thy sandals; for the 15
place whereon thou standest is sacred. By that, you may
know you are parting with a material sense of life and
happiness to win the spiritual sense of good. O learn to 18
lose with God! and you find Life eternal: you gain all.
To doubt this is implicit treason to divine decree.

The parable of "the ten virgins" serves to illustrate 21
the evil of inaction and delay. This parable is drawn
from the sad history of Vesta, — a little girl of eight
years, who takes the most solemn vow of celibacy for thirty 24
years, and is subject to terrible torture if the lamp she
tends is not replenished with oil day and night, so that the
flame never expires. The moral of the parable is pointed, 27
and the diction purely Oriental.

We learn from this parable that neither the cares of
this world nor the so-called pleasures or pains of mate- 30
rial sense are adequate to plead for the neglect of spiritual
light, that must be tended to keep aglow the flame of

1 devotion whereby to enter into the joy of divine Science demonstrated.

3   The foolish virgins had no oil in their lamps: their way was material; thus they were in doubt and darkness. They heeded not their sloth, their fading warmth 6 of action; hence the steady decline of spiritual light, until, the midnight gloom upon them, they must borrow the better-tended lamps of the faithful. By entering 9 the guest-chamber of Truth, and beholding the bridal of Life and Love, they would be wedded to a higher understanding of God. Each moment's fair expect- 12 ancy was to behold the bridegroom, the One "altogether lovely."

It was midnight: darkness profound brooded over 15 earth's lazy sleepers. With no oil in their lamps, no spiritual illumination to look upon him whom they had pierced, they heard the shout, "The bridegroom cometh!" 18 But how could they behold him? Hear that human cry: "Oh, lend us your oil! our lamps have gone out, — no light! earth's fables flee, and heaven is afar 21 off."

The door is shut. The wise virgins had no oil to spare, and they said to the foolish, "Go to them that sell, and 24 buy for yourselves." Seek Truth, and pursue it. It should cost you something: you are willing to pay for error and receive nothing in return; but if you pay the price of 27 Truth, you shall receive *all*.

"The children of this world are in their generation wiser than the children of light;" they watch the market, 30 acquaint themselves with the etiquette of the exchange, and are ready for the next move. How much more should we be faithful over the few things of Spirit, that are able

to make us wise unto salvation! Let us watch and pray 1
that we enter not into the temptation of ease in sin; and
let us not forget that others before us have laid upon the 3
altar all that we have to sacrifice, and have passed to
their reward. Too soon we cannot turn from disease
in the body to find disease in the mortal mind, and its cure, 6
in working for God. Thought must be made better, and
human life more fruitful, for the divine energy to move
it onward and upward. 9

Warmed by the sunshine of Truth, watered by the
heavenly dews of Love, the fruits of Christian Science
spring upward, and away from the sordid soil of self and 12
matter. Are we clearing the gardens of thought by uprooting the noxious weeds of passion, malice, envy, and
strife? Are we picking away the cold, hard pebbles of 15
selfishness, uncovering the secrets of sin and burnishing
anew the hidden gems of Love, that their pure perfection
shall appear? Are we feeling the vernal freshness and 18
sunshine of enlightened faith?

The weeds of mortal mind are not always destroyed
by the first uprooting; they reappear, like devastating 21
witch-grass, to choke the coming clover. O stupid gar-
dener! watch their reappearing, and tear them away from
their native soil, until no seedling be left to propagate — 24
and rot.

Among the manifold soft chimes that will fill the haunted
chambers of memory, this is the sweetest: "Thou hast 27
been faithful!"

1   TRUE PHILOSOPHY AND COMMUNION

It is related of Justin Martyr that, hearing of a Pythag-
3 orean professor of ethics, he expressed the wish to become one of his disciples. "Very well," the teacher
replied; "but have you studied music, astronomy, and
6 geometry, and do you think it possible for you to understand aught of that which leads to bliss, without having mastered the sciences that disengage the soul from
9 objects of sense, so rendering it a fit habitation for
the intelligences?" On Justin's confessing that he had
not studied those branches, he was dismissed by the
12 professor.

Alas for such a material science of life! Of what
avail would geometry be to a poor sinner struggling with
15 temptation, or to a man with the smallpox?

Ancient and modern philosophies are spoiled by lack
of Science. They would place Soul wholly inside of body,
18 intelligence in matter; and from error of premise would
seek a correct conclusion. Such philosophy can never
demonstrate the Science of Life, — the Science which
21 Paul understood when he spoke of willingness "to be
absent from the body, and present with the Lord." Such
philosophy is far from the rules of the mighty Nazarene
24 Prophet. His words, living in our hearts, were these:
"Whosoever shall not receive the kingdom of God as
a little child, shall in no wise enter therein." Not through
27 astronomy did he point out the way to heaven and the
reign of harmony.

We need the spirit of St. Paul, when he stood on Mars'
30 hill at Athens, bringing Christianity for the first time

into Europe. The Spirit bestows spiritual gifts, God's 1
presence and providence. St. Paul stood where Socrates
had stood four hundred years before, defending himself 3
against the charge of atheism; in the place where De-
mosthenes had pleaded for freedom in immortal strains
of eloquence.   6

We need the spirit of the pious Polycarp, who, when
the proconsul said to him, "I will set the beasts upon
you, unless you yield your religion," replied: "Let them 9
come; I cannot change from good to bad." Then they
bound him to the stake, set fire to the fagots, and his
pure and strong faith rose higher through the baptism 12
of flame.

Methinks the infidel was blind who said, "Christianity
is fit only for women and weak men;" but even infidels 15
may disagree. Bonaparte declared, "Ever since the
reign of Christianity began the loftiest intellects have had
a practical faith in God." Daniel Webster said, "My 18
heart has always assured and reassured me that Christianity must be a divine reality."

To turn the popular indignation against an advanced 21
form of religion, the pagan slanderers affirmed that
Christians took their infants to a place of worship in
order to offer them in sacrifice, — a baptism not of 24
water but of blood, thus distorting or misapprehending
the purpose of Christian sacraments. Christians met
in midnight feasts in the early days, and talked of the 27
crucified Saviour; thence arose the rumor that it was
a part of Christian worship to kill and eat a human
being.   30

Really, Christianity turned men away from the thought
of fleshly sacrifice, and directed them to spiritual attain-

1 ments. Life, not death, was and is the very centre of
its faith. Christian Science carries this thought even
3 higher, and insists on the demonstration of moral and
spiritual healing as eminent proof that God is understood
and illustrated.

6   ORIGIN OF EVIL

The origin of evil is the problem of ages. It confronts
each generation anew. It confronts Christian Science.
9 The question is often asked, If God created only the
good, whence comes the evil?

To this question Christian Science replies: Evil never
12 did exist as an entity. It is but a belief that there is an
opposite intelligence to God. This belief is a species of
idolatry, and is not more true or real than that an image
15 graven on wood or stone is God.

The mortal admission of the reality of evil perpetuates
faith in evil; and the Scriptures declare that "to whom
18 ye yield yourselves servants to obey, his servants ye
are." This leading, self-evident proposition of Christian
Science, that, good being real, its opposite is necessarily
21 unreal, needs to be grasped in all its divine requirements.

TRUTH VERSUS ERROR

"A word fitly spoken is like apples of gold in pictures
24 of silver." It is a rule in Christian Science never to repeat error unless it becomes requisite to bring out Truth.
Then lift the curtain, let in the light, and countermand

this first command of Solomon, "Answer not a fool accord- 1
ing to his folly, lest thou also be like unto him."

A distant rumbling and quivering of the earth foretell 3
the internal action of pent-up gas. To avoid danger from
this source people have to escape from their houses to the
open space. A conical cloud, hanging like a horoscope 6
in the air, foreshadows a cyclone. To escape from this
calamity people prepare shelter in caves of the earth.

They who discern the face of the skies cannot always 9
discern the mental signs of these times, and peer through
the opaque error. Where my vision begins and is clear,
theirs grows indistinct and ends. 12

There are diversities of operation by the same spirit.
Two individuals, with all the goodness of generous natures, advise me. One says, Go this way; the other 15
says, Take the opposite direction! Between the two I
stand still; or, accepting the premonition of one of them,
I follow his counsel, take a few steps, then halt. A true 18
sense not unfamiliar has been awakened. I see the way
now. The guardians of His presence go before me. I
enter the path. It may be smooth, or it may be rugged; 21
but it is always straight and narrow; and if it be up-
hill all the way, the ascent is easy and the summit can
be gained. 24

God is responsible for the mission of those whom He
has anointed. Those who know no will but His take
His hand, and from the night He leads to light. None 27
can say unto Him, What doest Thou?

The Christian Science Journal was the oldest and
only authenticated organ of Christian Science up to 30
1898. Loyal Scientists are targets for envy, rivalry,
slander; and whoever hits this mark is well paid by the

1 umpire. But the Scientists aim highest. They press forward towards the mark of a high calling. They recog-
3 nize the claims of the law and the gospel. They know that whatsoever a man soweth, that shall he reap. They infringe neither the books nor the business of others; and
6 with hearts overflowing with love for God, they help on the brotherhood of men. It is not *mine* but *Thine* they seek.

When God bids one uncover iniquity, in order to
9 exterminate it, one should lay it bare; and divine Love will bless this endeavor and those whom it reaches. "Nothing is hid that shall not be revealed."
12 It is only a question of time when God shall reveal His rod, and show the plan of battle. Error, left to itself, accumulates. Hence, Solomon's transverse command:
15 "Answer a fool according to his folly, lest he be wise in his own conceit."

To quench the growing flames of falsehood, once in
18 about seven years I have to repeat this, — that I use no drugs whatever, not even coffea (coffee), thea (tea), capsicum (red pepper); though every day, and especially at
21 dinner, I indulge in homœopathic doses of *Natrum muriaticum* (common salt).

When I found myself under this new *régime* of medi-
24 cine, the medicine of Mind, I wanted to satisfy my curiosity as to the effect of drugs on one who had lost all faith in them. Hence I tried several doses of medicine,
27 and so proved to myself that drugs have no beneficial effect on an individual in a proper state of mind.

I have by no means encouraged students of the Massa-
30 chusetts Metaphysical College to enter medical schools, and afterwards denied this and objected to their entering those schools. A student who consulted me on this sub-

ject, received my consent and even the offer of pecuniary 1
assistance to take lessons outside of my College, provided
he received these lessons of a certain regular-school physi- 3
cian, whose instructions included about twelve lessons,
three weeks' time, and the surgical part of midwifery. I
have students with the degree of M. D., who are skilful 6
obstetricians. Such a course with such a teacher would
not necessitate essential materialization of a student's
thought, nor detract from the metaphysical mode of 9
obstetrics taught in my College.

This student had taken the above-named course in
obstetrics when he consulted me on the feasibility of enter- 12
ing a medical school; and to this I objected on the ground
that it was inconsistent with Christian Science, which he
claimed to be practising; but I was willing, and said 15
so, that, notwithstanding my objection, he should do as
he deemed best, for I claim no jurisdiction over any students. He entered the medical school, and several other 18
students with him. My counsel to all of them was in
substance the same as the foregoing, and some of these
students have openly acknowledged this. 21

In answer to a question on the following subject, I
will state that I preached four years, and built up the
church, before I would accept the slightest remuneration. 24
When the church had sufficient members and means to
pay a salary, and refused to give me up or to receive my
gratuitous services, I accepted, for a time, fifteen dollars 27
each Sunday when I preached. I never received more
than this; and the contributions, when I preached,
doubled that amount. I have accepted no pay from my 30
church for about three years, and believe that I have
put into the church-fund about two thousand dollars of

1 my own contributions. I hold receipts for $1,489.50 paid in, and the balance was never receipted for.

3   I temporarily organized a secret society known as the P. M., the workings whereof were not "terrible and too shocking to relate." By and with advice of the very 6 student who brings up the question of this society, it was formed. The P. M. (Private Meeting) Society met only twice. The first subject given out for considera- 9 tion was this: "There is no Animal Magnetism." There was no advice given, no mental work, and there were no transactions at those meetings which I would hesi- 12 tate to have known. On the contrary, our deliberations were, as usual, Christian, and like my public instruction. The second P. M. convened in about one week from the 15 first. The subject given out at that meeting was, in substance, "God is All; there is none beside Him." This proved to be our last meeting. I dissolved the society, 18 and we have not met since. If harm could come from the consideration of these two topics, it was because of the misconception of those subjects in the mind that 21 handled them. An individual state of mind sometimes occasions effects on patients which are not in harmony with Science and the soundness of the argument used. 24 Hence it prevents the normal action, and the benefit that would otherwise accrue.

I issue no arguments, and cause none to be used in 27 mental practice, which consign people to suffering. On the contrary, I cannot serve two masters; therefore I teach the use of such arguments only as promote health 30 and spiritual growth. My life, consecrated to humanity through nameless suffering and sacrifice, furnishes its own proof of my practice.

I have sometimes called on students to test their ability 1
and meet the mental malpractice, so as to lift the burdens
imposed by students. 3

The fact is, that for want of time, and for the purpose
of blessing even my enemies, I neglect myself. I never
have practised by arguments which, perverted, are the 6
weapons of the silent mental malpractice. I have no skill
in occultism; and I could not if I would, and would not
if I could, harm any one through the mental method of 9
Mind-healing, or in any manner.

The late much-ado-about-nothing arose solely from
mental malicious practice, and the audible falsehood 12
designed to stir up strife between brethren, for the purpose
of placing Christian Science in the hands of aspirants
for place and power. These repeated attempts of mad 15
ambition may retard our Cause, but they never can place
it in the wrong hands and hold it there, nor benefit
mankind by such endeavors. 18

FALLIBILITY OF HUMAN CONCEPTS

Evil counterfeits good: it says, "I am Truth," though
it is a lie; it says, "I am Love," — but Love is spirit- 21
ual, and sensuous love is material, wherefore it is hate
instead of Love; for the five senses give to mortals pain,
sickness, sin, and death, — pleasure that is false, life that 24
leads unto death, joy that becomes sorrow. Love that is
not the procurator of happiness, declares itself the antipode of Love; and Love divine punishes the joys of this 27
false sense of love, chastens its affection, purifies it, and
turns it into the opposite channels.

Material life is the antipode of spiritual life; it mocks 30

1 the bliss of spiritual being; it is bereft of permanence and
peace.

3   When human sense is quickened to behold aright the
error, — the error of regarding Life, Truth, Love as
material and not spiritual, or as both material and spir-
6 itual, — it is able for the first time to discern the Science
of good.   But it must first see the error of its present
erroneous course, to be able to behold the facts of Truth
9 outside of the error; and, *vice versa,* when it discovers
the truth, this uncovers the error and quickens the true
consciousness of God, good.   May the human shadows of
12 thought lengthen as they approach the light, until they
are lost in light and no night is there!

In Science, sickness is healed upon the same Principle
15 and by the same rule that sin is healed.   To know the
supposed bodily belief of the patient and what has claimed
to produce it, enables the practitioner to act more under-
18 standingly in destroying this belief.   Thus it is in healing the moral sickness; the malicious mental operation
must be understood in order to enable one to destroy
21 it and its effects.   There is not sufficient spiritual power
in the human thought to heal the sick or the sinful.
Through the divine energies alone one must either get
24 out of himself and into God so far that his consciousness
is the reflection of the divine, or he must, through argument and the human consciousness of both evil and good,
27 overcome evil.

The only difference between the healing of sin and the
healing of sickness is, that sin must be *un*covered before
30 it can be destroyed, and the moral sense be aroused to
reject the sense of error; while sickness must be covered with the veil of harmony, and the consciousness be

allowed to rejoice in the sense that it has nothing to mourn 1
over, but something to forget.

Human concepts run in extremes; they are like the 3
action of sickness, which is either an excess of action or
not action enough; they are fallible; they are neither
standards nor models. 6

If one asks me, Is my concept of you right? I reply, The
human concept is always imperfect; relinquish your human
concept of me, or of any one, and find the divine, and you 9
have gained the right one — and never until then. People
give me too much attention of the misguided, fallible sort,
and this misrepresents one through malice or ignorance. 12

My brother was a manufacturer; and one day a workman in his mills, a practical joker, set a man who applied
for work, in the overseer's absence, to pour a bucket of 15
water every ten minutes on the regulator. When my
brother returned and saw it, he said to the jester, "You
must pay that man." Some people try to tend folks, as 18
if they should steer the regulator of mankind. God makes
us pay for tending the action that He adjusts.

The regulator is governed by the principle that makes 21
the machinery work rightly; and because it *is* thus governed, the folly of tending it is no mere jest. The divine
Principle carries on His harmony. 24

Now turn from the metaphor of the mill to the Mother's
four thousand children, most of whom, at about three
years of scientific age, set up housekeeping alone. Certain 27
students, being too much interested in themselves to think
of helping others, go their way. They do not love Mother,
but pretend to; they constantly go to her for help, interrupt 30
the home-harmony, criticise and disobey her; then "return
to their vomit," — world worship, pleasure seeking, and

1 sense indulgence, — meantime declaring they "never disobey Mother"! It exceeds my conception of human
3 nature. Sin in its very nature is marvellous! Who but a
moral idiot, sanguine of success in sin, can steal, and lie
and lie, and lead the innocent to doom? History needs it,
6 and it has the grandeur of the loyal, self-forgetful, faithful Christian Scientists to overbalance this foul stuff.

When the Mother's love can no longer promote peace
9 in the family, wisdom is not "justified of her children."
When depraved reason is preferred to revelation, error
to Truth, and evil to good, and sense seems sounder than
12 Soul, the children are tending the regulator; they are
indeed losing the knowledge of the divine Principle and
rules of Christian Science, whose fruits prove the nature
15 of their source. A little more grace, a motive made pure,
a few truths tenderly told, a heart softened, a character
subdued, a life consecrated, would restore the right action
18 of the mental mechanism, and make manifest the movement of body and soul in accord with God.

Instead of relying on the Principle of all that really
21 exists, — to govern His own creation, — self-conceit, ignorance, and pride would regulate God's action. Experience shows that humility is the first step in Christian
24 Science, wherein all is controlled, not by man or laws
material, but by wisdom, Truth, and Love.

27 Go gaze on the eagle, his eye on the sun,
  Fast gathering strength for a flight well begun,
  As rising he rests in a liberty higher
  Than genius inflated with worldly desire.

30 No tear dims his eye, nor his pinions lose power
  To gaze on the lark in her emerald bower —
  Whenever he soareth to fashion his nest,
33 No vision more bright than the dream in his breast.

THE WAY 1

The present stage of progress in Christian Science presents two opposite aspects, — a full-orbed promise, and 3 a gaunt want. The need, however, is not of the letter, but the spirit.

Less teaching and good healing is to-day the acme of 6 "well done;" a healing that is not guesswork, — chronic recovery ebbing and flowing, — but instantaneous cure. This absolute demonstration of Science must be revived. 9 To consummate this *desideratum*, mortal mind must pass through three stages of growth.

First, self-knowledge. The physician must know him- 12 self and understand the mental state of his patient. Error found out is two-thirds destroyed, and the last third pierces itself, for the remainder only stimulates and gives 15 scope to higher demonstration. To strike out right and left against the mist, never clears the vision; but to lift your head above it, is a sovereign panacea. Mental dark- 18 ness is senseless error, neither intelligence nor power, and its victim is responsible for its supposititious presence. "Cast the beam out of thine own eye." Learn what in 21 thine own mentality is unlike "the anointed," and cast it out; then thou wilt discern the error in thy patient's mind that makes his body sick, and remove it, and rest 24 like the dove from the deluge.

"Physician, heal thyself." Let no clouds of sin gather and fall in mist and showers from thine own mental 27 atmosphere. Hold thy gaze to the light, and the iris of faith, more beautiful than the rainbow seen from my window at the close of a balmy autumnal day, will span 30 thy heavens of thought.

1 A radiant sunset, beautiful as blessings when they take
their flight, dilates and kindles into rest. Thus will a
3 life corrected illumine its own atmosphere with spiritual
glow and understanding.

The pent-up elements of mortal mind need no terrible
6 detonation to free them. Envy, rivalry, hate need no
temporary indulgence that they be destroyed through
suffering; they should be stifled from lack of air and
9 freedom.

My students, with cultured intellects, chastened affections, and costly hopes, give promise of grand careers.
12 But they must remember that the seedtime is passed,
the harvest hour has come; and songs should ascend
from the mount of revelation, sweeter than the sound of
15 vintage bells.

The seed of Christian Science, which when sown was
"the least of all seeds," has sprung up, borne fruit, and
18 the birds of the air, the uplifted desires of the human
heart, have lodged in its branches. Now let my faithful
students carry the fruit of this tree into the rock-ribbed
21 nests of the raven's callow brood.

The second stage of mental development is humility.
This virtue triumphs over the flesh; it is the genius of
24 Christian Science. One can never go up, until one has
gone down in his own esteem. Humility is lens and
prism to the understanding of Mind-healing; it must be
27 had to understand our textbook; it is indispensable to
personal growth, and points out the chart of its divine
Principle and rule of practice.

30 Cherish humility, "watch," and "pray without ceasing," or you will miss the way of Truth and Love. Humility is no busybody: it has no moments for trafficking

in other people's business, no place for envy, no time for 1
idle words, vain amusements, and all the *et cetera* of the
ways and means of personal sense.   3

Let Christian Scientists minister to the sick; the schoolroom is the *dernier ressort*. Let them seek the lost sheep
who, having strayed from the true fold, have lost their 6
great Shepherd and yearn to find living pastures and
rest beside still waters. These long for the Christlikeness that is above the present status of religion and be- 9
yond the walks of common life, quite on the verge of
heaven. Without the cross and healing, Christianity has
no central emblem, no history.   12

The seeds of Truth fall by the wayside, on artless
listeners. They fall on stony ground and shallow soil.
The fowls of the air pick them up. Much of what has 15
been sown has withered away, but what remaineth has
fallen into the good and honest hearts and is bearing
fruit.   18

The third stage of mental growth is manifested in *love,*
the greatest of all stages and states of being; love that
is irrespective of self, rank, or following. For some time 21
it has been clear to my thought that those students of
Christian Science whose Christian characters and lives
recommend them, should receive full fellowship from us, 24
no matter who has taught them. If they have been taught
wrongly, they are not morally responsible for this, and
need special help. They are as lambs that have sought 27
the true fold and the great Shepherd, and strayed inno-
cently; hence we should be ready and glad to help them
and point the way.   30

Divine Love is the substance of Christian Science, the
basis of its demonstration, yea, its foundation and super-

1 structure. Love impels good works. Love is greatly
needed, and must be had to mark the way in divine
3 Science.

The student who heals by teaching and teaches by
healing, will graduate under divine honors, which are
6 the only appropriate seals for Christian Science. State
honors perish, and their gain is loss to the Christian
Scientist. They include for him at present naught but
9 tardy justice, hounded footsteps, false laurels. God
alone is his help, his shield and great reward. He that
seeketh aught besides God, loseth in Life, Truth, and
12 Love. All men shall be satisfied when they "awake in
His likeness," and they never should be until then. Human pride is human weakness. Self-knowledge, humility,
15 and love are divine strength. Christ's vestures are put
on only when mortals are "washed in the blood of the
Lamb;" we must walk in the way which Jesus marked
18 out, if we would reach the heaven-crowned summit of
Christian Science.

Be it understood that I do not require Christian Sci-
21 entists to stop teaching, to dissolve their organizations,
or to desist from organizing churches and associations.

The Massachusetts Metaphysical College, the first
24 and only College for teaching Christian Science Mind-
healing, after accomplishing the greatest work of the
ages, and at the pinnacle of prosperity, is closed. Let
27 Scientists who have grown to self-sacrifice do their
present work, awaiting, with staff in hand, God's
commands.

30 When students have fulfilled all the good ends of
organization, and are convinced that by leaving the
material forms thereof a higher spiritual unity is won,

then is the time to follow the example of the *Alma Mater*. 1
Material organization is requisite in the beginning; but
when it has done its work, the purely Christly method 3
of teaching and preaching must be adopted. On the same
principle, you continue the mental argument in the practice of Christian healing until you can cure without it 6
instantaneously, and through Spirit alone.

St. Paul says: "When I was a child, I spake as a
child, I understood as a child, I thought as a child: but 9
when I became a man, I put away childish things. For
now we see through a glass, darkly; but then face to
face." Growth is restricted by forcing humanity out of 12
the proper channels for development, or by holding it in
fetters.

For Jesus to walk the water was scientific, insomuch 15
as he was able to do this; but it is neither wisdom nor
Science for poor humanity to step upon the Atlantic until
we can walk on the water. 18

Peter's impetuosity was rebuked. He had to learn
from experience; so have we. The methods of our
Master were in advance of the period in which he per- 21
sonally appeared; but his example was right, and is
available at the right time. The *way* is absolute divine
Science: walk ye in it; but remember that Science is 24
demonstrated by degrees, and our demonstration rises
only as we rise in the scale of being.

SCIENCE AND PHILOSOPHY   27

Men give counsel; but they give not the wisdom to
profit by it. To ask wisdom of God, is the beginning of
wisdom. 30

1 Meekness, moderating human desire, inspires wisdom
and procures divine power. Human lives are yet un-
3 carved, — in the rough marble, encumbered with crude,
rude fragments, and awaiting the hammering, chiselling,
and transfiguration from His hand.

6 Great only as good, because fashioned divinely, were
those unpretentious yet colossal characters, Paul and
Jesus. Theirs were modes of mind cast in the moulds
9 of Christian Science: Paul's, by the supremely natural
transforming power of Truth; and the character of
Jesus, by his original scientific sonship with God. Phi-
12 losophy never has produced, nor can it reproduce, these
stars of the first magnitude — fixed stars in the heavens
of Soul. When shall earth be crowned with the true
15 knowledge of Christ?

When Christian Science has melted away the cloud of
false witnesses; and the dews of divine grace, fall-
18 ing upon the blighted flowers of fleeting joys, shall
lift every thought-leaflet Spiritward; and "Israel after
the flesh," who partaketh of its own altars, shall be
21 no more, — then, "the Israel according to Spirit"
shall fill earth with the divine energies, understanding,
and ever-flowing tides of spiritual sensation and con-
24 sciousness.

When mortal mind is silenced by the "still, small voice"
of Truth that regenerates philosophy and logic; and
27 Jesus, as the true idea of Him, is heard as of yore saying
to sensitive ears and dark disciples, "I came from the
Father," "Before Abraham was, I am," coexistent and
30 coeternal with God, — and this idea is understood, —
then will the earth be filled with the true knowledge of
Christ. No advancing modes of human mind made

Jesus; rather was it their subjugation, and the pure 1
heart that sees God.

When the belief in material origin, mortal mind, sen- 3
sual conception, dissolves through self-imposed suffering,
and its substances are found substanceless, — then its
miscalled life ends in death, and death itself is swallowed 6
up in Life, — spiritual Life, whose myriad forms are
neither material nor mortal.

When every form and mode of evil disappear to hu- 9
man thought, and mollusk and radiate are spiritual concepts testifying to one creator, — then, earth is full of
His glory, and Christian Science has overshadowed all 12
human philosophy, and being is understood in startling
contradiction of human hypotheses; and Socrates, Plato,
Kant, Locke, Berkeley, Tyndall, Darwin, and Spencer 15
sit at the feet of Jesus.

To this great end, Paul admonished, "Let us lay aside
every weight, and the sin which doth so easily beset us, 18
and let us run with patience the race that is set before
us, looking unto Jesus the author and finisher of our
faith." So shall mortals soar to final freedom, and rest 21
from the subtlety of speculative wisdom and human
woe.

God is the only Mind, and His manifestation is the 24
spiritual universe, including man and all eternal individuality. God, the only substance and divine Principle
of creation, is by no means a creative partner in the firm 27
of error, named matter, or mortal mind. He elucidates
His own idea, wherein Principle and idea, God and man,
are not one, but are inseparable as cause and effect. If 30
one, who could say which that "one" was?

His ways are not as our ways. The divine modes

1 and manifestations are not those of the material senses;
for instance, intelligent matter, or mortal mind, material
3 birth, growth, and decay: they are the forever-existing
realities of divine Science; wherein God and man are
perfect, and man's reason is at rest in God's wisdom, —
6 who comprehends and reflects all real mode, form, individuality, identity.

Scholastic dogma has made men blind. Christ's *logos*
9 gives sight to these blind, ears to these deaf, feet to these
lame, — physically, morally, spiritually. Theologians
make the mortal mistake of believing that God, having
12 made *all*, made evil; but the Scriptures declare that all
that He made was good. Then, was evil part and parcel
of His creation?
15   Philosophy hypothetically regards creation as its own
creator, puts cause into effect, and out of nothing would
create something, whose noumenon is mortal mind,
18 with its phenomenon matter, — an evil mind already
doomed, whose modes are material manifestations of
evil, and that continually, until self-extinguished by
21 suffering!

Here revelation must come to the rescue of mortals,
to remove this mental millstone that is dragging them
24 downward, and refute erring reason with the spiritual
cosmos and Science of Soul. We all must find shelter
from the storm and tempest in the tabernacle of Spirit.
27 Truth is won through Science or suffering: O vain mortals! which shall it be? And suffering has no reward,
except when it is necessary to prevent sin or reform
30 the sinner. And pleasure is no crime except when it
strengthens the influence of bad inclinations or lessens
the activities of virtue. The more nearly an erring so-

called mind approaches purity, the more conscious it becomes of its own unreality, and of the great reality of divine Mind and true happiness.

The "ego" that claims selfhood in error, and passes from molecule and monkey up to man, is no ego, but is simply the supposition that the absence of good is mind and makes men, — when its greatest flatterer, identification, is piqued by Him who compensateth vanity with nothingness, dust with dust!

The mythology of evil and mortality is but the material mode of a suppositional mind; while the immortal modes of Mind are spiritual, and pass through none of the changes of matter, or evil. Truth said, and said from the beginning, "Let us [Spirit] make man perfect;" and there is no other Maker: a perfect man would not desire to make himself imperfect, and God is not chargeable with imperfection. His modes declare the beauty of holiness, and His manifold wisdom shines through the visible world in glimpses of the eternal verities. Even through the mists of mortality is seen the brightness of His coming.

We must avoid the shoals of a sensual religion or philosophy that misguides reason and affection, and hold fast to the Principle of Christian Science as the Word that *is* God, Spirit, and Truth. This Word corrects the philosopher, confutes the astronomer, exposes the subtle sophist, and drives diviners mad. The Bible is the learned man's masterpiece, the ignorant man's dictionary, the wise man's directory.

I foresee and foresay that every advancing epoch of Truth will be characterized by a more spiritual apprehension of the Scriptures, that will show their marked

1 consonance with the textbook of Christian Science Mind-
healing, "Science and Health with Key to the Scriptures."
3 Interpreting the Word in the "new tongue," whereby
the sick are healed, naturally evokes new paraphrase
from the world of letters. "Wait patiently on the Lord,
6 and He will renew your strength." In return for individual sacrifice, what a recompense to have healed, through
Truth, the sick and sinful, made the public your friend,
9 and posterity your familiar!

Christian Science refutes everything that is not a
postulate of the divine Principle, God. It is the soul of
12 divine philosophy, and there is no other philosophy. It
is not a search after wisdom, it *is* wisdom: it is God's
right hand grasping the universe, — all time, space,
15 immortality, thought, extension, cause, and effect; constituting and governing all identity, individuality, law,
and power. It stands on this Scriptural platform:
18 that He made all that was made, and it is good, reflects
the divine Mind, is governed by it; and that nothing
apart from this Mind, one God, is self-created or evolves
21 the universe.

Human hypotheses predicate matter of Spirit and
evil of good; hence these opposites must either cooperate
24 or quarrel throughout time and eternity, — or until
this impossible partnership is dissolved. If Spirit is the
lawgiver to matter, and good has the same power or
27 modes as evil, it has the same consciousness, and there
is no absolute good. This error, carried to its ultimate,
would either extinguish God and His modes, or give
30 reality and power to evil *ad infinitum*.

Christian Science rends this veil of the temple of gods,
and reproduces the divine philosophy of Jesus and Paul.

This philosophy alone will bear the strain of time and 1
bring out the glories of eternity; for "other foundation can no man lay than that is laid," which is Christ, 3
Truth.

Human theories weighed in the balances of God are
found wanting; and their highest endeavors are to Science 6
what a child's love of pictures is to art. The school whose
schoolmaster is not Christ, gets things wrong, and is ignorant thereof.   9

If Christian Science lacked the proof of its goodness
and utility, it would destroy itself; for it rests alone on
demonstration. Its genius is right thinking and right 12
acting, physical and moral harmony; and the secret of
its success lies in supplying the universal need of better
health and better men.   15

Good health and a more spiritual religion form the
common want, and this want has worked out a moral
result; namely, that mortal mind is calling for what im- 18
mortal Mind alone can supply. If the uniform moral
and spiritual, as well as physical, effects of divine Science
were lacking, the demand would diminish; but it con- 21
tinues, and increases, which shows the real value of
Christian Science to the race. Even doctors agree that
infidelity, bigotry, or sham has never met the growing 24
wants of humanity.

As a literature, Christian metaphysics is hampered by
lack of proper terms in which to express what it means. 27
As a Science, it is held back by the common ignorance
of what it is and of what it does, — and more than all
else, by the impostors that come in its name. To be 30
appreciated, it must be conscientiously understood and
introduced.

1   If the Bible and "Science and Health with Key to the
Scriptures" had in our schools the time or attention that
3 human hypotheses consume, they would advance the
world.   True, it requires more study to understand and
demonstrate what they teach than to learn the doctrine
6 of theology, philosophy, or physics, because they contain and offer Science, with fixed Principle, given rule,
and unmistakable proof.

9   The Scriptures give the keynote of Christian Science
from Genesis to Revelation, and this is the prolonged
tone: "For   the   Lord   He   is   God,   and   there   is
12 *none beside Him."*   And   because   He   is   All-in-all,
He is in nothing unlike Himself;   and nothing that
worketh or maketh a lie is in Him, or can be divine con-
15 sciousness.

At this date, poor jaded humanity needs to get her
eyes open to a new style of imposition in the field of
18 medicine and of religion, and to "beware of the leaven
of the scribes and Pharisees," the doctrines of men, even
as Jesus admonished.   From first to last, evil insists on
21 the unity of good and evil as the purpose of God;   and
on drugs, electricity, and animal magnetism as modes
of medicine.   To a greater or less extent, all mortal con-
24 clusions start from this false premise, and they necessarily culminate in sickness, sin, disease, and death.
Erroneous doctrines never have abated and never will
27 abate dishonesty, self-will, envy, and lust.   To destroy
sin and its sequence, is the office of Christ, Truth, — according to His mode of Christian Science;   and this is
30 being done daily.

The false theories whose names are legion, gilded with
sophistry and what Jesus had not, namely, mere book-

learning, — letter without law, gospel, or demonstration, 1
— have no place in Christian Science. This Science requires man to be honest, just, pure; to love his neighbor 3
as himself, and to love God supremely.

Matter and evil are subjective states of error or mortal
mind. But Mind is immortal; and the fact of there 6
being no mortal mind, exposes the lie of suppositional
evil, showing that error is not Mind, substance, or
Life. Thus, whatever is wrongfully-minded will dis- 9
appear in the proportion that Science is understood,
and the reality of being — goodness and harmony — is
demonstrated. 12

Error says that knowing all things implies the necessity of knowing evil, that it dishonors God to claim that
He is ignorant of anything; but God says of this fruit 15
of the tree of knowledge of *both* good and evil, "In the
day that thou eatest thereof, thou shalt surely die." If
God is infinite good, He knows nothing but good; if He 18
did know aught else, He would not be infinite. Infinite
Mind knows nothing beyond Himself or Herself. To
good, evil is never present; for evil is a different state of 21
consciousness. It was not against evil, but against *knowing* evil, that God forewarned. He dwelleth in light;
and in the light He sees light, and cannot see darkness. 24
The opposite conclusion, that darkness dwelleth in light,
has neither precedent nor foundation in nature, in logic,
or in the character of Christ. 27

The senses would say that whatever saves from sin,
must know sin. Truth replies that God is too pure
to behold iniquity; and by virtue of His ignorance of 30
that which is not, He knoweth that which *is*, and
abideth in Himself, the only Life, Truth, and Love,

1 — and is reflected by a universe in His own image
and likeness.

3   Even so, Father, let the light that shineth in darkness, and the darkness comprehendeth it not, dispel this
illusion of the senses, open the eyes of the blind, and cause
6 the deaf to hear.

"Truth forever on the scaffold, Wrong forever on the throne.
    Yet that scaffold sways the future, and, behind the dim unknown,
9 Standeth God within the shadow, keeping watch above His own."
                                                        LOWELL

"TAKE HEED!"

12   We regret to be obliged to say that all are not metaphysicians, or Christian Scientists, who call themselves
so.   Charlatanism, fraud, and malice are getting into
15 the ranks of the good and pure, sending forth a poison
more deadly than the upas-tree in the eastern archi-
pelago. This evil obtains in the present false teaching
18 and false practice of the Science of treating disease through
Mind. The silent address of a mental malpractitioner
can only be portrayed in these words of the apostle,
21 "whisperers," and "the poison of asps is under their
tongue."
    Some of the mere puppets of the hour are playing
24 only for money, and at a fearful stake. Others, from
malice and envy, are working out the destinies of the
damned. But while the best, perverted, on the mortal
27 plane may become the worst, let us not forget that the
Lord reigns, and that this earth shall some time rejoice
in His supreme rule, — that the tired watchmen on the

walls of Zion, and the true Christian Scientist at the foot 1
of the mount of revelation, shall look up with shouts and
thanksgiving, — that God's law, as in divine Science, 3
shall be finally understood; and the gospel of glad tidings
bring "on earth peace, good will toward men."

THE CRY OF CHRISTMAS-TIDE   6

Metaphysics, not physics, enables us to stand erect
on sublime heights, surveying the immeasurable universe
of Mind, peering into the cause which governs all effects, 9
while we are strong in the unity of God and man. There
is "method" in the "madness" of this system, — since
madness it seems to many onlookers. This method sits 12
serene at the portals of the temple of thought, while
the leaders of materialistic schools indulge in mad
antics. Metaphysical healing seeks a wisdom that is 15
higher than a rhubarb tincture or an ipecacuanha pill.
This method is devout enough to trust Christ more than
it does drugs. 18
Meekly we kneel at our Master's feet, for even a crumb
that falleth from his table. We are hungry for Love,
for the white-winged charity that heals and saves; we 21
are tired of theoretic husks, — as tired as was the prodigal son of the carobs which he shared with the swine,
to whom he fed that wholesome but unattractive food. 24
Like him, we would find our Father's house again —
the perfect and eternal Principle of man. We thirst
for inspiring wine from the vine which our Father tends. 27
We crave the privilege of saying to the sick, when their

1 feebleness calls for help, "Rise and walk." We rejoice
to say, in the spirit of our Master, "Stretch forth thy
3 hand, and be whole!"

When the Pharisees saw Jesus do such deeds of mercy,
they went away and took counsel how they might remove
6 him. The antagonistic spirit of evil is still abroad; but
the greater spirit of Christ is also abroad, — risen from
the grave-clothes of tradition and the cave of ignorance.
9 Let the sentinels of Zion's watch-towers shout once
again, "Unto us a child is born, unto us a son is
given."

12 In different ages the divine idea assumes different
forms, according to humanity's needs. In this age it
assumes, more intelligently than ever before, the form
15 of Christian healing. This is the babe we are to cherish.
This is the babe that twines its loving arms about the
neck of omnipotence, and calls forth infinite care from
18 His loving heart.

BLIND LEADERS

What figure is less favorable than a wolf in sheep's
21 clothing? The braying donkey whose ears stick out is
less troublesome. What manner of man is it that has
discovered an improvement on Christian Science, a "met-
24 aphysical healing" by which error destroys error, and
would gather all sorts into a "national convention" by
the sophistry that such is the true fold for Christian heal-
27 ers, since the good shepherd cares for all?

Yes; the *good* Shepherd does care for all, and His
first care is to separate the sheep from the goats; and

this is among the first lessons on healing taught by our 1
great Master.

If, as the gentleman aforesaid states, large flocks of 3
metaphysicians are wandering about without a leader,
what has opened his eyes to see the need of taking them
out of the care of the great Shepherd, and behold the 6
remedy, to help them by his own leadership? Is it that
he can guide Christian Scientists better than they, through
the guidance of our common Father, can guide them- 9
selves? or is it that they are incapable of helping themselves thus?

I as their teacher can say, They know far more of 12
Christian Science than he who deprecates their condition
appears to, and my heart pleads for them to possess
more and more of Truth and Love; but mixing all grades 15
of persons is not productive of the better sort, although
he who has self-interest in this mixing is apt to propose it. 18

Whoever desires to say, "good right, and good wrong,"
has no truth to defend. It is a wise saying that "men
are known by their enemies." To sympathize in any 21
degree with error, is not to rectify it; but error always
strives to unite, in a definition of purpose, with Truth,
to give it buoyancy. What is under the mask, but error 24
in borrowed plumes?

"CHRIST AND CHRISTMAS"
An Illustrated Poem   27

This poem and its illustrations are as hopelessly original as is "Science and Health with Key to the Scrip-

1 tures." When the latter was first issued, critics declared
that it was incorrect, contradictory, unscientific, unchris-
3 tian; but those human opinions had not one feather's
weight in the scales of God. The fact remains, that
the textbook of Christian Science is transforming the
6 universe.

"Christ and Christmas" voices Christian Science
through song and object-lesson. In two weeks from the
9 date of its publication in December, 1893, letters extoll-
ing it were pouring in from artists and poets. A mother
wrote, "Looking at the pictures in your wonderful book
12 has healed my child."

Knowing that this book would produce a stir, I sought
the judgment of sound critics familiar with the works
15 of masters in France and Italy. From them came such
replies as the following: "The illustrations of your poem
are truly a work of art, and the artist seems quite familiar
18 with delineations from the old masters." I am delighted
to find "Christ and Christmas" in accord with the
ancient and most distinguished artists.

21 *The Christian Science Journal* gives no uncertain declaration concerning the spirit and mission of "Christ and
Christmas."

24 I aimed to reproduce, with reverent touch, the modest
glory of divine Science. Not by aid of foreign device
or environment could I copy art, — never having seen
27 the painter's masterpieces; but the *art* of Christian
Science, with true hue and character of the living God,
is akin to its *Science:* and Science and Health gives
30 scopes and shades to the shadows of divinity, thus imparting to humanity the true sense of meekness and
might.

One incident serves to illustrate the simple nature of art.

I insisted upon placing the serpent behind the woman in the picture "Seeking and Finding." My artist at the easel objected, as he often did, to my sense of Soul's expression through the brush; but, as usual, he finally yielded. A few days afterward, the following from Rotherham's translation of the New Testament was handed to me, — I had never before seen it: "And the serpent cast out of his mouth, *behind* the woman, water as a river, that he might cause her to be river-borne." Neither material finesse, standpoint, nor perspective guides the infinite Mind and spiritual vision that should, does, guide His children.

One great master clearly delineates Christ's appearing in the flesh, and his healing power, as clad not in soft raiment or gorgeous apparel; and when forced out of its proper channel, as living feebly, in kings' courts. This master's thought presents a sketch of Christianity's state, in the early part of the Christian era, as homelessness in a wilderness. But in due time Christianity entered into synagogues, and, as St. Mark writes, it has rich possession here, with houses and lands. In Genesis we read that God gave man dominion over all things; and this assurance is followed by Jesus' declaration, "All power is given unto me in heaven and in earth," and by his promise that the Christlike shall finally sit down at the right hand of the Father.

Christian Science is more than a prophet or a prophecy: it presents not words alone, but works, — the daily demonstration of Truth and Love. Its healing and sav-

1 ing power was so great a proof of Immanuel and the
realism of Christianity, that it caused even the publi-
3 cans to justify God. Although clad in panoply of power,
the Pharisees scorned the spirit of Christ in most of its
varied manifestations. To them it was cant and carica-
6 ture, — always the opposite of what it was. Keen and
alert was their indignation at whatever rebuked hypocrisy
and demanded Christianity in life and religion. In view
9 of this, Jesus said, "Wisdom is justified of all her
children."

Above the fogs of sense and storms of passion, Chris-
12 tian Science and its art will rise triumphant; ignorance,
envy, and hatred — earth's harmless thunder — pluck
not their heaven-born wings. Angels, with overtures,
15 hold charge over both, and announce their Principle and
idea.

It is most fitting that Christian Scientists memorize
18 the nativity of Jesus. To him who brought a great light
to all ages, and named his burdens light, homage is indeed due, — but is bankrupt. I never looked on my
21 ideal of the face of the Nazarite Prophet; but the one
illustrating my poem approximates it.

Extremists in every age either doggedly deny or fran-
24 tically affirm what is what: one renders not unto Cæsar
"the things that are Cæsar's;" the other sees "Helen's
beauty in a brow of Egypt."

27   Pictures are portions of one's ideal, but this ideal is
not one's personality. Looking behind the veil, he that
perceives a semblance between the thinker and his thought
30 on canvas, blames him not.

Because my ideal of an angel is a woman without
feathers on her wings, — is it less artistic or less natu-

ral? Pictures which present disordered phases of ma- 1
terial conceptions and personality blind with animality,
are not my concepts of angels. What is the material ego, 3
but the counterfeit of the spiritual?

The truest art of Christian Science is to be a Christian Scientist; and it demands more than a Raphael to 6
delineate *this* art.

The following is an extract from a letter reverting to
the illustrations of "Christ and Christmas": — 9

"In my last letter, I did not utter all I felt about the
wonderful new book you have given us. Years ago,
while in Italy, I studied the old masters and their great 12
works of art thoroughly, and so got quite an idea of
what constitutes true art. Then I spent two years in
Paris, devoting every moment to the study of music and 15
art.

"The first thing that impressed me in your illustrations was the conscientious application to detail, which 18
is the foundation of true art. From that, I went on to
study each illustration thoroughly, and to my amazement
and delight I find an almost identical resemblance, in 21
many things, to the old masters! In other words, the art
is perfect.

"The hands and feet of the figures — how many times 24
have I seen these hands and feet in Angelico's 'Jesus,'
or Botticelli's 'Madonna'!

"It gave me such a thrill of joy as no words can ex- 27
press, to see produced to-day that art — the only true
art — that we have identified with the old masters, and
mourned as belonging to them exclusively, — a thing of 30
the past, impossible of reproduction.

"All that I can say to you, as one who gives no mean

1 attention to such matters, is that the art is perfect. It
is the true art of the oldest, most revered, most authen-
3 tic Italian school, revived. I use the words *most au-
thentic* in the following sense: the face, figure, and
drapery of Jesus, very closely resemble in detail the
6 face, figure, and drapery of that Jesus portrayed by the
oldest of the old masters, and said to have been authen-
tic; the face having been taken by Fra Angelico from
9 Cæsar's Cameo, the figure and garments from a description, in *The Galaxy,* of a small sketch handed down
from the *living reality. Their* productions are expres-
12 sionless copies of an engraving cut in a stone. *Yours*
is a palpitating, living Saviour engraven on the heart.
You have given us back our Jesus, and in a much better
15 form."

SUNRISE AT PLEASANT VIEW

Who shall describe the brave splendor of a November
18 sky that this morning burst through the lattice for me,
on my bed? According to terrestrial calculations, above
the horizon, in the east, there rose one rod of rainbow
21 hues, crowned with an acre of eldritch ebony. Little
by little this topmost pall, drooping over a deeply dazzling sunlight, softened, grew gray, then gay, and glided
24 into a glory of mottled marvels. Fleecy, faint, fairy
blue and golden flecks came out on a background of
cerulean hue; while the lower lines of light kindled into
27 gold, orange, pink, crimson, violet; and diamond, topaz,
opal, garnet, turquoise, and sapphire spangled the gloom
in celestial space as with the brightness of His glory.
30 Then thought I, What are we, that He who fashions for-

ever such forms and hues of heaven, should move our
brush or pen to paint frail fairness or to weave a web
of words that glow with gladdening gleams of God, so
unapproachable, and yet so near and full of radiant relief
in clouds and darkness!

CHAPTER X

Inklings Historic

1 ABOUT the year 1862, while the author of this work
was at Dr. Vail's Hydropathic Institute in New
3 Hampshire, this occurred: A patient considered incurable left that institution, and in a few weeks returned
apparently well, having been healed, as he informed
6 the patients, by one Mr. P. P. Quimby of Portland,
Maine.

After much consultation among ourselves, and a struggle
9 with pride, the author, in company with several other
patients, left the water-cure, *en route* for the aforesaid
doctor in Portland. He proved to be a magnetic practi-
12 tioner. His treatment seemed at first to relieve her, but
signally failed in healing her case.

Having practised homœopathy, it never occurred to the
15 author to learn his practice, but she did ask him how
manipulation could benefit the sick. He answered kindly
and squarely, in substance, "Because it conveys *electricity*
18 to them." That was the sum of what he taught her of
his medical profession.

The readers of my books cannot fail to see that meta-
21 physical therapeutics, as in Christian Science, are farther
removed from such thoughts than the nebulous system
is from the earth.

After treating his patients, Mr. Quimby would retire 1
to an anteroom and write at his desk. I had a curiosity
to know if he indited anything pathological relative to 3
his patients, and asked if I could see his pennings on
my case. He immediately presented them. I read the
copy in his presence, and returned it to him. The com- 6
position was commonplace, mostly descriptive of the general appearance, height, and complexion of the individual,
and the nature of the case: it was not at all metaphysi- 9
cal or scientific; and from his remarks I inferred that
his writings usually ran in the vein of thought presented
by these. He was neither a scholar nor a metaphysician. 12
I never heard him say that matter was not as real as Mind,
or that electricity was not as potential or remedial, or
allude to God as the divine Principle of all healing. He 15
certainly had advanced views of his own, but they commingled error with truth, and were not Science. On
his rare humanity and sympathy one could write a 18
sonnet.

I had already experimented in medicine beyond the
basis of *materia medica,* — up to the highest attenuation 21
in homœopathy, thence to a mental standpoint not understood, and with phenomenally good results; [1] meanwhile, assiduously pondering the solution of this great 24
question: Is it matter, or is it Mind, that heals the
sick?

It was after Mr. Quimby's death that I discovered, 27
in 1866, the momentous facts relating to Mind and its
superiority over matter, and named my discovery Christian Science. Yet, there remained the difficulty of ad- 30
justing in the scale of Science a metaphysical *practice,*

[1] See Science and Health, p. 47, revised edition of 1890, and
pp. 152, 153 in late editions. 33

1 and settling the question, What shall be the outward
sign of such a practice: if a divine Principle alone heals,
3 what is the human modus for demonstrating this, — in
short, how can sinful mortals prove that a divine Principle
heals the sick, as well as governs the universe, time,
6 space, immortality, man?

When contemplating the majesty and magnitude of
this query, it looked as if centuries of spiritual growth
9 were requisite to enable me to elucidate or to demonstrate what I had discovered: but an unlooked-for,
imperative call for help impelled me to begin this stu-
12 pendous work at once, and teach the first student in
Christian Science. Even as when an accident, called
fatal to life, had driven me to discover the Science of
15 Life, I again, in faith, turned to divine help, — and commenced teaching.

My students at first practised in slightly differing
18 forms. Although *I* could heal mentally, without a sign
save the immediate recovery of the sick, my students'
patients, and people generally, called for a sign — a ma-
21 terial evidence wherewith to satisfy the sick that something was being done for them; and I said, "Suffer it
to be so now," for thus saith our Master. Experience,
24 however, taught me the impossibility of demonstrating
the Science of metaphysical healing by any outward form
of practice.

27   In April, 1883, a bill in equity was filed in the United
States Circuit Court in Boston, to restrain, by decree and
order of the Court, the unlawful publishing and use of an
30 infringing pamphlet printed and issued by a student of
Christian Science.

Answer was filed by the defendant, alleging that the

copyrighted works of Mrs. Eddy were not original with 1
her, but had been copied by her, or by her direction,
from manuscripts originally composed by Dr. P. P. 3
Quimby.

Testimony was taken on the part of Mrs. Eddy, the
defendant being present personally and by counsel. The 6
time for taking testimony on the part of the defendant
having nearly expired, he gave notice through his counsel that he should not put in testimony. Later, Mrs. 9
Eddy requested her lawyer to inquire of defendant's
counsel why he did not present evidence to support his
claim that Dr. Quimby was the author of her writings! 12
Accordingly, her counsel asked the defendant's counsel
this question, and he replied, in substance, "There is
no evidence to present." 15

The stipulation for a judgment and a decree in favor
of Mrs. Eddy was drawn up and signed by counsel.
It was ordered that the complainant (Mrs. Eddy) 18
recover of the defendant her cost of suit, taxed at
($113.09) one hundred thirteen and $\frac{9}{100}$ dollars.

A writ of injunction was issued under the seal of the 21
said Court, restraining the defendant from directly or
indirectly printing, publishing, selling, giving away,
distributing, or in any way or manner disposing of, 24
the enjoined pamphlet, on penalty of ten thousand
dollars.

The infringing books, to the number of thirty-eight 27
hundred or thereabouts, were put under the edge of
the knife, and their unlawful existence destroyed, in
Boston, Massachusetts. 30

It has been written that "nobody can be both founder
and discoverer of the same thing." If this declaration

1 were either a truism or a rule, my experience would
contradict it and prove an exception.

3   No works on the subject of Christian Science existed,
prior to my discovery of this Science. Before the publication of my first work on this doctrine, a few manu-
6 scripts of mine were in circulation. The discovery and
founding of Christian Science has cost more than thirty
years of unremitting toil and unrest; but, comparing those
9 with the joy of knowing that the sinner and the sick are
helped thereby, that time and eternity bear witness to
this gift of God to the race, I am the debtor.

12   In the latter half of the nineteenth century I discovered the Science of Christianity, and restored the first
patient healed in this age by Christian Science. I taught
15 the first student in Christian Science Mind-healing; was
author and publisher of the first books on this subject;
obtained the first charter for the first Christian Science
18 church, originated its form of government, and was its
first pastor. I donated to this church the land on which
in 1894 was erected the first church edifice of this de-
21 nomination in Boston; obtained the first and only charter
for a metaphysical medical college, — was its first and
only president; was editor and proprietor of the first
24 Christian Science periodical; organized the first Christian Scientist Association, wrote its constitution and by-
laws, — as also the constitution and by-laws of the
27 National Christian Science Association; and gave it
The Christian Science Journal; inaugurated our denominational form of Sunday services, Sunday School, and
30 the entire system of teaching and practising Christian
Science.

In 1895 I ordained that the Bible, and "Science and

Health with Key to the Scriptures," the Christian Science 1
textbook, be the pastor, on this planet, of all the churches
of the Christian Science denomination. This ordinance 3
took effect the same year, and met with the universal approval and support of Christian Scientists. Whenever
and wherever a church of Christian Science is established, 6
its pastor is the Bible and my book.

In 1896 it goes without saying, preeminent over ignorance or envy, that Christian Science *is founded by its* 9
discoverer, and built upon the rock of Christ. The elements of earth beat in vain against the immortal parapets
of this Science. Erect and eternal, it will go on with the 12
ages, go down the dim posterns of time unharmed, and
on every battle-field rise higher in the estimation of
thinkers and in the hearts of Christians. 15

CHAPTER XI

Poems

COME THOU

COME, in the minstrel's lay;
　　When two hearts meet,
　　And true hearts greet,
And all is morn and May.

Come Thou! and now, anew,
　　To thought and deed
　　Give sober speed,
Thy will to know, and do.

Stay! till the storms are o'er —
　　The cold blasts done,
　　The reign of heaven begun,
And Love, the evermore.

Be patient, waiting heart:
　　Light, Love divine
　　Is here, and thine;
You therefore cannot part.

"The seasons come and go:
　　Love, like the sea,
　　Rolls on with thee, —
But knows no ebb and flow.

"Faith, hope, and tears, triune,   1
  Above the sod
    Find peace in God,   3
And one eternal noon."

Oh, Thou hast heard my prayer;
  And I am blest!   6
    This is Thy high behest:
Thou, here and *everywhere*.

MEETING OF MY DEPARTED MOTHER AND HUSBAND   9

"Joy for thee, happy friend! thy bark is past
The dangerous sea, and safely moored at last —
    Beyond rough foam.   12
Soft gales celestial, in sweet music bore —
Spirit emancipate for this far shore —
    Thee to thy home.   15

"You've travelled long, and far from mortal joys,
To Soul's diviner sense, that spurns such toys,
    Brave wrestler, lone.   18
Now see thy ever-self; Life never fled;
Man is not mortal, never of the dead:
    The dark unknown.   21

"When hope soared high, and joy was eagle-plumed,
Thy pinions drooped; the flesh was weak, and doomed
    To pass away.   24
But faith triumphant round thy death-couch shed
Majestic forms; and radiant glory sped
    The dawning day.   27

1 "Intensely grand and glorious life's sphere, —
Beyond the shadow, infinite appear
3   Life, Love divine, —
Where mortal yearnings come not, sighs are stilled,
And home and peace and hearts are found and filled,
6   Thine, ever thine.

"Bearest thou no tidings from our loved on earth,
The toiler tireless for Truth's new birth
9   All-unbeguiled?
Our joy is gathered from her parting sigh:
This hour looks on her heart with pitying eye, —
12   What of my child?"

"When, severed by death's dream, I woke to Life,
She deemed I died, and could not know the strife
15   At first to fill
That waking with a love that steady turns
To God; a hope that ever upward yearns,
18   Bowed to His will.

"Years had passed o'er thy broken household band,
When angels beckoned me to this bright land,
21   With thee to meet.
She that has wept o'er thee, kissed my cold brow,
Rears the sad marble to our memory now,
24   In lone retreat.

"By the remembrance of her loyal life,
And parting prayer, I only know my wife,
27   Thy child, shall come —
Where farewells cloud not o'er our ransomed rest —
Hither to reap, with all the crowned and blest,
30   Of bliss the sum.

"When Love's rapt sense the heart-strings gently sweep, 1
With joy divinely fair, the high and deep,
                To call her home, 3
She shall mount upward unto purer skies;
We shall be waiting, in what glad surprise,
                Our spirits' own!" 6

LOVE

Brood o'er us with Thy shelt'ring wing,
    'Neath which our spirits blend 9
Like brother birds, that soar and sing,
    And on the same branch bend.
The arrow that doth wound the dove 12
Darts not from those who watch and love.

If thou the bending reed wouldst break
    By thought or word unkind, 15
Pray that his spirit you partake,
    Who loved and healed mankind:
Seek holy thoughts and heavenly strain, 18
That make men one in love remain.

Learn, too, that wisdom's rod is given
    For faith to kiss, and know; 21
That greetings glorious from high heaven,
    Whence joys supernal flow,
Come from that Love, divinely near, 24
Which chastens pride and earth-born fear,

1   Through God, who gave that word of might
        Which swelled creation's lay:
3   "Let there be light, and there was light."
        What chased the clouds away?
    'T was Love whose finger traced aloud
6   A bow of promise on the cloud.

    Thou to whose power our hope we give,
        Free us from human strife.
9   Fed by Thy love divine we live,
        For Love alone is Life;
    And life most sweet, as heart to heart
12   Speaks kindly when we meet and part.

WOMAN'S RIGHTS

    Grave on her monumental pile:
15   She won from vice, by virtue's smile,
        Her dazzling crown, her sceptred throne,
        Affection's wreath, a happy home;

18   The right to worship deep and pure,
        To bless the orphan, feed the poor;
        Last at the cross to mourn her Lord,
21   First at the tomb to hear his word:

        To fold an angel's wings below;
        And hover o'er the couch of woe;
24   To nurse the Bethlehem babe so sweet,
        The right to sit at Jesus' feet;

To form the bud for bursting bloom,   1
The hoary head with joy to crown;
In short, the right to work and pray,   3
"To point to heaven and lead the way."

THE MOTHER'S EVENING PRAYER

O gentle presence, peace and joy and power;   6
    O Life divine, that owns each waiting hour,
Thou Love that guards the nestling's faltering flight!
    Keep Thou my child on upward wing to-night.   9

Love is our refuge; only with mine eye
    Can I behold the snare, the pit, the fall:
His habitation high is here, and nigh,   12
    His arm encircles me, and mine, and all.

O make me glad for every scalding tear,
    For hope deferred, ingratitude, disdain!   15
Wait, and love more for every hate, and fear
    No ill, — since God is good, and loss is gain.

Beneath the shadow of His mighty wing;   18
    In that sweet secret of the narrow way,
Seeking and finding, with the angels sing:
    "Lo, I am with you alway," — watch and pray.   21

No snare, no fowler, pestilence or pain;
    No night drops down upon the troubled breast,
When heaven's aftersmile earth's tear-drops gain,   24
    And mother finds her home and heavenly rest.

JUNE

Whence are thy wooings, gentle June?
    Thou hast a Naiad's charm;
Thy breezes scent the rose's breath;
    Old Time gives thee her palm.
The lark's shrill song doth wake the dawn:
    The eve-bird's forest flute
Gives back some maiden melody,
    Too pure for aught so mute.

The fairy-peopled world of flowers,
    Enraptured by thy spell,
Looks love unto the laughing hours,
    Through woodland, grove, and dell;
And soft thy footstep falls upon
    The verdant grass it weaves;
To melting murmurs ye have stirred
    The timid, trembling leaves.

When sunshine beautifies the shower,
    As smiles through teardrops seen,
Ask of its June, the long-hushed heart,
    What hath the record been?
And thou wilt find that harmonies,
    In which the Soul hath part,
Ne'er perish young, like things of earth,
    In records of the heart.

WISH AND ITEM

Written to the Editor of the *Item*, Lynn, Mass.

I hope the heart that's hungry
  For things above the floor,
Will find within its portals
  An item rich in store;

That melancholy mortals
  Will count their mercies o'er,
And learn that Truth and wisdom
  Have many items more;

That when a wrong is done us,
  It stirs no thought of strife;
And Love becomes the substance,
  As item, of our life;

That every ragged urchin,
  With bare feet soiled or sore,
Share God's most tender mercies, —
  Find items at our door.

Then if we've done to others
  Some good ne'er told before,
When angels shall repeat it,
  'T will be an item more.

1   THE OAK ON THE MOUNTAIN'S SUMMIT

Oh, mountain monarch, at whose feet I stand, —
3 Clouds to adorn thy brow, skies clasp thy hand, —
Nature divine, in harmony profound,
With peaceful presence hath begirt thee round.

6 And thou, majestic oak, from yon high place
Guard'st thou the earth, asleep in night's embrace, —
And from thy lofty summit, pouring down
9 Thy sheltering shade, her noonday glories crown?

Whate'er thy mission, mountain sentinel,
To my lone heart thou art a power and spell;
12 A lesson grave, of life, that teacheth me
To love the Hebrew figure of a tree.

Faithful and patient be my life as thine;
15 As strong to wrestle with the storms of time;
As deeply rooted in a soil of love;
As grandly rising to the heavens above.

18   ISLE OF WIGHT

Written on receiving a painting of the Isle

Isle of beauty, thou art singing
21   To my sense a sweet refrain;
To my busy mem'ry bringing
        Scenes that I would see again.

Chief, the charm of thy reflecting,   1
  Is the moral that it brings;
Nature, with the mind connecting,   3
  Gives the artist's fancy wings.

Soul, sublime 'mid human *débris,*
  Paints the limner's work, I ween,   6
Art and Science, all unweary,
  Lighting up this mortal dream.

Work ill-done within the misty   9
  Mine of human thoughts, we see
Soon abandoned when the Master
  Crowns life's Cliff for such as we.   12

Students wise, he maketh now thus
  Those who fish in waters deep,
When the buried Master hails us   15
  From the shores afar, complete.

Art hath bathed this isthmus-lordling
  In a beauty strong and meek   18
As the rock, whose upward tending
  Points the plane of power to seek.

Isle of beauty, thou art teaching   21
  Lessons long and grand, to-night,
To my heart that would be bleaching
  To thy whiteness, Cliff of Wight.   24

HOPE

1
'T is borne on the zephyr at eventide's hour;
3 It falls on the heart like the dew on the flower, —
An infinite essence from tropic to pole,
The promise, the home, and the heaven of Soul.

6 Hope happifies life, at the altar or bower,
And loosens the fetters of pride and of power;
It comes through our tears, as the soft summer rain,
9 To beautify, bless, and make joyful again.

The harp of the minstrel, the treasure of time;
A rainbow of rapture, o'erarching, divine;
12 The God-given mandate that speaks from above, —
No place for earth's idols, but hope thou, and love.

RONDELET

15
"The flowers of June
The gates of memory unbar:
The flowers of June
18 Such old-time harmonies *re*tune,
I fain would keep the gates ajar, —
So full of sweet enchantment are
21
The flowers of June."

JAMES T. WHITE

TO MR. JAMES T. WHITE

1

Who loves not June
Is out of tune
With love and God;
The rose his rival reigns,
The stars reject his pains,
His home the clod!

3

6

And yet I trow,
When sweet *rondeau*
Doth play a part,
The curtain drops on June;
Veiled is the modest moon —
Hushed is the heart.

9

12

AUTUMN

Written in childhood, in a maple grove

15

Quickly earth's jewels disappear;
   The turf, whereon I tread,
Ere autumn blanch another year,
   May rest above my head.

18

Touched by the finger of decay
   Is every earthly love;
For joy, to shun my weary way,
   Is registered above.

21

The languid brooklets yield their sighs,
   A requiem o'er the tomb
Of sunny days and cloudless skies,
   Enhancing autumn's gloom.

24

27

1   The wild winds mutter, howl, and moan,
     To scare my woodland walk,
3   And frightened fancy flees, to roam
     Where ghosts and goblins stalk.

   The cricket's sharp, discordant scream
6   Fills mortal sense with dread;
   More sorrowful it scarce could seem;
     It voices beauty fled.

9   Yet here, upon this faded sod, —
     O happy hours and fleet, —
   When songsters' matin hymns to God
12   Are poured in strains so sweet,

   My heart unbidden joins rehearse;
     I hope it 's better made,
15   When mingling with the universe,
     Beneath the maple's shade.

CHRIST MY REFUGE

18   O'er waiting harpstrings of the mind
     There sweeps a strain,
   Low, sad, and sweet, whose measures bind
21   The power of pain,

   And wake a white-winged angel throng
     Of thoughts, illumed
24   By faith, and breathed in raptured song,
     With love perfumed.

Then His unveiled, sweet mercies show   1
    Life's burdens light.
I kiss the cross, and wake to know   3
    A world more bright.

And o'er earth's troubled, angry sea
    I see Christ walk,   6
And come to me, and tenderly,
    Divinely talk.

Thus Truth engrounds me on the rock,   9
    Upon Life's shore,
'Gainst which the winds and waves can shock,
    Oh, nevermore!   12

From tired joy and grief afar,
    And nearer Thee, —
Father, where Thine own children are,   15
    I love to be.

My prayer, some daily good to do
    To Thine, for Thee;   18
An offering pure of Love, whereto
    God leadeth me.

"FEED MY SHEEP"   21

Shepherd, show me how to go
    O'er the hillside steep,
How to gather, how to sow, —   24
    How to feed Thy sheep;

1   I will listen for Thy voice,
        Lest my footsteps stray;
3   I will follow and rejoice
        All the rugged way.

      Thou wilt bind the stubborn will,
6   Wound the callous breast,
      Make self-righteousness be still,
        Break earth's stupid rest.
9   Strangers on a barren shore,
        Lab'ring long and lone,
      We would enter by the door,
12   And Thou know'st Thine own;

      So, when day grows dark and cold,
        Tear or triumph harms,
15   Lead Thy lambkins to the fold,
        Take them in Thine arms;
      Feed the hungry, heal the heart,
18   Till the morning's beam;
      White as wool, ere they depart,
        Shepherd, wash them clean.

21   COMMUNION HYMN

Saw ye my Saviour? Heard ye the glad sound?
Felt ye the power of the Word?
24   'T was the Truth that made us free,
And was found by you and me
In the life and the love of our Lord.

Mourner, it calls you, — "Come to my bosom,   1
Love wipes your tears all away,
And will lift the shade of gloom,   3
And for you make radiant room
Midst the glories of one endless day."

Sinner, it calls you, — "Come to this fountain,   6
Cleanse the foul senses within;
'T is the Spirit that makes pure,
That exalts thee, and will cure   9
All thy sorrow and sickness and sin."

Strongest deliverer, friend of the friendless,
Life of all being divine: 12
Thou the Christ, and not the creed;
Thou the Truth in thought and deed;
Thou the water, the bread, and the wine.   15

LAUS DEO!

Written on laying the corner-stone of The Mother Church

Laus Deo, it is done!   18
Rolled away from loving heart
   Is a stone.
Lifted higher, we depart,   21
   Having one.

Laus Deo, — on this rock
(Heaven chiselled squarely good)   24
   Stands His church, —
God is Love, and understood
   By His flock.   27

1   *Laus Deo*, night star-lit
              Slumbers not in God's embrace;
3   Be awake;
              Like this stone, be in thy place:
                   Stand, not sit.

6   Grave, silent, steadfast stone,
              Dirge and song and shoutings low
                   In thy heart
9   Dwell serene, — and sorrow? No,
                   It has none,
                   Laus Deo!

12   A VERSE

MOTHER'S NEW YEAR GIFT TO THE LITTLE CHILDREN

              Father-Mother God,
15   Loving me, —
              Guard me when I sleep;
              Guide my little feet
18   Up to Thee.

              TO THE BIG CHILDREN

              Father-Mother good, lovingly
21   Thee I seek, —
                   Patient, meek,
              In the way Thou hast, —
24   Be it slow or fast,
                   Up to Thee.

CHAPTER XII

Testimonials

LETTERS FROM THOSE HEALED BY READING "SCIENCE AND HEALTH WITH KEY TO THE SCRIPTURES"

The Editor of *The Christian Science Journal* (Falmouth and St. Paul Streets, Boston, Mass.) holds the original of most of the letters that authenticate these.

IT is something more than a year and a half since I was cured of a complication of diseases through reading "Science and Health with Key to the Scriptures."

Becoming at an early age disgusted with drugs, I learned hygiene, and practised it faithfully for over twenty years; then I began to lose all faith in its efficacy, became greatly discouraged, and, as I had never been cured of a single ailment, I rapidly grew worse in health. Hearing of this, a dear sister brought me Science and Health. Her admonition was, "Now read it, E——; I have heard that just the reading of that book has been known to heal the sick."

I had read to, and through, the chapter on Healing and Teaching,[1] and was so deeply interested that I began reading that blessed chapter over again, — when I found I was cured of my dyspepsia, that I could use my strength in lifting without feeling the old distressing pain in my side, and also that the pain in the kidneys only came on

---

[1] Page 292 of the revised edition of 1890.

at night, waking me out of sleep. Then I began my first conscious treatments: of course I followed no formula, and I needed none. A cry for help, knowing it would be answered; precious texts from the Bible, which had already become like a new book to me; sweet assurance of faith by the witnessing Spirit; strong logical conclusions, learned from Science and Health: what a wealth of material! Before finishing the book, all tendency to my old aches and pains had left me, and I have been a strong, healthy woman ever since.

My first demonstration with another than myself was also before I had finished my first reading. My husband was cured of the belief of bilious fever by not over ten minutes' treatment; the fever and pain in head and limbs disappearing in that instantaneous way as soon as I could summon sufficient courage to offer my services in this, to us, new but glorious work. He slept soundly that night (the treatment was given about 10 A. M.), and ate and worked as usual the next day, with no symptoms of a relapse then or afterward. That was in March, 1888; in the following August I met in one of our Rocky Mountain berry patches a lady who complained so bitterly that I felt compelled to offer her treatment. Her words, when I visited her at her home during Christmas week, will give some idea of the result: —

"Yes, I am doing three women's work, — attending to my own and my son's housework, and caring for his wife and new-born babe; but I am equal to it, when I think of all the Lord has done for me! Why, Mrs. S., I was cured with that first treatment you gave me, I know; because I went out to gather berries that day and was caught in a drenching shower, — and for ten years before

I could not bear the least exposure without suffering from those dreadful headaches I told you about, and from dysentery, — but that day I had neither. I had once been laid out for dead, — lying there perfectly conscious, hearing my friends grieving over me, — but I did not want to come to, I suffered so. No, I never have any of those ailments. I am a well, hearty woman, — and that is not all. I had been seeking religion for more than twenty years, but I never knew how Christians felt till I told you I was cured that day on the camp-ground."

On the first of this year I was so blessed as to receive a course of lessons from one of our teacher's students. Now I am only trusting that the time will come when I may be enabled to teach others the way of Truth, as well as to add to the many demonstrations God has given me. — E. D. S.

A student of Christian Science was employed in the Massachusetts State Prison at Charlestown, to teach the prisoners to make shoes. He carried his copy of "Science and Health with Key to the Scriptures" and the *Journal* with him, and as he had the opportunity would tell the men what this wonderful truth could do for them, setting them free in a larger and higher sense than they had dreamed of.

We make extracts from a number of letters that one of the prisoners has written to those who are interesting themselves in this work.

"*Editor of The Christian Science Journal:* — At the prison, once a week, there are Christian papers given to the inmates. But none of those papers point out so clearly the fallibility of the mortal or carnal mind, and the infallibility of the divine Mind, as does the teaching of Christian Science.

"I was strangely blind and stupid. I loved sin, and it seemed as though I never would be able to forsake it. I did everything that would be expected of one entirely ignorant of God.

"I also had a complication of diseases. I could not begin to describe the medicines I have taken.

"I no longer look for material treatment, but humbly seek for the divine assistance of Jesus, through the way Christian Science has taught me. I am, indeed, an altered man. I now have no more doubt of the way of salvation than I have of the way to the prison workshop.

"I am very grateful to the students of Christian Science, for the interest they have taken in me and my fellow-prisoners. Their letters and books have been of great profit, and in accordance with their wish I have done what I could for the others.

"I gave the *Journal* to every man who would accept it, and related my experience to those who would listen. I told them they need go no farther than myself to see what the demonstration was; for not only have my eyes been healed, but many other ailments have disappeared.

"Some of the fellows told me I was becoming religiously insane, but acting upon your advice, I did not stop to argue with those opposed; and I am glad to be able to tell you that those who expressed interest were more than those who opposed.

"The chaplain told me I could keep Science and Health until I got through with it. I never should get through with that book, but, as others were waiting for it, I did not like to keep it too long. God bless the author!

"I need have no fear after leaving here; I feel that I can make an honest living. I can honestly add, that my bad reputation is largely due to my lack of education. What little I do know, I learned here and in the House of Correction. I tell you this, for I feel that I must be honest with the kind friends who have done so much for me.

"Providing I should not be paroled, I shall remain here until the 24th of next December. God bless you all. — J. C."

I am glad to tell how I was healed. Beliefs of consumption, dyspepsia, neuralgia, piles, tobacco, and bad language held me in bondage for many years. Doctors that were consulted did nothing to relieve me, and I constantly grew worse. Nearly two years ago a lady told me that if I would read a book called "Science and Health with Key to the Scriptures" I would be healed. I told her I would "go into it for all it is worth," and I have found that it is worth all. I got the book, and read day and night. I saw that it must be true, and believed that what I could not then understand would be made clear later.

After some days' reading I was affected with drowsiness, followed by vomiting. This lasted several hours; when I fell into a sleep, and awoke healed. The good I have received, and that I have been able to do in healing others, has all come from Science and Health. I received some instructions from teachers; but they did me more harm than good: I asked for bread, but they gave me a stone. I held to what I could understand of Science and Health; and the truth does not forsake me, but enables me to heal others.

Last February, I was called to treat a child that the M. D.'s said was dying from lung fever; after the third treatment the child got up and ran about, completely healed. Another child was brought to me, with rupture; after the second treatment the truss was thrown away. An aged lady was healed of heart disease and chills, in one treatment. These cases brought me many more, that were also healed.

The husband of a lady in the State Lunatic Asylum asked me to treat her; she had been for two years and a half in the asylum, and though taken home in this time once or twice, she had had to be taken back. After two weeks of absent treatment, the husband visited her, and the doctor reported great improvement during the preceding two weeks. At the end of another two weeks I went with the husband to the asylum, and the doctor told us that she was well enough to go home. The husband asked the doctor how it was that she had improved so rapidly, and he said that he could not account for it. We said nothing about the Christian Science treatment, and took the lady home. This was about a year ago, and she has remained perfectly well.

Many cases as striking as this can be referred to in this town, as evidence that Truth is the healer of sickness as well as of sin. — J. B. H.

No. I. A lady friend, who was found to have a severe attack of dysentery, was assured that such attacks could be cured without medicine, and advised to take no more. She was more than astonished at the result; for in less than an hour all pain and other symptoms of the trouble ceased, and she felt perfectly well the next day.

No. 2.   While she was visiting relatives in the country, an infant of theirs was attacked severely with croup, and appeared to be on the verge of suffocation, giving its parents much alarm.   The infant was taken in the arms of the lady, in thirty minutes was completely relieved, went to sleep, and awoke in good health the next morning.

No. 3.   The mother of this child was subsequently attacked with a scrofulous swelling on the neck, just under the ear, which was very painful and disfiguring; the side of the face, also, being badly swollen.   It was feared that this would develop into and undergo the usual phenomenon of abscess, as other similar swellings had done previously.   She had great faith in the metaphysical treatment, because of the experience which she had had with her baby, and wrote a letter describing her case.   This was immediately answered, and absent treatment was begun.   In twenty-four hours after receipt of the letter, to the astonishment of herself and family, the tumor had entirely disappeared: there was not a trace of it left;   although the day before it was fully as large as a hen's egg;   red, and tender to the touch.

These instances are only a few of the many cures which have been performed in this way, and they are mentioned simply to show what good work may be done by any earnest, conscientious person who has gained by reading my works the proper understanding of the Principle of Christian Science.

What a wonderful field for enlightenment and profit lies open to those who seek after Truth. Alas, that the feet of so few enter it!

Rev. M. B. G. Eddy: — Will you kindly spare me a few moments for the perusal of these lines from a stranger, — one who feels under a debt of gratitude to you, — for, through the divine Science brought to light by you, I have been "made whole." I have been cured of a malignant cancer since I began to study Christian Science, and have *demonstrated the truth* of it in a number of cases. I have only studied your good books, having been *unable* to take the lectures for want of means. I dare not think of these, for there is no prospect that I shall be in a position to take the course at all. I do not allow myself to complain, but cheerfully take up my books and study, and feel thankful for this light.

M. E. W., Cañon City, Col.

Dear Madam: — May I thank you for your book, "Science and Health with Key to the Scriptures," and say how much I owe to it — almost my very life — at a most critical time. . . .

If it were not for the heat of your American summers (I had nine attacks of dysentery in the last one), and the expense, I should dearly like to learn from you personally; but I must forego this, — at any rate, for the present. If you would write me what the cost would be for a course on divine metaphysics, I would try to manage it later on.

Meanwhile, I should be grateful if you would refer me to any one in this country who is interested similarly, for I get more kicks than halfpence in discussing it.

Your obliged friend, (REV.) I. G. W. BISHOP,

Bovington Vicarage, Hemel Hempstead,
Herts, England

Extract from a letter to Rev. M. B. G. Eddy

A gentleman here had hired all the most skilled doctors in the United States — nothing helped him. He was a ghost to look upon. I told him just to read my copies of your books. I talked to him, told him what he could do for himself if he but tried. He laughed at me. I was willing he should laugh, for it was very unusual for him to do this. He had your books two months, and last Sunday he returned them. I wish you could see him: *he is well.* He is happy, and told me he was going to write to you for the books for himself this week. — E. E. B.

Dear Madam: — I have been a sickly person all my life, until a few months ago, and was confined to my bed every little while. It was during one of many attacks that your book, "Science and Health with Key to the Scriptures," was handed me. I read it only a very short time, when I arose, well, went out into the kitchen, prepared a large dinner, and ate heartily of it.

I have been up and well ever since, — a marvel to my friends and family, and sometimes they can hardly believe it is I; and feeling so grateful, I must tell you of it. I wish everybody in the world would read your book, for all would be benefited by it.

Gratefully yours, ANNA M. SMITH

Dear Madam: — About seven years ago I was compelled to go to an oculist and have an operation performed upon my eyes. He fitted me with glasses, which I wore for a considerable time, and then removed; but the pain and difficulty returned, and I was obliged to go again to the oculist, who advised me never to take my glasses off again.

I continued wearing them for fully five years longer, until some time in last January, when, upon reading your book, "Science and Health with Key to the Scriptures," I again took them off. Since that time, though I have been in the courts reporting, and reading fine notes frequently, I have experienced no difficulty with my eyes.

Very respectfully,

WILLIAM A. SMITH, Wilmington, Del.

Dear Mrs. Eddy: — We have been studying "Science and Health with Key to the Scriptures" for a year, and I cannot tell you how much it has done for us; giving us health instead of sickness, and giving us such an understanding of God as we never had before. Christian Science was our only help two weeks ago, when our baby was born. My husband and myself were alone. I dressed myself the next day; commenced doing my work the third day, and am well and strong. It must be pleasing to you to know how much good your work is doing.

KITTIE BECK, Elmwood, Cass Co., Neb.

I was a helpless sufferer in August, 1883, and had been so for many years. The physicians said I had cancer of the uterus. I heard of your book, "Science and Health with Key to the Scriptures," bought a copy, began reading it, and a great light seemed to break through the darkness. I cried aloud in joy, "This is what I have been hungering for, these many years!" I studied it closely, and healed myself and several of my friends before I had taken instruction of any teacher.

            Mrs. S. A. McMahon, Wyandotte, Kans.

I was healed thoroughly of the belief of chronic hepatitis and kidney disease, by reading "Science and Health with Key to the Scriptures." I have never, to this day, had the slightest return of it.

            J. P. Filbert, Council Bluffs, Iowa

You, dear Mrs. Eddy, have saved my life, through Science and Health; and I feel that the patients healed through me should give the first thanks to God and to you. — Mrs. D. S. Harriman, Kansas City, Mo.

How grand your book, "Science and Health with Key to the Scriptures," is! It is a translation of Truth. No amount of money could buy the book of me, if I could not get another. No matter what suffering comes, physical or mental, I have only to take Science and Health, and almost invariably the first sentence brings relief. It seems to steady the thought. I do not think any student old enough to neglect reading it. When we think we are advanced far enough to let that book alone, then are we in danger.

MRS. ELLEN P. CLARK, Dorchester, Mass.

Many thanks for the good received from your books. When I commenced reading them, I was carrying about a very sick body. Your books have healed me. I am now in perfect health. People look at me with surprise, and say they do not understand it; but when they see the sick ones made well, they are not always willing to believe it.

MRS. JOSEPH TILLSON, South Hanson, Mass.

Rev. M. B. G. Eddy: — I add one more testimony of a cure from reading your book, "Science and Health with Key to the Scriptures." Five years ago I lay prostrate with piles and inflammation of the bowels. All the coating came off, apparently. A stricture was formed, beyond medical reach. I then lived in Chicago; one of the best physicians, who made a specialty of treating piles, attended me. The pain was relieved, but my bowels were inactive, and remained so until New Year's eve.

I determined to trust all to God, or die before I would take any more medicine, as I never had an action unless I took a free dose of some laxative. If I forgot to take the medicine one night, or allowed myself to be without it, I had a terrible sick headache for two or three days, and terrible backache. I never had backache at any other time, and the piles would be so much inflamed, in two days' time, that I could hardly tell where I suffered the worst.

Since I have learned to trust all to God, I have not had the least trouble with the piles, nor one twinge of the backache. I have an easy action of the bowels each morning. It was five days after I resolved to leave medicine alone, before a natural movement took place; and ever since I have been perfectly regular. It was a great effort for me to take that step, for I knew I was running the risk of throwing myself back into all misery, and perhaps into a worse state than before. By reading Science and Health, I learned that God was able to save the body as well as the soul, and I believed His promises were for me.

MATTIE E. MAYFIELD, Des Moines, Iowa

For the Cause of Truth, I submit the following testimonial for publication; may it bring *one* more, at least, into the fold of divine Science! The truth, as it is stated in "Science and Health with Key to the Scriptures," has done much towards making our home the abiding-place of peace and harmony. I now write of the wonderful demonstration of Truth over the birth of my baby boy, two weeks ago. Sunday, September 23, we went for a long drive of three hours; at night I retired at the usual hour; toward morning I was given a little warning; when I awoke at seven o'clock, the birth took place. Not more than ten minutes after, I ate a hearty breakfast, and then had a refreshing sleep; at ten o'clock walked across the room while my bed was dressed; at twelve took a substantial dinner; most of the afternoon sat up in bed, without any support but Truth; at six in the evening dressed myself and walked to the dining-room, and remained up for two hours. Next morning I arose at the usual hour, and have kept it up ever since, — was not confined to my bed one whole day. The second day was out walking in the yard, and the third day went for a drive in the morning and received callers in the afternoon. If it had not been for the presence of my young hopeful, it would have been hard to believe that there had so recently been a belief of a birth in the house; but then, I was sustained by Love, and had no belief of suffering to take my strength away. Before baby was two weeks old, I cooked, swept, ran the sewing machine, etc., assisting with the housework generally. How grateful I am for the obstetrics of this grand Science! Mothers need no longer listen to the whispering lies of the old serpent, for the law of mortal mind is broken by Truth.

MRS. DORA HOSSICK, Carrolton, Mo.

My wife and I have been healed by reading your book, "Science and Health with Key to the Scriptures." We both feel very grateful to you.

Five months ago my wife gave birth to a child, without pain or inconvenience, has done all the housework since, and has been every minute perfectly well. Neither she nor the child have been ill, — as was constantly the case with former children, — so we have thought it right to name the child Glover Eddy.

We have been reading Science and Health nearly

two years, and have sold several copies to others. We are reading the *Journal* also this year.

Yours respectfully, JOHN B. HOUSEL, Lincoln, Neb.

Dear Mother: — The most blessed of women! Oh, how I long to sit within range of your voice and hear the truth that comes to you from on high! for none could speak such wondrous thoughts as have come from your pen, except it be the Spirit that speaketh in you.

Two years ago last October, while laboring under a great strain of care and anxiety in regard to financial affairs, I heard of Christian Science. I borrowed "Science and Health with Key to the Scriptures," and began to read. I bless God that I was driven to it by such an extremity. After reading some one hundred and fifty pages, I was convinced that it was the truth for which I had searched during twenty years. While I was reading the chapter on Imposition and Demonstration,[1] I was healed of endometritis and prolapsus uteri of over twenty years' standing, pronounced incurable by eminent physicians. Professor Ludlam, the dean of Hahnemann Medical College, of Chicago, Ill., was one of my doctors.

Before I was healed, to walk seven or eight blocks would so fatigue me that it would take me a week to recover. I now started out and walked, and was on my feet all day and for several succeeding days, but felt no weariness from my labors.

I felt, after being healed, I must have a Science and Health of my own. I had no money to buy it, so earned

---

[1] Page 234, revised edition of 1890.

it by getting subscribers for the *Journal*. It has gone
with me everywhere I have been. I have been well ever
since.

I had suffered from bodily ailments, but they were
nothing compared to my mental trials. Grief, hatred,
jealousy, and revenge had well-nigh bereft me of reason.
I had lost a home of plenty, been reduced to almost abject
poverty, and had become a cheerless woman, — could
not smile without feeling I had sinned.

All my griefs and sorrows are now turned to joy, and
my hatred is changed to love. "Glory to God in the
highest, and on earth peace, good will toward men." I
read Science and Health, and all your other books, together with the New Testament, every minute I can
get. — E. B. C., Omaha, Neb.

I must add one more to your great pile of letters, to
tell you what your book, "Science and Health with Key
to the Scriptures," has done for me and my family. More
than a year ago, my husband was suffering from an injury
received about a year previous, and he went to Mrs. B. for
treatment. His shoulder had been fractured, his collar-
bone broken, and he had sustained internal injuries. Several M. D.'s had attended him, but had given him very
little relief. Mrs. B. treated him a short time, and he
received much benefit. He bought Science and Health.
From reading it, I was cured of a belief of chronic liver
complaint. I suffered so much from headaches and con-
stipation, and other beliefs, that I seldom ever saw a well
day; but, thanks to you and divine Principle, I now
seldom ever have a belief of feeling badly.

November 4th, last, I was confined. I was alone, because I knew no one whose thought was in harmony with Science. I thought I could get along without help, and I did. My little girl was sleeping in the same room with me, and after the birth she called a woman who was asleep upstairs, to take care of the baby. This woman was much frightened; but, on seeing how composed I was, she got over her fright. I was sitting up in bed, holding the child, and feeling as well as I ever did in my life. I never had seen a Scientist nor been treated, but got all my ideas from Science and Health. My baby was born on Sunday morning, and I got up Monday at noon, and stayed up. I never got along so well with a baby as I did with this one.

I am very thankful for the knowledge of Science I have gained through your book. I want so much to be a Scientist; but we are very poor. My husband is a brakeman on the railroad; and I have very little education. There is comfort in the thought that, if I can't be a Scientist, my children may be.

Yours with much love,   C. A. W., Lexington, Mo.

In the February *Journal* it appears there is some one who says that "Science and Health with Key to the Scriptures" is hard to understand, and who thinks she can explain it. Perhaps my experience with Science and Health may help some one who might otherwise take up this thought, and so be led away from the truth. After reading and studying it for some time, and talking to the Scientists I met in my travels, the thought came to me, "Why not try these truths on yourself?" I did so, and to my surprise and great joy I found immediate relief. Dyspepsia (the trouble of most commercial travellers), catarrh, and many lesser beliefs, left me, so that in a short time I was a *well man,* and by no other means than trusting to the Saviour's promises as explained in Science and Health. This took place while I was travelling about the country.

On my return home, I gave my wife treatments. In many instances the blessing came before the treatment was finished, and often we proved that only a thought of the power of Truth was sufficient to give relief.

One Sunday morning, soon after my return, a friend called and asked if I could give him anything to relieve his wife, who, he said, had been suffering for some days with rheumatism in her shoulder, so severely that she could neither dress alone nor comb her hair. I told him that the only medicine we had in the house was Christian Science. He laughed at the idea; but before he left, he asked if I would give his wife a treatment. I told him I was very young in Science, but if she wished it, I would. He went home, but returned immediately, saying she wished me to come. Then I asked help from the fountain of Truth, and started for my first treatment to be given away from home. When I left their room fifteen minutes later, she was shaking her hand high above her head, and exclaiming, "I am all right; I am well!" That was in November, 1887, and she has had no return of the belief since.

A friend told me that his son, twelve years old, had catarrh so badly that his breath was very offensive, his throat troubled him all the time, and that he had been deaf since he had the measles. In less than three weeks both beliefs vanished. This was a case of absent treatment. I could give you other cases, but I think I have said enough to prove that Science and Health *is not hard to understand,* for my work has all been done without my ever attending class.

                              H. H. B., New York City

A lady, with no other instructor than "Science and Health with Key to the Scriptures," has demonstrated beyond many who have taken numerous lessons. Persuaded, through her reading, of the allness of God, — and the perfectness of idea, — she would know nothing else. A daughter, so badly affected by poison oak (ivy) that for weeks death was feared from blood-poisoning, had recovered with a terrible dread of that plant. As the next season's picnic time drew near, she was regretting that she dared not go again. The mother, with her new-born faith in the Science of being, said, "Certainly you can go, for nothing can harm you." Assured by these words, the daughter went, and in her rambles fell into a mass of the dreaded plant; but trusting to the word of Truth, she thought nothing of it till one who knew of her previous trouble said, in her mother's presence, "See, her face is showing red already." But the mother was prompt in denial and assurance. Next morning, old symptoms were out in force, but they yielded at once and finally to the positive and uncompromising hold on Truth. Another daughter, that was thought too delicate to raise, from bronchial and nervous troubles, always dosed with medicine and wrapped in flannels, now runs free and well without either of these, winter and summer. The mother was recently attacked by mesmerism from the church that believed she was influencing her daughter to leave. She overcame by the same unwavering trust in God, seeing Truth clearer than ever before. Her demonstrations come through no form of treatment, but by letting the Spirit bear witness, — by the positive recognition and realization of no reality but ever-present good.

The other night her husband was attacked with an old belief, similar to one that some time before had ended in a congestive chill which the doctor thought very serious, and from which he had been a long time in recovering. The wife simply recognized no reality in the belief, and, seeing only perfect being, felt no fear. She did nothing, — no "treating" in the usual sense. There is nothing to do but to understand that all is harmony, always. He felt the presence that destroys the sense of evil, and next morning — there was nothing left to recover from.

A lady, while doing some starching, thoughtlessly put her hand into the scalding starch to wring out a collar. Recalled to mortal sense by the stinging pain, she immediately realized the all-power of God. At once the pain began to subside; and as she brushed off the scalding starch, she could see the blister-swelling go down till there was but a little redness to show for the accident; absorbed in her thankfulness, she mechanically wrung out the collar with the same hand, and with no sense of pain, thus verifying the demonstration. This woman (not reading English) only knows Science as she has received it from her practitioner during the treatments received within the last month. So much has come to her from Spirit through her loyalty to Christ, in so far as she could understand.

A case of ulcerated tooth and neuralgic belief would only partially yield after repeated treatments, till it was discovered that the patient was antagonizing Truth by holding the thought that her old remedy, laudanum, would give relief; treated from this standpoint, relief was immediate and final.

One morning after Rev. —— had been preaching to thousands for several days, he told them that he had never felt such a sense of depression nor had so little showing of results. Some Scientists hearing this, at once saw his trouble. He had been fearlessly exposing and denouncing evil; and it had turned on him, till the mesmerism was likely to overcome him entirely, for he did not understand the seeming power. The effect of the silent word to uplift and sustain, was very manifest that evening in his preaching, and was a beautiful demonstration of Science. He probably only felt Spirit-inspiration as he had not before, without a thought as to what had broken the evil spell; but we never know the what, or when, or where, of the harvest we can sow — "God giveth the increase." — E. H. B., Sacramento

I had two German patients who were anxious to have you publish "Science and Health with Key to the Scriptures" in their language. I advised them to buy it and try to read it. They commenced reading, and now can read all of Science and Health, but do not read well any other book or paper, and they do not need to. With great love. — M. H. P.

I sold three copies of "Science and Health with Key to the Scriptures" to friends, not long ago. One of them, fifty years of age, said to me, "I never had one day's sickness in my life; but after reading Science and Health I found that I was bruised and mangled, from the crown of my head to the soles of my feet. I have been reaching after something that, before reading Science and Health, seemed to me unattainable;" and with tears in her eyes, she rejoiced in the God of her salvation. Did not Jesus say, "If these should hold their peace, the stones would immediately cry out"?

P. L., Lexington, Ky.

For eight years I suffered terribly with my eyes; I could not read fifteen minutes without the most agonizing sick headache. Oculists called it a case of double vision, and said that the only chance for a cure lay in cutting the muscles of the eyes. This was done, but the pain was worse than before. One of the most famous oculists of New York said I would simply have to endure it for life, as it was a case of severe astigmatism.

I suffered so that my health gave way. A friend spoke to me of Christian Science, but I scoffed at the idea. Later on, in desperation, I asked her to lend me "Science and Health with Key to the Scriptures," thinking I might be able to read five minutes a day in it. I opened the book at the chapter on Physiology, and began. Time passed unnoticed: every page seemed illuminated. I said, "This is everything or nothing; if everything, then you need no glasses." I took off the heavy ground glasses, and went on. What a terrible headache I had the next morning! but I fought it with the truth laid down in the book. I said again, "This is everything or nothing," and the truth triumphed. The headache ceased, but I felt miserably. I recalled what was said about chemicalization, and persevered.

In four days my eyes were well; I read as many hours a day as I pleased; my strength returned. I conquered one belief after another, until now, strong and well, I meet every belief with confidence. "I will fear *no* evil: for *Thou* art with me." For two years I have realized the peace and confidence which the knowledge that God is all-powerful and always present alone can give. Feeling a great desire to spread Christian Science, that it may do the good to others that it has to me, not only physically but spiritually, I ask if you have any missionaries in the work. Being a member of the Episcopal Church, I have always sent what I could to help foreign missions through that church. Will it do the most good to continue so doing, as our foreign missionaries are devoted men, or have you Christian Science missionaries who devote their lives to the work?

An answer addressed to me, or published in the *Journal*, would help one who is seeking to do right.

Yours sincerely,   K. L. T.

I do wish to add my testimony of being healed by reading "Science and Health with Key to the Scriptures." I had been an invalid for over twenty years, and had given up all hope of ever being well again. I had read the book about six weeks, when it seemed I was made all over new, and I could "run, and not be weary; and . . . walk, and not faint." I did not understand it, but it was the savior from death unto life with me; I have remained well ever since I was healed, — more than five years ago. I commenced to treat others as soon as I was born anew into the kingdom of Truth. My patients were healed right along, before I had taken lessons in a class, and they have remained well to this day.

Christian Science has made me as young as a girl of sixteen. If this should meet the eye of any sufferers who may be led to go and do as I did, they will be healed. — N. A. E.

Language is inadequate when bearing grateful testimony to the book "Science and Health with Key to the Scriptures." By its simple reading, I was healed of ills which baffled the skill of specialists and all curatives that love and money could command. After eighteen years of invalidism, and eight years of scepticism, without hope, with no God, — except a First Cause, — I was given up to die.

A loving friend told me of this book, which was soon brought; and thirty-five pages of the first chapter were read to me that evening. The next morning I got up, walked, and read the book for myself.

I mention the chapter, for the reason that nearly two years have passed since those wonderful words of Life were first read to me, and *still* their sacred sweetness is ever the same. Now I exclaim, *God is* All!

MRS. MARY A. R.

It is impossible for me to keep still any longer. In 1885, when I had not known a well day in five years, "Science and Health with Key to the Scriptures" was placed in my hands by a dear lady who insisted upon my reading it, saying she believed it would heal me. Like many, I was afraid of it, — until I learned what it really was. The friend's words were verified. I *was* healed by the reading of the book, and for one year continued to read nothing whatever but the Bible and Science and Health. They were my constant study. Through the understanding gained, that *God is All,* I came to demonstrate with great success, and with but one thought, — for I knew nothing about giving a "treatment;" I wish I knew as little now, for I believe that healing in Christian Science is to be done in a moment. I became anxious to learn more, to study with the teacher, but funds would not allow, — and I thought to substitute a course in Chicago, perhaps. Every time I would speak of it, however, my dear mother would say, "You have Science and Health and the Bible, and God for your teacher — what more do you need? If I could not go to the teacher, I would not go to any one."

If I had only heeded the blessed counsel of Truth!

I went to Chicago, however, so full of confidence in Christian Science that I supposed every one who had studied with Mrs. Eddy must be right. Unfortunately, I took my course with a spiritualist who had been through two of her classes; discovered my mistake, and went to a mind-cure, — only to find the mistake repeated. Being an earnest seeker for Truth, I tried again to go to the Massachusetts Metaphysical College; but it was uncertain when there would be a class, so I took a course with one of Mrs. Eddy's students in Boston. The darkness now rolled away. Science and Health once more revealed the light to me as of old.

All this time, the mind-curers had me in view, and were sending me reading-matter; but, *praise the Lord!* Truth is victorious.

My dear brothers and sisters, let us be safely guided by the counsels of our Mother, in Science and Health! I, for one, am astounded that I was so led astray; but I did it all through ignorance, — and the *sincere* desire to know the truth and to *do* it, saved me.

Your sister in truth,   R. D.

I have been reading Science and Health for one year and a half, and have had some wonderful demonstrations. People here are antagonistic to the Science, and tell me that I am a "fit subject for the asylum." Physicians threaten me with arrest, also, but I walk straight on, knowing *well in whom I trust.*

E. I. R., Wauseon, Ohio

A little over two years ago, while living in Pittsburgh, my wife and I had Christian Science brought to our attention. We were at once interested, and bought a copy of "Science and Health with Key to the Scriptures."

At the time, Mrs. A—— was suffering with severe belief of astigmatism of the eyes. She had been treated by a number of specialists, during seven years, the last being the late Dr. Agnew of New York, who prescribed two sets of glasses. He said that he could do nothing more for her, as the trouble was organic; that she must wear glasses constantly; that if she attempted to go without, she would become either blind or insane. The glasses were in operation, and still life had become a burden from constant pain, when Christian Science came to our relief. Mrs. A—— had not in years read for two consecutive minutes, and could not use her eyes in sewing at all. The lady that told us of the Science, insisted that she *could* read Science and Health, which she actually did, — reading it through twice, and studying it carefully each time. After the second reading, there came the thought that she did not need the glasses, and she at once abandoned them, and went about her usual duties. In about two weeks from that day the eyes were perfectly healed, and are well and strong to-day.

E. G. A., New York City

My Dear Teacher: — Yours without date is at hand. Could you know out of what depths of material *débris* the first reading of the first volume of Science and Health, six years ago last December, lifted me, you would believe it had always been "all I could ask." It was *only* words from the pen of *uninspired* writers that gave me pain. As the revelation of the All-good appeared to me, all other books, all forms of religion, all methods of healing, to my sense became void. Chronic beliefs of disease of twenty years' standing, dimness of sight from the belief of age, all disappeared *instantly;* indeed, material life seemed a blank. The *why?* I could not explain, but this I did know, in this realm of the real I found joy, peace, rest, love to all, unbounded, unspeakable. Human language had lost its power of expression, for no words came to me; and in all this six years of bliss I still have found no words to tell my new-found life in God. The most chronic forms of disease have sometimes been healed instantly and without argument. With great love and gratitude. — M. H. P.

I take great comfort in reading "Science and Health with Key to the Scriptures," and will cling firmly to the light I have, knowing that more will be given me. While in Salt Lake City, I met at the hotel a lady who had been an invalid all her life. I talked with her about Christian Science, and loaned her Science and Health, together with the *Journals* I had with me. She had become very much discouraged, having lost all faith in doctors and medicine, and did not know where to turn next. She became very much absorbed in the book, feeling she had found salvation. She at once laid aside the glasses she was wearing, and now reads readily without them. She and her husband have accepted this truth beautifully. — Mrs. G. A. G., Ogden, Utah

On a trip through Mexico I met a woman who told me that, although she did not believe in Christian Science, on her way from Wisconsin, her home, she had bought a copy of Science and Health. When she reached M——, she met a minister from the North, whom the M. D.'s had sent there because of consumption, — they had given him two months to live. She gave him Science and Health, and while doing so, felt it was all absurd. The minister read it, and was healed *immediately*. Was not this a beautiful demonstration of the power of Truth, and good evidence that Science and Health is the word of God?

I had while in Mexico a glorious conquest over the fear of smallpox. There were hundreds of cases in some small towns where we were. After the fear was cast out, never a thought of it as real came to me or my husband, or troubled us in any way. On the street I met three men who were being taken to the pest-house with that loathsome disease. — F. W. C.

A lady to whom I sold "Science and Health with Key to the Scriptures," writes me: "My longing to know God has been answered in this book; and with the answer has come the healing." She is an intimate friend of Will Carleton, the poet. This is doing much good in the social circles. He has for a long time been interested, but his wife has declared it could not heal, and was not Christian. She will now be obliged to acknowledge this healing, for the lady above referred to has been, to sense, a great sufferer. — P. J. L.

Some of the experiences given in the *Journal* have been so helpful to me, I have been moved to give to its readers a little experience of my own, which occurred when I first began the study of "Science and Health with Key to the Scriptures."

I had already been healed of sick headache, almost instantly, by declaring that I was God's child, and, as God is perfect, His child must be perfect also. This had given me great happiness, and a quiet, peaceful state of mind I never had known before. My family did not seem to see anything good in Christian Science, but to me it was sacred.

One Monday morning, I awoke feeling very ill indeed. The morning was warm and sultry. I thought I certainly could not wash that day; but when I went downstairs, I found my daughter had made preparations for such work. I thought, "Well, if she feels like washing, I will not say anything; perhaps I shall get over this." After breakfast I went about my work, thinking I could lean against the tub and wash with more ease than I could do up the morning work. I tried to treat myself as I had done before, — tried to realize that "all is Mind, there is no matter;" that "God is All, there is nothing beside Him," but all to no purpose. I seemed to grow worse all the time. I did not want my family to know how badly I was feeling, and it was very humiliating to think that I must give up and go to bed.

All at once these questions came to me, as though spoken by some one, taking me away from my line of thought entirely: How is God an ever-present help? How does He know our earnest desires? Then, without waiting for me to think how, the answer came in the same way, God is conscious Mind. Instantly the thoughts came: Is God conscious of me? Can I be conscious of Him? I was healed instantly: every bad feeling was destroyed. I could see that the morning had not changed a particle, but I was oblivious of the weather. It did not seem that I had anything more to do with that washing. It was finished in good season, while I was "absent from the body, and present with the Lord."

That was the beginning of the battle with sin and self, but at the same time it was the dawning of the resurrection. Since then (over four years) I have had many experiences, some of which seem too sacred to give to the world. False literature has caused me much suffering; sorrow has visited my home; but, through all this, the light that came to me on that Monday morning — that new and precious sense of omnipresent Life, Truth, and Love — has never left me one moment. It was the light that cannot be hid.

Mrs. H. B. J., Cambridge, Ill.

HEALING

Four years ago I learned for the first time that there was a way to be healed through Christ. I had always been sick, but found no relief in drugs; still, I thought that if the Bible was true, God could heal me. So, when my attention was called to Christian Science, I at once bought "Science and Health with Key to the Scriptures," studied it, and began to improve in health. I seemed to see God so near and so dear, — so different from the God I had been taught to fear. I studied alone night and day, until I found I was healed, both physically and mentally.

Then came a desire to tell every one of this wonderful truth. I expected all to feel just as pleased as I did; but to my sorrow none would believe. Some, it is true, took treatment and were helped, but went on in the old way, without a word of thanks. But still I could not give up. I seemed to know that this was the way, and I had rather live it alone than to follow the crowd the other way. But as time passed, I had some good demonstrations of this Love that is our Life.

I am the only Scientist in Le Roy, as yet, but the good seed has been sown, and where the people once scoffed at this "silly new idea," they are becoming interested, and many have been healed, and some are asking about it. One dear old lady and I study the Bible Lessons every Tuesday afternoon. She came to call, and as we talked, she told me of her sickness of years' standing; and was healed during our talk, so that she has never felt a touch of the old trouble since.

One lady, whom I had never seen, was healed of consumption in six weeks' treatment. She had not left her bed in four months, and had been given up by many physicians.

MRS. FLORENCE WILLIAMS, Le Roy, Mich.

I like the *Journal* and *Quarterly,* and have many of Rev. Mary B. G. Eddy's works, which make my little world. I have a great desire to learn more of this Love that casts out all fear, and to work in this Science. It is the greatest pleasure I have, to talk this truth, as far as I understand it, to any who will listen; and am waiting for others to learn of this blessed Science.

I give my experience in reading "Science and Health with Key to the Scriptures" aloud to a little child. A letter published in the *Journal,* written by a lady who had relieved a two-year-old child by reading to her, first suggested this course to me. At the time, my little one was a trifle over a year old. I was trying to overcome for him a claim which, though not one of serious illness, was no small trial to me, because of its frequent occurrence and its seeming ability to baffle my efforts. One day as I sat near and treated him, it occurred to me to read aloud. I took up one of the older editions of Science and Health lying near, began at the words, "Brains can give no idea of God's man," and read on for two or three paragraphs, endeavoring— as the writer suggested — to understand it myself; yet thinking, perchance, the purer thought of the babe might grasp the underlying meaning sooner than I. So it proved. Before the disturbance felt by me had been calmed, the weary expression on the face of the child was replaced by one of evident relief.

When putting him to sleep, I had often repeated the spiritual interpretation of the Lord's Prayer. One night he was very restless, fretful, and cried a great deal, while I seemed unable to soothe him. At last I perceived that he was asking for something, and it dawned upon me that the Prayer might be his desire. I began repeating it aloud, endeavoring to *mean* it also. He turned over quietly, and in a few minutes was sweetly sleeping.

The last time my attention was specially called to this subject, was about a year after the first experience. Various hindrances had been allowed to keep me from

Science and Health all day; and it was toward evening when I recognized that material sense had been given predominance, and must be put down. I soon felt drawn to read the book. The little boy had seemed restless and somewhat disturbed all day; but without thinking specially of him, rather to assist in holding my own thought, I began to read aloud, "Consciousness constructs a better body, when it has conquered our fear of matter." In a minute or two a little hand had touched mine, and I looked down into a sweet face fairly radiant with smiles. I read it over. The child was evidently delighted, and was restful and happy all the rest of the day. — A. H. W., Deland, Florida

A week ago a friend wrote to me on business, and in the letter stated that his wife had been very ill for six weeks. At once the thought came, "Tell her to read the chapter on Healing, in Science and Health." In my answer to his letter I obeyed the thought. A few days after, I had occasion to call; found her much better, and *reading* Science and Health. They had done as directed, and had received the promise. — R., New York

The first allusion to Christian Science reached me in an article I read on that subject. Later, a friend came to visit me, bringing a copy of "Science and Health with Key to the Scriptures." For two weeks I read it eagerly; then I sent for a copy for myself. When it came, I began to study it. The Bible, of which I had had but a dim understanding, began to grow clearer. The light

grew brighter each day. Finally, I began to treat myself against ills that had bound me for twenty-eight
years. At the end of six weeks I was *healed,* much to the
amazement of all who knew me. From that time, my
desire was to help others out of their suffering, and to
talk this wonderful truth. After a while I took the class
lectures, and am doing what I can to spread this healing
gospel. — A. M. G.

Rev. Mary B. G. Eddy

My Dear Leader: — I will try to tell you how I was
led to Christian Science. Heretofore I have not tried to
lead a Christian life, but have always firmly believed
that if one truly desired and needed help, he would get
it from God by asking for it. I suffered, as I think but
very few have, for fourteen years; yet I did not think it
sufficient to warrant me in asking God to help me, until
I gave up all hope elsewhere, — and this occurred in the
spring of 1891. I then thought that the time had come
to commit myself to God. Being at home alone, after
going to bed I prayed God to deliver me from my torments, this sentence being the substance of my prayer,
"What shall I do to be saved?"

I repeated that sentence, I suppose, until I fell asleep.
About twelve o'clock at night, I saw a vision in the form
of a man with wings, standing at the foot of my bed, —
wings partly spread, — one arm hanging loosely at his
side, and one extended above his head. At the same
time there was a bright light shining in my room, which
made all objects shine like fire. I knew where I was,
and was not afraid. The vision (for such it was), after

looking directly at me for some time, spoke this one sentence, and then disappeared: "Do right, and thou shalt be saved."

I immediately tried to live according to that precept, and found relief in proportion to my understanding. I soon after learned of Christian Science. One of my brothers in Kansas, having been healed by it, persuaded me to buy "Science and Health with Key to the Scriptures," wherein I learned that the above precept was the key to Christian Science; that it is Christian Science to do right, and that nothing short of right living has any claim to the name.

I have been learning my way in Christian Science about one year, and have been successful in healing. I have all of your books, and am a subscriber for the *Journal* and *Quarterly Bible Lessons*. Some of the cases I have treated have yielded almost instantly. I am a stranger to you, but I have told you the truth, just as it occurred. Yours in truth,

SAM SCHROYER, Oklahoma City, Okla.

I desire to make known the great good I have received by reading the blessed book "Science and Health with Key to the Scriptures." Four years have now passed since I began to read it. It has been my only healer and teacher, as I never have had an opportunity to go through a class; but I find that the "Spirit of truth" will teach us all things if we will but practise well what we know. After two years and a half of study, I thought, as many beginners think, that I had travelled over the worst part of this narrow path.

Soon after, it came about that I was separated from every one who had ever heard of Christian Science; and, as I lived in the country, no one came to visit me for about eight months. At first, I thought the Lord had wrought a great evil. I had no one to talk to, but would take my Science and Health every morning, before going about my work, and read; yet mortal mind would say, "You can do no good, with no one to talk with." At last, one morning after listening to the serpent's voice, I looked out at the little wild flowers as they waved to and fro; they seemed to be a living voice, and this is what they said: "On earth peace, good will toward men." There was also a mocking-bird that would sit on the house and sing. For the first time, I realized that divine Love was the only friend I needed. Soon after, I sent the *Journal* to my nearest neighbor, by her little son who came to play with my children. Afterward she told me that when she began to read it she said to the family, "God has sent this book to me." Calling to see her one evening, I found her suffering from heart disease. I began talking to her about Christian Science, and in less than an hour she declared herself healed. She is to-day a happy woman. I would say to all suffering ones, that if you will buy a copy of this wonderful book, "Science and Health with Key to the Scriptures," by the Rev. Mary Baker G. Eddy, and study it, and practise its teachings, you will find it a pearl of great price.

MRS. FANNIE MEEKS, Bells, Grayson Co., Texas

On my arrival in New York, last July, my brother spoke to me of "Science and Health with Key to the

Scriptures;" and, coming in contact with a number of
Scientists, all wishing me to procure the book, I did so.
I read it through in the same manner in which I would
read any other book, to find out the contents.

Before I got to the end, having partly understood its
meaning, I began to demonstrate over old physical troubles, and they disappeared. A belt that I had worn for
over twelve years, I took off, and threw overboard (being
a seafaring man).

Up to that time I had been a constant smoker, and
chewed tobacco; but I gradually lost all pleasure in it,
and now look upon it with disgust.

I was brought up in the Lutheran doctrine, and when
a boy received a good knowledge of Scripture; but I
never understood it until explained to me in Science and
Health.   H. F. WITKOV,
            27 Needham Road, Liverpool, England

In a letter received a few days ago from one of my
absent patients, there was such a glorious testimonial
for Science and Health that I feel as if I ought to send
it in for the pages of our *Journal,* trusting it may be the
means of helping many others to turn for help and comfort, in every emergency, to this book.

In her letter, this lady says: "A few days since, I had
quite a serious claim attack me. I left my mending, took
Science and Health and read all the afternoon and evening; when all trace of the claim was gone, and I have
felt nothing of it since."

When this dear woman applied to Truth, she was a
great sufferer. Her gratitude knows no bounds. Many

chronic ailments, which have bound her with heavy chains for many years, are being removed one by one. It is such a sweet privilege to lead her out of this bondage of flesh, for she turns with such childlike trust and obedience to the book, and looks to that for aid in every trial and affliction. It is beautiful to see, and is a rebuke to some of us older in the thought, who depend so much on personality.

She is far away, in a little country town where Science has hardly been heard of; but she is so happy with her book that she has no desire for other reading.

I have always tried to show her that God was with her there as well as with us here; that in Him she possesses all; and that with her Bible and Science and Health no harm can befall her, for the remedy for every ill she has at hand. — Mrs. C. H. S., Woburn, Mass.

I have been an interested reader of the *Journal* for some time, and thought I would contribute my mite by giving one of my latest demonstrations in Christian Science.

An accident occurred as follows: Officers, while hunting for a criminal in thick underbrush, fired upon each other through mistake, and it was found that one was shot six times; two of the bullets passing through the abdomen, and one through the hips.

Two physicians who examined him had no hope. He asked me to help him. I took the case. Relief came almost instantly. I treated him for eight days; the fifth, I heard one of three physicians, who held a private consultation over my patient, ask him this question:

"Mr. F——, have you not got one bit of pain?" I was rewarded by hearing him answer, "No, sir; not the least bit." No one else seemed to have any hope for him; but I held firmly to the thought that God is an ever-present help, never doubting, and Christian Science has again won a victory. Many people call it a miracle, and it has set them to thinking.

The harvest is now ripe and ready for the reaper. I wish some good Christian Science teacher would come and help us. I can help in my own way, but am not advanced enough to lead and teach others. I have only studied Science and Health a little over a year, and have not been through a class yet.

S. G. SCHROYER, Oklahoma City, Oklahoma

I became interested in Christian Science through being healed. I had no faith in doctors, therefore would not consult any; but felt that something must be done, or I would soon follow a brother and sister who had passed on with the same claim. In my extremity I thought of the "great Physician," and took my case to Him, and realized that He alone could help me.

A relative, finding I would not consult a doctor or take any drug, gave me "Science and Health with Key to the Scriptures" to read; saying that, although a dear friend thought she was greatly helped by a Christian Scientist, he himself had no faith in that kind of treatment, and had no use for the book.

I had heard of the people called Christian Scientists, and of their textbook, Science and Health, but knew nothing about either; yet I wanted to know, and took

the book gladly, and was soon deeply interested in it.
It was a revelation to me. Although I could only understand it in part, I knew it was the truth, and the truth
was making me free. I felt that I had been bound and
in prison; and that now, one after another, the bonds
were being broken, and I was lifted into the pure air
and light of heaven. I was healed before I had read
half-way through the precious volume; for I was obliged
to read slowly, and some passages over and over again.
When I came to page 304, line 10 (47th edition), I then
and there felt that I must add my testimony, though
already there were "heaps upon heaps;" but since then,
I have tried to put the thought of those dark days away
from me, and only refer to them now in the hope that
some one who is bound may be released and brought
into the light of divine Love, which alone can heal, and
make us "every whit whole."

L. M. C., Brooklyn, N. Y.

I have been thinking for a long time that I would give
my experience in coming out of sickness into the knowledge of health by reading "Science and Health with Key
to the Scriptures."

I was sixty years old (as we mortals count time) before I ever read one word of Christian Science. On July
2, 1890, I met a Scientist who gave me a pamphlet called
"Christian Healing," by the Rev. Mary B. G. Eddy.
At that time I was almost helpless. This lady advised
me to buy Science and Health. I did so, and tried to
read it; but my hands were so lame I could not hold it,
and I let it fall to the floor so often that it became un-
bound, and I laid it away and resumed my medicine.

The following May, the Scientist visited in this city again. She advised me to burn all my medicines and to lean unreservedly on the promises of God. I took her advice; had my book rebound in three volumes, so I could hold it more easily, and now read it constantly, reading nothing else. Sometimes I would suffer intensely, then I would get a little better; then more suffering, and so on, until August, 1891, when all pain left me. I have had no return of it, and no disagreeable sensations of any kind, and am perfectly well in all respects.

Surely, if we will but trust our heavenly Father, He is sufficient for us. I hope some one of, or near, my age, who is afflicted, may read this and take courage; for I have *demonstrated* the fact that, by reading Science and Health, in connection with the Bible, and trying to follow the teaching therein, one in the autumn of life may be made over new. I am so thankful to God for my great recovery!

That remark of Sojourner Truth helps me to a better understanding of Life in God: "God is the great house that holds all His children; we dwell in Him as the fishes dwell in the seas." — P. T. P.

Until about one year ago, I had no thought of investigating Christian Science. Previous to that time it had been presented to me in such a way that I condemned it as unreasonable and absurd. At that time it was presented to me in a more reasonable light. I determined to divest myself of prejudice (as far as was possible) and investigate it, thinking that if there was anything in it, it was for me as well as others; that I surely needed

it, and if I found no good in it, I could then with some
show of reason condemn it.

I had been reading Science and Health about two
weeks, when one morning I wanted my cane. It had
been misplaced; and while looking for it the thought
came to me, If all is Mind, I need no cane. I went out
without it, have not used it at all since, and do not need
it as a support; but for a time I did miss it from my
hand. I had used it for years as a support to a very
lame back.

I before went much stooped, because it pained me to
straighten up; but from the time I laid my cane aside I
straightened up, free from pain. Occasionally I have a
slight pain in my back, but it is nothing to compare with
what it had been.

In a short time after laying my cane aside, my pipe
and tobacco went out into the street and have not returned. I had smoked for sixty-five years, and chewed
for fifty. I have no desire for either of them; in fact,
the smoke is offensive to me.

Many times before I had tried to quit, but the desire
for it was so strong that I would go back to it; and when
I tried to "taper off," I would make the taper end the
longest.

Many other physical claims have disappeared, and it
is a common thing for acquaintances to say when they
meet me, "You look better than I have seen you for
years; what have you been doing?" My reply is, I not
only look better, but feel better, and am better; and
Christian Science has done it.

With all this, I seem to have very little spiritual understanding of the truth; am endeavoring to get more, but

it seems slow.   If there is a shorter road to it than I have found, I should like to be directed to it.

J. S. M., Joplin, Mo.

Four years ago I was healed by reading "Science and Health with Key to the Scriptures."   The third day, one of my worst claims gave way.   The book was full of light, and disease vanished as naturally as darkness gives place to light, although it was about six months before I was entirely healed.

Seeing this truth in its purity, showed me where to take my stand; and in defending it I have the prince of this world to meet.   Mortal mind has even called me crazy; but what a blessing to know the nothingness of that mind, and that divine Principle governs all its ideas, and will place each where it belongs!

If our Master was persecuted, can his servants hope to escape?   I know in some degree what Paul meant when he said he rejoiced in tribulations, "for when I am weak, then am I strong."

Many claims that have baffled the skill of the physicians have disappeared through my understanding of Truth.   What a blessing that we can break the bread of Life to others, and so add to our crown of rejoicing!

S. E. R., Kansas City, Mo.

A dear little six-year old boy of my acquaintance was invited by his teacher, with the rest of his class in kindergarten school, to attend a picnic one afternoon.   He did not feel that he wanted to go; seemed dumpish, and according to mortal belief was not well; at noon, he said he wanted to go to sleep.

His mother took him in her lap and began to read to him from "Science and Health with Key to the Scriptures." Very soon he expressed a wish to go to the picnic, and did go. His father, happening to pass the place where the little ones were spending the afternoon, and somewhat surprised to see him playing, as happy and active as any there, called to him and asked, "How long did you sleep?" The little fellow replied, "I did not sleep at all; mamma read to me from Science and Health, and I was well in a minute." — K. L. H.

One evening I was calling on a neighbor, and somehow the subject of Christian Science came up. I asked her what it was, and what they believed.

She then told me of a friend of hers who had become a Christian Scientist. This friend had passed through great sorrow and disappointment; her health had failed her, and her cheerful disposition had entirely changed; she could talk of nothing but her troubles, and was a most unhappy woman. A few years ago she visited my neighbor, who, greatly surprised at her changed appearance, — for she was happy and well, — asked where her troubles were. The reply was, "I have no troubles. I have found true happiness; for I have become a Christian Scientist."

I became deeply interested, and asked if the students in Clinton had public meetings on Sundays. She replied that they had, and told me where they were.

The next Sunday, I went. All was quiet when I entered, for they were engaged in silent prayer. Soon they repeated the spiritual interpretation of the Lord's Prayer. I shall never forget the impression that made on me; all the next week I heard the leader's voice repeating the first sentence.

I was invited to come again, and did so. One of the ladies loaned me "Science and Health with Key to the Scriptures," and offered to get me one; which she did the next week. I have studied it in connection with the Bible. I have greatly improved in health, having had only one attack of a physical trouble which caused great suffering, since that time, and that was a year ago.

At first, I did not think anything about being healed, or of my physical infirmity. I only loved the sacred teaching. How true, that God's word does not return unto Him void! The words of truth that my neighbor's friend spoke to her, were what first awakened me. If the one who first hears it does not receive it, it goes to some one who is ready, and it takes root and bears fruit.

Mrs. G. H. I., Clinton, N. Y.

About three years ago I was near death's door, with various troubles; also, was seventy years old. I had a desire to know something of Christian Science.

I procured the textbook, and studied it with a desire to know the truth. At first all was dark; but light began slowly to come, and at the end of three months I found my physical claims all gone and my eyesight restored. At the end of three months more, I had gained thirty-five pounds in weight.

I had been an infidel, and the change from that came more slowly; but now I know that my Redeemer lives, and I am able by divine grace to make very convincing demonstrations. — J. S., Rudd, Iowa

For a long time I have felt that I must in some way express my great debt of gratitude for Christian Science. I know no better way to do so than to give an account, through the *Journal,* of some of the many blessings I have received as a result of our Leader's untiring toil and self-sacrificing love for suffering mortals, in giving to us the wonderful book, "Science and Health with Key to the Scriptures."

When I first heard of Christian Science, about six years ago, I was satisfied that it was the religion of Christ Jesus, because Jesus had so plainly said, "And these signs shall follow them that believe; In my name shall they cast out devils; . . . they shall lay hands on the sick, and they shall recover."

I had been a church-member since my girlhood, but was not satisfied that my belief would take me to heaven, as I did not have these "signs following" — and this had always troubled me; so, when I heard that an old acquaintance living at a distance had not only been raised from a dying condition to health, but her life had been changed and purified through Christian Science, I could hardly wait to know more of this Christlike religion which was casting out evils and healing the sick. I searched every bookstore in the city for Science and Health, at last found a copy, and was delighted to get hold of it, but little realized what a treasure it was to be to me and my household.

At first it was like Greek to me, and I could not understand much of it, but gleaned enough to keep on reading, and longed for some one to talk to me of it.

After I had been reading it about a year's time, I suddenly became almost blind. I knew no Scientist to go to, so went to physicians; they told me that my case was hopeless, that it was certain my sight never could be restored, and the probabilities were that I would soon be totally blind.

I felt sure that Christian Science would help me if I could only fully understand it; but there was no one from whom I could ask help, that I knew of. I gave all the time that I could use my eyes to studying Science and Health, — which at first was not more than five minutes two, and sometimes three, times a day; gradually my sight returned, until it was fully restored.

During this time God and the "little book" were my only help. My understanding was very limited; but like the prodigal son, I had turned away from the husks, towards my Father's house, and while I "was yet a great way off" my Father came to meet me. When this great cloud of darkness was banished by the light of Truth, could I doubt that Christian Science was indeed the "Comforter" that would lead us "into all truth"?

Again I lay at the point of death; but holding steadfastly to the truth, knowing, from the teaching of this precious book, that God is Life and there is no death, I was raised up to health, — restored to my husband and little children, all of whom I am thankful to say are now with me in Science.

I had no one to talk with on this subject, knew no one of whose understanding I felt sure enough to ask for help; but I was careful from the first not to read or inquire into anything except genuine Christian Science, and how thankful I am for it! Since then, I have been through a class.

I cannot express in words what Christian Science has done for my children, or my gratitude that the light of Truth has come to them in their innocent childhood, — healing all claims of sickness, and showing us how to overcome the more stubborn claims of sin. — L. F. B.

It is a little over one year since a very esteemed friend, of this city, invited me to partake of the heavenly manna contained in the revelation of "Science and Health with Key to the Scriptures." I had, up to that time, been for fifteen years a victim of hip-joint disease; this eventually confining me to my bed, where I had been ten months when the "book of prophecy" was opened for me. I was not long in finding the light I needed, — that gave "feet to the lame," enabling me now to go, move, and walk, where I will, without crutch or support of any description, save the staff of divine Science.

In proportion as my thoughts are occupied with the work in Science, does the peace and joy come inwardly that transforms the blight of error externally.

T. G. K., Tacoma, Wash.

I wish to acknowledge the blessings which Christian Science has brought to me through reading "Science and Health with Key to the Scriptures." My first demonstration was over the tobacco habit; I had smoked for at least fifteen years: I have now no desire for tobacco.

I was then healed of two claims which had bound me for ten years. My prayer is that I may be so filled with the truth that I can carry the message to my brother man.

F. W. K., Angelica, N. Y.

I take advantage of the great privilege granted us, to give my testimony for Christian Science through the pages of our much loved *Journal*. The blessing has been so bountiful that words can but poorly express my gratitude.

A little over six years ago, a relative came from Denver, Colorado, to visit us. She was a Christian Scientist, having herself been healed of a severe claim that M. D.'s, drugs, and climate could not relieve; and her husband having been in the drug business, she had had a chance to give them a fair trial.

My sister-in-law did not talk much on the subject, as I remember; but what was better, lived the truth before us as she realized it.

One day (a blessed day to me), I ventured to open Science and Health, and read the first sentence in the Preface. I closed the book, wondering what more it could contain, this seeming to cover the whole ground. When my sister-in-law returned to the room, I asked her if I might read it. Her reply was, "Yes; but begin at the first."

That night, after all had retired, I began to read; within forty-eight hours I destroyed all drugs, applications, etc., notwithstanding the fact that my husband had just paid fifty dollars to a travelling specialist for part of a treatment. With the drugs disappeared ailments of nine years' standing, which M. D.'s had failed to relieve.

I now understand that my sudden healing was due to my turning completely away from material methods; for I was convinced I should never use them again. I realized that God was my health, my strength, my Life, therefore All. As I read Science and Health, I wondered why others had not discerned this truth, — physicians, ministers, and others who had devoted their lives to benefit mankind. Yes! why? Because they had been seeking in the opposite direction to Truth, namely, for cause and effect in matter, when all cause and effect are mental.

I mention physicians and ministers, because one class claims to heal disease, the other claims to heal sin; but Christian Science heals physically and morally, — it contains all; "its leaves are for the healing of the nations."

L. B. A., Memphis, Tenn.

I was for years a great sufferer. I called doctor after doctor, getting no help. The last one, after treating me for one year, told me he would give me one year more to live.

One evening a near neighbor came in and asked me to go home with her; and as it was only a few steps, I did so.

She took up a new book, Science and Health, read me a few chapters, and then gave me some Christian Science tracts, which I read, and one of them I almost committed to memory.

I bought a copy of "Science and Health with Key to

452 Miscellaneous Writings

the Scriptures," and studied it carefully. I am healed of all those claims which troubled me so long. I was lifted out of darkness into light.

M. J. P., Burns, Oregon

Chicago, March 19, 1894

Rev. Mary B. G. Eddy, Boston, Mass.: — I wish to thank you for the true light that was revealed to me by reading your book, "Science and Health with Key to the Scriptures," and at once adopting its teaching. It was one year ago to-day that I put on the armor, determined never to surrender to the enemy; and you may know I have looked forward to this day with a great deal of pleasure, to show my friends that the Lord is constantly with me to help overcome all evil.

Some said, when I first started in this new path, "Wait until you get one of your stomach attacks, and you will change your mind." For months they have waited, and are beginning to see the truth in my actions, that speak for themselves, and show that all is *Mind.*

For nearly thirty years I had been a sufferer from throat and stomach troubles; bronchitis, dyspepsia, gas-tralgia, and gastritis, etc., were the terms applied by my physicians. About eighteen years of that time I was engaged in the drug business, had constant opportunities for consulting the best physicians, and took such medicine as I felt assured would cure me; but only to be disappointed each time.

The last few years I had been living on oatmeal crackers and hot water; suffering more or less all the time, and could not eat anything else without suffering intense pain. I felt as though I could not live many months more, and was getting ready to give up the fight when a dear friend and neighbor, Mrs. Corning, left a copy of Science and Health at our home. At first I did not care to read it; having been educated, for many years, in the belief that medicine can cure all diseases, I could not conceive of anything else to cure the sick.

One Sunday I had the curiosity to know something about this Christian Science, and read Science and Health. The more I read, the more interested I became, and finally said to myself, "I will try it." I took a large porous plaster and four thicknesses of flannel off my stomach, and threw them in the corner, saying, "Now it shall be Mind over matter; no more matter over Mind." I filled a large basket full of bottles containing medicine, and put it in the shed (where all medicine should be). From that day I have eaten of everything on the table, and all I wished. Coffee was my worst enemy, and I had not tasted it for years without suffering untold agony. Several days passed before I cared to drink it; then, one morning, I told my family I would commence to use it; I did, and have used it every day since, and don't know that I have a stomach, as it never has caused me any trouble since that morning.

I am happy to say I have not used a drop of any kind of medicine, internally or externally, from that day, and *I know that all is Mind.* I read the Bible and Science and Health nearly every day, thanking the Lord for the years of suffering which have led me to the truth as taught by our Saviour; for I feel it was only through its victory over the suffering that the truth could have been revealed in my case.

I have had some demonstrations to make over error, but each time it becomes easier. God is ever present and ready to help me, and I trust in Him; my faith is planted on a rock that is immovable.

Yours truly,   FRANK S. EBERHART

P. S. If you think this letter, or any part of it, will help some one out of darkness into the light of Truth, you are at liberty to have it published.

Having so many occupations and interruptions, I have not found time to read "Science and Health with Key to the Scriptures" sufficiently, but will not on that account delay thanking you for its excellence.

HENRY W. LONGFELLOW, Cambridge, Mass.

I am an old-school practitioner; have served as surgeon in two European wars; practised medicine for about ten years in New York city and Brooklyn, until my health compelled me to relinquish my profession. I became a victim of the morphia habit, taking daily thirty grains of that drug. My physicians declared me consumptive, and abandoned all hopes of recovery. Shortly after this I made the acquaintance of a student of the author of "Science and Health with Key to the Scriptures," who presented me with her works; and as drugs did me no good, I stopped taking any whatever, save morphia, without which I thought it impossible to get along, and to my astonishment began to gain in flesh, and my ambition returning in proportion. I finally felt that I would stop my loathsome habit of morphia-eating, and did so in one week, without any discomfort worth mentioning. For a test I administered one fourth of a grain of morphia to the aforesaid Scientist, hypodermically, without the slightest physiological effect, clearly proving the existence of metaphysical laws. I have read Science and Health carefully, and consider my present improved health solely due to mental influence.

OTTO ANDERSON, M. D., Cincinnati, Ohio

The profound truths which you announce, sustained by facts of the immortal life, give to your work the seal of inspiration — reaffirm in modern phrase the Christian revelations. In times like these, so sunk in sensualism, I hail with joy your voice, speaking an assured word for God and immortality, and my joy is heightened that these words are of woman's divinings.

A. BRONSON ALCOTT, Concord, Mass.

I was sick six years; tried many physicians and remedies, but received no lasting benefit from any of them, and concluded I must remain sick the rest of my life. In this condition, I purchased the book "Science and Health with Key to the Scriptures," read it, was deeply interested, and noticed that my health began to improve; and the more I read the book, the better I became in health. This I can say truly: it did more for my health than all the physicians and remedies that I had ever tried. — DR. S. G. TODD, 11 School St., Newburyport

I had been a nervous sufferer for nine years; had a belief of incurable disease of the heart, and was subject to severe nervous prostration if I became the least weary. I was told that if I should read your books they would cure me. I commenced reading them: in ten days I was surprised to find myself overcoming my nervous spasms without the aid of medicine; and ever since then I have been improving, and I now can walk twenty miles without fatigue, and have been able to rise above all ailments.

MRS. JULIA A. B. DAVIS,
Central Village, Westport, Mass.

I would inform my friends and the public, that after twelve years of sickness I am restored to health; and, with renewed vigor and keen enjoyment, take up the pleasures and duties of life once more; all labor now seems less arduous, and all happiness more perfect. To Christian Science, as taught in "Science and Health with Key to the Scriptures," I am indebted for my restoration. I can cordially recommend this book to all.

ROSE A. WIGGLESWORTH, Lowell, Mass.

When I commenced reading "Science and Health with Key to the Scriptures," I could sit up but a very short time, and could not eat the most simple food without great distress. In a few days there was a great change, and I have been growing better ever since.

E. D. RICHARDSON, Merrimac, Mass.

I have not been as well for years as I have been since reading "Science and Health with Key to the Scriptures," all of which I impute to its teaching.

(MRS.) MARY A. WILLIAMS, Freeport, Ill.

Had been in ill-health for several years; had been confined to my bed three months, when I got your book and read it. At first I was unable to read it myself, and others read it to me, and the truth revealed in your book restored me to health.

(Col.) E. J. Smith, Washington, D. C.

I have been perusing with great interest your work on metaphysical Science, for the last four months, and to great advantage; you make the path to health so plain, that a wayfaring man, though a fool, cannot err therein.

R. I. Barker, Bethel, Me.

"Science and Health with Key to the Scriptures" "is a lamp unto my feet, and a light unto my path;" your missiles of Mind have battered down the illusions of sense, allowing Life to appear an eternal monument, whose spirited hieroglyphics, Truth and Love, unlike those cut in marble, shall grow more luminous to consciousness as sickness, sin and death fade out of belief.

Arthur T. Buswell,
Office of Associated Charities, Cincinnati, O.

"Science and Health with Key to the Scriptures" is beautiful in its form of thought and expression. I have perused it with interest. Your book tends to lead us to new thoughts and practices in the healing art, and for many maladies I have no doubt the treatment your excellent work introduces will be the only remedy.

(Col.) Rob't B. Caverly, Centralville, Mass.

Undoubtedly "Science and Health with Key to the Scriptures" is the greatest and grandest book ever published; and that by pulpit and press it will be so acknowledged, is only a question of time. Yours has, indeed, been a pioneer work, and will be; and I believe that you, of all the millions, are selected and chosen because of your peculiar fitness for this great work — this grand work of opening the gates and leading the way, that fallen humanity may follow step by step; reach up to Christ, and be made whole! That all this should be systematized and proven with mathematical precision, — that there can be no guesswork or quackery, — is simply astounding. Science and Health has given me a new impetus heavenward.

M. A. HINKLEY, Williamsport, Pa.

The book "Science and Health with Key to the Scriptures" is the most wonderful work that has been written in the past five thousand years. I wish you could get ten dollars per copy. I am of the opinion that I can heal the sick on its basis, from reading the work.

H. D. DEXTER, M. D., Dundee, N. Y.

Rev. Mary B. G. Eddy's book, "Science and Health with Key to the Scriptures," has been duly catalogued and placed on our shelves for use. In behalf of the trustees, let me convey cordial thanks to the earnest-minded author for this interesting contribution. My own idea is, that the power of Mind or Spirit is supreme in character, and destined to supremacy over all that is adverse to divine order.   WILLIAM H. KIMBALL,
Librarian New Hampshire State Library

I am reading the work, "Science and Health with Key to the Scriptures," for the third time; and I am convinced of the truth of the Science of which it treats, — instructing us how to attain holiness of heart, purity of life, and the sublime ascendency of soul over body.

C. CLEMENT, McMinnville, Warren Co., Tenn.

I was sick for a number of years with what some of the most skilful physicians pronounced an incurable disease. The more I tried to get help, the worse I became, until a life of pain and helplessness seemed unavoidable. Two years ago I heard of "Science and Health with Key to the Scriptures," began reading it and trying to live up to its teachings. At first, my beliefs were so strong I made but little progress; but gradually my disease gave way, and finally disappeared, and to-day I am a well woman. I cannot express the gratitude I feel for what the light shining through the teachings of that book did for me.

(MRS.) EMILY T. HOWE, Norway, Me.

I have been reading "Science and Health with Key to the Scriptures," and feasting — like a starving, shipwrecked mariner, on the food that was to sustain him — on truths which ages to come will appreciate, understand, and accept. Many of the theories which at first appear abstruse and obscure, at length become clear and lucid. The candle of intellect requires occasional snuffing to throw the clear light of penetration on the page.

(MRS.) S. A. ORNE, Malden, Mass.

The mother of a little girl about eight years old told me her child was having a severe attack of cold, and was delicate and easy to take cold. I told her the little girl would be all right; not to give her any medicine, but read Science and Health to her. When I next saw the mother, she told me the little girl was entirely well; that the cold had all disappeared, and with it a claim of night-sweats that the child had been under for more than a year. The little girl had been out sliding down-hill in the snow a number of times; had her feet very wet, but it did not affect her at all. They were all pleased, — especially the child; her face was beaming with happiness and smiles. This is just one little instance of the good that comes from reading Science and Health.

T. W. H.

OPINIONS OF THE PRESS

This is, perhaps, the most remarkable book on health, in some respects, which has appeared in this country. The author evidently discards physiology, hygiene, mesmerism, magnetism, and every form of medication, bathing, dieting, etc., — all go by the board; no medicine, manipulation, or external applications are permitted; everything is done through the mind. Applied to certain conditions, this method has great value: even the reading of the author's book has cured hopeless cases. The author claims that her methods are those used by Christ and his apostles, and she has established a church and school to propagate them. — *Herald of Health,* N. Y. (M. L. HOLBROOK, *Publisher*)

The Christian Scientists claim that the power of healing is not lost, and have supported that claim by induc-
ing cures astonishingly like those quoted from the New
Testament. And even more good they hope to achieve,
as this power which they possess is better understood
and the new light gains strength in the world. Experience has taught us that the nearer we approach to the
source of a report of miraculous power, the smaller does
the wonder grow. In the instance of the Christian Scientists, the result has been rather the reverse; if third
parties have related a remarkable circumstance, the person
of whom the fact was alleged has been found to make
the assertion still stronger. — *Boston Sunday Globe*

"Science and Health with Key to the Scriptures," by
Mary Baker G. Eddy, President of the Massachusetts
Metaphysical College, is a remarkable publication,
claiming to elucidate the influence of mentality over
matter. Mrs. Eddy announces herself as the discoverer
of this metaphysical Science, and receives students, to
whom she imparts so much of her metaphysics as their
minds are capable of receiving. The volumes are a
vigorous protest against the materialism of our modern
scientists, Darwin, Huxley, Tyndall, etc. Her Science
of Mind was first self-applied: having been ill and treated
by doctors of the various schools without benefit, she
discovered the grand Principle of all healing to be God,
or Mind. Relying on this Principle alone, she regained
her health, and for the last sixteen years has taught
this theory to others, and has healed the sick in all cases
where the patient's mentality was sufficiently strong to

understand her teachings and act upon them. — *Brooklyn Eagle*

The book "Science and Health with Key to the Scriptures" is certainly original, and contains much that will do good. The reader will find this work not influenced by superstition or pride, but striking out boldly, — full of self-sacrifice and love towards God and man. — *Christian Advocate*, Buffalo, N. Y.

The doctrines of "Science and Health with Key to the Scriptures" are high and pure, wholly free from those vile theories about love and marriage which have been so prevalent among the spiritualists. This new sect devotes itself to a study of the Bible, and a practice of curing disease without mesmerism or spiritualism. It treats Darwin and materialists with a lofty scorn. — *Springfield Republican*

"Science and Health with Key to the Scriptures" is indisputably a wonderful work. It has no equal. No one can read the book and not be benefited by it in mind and body. The work is endorsed by some of the best men of the age. — *Star-Spangled Banner*

We shall watch with keen interest the promised results of "Science and Health with Key to the Scriptures." The work shows how the body can be cured, and how a better state of Christianity can be introduced (which is certainly very desirable). It likewise has a hard thrust at spiritualism; and, taken altogether, it is a very rare book. — *Boston Investigator*

The author of "Science and Health with Key to the Scriptures," which is attracting much attention, shows her ability to defend her cause with vigor. —*Boston Weekly Journal*

(*By permission*)

HOW TO UNDERSTAND SCIENCE AND HEALTH

My Dear Friend H.: — Your good letter of the 26th ult. came duly to hand several days ago, and I am not greatly surprised at its contents. You say, in substance, that you procured the book, "Science and Health with Key to the Scriptures," which I recommended, and that to your surprise and disgust you found it to be a work on faith-cure, and ask by what process of reasoning I could possibly bring myself to adopt or accept such visionary theories. In answer to your very natural question, I will try, in my own way, to give you what appears to me to be a reason for the hope that is in me.

My religious views of fifteen years ago are too familiar to you to need any exposition at my hands at this time. Suffice it to say that the religion of the Bible, as taught by the churches, to my mind appeared to be self-contradictory and confusing, and their explanations failed to explain. During the next eleven years my convictions underwent little change. I read everything that came in my way that had any bearing upon, or pretended in any degree to explain, the problem of life; and while I gained some knowledge of a general nature, I was no nearer the solution of life's problem than when I began my investigations years ago, and I had given up all hope of ever being able to come to a knowledge of the truth, or a satisfactory explanation of the enigma of life.

In all my intellectual wanderings I had never lost my belief in a great First Cause, which I was as well satisfied to call God as anything else; but the orthodox explanations of His or its nature and power were to my mind such a mixture of truth and error, that I could not tell where fact left off and fancy began. The whole effort of the pulpit being put forth, seemed directed to the impossible task of harmonizing the teachings of Jesus Christ with the wisdom of the world; and the whole tendency of our religious education was to befog the intellect and produce scepticism in a mind that presumed to think for itself and to inquire into the why and the wherefore. I fully believe that the agnosticism of yourself and myself was produced by the futile attempt to mix and harmonize the wisdom of the world with the philosophy of the Christ.

In my investigations into the researches of the savants and philosophers I found neither any satisfactory explanation of things as they seemed to exist, nor any solution of the great and all-absorbing question, "What is Truth?" Their premises appeared to be sound, and their reasonings faultless; but in the nature of things, no final conclusion of the whole matter could be reached from premises based wholly on material knowledge. They could explain "matter" and its properties to their own satisfaction, but the intelligence that lay behind or beyond it, and which was manifested in and through it, was to them as much of a mystery as it was to the humblest of God's creatures. They could prove pretty conclusively that many of the generally accepted theories had no basis in fact; but they left us as much in the dark regarding Life and its governing Principle as had the divines before them.

About four years ago, while still in the mental condition above indicated, my attention was called to what at that time appeared to me to be a new phase of spiritism, and which was called by those who professed to believe in it, *Christian Science*. I thought that I had given some attention to about all the *isms* that ever existed, and that this was only another phantasm of some religionist lost in the labyrinths of mental hallucination.

In my reflections at that time it seemed to me that life was an incomprehensible enigma; that the creator had placed us on this earth, and left us entirely in the dark as to His purpose in so doing. We seemed to be cast upon the ocean of time, and left to drift aimlessly about, with no exact knowledge of what was required of us or how to attain unto the truth, which must certainly have an existence somewhere. It seemed to me that in the very nature of things there must be a great error somewhere in our understanding, or that the creator Himself had slipped a cog when He fitted all things into their proper spheres. That there had been a grand mistake somewhere I had no doubt; but I still had doubt enough of my own capabilities and understanding to believe that the mistake, whatever it was, was in me and not in the creator. I knew that, in a fair measure at least, I had an honest desire to live aright, as it was given me to see the right, and to strive to some extent to do the will of God, if I could only know certainly just what it was.

While in this frame of mind, I inwardly appealed to the great unseen power to enlighten my understanding, and to lead me into a knowledge of the truth, promising mentally to follow wherever it might lead, if I could only do so understandingly.

My wife had been investigating Christian Science to some extent, but knowing my natural antipathy to such vagaries, as I then thought them, had said very little to me about it; but one day, while discussing the mysteries of life with a judge of one of our courts, he asked me whether I had ever looked into the teachings of the Christian Scientists. I told him that I had not, and he urged me very strongly to do so. He claimed to have investigated their teachings, and said that he had become a thorough believer in them. This aroused my curiosity, and I procured the book called "Science and Health with Key to the Scriptures," and read it. Before reading very far in it, I became pretty thoroughly nauseated with what I thought the chimerical ideas of the author, but kept on reading, — more because I had promised to read the book than because of interest in its teachings; but before I had gotten through with it, I did become interested in the Principle that I thought I discovered the author was striving to elucidate; and when I got through it, I began again and reread it very carefully. When I had finished reading this book the second time, I had become thoroughly convinced that her explanation of the religion taught by Jesus Christ, and what he did teach, afforded the only explanation which, to my mind, came anywhere near harmonizing and making cohesive what had always seemed contradictory and inexplicable in the Bible. I became satisfied that I had found the truth for which I had long been seeking, and I arose from the reading of the book a changed man; doubt and uncertainty had fled, and my mind has never been troubled with a serious doubt upon the subject from that day to this.

I do not pretend to have acquired the power it is claimed we may attain to; but I am satisfied that the fault is in me, and not in the Principle. I think I can almost hear you ask, What! do you believe in miracles? I answer unhesitatingly, Yes; I believe in the manifestations of the power of Mind which the world calls miraculous; but which those who claim to understand the Principle through which the works are done, seem to think not unnatural, but only the logical result of the application of a known Principle.

It always did seem to me that Truth should be self-evident, or at least susceptible of unmistakable proof, — which all religions seemed to lack, at least in so far as I had known them. I now remember that Jesus furnished unmistakable proofs of the truth of his teachings, by his manifestations of the power of Mind, or, as some might call it, Spirit; which power he plainly taught would be acquired by those who believed in the Principle which he taught, and which manifestations would follow as signs that an understanding of his philosophy had been reached. It does seem to me, that where the signs do not follow professing Christians which Christ said should follow them, there must be something wrong, either in his teachings or their understanding of them; and to say the least, the foundations of their faith require a careful re-examination, with a view to harmonizing them with the plain teachings of the Christ in whose footsteps they profess to follow.

I never could understand how God could be ever-present as a personal Being, but I think I can and do understand how divine Principle can pervade every thing and place.

I never could understand how heaven could be a place with gorgeous fittings, but I think I can and do understand how it might be a spiritual (or if you please mental) condition. Jesus said, "The kingdom of God cometh not with observation: neither shall they say, Lo here! or, lo there! for, behold, the kingdom of God is within you."

"Knowledge (or understanding) is power." Since adopting the views of life as set forth in "Science and Health with Key to the Scriptures," I have seen proofs of what can be accomplished through a knowledge of the truth, which to my mind amount to demonstrations, and which no longer seem incredible, but which I do not ask another to accept upon my statements. Every one must see or feel for himself in order to be convinced; but I am satisfied that any who will lay aside their preconceived notions, and deal honestly with themselves and the light they have, will come to a knowledge of the truth as illustrated in the teachings and life of Jesus Christ; that is, that Mind, or Soul, or whatever you may be pleased to call it, is the real Ego, or self, and that mortal mind with its body is the unreal and vanishing, and eventually goes back to its native nothingness.

Truth is, and ever has been, simple; and because of its utter simplicity, we in our pride and selfishness have been looking right over it. We have been keeping our eyes turned toward the sky, scanning the heavens with a far-off gaze in search of light, expecting to see the truth blaze forth like some great comet, or in some extraordinary manner; and when, instead of coming in great pomp and splendor, it appears in the simpleness of demonstration, we are staggered at it, and refuse to accept it; our intellectual pride is shocked, and we are sure that there has been some mistake. Human nature is ever the same. The Jews were looking for something transcendently wonderful, and the absence of it made the Christ, Truth, to them a stumbling-block. It was foolishness to the Greeks, who excelled in the worldly wisdom of that day; but in all ages of the world it has ever been the power of God to them that believe, not blindly, but because of an enlightened understanding.

I always did think that there was something beautiful in the philosophy of life as taught by Jesus Christ, but that it was impracticable and not susceptible of application to the affairs of life in a world constituted as this appeared to be. As I now view it, that belief was the result of ignorance of the real power that "moves the universe," — too much faith in matter or effect, and not enough in Mind or cause, which is God.

To one who can accept the truth that all causation is in Mind, and who therefore begins to look away from matter and into Mind, or Spirit, for all that is real and eternal, and for all that produces anything that is lasting, the doubts and petty annoyances of life become dissolved in the light of a better understanding, which has been refined in the crucible of charity and love; and they fade away into the nothingness from whence they came, never having had any existence in fact, being only the inventions of erring human belief.

Read the teachings of the Christ from a Christian Science standpoint, and they no longer appear vague and mystical, but become luminous and powerful, — and, let me say, intelligible.

It is true, as you intimate, that this theory of life is much more generally accepted by women than by men, and it may be true that as a rule their reasoning is much less rigid in its nature than that of the sterner sex, and that they may be liable to scan their premises less keenly; but may it not also be true, that they are of finer texture and more spiritual in their natures, and that they may be just as likely to arrive at the truth through their intuitions, in connection with their logic, as we are through the more rugged courses? If it be true that man is the more logical, the fallibility of our own reasonings very frequently becomes painfully apparent even to ourselves, and they are therefore not the safest gauge by which to judge others.

I believe, myself, that when it comes to standing up for Truth in the face of the world, and possibly at the sacrifice of position and popularity, women possess the necessary courage in a much greater degree than do men.

I had not intended to weary you with such a long

letter, but after getting into the subject, I hardly knew where to stop.   As an old and loved friend, I have given you a glimpse of my inner life, because I hardly knew how to explain my mental condition to you in any other way. . . .

Retrospection and Introspection

Retrospection and Introspection

by MARY BAKER EDDY
Discoverer and Founder of Christian Science
and Author of Science and Health
with Key to the Scriptures

Marcas Registradas

Published by The First Church of Christ, Scientist, in Boston, Massachusetts, U.S.A.

*The facsimile of the signature of Mary Baker Eddy
and the design of the Cross and Crown seal are
trademarks of The Christian Science Board of Directors,
registered in the United States and other countries.*

Contents

Contents

Retrospection and Introspection

Ancestral Shadows

MY ancestors, according to the flesh, were from both Scotland and England, my great-grandfather, on my father's side, being John McNeil of Edinburgh.

His wife, my great-grandmother, was Marion Moor, and her family is said to have been in some way related to Hannah More, the pious and popular English authoress of a century ago.

I remember reading, in my childhood, certain manuscripts containing Scriptural sonnets, besides other verses and enigmas which my grandmother said were written by my great-grandmother. But because my great-grandmother wrote a stray sonnet and an occasional riddle, it was no sign that she inherited a spark from Hannah More, or was her relative.

John and Marion Moor McNeil had a daughter, who perpetuated her mother's name. This second Marion McNeil in due time was married to an Englishman, named Joseph Baker, and so became my paternal grandmother, the Scotch and English elements thus mingling in her children.

Mrs. Marion McNeil Baker was reared among the Scotch Covenanters, and had in her character that sturdy Calvinistic devotion to Protestant liberty which gave those religionists the poetic daring and pious picturesqueness which we find so graphically set forth in the pages of Sir Walter Scott and in John Wilson's sketches.

Joseph Baker and his wife, Marion McNeil, came to America seeking "freedom to worship God;" though they could hardly have crossed the Atlantic more than a score of years prior to the Revolutionary period.

With them they brought to New England a heavy sword, encased in a brass scabbard, on which was inscribed the name of a kinsman upon whom the weapon had been bestowed by Sir William Wallace, from whose patriotism and bravery comes that heart-stirring air, "Scots wha hae wi' Wallace bled."

My childhood was also gladdened by one of my Grandmother Baker's books, printed in olden type and replete with the phraseology current in the seventeenth and eighteenth centuries.

Among grandmother's treasures were some newspapers, yellow with age. Some of these, however, were not very ancient, nor had they crossed the ocean; for they were American newspapers, one of which contained a full account of the death and burial of George Washington.

A relative of my Grandfather Baker was General Henry Knox of Revolutionary fame. I was fond of listening, when a child, to grandmother's stories about General Knox, for whom she cherished a high regard.

In the line of my Grandmother Baker's family was the

late Sir John Macneill, a Scotch knight, who was promi- 1
nent in British politics, and at one time held the position
of ambassador to Persia.   3

My grandparents were likewise connected with Capt.
John Lovewell of Dunstable, New Hampshire, whose
gallant leadership and death, in the Indian troubles of 6
1722–1725, caused that prolonged contest to be known
historically as Lovewell's War.

A cousin of my grandmother was John Macneil, the 9
New Hampshire general who fought at Lundy's Lane,
and won distinction in 1814 at the neighboring battle of
Chippewa, towards the close of the War of 1812.   12

Autobiographic Reminiscences

1 THIS venerable grandmother had thirteen children,
the youngest of whom was my father, Mark Baker,
3 who inherited the homestead, and with his brother, James
Baker, he inherited my grandfather's farm of about five
hundred acres, lying in the adjoining towns of Concord
6 and Bow, in the State of New Hampshire.

One hundred acres of the old farm are still cultivated
and owned by Uncle James Baker's grandson, brother of
9 the Hon. Henry Moore Baker of Washington, D. C.

The farm-house, situated on the summit of a hill, commanded a broad picturesque view of the Merrimac River
12 and the undulating lands of three townships. But change
has been busy. Where once stretched broad fields of
bending grain waving gracefully in the sunlight, and
15 orchards of apples, peaches, pears, and cherries shone
richly in the mellow hues of autumn, — now the lone night-
bird cries, the crow caws cautiously, and wandering winds
18 sigh low requiems through dark pine groves. Where
green pastures bright with berries, singing brooklets,
beautiful wild flowers, and flecked with large flocks and
21 herds, covered areas of rich acres, — now the scrub-oak,
poplar, and fern flourish.

The wife of Mark Baker was Abigail Barnard Ambrose,
24 daughter of Deacon Nathaniel Ambrose of Pembroke, a

small town situated near Concord, just across the bridge, 1
on the left bank of the Merrimac River.

Grandfather Ambrose was a very religious man, and 3
gave the money for erecting the first Congregational
Church in Pembroke.

In the Baker homestead at Bow I was born, the young- 6
est of my parents' six children and the object of their
tender solicitude.

During my childhood my parents removed to Tilton, 9
eighteen miles from Concord, and there the family remained until the names of both father and mother were
inscribed on the stone memorials in the Park Cemetery 12
of that beautiful village.

My father possessed a strong intellect and an iron will.
Of my mother I cannot speak as I would, for memory 15
recalls qualities to which the pen can never do justice.
The following is a brief extract from the eulogy of the Rev.
Richard S. Rust, D. D., who for many years had re- 18
sided in Tilton and knew my sainted mother in all the
walks of life.

The character of Mrs. Abigail Ambrose Baker was distin- 21
guished for numerous excellences. She possessed a strong
intellect, a sympathizing heart, and a placid spirit. Her
presence, like the gentle dew and cheerful light, was felt by 24
all around her. She gave an elevated character to the tone of
conversation in the circles in which she moved, and directed
attention to themes at once pleasing and profitable. 27

As a mother, she was untiring in her efforts to secure the
happiness of her family. She ever entertained a lively sense
of the parental obligation, especially in regard to the educa- 30

1 tion of her children. The oft-repeated impressions of that
sainted spirit, on the hearts of those especially entrusted to her
3 watch-care, can never be effaced, and can hardly fail to induce
them to follow her to the brighter world. Her life was a
living illustration of Christian faith.

6   My childhood's home I remember as one with the open
hand. The needy were ever welcome, and to the clergy
were accorded special household privileges.
9   Among the treasured reminiscences of my much respected parents, brothers, and sisters, is the memory of
my second brother, Albert Baker, who was, next to my
12 mother, the very dearest of my kindred. To speak of his
beautiful character as I cherish it, would require more
space than this little book can afford.
15   My brother Albert was graduated at Dartmouth College in 1834, and was reputed one of the most talented,
close, and thorough scholars ever connected with that
18 institution. For two or three years he read law at Hills-
borough, in the office of Franklin Pierce, afterwards President of the United States; but later Albert spent a year
21 in the office of the Hon. Richard Fletcher of Boston.
He was consequently admitted to the bar in two States,
Massachusetts and New Hampshire. In 1837 he suc-
24 ceeded to the law-office which Mr. Pierce had occupied,
and was soon elected to the Legislature of his native State,
where he served the public interests faithfully for two
27 consecutive years. Among other important bills which
were carried through the Legislature by his persistent energy was one for the abolition of imprisonment for debt.
30   In 1841 he received further political preferment, by

nomination to Congress on a majority vote of seven 1
thousand, — it was the largest vote of the State; but he
passed away at the age of thirty-one, after a short illness, 3
before his election.   His noble political antagonist, the
Hon. Isaac Hill, of Concord, wrote of my brother as
follows: —   6

   Albert Baker was a young man of uncommon promise.
Gifted with the highest order of intellectual powers, he trained
and schooled them by intense and almost incessant study 9
throughout his short life.   He was fond of investigating abstruse and metaphysical principles, and he never forsook
them until he had explored their every nook and corner, 12
however hidden and remote.   Had life and health been spared
to him, he would have made himself one of the most distinguished men in the country.   As a lawyer he was able and 15
learned, and in the successful practice of a very large business.
He was noted for his boldness and firmness, and for his powerful advocacy of the side he deemed right.   His death will be 18
deplored, with the most poignant grief, by a large number of
friends, who expected no more than they realized from his
talents and acquirements.   This sad event will not be soon 21
forgotten.   It blights too many hopes; it carries with it too
much of sorrow and loss.   It is a public calamity.

Voices Not Our Own

1 MANY peculiar circumstances and events connected
with my childhood throng the chambers of memory.
3 For some twelve months, when I was about eight years
old, I repeatedly heard a voice, calling me distinctly by
name, three times, in an ascending scale. I thought this
6 was my mother's voice, and sometimes went to her, be-
seeching her to tell me what she wanted. Her answer was
always, "Nothing, child! What do you mean?" Then
9 I would say, "Mother, who *did* call me? I heard somebody call *Mary,* three times!" This continued until I
grew discouraged, and my mother was perplexed and
12 anxious.

One day, when my cousin, Mehitable Huntoon, was
visiting us, and I sat in a little chair by her side, in the
15 same room with grandmother, — the call again came, so
loud that Mehitable heard it, though I had ceased to
notice it. Greatly surprised, my cousin turned to me and
18 said, "Your mother is calling you!" but I answered not,
till again the same call was thrice repeated. Mehitable
then said sharply, "Why don't you go? your mother is
21 calling you!" I then left the room, went to my mother,
and once more asked her if she had summoned me? She
answered as always before. Then I earnestly declared
24 my cousin had heard the voice, and said that mother

8

wanted me. Accordingly she returned with me to grand- 1
mother's room, and led my cousin into an adjoining apartment. The door was ajar, and I listened with bated 3
breath. Mother told Mehitable all about this mysterious
voice, and asked if she really did hear Mary's name pronounced in audible tones. My cousin answered quickly, 6
and emphasized her affirmation.

That night, before going to rest, my mother read to me
the Scriptural narrative of little Samuel, and bade me, 9
when the voice called again, to reply as he did, "Speak,
Lord; for Thy servant heareth." The voice came; but
I was afraid, and did not answer. Afterward I wept, and 12
prayed that God would forgive me, resolving to do, next
time, as my mother had bidden me. When the call came
again I did answer, in the words of Samuel, but never 15
again to the material senses was that mysterious call
repeated.

Is it not much that I may worship Him,   18
  With naught my spirit's breathings to control,
And feel His presence in the vast and dim
  And whispering woods, where dying thunders roll 21
From the far cataracts? Shall I not rejoice
That I have learned at last to know His voice
  From man's? — I will rejoice! My soaring soul 24
Now hath redeemed her birthright of the day,
And won, through clouds, to Him, her own unfettered way!
             — Mrs. Hemans 27

Early Studies

1 MY father was taught to believe that my brain was too large for my body and so kept me much out of 3 school, but I gained book-knowledge with far less labor than is usually requisite. At ten years of age I was as familiar with Lindley Murray's Grammar as with the 6 Westminster Catechism; and the latter I had to repeat every Sunday. My favorite studies were natural philosophy, logic, and moral science. From my brother Al-9 bert I received lessons in the ancient tongues, Hebrew, Greek, and Latin. My brother studied Hebrew during his college vacations. After my discovery of Christian 12 Science, most of the knowledge I had gleaned from schoolbooks vanished like a dream.

Learning was so illumined, that grammar was eclipsed. 15 Etymology was divine history, voicing the idea of God in man's origin and signification. Syntax was spiritual order and unity. Prosody, the song of angels, and no earthly 18 or inglorious theme.

Girlhood Composition

FROM childhood I was a verse-maker. Poetry suited 1
my emotions better than prose. The following is
one of my girlhood productions. 3

ALPHABET AND BAYONET

If fancy plumes aerial flight,
   Go fix thy restless mind 6
On learning's lore and wisdom's might,
   And live to bless mankind.
The sword is sheathed, 't is freedom's hour, 9
   No despot bears misrule,
Where knowledge plants the foot of power
   In our God-blessed free school. 12

Forth from this fount the streamlets flow,
   That widen in their course.
Hero and sage arise to show 15
   Science the mighty source,
And laud the land whose talents rock
   The cradle of her power, 18
And wreaths are twined round Plymouth Rock,
   From erudition's bower.

Farther than feet of chamois fall, 21
   Free as the generous air,

1   Strains nobler far than clarion call
     Wake freedom's welcome, where
3   Minerva's silver sandals still
     Are loosed, and not effete;
     Where echoes still my day-dreams thrill,
6   Woke by her fancied feet.

Theological Reminiscence

AT the age of twelve [1] I was admitted to the Congre- 1
gational (Trinitarian) Church, my parents having
been members of that body for a half-century. In connec- 3
tion with this event, some circumstances are noteworthy.
Before this step was taken, the doctrine of unconditional
election, or predestination, greatly troubled me; for I 6
was unwilling to be saved, if my brothers and sisters were
to be numbered among those who were doomed to perpetual banishment from God. So perturbed was I by the 9
thoughts aroused by this erroneous doctrine, that the
family doctor was summoned, and pronounced me stricken
with fever. 12

My father's relentless theology emphasized belief in a
final judgment-day, in the danger of endless punishment,
and in a Jehovah merciless towards unbelievers; and of 15
these things he now spoke, hoping to win me from dreaded
heresy.

My mother, as she bathed my burning temples, bade 18
me lean on God's love, which would give me rest, if I
went to Him in prayer, as I was wont to do, seeking His
guidance. I prayed; and a soft glow of ineffable joy came 21
over me. The fever was gone, and I rose and dressed
myself, in a normal condition of health. Mother saw this,
and was glad. The physician marvelled; and the "hor- 24

[1] See Page 311, Lines 12 to 17, "The First Church of Christ,
Scientist, and Miscellany."

13

1 rible decree" of predestination — as John Calvin rightly called his own tenet — forever lost its power over me.

3   When the meeting was held for the examination of candidates for membership, I was of course present. The pastor was an old-school expounder of the strictest Pres-
6 byterian doctrines. He was apparently as eager to have unbelievers in these dogmas lost, as he was to have elect believers converted and rescued from perdition; for both
9 salvation and condemnation depended, according to his views, upon the good pleasure of infinite Love. However, I was ready for his doleful questions, which I answered with-
12 out a tremor, declaring that never could I unite with the church, if assent to this doctrine was essential thereto.

Distinctly do I recall what followed. I stoutly main-
15 tained that I was willing to trust God, and take my chance of spiritual safety with my brothers and sisters, — not one of whom had then made any profession of religion, —
18 even if my creedal doubts left me outside the doors. The minister then wished me to tell him when I had experienced a change of heart; but tearfully I had to respond
21 that I could not designate any precise time. Nevertheless, he persisted in the assertion that I *had* been truly regenerated, and asked me to say how I felt when the new light
24 dawned within me. I replied that I could only answer him in the words of the Psalmist: "Search me, O God, and know my heart: try me, and know my thoughts:
27 and see if there be any wicked way in me, and lead me in the way everlasting."

This was so earnestly said, that even the oldest church-
30 members wept. After the meeting was over they came

and kissed me. To the astonishment of many, the good ₁
clergyman's heart also melted, and he received me into
their communion, and my protest along with me. My con- ₃
nection with this religious body was retained till I founded
a church of my own, built on the basis of Christian Science,
"Jesus Christ himself being the chief corner-stone." ₆

In confidence of faith, I could say in David's words,
"I will go in the strength of the Lord God: I will make
mention of Thy righteousness, even of Thine only. O ₉
God, Thou hast taught me from my youth: and hitherto have I declared Thy wondrous works." (Psalms lxxi.
16, 17.) ₁₂

In the year 1878 I was called to preach in Boston at the
Baptist Tabernacle of Rev. Daniel C. Eddy, D. D., — by
the pastor of this church. I accepted the invitation and ₁₅
commenced work.

The congregation so increased in number the pews were
not sufficient to seat the audience and benches were used ₁₈
in the aisles. At the close of my engagement we parted
in Christian fellowship, if not in full unity of doctrine.

Our last vestry meeting was made memorable by elo- ₂₁
quent addresses from persons who feelingly testified to
having been healed through my preaching. Among other
diseases cured they specified cancers. The cases described ₂₄
had been treated and given over by physicians of the popular schools of medicine, but I had not heard of these cases
till the persons who divulged their secret joy were healed. ₂₇
A prominent churchman agreeably informed the congregation that many others present had been healed under
my preaching, but were too timid to testify in public. ₃₀

1   One memorable Sunday afternoon, a soprano, — clear, strong, sympathetic, — floating up from the pews, caught
3 my ear. When the meeting was over, two ladies pushing their way through the crowd reached the platform. With tears of joy flooding her eyes — for she was a mother —
6 one of them said, "Did you hear my daughter sing? Why, she has not sung before since she left the choir and was in consumption! When she entered this church one hour
9 ago she could not speak a loud word, and now, oh, thank God, she is healed!"

It was not an uncommon occurrence in my own church
12 for the sick to be healed by my sermon. Many pale cripples went into the church leaning on crutches who went out carrying them on their shoulders. "And these signs shall
15 follow them that believe."

The charter for The Mother Church in Boston was obtained June, 1879,[1] and the same month the members,
18 twenty-six in number, extended a call to Mary B. G. Eddy to become their pastor. She accepted the call, and was ordained A. D. 1881.

[1] This statement appears to be based upon the Annual Report of the Secretary of The Christian Scientist Association, read at its meeting, January 15, 1880, in which June is named as the month in which the charter for The Mother Church was obtained, instead of August 23, 1879, the correct date.

The Country-seat

Written in youth, while visiting a family friend in the beautiful 1
suburbs of Boston.

WILD spirit of song, — midst the zephyrs at play 3
In bowers of beauty, — I bend to thy lay,
And woo, while I worship in deep sylvan spot,
The Muses' soft echoes to kindle the grot. 6
Wake chords of my lyre, with musical kiss,
To vibrate and tremble with accents of bliss.

Here morning peers out, from her crimson repose, 9
On proud Prairie Queen and the modest Moss-rose;
And vesper reclines — when the dewdrop is shed
On the heart of the pink — in its odorous bed; 12
But Flora has stolen the rainbow and sky,
To sprinkle the flowers with exquisite dye.

Here fame-honored hickory rears his bold form, 15
And bares a brave breast to the lightning and storm,
While palm, bay, and laurel, in classical glee,
Chase tulip, magnolia, and fragrant fringe-tree; 18
And sturdy horse-chestnut for centuries hath given
Its feathery blossom and branches to heaven.

1 Here is life! Here is youth! Here the poet's world-
   wish, —
3 Cool waters at play with the gold-gleaming fish;
   While cactus a mellower glory receives
   From light colored softly by blossom and leaves;
6 And nestling alder is whispering low,
   In lap of the pear-tree, with musical flow.[1]

   Dark sentinel hedgerow is guarding repose,
9 Midst grotto and songlet and streamlet that flows
   Where beauty and perfume from buds burst away,
   And ope their closed cells to the bright, laughing day;
12 Yet, dwellers in Eden, earth yields you her tear, —
   Oft plucked for the banquet, but laid on the bier.

   Earth's beauty and glory delude as the shrine
15 Or fount of real joy and of visions divine;
   But hope, as the eaglet that spurneth the sod,
   May soar above matter, to fasten on God,
18 And freely adore all His spirit hath made,
   Where rapture and radiance and glory ne'er fade.

   Oh, give me the spot where affection may dwell
21 In sacred communion with home's magic spell!
   Where flowers of feeling are fragrant and fair,
   And those we most love find a happiness rare;
24 But clouds are a presage, — they darken my lay:
   This life is a shadow, and hastens away.

[1] An alder growing from the bent branch of a pear-tree.

Marriage and Parentage

IN 1843 I was united to my first husband, Colonel George 1
Washington Glover of Charleston, South Carolina,
the ceremony taking place under the paternal roof in 3
Tilton.

After parting with the dear home circle I went with
him to the South; but he was spared to me for only one 6
brief year. He was in Wilmington, North Carolina, on
business, when the yellow-fever raged in that city, and was
suddenly attacked by this insidious disease, which in his 9
case proved fatal.

My husband was a freemason, being a member in Saint
Andrew's Lodge, Number 10, and of Union Chapter, Num- 12
ber 3, of Royal Arch masons. He was highly esteemed
and sincerely lamented by a large circle of friends and acquaintances, whose kindness and sympathy helped to sup- 15
port me in this terrible bereavement. A month later I
returned to New Hampshire, where, at the end of four
months, my babe was born. 18

Colonel Glover's tender devotion to his young bride
was remarked by all observers. With his parting breath
he gave pathetic directions to his brother masons about 21
accompanying her on her sad journey to the North. Here
it is but justice to record, they performed their obligations
most faithfully. 24

19

1   After returning to the paternal roof I lost all my husband's property, except what money I had brought with
3   me; and remained with my parents until after my mother's decease.

A few months before my father's second marriage, to
6   Mrs. Elizabeth Patterson Duncan, sister of Lieutenant-Governor George W. Patterson of New York, my little son, about four years of age, was sent away from me, and
9   put under the care of our family nurse, who had married, and resided in the northern part of New Hampshire.   I had no training for self-support, and my home I regarded
12 as very precious.   The night before my child was taken from me, I knelt by his side throughout the dark hours, hoping for a vision of relief from this trial.   The follow-
15 ing lines are taken from my poem, "Mother's Darling," written after this separation: —

Thy smile through tears, as sunshine o'er the sea,
18   Awoke new beauty in the surge's roll!
Oh, life is dead, bereft of all, with thee, —
         Star of my earthly hope, babe of my soul.

21 My second marriage was very unfortunate, and from it I was compelled to ask for a bill of divorce, which was granted me in the city of Salem, Massachusetts.
24 My dominant thought in marrying again was to get back my child, but after our marriage his stepfather was not willing he should have a home with me.   A plot was
27 consummated for keeping us apart.   The family to whose care he was committed very soon removed to what was then regarded as the Far West.

After his removal a letter was read to my little son, 1
informing him that his mother was dead and buried.
Without my knowledge a guardian was appointed him, and 3
I was then informed that my son was lost. Every means
within my power was employed to find him, but without
success. We never met again until he had reached the 6
age of thirty-four, had a wife and two children, and by a
strange providence had learned that his mother still lived,
and came to see me in Massachusetts. 9

Meanwhile he had served as a volunteer throughout
the war for the Union, and at its expiration was appointed
United States Marshal of the Territory of Dakota. 12

It is well to know, dear reader, that our material, mortal
history is but the record of dreams, not of man's real existence, and the dream has no place in the Science of being. 15
It is "as a tale that is told," and "as the shadow when it
declineth." The heavenly intent of earth's shadows is to
chasten the affections, to rebuke human consciousness and 18
turn it gladly from a material, false sense of life and happiness, to spiritual joy and true estimate of being.

The awakening from a false sense of life, substance, and 21
mind in matter, is as yet imperfect; but for those lucid
and enduring lessons of Love which tend to this result,
I bless God. 24

Mere historic incidents and personal events are frivo-
lous and of no moment, unless they illustrate the ethics of
Truth. To this end, but only to this end, such narrations 27
may be admissible and advisable; but if spiritual conclusions are separated from their premises, the *nexus* is
lost, and the argument, with its rightful conclusions, be- 30

1 comes correspondingly obscure. The human history needs
to be revised, and the material record expunged.

3   The Gospel narratives bear brief testimony even to the
life of our great Master. His spiritual noumenon and
phenomenon silenced portraiture. Writers less wise than
6 the apostles essayed in the Apocryphal New Testament
a legendary and traditional history of the early life of
Jesus. But St. Paul summarized the character of Jesus
9 as the model of Christianity, in these words: "Consider
him that endured such contradiction of sinners against
himself." "Who for the joy that was set before him en-
12 dured the cross, despising the shame, and is set down
at the right hand of the throne of God."

It may be that the mortal life-battle still wages, and
15 must continue till its involved errors are vanquished by
victory-bringing Science; but this triumph will come!
God is over all. He alone is our origin, aim, and being.
18 The real man is not of the dust, nor is he ever created
through the flesh; for his father and mother are the one
Spirit, and his brethren are all the children of one parent,
21 the eternal good.

Emergence into Light

THE trend of human life was too eventful to leave me 1
undisturbed in the illusion that this so-called life
could be a real and abiding rest. All things earthly must 3
ultimately yield to the irony of fate, or else be merged
into the one infinite Love.

As these pungent lessons became clearer, they grew 6
sterner. Previously the cloud of mortal mind seemed to
have a silver lining; but now it was not even fringed with
light. Matter was no longer spanned with its rainbow 9
of promise. The world was dark. The oncoming hours
were indicated by no floral dial. The senses could not
prophesy sunrise or starlight. 12

Thus it was when the moment arrived of the heart's
bridal to more spiritual existence. When the door opened,
I was waiting and watching; and, lo, the bridegroom 15
came! The character of the Christ was illuminated by
the midnight torches of Spirit. My heart knew its Redeemer. He whom my affections had diligently sought 18
was as the One "altogether lovely," as "the chiefest,"
the only, "among ten thousand." Soulless famine had
fled. Agnosticism, pantheism, and theosophy were void. 21
Being was beautiful, its substance, cause, and currents
were God and His idea. I had touched the hem of Christian Science. 24

23

The Great Discovery

1 IT was in Massachusetts, in February, 1866, and after
the death of the magnetic doctor, Mr. P. P. Quimby,
3 whom spiritualists would associate therewith, but who
was in no wise connected with this event, that I discovered the Science of divine metaphysical healing which I
6 afterwards named Christian Science. The discovery came
to pass in this way. During twenty years prior to my
discovery I had been trying to trace all physical effects to
9 a mental cause; and in the latter part of 1866 I gained
the scientific certainty that all causation was Mind, and
every effect a mental phenomenon.

12 My immediate recovery from the effects of an injury
caused by an accident, an injury that neither medicine nor
surgery could reach, was the falling apple that led me to
15 the discovery how to be well myself, and how to make
others so.

Even to the homœopathic physician who attended me,
18 and rejoiced in my recovery, I could not then explain the
modus of my relief. I could only assure him that the divine
Spirit had wrought the miracle — a miracle which later
21 I found to be in perfect scientific accord with divine law.

I then withdrew from society about three years, — to
ponder my mission, to search the Scriptures, to find the
24 Science of Mind that should take the things of God and

show them to the creature, and reveal the great curative 1
Principle, — Deity.

The Bible was my textbook. It answered my questions 3
as to how I was healed; but the Scriptures had to me a
new meaning, a new tongue. Their spiritual signification appeared; and I apprehended for the first time, in 6
their spiritual meaning, Jesus' teaching and demonstration, and the Principle and rule of spiritual Science and
metaphysical healing, — in a word, Christian Science. 9

I named it *Christian,* because it is compassionate,
helpful, and spiritual. God I called *immortal Mind.* That
which sins, suffers, and dies, I named *mortal mind.* The 12
physical senses, or sensuous nature, I called *error* and
shadow. Soul I denominated *substance,* because Soul
alone is truly substantial. God I characterized as individ- 15
ual entity, but His corporeality I denied. The real I
claimed as eternal; and its antipodes, or the temporal,
I described as unreal. Spirit I called the *reality;* and 18
matter, the *unreality.*

I knew the human conception of God to be that He was
a physically personal being, like unto man; and that the 21
five physical senses are so many witnesses to the physical
personality of mind and the real existence of matter; but
I learned that these material senses testify falsely, that 24
matter neither sees, hears, nor feels Spirit, and is therefore
inadequate to form any proper conception of the infinite
Mind. "If I bear witness of myself, my witness is not 27
true." (John v. 31.)

I beheld with ineffable awe our great Master's purpose
in not questioning those he healed as to their disease or 30

1 its symptoms, and his marvellous skill in demanding
neither obedience to hygienic laws, nor prescribing drugs
3 to support the divine power which heals. Adoringly I
discerned the Principle of his holy heroism and Christian
example on the cross, when he refused to drink the "vine-
6 gar and gall," a preparation of poppy, or aconite, to allay
the tortures of crucifixion.

Our great Way-shower, steadfast to the end in his obedi-
9 ence to God's laws, demonstrated for all time and peoples
the supremacy of good over evil, and the superiority of
Spirit over matter.

12   The miracles recorded in the Bible, which had before
seemed to me supernatural, grew divinely natural and ap-
prehensible; though uninspired interpreters ignorantly
15 pronounce Christ's healing miraculous, instead of seeing
therein the operation of the divine law.

Jesus of Nazareth was a natural and divine Scientist.
18 He was so before the material world saw him. He who
antedated Abraham, and gave the world a new date in the
Christian era, was a Christian Scientist, who needed no
21 discovery of the Science of being in order to rebuke the
evidence. To one "born of the flesh," however, divine
Science must be a discovery. Woman must give it birth.
24 It must be begotten of spirituality, since none but the pure
in heart can see God, — the Principle of all things pure;
and none but the "poor in spirit" could first state this
27 Principle, could know yet more of the nothingness of matter and the allness of Spirit, could utilize Truth, and absolutely reduce the demonstration of being, in Science, to
30 the apprehension of the age.

I wrote also, at this period, comments on the Scriptures, 1
setting forth their spiritual interpretation, the Science of
the Bible, and so laid the foundation of my work called 3
Science and Health, published in 1875.

If these notes and comments, which have never been
read by any one but myself, were published, it would 6
show that after my discovery of the absolute Science
of Mind-healing, like all great truths, this spiritual
Science developed itself to me until Science and 9
Health was written. These early comments are valuable to me as waymarks of progress, which I would not
have effaced.   12

Up to that time I had not fully voiced my discovery. Naturally, my first jottings were but efforts to
express in feeble diction Truth's ultimate. In Longfellow's 15
language, —

> But the feeble hands and helpless,
> Groping blindly in the darkness,   18
> Touch God's right hand in that darkness,
> And are lifted up and strengthened.

As sweet music ripples in one's first thoughts of it like 21
the brooklet in its meandering midst pebbles and rocks,
before the mind can duly express it to the ear, — so the
harmony of divine Science first broke upon my sense, 24
before gathering experience and confidence to articulate
it. Its natural manifestation is beautiful and euphonious,
but its written expression increases in power and perfection 27
under the guidance of the great Master.

The divine hand led me into a new world of light and
Life, a fresh universe — old to God, but new to His "little 30

1 one." It became evident that the divine Mind alone must
answer, and be found as the Life, or Principle, of all being;
3 and that one must acquaint himself with God, if he would
be at peace. He must be ours practically, guiding our
every thought and action; else we cannot understand
6 the omnipresence of good sufficiently to demonstrate,
even in part, the Science of the perfect Mind and divine
healing.

9   I had learned that thought must be spiritualized, in
order to apprehend Spirit. It must become honest, unselfish, and pure, in order to have the least understanding
12 of God in divine Science. The first must become last.
Our reliance upon material things must be transferred to
a perception of and dependence on spiritual things. For
15 Spirit to be supreme in demonstration, it must be supreme
in our affections, and we must be clad with divine power.
Purity, self-renunciation, faith, and understanding must
18 reduce all things real to their own mental denomination, Mind, which divides, subdivides, increases, diminishes, constitutes, and sustains, according to the law of
21 God.

   I had learned that Mind reconstructed the body, and
that nothing else could. How it was done, the spiritual
24 Science of Mind must reveal. It was a mystery to me
then, but I have since understood it. All Science is a
revelation. Its Principle is divine, not human, reaching
27 higher than the stars of heaven.

   Am I a believer in spiritualism? I believe in no *ism*.
This is my endeavor, to be a Christian, to assimilate the
30 character and practice of the anointed; and no motive

can cause a surrender of this effort. As I understand it, 1
spiritualism is the antipode of Christian Science. I esteem
all honest people, and love them, and hold to loving our 3
enemies and doing good to them that "despitefully use
you and persecute you."

Foundation Work

1 AS the pioneer of Christian Science I stood alone in
this conflict, endeavoring to smite error with the
3 falchion of Truth. The rare bequests of Christian Science
are costly, and they have won fields of battle from which
the dainty borrower would have fled. Ceaseless toil, self-
6 renunciation, and love, have cleared its pathway.

The motive of my earliest labors has never changed.
It was to relieve the sufferings of humanity by a sanitary
9 system that should include all moral and religious reform.

It is often asked why Christian Science was revealed to
me as one intelligence, analyzing, uncovering, and annihi-
12 lating the false testimony of the physical senses. Why was
this conviction necessary to the right apprehension of the
invincible and infinite energies of Truth and Love, as con-
15 trasted with the foibles and fables of finite mind and material existence.

The answer is plain. St. Paul declared that the law
18 was the schoolmaster, to bring him to Christ. Even so
was I led into the mazes of divine metaphysics through
the gospel of suffering, the providence of God, and the
21 cross of Christ. No one else can drain the cup which I
have drunk to the dregs as the Discoverer and teacher of
Christian Science; neither can its inspiration be gained
24 without tasting this cup.

The loss of material objects of affection sunders the 1
dominant ties of earth and points to heaven. Nothing
can compete with Christian Science, and its demonstra- 3
tion, in showing this solemn certainty in growing freedom
and vindicating "the ways of God" to man. The absolute proof and self-evident propositions of Truth are im- 6
measurably paramount to rubric and dogma in proving
the Christ.

From my very childhood I was impelled, by a hunger 9
and thirst after divine things, — a desire for something
higher and better than matter, and apart from it, — to
seek diligently for the knowledge of God as the one great 12
and ever-present relief from human woe. The first spontaneous motion of Truth and Love, acting through Christian Science on my roused consciousness, banished at once 15
and forever the fundamental error of faith in things material; for this trust is the unseen sin, the unknown foe, —
the heart's untamed desire which breaketh the divine com- 18
mandments. As says St. James: "Whosoever shall keep
the whole law, and yet offend in one point, he is guilty
of all."   21

Into mortal mind's material obliquity I gazed, and stood
abashed. Blanched was the cheek of pride. My heart
bent low before the omnipotence of Spirit, and a tint of 24
humility, soft as the heart of a moonbeam, mantled the
earth. Bethlehem and Bethany, Gethsemane and Calvary,
spoke to my chastened sense as by the tearful lips of a 27
babe. Frozen fountains were unsealed. Erudite systems
of philosophy and religion melted, for Love unveiled the
healing promise and potency of a present spiritual *afflatus*. 30

1 It was the gospel of healing, on its divinely appointed
human mission, bearing on its white wings, to my appre-
3 hension, "the beauty of holiness," — even the possibilities of spiritual insight, knowledge, and being.

Early had I learned that whatever is loved materially,
6 as mere corporeal personality, is eventually lost. "For
whosoever will save his life shall lose it," saith the Master.
Exultant hope, if tinged with earthliness, is crushed as the
9 moth.

What is termed mortal and material existence is graphically defined by Calderon, the famous Spanish poet, who
12 wrote, —

> What is life? 'T is but a madness.
> What is life? A mere illusion,
> 15   Fleeting pleasure, fond delusion,
> Short-lived joy, that ends in sadness,
> Whose most constant substance seems
> 18   But the dream of other dreams.

Medical Experiments

THE physical side of this research was aided by hints from homœopathy, sustaining my final conclusion that mortal belief, instead of the drug, governed the action of material medicine.

I wandered through the dim mazes of *materia medica*, till I was weary of "scientific guessing," as it has been well called. I sought knowledge from the different schools, — allopathy, homœopathy, hydropathy, electricity, and from various humbugs, — but without receiving satisfaction.

I found, in the two hundred and sixty-two remedies enumerated by Jahr, one pervading secret; namely, that the less material medicine we have, and the more Mind, the better the work is done; a fact which seems to prove the Principle of Mind-healing. One drop of the thirtieth attenuation of *Natrum muriaticum,* in a tumbler-full of water, and one teaspoonful of the water mixed with the faith of ages, would cure patients not affected by a larger dose. The drug disappears in the higher attenuations of homœopathy, and matter is thereby rarefied to its fatal essence, mortal mind; but immortal Mind, the curative Principle, remains, and is found to be even more active.

The mental virtues of the material methods of medicine, when understood, were insufficient to satisfy my doubts

1 as to the honesty or utility of using a material curative. I
must know more of the unmixed, unerring source, in order
3 to gain the Science of Mind, the All-in-all of Spirit, in
which matter is obsolete. Nothing less could solve the
mental problem. If I sought an answer from the medical
6 schools, the reply was dark and contradictory. Neither
ancient nor modern philosophy could clear the clouds, or
give me one distinct statement of the spiritual Science of
9 Mind-healing. Human reason was not equal to it.

I claim for healing scientifically the following advantages: *First:* It does away with all material medicines,
12 and recognizes the antidote for all sickness, as well as sin,
in the immortal Mind; and mortal mind as the source of
all the ills which befall mortals. *Second:* It is more effec-
15 tual than drugs, and cures when they fail, or only relieve;
thus proving the superiority of metaphysics over physics.
Third: A person healed by Christian Science is not only
18 healed of his disease, but he is advanced morally and
spiritually. The mortal body being but the objective state
of the mortal mind, this mind must be renovated to im-
21 prove the body.

First Publication

IN 1870 I copyrighted the first publication on spirit- 1
ual, scientific Mind-healing, entitled "The Science of
Man." This little book is converted into the chapter on 3
Recapitulation in Science and Health. It was so new —
the basis it laid down for physical and moral health was
so hopelessly original, and men were so unfamiliar with 6
the subject — that I did not venture upon its publication
until later, having learned that the merits of Christian
Science must be proven before a work on this subject 9
could be profitably published.

The truths of Christian Science are not interpolations
of the Scriptures, but the spiritual interpretations thereof. 12
Science is the prism of Truth, which divides its rays and
brings out the hues of Deity. Human hypotheses have
darkened the glow and grandeur of evangelical religion. 15
When speaking of his true followers in every period, Jesus
said, "*They* shall lay hands on the sick, and they shall
recover." There is no authority for querying the authen- 18
ticity of this declaration, for it already was and is demonstrated as practical, and its claim is substantiated, — a
claim too immanent to fall to the ground beneath the stroke 21
of artless workmen.

Though a man were girt with the Urim and Thummim
of priestly office, and denied the perpetuity of Jesus' com- 24

35

1 mand, "Heal the sick," or its application in all time to
those who understand Christ as the Truth and the Life,
3 that man would not expound the gospel according to
Jesus.

Five years after taking out my first copyright, I taught
6 the Science of Mind-healing, *alias* Christian Science, by
writing out my manuscripts for students and distributing them unsparingly. This will account for certain pub-
9 lished and unpublished manuscripts extant, which the
evil-minded would insinuate did not originate with me.

The Precious Volume

THE first edition of my most important work, Science 1
and Health, containing the complete statement of
Christian Science, — the term employed by me to express 3
the divine, or spiritual, Science of Mind-healing, was published in 1875.

When it was first printed, the critics took pleasure in 6
saying, "This book is indeed wholly original, but it will
never be read."

The first edition numbered one thousand copies. In 9
September, 1891, it had reached sixty-two editions.

Those who formerly sneered at it, as foolish and ec-
centric, now declare Bishop Berkeley, David Hume, Ralph 12
Waldo Emerson, or certain German philosophers, to have
been the originators of the Science of Mind-healing as
therein stated. 15

Even the Scriptures gave no direct interpretation of the
scientific basis for demonstrating the spiritual Principle
of healing, until our heavenly Father saw fit, through the 18
Key to the Scriptures, in Science and Health, to unlock
this "mystery of godliness."

My reluctance to give the public, in my first edition of 21
Science and Health, the chapter on Animal Magnetism,
and the divine purpose that this should be done, may
have an interest for the reader, and will be seen in the fol- 24

1 lowing circumstances. I had finished that edition as far
as that chapter, when the printer informed me that he
3 could not go on with my work. I had already paid
him seven hundred dollars, and yet he stopped my work.
All efforts to persuade him to finish my book were in
6 vain.

After months had passed, I yielded to a constant conviction that I must insert in my last chapter a partial
9 history of what I had already observed of mental malpractice. Accordingly, I set to work, contrary to my inclination, to fulfil this painful task, and finished my copy
12 for the book. As it afterwards appeared, although I had
not thought of such a result, my printer resumed his work
at the same time, finished printing the copy he had on
15 hand, and then started for Lynn to see me. The afternoon that he left Boston for Lynn, I started for Boston
with my finished copy. We met at the Eastern depot in
18 Lynn, and were both surprised, — I to learn that he had
printed all the copy on hand, and had come to tell me he
wanted more, — he to find me *en route* for Boston, to give
21 him the closing chapter of my first edition of Science and
Health. Not a word had passed between us, audibly or
mentally, while this went on. I had grown disgusted
24 with my printer, and become silent. He had come to
a standstill through motives and circumstances unknown
to me.

27   Science and Health is the textbook of Christian Science.
Whosoever learns the letter of this book, must also gain
its spiritual significance, in order to demonstrate Christian
30 Science.

When the demand for this book increased, and people 1
were healed simply by reading it, the copyright was infringed. I entered a suit at law, and my copyright was 3
protected.

Recuperative Incident

1 THROUGH four successive years I healed, preached, and taught in a general way, refusing to take any 3 pay for my services and living on a small annuity.

At one time I was called to speak before the Lyceum Club, at Westerly, Rhode Island. On my arrival my 6 hostess told me that her next-door neighbor was dying. I asked permission to see her. It was granted, and with my hostess I went to the invalid's house.

9 The physicians had given up the case and retired. I had stood by her side about fifteen minutes when the sick woman rose from her bed, dressed herself, and was well. 12 Afterwards they showed me the clothes already prepared for her burial; and told me that her physicians had said the diseased condition was caused by an injury received 15 from a surgical operation at the birth of her last babe, and that it was impossible for her to be delivered of another child. It is sufficient to add her babe was safely born, 18 and weighed twelve pounds. The mother afterwards wrote to me, "I never before suffered so little in child-birth."

21 This scientific demonstration so stirred the doctors and clergy that they had my notices for a second lecture pulled down, and refused me a hearing in their halls and churches. 24 This circumstance is cited simply to show the opposition

which Christian Science encountered a quarter-century 1
ago, as contrasted with its present welcome into the sick-
room.   3

Many were the desperate cases I instantly healed,
"without money and without price," and in most instances
without even an acknowledgment of the benefit.   6

A True Man

1 MY last marriage was with Asa Gilbert Eddy, and was a blessed and spiritual union, solemnized at 3 Lynn, Massachusetts, by the Rev. Samuel Barrett Stewart, in the year 1877. Dr. Eddy was the first student publicly to announce himself a Christian Scientist, and place these 6 symbolic words on his office sign. He forsook all to follow in this line of light. He was the first organizer of a Christian Science Sunday School, which he superintended. He 9 also taught a special Bible-class; and he lectured so ably on Scriptural topics that clergymen of other denominations listened to him with deep interest. He was remark- 12 ably successful in Mind-healing, and untiring in his chosen work. In 1882 he passed away, with a smile of peace and love resting on his serene countenance. "Mark the per- 15 fect *man,* and behold the upright: for the end of *that* man *is* peace." (Psalms xxxvii. 37.)

College and Church

IN 1867 I introduced the first purely metaphysical sys- 1
tem of healing since the apostolic days. I began by
teaching one student Christian Science Mind-healing. 3
From this seed grew the Massachusetts Metaphysical
College in Boston, chartered in 1881. No charter was
granted for similar purposes after 1883. It is the only 6
College, hitherto, for teaching the pathology of spiritual
power, *alias* the Science of Mind-healing.

My husband, Asa G. Eddy, taught two terms in my 9
College. After I gave up teaching, my adopted son,
Ebenezer J. Foster-Eddy, a graduate of the Hahnemann
Medical College of Philadelphia, and who also received a 12
certificate from Dr. W. W. Keen's (allopathic) Philadelphia
School of Anatomy and Surgery, — having renounced his
material method of practice and embraced the teach- 15
ings of Christian Science, taught the Primary, Normal,
and Obstetric class one term. Gen. Erastus N. Bates
taught one Primary class, in 1889, after which I judged 18
it best to close the institution. These students of mine
were the only assistant teachers in the College.

The first Christian Scientist Association was organized 21
by myself and six of my students in 1876, on the Centen-
nial Day of our nation's freedom. At a meeting of the
Christian Scientist Association, on April 12, 1879, it was 24

1 voted to organize a church to commemorate the words
and works of our Master, a Mind-healing church, without
3 a creed, to be called the Church of Christ, Scientist, the
first such church ever organized.   The charter for this
church was obtained in June, 1879,[1] and during the same
6 month the members, twenty-six in number, extended a
call to me to become their pastor.   I accepted the call,
and was ordained in 1881, though I had preached five
9 years before being ordained.

When I was its pastor, and in the pulpit every Sunday,
my church increased in members, and its spiritual growth
12 kept pace with its increasing popularity; but when obliged,
because of accumulating work in the College, to preach
only occasionally, no student, at that time, was found able
15 to maintain the church in its previous harmony and
prosperity.

Examining the situation prayerfully and carefully, noting
18 the church's need, and the predisposing and exciting cause
of its condition, I saw that the crisis had come when much
time and attention must be given to defend this church
21 from the envy and molestation of other churches, and
from the danger to its members which must always lie in
Christian warfare.   At this juncture I recommended that
24 the church be dissolved.   No sooner were my views made
known, than the proper measures were adopted to carry
them out, the votes passing without a dissenting voice.
27   This measure was immediately followed by a great re-
vival of mutual love, prosperity, and spiritual power.

The history of that hour holds this true record.   Add-
30 ing to its ranks and influence, this spiritually organized

[1] Steps were taken to promote the Church of Christ, Scientist, in April, May,
and June; formal organization was accomplished and the charter obtained in
August, 1879.

Church of Christ, Scientist, in Boston, still goes on. A 1
new light broke in upon it, and more beautiful became
the garments of her who "bringeth good tidings, that pub- 3
lisheth peace."

Despite the prosperity of my church, it was learned
that material organization has its value and peril, and that 6
organization is requisite only in the earliest periods in
Christian history. After this material form of cohesion
and fellowship has accomplished its end, continued organi- 9
zation retards spiritual growth, and should be laid off, —
even as the corporeal organization deemed requisite in
the first stages of mortal existence is finally laid off, in 12
order to gain spiritual freedom and supremacy.

From careful observation and experience came my clue
to the uses and abuses of organization. Therefore, in ac- 15
cord with my special request, followed that noble, unprecedented action of the Christian Scientist Association
connected with my College when dissolving that organiza- 18
tion, — in forgiving enemies, returning good for evil, in
following Jesus' command, "Whosoever shall smite thee
on thy right cheek, turn to him the other also." I saw 21
these fruits of Spirit, long-suffering and temperance, fulfil the law of Christ in righteousness. I also saw that
Christianity has withstood less the temptation of popularity 24
than of persecution.

"Feed My Sheep"

Lines penned when I was pastor of the Church of Christ, Scientist, in Boston.

SHEPHERD, show me how to go
O'er the hillside steep,
How to gather, how to sow, —
How to feed Thy sheep;
I will listen for Thy voice,
Lest my footsteps stray;
I will follow and rejoice
All the rugged way.

Thou wilt bind the stubborn will,
Wound the callous breast,
Make self-righteousness be still,
Break earth's stupid rest.
Strangers on a barren shore,
Lab'ring long and lone,
We would enter by the door,
And Thou know'st Thine own.

So, when day grows dark and cold,
Tear or triumph harms,
Lead Thy lambkins to the fold,
Take them in Thine arms;
Feed the hungry, heal the heart,
Till the morning's beam;
White as wool, ere they depart,
Shepherd, wash them clean.

College Closed

THE apprehension of what has been, and must be, the 1
final outcome of material organization, which wars
with Love's spiritual compact, caused me to dread the 3
unprecedented popularity of my College. Students from
all over our continent, and from Europe, were flooding
the school. At this time there were over three hundred 6
applications from persons desiring to enter the College,
and applicants were rapidly increasing. Example had
shown the dangers arising from being placed on earthly 9
pinnacles, and Christian Science shuns whatever involves
material means for the promotion of spiritual ends.

In view of all this, a meeting was called of the Board 12
of Directors of my College, who, being informed of
my intentions, unanimously voted that the school be
discontinued. 15

A Primary class student, richly imbued with the spirit
of Christ, is a better healer and teacher than a Normal
class student who partakes less of God's love. After hav- 18
ing received instructions in a Primary class from me, or
a loyal student, and afterwards studied thoroughly Science
and Health, a student can enter upon the gospel work of 21
teaching Christian Science, and so fulfil the command of
Christ. But before entering this field of labor he must
have studied the latest editions of my works, be a good 24
Bible scholar and a consecrated Christian.

1 The Massachusetts Metaphysical College drew its
breath from me, but I was yearning for retirement. The
3 question was, Who else could sustain this institute, under
all that was aimed at its vital purpose, the establishment
of *genuine* Christian Science healing? My conscientious
6 scruples about diplomas, the recent experience of the
church fresh in my thoughts, and the growing conviction
that every one should build on his own foundation, sub-
9 ject to the one builder and maker, God, — all these considerations moved me to close my flourishing school, and
the following resolutions were passed: —

12 At a special meeting of the Board of the Metaphysical
College Corporation, Oct. 29, 1889, the following are some
of the resolutions which were presented and passed
15 unanimously: —

WHEREAS, The Massachusetts Metaphysical College,
chartered in January, 1881, for medical purposes, to give
18 instruction in scientific methods of mental healing on a purely
practical basis, to impart a thorough understanding of metaphysics, to restore health, hope, and harmony to man, — has
21 fulfilled its high and noble destiny, and sent to all parts of our
country, and into foreign lands, students instructed in Christian Science Mind-healing, to meet the demand of the age for
24 something higher than physic or drugging; and

WHEREAS, The material organization was, in the beginning
in this institution, like the baptism of Jesus, of which he said,
27 "Suffer it to be so now," though the teaching was a purely
spiritual and scientific impartation of Truth, whose Christly
spirit has led to higher ways, means, and understanding, — the
30 President, the Rev. Mary B. G. Eddy, at the height of pros-

perity in the institution, which yields a large income, is willing 1
to sacrifice all for the advancement of the world in Truth and
Love; and 3

WHEREAS, Other institutions for instruction in Christian
Science, which are working out their periods of organization,
will doubtless follow the example of the *Alma Mater* after 6
having accomplished the worthy purpose for which they were
organized, and the hour has come wherein the great need is
for more of the spirit instead of the letter, and Science and 9
Health is adapted to work this result; and

WHEREAS, The fundamental principle for growth in Christian Science is spiritual formation first, last, and always, while 12
in human growth material organization is first; and

WHEREAS, Mortals must learn to lose their estimate
of the powers that are not ordained of God, and attain 15
the bliss of loving unselfishly, working patiently, and con-
quering all that is unlike Christ and the example he gave;
therefore 18

Resolved, That we thank the State for its charter, which is
the only one ever granted to a *legal college* for teaching the
Science of Mind-healing; that we thank the public for its 21
liberal patronage. And everlasting gratitude is due to the
President, for her great and noble work, which we believe
will prove a healing for the nations, and bring all men to a 24
knowledge of the true God, uniting them in one common
brotherhood.

After due deliberation and earnest discussion it was unani- 27
mously voted: That as all debts of the corporation have been
paid, it is deemed best to dissolve this corporation, and the
same is hereby dissolved. 30

C. A. FRYE, *Clerk*

1   When God impelled me to set a price on my instruction
in Christian Science Mind-healing, I could think of no
3 financial equivalent for an impartation of a knowledge of
that divine power which heals; but I was led to name three
hundred dollars as the price for each pupil in one course
6 of lessons at my College, — a startling sum for tuition
lasting barely three weeks. This amount greatly troubled
me. I shrank from asking it, but was finally led, by a
9 strange providence, to accept this fee.

God has since shown me, in multitudinous ways, the
wisdom of this decision; and I beg disinterested people
12 to ask my loyal students if they consider three hundred
dollars any real equivalent for my instruction during
twelve half-days, or even in half as many lessons. Never-
15 theless, my list of indigent charity scholars is very large,
and I have had as many as seventeen in one class.

Loyal students speak with delight of their pupilage,
18 and of what it has done for them, and for others through
them. By loyalty in students I mean this, — allegiance
to God, subordination of the human to the divine, stead-
21 fast justice, and strict adherence to divine Truth and
Love.

I see clearly that students in Christian Science should,
24 at present, continue to organize churches, schools, and
associations for the furtherance and unfolding of Truth,
and that my necessity is not necessarily theirs; but it was
27 the Father's opportunity for furnishing a new rule of order
in divine Science, and the blessings which arose therefrom.
Students are not environed with such obstacles as were
30 encountered in the beginning of pioneer work.

In December, 1889, I gave a lot of land in Boston to my   1
student, Mr. Ira O. Knapp of Roslindale, — valued in
1892 at about twenty thousand dollars, and rising in value,   3
— to be appropriated for the erection, and building on
the premises thereby conveyed, of a church edifice to be
used as a temple for Christian Science worship.   6

General Associations, and Our Magazine

1 FOR many successive years I have endeavored to find new ways and means for the promotion and expan-
3 sion of scientific Mind-healing, seeking to broaden its channels and, if possible, to build a hedge round about it that should shelter its perfections from the contaminat-
6 ing influences of those who have a small portion of its letter and less of its spirit. At the same time I have worked to provide a home for every true seeker and honest
9 worker in this vineyard of Truth.

To meet the broader wants of humanity, and provide folds for the sheep that were without shepherds, I sug-
12 gested to my students, in 1886, the propriety of forming a National Christian Scientist Association. This was immediately done, and delegations from the Christian
15 Scientist Association of the Massachusetts Metaphysical College, and from branch associations in other States, met in general convention at New York City, February
18 11, 1886.

The first official organ of the Christian Scientist Association was called *Journal of Christian Science*. I started
21 it, April, 1883, as editor and publisher.

To the National Christian Scientist Association, at its meeting in Cleveland, Ohio, June, 1889, I sent a letter,

presenting to its loyal members *The Christian Science* 1
Journal, as it was now called, and the funds belonging
thereto. This monthly magazine had been made success- 3
ful and prosperous under difficult circumstances, and was
designed to bear aloft the standard of genuine Christian
Science. 6

Faith-cure

1 IT is often asked, Why are faith-cures sometimes more
  speedy than some of the cures wrought through Chris-
3 tian Scientists? Because faith is belief, and not understanding; and it is easier to believe, than to understand
  spiritual Truth. It demands less cross-bearing, self-
6 renunciation, and divine Science to admit the claims of
  the corporeal senses and appeal to God for relief through
  a humanized conception of His power, than to deny these
9 claims and learn the divine way, — drinking Jesus' cup,
  being baptized with his baptism, gaining the end through
  persecution and purity.
12   Millions are believing in God, or good, without bearing
  the fruits of goodness, not having reached its Science.
  Belief is virtually blindness, when it admits Truth with-
15 out understanding it. Blind belief cannot say with the
  apostle, "I know whom I have believed." There is danger
  in this mental state called belief; for if Truth is admitted,
18 but not understood, it may be lost, and error may enter
  through this same channel of ignorant belief. The faith-
  cure has devout followers, whose Christian practice is far
21 in advance of their theory.
     The work of healing, in the Science of Mind, is the most
  sacred and salutary power which can be wielded. My
24 Christian students, impressed with the true sense of the

great work before them, enter this strait and narrow path, 1
and work conscientiously.

Let us follow the example of Jesus, the master Meta- 3
physician, and gain sufficient knowledge of error to destroy
it with Truth. Evil is not mastered by evil; it can only
be overcome with good. This brings out the nothingness 6
of evil and the eternal somethingness, vindicates the divine
Principle, and improves the race of Adam.

Foundation-stones

1 THE following ideas of Deity, antagonized by finite
theories, doctrines, and hypotheses, I found to be
3 demonstrable rules in Christian Science, and that we
must abide by them.

Whatever diverges from the one divine Mind, or God,
6 — or divides Mind into minds, Spirit into spirits, Soul
into souls, and Being into beings, — is a misstatement
of the unerring divine Principle of Science, which inter-
9 rupts the meaning of the omnipotence, omniscience, and
omnipresence of Spirit, and is of human instead of divine
origin.

12 War is waged between the evidences of Spirit and the
evidences of the five physical senses; and this contest
must go on until peace be declared by the final triumph
15 of Spirit in immutable harmony. Divine Science disclaims
sin, sickness, and death, on the basis of the omnipotence
and omnipresence of God, or divine good.

18 All consciousness is Mind, and Mind is God. Hence
there is but one Mind; and that one is the infinite good,
supplying all Mind by the reflection, not the subdivision,
21 of God. Whatever else claims to be mind, or consciousness,
is untrue. The sun sends forth light, but not suns; so
God reflects Himself, or Mind, but does not subdivide
24 Mind, or good, into minds, good and evil. Divine Sci-

ence demands mighty wrestlings with mortal beliefs, as 1
we sail into the eternal haven over the unfathomable
sea of possibilities. 3

Neither ancient nor modern philosophy furnishes a
scientific basis for the Science of Mind-healing. Plato
believed he had a soul, which must be doctored in order 6
to heal his body. This would be like correcting the principle of music for the purpose of destroying discord. Principle is right; it is practice that is wrong. Soul is right; 9
it is the flesh that is evil. Soul is the synonym of Spirit,
God; hence there is but one Soul, and that one is infinite.
If that pagan philosopher had known that physical sense, 12
not Soul, causes all bodily ailments, his philosophy would
have yielded to Science.

Man shines by borrowed light. He reflects God as 15
his Mind, and this reflection is substance, — the substance
of good. Matter is substance in error, Spirit is substance
in Truth. 18

Evil, or error, is not Mind; but infinite Mind is sufficient
to supply all manifestations of intelligence. The notion
of more than one Mind, or Life, is as unsatisfying as it is 21
unscientific. All must be of God, and not our own, separated from Him.

Human systems of philosophy and religion are depart- 24
ures from Christian Science. Mistaking divine Principle
for corporeal personality, ingrafting upon one First Cause
such opposite effects as good and evil, health and sickness, 27
life and death; making mortality the status and rule of
divinity, — such methods can never reach the perfection
and demonstration of metaphysical, or Christian Science. 30

1   Stating the divine Principle, omnipotence (*omnis potens*), and then departing from this statement and taking the
3 rule of finite matter, with which to work out the problem of infinity or Spirit, — all this is like trying to compensate for the absence of omnipotence by a physical, false, and
6 finite substitute.

With our Master, life was not merely a sense of existence, but an accompanying sense of power that subdued
9 matter and brought to light immortality, insomuch that the people "were astonished at his doctrine: for he taught them as one having authority, and not as the scribes."
12 Life, as defined by Jesus, had no beginning; it was not the result of organization, or infused into matter; it was Spirit.

The Great Revelation

CHRISTIAN SCIENCE reveals the grand verity, that 1
to believe man has a finite and erring mind, and
consequently a mortal mind and soul and life, is error. 3
Scientific terms have no contradictory significations.

In Science, Life is not temporal, but eternal, without
beginning or ending. The word *Life* never means that 6
which is the source of death, and of good and evil. Such
an inference is unscientific. It is like saying that addition
means subtraction in one instance and addition in an- 9
other, and then applying this rule to a demonstration of
the science of numbers; even as mortals apply finite terms
to God, in demonstration of infinity. *Life* is a term used 12
to indicate Deity; and every other name for the Supreme
Being, if properly employed, has the signification of
Life. Whatever errs is mortal, and is the antipodes of 15
Life, or God, and of health and holiness, both in idea
and demonstration.

Christian Science reveals Mind, the only living and true 18
God, and all that is made by Him, Mind, as harmonious,
immortal, and spiritual: the five material senses define
Mind and matter as distinct, but mutually dependent, 21
each on the other, for intelligence and existence. Science
defines man as immortal, as coexistent and coeternal with
God, as made in His own image and likeness; material 24

1 sense defines life as something apart from God, beginning
and ending, and man as very far from the divine likeness.
3 Science reveals Life as a complete sphere, as eternal, self-
existent Mind; material sense defines life as a broken
sphere, as organized matter, and mind as something sep-
6 arate from God.   Science reveals Spirit as All, averring
that there is nothing beside God; material sense says that
matter, His antipode, is something besides God. Material
9 sense adds that the divine Spirit created matter, and that
matter and evil are as real as Spirit and good.

Christian Science reveals God and His idea as the All
12 and Only.   It declares that evil is the absence of good;
whereas, good is God ever-present, and therefore evil is
unreal and good is all that is real. Christian Science saith
15 to the wave and storm, "Be still," and there is a great
calm.   Material sense asks, in its ignorance of Science,
"When will the raging of the material elements cease?"
18 Science saith to all manner of disease, "Know that God
is all-power and all-presence, and there is nothing beside
Him;" and the sick are healed. Material sense saith,
21 "Oh, when will my sufferings cease? Where is God?
Sickness is something besides Him, which He cannot, or
does not, heal."

24   Christian Science is the only sure basis of harmony.
Material sense contradicts Science, for matter and its
so-called organizations take no cognizance of the spir-
27 itual facts of the universe, or of the real man and God.
Christian Science declares that there is but one Truth,
Life, Love, but one Spirit, Mind, Soul. Any attempt
30 to divide these arises from the fallibility of sense, from

mortal man's ignorance, from enmity to God and divine 1
Science.

Christian Science declares that sickness is a belief, a 3
latent fear, made manifest on the body in different forms
of fear or disease. This fear is formed unconsciously in
the silent thought, as when you awaken from sleep and 6
feel ill, experiencing the effect of a fear whose existence
you do not realize; but if you fall asleep, actually conscious of the truth of Christian Science, — namely, that 9
man's harmony is no more to be invaded than the rhythm
of the universe, — you cannot awake in fear or suffering
of any sort. 12

Science saith to fear, "You are the cause of all sickness; but you are a self-constituted falsity, — you are
darkness, nothingness. You are without 'hope, and with- 15
out God in the world.' You do not exist, and have no
right to exist, for 'perfect Love casteth out fear.'"

God is everywhere. "There is no speech nor language, 18
where their voice is not heard;" and this voice is Truth
that destroys error and Love that casts out fear.

Christian Science reveals the fact that, if suffering exists, 21
it is in the mortal mind only, for matter has no sensation
and cannot suffer.

If you rule out every sense of disease and suffering from 24
mortal mind, it cannot be found in the body.

Posterity will have the right to demand that Christian
Science be stated and demonstrated in its godliness and 27
grandeur, — that however little be taught or learned, that
little shall be right. Let there be milk for babes, but let
not the milk be adulterated. Unless this method be pur- 30

1 sued, the Science of Christian healing will again be lost,
and human suffering will increase.

3   Test Christian Science by its effect on society, and you
will find that the views here set forth — as to the illusion
of sin, sickness, and death — bring forth better fruits of
6 health, righteousness, and Life, than *a belief in their reality
has ever done*. A demonstration of the *unreality* of evil
destroys evil.

Sin, Sinner, and Ecclesiasticism

WHY do Christian Scientists say God and His idea 1
are the only realities, and then insist on the need
of healing sickness and sin? Because Christian Science 3
heals sin as it heals sickness, by establishing the recognition that God *is All,* and there is none beside Him, — that
all is good, and there is in reality no evil, neither sickness 6
nor sin. We attack the sinner's belief in the pleasure of
sin, *alias* the reality of sin, which makes him a sinner, in
order to destroy this belief and save him from sin; and 9
we attack the belief of the sick in the reality of sickness,
in order to heal them. When we deny the authority of
sin, we begin to sap it; for this denunciation must precede 12
its destruction.

God is good, hence goodness is something, for it represents God, the Life of man. Its opposite, nothing, 15
named *evil,* is nothing but a conspiracy against man's
Life and goodness. Do you not feel bound to expose this
conspiracy, and so to save man from it? Whosoever 18
covers iniquity becomes accessory to it. Sin, as a claim,
is more dangerous than sickness, more subtle, more difficult to heal. 21

St. Augustine once said, "The devil is but the ape of
God." Sin is worse than sickness; but recollect that it
encourages sin to say, "There is no sin," and leave the 24
subject there.

1 Sin ultimates in sinner, and in this sense they are one. You cannot separate sin from the sinner, nor the sinner 3 from his sin. The sin is the sinner, and *vice versa*, for such is the unity of evil; and together both sinner and sin will be destroyed by the supremacy of good. This, how- 6 ever, does not annihilate man, for to efface sin, *alias* the sinner, brings to light, makes apparent, the real man, even God's "image and likeness." Need it be said that 9 any opposite theory is heterodox to divine Science, which teaches that good is equally *one* and *all*, even as the opposite claim of evil is one.

12 In Christian Science the fact is made obvious that the sinner and the sin are alike simply nothingness; and this view is supported by the Scripture, where the Psalmist 15 saith: "He shall go to the generation of his fathers; they shall never see light. Man that is in honor, and understandeth not, is like the beasts that perish." God's ways 18 and works and thoughts have never changed, either in Principle or practice.

Since there is in belief an illusion termed sin, which 21 must be met and mastered, we classify sin, sickness, and death as illusions. They are supposititious claims of error; and error being a false claim, they are no claims 24 at all. It is scientific to abide in conscious harmony, in health-giving, deathless Truth and Love. To do this, mortals must first open their eyes to all the illusive forms, 27 methods, and subtlety of error, in order that the illusion, error, may be destroyed; if this is not done, mortals will become the victims of error.

30 If evangelical churches refuse fellowship with the

Church of Christ, Scientist, or with Christian Science, 1
they must rest their opinions of Truth and Love on
the evidences of the physical senses, rather than on 3
the teaching and practice of Jesus, or the works of the
Spirit.

Ritualism and dogma lead to self-righteousness and 6
bigotry, which freeze out the spiritual element. Pharisa-
ism killeth; Spirit giveth Life. The odors of persecution,
tobacco, and alcohol are not the sweet-smelling savor of 9
Truth and Love. Feasting the senses, gratification of
appetite and passion, have no warrant in the gospel or
the Decalogue. Mortals must take up the cross if they 12
would follow Christ, and worship the Father "in spirit
and in truth."

The Jewish religion was not spiritual; hence Jesus 15
denounced it. If the religion of to-day is constituted of
such elements as of old ruled Christ out of the synagogues,
it will continue to avoid whatever follows the example of 18
our Lord and prefers Christ to creed. Christian Science
is the pure evangelic truth. It accords with the trend and
tenor of Christ's teaching and example, while it demon- 21
strates the power of Christ as taught in the four Gospels.
Truth, casting out evils and healing the sick; Love, fulfilling the law and keeping man unspotted from the world, 24
— these practical manifestations of Christianity constitute
the only evangelism, and they need no creed.

As well expect to determine, without a telescope, the 27
magnitude and distance of the stars, as to expect to obtain
health, harmony, and holiness through an unspiritual and
unhealing religion. Christianity reveals God as ever- 30

1 present Truth and Love, to be utilized in healing the sick,
in casting out error, in raising the dead.
3   Christian Science gives vitality to religion, which is no
longer buried in materiality. It raises men from a material
sense into the spiritual understanding and scientific demon-
6 stration of God.

The Human Concept

SIN existed as a false claim before the human concept 1
of sin was formed; hence one's concept of error is
not the whole of error. The human thought does not 3
constitute sin, but *vice versa,* sin constitutes the human or
physical concept.

Sin is both concrete and abstract. Sin was, and *is,* the 6
lying supposition that life, substance, and intelligence are
both material and spiritual, and yet are separate from
God. The first iniquitous manifestation of sin was a 9
finity. The finite was self-arrayed against the infinite,
the mortal against immortality, and a sinner was the
antipode of God. 12

Silencing self, *alias* rising above corporeal personality,
is what reforms the sinner and destroys sin. In the ratio
that the testimony of material personal sense ceases, sin 15
diminishes, until the false claim called sin is finally lost
for lack of witness.

The sinner created neither himself nor sin, but sin 18
created the sinner; that is, error made its man mortal,
and this mortal was the image and likeness of evil, not of
good. Therefore the lie was, and *is,* collective as well as 21
individual. It was in no way contingent on Adam's
thought, but supposititiously self-created. In the words
of our Master, it, the "devil" (*alias* evil), "was a liar, and 24
the father of it."

1 This mortal material concept was never a creator, although as a serpent it claimed to originate in the name of
3 "the Lord," or good, — original evil; second, in the name of human concept, it claimed to beget the offspring of evil, *alias* an evil offspring. However, the human concept
6 never was, neither indeed can be, the father of man. Even the spiritual idea, or ideal man, is not a parent, though he reflects the infinity of good. The great differ-
9 ence between these opposites is, that the human material concept is *unreal*, and the divine concept or idea is spiritually real. One is false, while the other is true. One is
12 temporal, but the other is eternal.

Our Master instructed his students to "call no man your father upon the earth: for one is your Father, which
15 is in heaven." (Matt. xxiii. 9.)

Science and Health, the textbook of Christian Science, treats of the human concept, and the transference of
18 thought, as follows: —

"How can matter originate or transmit mind? We answer that it cannot. Darkness and doubt encompass
21 thought, so long as it bases creation on materiality" (p. 551).

"In reality there is no *mortal* mind, and consequently
24 no transference of mortal thought and will-power. Life and being are of God. In Christian Science, man can do no harm, for scientific thoughts are true thoughts, passing
27 from God to man" (pp. 103, 104).

"Man is the offspring of Spirit. The beautiful, good, and pure constitute his ancestry. His origin is not, like

that of mortals, in brute instinct, nor does he pass through 1
material conditions prior to reaching intelligence. Spirit
is his primitive and ultimate source of being; God is his 3
Father, and Life is the law of his being" (p. 63).

"The parent of all human discord was the Adam-
dream, the deep sleep, in which originated the delusion 6
that life and intelligence proceeded from and passed into
matter. This pantheistic error, or so-called *serpent,* insists still upon the opposite of Truth, saying, 'Ye shall be 9
as gods;' that is, I will make error as real and eternal as
Truth. . . . 'I will put spirit into what I call matter, and
matter shall seem to have life as much as God, Spirit, 12
who *is* the only Life.' This error has proved itself to be
error. Its life is found to be not Life, but only a transient,
false sense of an existence which ends in death" (pp. 306, 15
307).

"When will the error of believing that there is life in
matter, and that sin, sickness, and death are creations of 18
God, be unmasked? When will it be understood that
matter has no intelligence, life, nor sensation, and that
the opposite belief is the prolific source of all suffering? 21
God created all through Mind, and made all perfect and
eternal. Where then is the necessity for recreation or
procreation?" (p. 205). 24

"Above error's awful din, blackness, and chaos, the
voice of Truth still calls: 'Adam, where art thou? Consciousness, where art thou? Art thou dwelling in the be- 27
lief that mind is in matter, and that evil is mind, or art
thou in the living faith that there is and can be but one
God, and keeping His commandment?'" (pp. 307, 308). 30

1   "Mortal mind inverts the true likeness, and confers animal names and natures upon its own misconceptions.
3 Ignorant of the origin and operations of mortal mind, — that is, ignorant of itself, — this so-called mind puts forth its own qualities, and claims God as their author; . . .
6 usurps the deific prerogatives and is an attempted infringement on infinity" (pp. 512, 513).

We do not question the authenticity of the Scriptural
9 narrative of the Virgin-mother and Bethlehem babe, and the Messianic mission of Christ Jesus; but in our time no Christian Scientist will give chimerical wings to his
12 imagination, or advance speculative theories as to the recurrence of such events.

No person can take the individual place of the Virgin
15 Mary. No person can compass or fulfil the individual mission of Jesus of Nazareth. No person can take the place of the author of Science and Health, the Discoverer
18 and Founder of Christian Science. Each individual must fill his own niche in time and eternity.

The second appearing of Jesus is, unquestionably, the
21 spiritual advent of the advancing idea of God, as in Christian Science.

And the scientific ultimate of this God-idea must be,
24 will be, forever individual, incorporeal, and infinite, even the reflection, "image and likeness," of the infinite God.

The right teacher of Christian Science lives the truth he
27 teaches. Preeminent among men, he virtually stands at the head of all sanitary, civil, moral, and religious reform. Such a post of duty, unpierced by vanity, exalts a mortal

beyond human praise, or monuments which weigh dust, 1
and humbles him with the tax it raises on calamity to open
the gates of heaven. It is not the forager on others' wis- 3
dom that God thus crowns, but he who is obedient to the
divine command, "Render to Cæsar the things that are
Cæsar's, and to God the things that are God's." 6

Great temptations beset an ignorant or an unprincipled
mind-practice in opposition to the straight and narrow
path of Christian Science. Promiscuous mental treat- 9
ment, without the consent or knowledge of the individual
treated, is an error of much magnitude. People unaware
of the indications of mental treatment, know not what is 12
affecting them, and thus may be robbed of their individual
rights, — freedom of choice and self-government. Who is
willing to be subjected to such an influence? Ask the un- 15
bridled mind-manipulator if he would consent to this; and
if not, then he is knowingly transgressing Christ's command. He who secretly manipulates mind without the 18
permission of man or God, is not dealing justly and
loving mercy, according to pure and undefiled religion.

Sinister and selfish motives entering into mental practice 21
are dangerous incentives; they proceed from false convictions and a fatal ignorance. These are the tares growing side by side with the wheat, that must be recognized, 24
and uprooted, before the wheat can be garnered and
Christian Science demonstrated.

Secret mental efforts to obtain help from one who is 27
unaware of this attempt, demoralizes the person who does
this, the same as other forms of stealing, and will end in
destroying health and morals. 30

1   In the practice of Christian Science one cannot impart
a mental influence that hazards another's happiness, nor
3 interfere with the rights of the individual. To disregard
the welfare of others is contrary to the law of God; therefore it deteriorates one's ability to do good, to benefit
6 himself and mankind.

  The Psalmist vividly portrays the result of secret faults,
presumptuous sins, and self-deception, in these words:
9 "How are they brought into desolation, as in a moment!
They are utterly consumed with terrors."

Personality

THE immortal man being spiritual, individual, and 1
eternal, his mortal opposite must be material, corporeal, and temporal. Physical personality is finite; but 3
God is infinite. He is without materiality, without finiteness of form or Mind.

Limitations are put off in proportion as the fleshly 6
nature disappears and man is found in the reflection of
Spirit.

This great fact leads into profound depths. The mate- 9
rial human concept grew beautifully less as I floated into
more spiritual latitudes and purer realms of thought.

From that hour personal corporeality became less to 12
me than it is to people who fail to appreciate individual
character. I endeavored to lift thought above physical
personality, or selfhood in matter, to man's spiritual in- 15
dividuality in God, — in the true Mind, where sensible
evil is lost in supersensible good. This is the only way
whereby the false personality is laid off.   18

He who clings to personality, or perpetually warns you
of "personality," wrongs it, or terrifies people over it,
and is the sure victim of his own corporeality. Constantly 21
to scrutinize physical personality, or accuse people of being
unduly personal, is like the sick talking sickness. Such
errancy betrays a violent and egotistical personality, 24

1 increases one's sense of corporeality, and begets a fear of
the senses and a perpetually egotistical sensibility.

3   He who does this is ignorant of the meaning of the word
personality, and defines it by his own *corpus sine pectore*
(soulless body), and fails to distinguish the individual, or
6 real man from the false sense of corporeality, or egotistic
self.

My own corporeal personality afflicteth me not wittingly;
9 for I desire never to think of it, and it cannot think
of me.

Plagiarism

THE various forms of book-borrowing without credit 1 spring from this ill-concealed question in mortal mind, Who shall be greatest? This error violates the 3 law given by Moses, it tramples upon Jesus' Sermon on the Mount, it does violence to the ethics of Christian Science. 6

Why withhold my name, while appropriating my language and ideas, but give credit when citing from the works of other authors? 9

Life and its ideals are inseparable, and one's writings on ethics, and demonstration of Truth, are not, cannot be, understood or taught by those who persistently misunder- 12 stand or misrepresent the author. Jesus said, "For there is no man which shall do a miracle in my name, that can lightly speak evil of me." 15

If one's spiritual ideal is comprehended and loved, the borrower from it is embraced in the author's own mental mood, and is therefore *honest*. The Science of Mind ex- 18 cludes opposites, and rests on unity.

It is proverbial that dishonesty retards spiritual growth and strikes at the heart of Truth. If a student at Harvard 21 College has studied a textbook written by his teacher, is he entitled, when he leaves the University, to write out as his own the substance of this textbook? There is no war- 24 rant in common law and no permission in the gospel

1 for plagiarizing an author's ideas and their words. Christian Science is not copyrighted; nor would pro-
3 tection by copyright be requisite, if mortals obeyed God's law of *manright*. A student can write volumi- nous works on Science without trespassing, if he writes
6 honestly, and he cannot dishonestly compose *Christian Science*. The Bible is not stolen, though it is cited, and quoted deferentially.

9   Thoughts touched with the Spirit and Word of Christian Science gravitate naturally toward Truth. Therefore the mind to which this Science was revealed must have risen
12 to the altitude which perceived a light beyond what others saw.

   The spiritually minded meet on the stairs which lead up
15 to spiritual love. This affection, so far from being per- sonal worship, fulfils the law of Love which Paul enjoined upon the Galatians. This is the Mind "which was also
18 in Christ Jesus," and knows no material limitations. It is the unity of good and bond of perfectness. This just affec- tion serves to constitute the Mind-healer a wonder-worker,
21 — as of old, on the Pentecost Day, when the disciples were of one accord.

   He who gains the God-crowned summit of Christian
24 Science never abuses the corporeal personality, but up- lifts it. He thinks of every one in his real quality, and sees each mortal in an impersonal depict.

27   I have long remained silent on a growing evil in plagi- arism; but if I do not insist upon the strictest observance of moral law and order in Christian Scientists, I become

responsible, as a teacher, for laxity in discipline and law- 1
lessness in literature. Pope was right in saying, "An
honest man's the noblest work of God;" and Ingersoll's 3
repartee has its moral: "An honest God's the noblest
work of man."

Admonition

THE neophyte in Christian Science acts like a diseased physique, — being too fast or too slow. He is inclined to do either too much or too little. In healing and teaching the student has not yet achieved the entire wisdom of Mind-practice. The textual explanation of this practice is complete in Science and Health; and scientific practice makes perfect, for it is governed by its Principle, and not by human opinions; but carnal and sinister motives, entering into this practice, will prevent the demonstration of Christian Science.

I recommend students not to read so-called scientific works, antagonistic to Christian Science, which advocate materialistic systems; because such works and words becloud the right sense of metaphysical Science.

The rules of Mind-healing are wholly Christlike and spiritual. Therefore the adoption of a worldly policy or a resort to subterfuge in the statement of the Science of Mind-healing, or any name given to it other than Christian Science, or an attempt to demonstrate the facts of this Science other than is stated in Science and Health — is a departure from the Science of Mind-healing. To becloud mortals, or for yourself to hide from God, is to conspire against the blessings otherwise conferred, against your own success and final happiness, against the progress of

the human race as well as against *honest* metaphysical 1
theory and practice.

Not by the hearing of the ear is spiritual truth learned 3
and loved; nor cometh this apprehension from the experiences of others. We glean spiritual harvests from our
own material losses. In this consuming heat false images 6
are effaced from the canvas of mortal mind; and thus does
the material pigment beneath fade into invisibility.

The signs for the wayfarer in divine Science lie in meek- 9
ness, in unselfish motives and acts, in shuffling off scholastic
rhetoric, in ridding the thought of effete doctrines, in the
purification of the affections and desires. 12

Dishonesty, envy, and mad ambition are "lusts of the
flesh," which uproot the germs of growth in Science and
leave the inscrutable problem of being unsolved. Through 15
the channels of material sense, of worldly policy, pomp,
and pride, cometh no success in Truth. If beset with misguided emotions, we shall be stranded on the quicksands 18
of worldly commotion, and practically come short of the
wisdom requisite for teaching and demonstrating the
victory over self and sin. 21

Be temperate in thought, word, and deed. Meekness
and temperance are the jewels of Love, set in wisdom.
Restrain untempered zeal. "Learn to labor and to wait." 24
Of old the children of Israel were saved by patient waiting.

"The kingdom of heaven suffereth violence, and the
violent take it by force!" said Jesus. Therefore are 27
its spiritual gates not captured, nor its golden streets
invaded.

We recognize this kingdom, the reign of harmony 30

1 within us, by an unselfish affection or love, for this is the
pledge of divine good and the insignia of heaven. This
3 also is proverbial, that though eternal justice be graciously
gentle, yet it may seem severe.

For whom the Lord loveth He chasteneth,

6   And scourgeth every son whom He receiveth.

As the poets in different languages have expressed it: —

Though the mills of God grind slowly,

9   Yet they grind exceeding small;

Though with patience He stands waiting,

    With exactness grinds He all.

12 Though the divine rebuke is effectual to the pulling
down of sin's strongholds, it may stir the human heart to
resist Truth, before this heart becomes obediently recep-
15 tive of the heavenly discipline. If the Christian Scientist
recognize the mingled sternness and gentleness which
permeate justice and Love, he will not scorn the timely re-
18 proof, but will so absorb it that this warning will be within
him a spring, welling up into unceasing spiritual rise and
progress. Patience and obedience win the golden scholar-
21 ship of experimental tuition.

The kindly shepherd of the East carries his lambs in his
arms to the sheepcot, but the older sheep pass into the fold
24 under his compelling rod. He who sees the door and turns
away from it, is guilty, while innocence strayeth yearningly.

There are no greater miracles known to earth than per-
27 fection and an unbroken friendship. We love our friends,
but ofttimes we lose them in proportion to our affection.
The sacrifices made for others are not infrequently met by

envy, ingratitude, and enmity, which smite the heart and 1
threaten to paralyze its beneficence. The unavailing tear
is shed both for the living and the dead. 3

Nothing except sin, in the students themselves, can
separate them from me. Therefore we should guard
thought and action, keeping them in accord with Christ, 6
and our friendship will surely continue.

The letter of the law of God, separated from its spirit,
tends to demoralize mortals, and must be corrected by a 9
diviner sense of liberty and light. The spirit of Truth ex-
tinguishes false thinking, feeling, and acting; and falsity
must thus decay, ere spiritual sense, affectional conscious- 12
ness, and genuine goodness become so apparent as to be
well understood.

After the supreme advent of Truth in the heart, there 15
comes an overwhelming sense of error's vacuity, of the
blunders which arise from wrong apprehension. The enlightened heart loathes error, and casts it aside; or else 18
that heart is consciously untrue to the light, faithless to
itself and to others, and so sinks into deeper darkness.
Said Jesus: "If the light that is in thee be darkness, how 21
great is that darkness!" and Shakespeare puts this pious
counsel into a father's mouth: —

> This above all: To thine own self be true; 24
> And it must follow, as the night the day,
> Thou canst not then be false to any man.

A realization of the shifting scenes of human happiness, 27
and of the frailty of mortal anticipations, — such as first
led me to the feet of Christian Science, — seems to be requisite at every stage of advancement. Though our first les- 30

1 sons are changed, modified, broadened, yet their core is
constantly renewed; as the law of the chord remains
3 unchanged, whether we are dealing with a simple Latour
exercise or with the vast Wagner Trilogy.

A general rule is, that my students should not allow their
6 movements to be controlled by other students, even if they
are teachers and practitioners of the same blessed faith.
The exception to this rule should be very rare.
9 The widest power and strongest growth have always
been attained by those loyal students who rest on divine
Principle for guidance, not on themselves; and who locate
12 permanently in one section, and adhere to the orderly
methods herein delineated.

At this period my students should locate in large cities,
15 in order to do the greatest good to the greatest number, and
therein abide. The population of our principal cities is
ample to supply many practitioners, teachers, and preachers
18 with work. This fact interferes in no way with the prosperity of each worker; rather does it represent an accumulation of power on his side which promotes the ease and
21 welfare of the workers. Their liberated capacities of mind
enable Christian Scientists to consummate much good or
else evil; therefore their examples either excel or fall short
24 of other religionists; and they must be found dwelling
together in harmony, if even they compete with ecclesiastical fellowship and friendship.
27 It is often asked which revision of Science and Health is
the best. The arrangement of my last revision, in 1890,
makes the subject-matter clearer than any previous edition,
30 and it is therefore better adapted to spiritualize thought

and elucidate scientific healing and teaching. It has 1
already been proven that this volume is accomplishing the
divine purpose to a remarkable degree. The wise Chris- 3
tian Scientist will commend students and patients to the
teachings of this book, and the healing efficacy thereof,
rather than try to centre their interest on himself. 6

Students whom I have taught are seldom benefited by
the teachings of other students, for scientific foundations
are already laid in their minds which ought not to be tam- 9
pered with. Also, they are prepared to receive the infinite
instructions afforded by the Bible and my books, which
mislead no one and are their best guides. 12

The student may mistake in his conception of Truth, and
this error, in an honest heart, is sure to be corrected. But
if he misinterprets the text to his pupils, and communicates, 15
even unintentionally, his misconception of Truth, thereafter he will find it more difficult to rekindle his own light
or to enlighten them. Hence, as a rule, the student should 18
explain only Recapitulation, the chapter for the class-room,
and leave Science and Health to God's daily interpretation.

Christian Scientists should take their textbook into the 21
schoolroom the same as other teachers; they should ask
questions from it, and be answered according to it, — occasionally reading aloud from the book to corroborate what 24
they teach. It is also highly important that their pupils
study each lesson before the recitation.

That these essential points are ever omitted, is anoma- 27
lous, when we consider the necessity of thoroughly understanding Science, and the present liability of deviating
from absolute Christian Science. 30

1   Centuries will intervene before the statement of the inexhaustible topics of Science and Health is sufficiently under-
3 stood to be fully demonstrated.

The teacher himself should continue to study this textbook, and to spiritualize his own thoughts and human life
6 from this open fount of Truth and Love.

He who sees clearly and enlightens other minds most readily, keeps his own lamp trimmed and burning.
9 Throughout his entire explanations he strictly adheres to the teachings in the chapter on Recapitulation. When closing the class, each member should own a copy of
12 Science and Health, and continue to study and assimilate this inexhaustible subject — Christian Science.

The opinions of men cannot be substituted for God's
15 revelation. In times past, arrogant pride, in attempting to steady the ark of Truth, obscured even the power and glory of the Scriptures, — to which Science and Health is
18 the Key.

That teacher does most for his students who divests himself most of pride and self, and by reason thereof is able to
21 empty his students' minds of error, that they may be filled with Truth. Thus doing, posterity will call him blessed, and the tired tongue of history be enriched.
24   The less the teacher personally controls other minds, and the more he trusts them to the divine Truth and Love, the better it will be for both teacher and student.
27   A teacher should take charge only of his own pupils and patients, and of those who voluntarily place themselves under his direction; he should avoid leaving his own regu-
30 lar institute or place of labor, or expending his labor where

there are other teachers who should be specially responsible 1
for doing their own work well.

Teachers of Christian Science will find it advisable to 3
band together their students into associations, to continue
the organization of churches, and at present they can
employ any other organic operative method that may 6
commend itself as useful to the Cause and beneficial to
mankind.

Of this also rest assured, that books and teaching are but 9
a ladder let down from the heaven of Truth and Love, upon
which angelic thoughts ascend and descend, bearing on
their pinions of light the Christ-spirit. 12

Guard yourselves against the subtly hidden suggestion
that the Son of man will be glorified, or humanity benefited,
by any deviation from the order prescribed by supernal 15
grace. Seek to occupy no position whereto you do not feel
that God ordains you. Never forsake your post without
due deliberation and light, but always wait for God's finger 18
to point the way. The loyal Christian Scientist is incapable
alike of abusing the practice of Mind-healing or of healing
on a material basis. 21

The tempter is vigilant, awaiting only an opportunity
to divide the ranks of Christian Science and scatter the
sheep abroad; but "if God be for us, who can be against 24
us?" The Cause, *our* Cause, is highly prosperous, rapidly
spreading over the globe; and the morrow will crown the
effort of to-day with a diadem of gems from the New 27
Jerusalem.

Exemplification

1 TO energize wholesome spiritual warfare, to rebuke
vainglory, to offset boastful emptiness, to crown
3 patient toil, and rejoice in the spirit and power of Christian
Science, we must ourselves be true. There is but one way
of *doing* good, and that is to *do* it! There is but one way of
6 *being* good, and that is to *be* good!

Art thou still unacquainted with thyself? Then be introduced to this self. "Know thyself!" as said the classic
9 Grecian motto. Note well the falsity of this mortal self!
Behold its vileness, and remember this poverty-stricken
"stranger that is within thy gates." Cleanse every stain
12 from this wanderer's soiled garments, wipe the dust from
his feet and the tears from his eyes, that you may behold
the real man, the fellow-saint of a holy household. There
15 should be no blot on the escutcheon of our Christliness
when we offer our gift upon the altar.

A student desiring growth in the knowledge of Truth,
18 can and will obtain it by taking up his cross and following
Truth. If he does this not, and another one undertakes to
carry his burden and do his work, the duty will *not be*
21 *accomplished*. No one can save himself without God's
help, and God will help each man who performs his own
part. After this manner and in no other way is every
24 man cared for and blessed. To the unwise helper our

Master said, "Follow me; and let the dead bury their dead." 1

The poet's line, "Order is heaven's first law," is so eternally true, so axiomatic, that it has become a truism; and 3 its wisdom is as obvious in religion and scholarship as in astronomy or mathematics. 6

Experience has taught me that the rules of Christian Science can be far more thoroughly and readily acquired by regularly settled and systematic workers, than by unsettled and spasmodic efforts. Genuine Christian Scientists are, or should be, the most systematic and law-abiding people on earth, because their religion demands implicit 12 adherence to fixed rules, in the orderly demonstration thereof. Let some of these rules be here stated.

First: Christian Scientists are to "heal the sick" as the 15 Master commanded.

In so doing they must follow the divine order as prescribed by Jesus, — never, in any way, to trespass upon 18 the rights of their neighbors, but to obey the celestial injunction, "Whatsoever ye would that men should do to you, do ye even so to them." 21

In this orderly, scientific dispensation healers become a law unto themselves. They feel their own burdens less, and can therefore bear the weight of others' burdens, since 24 it is only through the lens of their unselfishness that the sunshine of Truth beams with such efficacy as to dissolve error. 27

It is already understood that Christian Scientists will not receive a patient who is under the care of a regular physician, until he has done with the case and different aid 30

1 is sought. The same courtesy should be observed in the professional intercourse of Christian Science healers with
3 one another.

Second: Another command of the Christ, his prime command, was that his followers should "raise the dead."
6 He lifted his own body from the sepulchre. In him, Truth called the physical man from the tomb to health, and the so-called dead forthwith emerged into a higher manifesta-
9 tion of Life.

The spiritual significance of this command, "Raise the dead," most concerns mankind. It implies such an eleva-
12 tion of the understanding as will enable thought to apprehend the living beauty of Love, its practicality, its divine energies, its health-giving and life-bestowing qualities, —
15 yea, its power to demonstrate immortality. This end Jesus achieved, both by example and precept.

Third: This leads inevitably to a consideration of an-
18 other part of Christian Science work, — a part which concerns us intimately, — preaching the gospel.

This evangelistic duty should not be so warped as to
21 signify that we must or may go, uninvited, to work in other vineyards than our own. One would, or should, blush to enter unasked another's pulpit, and preach without the
24 consent of the stated occupant of that pulpit. The Lord's command means this, that we should adopt the spirit of the Saviour's ministry, and abide in such a spiritual atti-
27 tude as will draw men unto us. Itinerancy should not be allowed to clip the wings of divine Science. Mind demonstrates omnipresence and omnipotence, but Mind revolves
30 on a spiritual axis, and its power is displayed and its pres-

ence felt in eternal stillness and immovable Love. The 1
divine potency of this spiritual mode of Mind, and the hindrance opposed to it by material motion, is proven beyond 3
a doubt in the practice of Mind-healing.

In those days preaching and teaching were substantially
one. There was no church preaching, in the modern sense 6
of the term. Men assembled in the one temple (at Jerusalem) for sacrificial ceremonies, not for sermons. Into
the synagogues, scattered about in cities and villages, they 9
went for liturgical worship, and instruction in the Mosaic
law. If one worshipper preached to the others, he did so
informally, and because he was bidden to this privileged 12
duty at that particular moment. It was the custom to pay
this hortatory compliment to a stranger, or to a member
who had been away from the neighborhood; as Jesus was 15
once asked to exhort, when he had been some time absent
from Nazareth but once again entered the synagogue which
he had frequented in childhood.   18

Jesus' method was to instruct his own students; and he
watched and guarded them unto the end, even according
to his promise, "Lo, I am with you alway!" Nowhere in 21
the four Gospels will Christian Scientists find any precedent for employing another student to take charge of
their students, or for neglecting their own students, in 24
order to enlarge their sphere of action.

Above all, trespass not intentionally upon other people's
thoughts, by endeavoring to influence other minds to any 27
action not first made known to them or sought by them.
Corporeal and selfish influence is human, fallible, and temporary; but incorporeal impulsion is divine, infallible, and 30

1 eternal. The student should be most careful not to thrust
aside Science, and shade God's window which lets in light,
3 or seek to stand in God's stead.

Does the faithful shepherd forsake the lambs, — retaining his salary for tending the home flock while he is serving
6 another fold? There is no evidence to show that Jesus
ever entered the towns whither he sent his disciples; no
evidence that he there taught a few hungry ones, and then
9 left them to starve or to stray. To these selected ones (like
"the elect lady" to whom St. John addressed one of his
epistles) he gave personal instruction, and gave in plain
12 words, until they were able to fulfil his behest and depart
on their united pilgrimages. This he did, even though
one of the twelve whom he kept near himself betrayed
15 him, and others forsook him.

The true mother never willingly neglects her children
in their early and sacred hours, consigning them to the care
18 of nurse or stranger. Who can feel and comprehend the
needs of her babe like the ardent mother? What other
heart yearns with her solicitude, endures with her patience,
21 waits with her hope, and labors with her love, to promote
the welfare and happiness of her children? Thus must the
Mother in Israel give all her hours to those first sacred
24 tasks, till her children can walk steadfastly in wisdom's
ways.

One of my students wrote to me: "I believe the proper
27 thing for us to do is to follow, as nearly as we can, in the
path you have pursued!" It is gladdening to find, in such
a student, one of the children of light. It is safe to leave
30 with God the government of man. He appoints and He

anoints His Truth-bearers, and God is their sure defense 1
and refuge.

The parable of "the prodigal son" is rightly called "the 3
pearl of parables," and our Master's greatest utterance may
well be called "the diamond sermon." No purer and more
exalted teachings ever fell upon human ears than those con- 6
tained in what is commonly known as the Sermon on the
Mount, — though this name has been given it by compilers
and translators of the Bible, and not by the Master him- 9
self or by the Scripture authors. Indeed, this title really
indicates more the Master's mood, than the material
locality. 12

Where did Jesus deliver this great lesson — or, rather,
this series of great lessons — on humanity and divinity?
On a hillside, near the sloping shores of the Lake of Gali- 15
lee, where he spake primarily to his immediate disciples.

In this simplicity, and with such fidelity, we see Jesus
ministering to the spiritual needs of all who placed them- 18
selves under his care, always leading them into the divine
order, under the sway of his own perfect understanding.
His power over others was spiritual, not corporeal. To the 21
students whom he had chosen, his immortal teaching was
the bread of Life. When *he* was with them, a fishing-boat
became a sanctuary, and the solitude was peopled with 24
holy messages from the All-Father. The grove became
his class-room, and nature's haunts were the Messiah's
university. 27

What has this hillside priest, this seaside teacher, done
for the human race? Ask, rather, what has he *not* done.
His holy humility, unworldliness, and self-abandonment 30

1 wrought infinite results. The method of his religion was
not too simple to be sublime, nor was his power so exalted
3 as to be unavailable for the needs of suffering mortals,
whose wounds he healed by Truth and Love.

His order of ministration was "first the blade, then the
6 ear, after that the full corn in the ear." May we unloose
the latchets of his Christliness, inherit his legacy of love,
and reach the fruition of his promise: "If ye abide in me,
9 and my words abide in you, ye shall ask what ye will, and
it shall be done unto you."

Waymarks

IN the first century of the Christian era Jesus went about 1
doing good. The evangelists of those days wandered
about. Christ, or the spiritual idea, appeared to human 3
consciousness as the man Jesus. At the present epoch
the human concept of Christ is based on the incorporeal
divine Principle of man, and Science has elevated this idea 6
and established its rules in consonance with their Principle.
Hear this saying of our Master, "And I, if I be lifted up
from the earth, will draw all men unto me." 9

The ideal of God is no longer impersonated as a waif or
wanderer; and Truth is not fragmentary, disconnected, un-
systematic, but concentrated and immovably fixed in Princi- 12
ple. The best spiritual type of Christly method for uplifting
human thought and imparting divine Truth, is stationary
power, stillness, and strength; and when this spiritual ideal 15
is made our own, it becomes the model for human action.

St. Paul said to the Athenians, "For in Him we live,
and move, and have our being." This statement is in sub- 18
stance identical with my own: "There is no life, truth,
substance, nor intelligence in matter." It is quite clear
that as yet this grandest verity has not been fully demon- 21
strated, but it is nevertheless true. If Christian Science
reiterates St. Paul's teaching, we, as Christian Scientists,
should give to the world convincing proof of the validity of 24

1 this scientific statement of being. Having perceived, in advance of others, this scientific fact, we owe to ourselves 3 and to the world a struggle for its demonstration.

At some period and in some way the conclusion must be met that whatsoever seems true, and yet contradicts divine 6 Science and St. Paul's text, must be and is false; and that whatsoever seems to be good, and yet errs, though acknowledging the true way, is really evil.

9   As dross is separated from gold, so Christ's baptism of fire, his purification through suffering, consumes whatsoever is of sin. Therefore this purgation of divine mercy, 12 destroying all error, leaves no flesh, no matter, to the mental consciousness.

When all fleshly belief is annihilated, and every spot and 15 blemish on the disk of consciousness is removed, then, and not till then, will immortal Truth be found true, and scientific teaching, preaching, and practice be essentially one. 18 "Happy is he that condemneth not himself in that thing which he alloweth. . . . for whatsoever is not of faith is sin." (Romans xiv. 22, 23.)

21   There is no "lo here! or lo there!" in divine Science; its manifestation must be "the same yesterday, and to-day, and forever," since Science is eternally one, and 24 unchanging, in Principle, rule, and demonstration.

I am persuaded that only by the modesty and distinguishing affection illustrated in Jesus' career, can Chris- 27 tian Scientists aid the establishment of Christ's kingdom on the earth. In the first century of the Christian era Jesus' teachings bore much fruit, and the Father was glorified 30 therein. In this period and the forthcoming centuries,

watered by dews of divine Science, this "tree of life" will 1
blossom into greater freedom, and its leaves will be "for
the healing of the nations." 3

> Ask God to give thee skill
>   In comfort's art:
> That thou may'st consecrated be 6
>   And set apart
> Unto a life of sympathy.
> For heavy is the weight of ill 9
>   In every heart;
> And comforters are needed much
>   Of Christlike touch. 12
>
> — A. E. HAMILTON

Unity
of
Good

Unity
of
Good

by MARY BAKER EDDY
*Discoverer and Founder of Christian Science
and Author of Science and Health
with Key to the Scriptures*

Marcas Registradas

Published by The First Church of Christ, Scientist, in Boston, Massachusetts, U.S.A.

Contents

Contents

Unity of Good

Caution in the Truth

PERHAPS no doctrine of Christian Science rouses so 1
much natural doubt and questioning as this, that
God knows no such thing as sin. Indeed, this may be set 3
down as one of the "things hard to be understood," such
as the apostle Peter declared were taught by his fellow-
apostle Paul, "which they that are unlearned and unstable 6
wrest . . . unto their own destruction." (2 Peter iii. 16.)

Let us then reason together on this important subject,
whose statement in Christian Science may justly be char- 9
acterized as *wonderful.*

Does God know or behold sin, sickness, and death?

The nature and character of God is so little appre- 12
hended and demonstrated by mortals, that I counsel my
students to defer this infinite inquiry, in their discussions
of Christian Science. In fact, they had better leave the 15
subject untouched, until they draw nearer to the divine
character, and are practically able to testify, by their lives,
that as they come closer to the true understanding of God 18
they lose all sense of error.

1

1   The Scriptures declare that God is too pure to behold iniquity (Habakkuk i. 13); but they also declare that
3 God pitieth them who fear Him; that there is no place where His voice is not heard; that He is "a very present help in trouble."

6   The sinner has no refuge from sin, except in God, who is his salvation. We must, however, realize God's presence, power, and love, in order to be saved from sin. This
9 realization takes away man's fondness for sin and his pleasure in it; and, lastly, it removes the pain which accrues to him from it. Then follows this, as the *finale* in
12 Science: The sinner loses his sense of sin, and gains a higher sense of God, in whom there is no sin.

The true man, really *saved*, is ready to testify of God
15 in the infinite penetration of Truth, and can affirm that the Mind which is good, or God, has no knowledge of sin.

In the same manner the sick lose their sense of sickness,
18 and gain that spiritual sense of harmony which contains neither discord nor disease.

According to this same rule, in divine Science, the
21 dying — if they die in the Lord — awake from a sense of death to a sense of Life in Christ, with a knowledge of Truth and Love beyond what they possessed before; be-
24 cause their lives have grown so far toward the stature of manhood in Christ Jesus, that they are ready for a spiritual transfiguration, through their affections and under-
27 standing.

Those who reach this transition, called *death*, without

having rightly improved the lessons of this primary school 1
of mortal existence, — and still believe in matter's reality,
pleasure, and pain, — are not ready to understand im- 3
mortality. Hence they awake only to another sphere of
experience, and must pass through another probationary
state before it can be truly said of them: "Blessed are the 6
dead which die in the Lord."

They upon whom the second death, of which we read
in the Apocalypse (Revelation xx. 6), hath no power, are 9
those who have obeyed God's commands, and have
washed their robes white through the sufferings of the
flesh and the triumphs of Spirit. Thus they have reached 12
the goal in divine Science, by knowing Him in whom they
have believed. This knowledge is not the forbidden fruit
of sin, sickness, and death, but it is the fruit which grows 15
on the "tree of life." This is the understanding of God,
whereby man is found in the image and likeness of
good, not of evil; of health, not of sickness; of Life, not 18
of death.

God is All-in-all. Hence He is in Himself only, in His
own nature and character, and is perfect being, or con- 21
sciousness. He is all the Life and Mind there is or can be.
Within Himself is every embodiment of Life and Mind.

If He is All, He can have no consciousness of anything 24
unlike Himself; because, if He is omnipresent, there can
be nothing outside of Himself.

Now this self-same God is our helper. He pities us. 27
He has mercy upon us, and guides every event of our

1 careers. He is near to them who adore Him. To understand Him, without a single taint of our mortal, finite sense
3 of sin, sickness, or death, is to approach Him and become
like Him.

Truth is God, and in God's law. This law declares
6 that Truth is All, and there is no error. This law of Truth
destroys every phase of error. To gain a temporary consciousness of God's law is to feel, in a certain finite human
9 sense, that God comes to us and pities us; but the attainment of the understanding of His presence, through the
Science of God, destroys our sense of imperfection, or
12 of His absence, through a diviner sense that God is all
true consciousness; and this convinces us that, as we
get still nearer Him, we must forever lose our own con-
15 sciousness of error.

But how could we lose all consciousness of error, if God
be conscious of it? God has not forbidden man to know
18 Him; on the contrary, the Father bids man have the
same Mind "which was also in Christ Jesus," — which
was certainly the divine Mind; but God does forbid man's
21 acquaintance with evil. Why? Because evil is no part
of the divine knowledge.

John's Gospel declares (xvii. 3) that "life eternal" con-
24 sists in the knowledge of the only true God, and of Jesus
Christ, whom He has sent. Surely from such an understanding of Science, such knowing, the vision of sin is
27 wholly excluded.

Nevertheless, at the present crude hour, no wise men or

women will rudely or prematurely agitate a theme involv- 1
ing the All of infinity.

Rather will they rejoice in the small understanding 3
they have already gained of the wholeness of Deity, and
work gradually and gently up toward the perfect thought
divine. This meekness will increase their apprehension 6
of God, because their mental struggles and pride of opinion will proportionately diminish.

Every one should be encouraged not to accept any per- 9
sonal opinion on so great a matter, but to seek the divine
Science of this question of Truth by following upward individual convictions, undisturbed by the frightened sense of 12
any need of attempting to solve every Life-problem in a day.

"Great is the mystery of godliness," says Paul; and
mystery involves the unknown. No stubborn purpose to 15
force conclusions on this subject will unfold in us a higher
sense of Deity; neither will it promote the Cause of Truth
or enlighten the individual thought. 18

Let us respect the rights of conscience and the liberty
of the sons of God, so letting our "moderation be known
to all men." Let no enmity, no untempered controversy, 21
spring up between Christian Science students and Christians who wholly or partially differ from them as to the
nature of sin and the marvellous unity of man with God 24
shadowed forth in scientific thought. Rather let the
stately goings of this wonderful part of Truth be left to
the supernal guidance. 27

"These are but parts of Thy ways," says Job; and the

1 whole is greater than its parts. Our present understanding
is but "the seed within itself," for it is divine Science,
3 "bearing fruit after its kind."

Sooner or later the whole human race will learn that, in
proportion as the spotless selfhood of God is understood,
6 human nature will be renovated, and man will receive a
higher selfhood, derived from God, and the redemption
of mortals from sin, sickness, and death be established on
9 everlasting foundations.

The Science of physical harmony, as now presented to
the people in divine light, is radical enough to promote
12 as forcible collisions of thought as the age has strength
to bear. Until the heavenly law of health, according to
Christian Science, is firmly grounded, even the thinkers
15 are not prepared to answer intelligently leading questions
about God and sin, and the world is far from ready to
assimilate such a grand and all-absorbing verity concern-
18 ing the divine nature and character as is embraced in the
theory of God's blindness to error and ignorance of sin.
No wise mother, though a graduate of Wellesley College,
21 will talk to her babe about the problems of Euclid.

Not much more than a half-century ago the assertion
of universal salvation provoked discussion and horror,
24 similar to what our declarations about sin and Deity must
arouse, if hastily pushed to the front while the platoons of
Christian Science are not yet thoroughly drilled in the
27 plainer manual of their spiritual armament. "Wait
patiently on the Lord;" and in less than another fifty

years His name will be magnified in the apprehension of 1
this new subject, as already He is glorified in the wide
extension of belief in the impartial grace of God, — 3
shown by the changes at Andover Seminary and in multitudes of other religious folds.

Nevertheless, though I thus speak, and from my heart 6
of hearts, it is due both to Christian Science and myself
to make also the following statement: When I have most
clearly seen and most sensibly felt that the infinite recog- 9
nizes no disease, this has not separated me from God, but
has so bound me to Him as to enable me instantaneously to
heal a cancer which had eaten its way to the jugular vein. 12

In the same spiritual condition I have been able to re-
place dislocated joints and raise the dying to instantaneous
health. People are now living who can bear witness to 15
these cures. Herein is my evidence, from on high, that
the views here promulgated on this subject are correct.

Certain self-proved propositions pour into my waiting 18
thought in connection with these experiences; and here is
one such conviction: that an acknowledgment of the perfection of the infinite Unseen confers a power nothing else 21
can. An incontestable point in divine Science is, that
because God is All, a realization of this fact dispels even
the sense or consciousness of sin, and brings us nearer to 24
God, bringing out the highest phenomena of the All-
Mind.

Seedtime and Harvest

1 LET another query now be considered, which gives much trouble to many earnest thinkers before Science 3 answers it.

Is anything real of which the physical senses are cognizant?

Everything is as real as you make it, and no more so. 6 What you see, hear, feel, is a mode of consciousness, and can have no other reality than the sense you entertain of it.

9 It is dangerous to rest upon the evidence of the senses, for this evidence is not absolute, and therefore not real, in our sense of the word. All that is beautiful and good 12 in your individual consciousness is permanent. That which is not so is illusive and fading. My insistence upon a proper understanding of the unreality of matter and 15 evil arises from their deleterious effects, physical, moral, and intellectual, upon the race.

All forms of error are uprooted in Science, on the same 18 basis whereby sickness is healed, — namely, by the establishment, through reason, revelation, and Science, of the nothingness of every claim of error, even the doc- 21 trine of heredity and other physical causes. You demonstrate the process of Science, and it proves my view

8

conclusively, that mortal mind is the cause of all disease. 1
Destroy the mental sense of the disease, and the disease
itself disappears. Destroy the sense of sin, and sin itself 3
disappears.

Material and sensual consciousness are mortal. Hence
they must, some time and in some way, be reckoned un- 6
real. That time has partially come, or my words would
not have been spoken. Jesus has made the way plain,
— so plain that all are without excuse who walk not in 9
it; but this way is not the path of physical science, human
philosophy, or mystic psychology.

The talent and genius of the centuries have wrongly 12
reckoned. They have not based upon revelation their
arguments and conclusions as to the source and resources
of being, — its combinations, phenomena, and outcome, 15
— but have built instead upon the sand of human reason.
They have not accepted the simple teaching and life of
Jesus as the only true solution of the perplexing problem 18
of human existence.

Sometimes it is said, by those who fail to understand
me, that I *monopolize;* and this is said because ideas 21
akin to mine have been held by a few spiritual thinkers in all ages. So they have, but in a far different
form. Healing has gone on continually; yet healing, as 24
I teach it, has not been practised since the days of
Christ.

What is the cardinal point of the difference in my meta- 27
physical system? This: that *by knowing the unreality of*

1 *disease, sin, and death,* you demonstrate the allness of God.
This difference wholly separates my system from all others.
3 The reality of these so-called existences I deny, because
they are not to be found in God, and this system is built
on Him as the sole cause. It would be difficult to name
6 any previous teachers, save Jesus and his apostles, who
have thus taught.

If there be any *monopoly* in my teaching, it lies in this
9 utter reliance upon the one God, to whom belong all
things.

Life is God, or Spirit, the supersensible eternal. The
12 universe and man are the spiritual phenomena of this one
infinite Mind. Spiritual phenomena never converge toward
aught but infinite Deity. Their gradations are spiritual
15 and divine; they cannot collapse, or lapse into their opposites, for God is their divine Principle. They live,
because He lives; and they are eternally perfect, because
18 He is perfect, and governs them in the Truth of divine
Science, whereof God is the Alpha and Omega, the centre
and circumference.
21 To attempt the calculation of His mighty ways, from
the evidence before the material senses, is fatuous. It is
like commencing with the minus sign, to learn the prin-
24 ciple of positive mathematics.

God was not in the whirlwind. He is not the blind
force of a material universe. Mortals must learn this;
27 unless, pursued by their fears, they would endeavor to
hide from His presence under their own falsities, and call

in vain for the mountains of unholiness to shield them 1
from the penalty of error.

Jesus taught us to walk *over*, not *into* or *with*, the cur- 3
rents of matter, or mortal mind. His teachings beard
the lions in their dens. He turned the water into wine,
he commanded the winds, he healed the sick, — all in 6
direct opposition to human philosophy and so-called
natural science. He annulled the laws of matter, showing
them to be laws of mortal mind, not of God. He showed 9
the need of changing this mind and its abortive laws. He
demanded a change of consciousness and evidence, and
effected this change through the higher laws of God. 12
The palsied hand moved, despite the boastful sense of
physical law and order. Jesus stooped not to human
consciousness, nor to the evidence of the senses. He 15
heeded not the taunt, "That withered hand looks very
real and feels very real;" but he cut off this vain boasting and destroyed human pride by taking away the ma- 18
terial evidence. If his patient was a theologian of some
bigoted sect, a physician, or a professor of natural philosophy, — according to the ruder sort then prevalent, — 21
he never thanked Jesus for restoring his senseless hand;
but neither red tape nor indignity hindered the divine
process. Jesus required neither cycles of time nor thought 24
in order to mature fitness for perfection and its possibilities. He said that the kingdom of heaven is here, and
is included in Mind; that while ye say, There are yet four 27
months, and *then* cometh the harvest, I say, Look up,

1 not down, for your fields are already white for the harvest;
and gather the harvest by mental, not material processes.
3 The laborers are few in this vineyard of Mind-sowing and
reaping; but let them apply to the waiting grain the curv-
ing sickle of Mind's eternal circle, and bind it with bands
6 of Soul.

The Deep Things of God

SCIENCE reverses the evidence of the senses in the- 1
ology, on the same principle that it does in astronomy.
Popular theology makes God tributary to man, coming at 3
human call; whereas the reverse is true in Science. Men
must approach God reverently, doing their own work in
obedience to divine law, if they would fulfil the intended 6
harmony of being.

The principle of music knows nothing of discord. God
is harmony's selfhood. His universal laws, His unchange- 9
ableness, are not infringed in ethics any more than in
music. To Him there is no moral inharmony; as we shall
learn, proportionately as we gain the true understanding 12
of Deity. If God could be conscious of sin, His infinite
power would straightway reduce the universe to chaos.

If God has any real knowledge of sin, sickness, and 15
death, they must be eternal; since He is, in the very
fibre of His being, "without beginning of years or end of
days." If God knows that which is not permanent, it 18
follows that He knows something which He must learn
to *unknow*, for the benefit of our race.

Such a view would bring us upon an outworn theological 21

13

1 platform, which contains such planks as the divine repentance, and the belief that God must one day do His
3 work over again, because it was not at first done
aright.

Can it be seriously held, by any thinker, that long after
6 God made the universe, — earth, man, animals, plants,
the sun, the moon, and "the stars also," — He should so
gain wisdom and power from past experience that He
9 could vastly improve upon His own previous work, — as
Burgess, the boatbuilder, remedies in the Volunteer the
shortcomings of the Puritan's model?

12 Christians are commanded to *grow in grace*. Was it
necessary for God to grow in grace, that He might rectify
His spiritual universe?

15 The Jehovah of limited Hebrew faith might need
repentance, because His created children proved sinful;
but the New Testament tells us of "the Father of lights,
18 with whom is no variableness, neither shadow of turning."
God is not the shifting vane on the spire, but the
corner-stone of living rock, firmer than everlasting hills.

21 As God is Mind, if this Mind is familiar with evil, all
cannot be good therein. Our infinite model would be
taken away. What is in eternal Mind must be reflected
24 in man, Mind's image. How then could man escape, or
hope to escape, from a knowledge which is everlasting in
his creator?

27 God never said that man would become better by learning to distinguish evil from good, — but the contrary, that

by this knowledge, by man's first disobedience, came 1
"death into the world, and all our woe."

"Shall mortal man be more just than God?" asks the 3
poet-patriarch. May men rid themselves of an incubus
which God never can throw off? Do mortals know more
than God, that they may declare Him absolutely cognizant 6
of sin?

God created all things, and pronounced them good.
Was evil among these good things? Man is God's child 9
and image. If God knows evil, so must man, or the likeness is incomplete, the image marred.

If man must be destroyed by the knowledge of evil, 12
then his destruction comes through the very knowledge
caught from God, and the creature is punished for his
likeness to his creator.   15

God is commonly called the *sinless,* and man the *sinful;*
but if the thought of sin could be possible in Deity, would
Deity then be sinless? Would God not of necessity take 18
precedence as the infinite sinner, and human sin become
only an echo of the divine?

Such vagaries are to be found in heathen religious his- 21
tory. There are, or have been, devotees who worship not
the good Deity, who will not harm them, but the bad
deity, who seeks to do them mischief, and whom there- 24
fore they wish to bribe with prayers into quiescence,
as a criminal appeases, with a money-bag, the venal
officer.   27

Surely this is no Christian worship! In Christianity,

1 man bows to the infinite perfection which he is bidden to
imitate.   In Truth, such terms as *divine sin* and *infinite*
3 *sinner* are unheard-of contradictions, — absurdities; but
would they be sheer nonsense, if God has, or can have,
a real knowledge of sin?

Ways Higher than Our Ways

ALIE has only one chance of successful deception, — to be accounted true. Evil seeks to fasten all error upon God, and so make the lie seem part of eternal Truth. 3

Emerson says, "Hitch your wagon to a star." I say, Be allied to the deific power, and all that is good will aid your journey, as the stars in their courses fought against 6 Sisera. (Judges v. 20.) Hourly, in Christian Science, man thus weds himself with God, or rather he ratifies a union predestined from all eternity; but evil ties its wagon- 9 load of offal to the divine chariots, — or seeks so to do, — that its vileness may be christened purity, and its darkness get consolation from borrowed scintillations. 12

Jesus distinctly taught the arrogant Pharisees that, from the beginning, their father, the devil, was the would-be murderer of Truth. A right apprehension of the wonder- 15 ful utterances of him who "spake as never man spake," would despoil error of its borrowed plumes, and transform the universe into a home of marvellous light, — "a 18 consummation devoutly to be wished."

Error says God must know evil because He knows all things; but Holy Writ declares God told our first parents 21 that in the day when they should partake of the fruit of evil, they must surely die. Would it not absurdly follow

17

1 that God must perish, if He knows evil and evil necessarily leads to extinction?   Rather let us think of God as
3 saying, I am infinite good; therefore I know not evil.
Dwelling in light, I can see only the brightness of My
own glory.

6   Error may say that God can never save man from sin,
if He knows and sees it not; but God says, I am too pure
to behold iniquity, and destroy everything that is unlike
9 Myself.

Many fancy that our heavenly Father reasons thus:
If pain and sorrow were not in My mind, I could not
12 remedy them, and wipe the tears from the eyes of My children. Error says you must know grief in order to console
it. Truth, God, says you oftenest console others in
15 troubles that you have not. Is not our comforter always
from outside and above ourselves?

God says, I show My pity through divine law, not
18 through human. It is My sympathy with and My knowledge of harmony (not inharmony) which alone enable Me
to rebuke, and eventually destroy, every supposition of
21 discord.

Error says God must know death in order to strike at
its root; but God saith, I am ever-conscious Life, and
24 thus I conquer death; for to be ever conscious of Life is
to be never conscious of death. I am All. A knowledge
of aught beside Myself is impossible.

27   If such knowledge of evil were possible to God, it would
lower His rank.

With God, *knowledge* is necessarily *foreknowledge;* and 1
foreknowledge and *foreordination* must be one, in an infinite Being. What Deity *foreknows,* Deity must *fore-* 3
ordain; else He is not omnipotent, and, like ourselves,
He foresees events which are contrary to His creative will,
yet which He cannot avert.   6

If God knows evil at all, He must have had foreknowledge thereof; and if He foreknew it, He must virtually
have intended it, or ordered it aforetime, — foreordained 9
it; else how could it have come into the world?

But this we cannot believe of God; for if the supreme
good could predestine or foreknow evil, there would be 12
sin in Deity, and this would be the end of infinite moral
unity. "If therefore the light that is in thee be darkness,
how great is that darkness!" On the contrary, evil is 15
only a delusive deception, without any actuality which
Truth can know.

Rectifications

1 HOW is a mistake to be rectified? By reversal or revision, — by seeing it in its proper light, and then
3 turning it or turning from it.

We undo the statements of error by reversing them.

Through these three statements, or misstatements, evil
6 comes into authority: —

First: The Lord created it.

Second: The Lord knows it.

9 *Third:* I am afraid of it.

By a reverse process of argument evil must be dethroned: —

12 *First:* God never made evil.

Second: He knows it not.

Third: We therefore need not fear it.

15 Try this process, dear inquirer, and so reach that perfect Love which "casteth out fear," and then see if this Love does not destroy in you all hate and the sense of evil.
18 You will awake to the perception of God as All-in-all. You will find yourself losing the knowledge and the operation of sin, proportionably as you realize the divine in-
21 finitude and believe that He can see nothing outside of His own focal distance.

20

A Colloquy

IN Romans (ii. 15) we read the apostle's description of 1
mental processes wherein human thoughts are "the
mean while accusing or else excusing one another." If we 3
observe our mental processes, we shall find that we are
perpetually arguing with ourselves; yet each mortal is
not two personalities, but one. 6

In like manner good and evil talk to one another; yet
they are not two but one, for evil is naught, and good only
is reality. 9

Evil. God hath said, "Ye shall eat of every tree of the
garden." If you do not, your intellect will be circum-
scribed and the evidence of your personal senses be de- 12
nied. This would antagonize individual consciousness
and existence.

Good. The Lord is God. With Him is no conscious- 15
ness of evil, because there is nothing beside Him or
outside of Him. Individual consciousness in man is
inseparable from good. There is no sensible matter, no 18
sense in matter; but there is a spiritual sense, a sense of
Spirit, and this is the only consciousness belonging to true
individuality, or a divine sense of being. 21

21

1   *Evil.* Why is this so?

Good. Because man is made after God's eternal like-
3 ness, and this likeness consists in a sense of harmony and
immortality, in which no evil can possibly dwell. You
may eat of the fruit of Godlikeness, but as to the fruit of
6 ungodliness, which is opposed to Truth, — ye shall not
touch it, lest ye die.

Evil. But I would taste and know error for myself.

9   *Good.* Thou shalt not admit that error is something
to know or be known, to eat or be eaten, to see or be seen,
to feel or be felt. To admit the existence of error would
12 be to admit the truth of a lie.

Evil. But there is something besides good. God
knows that a knowledge of this something is essential to
15 happiness and life. A lie is as genuine as Truth, though
not so legitimate a child of God. Whatever exists must
come from God, and be important to our knowledge.
18 Error, even, is His offspring.

Good. Whatever cometh not from the eternal Spirit,
has its origin in the physical senses and material brains,
21 called *human intellect* and *will-power,* — *alias* intelligent
matter.

In Shakespeare's tragedy of King Lear, it was the

traitorous and cruel treatment received by old Gloster 1
from his bastard son Edmund which makes true the lines:

> The gods are just, and of our pleasant vices 3
> Make instruments to scourge us.

His lawful son, Edgar, was to his father ever loyal. Now
God has no bastards to turn again and rend their Maker. 6
The divine children are born of law and order, and Truth
knows only such.

How well the Shakespearean tale agrees with the word 9
of Scripture, in Hebrews xii. 7, 8: "If ye endure chasten-
ing, God dealeth with you as with sons; for what son is
he whom the father chasteneth not? But if ye be with- 12
out chastisement, whereof all are partakers, then are ye
bastards, and not sons."

The doubtful or spurious evidence of the senses is not 15
to be admitted, — especially when they testify concerning Spirit, whereof they are confessedly incompetent to
speak. 18

Evil. But mortal mind and sin really exist!

Good. How can they exist, unless God has created
them? And how can He create anything so wholly unlike 21
Himself and foreign to His nature? An evil material mind,
so-called, can conceive of God only as like itself, and
knowing both evil and good; but a purely good and 24
spiritual consciousness has no sense whereby to cognize

1 evil. Mortal mind is the opposite of immortal Mind, and
sin the opposite of goodness. I am the infinite All. From
3 me proceedeth all Mind, all consciousness, all individuality, all being. My Mind is divine good, and cannot
drift into evil. To believe in minds many is to depart
6 from the supreme sense of harmony. Your assumptions
insist that there is more than the one Mind, more than the
one God; but verily I say unto you, God is All-in-all;
9 and you can never be outside of His oneness.

Evil. I am a finite consciousness, a material individuality, — a mind in matter, which is both evil and good.

12 *Good.* All consciousness is Mind; and Mind is God, —
an infinite, and not a finite consciousness. This consciousness is reflected in individual consciousness, or man, whose
15 source is infinite Mind. There is no really finite mind, no
finite consciousness. There is no material substance, for
Spirit is all that endureth, and hence is the only substance.
18 There is, can be, no evil mind, because Mind is God.
God and His ideas — that is, God and the universe —
constitute all that exists. Man, as God's offspring, must
21 be spiritual, perfect, eternal.

Evil. I am something separate from good or God. I
am substance. My mind is more than matter. In my
24 mortal mind, matter becomes conscious, and is able to see,
taste, hear, feel, smell. Whatever matter thus affirms is

mainly correct. If you, O good, deny this, then I deny 1
your truthfulness. If you say that matter is unconscious,
you stultify my intellect, insult my conscience, and dispute 3
self-evident facts; for nothing can be clearer than the
testimony of the five senses.

Good. Spirit is the only substance. Spirit is God, and 6
God is good; hence good is the only substance, the only
Mind. Mind is not, cannot be, in matter. It sees, hears,
feels, tastes, smells as Mind, and not as matter. Matter 9
cannot talk; and hence, whatever it appears to say of
itself is a lie. This lie, that Mind can be in matter, —
claiming to be something beside God, denying Truth and 12
its demonstration in Christian Science, — this lie I declare
an illusion. This denial enlarges the human intellect by
removing its evidence from sense to Soul, and from finite- 15
ness into infinity. It honors conscious human individuality by showing God as its source.

Evil. I am a creator, — but upon a material, not a 18
spiritual basis. I give life, and I can destroy life.

Good. Evil is not a creator. God, good, is the only
creator. Evil is not conscious or conscientious Mind; it 21
is not individual, not actual. Evil is not spiritual, and
therefore has no groundwork in Life, whose only source
is Spirit. The elements which belong to the eternal All, — 24
Life, Truth, Love, — evil can never take away.

1   *Evil.* I am intelligent matter; and matter is egoistic,
having its own innate selfhood and the capacity to evolve
3 mind.   God is in matter, and matter reproduces God.
From Him come my forms, near or remote.   This is my
honor, that God is my author, authority, governor, dis-
6 poser.   I am proud to be in His outstretched hands, and
I shirk all responsibility for myself as evil, and for my
varying manifestations.

9   *Good.* You mistake, O evil! God is not your authority
and law.   Neither is He the author of the material changes,
the *phantasma,* a belief in which leads to such teaching
12 as we find in the hymn-verse so often sung in church: —

> Chance and change are busy ever,
> Man decays and ages move;
15 But His mercy waneth never, —
> God is wisdom, God is love.

Now if it be true that God's power *never waneth,* how
18 can it be also true that *chance* and *change* are universal
factors, — that *man decays?*   Many ordinary Christians
protest against this stanza of Bowring's, and its sentiment
21 is foreign to Christian Science.   If God be *changeless goodness,* as sings another line of this hymn, what place has
chance in the divine economy?   Nay, there is in God
24 naught fantastic.   All is real, all is serious.   The phan-
tasmagoria is a product of human dreams.

The Ego

FROM various friends comes inquiry as to the meaning 1
of a word employed in the foregoing colloquy.

There are two English words, often used as if they were 3
synonyms, which really have a shade of difference between
them.

An *egotist* is one who talks much of himself. *Egotism* 6
implies vanity and self-conceit.

Egoism is a more philosophical word, signifying a
passionate love of self, which doubts all existence except 9
its own. An *egoist,* therefore, is one uncertain of everything except his own existence.

Applying these distinctions to evil and God, we shall 12
find that evil is *egotistic,* — boastful, but fleeing like a
shadow at daybreak; while God is *egoistic,* knowing only
His own all-presence, all-knowledge, all-power. 15

Soul

1 WE read in the Hebrew Scriptures, "The soul that sinneth, it shall die."

3 What is Soul? Is it a reality within the mortal body? Who can prove that? Anatomy has not descried nor described Soul. It was never touched by the scalpel nor 6 cut with the dissecting-knife. The five physical senses do not cognize it.

Who, then, dares define Soul as something within man? 9 As well might you declare some old castle to be peopled with demons or angels, though never a light or form was discerned therein, and not a spectre had ever been seen 12 going in or coming out.

The common hypotheses about souls are even more vague than ordinary material conjectures, and have less 15 basis; because material theories are built on the evidence of the material senses.

Soul must be God; since we learn Soul only as we learn 18 God, by spiritualization. As the five senses take no cognizance of Soul, so they take no cognizance of God. Whatever cannot be taken in by mortal mind — by human 21 reflection, reason, or belief — must be the unfathomable Mind, which "eye hath not seen, nor ear heard." Soul

28

stands in this relation to every hypothesis as to its human 1
character.

If Soul sins, it is a sinner, and Jewish law condemned 3
the sinner to death, — as does all criminal law, to a certain extent.

Spirit never sins, because Spirit is God. Hence, as 6
Spirit, Soul is sinless, and is God. Therefore there is,
there can be, no spiritual death.

Transcending the evidence of the material senses, 9
Science declares God to be the Soul of all being, the only
Mind and intelligence in the universe. There is but one
God, one Soul, or Mind, and that one is infinite, supplying 12
all that is absolutely immutable and eternal, — Truth,
Life, Love.

Science reveals Soul as that which the senses cannot 15
define from any standpoint of their own. What the physical senses miscall soul, Christian Science defines as material sense; and herein lies the discrepancy between the 18
true Science of Soul and that material sense of a soul which
that very sense declares can never be seen or measured or
weighed or touched by physicality. 21

Often we can elucidate the deep meaning of the Scriptures by reading *sense* instead of *soul,* as in the Forty-
second Psalm: "Why art thou cast down, O my soul 24
[sense]? . . . Hope thou in God [Soul]: for I shall yet
praise Him, who is the health of my countenance, and
my God [my Soul, immortality]." 27

The Virgin-mother's sense being uplifted to behold

1 Spirit as the sole origin of man, she exclaimed, "My soul
[spiritual sense] doth magnify the Lord."

3   Human language constantly uses the word *soul* for
sense. This it does under the delusion that the senses can
reverse the spiritual facts of Science, whereas Science re-
6 verses the testimony of the material senses.

Soul is Life, and being spiritual Life, never sins. Material sense is the so-called material life. Hence this lower
9 sense sins and suffers, according to material belief, till
divine understanding takes away this belief and restores
Soul, or spiritual Life. "He restoreth my soul," says
12 David.

In his first epistle to the Corinthians (xv. 45) Paul writes:
"The first man Adam was made a living soul; the last
15 Adam was made a quickening spirit." The apostle refers to the second Adam as the Messiah, our blessed
Master, whose interpretation of God and His creation —
18 by restoring the spiritual sense of man as immortal instead
of mortal — made humanity victorious over death and the
grave.

21   When I discovered the power of Spirit to break the
cords of matter, through a change in the mortal sense of
things, then I discerned the last Adam as a quickening
24 Spirit, and understood the meaning of the declaration of
Holy Writ, "The first shall be last," — the living Soul
shall be found a quickening Spirit; or, rather, shall reflect
27 the Life of the divine Arbiter.

There is no Matter

"GOD is a Spirit" (or, more accurately translated, 1
"God is Spirit"), declares the Scripture (John iv.
24), "and they that worship Him must worship Him in 3
spirit and in truth."

If God is Spirit, and God is All, surely there can be no
matter; for the divine All must be Spirit. 6

The tendency of Christianity is to spiritualize thought
and action. The demonstrations of Jesus annulled the
claims of matter, and overruled laws material as emphati- 9
cally as they annihilated sin.

According to Christian Science, the *first* idolatrous claim
of sin is, that matter exists; the *second,* that matter is 12
substance; the *third,* that matter has intelligence; and
the *fourth,* that matter, being so endowed, produces life
and death. 15

Hence my conscientious position, in the denial of matter,
rests on the fact that matter usurps the authority of God,
Spirit; and the nature and character of matter, the anti- 18
pode of Spirit, include all that denies and defies Spirit, in
quantity or quality.

This subject can be enlarged. It can be shown, in 21
detail, that evil does not obtain in Spirit, God; and that
God, or good, is Spirit alone; whereas, evil *does,* accord-

1 ing to belief, obtain in matter; and that evil is a false
claim, — false to God, false to Truth and Life. Hence
3 the claim of matter usurps the prerogative of God, saying,
"I am a creator. God made me, and I make man and
the material universe."

6   Spirit is the only creator, and man, including the universe, is His spiritual concept. By matter is commonly
meant mind, — not the highest Mind, but a false form of
9 mind. This so-called mind and matter cannot be separated in origin and action.

What is this mind? It is not the Mind of Spirit; for
12 spiritualization of thought destroys all sense of matter as
substance, Life, or intelligence, and enthrones God in
the eternal qualities of His being.

15 This lower, misnamed mind is a false claim, a suppositional mind, which I prefer to call *mortal mind.* True
Mind is immortal. This mortal mind declares itself ma-
18 terial, in sin, sickness, and death, virtually saying, "I am
the opposite of Spirit, of holiness, harmony, and Life."

To this declaration Christian Science responds, even
21 as did our Master: "You were a murderer from the beginning. The truth abode not in you. You are a liar, and
the father of it." Here it appears that a *liar* was in the
24 neuter gender, — neither masculine nor feminine. Hence
it was not man (the image of God) who lied, but the false
claim to personality, which I call *mortal mind;* a claim
27 which Christian Science uncovers, in order to demonstrate
the falsity of the claim.

There are lesser arguments which prove matter to be 1
identical with mortal mind, and this mind a lie.

The physical senses (matter really having no sense) 3
give the only pretended testimony there can be as to the
existence of a substance called *matter*. Now these senses,
being material, can only testify from their own evidence, 6
and concerning themselves; yet we have it on divine
authority: "If I bear witness of myself, my witness is
not true." (John v. 31.) 9

In other words: matter testifies of itself, "I am matter;"
but unless matter is mind, it cannot talk or testify; and
if it is mind, it is certainly not the Mind of Christ, not 12
the Mind that is identical with Truth.

Brain, thus assuming to testify, is only matter within
the skull, and is believed to be mind only through error 15
and delusion. Examine that form of matter called *brains*,
and you find no mind therein. Hence the logical sequence,
that there is in reality neither matter nor mortal mind, 18
but that the self-testimony of the physical senses is
false.

Examine these witnesses for error, or falsity, and 21
observe the foundations of their testimony, and you will
find them divided in evidence, mocking the Scripture
(Matthew xviii. 16), "In the mouth of two or three wit- 24
nesses every word may be established."

Sight. Mortal mind declares that matter sees through
the organizations of matter, or that mind sees by means 27

1 of matter. Disorganize the so-called material structure, and then mortal mind says, "I cannot see;" and declares 3 that matter is the master of mind, and that non-intelligence governs. Mortal mind admits that it sees only material images, pictured on the eye's retina.

6   What then is the line of the syllogism? It must be this: That matter is not seen; that mortal mind cannot see without matter; and therefore that the whole function 9 of material sight is an illusion, a lie.

Here comes in the summary of the whole matter, wherewith we started: that God is All, and God is Spirit; there-12 fore there is nothing but Spirit; and consequently there is no matter.

Touch. Take another train of reasoning. Mortal mind 15 says that matter cannot feel matter; yet put your finger on a burning coal, and the nerves, material nerves, *do* feel matter.

18   Again I ask: What evidence does mortal mind afford that matter is substantial, is hot or cold? Take away mortal mind, and matter could not feel what it calls *sub-*21 *stance.* Take away matter, and mortal mind could not cognize its own so-called substance, and this so-called mind would have no identity. Nothing would remain to 24 be seen or felt.

What is substance? What is the reality of God and the universe? Immortal Mind is the real substance,— Spirit, 27 Life, Truth, and Love.

Taste. Mortal mind says, "I taste; and this is sweet, 1
this is sour." Let mortal mind change, and say that sour
is sweet, and *so* it would be. If every mortal mind believed 3
sweet to be sour, it would be so; for the qualities of matter
are but qualities of mortal mind. Change the mind, and
the quality changes. Destroy the belief, and the quality 6
disappears.

The so-called material senses are found, upon examination, to be mortally mental, instead of material. Reduced 9
to its proper denomination, matter is mortal mind; yet,
strictly speaking, there is no mortal mind, for Mind is
immortal, and is not matter, but Spirit.   12

Force. What is gravitation? Mortal mind says gravitation is a material power, or force. I ask, Which was
first, matter or power? That which was first was God, 15
immortal Mind, the Parent of *all.* But God is Truth,
and the forces of Truth are moral and spiritual, not physical. They are not the merciless forces of matter. What 18
then *are* the so-called forces of matter? They are the
phenomena of mortal mind, and matter and mortal
mind are one; and this one is a misstatement of Mind, 21
God.

A molecule, as matter, is not formed by Spirit; for
Spirit is *spiritual* consciousness alone. Hence this spiritual 24
consciousness can form nothing unlike itself, Spirit, and
Spirit is the only creator. The material atom is an outlined falsity of consciousness, which can gather additional 27

1 evidence of consciousness and life only as it adds lie to lie.
This process it names material attraction, and endows
3 with the double capacity of creator and creation.

From the beginning this lie was the false witness against
the fact that Spirit is All, beside which there is no other
6 existence. The use of a lie is that it unwittingly confirms
Truth, when handled by Christian Science, which reverses
false testimony and gains a knowledge of God from op-
9 posite facts, or phenomena.

This whole subject is met and solved by Christian
Science according to Scripture. Thus we see that Spirit
12 is Truth and eternal reality; that matter is the opposite
of Spirit, — referred to in the New Testament as the flesh
at war with Spirit; hence, that matter is erroneous, tran-
15 sitory, unreal.

A further proof of this is the demonstration, according
to Christian Science, that by the reduction and the rejec-
18 tion of the claims of matter (instead of acquiescence
therein) man is improved physically, mentally, morally,
spiritually.

21   To deny the existence or reality of matter, and yet
admit the reality of moral evil, sin, or to say that the
divine Mind is conscious of evil, yet is not conscious of
24 matter, is erroneous. This error stultifies the logic of
divine Science, and must interfere with its practical
demonstration.

Is There no Death?

JESUS not only declared himself "the way" and "the 1
truth," but also "the life." God is Life; and as
there is but one God, there can be but one Life. Must 3
man die, then, in order to inherit eternal life and enter
heaven?

Our Master said, "The kingdom of heaven is at hand." 6
Then God and heaven, or Life, are present, and death is
not the real stepping-stone to Life and happiness. They
are now and here; and a change in human consciousness, 9
from sin to holiness, would reveal this wonder of being.
Because God is ever present, no boundary of time can
separate us from Him and the heaven of His presence; 12
and because God is Life, all Life is eternal.

Is it unchristian to believe there is no death? Not
unless it be a sin to believe that God is Life and All-in-all. 15
Evil and disease do not testify of Life and God.

Human beings are physically mortal, but spiritually
immortal. The evil accompanying physical personality 18
is illusive and mortal; but the good attendant upon spiritual individuality is immortal. Existing here and now,
this unseen individuality is real and eternal. The so- 21
called material senses, and the mortal mind which is mis-

1 named *man*, take no cognizance of spiritual individuality,
which manifests immortality, whose Principle is God.

3   To God alone belong the indisputable realities of being.
Death is a contradiction of Life, or God; therefore it is
not in accordance with His law, but antagonistic thereto.

6   Death, then, is error, opposed to Truth, — even the
unreality of mortal mind, not the reality of that Mind
which is Life.   Error has no life, and is virtually without
9 existence.   Life is real; and all is real which proceeds
from Life and is inseparable from it.

It is unchristian to believe in the transition called *ma-*
12 *terial death*, since matter has no life, and such misbelief
must enthrone another power, an imaginary life, above
the living and true God.   A material sense of life robs
15 God, by declaring that not He alone is Life, but that something else also is life, — thus affirming the existence and
rulership of more gods than one.   This idolatrous and
18 false sense of life is all that dies, or appears to die.

The opposite understanding of God brings to light
Life and immortality.   Death has no quality of Life; and
21 no divine fiat commands us to believe in aught which is
unlike God, or to deny that He is Life eternal.

Life as God, moral and spiritual good, is not seen in
24 the mineral, vegetable, or animal kingdoms.   Hence the
inevitable conclusion that Life is not in these kingdoms,
and that the popular views to this effect are not up to the
27 Christian standard of Life, or equal to the reality of being,
whose Principle is God.

When "the Word" is "made flesh" among mortals, 1
the Truth of Life is rendered practical on the body.
Eternal Life is partially understood; and sickness, sin, 3
and death yield to holiness, health, and Life, — that is,
to God. The lust of the flesh and the pride of physical
life must be quenched in the divine essence, — that om- 6
nipotent Love which annihilates hate, that Life which
knows no death.

"Who hath believed our report?" Who understands 9
these sayings? He to whom the arm of the Lord is revealed. He loves them from whom divine Science removes
human weakness by divine strength, and who unveil the 12
Messiah, whose name is Wonderful.

Man has no underived power. That selfhood is false
which opposes itself to God, claims another father, and 15
denies spiritual sonship; but as many as receive the knowledge of God in Science must reflect, in some degree, the
power of Him who gave and giveth man dominion over 18
all the earth.

As soldiers of the cross we must be brave, and let Science
declare the immortal status of man, and deny the evidence 21
of the material senses, which testify that man dies.

As the image of God, or Life, man forever reflects and
embodies Life, not death. The material senses testify 24
falsely. They presuppose that God is good and that man
is evil, that Deity is deathless, but that man dies, losing
the divine likeness. 27

Science and material sense conflict at all points, from

1 the revolution of the earth to the fall of a sparrow. It is
mortality only that dies.

3   To say that you and I, as mortals, will not enter this
dark shadow of material sense, called *death,* is to assert
what we have not proved; but man in Science never dies.
6 Material sense, or the belief of life in matter, must perish,
in order to prove man deathless.

As Truth supersedes error, and bears the fruits of Love,
9 this understanding of Truth subordinates the belief in
death, and demonstrates Life as imperative in the divine
order of being.

12   Jesus declares that they who believe his sayings will
never die; therefore mortals can no more receive everlasting life by believing in death, than they can become
15 perfect by believing in imperfection and living imperfectly.

Life is God, and God is good. Hence Life abides in
man, if man abides in good, if he lives in God, who holds
18 Life by a spiritual and not by a material sense of being.

A sense of death is not requisite to a proper or true
sense of Life, but beclouds it. Death can never alarm or
21 even appear to him who fully understands Life. The
death-penalty comes through our ignorance of Life, — of
that which is without beginning and without end, — and
24 is the punishment of this ignorance.

Holding a material sense of Life, and lacking the spiritual sense of it, mortals die, in belief, and regard all things
27 as temporal. A sense material apprehends nothing strictly
belonging to the nature and office of Life. It conceives

and beholds nothing but mortality, and has but a feeble 1
concept of immortality.

In order to reach the true knowledge and consciousness 3
of Life, we must learn it of good.   Of evil we can never
learn it, because sin shuts out the real sense of Life, and
brings in an unreal sense of suffering and death.   6

Knowledge of evil, or belief in it, involves a loss of the
true sense of good, God; and to know death, or to believe
in it, involves a temporary loss of God, the infinite and 9
only Life.

Resurrection from the dead (that is, from the belief in
death) must come to all sooner or later; and they who 12
have part in this resurrection are they upon whom the
second death has no power.

The sweet and sacred sense of the permanence of man's 15
unity with his Maker can illumine our present being with
a continual presence and power of good, opening wide
the portal from death into Life; and when this Life shall 18
appear "we shall be like Him," and we shall go to the
Father, not through death, but through Life; not through
error, but through Truth.   21

All Life is Spirit, and Spirit can never dwell in its antagonist, matter.   Life, therefore, is deathless, because God
cannot be the opposite of Himself.   In Christian Science 24
there is no matter; hence matter neither lives nor dies.
To the senses, matter appears to both live and die, and
these phenomena appear to go on *ad infinitum;* but such 27
a theory implies perpetual disagreement with Spirit.

1　　Life, God, being everywhere, it must follow that death can be nowhere; because there is no place left for it.

3　　Soul, Spirit, is deathless. Matter, sin, and death are not the outcome of Spirit, holiness, and Life. What then are matter, sin, and death? They can be nothing except 6 the results of material consciousness; but material consciousness can have no real existence, because it is not a living — that is to say, a divine and intelligent — reality.

9　　That man must be vicious before he can be virtuous, dying before he can be deathless, material before he can be spiritual, is an error of the senses; for the very opposite 12 of this error is the genuine Science of being.

Man, in Science, is as perfect and immortal now, as when "the morning stars sang together, and all the sons 15 of God shouted for joy."

With Christ, Life was not merely a sense of existence, but a sense of might and ability to subdue material conditions. 18 ditions. No wonder "people were astonished at his doctrine; for he taught them as one having authority, and not as the scribes."

21　　As defined by Jesus, Life had no beginning; nor was it the result of organization, or of an infusion of power into matter. To him, Life was Spirit.

24　　Truth, defiant of error or matter, is Science, dispelling a false sense and leading man into the true sense of selfhood and Godhood; wherein the mortal does not develop 27 the immortal, nor the material the spiritual, but wherein true manhood and womanhood go forth in the radiance

of eternal being and its perfections, unchanged and 1
unchangeable.

This generation seems too material for any strong dem- 3
onstration over death, and hence cannot bring out the
infinite reality of Life, — namely, that there is no death,
but only Life. The present mortal sense of being is too 6
finite for anchorage in infinite good, God, because mortals
now believe in the possibility that Life can be evil.

The achievement of this ultimatum of Science, com- 9
plete triumph over death, requires time and immense
spiritual growth.

I have by no means spoken of myself, I *cannot* speak 12
of myself as "sufficient for these things." I insist only
upon the fact, as it exists in divine Science, that man dies
not, and on the words of the Master in support of this 15
verity, — words which can never "pass away till all be
fulfilled."

Because of these profound reasons I urge Christians 18
to have more faith in living than in dying. I exhort them
to accept Christ's promise, and unite the influence of their
own thoughts with the power of his teachings, in the 21
Science of being. This will interpret the divine power to
human capacity, and enable us to *apprehend*, or lay hold
upon, "that for which," as Paul says in the third chapter 24
of Philippians, we are also "apprehended of [or grasped
by] Christ Jesus," — the ever-present Life which knows
no death, the omnipresent Spirit which knows no matter. 27

Personal Statements

1 MANY misrepresentations are made concerning my
doctrines, some of which are as unkind and unjust
3 as they are untrue; but I can only repeat the Master's
words: "They know not what they do."

The foundations of these assertions, like the structure
6 raised thereupon, are vain shadows, repeating — if the
popular couplet may be so paraphrased —

The old, old story,
9 Of *Satan* and his *lie*.

In the days of Eden, humanity was misled by a false
personality, — a talking snake, — according to Biblical
12 history. This pretender taught the opposite of Truth.
This abortive ego, this fable of error, is laid bare in
Christian Science.

15 Human theories call, or miscall, this evil a child of God.
Philosophy would multiply and subdivide personality into
everything that exists, whether expressive or not expressive
18 of the Mind which is God. Human wisdom says of evil,
"The Lord knows it!" thus carrying out the serpent's
assurance: "In the day ye eat thereof [when you, lie, get
21 the floor], then your eyes shall be opened [you shall be
conscious matter], and ye shall be as gods, knowing good

44

and evil [you shall believe a lie, and this lie shall seem 1
truth]."

Bruise the head of this serpent, as Truth and "the 3
woman" are doing in Christian Science, and it stings
your heel, rears its crest proudly, and goes on saying, "Am
I not myself? Am I not mind and matter, person and 6
thing?" We should answer: "Yes! you are indeed yourself, and need most of all to be rid of this self, for it is
very far from God's likeness." 9

The egotist must come down and learn, in humility,
that God never made evil. An evil ego, and his assumed
power, are falsities. These falsities need a denial. The 12
falsity is the teaching that matter can be conscious; and
conscious matter implies pantheism. This pantheism I
unveil. I try to show its all-pervading presence in certain 15
forms of theology and philosophy, where it becomes error's
affirmative to Truth's negative. Anatomy and physiology
make mind-matter a habitant of the cerebellum, whence 18
it telegraphs and telephones over its own body, and goes
forth into an imaginary sphere of its own creation and
limitation, until it finally dies in order to better itself. 21
But Truth never dies, and death is not the goal which
Truth seeks.

The evil ego has but the visionary substance of matter. 24
It lacks the substance of Spirit, — Mind, Life, Soul. Mortal mind is self-creative and self-sustained, until it becomes
non-existent. It has no origin or existence in Spirit, im- 27
mortal Mind, or good. Matter is not truly conscious; and

1 mortal error, called *mind,* is not Godlike. These are the
shadowy and false, which neither think nor speak.

3 All Truth is from inspiration and revelation, — from
Spirit, not from flesh.

We do not see much of the real man here, for he is
6 God's man; while ours is man's man.

I do not deny, I maintain, the individuality and reality
of man; but I do so on a divine Principle, not based on a
9 human conception and birth. The scientific man and his
Maker are here; and you would be none other than this
man, if you would subordinate the fleshly perceptions to
12 the spiritual sense and source of being.

Jesus said, "I and my Father are one." He taught no
selfhood as existent in matter. In his identity there is no
15 evil. Individuality and Life were real to him only as
spiritual and good, not as material or evil. This incensed
the rabbins against Jesus, because it was an indignity to
18 their personality; and this personality they regarded as
both good and evil, as is still claimed by the worldly-wise.
To them evil was even more the ego than was the good.
21 Sin, sickness, and death were evil's concomitants. This
evil ego they believed must extend throughout the universe, as being equally identical and self-conscious with
24 God. This ego was in the earthquake, thunderbolt, and
tempest.

The Pharisees fought Jesus on this issue. It furnished
27 the battle-ground of the past, as it does of the present.
The fight was an effort to enthrone evil. Jesus assumed

the burden of disproof by destroying sin, sickness, and 1
death, to sight and sense.

Nowhere in Scripture is evil connected with good, the 3
being of God, and with every passing hour it is losing its
false claim to existence or consciousness. All that can
exist is God and His idea. 6

Credo

1 IT is fair to ask of every one a reason for the faith within.
Though it be but to repeat my twice-told tale, — nay,
3 the tale already told a hundred times, — yet ask, and I
will answer.

Do you believe in God?

6 I believe more in Him than do most Christians, for I
have no faith in any other thing or being. He sustains
my individuality. Nay, more — He *is* my individuality
9 and my Life. Because He lives, I live. He heals all my
ills, destroys my iniquities, deprives death of its sting, and
robs the grave of its victory.

12 To me God is All. He is best understood as Supreme
Being, as infinite and conscious Life, as the affectionate
Father and Mother of all He creates; but this divine
15 Parent no more enters into His creation than the human
father enters into his child. His creation is not the Ego,
but the reflection of the Ego. The Ego is God Himself,
18 the infinite Soul.

I believe that of which I am conscious through the
understanding, however faintly able to demonstrate Truth
21 and Love.

48

Do you believe in man? 1

I believe in the individual man, for I understand that man is as definite and eternal as God, and that man is 3 coexistent with God, as being the eternally divine idea. This is demonstrable by the simple appeal to human consciousness. 6

But I believe less in the sinner, wrongly named *man.* The more I understand true humanhood, the more I see it to be sinless, — as ignorant of sin as is the perfect Maker. 9

To me the reality and substance of being are *good,* and nothing else. Through the eternal reality of existence I reach, in thought, a glorified consciousness of the only 12 living God and the genuine man. So long as I hold evil in consciousness, I cannot be wholly good.

You cannot simultaneously serve the mammon of 15 materiality and the God of spirituality. There are not two realities of being, two opposite states of existence. One should appear real to us, and the other unreal, or we 18 lose the Science of being. Standing in no basic Truth, we make "the worse appear the better reason," and the unreal masquerades as the real, in our thought. 21

Evil is without Principle. Being destitute of Principle, it is devoid of Science. Hence it is undemonstrable, without proof. This gives me a clearer right to call evil a nega- 24 tion, than to affirm it to be something which God sees and knows, but which He straightway commands mortals to shun or relinquish, lest it destroy them. This notion of 27

1 the destructibility of Mind implies the possibility of its
defilement; but how can infinite Mind be defiled?

3 *Do you believe in matter?*

I believe in matter only as I believe in evil, that it is
something to be denied and destroyed to human conscious-
6 ness, and is unknown to the Divine. We should watch
and pray that we enter not into the temptation of pantheistic belief in matter as sensible mind. We should sub-
9 jugate it as Jesus did, by a dominant understanding of
Spirit.

At best, matter is only a phenomenon of mortal mind,
12 of which evil is the highest degree; but really there is no
such thing as *mortal mind,* — though we are compelled
to use the phrase in the endeavor to express the underlying
15 thought.

In reality there are no material states or stages of consciousness, and matter has neither Mind nor sensation.
18 Like evil, it is destitute of Mind, for Mind is God.

The less consciousness of evil or matter mortals have,
the easier it is for them to evade sin, sickness, and death,
21 — which are but states of false belief, — and awake from
the troubled dream, a consciousness which is without
Mind or Maker.

24 Matter and evil cannot be conscious, and consciousness
should not be evil. Adopt this rule of Science, and you
will discover the material origin, growth, maturity, and
27 death of sinners, as the history of man, disappears, and the

everlasting facts of being appear, wherein man is the re- 1
flection of immutable good.

Reasoning from false premises, — that Life is material, 3
that immortal Soul is sinful, and hence that sin is eternal,
— the reality of being is neither seen, felt, heard, nor understood. Human philosophy and human reason can 6
never make one hair white or black, except in belief;
whereas the demonstration of God, as in Christian Science,
is gained through Christ as perfect manhood. 9

In pantheism the world is bereft of its God, whose
place is ill supplied by the pretentious usurpation, by
matter, of the heavenly sovereignty. 12

What say you of woman?

Man is the generic term for all humanity. Woman is
the highest species of man, and this word is the generic 15
term for all women; but not one of all these individualities
is an Eve or an Adam. They have none of them lost their
harmonious state, in the economy of God's wisdom and 18
government.

The Ego is divine consciousness, eternally radiating
throughout all space in the idea of God, good, and not of 21
His opposite, evil. The Ego is revealed as Father, Son,
and Holy Ghost; but the full Truth is found only in
divine Science, where we see God as Life, Truth, and 24
Love. In the scientific relation of man to God, man is
reflected not as human soul, but as the divine ideal, whose
Soul is not in body, but is God, — the divine Principle of 27

1 man. Hence Soul is sinless and immortal, in contradistinction to the supposition that there can be sinful souls or
3 immortal sinners.

This Science of God and man is the Holy Ghost, which
reveals and sustains the unbroken and eternal harmony
6 of both God and the universe. It is the kingdom of heaven,
the ever-present reign of harmony, already with us. Hence
the need that human consciousness should become divine,
9 in the coincidence of God and man, in contradistinction
to the false consciousness of both good and evil, God and
devil, — of man separated from his Maker. This is the
12 precious redemption of soul, as mortal sense, through
Christ's immortal sense of Truth, which presents Truth's
spiritual idea, *man* and *woman*.

15   *What say you of evil?*

God is not the so-called ego of evil; for evil, as a supposition, is the father of itself, — of the material world,
18 the flesh, and the devil. From this falsehood arise the
self-destroying elements of this world, its unkind forces,
its tempests, lightnings, earthquakes, poisons, rabid
21 beasts, fatal reptiles, and mortals.

Why are earth and mortals so elaborate in beauty, color,
and form, if God has no part in them? By the law of
24 opposites. The most beautiful blossom is often poisonous,
and the most beautiful mansion is sometimes the home of
vice. The senses, not God, Soul, form the condition of
27 beautiful evil, and the supposed modes of self-conscious

matter, which make a beautiful lie. Now a lie takes its 1
pattern from Truth, by reversing Truth. So evil and all
its forms are inverted good. God never made them; but 3
the lie must say He made them, or it would not be evil.
Being a lie, it would be truthful to call itself a lie; and by
calling the knowledge of evil good, and greatly to be de- 6
sired, it constitutes the lie an evil.

The reality and individuality of man are good and God-
made, and they are here to be seen and demonstrated; it 9
is only the evil belief that renders them obscure.

Matter and evil are anti-Christian, the antipodes of
Science. To say that Mind is material, or that evil is 12
Mind, is a misapprehension of being, — a mistake which
will die of its own delusion; for being self-contradictory,
it is also self-destructive. The harmony of man's being is 15
not built on such false foundations, which are no more
logical, philosophical, or scientific than would be the assertion that the rule of addition is the rule of subtraction, 18
and that sums done under both rules would have one
quotient.

Man's individuality is not a mortal mind or sinner; or 21
else he has lost his true individuality as a perfect child of
God. Man's Father is not a mortal mind and a sinner;
or else the immortal and unerring Mind, God, is not his 24
Father; but God *is* man's origin and loving Father,
hence that saying of Jesus, "Call no man your father
upon the earth: for one is your Father, which is in 27
heaven."

1   The bright gold of Truth is dimmed by the doctrine of
mind in matter.

3   To say there *is* a false claim, called *sickness,* is to admit
all there is of sickness; for it is nothing but a false claim.
To be healed, one must lose sight of a false claim. If the
6 claim be present to the thought, then disease becomes as
tangible as any reality. To regard sickness as a false
claim, is to abate the fear of it; but this does not destroy
9 the so-called fact of the *claim.* In order to be whole, we
must be insensible to every claim of error.

As with sickness, so is it with sin. To admit that sin
12 has any claim whatever, just or unjust, is to admit a dangerous fact. Hence the fact must be denied; for if sin's
claim be allowed in any degree, then sin destroys the
15 *at-one-ment,* or oneness with God, — a unity which sin
recognizes as its most potent and deadly enemy.

If God knows sin, even as a false claimant, then ac-
18 quaintance with that claimant becomes legitimate to
mortals, and this knowledge would not be forbidden; but
God forbade man to know evil at the very beginning,
21 when Satan held it up before man as something desirable
and a distinct addition to human wisdom, because the
knowledge of evil would make man a god, — a representa-
24 tion that God both knew and admitted the dignity of evil.

Which is right, — God, who condemned the knowledge
of sin and disowned its acquaintance, or the serpent, who
27 pushed that claim with the glittering audacity of diabolical
and sinuous logic?

Suffering from Others' Thoughts

JESUS accepted the one fact whereby alone the rule of Life can be demonstrated, — namely, that there is no death.

In his real self he bore no infirmities. Though "a man of sorrows, and acquainted with grief," as Isaiah says of him, he bore not *his* sins, but *ours,* "in his own body on the tree." "He was bruised for *our* iniquities; . . . and with his stripes we are healed."

He was the Way-shower; and Christian Scientists who would demonstrate "the way" must keep close to his path, that they may win the prize. "The way," in the flesh, is the suffering which leads out of the flesh. "The way," in Spirit, is "the way" of Life, Truth, and Love, redeeming us from the false sense of the flesh and the wounds it bears. This threefold Messiah reveals the self-destroying ways of error and the life-giving way of Truth.

Job's faith and hope gained him the assurance that the so-called sufferings of the flesh are unreal. We shall learn how false are the pleasures and pains of material sense, and behold the truth of being, as expressed in his conviction, "Yet in my flesh shall I see God;" that is, Now and here shall I behold God, divine Love.

55

1 The chaos of mortal mind is made the stepping-stone to the cosmos of immortal Mind.

3 If Jesus suffered, as the Scriptures declare, it must have been from the mentality of others; since all suffering comes from mind, not from matter, and there could be 6 no sin or suffering in the Mind which is God. Not his own sins, but the sins of the world, "crucified the Lord of glory," and "put him to an open shame."

9 Holding a quickened sense of false environment, and suffering from mentality in opposition to Truth, are significant of that state of mind which the actual understanding 12 of Christian Science first eliminates and then destroys.

In the divine order of Science every follower of Christ shares his cup of sorrows. He also suffereth in the flesh, 15 and from the mentality which opposes the law of Spirit; but the divine law is supreme, for it freeth him from the law of sin and death.

18 Prophets and apostles suffered from the thoughts of others. Their conscious being was not fully exempt from physicality and the sense of sin.

21 Until he awakes from his delusion, he suffers least from sin who is a hardened sinner. The hypocrite's affections must first be made to fret in their chains; and the pangs 24 of hell must lay hold of him ere he can change from flesh to Spirit, become acquainted with that Love which is without dissimulation and endureth all things. Such 27 mental conditions as ingratitude, lust, malice, hate, constitute the miasma of earth. More obnoxious than

Chinese stenchpots are these dispositions which offend 1
the spiritual sense.

Anatomically considered, the design of the material 3
senses is to warn mortals of the approach of danger by
the pain they feel and occasion; but as this sense disappears it foresees the impending doom and foretells the 6
pain. Man's refuge is in spirituality, "under the shadow
of the Almighty."

The cross is the central emblem of human history. 9
Without it there is neither temptation nor glory. When
Jesus turned and said, "Who hath touched me?" he
must have felt the influence of the woman's thought; for 12
it is written that he felt that "virtue had gone out of him."
His pure consciousness was discriminating, and rendered
this infallible verdict; but he neither held her error by 15
affinity nor by infirmity, for it was detected and dismissed.

This gospel of suffering brought life and bliss. This
is earth's Bethel in stone, — its pillow, supporting the 18
ladder which reaches heaven.

Suffering was the confirmation of Paul's faith. Through
"a thorn in the flesh" he learned that spiritual grace was 21
sufficient for him.

Peter rejoiced that he was found worthy to suffer for
Christ; because to suffer with him is to reign with him. 24

Sorrow is the harbinger of joy. Mortal throes of anguish
forward the birth of immortal being; but divine Science
wipes away all tears. 27

The only conscious existence in the flesh is error of some

1 sort, — sin, pain, death, — a false sense of life and happiness. Mortals, if at ease in so-called existence, are in their
3 native element of error, and must become *dis-eased,* disquieted, before error is annihilated.

Jesus walked with bleeding feet the thorny earth-road,
6 treading "the winepress alone." His persecutors said
mockingly, "Save thyself, and come down from the cross."
This was the very thing he *was* doing, coming down from
9 the cross, saving himself after the manner that he had
taught, by the law of Spirit's supremacy; and this was
done through what is humanly called *agony.*
12   Even the ice-bound hypocrite melts in fervent heat,
before he apprehends Christ as "the way." The Master's
sublime triumph over all mortal mentality was immortal-
15 ity's goal. He was too wise not to be willing to test the
full compass of human woe, being "in all points tempted
like as we are, yet without sin."
18   Thus the absolute unreality of sin, sickness, and death
was revealed, — a revelation that beams on mortal sense
as the midnight sun shines over the Polar Sea.

The Saviour's Mission

IF there is no reality in evil, why did the Messiah come 1
to the world, and from what evils was it his purpose
to save humankind? How, indeed, is he a Saviour, if 3
the evils from which he saves are nonentities?

Jesus came to earth; but the Christ (that is, the divine
idea of the divine Principle which made heaven and earth) 6
was never absent from the earth and heaven; hence the
phraseology of Jesus, who spoke of the Christ as one who
came down from heaven, yet as "the Son of man *which* 9
is in heaven." (John iii. 13.) By this we understand
Christ to be the divine idea brought to the flesh in the son
of Mary.   12

Salvation is as eternal as God. To mortal thought
Jesus appeared as a child, and grew to manhood, to suffer
before Pilate and on Calvary, because he could reach and 15
teach mankind only through this conformity to mortal
conditions; but Soul never saw the Saviour come and go,
because the divine idea is always present.   18

Jesus came to rescue men from these very illusions to
which he seemed to conform: from the illusion which
calls sin real, and man a sinner, needing a Saviour; the 21
illusion which calls sickness real, and man an invalid,
needing a physician; the illusion that death is as real as

1 Life. From such thoughts — mortal inventions, one and all — Christ Jesus came to save men, through ever-present 3 and eternal good.

Mortal man is a kingdom divided against itself. With the same breath he articulates truth and error. We say 6 that God is All, and there is none beside Him, and then talk of sin and sinners as real. We call God omnipotent and omnipresent, and then conjure up, from the dark 9 abyss of nothingness, a powerful presence named *evil*. We say that harmony is real, and inharmony is its opposite, and therefore unreal; yet we descant upon sickness, sin, 12 and death as realities.

With the tongue "bless we God, even the Father; and therewith curse we men, who are made after the simili- 15 tude [human concept] of God. Out of the same mouth proceedeth blessing and cursing. My brethren, these things ought not so to be." (James iii. 9, 10.) Mortals 18 are free moral agents, to choose whom they would serve. If God, then let them serve Him, and He will be unto them All-in-all.

21 If God is ever present, He is neither absent from Him-self nor from the universe. Without Him, the universe would disappear, and space, substance, and immortality 24 be lost. St. Paul says, "And if Christ be not raised, your faith is vain; ye are yet in your sins." (1 Corinthians xv. 17.) Christ cannot come to mortal and material sense, 27 which sees not God. This false sense of substance must yield to His eternal presence, and so dissolve. Rising

above the false, to the true evidence of Life, is the resur- 1
rection that takes hold of eternal Truth.   Coming and
going belong to mortal consciousness.   God is "the same 3
yesterday, and to-day, and forever."

To material sense, Jesus first appeared as a helpless
human babe; but to immortal and spiritual vision he was 6
one with the Father, even the eternal idea of God, that
was — and is — neither young nor old, neither dead nor
risen.   The mutations of mortal sense are the evening and 9
the morning of human thought, — the twilight and dawn
of earthly vision, which precedeth the nightless radiance
of divine Life.   Human perception, advancing toward 12
the apprehension of its nothingness, halts, retreats, and
again goes forward; but the divine Principle and Spirit
and spiritual man are unchangeable, — neither advancing, 15
retreating, nor halting.

Our highest sense of infinite good in this mortal sphere
is but the sign and symbol, not the substance of good. 18
Only faith and a feeble understanding make the earthly
acme of human sense.   "The life which I now live in the
flesh I live by the faith of the Son of God."   (Galatians 21
ii. 20.)

Christian Science is both demonstration and fruition,
but how attenuated are our demonstration and realization 24
of this Science!   Truth, in divine Science, is the stepping-
stone to the understanding of God;   but the broken and
contrite heart soonest discerns this truth, even as the help- 27
less sick are soonest healed by it.   Invalids say, "I have

1 recovered from sickness;" when the fact really remains, in divine Science, that they never were sick.

3   The Christian saith, "Christ (God) died for me, and came to save me;" yet God dies not, and is the ever-presence that neither comes nor goes, and man is forever
6 His image and likeness. "The things which are seen are temporal; but the things which are not seen are eternal." (2 Corinthians iv. 18.) This is the mystery of godliness
9 — that God, good, is never absent, and there is none beside good. Mortals can understand this only as they reach the Life of good, and learn that there is no Life in evil.
12 Then shall it appear that the true ideal of omnipotent and ever-present good is an ideal wherein and wherefor there is no evil. Sin exists only as a sense, and not as Soul.
15 Destroy this sense of sin, and sin disappears. Sickness, sin, or death is a false sense of Life and good. Destroy this trinity of error, and you find Truth.

18   In Science, Christ never died. In material sense Jesus died, and lived. The fleshly Jesus seemed to die, though he did not. The Truth or Life in divine Science — un-
21 disturbed by human error, sin, and death — saith forever, "I am the living God, and man is My idea, never in matter, nor resurrected from it." "Why seek ye the living among
24 the dead? He is not here, but is risen." (Luke xxiv. 5, 6.) Mortal sense, confining itself to matter, is all that can be buried or resurrected.

27   Mary had risen to discern faintly God's ever-presence, and that of His idea, man; but her mortal sense, revers-

ing Science and spiritual understanding, interpreted this 1
appearing as a risen Christ. The I AM was neither buried
nor resurrected. The Way, the Truth, and the Life were 3
never absent for a moment. This trinity of Love lives
and reigns forever. Its kingdom, not apparent to material
sense, never disappeared to spiritual sense, but remained 6
forever in the Science of being. The so-called appearing,
disappearing, and reappearing of ever-presence, in whom
is no variableness or shadow of turning, is the false human 9
sense of that light which shineth in darkness, and the
darkness comprehendeth it not.

Summary

1 ALL that *is,* God created. If sin has any pretense of existence, God is responsible therefor; but there is
3 no reality in sin, for God can no more behold it, or acknowledge it, than the sun can coexist with darkness.

To build the individual spiritual sense, conscious of
6 only health, holiness, and heaven, on the foundations of an eternal Mind which is conscious of sickness, sin, and death, is a moral impossibility; for "other foundation
9 can no man lay than that is laid." (1 Corinthians iii. 11.) The nearer we approximate to such a Mind, even if it were (or could be) God, the more real those mind-pictures would
12 become to us; until the hope of ever eluding their dread presence must yield to despair, and the haunting sense of evil forever accompany our being.

15 Mortals may climb the smooth glaciers, leap the dark fissures, scale the treacherous ice, and stand on the summit of Mont Blanc; but they can never turn back what
18 Deity knoweth, nor escape from identification with what dwelleth in the eternal Mind.

Pulpit and Press

Pulpit and Press

by MARY BAKER EDDY
*Discoverer and Founder of Christian Science
and Author of Science and Health
with Key to the Scriptures*

Marcas Registradas

Published by The First Church of Christ, Scientist, in Boston, Massachusetts, U.S.A.

To
THE DEAR TWO THOUSAND AND SIX HUNDRED CHILDREN

*whose contributions of $4,460[1] were devoted
to the Mother's Room in The First Church
of Christ, Scientist, Boston, this unique
book is tenderly dedicated by*

MARY BAKER EDDY

[1] See footnote on page nine

Preface

THIS volume contains scintillations from press and 1
pulpit — utterances which epitomize the story of the
birth of Christian Science, in 1866, and its progress 3
during the ensuing thirty years. Three quarters of a
century hence, when the children of to-day are the elders
of the twentieth century, it will be interesting to have 6
not only a record of the inclination given their own
thoughts in the latter half of the nineteenth century,
but also a registry of the rise of the mercury in the glass 9
of the world's opinion.

It will then be instructive to turn backward the telescope of that advanced age, with its lenses of more 12
spiritual mentality, indicating the gain of intellectual
momentum, on the early footsteps of Christian Science
as planted in the pathway of this generation; to note 15
the impetus thereby given to Christianity; to con the
facts surrounding the cradle of this grand verity — that
the sick are healed and sinners saved, not by matter, but 18
by Mind; and to scan further the features of the vast
problem of eternal life, as expressed in the absolute
power of Truth and the actual bliss of man's existence 21
in Science.

MARY BAKER EDDY

February, 1895   24

vii

Contents

CLIPPINGS FROM NEWSPAPERS

Contents

Pulpit and Press

Dedicatory Sermon

BY REV. MARY BAKER EDDY

First Pastor of The First Church of Christ, Scientist, Boston, Mass.
Delivered January 6, 1895

TEXT: *They shall be abundantly satisfied with the fatness of Thy* 1
house; and Thou shalt make them drink of the river of Thy pleasures.
— PSALMS xxxvi. 8.
3

A NEW year is a nursling, a babe of time, a prophecy
and promise clad in white raiment, kissed — and
encumbered with greetings — redolent with grief and 6
gratitude.

An old year is time's adult, and 1893 was a distinguished
character, notable for good and evil. Time past and time 9
present, both, may pain us, but time *improved* is eloquent in God's praise. For due refreshment garner the
memory of 1894; for if wiser by reason of its large lessons, 12
and records deeply engraven, great is the value thereof.

Pass on, returnless year!
The path behind thee is with glory crowned; 15
This spot whereon thou troddest was holy ground;
Pass proudly to thy bier!

To-day, being with you in spirit, what need that I should 18
be present *in propria persona?* Were I present, methinks

1

1 I should be much like the Queen of Sheba, when she saw
the house Solomon had erected. In the expressive language
3 of Holy Writ, "There was no more spirit in her;" and
she said, "Behold, the half was not told me: thy wisdom
and prosperity exceedeth the fame which I heard." Both
6 without and within, the spirit of beauty dominates The
Mother Church, from its mosaic flooring to the soft shimmer of its starlit dome.

9   Nevertheless, there is a thought higher and deeper than
the edifice. Material light and shade are temporal, not
eternal. Turning the attention from sublunary views,
12 however enchanting, think for a moment with me of the
house wherewith "they shall be abundantly satisfied," —
even the "house not made with hands, eternal in the
15 heavens." With the mind's eye glance at the direful
scenes of the war between China and Japan. Imagine
yourselves in a poorly barricaded fort, fiercely besieged
18 by the enemy. Would you rush forth single-handed to
combat the foe? Nay, would you not rather strengthen
your citadel by every means in your power, and remain
21 within the walls for its defense? Likewise should we do
as metaphysicians and Christian Scientists. The real
house in which "we live, and move, and have our being"
24 is Spirit, God, the eternal harmony of infinite Soul. The
enemy we confront would overthrow this sublime fortress,
and it behooves us to defend our heritage.

27   How can we do this Christianly scientific work? By
intrenching ourselves in the knowledge that our true
temple is no human fabrication, but the superstructure
30 of Truth, reared on the foundation of Love, and pinnacled

in Life. Such being its nature, how can our godly temple 1
possibly be demolished, or even disturbed? Can eternity
end? Can Life die? Can Truth be uncertain? Can 3
Love be less than boundless? Referring to this temple,
our Master said: "Destroy this temple, and in three days
I will raise it up." He also said: "The kingdom of God 6
is within you." Know, then, that you possess sovereign
power to think and act rightly, and that nothing can dispossess you of this heritage and trespass on Love. If you 9
maintain this position, who or what can cause you to sin
or suffer? Our surety is in our confidence that we are
indeed dwellers in Truth and Love, man's eternal mansion. 12
Such a heavenly assurance ends all warfare, and bids tumult cease, for the good fight we have waged is over, and
divine Love gives us the true sense of victory. "They 15
shall be abundantly satisfied with the fatness of Thy house;
and Thou shalt make them drink of the river of Thy
pleasures." No longer are we of the church militant, but 18
of the church triumphant; and with Job of old we exclaim, "Yet in my flesh shall I see God." The river of
His pleasures is a tributary of divine Love, whose living 21
waters have their source in God, and flow into everlasting
Life. We drink of this river when all human desires are
quenched, satisfied with what is pleasing to the divine 24
Mind.

Perchance some one of you may say, "The evidence of
spiritual verity in me is so small that I am afraid. I feel 27
so far from victory over the flesh that to reach out for a
present realization of my hope savors of temerity. Because of my own unfitness for such a spiritual animus my 30

1 strength is naught and my faith fails." O thou "weak
and infirm of purpose." Jesus said, "Be not afraid"!

3   "What if the little rain should say,
         'So small a drop as I
         Can ne'er refresh a drooping earth,
6   I'll tarry in the sky.'"

Is not a man metaphysically and mathematically number one, a unit, and therefore whole number, governed
9 and protected by his divine Principle, God? You have
simply to preserve a scientific, positive sense of unity with
your divine source, and daily demonstrate this. Then you
12 will find that one is as important a factor as duodecillions
in being and doing right, and thus demonstrating deific
Principle. A dewdrop reflects the sun. Each of Christ's
15 little ones reflects the infinite One, and therefore is the
seer's declaration true, that "one on God's side is a
majority."

18   A single drop of water may help to hide the stars, or
crown the tree with blossoms.

Who lives in good, lives also in God, — lives in all Life,
21 through all space. His is an individual kingdom, his diadem a crown of crowns. His existence is deathless, forever unfolding its eternal Principle. Wait patiently on
24 illimitable Love, the lord and giver of Life. *Reflect this
Life,* and with it cometh the full power of being. "They
shall be abundantly satisfied with the fatness of Thy
27 house."

In 1893 the World's Parliament of Religions, held in
Chicago, used, in all its public sessions, my form of prayer

since 1866; and one of the very clergymen who had pub- 1
licly proclaimed me "the prayerless Mrs. Eddy," offered
his audible adoration in the words I use, besides listening 3
to an address on Christian Science from my pen, read by
Judge S. J. Hanna, in that unique assembly.

When the light of one friendship after another passes 6
from earth to heaven, we kindle in place thereof the glow
of some deathless reality. Memory, faithful to goodness,
holds in her secret chambers those characters of holiest 9
sort, bravest to endure, firmest to suffer, soonest to renounce. Such was the founder of the Concord School of
Philosophy — the late A. Bronson Alcott. 12

After the publication of "Science and Health with Key
to the Scriptures," his athletic mind, scholarly and serene,
was the first to bedew my hope with a drop of humanity. 15
When the press and pulpit cannonaded this book, he
introduced himself to its author by saying, "I have come
to comfort you." Then eloquently paraphrasing it, and 18
prophesying its prosperity, his conversation with a beauty
all its own reassured me. *That prophecy is fulfilled.*

This book, in 1895, is in its ninety-first edition of one 21
thousand copies. It is in the public libraries of the principal cities, colleges, and universities of America; also
the same in Great Britain, France, Germany, Russia, 24
Italy, Greece, Japan, India, and China; in the Oxford
University and the Victoria Institute, England; in the
Academy of Greece, and the Vatican at Rome. 27

This book is the leaven fermenting religion; it is
palpably working in the sermons, Sunday Schools, and
literature of our and other lands. This spiritual chemi- 30

1 calization is the upheaval produced when Truth is neutralizing error and impurities are passing off. And it will
3 continue till the antithesis of Christianity, engendering the
limited forms of a national or tyrannical religion, yields to
the church established by the Nazarene Prophet and main-
6 tained on the spiritual foundation of Christ's healing.

Good, the Anglo-Saxon term for God, unites Science to
Christianity. It presents to the understanding, not matter,
9 but Mind; not the deified drug, but the goodness of God —
healing and saving mankind.

The author of "Marriage of the Lamb," who made the
12 mistake of thinking she caught her notions from my book,
wrote to me in 1894, "Six months ago your book, Science
and Health, was put into my hands. I had not read three
15 pages before I realized I had found that for which I had
hungered since girlhood, and was healed instantaneously
of an ailment of seven years' standing. I cast from me the
18 false remedy I had vainly used, and turned to the 'great
Physician.' I went with my husband, a missionary to
China, in 1884. He went out under the auspices of the
21 Methodist Episcopal Church. I feel the truth is leading
us to return to Japan."

Another brilliant enunciator, seeker, and servant of
24 Truth, the Rev. William R. Alger of Boston, signalled
me kindly as my lone bark rose and fell and rode the rough
sea. At a *conversazione* in Boston, he said, "You may
27 find in Mrs. Eddy's metaphysical teachings more than is
dreamt of in your philosophy."

Also that renowned apostle of anti-slavery, Wendell
30 Phillips, the native course of whose mind never swerved

from the chariot-paths of justice, speaking of my work, 1
said: "Had I young blood in my veins, I would help that
woman." 3

I love Boston, and especially the laws of the State whereof this city is the capital. To-day, as of yore, her laws
have befriended progress. 6

Yet when I recall the past, — how the gospel of healing
was simultaneously praised and persecuted in Boston, —
and remember also that God is just, I wonder whether, 9
were our dear Master in our New England metropolis at
this hour, he would not weep over it, as he wept over
Jerusalem! O ye tears! Not in vain did ye flow. Those 12
sacred drops were but enshrined for future use, and God
has now unsealed their receptacle with His outstretched
arm. Those crystal globes made morals for mankind. 15
They will rise with joy, and with power to wash away, in
floods of forgiveness, every crime, even when mistakenly
committed in the name of religion. 18

An unjust, unmerciful, and oppressive priesthood must
perish, for false prophets in the present as in the past
stumble onward to their doom; while their tabernacles 21
crumble with dry rot. "God is not mocked," and "the
word of the Lord endureth forever."

I have ordained the Bible and the Christian Science 24
textbook, "Science and Health with Key to the Scriptures,"
as pastor of The First Church of Christ, Scientist, in
Boston, — so long as this church is satisfied with this 27
pastor. This is my first ordination. "They shall be
abundantly satisfied with the fatness of Thy house; and
Thou shalt make them drink of the river of Thy pleasures." 30

1   All praise to the press of America's Athens, — and
throughout our land the press has spoken out historically,
3 impartially. Like the winds telling tales through the
leaves of an ancient oak, unfallen, may our church chimes
repeat my thanks to the press.

6   Notwithstanding the perplexed condition of our nation's finances, the want and woe with millions of dollars
unemployed in our money centres, the Christian Scientists,
9 within fourteen months, responded to the call for this
church with $191,012. Not a mortgage was given nor a
loan solicited, and the donors all touchingly told their
12 privileged joy at helping to build The Mother Church.
There was no urging, begging, or borrowing; only the
need made known, and forth came the money, or dia-
15 monds, which served to erect this "miracle in stone."
Even the children vied with their parents to meet the
demand. Little hands, never before devoted to menial
18 services, shoveled snow, and babes gave kisses to earn a
few pence toward this consummation. Some of these
lambs my prayers had christened, but Christ will rechristen
21 them with his own new name. "Out of the mouths of
babes and sucklings Thou hast perfected praise." The
resident youthful workers were called "Busy Bees."
24   Sweet society, precious children, your loving hearts and
deft fingers distilled the nectar and painted the finest
flowers in the fabric of this history, — even its centre-piece,
27 — Mother's Room in The First Church of Christ, Scientist, in Boston. The children are destined to witness
results which will eclipse Oriental dreams. They belong
30 to the twentieth century. By juvenile aid, into the build-

ing fund have come $4,460.[1] Ah, children, you are the
bulwarks of freedom, the cement of society, the hope of
our race!

Brothers of the Christian Science Board of Directors,
when your tireless tasks are done — well done — no Del-
phian lyre could break the full chords of such a rest. May
the altar you have built never be shattered in our hearts,
but justice, mercy, and love kindle perpetually its fires.

It was well that the brother whose appliances warm
this house, warmed also our perishless hope, and nerved
its grand fulfilment. Woman, true to her instinct, came
to the rescue as sunshine from the clouds; so, when man
quibbled over an architectural exigency, a woman climbed
with feet and hands to the top of the tower, and helped
settle the subject.

After the loss of our late lamented pastor, Rev. D. A.
Easton, the church services were maintained by excellent
sermons from the editor of *The Christian Science Journal*
(who, with his better half, is a very whole man), together
with the Sunday School giving this flock "drink from the
river of His pleasures." O glorious hope and blessed assurance, "it is your Father's good pleasure to give you the
kingdom." Christians rejoice in secret, they have a bounty
hidden from the world. Self-forgetfulness, purity, and
love are treasures untold — constant prayers, prophecies,
and anointings. Practice, not profession, — goodness, not
doctrines, — spiritual understanding, not mere belief,
gain the ear and right hand of omnipotence, and call down
blessings infinite. "Faith without works is dead." The
foundation of enlightened faith is Christ's teachings and

---

[1] This sum was increased to $5,568.51 by contributions which reached the Treas-
urer after the Dedicatory Services.

1 *practice.* It was our Master's self-immolation, his life-
giving love, healing both mind and body, that raised the
3 deadened conscience, paralyzed by inactive faith, to a
quickened sense of mortal's necessities, — and God's
power and purpose to supply them. It was, in the words
6 of the Psalmist, He "who forgiveth all thine iniquities;
who healeth all thy diseases."

Rome's fallen fanes and silent Aventine is glory's tomb;
9 her pomp and power lie low in dust. Our land, more
favored, had its Pilgrim Fathers. On shores of solitude,
at Plymouth Rock, they planted a nation's heart, — the
12 rights of conscience, imperishable glory. No dream of
avarice or ambition broke their exalted purpose, theirs
was the wish to reign in hope's reality — the realm of
15 Love.

Christian Scientists, you have planted your standard
on the rock of Christ, the true, the spiritual idea, — the
18 chief corner-stone in the house of our God. And our
Master said: "The stone which the builders rejected, the
same is become the head of the corner." If you are less
21 appreciated to-day than your forefathers, wait — for if
you are as devout as they, and more scientific, as progress
certainly demands, your plant is immortal. Let us rejoice
24 that chill vicissitudes have not withheld the timely shelter
of this house, which descended like day-spring from on
high.
27 Divine presence, breathe Thou Thy blessing on every
heart in this house. Speak out, O soul! This is the new-
born of Spirit, this is His redeemed; this, His beloved.
30 May the kingdom of God within you, — with you alway, —

reascending, bear you outward, upward, heavenward. 1
May the sweet song of silver-throated singers, making
melody more real, and the organ's voice, as the sound of 3
many waters, and the Word spoken in this sacred temple
dedicated to the ever-present God — mingle with the joy
of angels and rehearse your hearts' holy intents. May all 6
whose means, energies, and prayers helped erect The
Mother Church, find within it home, and *heaven*.

Christian Science Textbook

1   The following selections from "Science and Health
with Key to the Scriptures," pages 568–571, were read
3 from the platform.   The impressive stillness of the audience indicated close attention.

     Revelation xii. 10–12. And I heard a loud voice saying in
6 heaven, Now is come salvation, and strength, and the kingdom of our God, and the power of His Christ: for the accuser
of our brethren is cast down, which accused them before our
9 God day and night.   And they overcame him by the blood
of the Lamb, and by the word of their testimony; and they
loved not their lives unto the death.   Therefore rejoice, ye
12 heavens, and ye that dwell in them.   Woe to the inhabiters
of the earth and of the sea! for the devil is come down unto
you, having great wrath, because he knoweth that he hath
15 but a short time.

    For victory over a single sin, we give thanks and mag-
nify the Lord of Hosts.   What shall we say of the mighty
18 conquest over all sin?   A louder song, sweeter than has
ever before reached high heaven, now rises clearer and
nearer to the great heart of Christ; for the accuser is not
21 there, and Love sends forth her primal and everlasting
strain.   Self-abnegation, by which we lay down all for
Truth, or Christ, in our warfare against error, is a rule in
24 Christian Science.   This rule clearly interprets God as

12

divine Principle, — as Life, represented by the Father; 1
as Truth, represented by the Son; as Love, represented
by the Mother. Every mortal at some period, here or here- 3
after, must grapple with and overcome the mortal belief
in a power opposed to God.

The Scripture, "Thou hast been faithful over a few 6
things, I will make thee ruler over many," is literally fulfilled, when we are conscious of the supremacy of Truth,
by which the nothingness of error is seen; and we know 9
that the nothingness of error is in proportion to its wickedness. He that touches the hem of Christ's robe and masters
his mortal beliefs, animality, and hate, rejoices in the proof 12
of healing, — in a sweet and certain sense that God is
Love. Alas for those who break faith with divine Science
and fail to strangle the serpent of sin as well as of sickness! 15
They are dwellers still in the deep darkness of belief.
They are in the surging sea of error, not struggling to lift
their heads above the drowning wave.   18

What must the end be? They must eventually expiate
their sin through suffering. The sin, which one has made
his bosom companion, comes back to him at last with 21
accelerated force, for the devil knoweth his time is short.
Here the Scriptures declare that evil is temporal, not
eternal. The dragon is at last stung to death by his own 24
malice; but how many periods of torture it may take to
remove all sin, must depend upon sin's obduracy.

Revelation xii. 13. And when the dragon saw that he was 27
cast unto the earth, he persecuted the woman which brought
forth the man child.

1   The march of mind and of honest investigation will bring the hour when the people will chain, with fetters of 3 some sort, the growing occultism of this period. The present apathy as to the tendency of certain active yet unseen mental agencies will finally be shocked into another 6 extreme mortal mood, — into human indignation; for one extreme follows another.

    Revelation xii. 15, 16. And the serpent cast out of his 9 mouth water as a flood, after the woman, that he might cause her to be carried away of the flood. And the earth helped the woman, and the earth opened her mouth, and 12 swallowed up the flood which the dragon cast out of his mouth.

    Millions of unprejudiced minds — simple seekers for 15 Truth, weary wanderers, athirst in the desert — are waiting and watching for rest and drink. Give them a cup of cold water in Christ's name, and never fear the conse- 18 quences. What if the old dragon should send forth a new flood to drown the Christ-idea? He can neither drown your voice with its roar, nor again sink the world into the 21 deep waters of chaos and old night. In this age the earth will help the woman; the spiritual idea will be understood. Those ready for the blessing you impart will give thanks. 24 The waters will be pacified, and Christ will command the wave.

    When God heals the sick or the sinning, they should 27 know the great benefit which Mind has wrought. They should also know the great delusion of mortal mind, when it makes them sick or sinful. Many are willing to open

the eyes of the people to the power of good resident in 1
divine Mind, but they are not so willing to point out the
evil in human thought, and expose evil's hidden mental 3
ways of accomplishing iniquity.

Why this backwardness, since exposure is necessary to
ensure the avoidance of the evil?   Because people like 6
you better when you tell them their virtues than when you
tell them their vices.   It requires the spirit of our blessed
Master to tell a man his faults, and so risk human dis- 9
pleasure for the sake of doing right and benefiting our
race.   Who is telling mankind of the foe in ambush?   Is
the informer one who sees the foe?   If so, listen and be 12
wise.   Escape from evil, and designate those as unfaithful
stewards who have seen the danger and yet have given
no warning.   15

At all times and under all circumstances, overcome evil
with good. Know thyself, and God will supply the wisdom
and the occasion for a victory over evil.   Clad in the 18
panoply of Love, human hatred cannot reach you.   The
cement of a higher humanity will unite all interests in the
one divinity.   21

Hymns

BY REV. MARY BAKER EDDY

1   [Set to the Church Chimes and Sung on This Occasion]

LAYING THE CORNER-STONE

3   *Laus Deo,* it is done!
Rolled away from loving heart
Is a stone.
6   Joyous, risen, we depart
Having one.

Laus Deo, — on this rock
9   (Heaven chiselled squarely good)
Stands His church, —
God is Love, and understood
12   By His flock.

Laus Deo, night starlit
Slumbers not in God's embrace;
15   Then, O man!
Like this stone, be in thy place;
Stand, not sit.

18   Cold, silent, stately stone,
Dirge and song and shoutings low,
In thy heart
21   Dwell serene, — and sorrow?   No,
It has none,
Laus Deo!

16

"FEED MY SHEEP" 1

Shepherd, show me how to go
  O'er the hillside steep, 3
How to gather, how to sow, —
  How to feed Thy sheep;
I will listen for Thy voice, 6
  Lest my footsteps stray;
I will follow and rejoice
  All the rugged way. 9

Thou wilt bind the stubborn will,
  Wound the callous breast,
Make self-righteousness be still, 12
  Break earth's stupid rest.
Strangers on a barren shore,
  Lab'ring long and lone — 15
We would enter by the door,
  And Thou know'st Thine own.

So, when day grows dark and cold, 18
  Tear or triumph harms,
Lead Thy lambkins to the fold,
  Take them in Thine arms; 21
Feed the hungry, heal the heart,
  Till the morning's beam;
White as wool, ere they depart — 24
  Shepherd, wash them clean.

CHRIST MY REFUGE

O'er waiting harpstrings of the mind
    There sweeps a strain,
Low, sad, and sweet, whose measures bind
    The power of pain.

And wake a white-winged angel throng
    Of thoughts, illumed
By faith, and breathed in raptured song,
    With love perfumed.

Then His unveiled, sweet mercies show
    Life's burdens light.
I kiss the cross, and wake to know
    A world more bright.

And o'er earth's troubled, angry sea
    I see Christ walk,
And come to me, and tenderly,
    Divinely talk.

Thus Truth engrounds me on the rock,
    Upon Life's shore;
'Gainst which the winds and waves can shock,
    Oh, nevermore!

From tired joy and grief afar,
    And nearer Thee, —
Father, where Thine own children are,
    I love to be.

My prayer, some daily good to do   1
    To Thine, for Thee;
An offering pure of Love, whereto   3
    God leadeth me.

Note

BY REV. MARY BAKER EDDY

1   The land whereon stands The First Church of Christ, Scientist, in Boston, was first purchased by the church 3 and society. Owing to a heavy loss, they were unable to pay the mortgage; therefore I paid it, and through trustees gave back the land to the church.

6   In 1892 I had to recover the land from the trustees, reorganize the church, and reobtain its charter — not, however, through the State Commissioner, who refused to 9 grant it, but by means of a statute of the State, and through Directors regive the land to the church. In 1895 I reconstructed my original system of ministry and church gov- 12 ernment. Thus committed to the providence of God, the prosperity of this church is unsurpassed.

  From first to last The Mother Church seemed type and 15 shadow of the warfare between the flesh and Spirit, even that shadow whose substance is the divine Spirit, imperatively propelling the greatest moral, physical, civil, 18 and religious reform ever known on earth. In the words of the prophet: "The shadow of a great rock in a weary land."

21   This church was dedicated on January 6, anciently one of the many dates selected and observed in the East as the day of the birth and baptism of our master Metaphysician, 24 Jesus of Nazareth.

20

Christian Scientists, their children and grandchildren 1
to the latest generations, inevitably love one another with
that love wherewith Christ loveth us; a love unselfish, 3
unambitious, impartial, universal, — that loves only because it *is* Love. Moreover, they love their enemies, even
those that hate them. This we all must do to be Christian 6
Scientists in spirit and in truth. I long, and live, to see
this love demonstrated. I am seeking and praying for it
to inhabit my own heart and to be made manifest in my 9
life. Who will unite with me in this pure purpose, and
faithfully struggle till it be accomplished? Let this be our
Christian endeavor society, which Christ organizes and 12
blesses.

While we entertain due respect and fellowship for what
is good and doing good in all denominations of religion, 15
and shun whatever would isolate us from a true sense of
goodness in others, we cannot serve mammon.

Christian Scientists are really united to only that which 18
is Christlike, but they are not indifferent to the welfare of
any one. To perpetuate a cold distance between our denomination and other sects, and close the door on church 21
or individuals — however much this is done to us — is
not Christian Science. Go not into the way of the un-
christly, but wheresoever you recognize a clear expression 24
of God's likeness, there abide in confidence and hope.

Our unity with churches of other denominations must
rest on the spirit of Christ calling us together. It cannot 27
come from any other source. Popularity, self-aggrandizement, aught that can darken in any degree our spirituality,
must be set aside. Only what feeds and fills the sentiment 30

1 with unworldliness, can give peace and good will towards
men.

3 All Christian churches have one bond of unity, one
nucleus or point of convergence, one prayer, — the Lord's
Prayer. It is matter for rejoicing that we unite in love,
6 and in this sacred petition with every praying assembly
on earth, — "Thy kingdom come. Thy will be done in
earth, as it is in heaven."

9 If the lives of Christian Scientists attest their fidelity
to Truth, I predict that in the twentieth century every
Christian church in our land, and a few in far-off lands,
12 will approximate the understanding of Christian Science
sufficiently to heal the sick in his name. Christ will give
to Christianity his new name, and Christendom will be
15 classified as Christian Scientists.

When the doctrinal barriers between the churches are
broken, and the bonds of peace are cemented by spiritual
18 understanding and Love, there will be unity of spirit, and
the healing power of Christ will prevail. Then shall Zion
have put on her most beautiful garments, and her waste
21 places budded and blossomed as the rose.

Clippings from Newspapers

[*Daily Inter-Ocean*, Chicago, December 31, 1894] 1

MARY BAKER EDDY

COMPLETION OF THE FIRST CHURCH OF CHRIST, SCIENTIST, BOSTON 3
— "OUR PRAYER IN STONE" — DESCRIPTION OF THE MOST
UNIQUE STRUCTURE IN ANY CITY — A BEAUTIFUL TEMPLE
AND ITS FURNISHINGS — MRS. EDDY'S WORK AND HER IN- 6
FLUENCE

Boston, Mass., December 28. — *Special Correspond-*
ence. — The "great awakening" of the time of Jonathan 9
Edwards has been paralleled during the last decade by a
wave of idealism that has swept over the country, manifesting itself under several different aspects and under 12
various names, but each having the common identity of
spiritual demand. This movement, under the guise of
Christian Science, and ingenuously calling out a closer 15
inquiry into Oriental philosophy, prefigures itself to us
as one of the most potent factors in the social evolution
of the last quarter of the nineteenth century. History 18
shows the curious fact that the closing years of every century are years of more intense life, manifested in unrest
or in aspiration, and scholars of special research, like 21
Prof. Max Muller, assert that the end of a cycle, as is the
latter part of the present century, is marked by peculiar
intimations of man's immortal life. 24

23

1   The completion of the first Christian Science church erected in Boston strikes a keynote of definite attention.

3 This church is in the fashionable Back Bay, between Commonwealth and Huntington Avenues. It is one of the most beautiful, and is certainly the most unique struc-

6 ture in any city. The First Church of Christ, Scientist, as it is officially called, is termed by its Founder, "Our prayer in stone." It is located at the intersection of Nor-

9 way and Falmouth Streets, on a triangular plot of ground, the design a Romanesque tower with a circular front and an octagonal form, accented by stone porticos and turreted

12 corners. On the front is a marble tablet, with the following inscription carved in bold relief: —

"The First Church of Christ, Scientist, erected Anno

15 Domini 1894. A testimonial to our beloved teacher, the Rev. Mary Baker Eddy, Discoverer and Founder of Christian Science; author of "Science and Health

18 with Key to the Scriptures;" president of the Massachusetts Metaphysical College, and the first pastor of this denomination."

21   *The Church Edifice*

The church is built of Concord granite in light gray, with trimmings of the pink granite of New Hampshire,

24 Mrs. Eddy's native State. The architecture is Romanesque throughout. The tower is one hundred and twenty feet in height and twenty-one and one half feet square. The en-

27 trances are of marble, with doors of antique oak richly carved. The windows of stained glass are very rich in

pictorial effect. The lighting and cooling of the church — for cooling is a recognized feature as well as heating — are done by electricity, and the heat generated by two large boilers in the basement is distributed by the four systems with motor electric power. The partitions are of iron; the floors of marble in mosaic work, and the edifice is therefore as literally fire-proof as is conceivable. The principal features are the auditorium, seating eleven hundred people and capable of holding fifteen hundred; the "Mother's Room," designed for the exclusive use of Mrs. Eddy; the "directors' room," and the vestry. The girders are all of iron, the roof is of terra cotta tiles, the galleries are in plaster relief, the window frames are of iron, coated with plaster; the staircases are of iron, with marble stairs of rose pink, and marble approaches.

The vestibule is a fitting entrance to this magnificent temple. In the ceiling is a sunburst with a seven-pointed star, which illuminates it. From this are the entrances leading to the auditorium, the "Mother's Room," and the directors' room.

The auditorium is seated with pews of curly birch, up-holstered in old rose plush. The floor is in white Italian mosaic, with frieze of the old rose, and the wainscoting repeats the same tints. The base and cap are of pink Tennessee marble. On the walls are bracketed oxidized silver lamps of Roman design, and there are frequent illuminated texts from the Bible and from Mrs. Eddy's "Science and Health with Key to the Scriptures" im-panelled. A sunburst in the centre of the ceiling takes the place of chandeliers. There is a disc of cut glass in

1 decorative designs, covering one hundred and forty-four
electric lights in the form of a star, which is twenty-one
3 inches from point to point, the centre being of pure white
light, and each ray under prisms which reflect the rainbow
tints. The galleries are richly panelled in relief work.
6 The organ and choir gallery is spacious and rich beyond
the power of words to depict. The platform — corresponding to the chancel of an Episcopal church — is a
9 mosaic work, with richly carved seats following the sweep
of its curve, with a lamp stand of the Renaissance period
on either end, bearing six richly wrought oxidized silver
12 lamps, eight feet in height. The great organ comes from
Detroit. It is one of vast compass, with Æolian attachment, and cost eleven thousand dollars. It is the gift of
15 a single individual — a votive offering of gratitude for the
healing of the wife of the donor.

The chime of bells includes fifteen, of fine range and
18 perfect tone.

The "Mother's Room"

The "Mother's Room" is approached by an entrance of
21 Italian marble, and over the door, in large golden letters on
a marble tablet, is the word "Love." In this room the
mosaic marble floor of white has a Romanesque border and
24 is decorated with sprays of fig leaves bearing fruit. The
room is toned in pale green with relief in old rose. The
mantel is of onyx and gold. Before the great bay window
27 hangs an Athenian lamp over two hundred years old,
which will be kept always burning day and night.[1] Lead-

---

[1] At Mrs. Eddy's request the lamp was not kept burning.

ing off the "Mother's Room" are toilet apartments, with 1
full-length French mirrors and every convenience.

The directors' room is very beautiful in marble ap- 3
proaches and rich carving, and off this is a vault for the
safe preservation of papers.

The vestry seats eight hundred people, and opening from 6
it are three large class-rooms and the pastor's study.

The windows are a remarkable feature of this temple.
There are no "memorial" windows; the entire church is a 9
testimonial, not a memorial — a point that the members
strongly insist upon.

In the auditorium are two rose windows — one repre- 12
senting the heavenly city which "cometh down from God
out of heaven," with six small windows beneath, emblematic of the six water-pots referred to in John ii. 6. The 15
other rose window represents the raising of the daughter
of Jairus. Beneath are two small windows bearing palms
of victory, and others with lamps, typical of Science and 18
Health.

Another great window tells its pictorial story of the four
Marys — the mother of Jesus, Mary anointing the head of 21
Jesus, Mary washing the feet of Jesus, Mary at the resurrection; and the woman spoken of in the Apocalypse,
chapter 12, God-crowned. 24

One more window in the auditorium represents the
raising of Lazarus.

In the gallery are windows representing John on the 27
Isle of Patmos, and others of pictorial significance. In
the "Mother's Room" the windows are of still more unique
interest. A large bay window, composed of three separate 30

1 panels, is designed to be wholly typical of the work of Mrs.
Eddy. The central panel represents her in solitude and
3 meditation, searching the Scriptures by the light of a single
candle, while the star of Bethlehem shines down from above.
Above this is a panel containing the Christian Science seal,
6 and other panels are decorated with emblematic designs,
with the legends, "Heal the Sick," "Raise the Dead,"
"Cleanse the Lepers," and "Cast out Demons."
9 The cross and the crown and the star are presented in
appropriate decorative effect. The cost of this church is
two hundred and twenty-one thousand dollars, exclusive
12 of the land — a gift from Mrs. Eddy — which is valued
at some forty thousand dollars.

The Order of Service

15 The order of service in the Christian Science Church
does not differ widely from that of any other sect, save that
its service includes the use of Mrs. Eddy's book, entitled
18 "Science and Health with Key to the Scriptures," in perhaps equal measure to its use of the Bible. The reading
is from the two alternately; the singing is from a compila-
21 tion called the "Christian Science Hymnal," but its songs
are for the most part those devotional hymns from Herbert,
Faber, Robertson, Wesley, Bowring, and other recog-
24 nized devotional poets, with selections from Whittier and
Lowell, as are found in the hymn-books of the Unitarian
churches. For the past year or two Judge Hanna, for-
27 merly of Chicago, has filled the office of pastor to the
church in this city, which held its meetings in Chickering

Hall, and later in Copley Hall, in the new Grundmann 1
Studio Building on Copley Square. Preceding Judge
Hanna were Rev. D. A. Easton and Rev. L. P. Norcross, 3
both of whom had formerly been Congregational clergymen. The organizer and first pastor of the church here
was Mrs. Eddy herself, of whose work I shall venture to 6
speak, a little later, in this article.

Last Sunday I gave myself the pleasure of attending the
service held in Copley Hall. The spacious apartment was 9
thronged with a congregation whose remarkable earnestness impressed the observer. There was no straggling
of late-comers. Before the appointed hour every seat in the 12
hall was filled and a large number of chairs pressed into
service for the overflowing throng. The music was spirited,
and the selections from the Bible and from Science and 15
Health were finely read by Judge Hanna. Then came his
sermon, which dealt directly with the command of Christ
to "heal the sick, raise the dead, cleanse the lepers, cast 18
out demons." In his admirable discourse Judge Hanna
said that while all these injunctions could, under certain
conditions, be interpreted and fulfilled literally, the 21
special lesson was to be taken spiritually — to cleanse the
leprosy of sin, to cast out the demons of evil thought.
The discourse was able, and helpful in its suggestive 24
interpretation.

The Church Members

Later I was told that almost the entire congregation was 27
composed of persons who had either been themselves, or

1 had seen members of their own families, healed by Christian Science treatment; and I was further told that once
3 when a Boston clergyman remonstrated with Judge Hanna
for enticing a separate congregation rather than offering
their strength to unite with churches already established —
6 I was told he replied that the Christian Science Church did
not recruit itself from other churches, but from the graveyards! The church numbers now four thousand members;
9 but this estimate, as I understand, is not limited to the
Boston adherents, but includes those all over the country.
The ceremonial of uniting is to sign a brief "confession of
12 faith," written by Mrs. Eddy, and to unite in communion,
which is not celebrated by outward symbols of bread and
wine, but by uniting in silent prayer.
15   The "confession of faith" includes the declaration that
the Scriptures are the guide to eternal Life; that there is a
Supreme Being, and His Son, and the Holy Ghost, and
18 that man is made in His image. It affirms the atonement;
it recognizes Jesus as the teacher and guide to salvation;
the forgiveness of sin by God, and affirms the power of
21 Truth over error, and the need of living faith at the
moment to realize the possibilities of the divine Life.
The entire membership of Christian Scientists throughout
24 the world now exceeds two hundred thousand people. The
church in Boston was organized by Mrs. Eddy, and the
first meeting held on April 12, 1879. It opened with
27 twenty-six members, and within fifteen years it has grown
to its present impressive proportions, and has now its own
magnificent church building, costing over two hundred
30 thousand dollars, and entirely paid for when its consecra-

tion service on January 6 shall be celebrated. This is 1
certainly a very remarkable retrospect.

Rev. Mary Baker Eddy, the Founder of this denomina- 3
tion and Discoverer of Christian Science, as they term her
work in affirming the present application of the principles
asserted by Jesus, is a most interesting personality. At 6
the risk of colloquialism, I am tempted to "begin at the
beginning" of my own knowledge of Mrs. Eddy, and take,
as the point of departure, my first meeting with her and 9
the subsequent development of some degree of familiarity
with the work of her life which that meeting inaugurated
for me. 12

Mrs. Eddy

It was during some year in the early '80's that I became
aware — from that close contact with public feeling result- 15
ing from editorial work in daily journalism — that the
Boston atmosphere was largely thrilled and pervaded by a
new and increasing interest in the dominance of mind over 18
matter, and that the central figure in all this agitation was
Mrs. Eddy. To a note which I wrote her, begging the
favor of an interview for press use, she most kindly replied, 21
naming an evening on which she would receive me. At
the hour named I rang the bell at a spacious house on
Columbus Avenue, and I was hardly more than seated be- 24
fore Mrs. Eddy entered the room. She impressed me as
singularly graceful and winning in bearing and manner,
and with great claim to personal beauty. Her figure was 27
tall, slender, and as flexible in movement as that of a Del-

1 sarte disciple; her face, framed in dark hair and lighted
by luminous blue eyes, had the transparency and rose-flush
3 of tint so often seen in New England, and she was magnetic,
earnest, impassioned. No photographs can do the least
justice to Mrs. Eddy, as her beautiful complexion and
6 changeful expression cannot thus be reproduced. At once
one would perceive that she had the temperament to dominate, to lead, to control, not by any crude self-assertion, but
9 a spiritual animus. Of course such a personality, with the
wonderful tumult in the air that her large and enthusiastic
following excited, fascinated the imagination. What had
12 she originated? I mentally questioned this modern St.
Catherine, who was dominating her followers like any ab-
bess of old. She told me the story of her life, so far as out-
15 ward events may translate those inner experiences which
alone are significant.

Mary Baker was the daughter of Mark and Abigail
18 (Ambrose) Baker, and was born in Concord, N. H., somewhere in the early decade of 1820–'30. At the time I met
her she must have been some sixty years of age, yet she had
21 the coloring and the elastic bearing of a woman of thirty,
and this, she told me, was due to the principles of Christian Science. On her father's side Mrs. Eddy came from
24 Scotch and English ancestry, and Hannah More was a
relative of her grandmother. Deacon Ambrose, her mater-
nal grandfather, was known as a "godly man," and her
27 mother was a religious enthusiast, a saintly and consecrated
character. One of her brothers, Albert Baker, graduated
at Dartmouth and achieved eminence as a lawyer.

Mrs. Eddy as a Child   1

As a child Mary Baker saw visions and dreamed dreams. When eight years of age she began, like Jeanne d'Arc, to 3 hear "voices," and for a year she heard her name called distinctly, and would often run to her mother questioning if she were wanted. One night the mother related to her 6 the story of Samuel, and bade her, if she heard the voice again to reply as he did: "Speak, Lord, for Thy servant heareth." The call came, but the little maid was afraid 9 and did not reply. This caused her tears of remorse and she prayed for forgiveness, and promised to reply if the call came again. It came, and she answered as her mother had 12 bidden her, and after that it ceased.

These experiences, of which Catholic biographies are full, and which history not infrequently emphasizes, cer- 15 tainly offer food for meditation. Theodore Parker related that when he was a lad, at work in a field one day on his father's farm at Lexington, an old man with a snowy beard 18 suddenly appeared at his side, and walked with him as he worked, giving him high counsel and serious thought. All inquiry in the neighborhood as to whence the stranger 21 came or whither he went was fruitless; no one else had seen him, and Mr. Parker always believed, so a friend has told me, that his visitor was a spiritual form from another 24 world. It is certainly true that many and many persons, whose life has been destined to more than ordinary achieve- ment, have had experiences of voices or visions in their 27 early youth.

1   At an early age Miss Baker was married to Colonel
Glover, of Charleston, S. C., who lived only a year. She
3 returned to her father's home — in 1844 — and from that
time until 1866 no special record is to be made.

In 1866, while living in Lynn, Mass., Mrs. Eddy
6 met with a severe accident, and her case was pronounced hopeless by the physicians. There came a
Sunday morning when her pastor came to bid her good-
9 by before proceeding to his morning service, as there was
no probability that she would be alive at its close. During
this time she suddenly became aware of a divine illumina-
12 tion and ministration. She requested those with her to
withdraw, and reluctantly they did so, believing her de-
lirious. Soon, to their bewilderment and fright, she walked
15 into the adjoining room, "and they thought I had died,
and that it was my apparition," she said.

The Principle of Divine Healing

18   From that hour dated her conviction of the Principle of
divine healing, and that it is as true to-day as it was in the
days when Jesus of Nazareth walked the earth. "I felt
21 that the divine Spirit had wrought a miracle," she said, in
reference to this experience. "How, I could not tell, but
later I found it to be in perfect scientific accord with the
24 divine law." From 1866–'69 Mrs. Eddy withdrew from the
world to meditate, to pray, to search the Scriptures.

"During this time," she said, in reply to my questions,
27 "the Bible was my only textbook. It answered my questions as to the process by which I was restored to health;

it came to me with a new meaning, and suddenly I appre- 1
hended the spiritual meaning of the teaching of Jesus and
the Principle and the law involved in spiritual Science 3
and metaphysical healing — in a word — Christian
Science."

Mrs. Eddy came to perceive that Christ's healing was not 6
miraculous, but was simply a natural fulfilment of divine
law — a law as operative in the world to-day as it was
nineteen hundred years ago. "Divine Science is begotten 9
of spirituality," she says, "since only the 'pure in heart'
can see God."

In writing of this experience, Mrs. Eddy has said: — 12
"I had learned that thought must be spiritualized in
order to apprehend Spirit. It must become honest, unselfish, and pure, in order to have the least understanding 15
of God in divine Science. The first must become last.
Our reliance upon material things must be transferred to
a perception of and dependence on spiritual things. For 18
Spirit to be supreme in demonstration, it must be supreme
in our affections, and we must be clad with divine power.
I had learned that Mind reconstructed the body, and that 21
nothing else could. All Science is a revelation."

Through homœopathy, too, Mrs. Eddy became convinced of the Principle of Mind-healing, discovering that 24
the more attenuated the drug, the more potent was its
effects.

In 1877 Mrs. Glover married Dr. Asa Gilbert Eddy, of 27
Londonderry, Vermont, a physician who had come into
sympathy with her own views, and who was the first to
place "Christian Scientist" on the sign at his door. Dr. 30

1 Eddy died in 1882, a year after her founding of the Metaphysical College in Boston, in which he taught.

3   The work in the Metaphysical College lasted nine years,
and it was closed (in 1889) in the very zenith of its prosperity, as Mrs. Eddy felt it essential to the deeper founda-
6 tion of her religious work to retire from active contact with
the world.   To this College came hundreds and hundreds
of students, from Europe as well as this country.   I was
9 present at the class lectures now and then, by Mrs. Eddy's
kind invitation, and such earnestness of attention as was
given to her morning talks by the men and women present
12 I never saw equalled.

Mrs. Eddy's Personality

On the evening that I first met Mrs. Eddy by her hos-
15 pitable courtesy, I went to her peculiarly fatigued.   I came
away in a state of exhilaration and energy that made me
feel I could have walked any conceivable distance.   I have
18 met Mrs. Eddy many times since then, and always with
this experience repeated.

Several years ago Mrs. Eddy removed from Columbus
21 to Commonwealth Avenue, where, just beyond Massachusetts Avenue, at the entrance to the Back Bay Park,
she bought one of the most beautiful residences in Boston.
24 The interior is one of the utmost taste and luxury, and the
house is now occupied by Judge and Mrs. Hanna, who are
the editors of *The Christian Science Journal,* a monthly
27 publication, and to whose courtesy I am much indebted
for some of the data of this paper.   "It is a pleasure to

give any information for *The Inter-Ocean*," remarked 1
Mrs. Hanna, "for it is the great daily that is so fair and so
just in its attitude toward all questions." 3

The increasing demands of the public on Mrs. Eddy
have been, it may be, one factor in her removal to Concord,
N. H., where she has a beautiful residence, called Pleasant 6
View. Her health is excellent, and although her hair is
white, she retains in a great degree her energy and power;
she takes a daily walk and drives in the afternoon. She 9
personally attends to a vast correspondence; superin-
tends the church in Boston, and is engaged on further
writings on Christian Science. In every sense she is the 12
recognized head of the Christian Science Church. At the
same time it is her most earnest aim to eliminate the element of personality from the faith. "On this point, Mrs. 15
Eddy feels very strongly," said a gentleman to me on
Christmas eve, as I sat in the beautiful drawing-room,
where Judge and Mrs. Hanna, Miss Elsie Lincoln, the 18
soprano for the choir of the new church, and one or two
other friends were gathered.

"Mother feels very strongly," he continued, "the danger 21
and the misfortune of a church depending on any one
personality. It is difficult not to centre too closely around
a highly gifted personality." 24

The First Association

The first Christian Scientist Association was organized
on July 4, 1876, by seven persons, including Mrs. Eddy. 27
In April, 1879, the church was founded with twenty-six

1 members, and its charter obtained the following June.[1]
Mrs. Eddy had preached in other parishes for five years
3 before being ordained in this church, which ceremony
took place in 1881.

The first edition of Mrs. Eddy's book, Science and
6 Health, was issued in 1875. During these succeeding
twenty years it has been greatly revised and enlarged, and
it is now in its ninety-first edition. It consists of fourteen
9 chapters, whose titles are as follows: "Science, Theology,
Medicine," "Physiology," "Footsteps of Truth," "Creation," "Science of Being," "Christian Science and Spirit-
12 ualism," "Marriage," "Animal Magnetism," "Some
Objections Answered," "Prayer," "Atonement and Eucharist," "Christian Science Practice," "Teaching Chris-
15 tian Science," "Recapitulation." Key to the Scriptures,
Genesis, Apocalypse, and Glossary.

The Christian Scientists do not accept the belief we call
18 spiritualism. They believe those who have passed the
change of death are in so entirely different a plane of consciousness that between the embodied and disembodied
21 there is no possibility of communication.

They are diametrically opposed to the philosophy of
Karma and of reincarnation, which are the tenets of
24 theosophy. They hold with strict fidelity to what they
believe to be the literal teachings of Christ.

Yet each and all these movements, however they may
27 differ among themselves, are phases of idealism and manifestations of a higher spirituality seeking expression.

It is good that each and all shall prosper, serving those
30 who find in one form of belief or another their best aid

---

[1] Steps were taken to promote the Church of Christ, Scientist, in April, May,
and June; formal organization was accomplished and the charter obtained in
August, 1879.

and guidance, and that all meet on common ground in the   1
great essentials of love to God and love to man as a signal
proof of the divine origin of humanity which finds no rest   3
until it finds the peace of the Lord in spirituality.   They
all teach that one great truth, that

> God's greatness flows around our incompleteness,   6
> Round our restlessness, His rest.
>   ELIZABETH BARRETT BROWNING

———————

   I add on the following page a little poem that I con-   9
sider superbly sweet — from my friend, Miss Whiting,
the talented author of "The World Beautiful." — M. B.
EDDY   12

AT THE WINDOW

[Written for the *Traveller*]

The sunset, burning low,   15
   Throws o'er the Charles its flood of golden light.
Dimly, as in a dream, I watch the flow
   Of waves of light.   18

The splendor of the sky
   Repeats its glory in the river's flow;
And sculptured angels, on the gray church tower,   21
   Gaze on the world below.

Dimly, as in a dream,
   I see the hurrying throng before me pass,   24
But 'mid them all I only see *one* face,
   Under the meadow grass.

1   Ah, love!   I only know
          How thoughts of you forever cling to me:
3   I wonder how the seasons come and go
          Beyond the sapphire sea?

                                      LILIAN WHITING

6 April 15, 1888

[*Boston Herald*, January 7, 1895]

[Extract]

9 A TEMPLE GIVEN TO GOD — DEDICATION OF THE
MOTHER CHURCH OF CHRISTIAN SCIENCE

NOVEL METHOD OF ENABLING SIX THOUSAND BELIEVERS TO
12   ATTEND THE EXERCISES — THE SERVICE REPEATED FOUR
TIMES — SERMON BY REV. MARY BAKER EDDY, FOUNDER OF
THE DENOMINATION — BEAUTIFUL ROOM WHICH THE CHILDREN
15   BUILT

With simple ceremonies, four times repeated, in the
presence of four different congregations, aggregating
18 nearly six thousand persons, the unique and costly edifice
erected in Boston at Norway and Falmouth Streets as a
home for The First Church of Christ, Scientist, and a
21 testimonial to the Discoverer and Founder of Christian
Science, Rev. Mary Baker Eddy, was yesterday dedicated
to the worship of God.

The structure came forth from the hands of the artisans 1
with every stone paid for — with an appeal, not for more
money, but for a cessation of the tide of contributions 3
which continued to flow in after the full amount needed
was received. From every State in the Union, and from
many lands, the love-offerings of the disciples of Christian 6
Science came to help erect this beautiful structure, and
more than four thousand of these contributors came to
Boston, from the far-off Pacific coast and the Gulf States 9
and all the territory that lies between, to view the new-
built temple and to listen to the Message sent them by
the teacher they revere. 12

From all New England the members of the denomination gathered; New York sent its hundreds, and even
from the distant States came parties of forty and fifty. 15
The large auditorium, with its capacity for holding from
fourteen hundred to fifteen hundred persons, was hopelessly
incapable of receiving this vast throng, to say nothing of 18
nearly a thousand local believers. Hence the service was
repeated until all who wished had heard and seen; and
each of the four vast congregations filled the church to 21
repletion.

At 7:30 a. m. the chimes in the great stone tower, which
rises one hundred and twenty-six feet above the earth, 24
rung out their message of "On earth peace, good will
toward men."

Old familiar hymns — "All hail the power of Jesus' 27
name," and others such — were chimed until the hour for
the dedication service had come.

At 9 a. m. the first congregation gathered. Before this 30

service had closed the large vestry room and the spacious lobbies and the sidewalks around the church were all filled with a waiting multitude. At 10:30 o'clock another service began, and at noon still another. Then there was an intermission, and at 3 p. m. the service was repeated for the last time.

There was scarcely even a minor variation in the exercises at any one of these services. At 10:30 a. m., however, the scene was rendered particularly interesting by the presence of several hundred children in the central pews. These were the little contributors to the building fund, whose money was devoted to the "Mother's Room," a superb apartment intended for the sole use of Mrs. Eddy. These children are known in the church as the "Busy Bees," and each of them wore a white satin badge with a golden beehive stamped upon it, and beneath the beehive the words, "Mother's Room," in gilt letters.

The pulpit end of the auditorium was rich with the adornment of flowers. On the wall of the choir gallery above the platform, where the organ is to be hereafter placed, a huge seven-pointed star was hung — a star of lilies resting on palms, with a centre of white immortelles, upon which in letters of red were the words: "Love-Children's Offering — 1894."

In the choir and the steps of the platform were potted palms and ferns and Easter lilies. The desk was wreathed with ferns and pure white roses fastened with a broad ribbon bow. On its right was a large basket of white carnations resting on a mat of palms, and on its left a vase filled with beautiful pink roses.

Two combined choirs — that of First Church of Christ, 1
Scientist, of New York, and the choir of the home church,
numbering thirty-five singers in all — led the singing, 3
under the direction, respectively, of Mr. Henry Lincoln
Case and Miss Elsie Lincoln.

Judge S. J. Hanna, editor of *The Christian Science* 6
Journal, presided over the exercises. On the platform
with him were Messrs. Ira O. Knapp, Joseph Armstrong,
Stephen A. Chase, and William B. Johnson, who compose 9
the Board of Directors, and Mrs. Henrietta Clark Bemis,
a distinguished elocutionist, and a native of Concord, New
Hampshire.   12

The utmost simplicity marked the exercises. After an
organ voluntary, the hymn, *"Laus Deo,* it is done!"
written by Mrs. Eddy for the corner-stone laying last 15
spring, was sung by the congregation. Selections from the
Scriptures and from "Science and Health with Key to the
Scriptures," were read by Judge Hanna and Dr. Eddy.   18

A few minutes of silent prayer came next, followed by
the recitation of the Lord's Prayer, with its spiritual interpretation as given in the Christian Science textbook. 21

The sermon prepared for the occasion by Mrs. Eddy,
which was looked forward to as the chief feature of the
dedication, was then read by Mrs. Bemis. Mrs. Eddy 24
remained at her home in Concord, N. H., during the day,
because, as heretofore stated in *The Herald,* it is her
custom to discourage among her followers that sort of 27
personal worship which religious teachers so often receive.

Before presenting the sermon, Mrs. Bemis read the following letter from a former pastor of the church: —   30

1 "To Rev. Mary Baker Eddy

"*Dear Teacher, Leader, Guide:* — '*Laus Deo,* it is done!'
3 At last you begin to see the fruition of that you have worked, toiled, prayed for. The 'prayer in stone' is accomplished. Across two thousand miles of space, as mortal sense puts
6 it, I send my hearty congratulations. You are fully occupied, but I thought you would willingly pause for an instant to receive this brief message of congratulation.
9 Surely it marks an era in the blessed onward work of Christian Science. It is a most auspicious hour in your eventful career. While we all rejoice, yet the mother in
12 Israel, alone of us all, comprehends its full significance.

"Yours lovingly,

"LANSON P. NORCROSS"

15   [*Boston Sunday Globe,* January 6, 1895]

[Extract]

STATELY HOME FOR BELIEVERS IN GOSPEL HEALING —
18   A WOMAN OF WEALTH WHO DEVOTES ALL TO HER CHURCH WORK

Christian Science has shown its power over its students,
21 as they are called, by building a church by voluntary contributions, the first of its kind; a church which will be dedicated to-day with a quarter of a million dollars ex-
24 pended and free of debt.

The money has flowed in from all parts of the United States and Canada without any special appeal, and it kept
27 coming until the custodian of funds cried "enough" and refused to accept any further checks by mail or otherwise.

Men, women, and children lent a helping hand, some 1
giving a mite and some substantial sums. Sacrifices were
made in many an instance which will never be known in 3
this world.

Christian Scientists not only say that they can effect
cures of disease and erect churches, but add that they can 6
get their buildings finished on time, even when the feat
seems impossible to mortal senses. Read the following,
from a publication of the new denomination: —   9

"One of the grandest and most helpful features of this
glorious consummation is this: that one month before the
close of the year every evidence of material sense declared 12
that the church's completion within the year 1894 transcended human possibility. The predictions of workman
and onlooker alike were that it could not be completed 15
before April or May of 1895. Much was the ridicule
heaped upon the hopeful, trustful ones, who declared and
repeatedly asseverated to the contrary. This is indeed, 18
then, a scientific demonstration. It has proved, in most
striking manner, the oft-repeated declarations of our
textbooks, that the evidence of the mortal senses is 21
unreliable."

A week ago Judge Hanna withdrew from the pastorate
of the church, saying he gladly laid down his responsibili- 24
ties to be succeeded by the grandest of ministers — the
Bible and "Science and Health with Key to the Scriptures." This action, it appears, was the result of rules 27
made by Mrs. Eddy. The sermons hereafter will consist
of passages read from the two books by Readers, who will
be elected each year by the congregation.   30

1   A story has been abroad that Judge Hanna was so eloquent and magnetic that he was attracting listeners who
3 came to hear him preach, rather than in search of the
truth as taught.   Consequently the new rules were formulated. But at Christian Science headquarters this is denied;
6 Mrs. Eddy says the words of the judge speak to the point,
and that no such inference is to be drawn therefrom.

In Mrs. Eddy's personal reminiscences, which are pub-
9 lished under the title of "Retrospection and Introspection,"
much is told of herself in detail that can only be touched
upon in this brief sketch.

12   Aristocratic to the backbone, Mrs. Eddy takes delight
in going back to the ancestral tree and in tracing those
branches which are identified with good and great names
15 both in Scotland and England.

Her family came to this country not long before the
Revolution. Among the many souvenirs that Mrs. Eddy
18 remembers as belonging to her grandparents was a heavy
sword, encased in a brass scabbard, upon which had been
inscribed the name of the kinsman upon whom the sword
21 had been bestowed by Sir William Wallace of mighty
Scottish fame.

Mrs. Eddy applied herself, like other girls, to her studies,
24 though perhaps with an unusual zest, delighting in philosophy, logic, and moral science, as well as looking into the
ancient languages, Hebrew, Greek, and Latin.

27   Her last marriage was in the spring of 1877, when, at
Lynn, Mass., she became the wife of Asa Gilbert Eddy.
He was the first organizer of a Christian Science Sunday
30 School, of which he was the superintendent, and later he

attracted the attention of many clergymen of other de- 1
nominations by his able lectures upon Scriptural topics.
He died in 1882.   3

Mrs. Eddy is known to her circle of pupils and admirers
as the editor and publisher of the first official organ of this
sect. It was called the *Journal of Christian Science*, and 6
has had great circulation with the members of this fast-
increasing faith.

In recounting her experiences as the pioneer of Chris- 9
tian Science, she states that she sought knowledge concerning the physical side in this research through the different
schools of allopathy, homœopathy, and so forth, without 12
receiving any real satisfaction. No ancient or modern
philosophy gave her any distinct statement of the Science
of Mind-healing. She claims that no human reason has 15
been equal to the question. And she also defines carefully the difference in the theories between faith-cure and
Christian Science, dwelling particularly upon the terms 18
belief and understanding, which are the key words respectively used in the definitions of these two healing arts.

Besides her Boston home, Mrs. Eddy has a delightful 21
country home one mile from the State House of New
Hampshire's quiet capital, an easy driving distance for
her when she wishes to catch a glimpse of the world. But 24
for the most part she lives very much retired, driving rather
into the country, which is so picturesque all about Concord and its surrounding villages.   27

The big house, so delightfully remodelled and modern-
ized from a primitive homestead that nothing is left excepting the angles and pitch of the roof, is remarkably 30

well placed upon a terrace that slopes behind the buildings, while they themselves are in the midst of green stretches of lawns, dotted with beds of flowering shrubs, with here and there a fountain or summer-house.

Mrs. Eddy took the writer straight to her beloved "lookout" — a broad piazza on the south side of the second story of the house, where she can sit in her swinging chair, revelling in the lights and shades of spring and summer greenness. Or, as just then, in the gorgeous October coloring of the whole landscape that lies below, across the farm, which stretches on through an intervale of beautiful meadows and pastures to the woods that skirt the valley of the little truant river, as it wanders eastward.

It pleased her to point out her own birthplace. Straight as the crow flies, from her piazza, does it lie on the brow of Bow hill, and then she paused and reminded the reporter that Congressman Baker from New Hampshire, her cousin, was born and bred in that same neighborhood. The photograph of Hon. Hoke Smith, another distinguished relative, adorned the mantel.

Then my eye caught her family coat of arms and the diploma given her by the Society of the Daughters of the Revolution.

The natural and lawful pride that comes with a tincture of blue and brave blood, is perhaps one of her characteristics, as is many another well-born woman's. She had a long list of worthy ancestors in Colonial and Revolutionary days, and the McNeils and General Knox figure largely in her genealogy, as well as the hero who killed the ill-starred Paugus.

This big, sunny room which Mrs. Eddy calls her den — 1
or sometimes "Mother's room," when speaking of her
many followers who consider her their spiritual Leader — 3
has the air of hospitality that marks its hostess herself.
Mrs. Eddy has hung its walls with reproductions of some
of Europe's masterpieces, a few of which had been the 6
gifts of her loving pupils.

Looking down from the windows upon the tree-tops
on the lower terrace, the reporter exclaimed: "You have 9
lived here only four years, and yet from a barren waste
of most unpromising ground has come forth all this
beauty!"   12

"Four years!" she ejaculated; "two and a half, only
two and a half years." Then, touching my sleeve and
pointing, she continued: "Look at those big elms! I had 15
them brought here in warm weather, almost as big as they
are now, and not one died."

Mrs. Eddy talked earnestly of her friendships. . . . 18
She told something of her domestic arrangements, of how
she had long wished to get away from her busy career in
Boston, and return to her native granite hills, there to 21
build a substantial home that should do honor to that
precinct of Concord.

She chose the stubbly old farm on the road from Con- 24
cord, within one mile of the "Eton of America," St. Paul's
School. Once bought, the will of the woman set at work,
and to-day a strikingly well-kept estate is the first impres- 27
sion given to the visitor as he approaches Pleasant View.

She employs a number of men to keep the grounds and
farm in perfect order, and it was pleasing to learn that this 30

1 rich woman is using her money to promote the welfare of industrious workmen, in whom she takes a vital interest. 3 Mrs. Eddy believes that "the laborer is worthy of his hire," and, moreover, that he deserves to have a home and family of his own. Indeed, one of her motives in buying 6 so large an estate was that she might do something for the toilers, and thus add her influence toward the advancement of better home life and citizenship.

_____

9 [*Boston Transcript*, December 31, 1894]

[Extract]

The growth of Christian Science is properly marked by 12 the erection of a visible house of worship in this city, which will be dedicated to-morrow. It has cost two hundred thousand dollars, and no additional sums outside of the 15 subscriptions are asked for. This particular phase of religious belief has impressed itself upon a large and increasing number of Christian people, who have been 18 tempted to examine its principles, and doubtless have been comforted and strengthened by them. Any new movement will awaken some sort of interest. There are many 21 who have worn off the novelty and are thoroughly carried away with the requirements, simple and direct as they are, of Christian Science. The opposition against it from the 24 so-called orthodox religious bodies keeps up a while, but after a little skirmishing, finally subsides. No one religious body holds the whole of truth, and whatever is likely to 27 show even some one side of it will gain followers and live down any attempted repression.

Christian Science does not strike all as a system of truth. 1
If it did, it would be a prodigy. Neither does the Christian
faith produce the same impressions upon all. Freedom to 3
believe or to dissent is a great privilege in these days. So
when a number of conscientious followers apply themselves
to a matter like Christian Science, they are enjoying that 6
liberty which is their inherent right as human beings, and
though they cannot escape censure, yet they are to be
numbered among the many pioneers who are searching 9
after religious truth. There is really nothing settled.
Every truth is more or less in a state of agitation. The
many who have worked in the mine of knowledge are glad 12
to welcome others who have different methods, and with
them bring different ideas.

It is too early to predict where this movement will go, 15
and how greatly it will affect the well-established methods.
That it has produced a sensation in religious circles, and
called forth the implements of theological warfare, is very 18
well known. While it has done this, it may, on the other
hand, have brought a benefit. Ere this many a new project
in religious belief has stirred up feeling, but as time has 21
gone on, compromises have been welcomed.

The erection of this temple will doubtless help on the
growth of its principles. Pilgrims from everywhere will go 24
there in search of truth, and some may be satisfied and some
will not. Christian Science cannot absorb the world's
thought. It may get the share of attention it deserves, but 27
it can only aspire to take its place alongside other great
demonstrations of religious belief which have done something good for the sake of humanity. 30

1   Wonders will never cease.   Here is a church whose
treasurer has to send out word that no sums except those
3 already subscribed can be received!   The Christian
Scientists have a faith of the mustard-seed variety.
What a pity some of our practical Christian folk have not a
6 faith approximate to that of these "impractical" Christian
Scientists.

[*Jackson Patriot*, Jackson, Mich., January 20, 1895]

9   [Extract]

CHRISTIAN SCIENCE

The erection of a massive temple in Boston by Christian
12 Scientists, at a cost of over two hundred thousand dollars,
love-offerings of the disciples of Mary Baker Eddy, reviver
of the ancient faith and author of the textbook from which,
15 with the New Testament at the foundation, believers
receive light, health, and strength, is evidence of the rapid
growth of the new movement.   We call it new.   It is not.
18 The name Christian Science alone is new.   At the beginning of Christianity it was taught and practised by Jesus
and his disciples.   The Master was the great healer.   But
21 the wave of materialism and bigotry that swept over the
world for fifteen centuries, covering it with the blackness
of the Dark Ages, nearly obliterated all vital belief in his
24 teachings.   The Bible was a sealed book.   Recently a
revived belief in what he taught is manifest, and Christian
Science is one result.   No new doctrine is proclaimed, but

there is the fresh development of a Principle that was put 1
into practice by the Founder of Christianity nineteen hundred years ago, though practised in other countries at an 3
earlier date. "The thing that hath been, it is that which
shall be; and that which is done is that which shall be
done: and there is no new thing under the sun." 6

The condition which Jesus of Nazareth, on various
occasions during the three years of his ministry on earth,
declared to be essential, in the mind of both healer and 9
patient, is contained in the one word — *faith*. Can drugs
suddenly cure leprosy? When the ten lepers were cleansed
and one returned to give thanks in Oriental phrase, Jesus 12
said to him: "Arise, go thy way: thy faith hath made thee
whole." That was Christian Science. In his "Law of
Psychic Phenomena" Hudson says: "That word, more 15
than any other, expresses the whole law of human felicity
and power in this world, and of salvation in the world to
come. It is that attribute of mind which elevates man 18
above the level of the brute, and gives dominion over the
physical world. It is the essential element of success in
every field of human endeavor. It constitutes the power 21
of the human soul. When Jesus of Nazareth proclaimed
its potency from the hilltops of Palestine, he gave to mankind the key to health and heaven, and earned the title 24
of Saviour of the World." Whittier, grandest of mystic
poets, saw the truth: —

> That healing gift he lends to them 27
> Who use it in his name;
> The power that filled his garment's hem
> Is evermore the same. 30

1   Again, in a poem entitled "The Master," he wrote: —

>   The healing of his seamless dress
> 3   Is by our beds of pain;
>   We touch him in life's throng and press,
>   And we are whole again.[1]

6   That Jesus operated in perfect harmony with natural
law, not in defiance, suppression, or violation of it, we cannot doubt. The perfectly natural is the perfectly spiritual.
9 Jesus enunciated and exemplified the Principle; and,
obviously, the conditions requisite in psychic healing
to-day are the same as were necessary in apostolic times.
12 We accept the statement of Hudson: "There was no law
of nature violated or transcended. On the contrary, the
whole transaction was in perfect obedience to the laws of
15 nature. He understood the law perfectly, as no one before
him understood it; and in the plenitude of his power he
applied it where the greatest good could be accomplished."
18 A careful reading of the accounts of his healings, in the
light of modern science, shows that he observed, in his
practice of mental therapeutics, the conditions of environ-
21 ment and harmonious influence that are essential to success.
In the case of Jairus' daughter they are fully set forth.
He kept the unbelievers away, "put them all out," and
24 permitting only the father and mother, with his closest
friends and followers, Peter, James, and John, in the
chamber with him, and having thus the most perfect
27 obtainable environment, he raised the daughter to life.

---

[1] NOTE: — About 1868, the author of Science and Health healed
Mr. Whittier with one visit, at his home in Amesbury, of incipient
30 pulmonary consumption. — M. B. EDDY

"Not in blind caprice of will,
 Not in cunning sleight of skill,
 Not for show of power, was wrought
 Nature's marvel in thy thought."

In a previous article we have referred to cyclic changes
that came during the last quarter of preceding centuries.
Of our remarkable nineteenth century not the least eventful circumstance is the advent of Christian Science.
That it should be the work of a woman is the natural outcome of a period notable for her emancipation from many
of the thraldoms, prejudices, and oppressions of the past.
We do not, therefore, regard it as a mere coincidence that
the first edition of Mrs. Eddy's Science and Health should
have been published in 1875. Since then she has revised
it many times, and the ninety-first edition is announced.
Her discovery was first called, "The Science of Divine
Metaphysical Healing." Afterward she selected the name
Christian Science. It is based upon what is held to be
scientific certainty, namely, — that all causation is of
Mind, every effect has its origin in desire and thought.
The theology — if we may use the word — of Christian
Science is contained in the volume entitled "Science and
Health with Key to the Scriptures."

The present Boston congregation was organized
April 12, 1879, and has now over four thousand members.
It is regarded as the parent organization, all others being
branches, though each is entirely independent in the
management of its own affairs. Truth is the sole recognized
authority. Of actual members of different congregations
there are between one hundred thousand and two hundred

1 thousand.   One or more organized societies have sprung
up in New York, Chicago, Buffalo, Cleveland, Cincin-
3 nati, Philadelphia, Detroit, Toledo, Milwaukee, Madison,
Scranton, Peoria, Atlanta, Toronto, and nearly every other
centre of population, besides a large and growing number
6 of receivers of the faith among the members of all the
churches and non-church-going people.   In some churches
a majority of the members are Christian Scientists, and, as
9 a rule, are the most intelligent.

Space does not admit of an elaborate presentation on the
occasion of the erection of the temple, in Boston, the
12 dedication taking place on the 6th of January, of one of
the most remarkable, helpful, and powerful movements
of the last quarter of the century.   Christian Science
15 has brought hope and comfort to many weary souls.   It
makes people better and happier.   Welding Christianity
and Science, hitherto divorced because dogma and truth
18 could not unite, was a happy inspiration.

> "And still we love the evil cause,
> And of the just effect complain;
> 21   We tread upon life's broken laws,
> And mourn our self-inflicted pain."

[*The Outlook*, New York, January 19, 1895]

24   A CHRISTIAN SCIENCE CHURCH

A great Christian Science church was dedicated in Boston on Sunday, the 6th inst.   It is located at Norway and
27 Falmouth Streets, and is intended to be a testimonial to

the Discoverer and Founder of Christian Science, the 1
Rev. Mary Baker Eddy. The building is fire-proof, and
cost over two hundred thousand dollars. It is entirely 3
paid for, and contributions for its erection came from every
State in the Union, and from many lands. The auditorium
is said to seat between fourteen and fifteen hundred, and 6
was thronged at the four services on the day of dedication.
The sermon, prepared by Mrs. Eddy, was read by Mrs.
Bemis. It rehearsed the significance of the building, and 9
reenunciated the truths which will find emphasis there.
From the description we judge that it is one of the most
beautiful buildings in Boston, and, indeed, in all New 12
England. Whatever may be thought of the peculiar tenets
of the Christian Scientists, and whatever difference of
opinion there may be concerning the organization of such 15
a church, there can be no question but that the adherents
of this church have proved their faith by their works.

[*American Art Journal*, New York, January 26, 1895]   18

"OUR PRAYER IN STONE"

Such is the excellent name given to a new Boston church.
Few people outside its own circles realize how extensive is 21
the belief in Christian Science. There are several sects of
mental healers, but this new edifice on Back Bay, just off
Huntington Avenue, not far from the big Mechanics 24
Building and the proposed site of the new Music Hall,
belongs to the followers of Rev. Mary Baker Glover Eddy,
a lady born of an old New Hampshire family, who, after 27

1 many vicissitudes, found herself in Lynn, Mass., healed by
the power of divine Mind, and thereupon devoted herself
3 to imparting this faith to her fellow-beings. Coming to
Boston about 1880, she began teaching, gathered an
association of students, and organized a church. For
6 several years past she has lived in Concord, N. H., near
her birthplace, owning a beautiful estate called Pleasant
View; but thousands of believers throughout this country
9 have joined The Mother Church in Boston, and have now
erected this edifice at a cost of over two hundred thousand
dollars, every bill being paid.
12 Its appearance is shown in the pictures we are permitted
to publish. In the belfry is a set of tubular chimes. Inside
is a basement room, capable of division into seven excellent
15 class-rooms, by the use of movable partitions. The main
auditorium has wide galleries, and will seat over a thousand
in its exceedingly comfortable pews. Scarcely any wood-
18 work is to be found. The floors are all mosaic, the steps
marble, and the walls stone. It is rather dark, often too
much so for comfortable reading, as all the windows are of
21 colored glass, with pictures symbolic of the tenets of the
organization. In the ceiling is a beautiful sunburst window.
Adjoining the chancel is a pastor's study; but for an
24 indefinite time their prime instructor has ordained that the
only pastor shall be the Bible, with her book, called
"Science and Health with Key to the Scriptures." In the
27 tower is a room devoted to her, and called "Mother's
Room," furnished with all conveniences for living, should
she wish to make it a home by day or night. Therein is
30 a portrait of her in stained glass; and an electric light,

behind an antique lamp, kept perpetually burning[1] in her   1
honor; though she has not yet visited her temple, which
was dedicated on New Year's Sunday in a somewhat novel   3
way.

There was no special sentence or prayer of consecration,
but continuous services were held from nine to four o'clock,   6
every hour and a half, so long as there were attendants;
and some people heard these exercises four times repeated.
The printed program was for some reason not followed,   9
certain hymns and psalms being omitted. There was singing by a choir and congregation. The *Pater Noster* was
repeated in the way peculiar to Christian Scientists, the   12
congregation repeating one sentence and the leader responding with its parallel interpretation by Mrs. Eddy.
Antiphonal paragraphs were read from the book of   15
Revelation and her work respectively. The sermon,
prepared by Mrs. Eddy, was well adapted for its purpose,
and read by a professional elocutionist, not an adherent of   18
the order, Mrs. Henrietta Clark Bemis, in a clear emphatic
style. The solo singer, however, was a Scientist, Miss Elsie
Lincoln; and on the platform sat Joseph Armstrong,   21
formerly of Kansas, and now the business manager of the
Publishing Society, with the other members of the Christian
Science Board of Directors — Ira O. Knapp, Edward P.   24
Bates, Stephen A. Chase, — gentlemen officially connected
with the movement. The children of believing families
collected the money for the Mother's Room, and seats were   27
especially set apart for them at the second dedicatory
service. Before one service was over and the auditors left
by the rear doors, the front vestibule and street (despite   30

---

[1] At Mrs. Eddy's request the lamp was not kept burning.

1 the snowstorm) were crowded with others, waiting for admission.

3   On the next Sunday the new order of service went into operation. There was no address of any sort, no notices, no explanation of Bible or their textbook. Judge 6 Hanna, who was a Colorado lawyer before coming into this work, presided, reading in clear, manly, and intelligent tones, the *Quarterly* Bible Lesson, which happened 9 that day to be on Jesus' miracle of loaves and fishes. Each paragraph he supplemented first with illustrative Scripture parallels, as set down for him, and then by pas-12 sages selected for him from Mrs. Eddy's book. The place was again crowded, many having remained over a week from among the thousands of adherents who had come 15 to Boston for this auspicious occasion from all parts of the country. The organ, made by Farrand & Votey in Detroit, at a cost of eleven thousand dollars, is the gift of 18 a wealthy Universalist gentleman, but was not ready for the opening. It is to fill the recess behind the spacious platform, and is described as containing pneumatic wind-21 chests throughout, and having an Æolian attachment. It is of three-manual compass, C. C. C. to C. 4, 61 notes; and pedal compass, C. C. C. to F. 30. The great organ 24 has double open diapason (stopped bass), open diapason, dulciana, viola di gamba, doppel flute, hohl flute, octave, octave quint, superoctave, and trumpet, — 61 pipes each. 27 The swell organ has bourdon, open diapason, salicional, æoline, stopped diapason, gemshorn, flute harmonique, flageolet, cornet — 3 ranks, 183, — cornopean, oboe, vox 30 humana — 61 pipes each. The choir organ, enclosed in

separate swell-box, has geigen principal, dolce, concert 1
flute, quintadena, fugara, flute d'amour, piccolo harmonique, clarinet, — 61 pipes each. The pedal organ has 3
open diapason, bourdon, lieblich gedeckt (from stop 10),
violoncello-wood, — 30 pipes each. Couplers: swell to
great; choir to great; swell to choir; swell to great oc- 6
taves, swell to great sub-octaves; choir to great sub-
octaves; swell octaves; swell to pedal; great to pedal;
choir to pedal. Mechanical accessories: swell tremulant, 9
choir tremulant, bellows signal; wind indicator. Pedal
movements: three affecting great and pedal stops, three
affecting swell and pedal stops; great to pedal reversing 12
pedal; crescendo and full organ pedal; balanced great
and choir pedal; balanced swell pedal.

Beautiful suggestions greet you in every part of this 15
unique church, which is practical as well as poetic, and
justifies the name given by Mrs. Eddy, which stands at
the head of this sketch.   J. H. W.   18

[*Boston Journal*, January 7, 1895]

CHIMES RANG SWEETLY

Much admiration was expressed by all those fortunate 21
enough to listen to the first peal of the chimes in the tower
of The First Church of Christ, Scientist, corner of Falmouth and Norway Streets, dedicated yesterday. The 24
sweet, musical tones attracted quite a throng of people,
who listened with delight.

The chimes were made by the United States Tubular 27

1 Bell Company, of Methuen, Mass., and are something
of a novelty in this country, though for some time well
3 and favorably known in the Old Country, especially in
England.

They are a substitution of tubes of drawn brass for the
6 heavy cast bells of old-fashioned chimes. They have the
advantage of great economy of space, as well as of cost, a
chime of fifteen bells occupying a space not more than
9 five by eight feet.

Where the old-fashioned chimes required a strong man
to ring them, these can be rung from an electric keyboard,
12 and even when rung by hand require but little muscular
power to manipulate them and call forth all the purity
and sweetness of their tones. The quality of tone is some-
15 thing superb, being rich and mellow. The tubes are carefully tuned, so that the harmony is perfect. They have
all the beauties of a great cathedral chime, with infinitely
18 less expense.

There is practically no limit to the uses to which these
bells may be put. They can be called into requisition in
21 theatres, concert halls, and public buildings, as they range
in all sizes, from those described down to little sets of
silver bells that might be placed on a small centre table.

[*The Republic*, Washington, D. C., February 2, 1895]   1

[Extract]

CHRISTIAN SCIENCE   3

MARY BAKER EDDY THE "MOTHER" OF THE IDEA — SHE HAS AN
   IMMENSE FOLLOWING THROUGHOUT THE UNITED STATES, AND
   A CHURCH COSTING $250,000 WAS RECENTLY BUILT IN HER   6
   HONOR AT BOSTON

"My faith has the strength to nourish trees as well as
souls," was the remark Rev. Mary Baker Eddy, the   9
"Mother" of Christian Science, made recently as she
pointed to a number of large elms that shade her delightful country home in Concord, N. H. "I had them brought   12
here in warm weather, almost as big as they are now, and
not one died." This is a remarkable statement, but it is
made by a remarkable woman, who has originated a new   15
phase of religious belief, and who numbers over one hundred thousand intelligent people among her devoted
followers.   18
    The great hold she has upon this army was demon-
strated in a very tangible and material manner recently,
when "The First Church of Christ, Scientist," erected at   21
a cost of two hundred and fifty thousand dollars, was
dedicated in Boston. This handsome edifice was paid
for before it was begun, by the voluntary contributions of   24
Christian Scientists all over the country, and a tablet im-
bedded in its wall declares that it was built as "a testimonial to our beloved teacher, Rev. Mary Baker Eddy,   27

1 Discoverer and Founder of Christian Science, author of
its textbook, 'Science and Health with Key to the Scrip-
3 tures,' president of the Massachusetts Metaphysical College, and the first pastor of this denomination."

There is usually considerable difficulty in securing suffi-
6 cient funds for the building of a new church, but such was
not the experience of Rev. Mary Baker Eddy. Money
came freely from all parts of the United States. Men,
9 women, and children contributed, some giving a pittance,
others donating large sums. When the necessary amount
was raised, the custodian of the funds was compelled to
12 refuse further contributions, in order to stop the continued
inflow of money from enthusiastic Christian Scientists.

Mrs. Eddy says she discovered Christian Science in
15 1866. She studied the Scriptures and the sciences, she
declares, in a search for the great curative Principle. She
investigated allopathy, homœopathy, and electricity, with-
18 out finding a clew; and modern philosophy gave her no
distinct statement of the Science of Mind-healing. After
careful study she became convinced that the curative
21 Principle was the Deity.

[*New York Tribune*, February 7, 1895]

[Extract]

24 Boston has just dedicated the first church of the Christian Scientists, in commemoration of the Founder of that
sect, the Rev. Mary Baker Eddy, drawing together six
27 thousand people to participate in the ceremonies, showing

that belief in that curious creed is not confined to its 1
original apostles and promulgators, but that it has pene-
trated what is called the New England mind to an un- 3
looked-for extent. In inviting the Eastern churches and
the Anglican fold to unity with Rome, the Holy Father
should not overlook the Boston sect of Christian Scientists, 6
which is rather small and new, to be sure, but is undoubtedly an interesting faith and may have a future before it,
whatever attitude Rome may assume toward it.   9

[*Journal*, Kansas City, Mo., January 10, 1895]

[Extract]

GROWTH OF A FAITH   12

Attention is directed to the progress which has been
made by what is called Christian Science by the dedication
at Boston of "The First Church of Christ, Scientist." 15
It is a most beautiful structure of gray granite, and its
builders call it their "prayer in stone," which suggests
to recollection the story of the cathedral of Amiens, whose 18
architectural construction and arrangement of statuary
and paintings made it to be called the Bible of that city.
The Frankish church was reared upon the spot where, in 21
pagan times, one bitter winter day, a Roman soldier parted
his mantle with his sword and gave half of the garment to
a naked beggar; and so was memorialized in art and 24
stone what was called the divine spirit of giving, whose un-
believing exemplar afterward became a saint. The Boston
church similarly expresses the faith of those who believe 27

1 in what they term the divine art of healing, which, to their
minds, exists as much to-day as it did when Christ healed
3 the sick.

The first church organization of this faith was founded
fifteen years ago with a membership of only twenty-six,
6 and since then the number of believers has grown with
remarkable rapidity, until now there are societies in every
part of the country. This growth, it is said, proceeds
9 more from the graveyards than from conversions from
other churches, for most of those who embrace the faith
claim to have been rescued from death miraculously under
12 the injunction to "heal the sick, cleanse the lepers, raise
the dead, cast out demons." They hold with strict fidelity
to what they conceive to be the literal teachings of the
15 Bible as expressed in its poetical and highly figurative
language.

Altogether the belief and service are well suited to
18 satisfy a taste for the mystical which, along many lines, has
shown an uncommon development in this country during
the last decade, and which is largely Oriental in its choice.
21 Such a rapid departure from long respected views as is
marked by the dedication of this church, and others of
kindred meaning, may reasonably excite wonder as to
24 how radical is to be this encroachment upon prevailing
faiths, and whether some of the pre-Christian ideas of
the Asiatics are eventually to supplant those in company
27 with which our civilization has developed.

[*Montreal Daily Herald*, Saturday, February 2, 1895]   1

[Extract]

CHRISTIAN SCIENCE   3

SKETCH OF ITS ORIGIN AND GROWTH — THE MONTREAL BRANCH

"If you would found a new faith, go to Boston," has been said by a great American writer. This is no idle 6 word, but a fact borne out by circumstances. Boston can fairly claim to be the hub of the logical universe, and an accurate census of the religious faiths which are to be 9 found there to-day would probably show a greater number of them than even Max O'Rell's famous enumeration of John Bull's creeds.   12

Christian Science, or the Principle of divine healing, is one of those movements which seek to give expression to a higher spirituality. Founded twenty-five years ago, 15 it was still practically unknown a decade since, but to-day it numbers over a quarter of a million of believers, the majority of whom are in the United States, and is rapidly 18 growing. In Canada, also, there is a large number of members. Toronto and Montreal have strong churches, comparatively, while in many towns and villages single 21 believers or little knots of them are to be found.

It was exactly one hundred years from the date of the Declaration of Independence, when on July 4, 1876, the 24 first Christian Scientist Association was organized by seven persons, of whom the foremost was Mrs. Eddy. The church was founded in April, 1879, with twenty-six 27 members, and a charter was obtained two months later.

1 Mrs. Eddy assumed the pastorship of the church during
its early years, and in 1881 was ordained, being now known
3 as the Rev. Mary Baker Eddy.

The Massachusetts Metaphysical College was founded
by Mrs. Eddy in 1881, and here she taught the principles
6 of the faith for nine years. Students came to it in hundreds from all parts of the world, and many are now pastors
or in practice. The college was closed in 1889, as Mrs.
9 Eddy felt it necessary for the interests of her religious work
to retire from active contact with the world. She now
lives in a beautiful country residence in her native State.

———————

12　　　　[*The American*, Baltimore, Md., January 14, 1895]

[Extract]

MRS. EDDY'S DISCIPLES

15　　It is not generally known that a Christian Science congregation was organized in this city about a year ago. It
now holds regular services in the parlor of the residence
18 of the pastor, at 1414 Linden Avenue. The dedication in
Boston last Sunday of the Christian Science church, called
The Mother Church, which cost over two hundred thou-
21 sand dollars, adds interest to the Baltimore organization.
There are many other church edifices in the United States
owned by Christian Scientists. Christian Science was
24 founded by Mrs. Mary Baker Eddy. The Baltimore congregation was organized at a meeting held at the present
location on February 27, 1894.

Dr. Hammond, the pastor, came to Baltimore about 1
three years ago to organize this movement. Miss Cross
came from Syracuse, N. Y., about eighteen months ago. 3
Both were under the instruction of Mrs. Mary Baker
Eddy, the Founder of the movement.

Dr. Hammond says he was converted to Christian Sci- 6
ence by being cured by Mrs. Eddy of a physical ailment
some twelve years ago, after several doctors had pronounced
his case incurable. He says they use no medicines, but 9
rely on Mind for cure, believing that disease comes from
evil and sick-producing thoughts, and that, if they can so
fill the mind with good thoughts as to leave no room there 12
for the bad, they can work a cure. He distinguishes Christian Science from the faith-cure, and added: "This Christian Science really is a return to the ideas of primitive 15
Christianity. It would take a small book to explain fully
all about it, but I may say that the fundamental idea is that
God is Mind, and we interpret the Scriptures wholly from 18
the spiritual or metaphysical standpoint. We find in this
view of the Bible the power fully developed to heal the
sick. It is not faith-cure, but it is an acknowledgment of 21
certain Christian and scientific laws, and to work a cure the
practitioner must understand these laws aright. The
patient may gain a better understanding than the Church 24
has had in the past. All churches have prayed for the cure
of disease, but they have not done so in an intelligent manner, understanding and demonstrating the Christ-healing." 27

1   [*The Reporter*, Lebanon, Ind., January 18, 1895]

[Extract]

3   DISCOVERED CHRISTIAN SCIENCE

Remarkable Career of Rev. Mary Baker Eddy, Who Has
Over One Hundred Thousand Followers

6   Rev. Mary Baker Eddy, Discoverer and Founder of
Christian Science, author of its textbook, "Science and
Health with Key to the Scriptures," president of the Mas-
9 sachusetts Metaphysical College, and first pastor of the
Christian Science denomination, is without doubt one of
the most remarkable women in America. She has within a
12 few years founded a sect that has over one hundred thousand converts, and very recently saw completed in Boston,
as a testimonial to her labors, a handsome fire-proof church
15 that cost two hundred and fifty thousand dollars and was
paid for by Christian Scientists all over the country.

   Mrs. Eddy asserts that in 1866 she became certain that
18 "all causation was Mind, and every effect a mental phenomenon." Taking her text from the Bible, she endeavored in vain to find the great curative Principle — the Deity
21 — in philosophy and schools of medicine, and she concluded that the way of salvation demonstrated by Jesus
was the power of Truth over all error, sin, sickness, and
24 death. Thus originated the divine or spiritual Science of
Mind-healing, which she termed Christian Science. She
has a palatial home in Boston and a country-seat in
27 Concord, N. H. The Christian Science Church has a

membership of four thousand, and eight hundred of the 1
members are Bostonians.

———

[*N. Y. Commercial Advertiser*, January 9, 1895]   3

The idea that Christian Science has declined in popularity is not borne out by the voluntary contribution of a
quarter of a million dollars for a memorial church for Mrs. 6
Eddy, the inventor of this cure.   The money comes from
Christian Science believers exclusively.

———

[*The Post*, Syracuse, New York, February 1, 1895]   9

DO NOT BELIEVE SHE WAS DEIFIED

CHRISTIAN SCIENTISTS OF SYRACUSE SURPRISED AT THE NEWS
ABOUT MRS. MARY BAKER EDDY, FOUNDER OF THE FAITH   12

Christian Scientists in this city, and in fact all over the
country, have been startled and greatly discomfited over
the announcements in New York papers that Mrs. Mary 15
Baker G. Eddy, the acknowledged Christian Science
Leader, has been exalted by various dignitaries of the
faith. . . .   18

It is well known that Mrs. Eddy has resigned herself
completely to the study and foundation of the faith to which
many thousands throughout the United States are now so 21
entirely devoted.   By her followers and cobelievers she is
unquestionably looked upon as having a divine mission to

1 fulfil, and as though inspired in her great task by supernatural power.

3   For the purpose of learning the feeling of Scientists in this
city toward the reported deification of Mrs. Eddy, a *Post*
reporter called upon a few of the leading members of the
6 faith yesterday and had a number of very interesting conversations upon the subject.

Mrs. D. W. Copeland of University Avenue was one of
9 the first to be seen. Mrs. Copeland is a very pleasant and
agreeable lady, ready to converse, and evidently very much
absorbed in the work to which she has given so much of
12 her attention. Mrs. Copeland claims to have been healed
a number of years ago by Christian Scientists, after she
had practically been given up by a number of well-known
15 physicians.

"And for the past eleven years," said Mrs. Copeland,
"I have not taken any medicine or drugs of any kind, and
18 yet have been perfectly well."

In regard to Mrs. Eddy, Mrs. Copeland said that she
was the Founder of the faith, but that she had never
21 claimed, nor did she believe that Mrs. Lathrop had, that
Mrs. Eddy had any power other than that which came
from God and through faith in Him and His teachings.

24   "The power of Christ has been dormant in mankind for
ages," added the speaker, "and it was Mrs. Eddy's mission
to revive it. In our labors we take Christ as an example,
27 going about doing good and healing the sick. Christ has
told us to do his work, naming as one great essential that
we have faith in him.

30   "Did you ever hear of Jesus' taking medicine himself, or

giving it to others?" inquired the speaker. "Then why 1
should we worry ourselves about sickness and disease?
If we become sick, God will care for us, and will send to 3
us those who have faith, who believe in His unlimited and
divine power. Mrs. Eddy was strictly an ardent follower
after God. She had faith in Him, and she cured herself of 6
a deathly disease through the mediation of her God. Then
she secluded herself from the world for three years and
studied and meditated over His divine Word. She delved 9
deep into the Biblical passages, and at the end of the period
came from her seclusion one of the greatest Biblical scholars of the age. Her mission was then the mission of a 12
Christian, to do good and heal the sick, and this duty she
faithfully performed. She of herself had no power. But
God has fulfilled His promises to her and to the world. 15
If you have faith, you can move mountains."

Mrs. Henrietta N. Cole is also a very prominent member
of the church. When seen yesterday she emphasized her- 18
self as being of the same theory as Mrs. Copeland. Mrs.
Cole has made a careful and searching study in the beliefs
of Scientists, and is perfectly versed in all their beliefs and 21
doctrines. She stated that man of himself has no power,
but that all comes from God. She placed no credit whatever in the reports from New York that Mrs. Eddy has 24
been accredited as having been deified. She referred the
reporter to the large volume which Mrs. Eddy had herself
written, and said that no more complete and yet concise 27
idea of her belief could be obtained than by a perusal of it.

1   [*New York Herald*, February 6, 1895]

MRS. EDDY SHOCKED

3   [By Telegraph to the *Herald*]

Concord, N. H., February 4, 1895. — The article published in the *Herald* on January 29, regarding a statement 6 made by Mrs. Laura Lathrop, pastor of the Christian Science congregation that meets every Sunday in Hodgson Hall, New York, was shown to Mrs. Mary Baker Eddy, 9 the Christian Science "Discoverer," to-day.

Mrs. Eddy preferred to prepare a written answer to the interrogatory, which she did in this letter, addressed to the 12 editor of the *Herald:* —

"A despatch is given me, calling for an interview to answer for myself, 'Am I the second Christ?'

15   "Even the question shocks me. What I am is for God to declare in His infinite mercy. As it is, I claim nothing more than what I am, the Discoverer and Founder of 18 Christian Science, and the blessing it has been to mankind which eternity enfolds.

"I think Mrs. Lathrop was not understood. If she said 21 aught with intention to be thus understood, it is not what I have taught her, and not at all as I have heard her talk.

"My books and teachings maintain but one conclusion 24 and statement of the Christ and the deification of mortals.

"Christ is individual, and one with God, in the sense of divine Love and its compound divine ideal.

27   "There was, is, and never can be but one God, one

Christ, one Jesus of Nazareth. Whoever in any age expresses most of the spirit of Truth and Love, the Principle of God's idea, has most of the spirit of Christ, of that Mind which was in Christ Jesus.

"If Christian Scientists find in my writings, teachings, and example a greater degree of this spirit than in others, they can justly declare it. But to think or speak of me in any manner as a Christ, is sacrilegious. Such a statement would not only be false, but the absolute antipode of Christian Science, and would savor more of heathenism than of my doctrines.

"MARY BAKER EDDY"

[*The Globe*, Toronto, Canada, January 12, 1895]

[Extract]

CHRISTIAN SCIENTISTS

DEDICATION TO THE FOUNDER OF THE ORDER OF A BEAUTIFUL CHURCH AT BOSTON — MANY TORONTO SCIENTISTS PRESENT

The Christian Scientists of Toronto, to the number of thirty, took part in the ceremonies at Boston last Sunday and for the day or two following, by which the members of that faith all over North America celebrated the dedication of the church constructed in the great New England capital as a testimonial to the Discoverer and Founder of Christian Science, Rev. Mary Baker Eddy.

The temple is believed to be the most nearly fire-proof church structure on the continent, the only combustible

1 material used in its construction being that used in the
doors and pews. A striking feature of the church is a
3 beautiful apartment known as the "Mother's Room,"
which is approached through a superb archway of Italian
marble set in the wall. The furnishing of the "Mother's
6 Room" is described as "particularly beautiful, and blends
harmoniously with the pale green and gold decoration of the
walls. The floor is of mosaic in elegant designs, and two
9 alcoves are separated from the apartment by rich hangings
of deep green plush, which in certain lights has a shimmer
of silver. The furniture frames are of white mahogany
12 in special designs, elaborately carved, and the upholstery
is in white and gold tapestry. A superb mantel of Mexican
onyx with gold decoration adorns the south wall, and before
15 the hearth is a large rug composed entirely of skins of the
eider-down duck, brought from the Arctic regions. Pictures and bric-a-brac everywhere suggest the tribute of
18 loving friends. One of the two alcoves is a retiring-room
and the other a lavatory in which the plumbing is all
heavily plated with gold."

---

21 [*Evening Monitor*, Concord, N. H., February 27, 1895]

AN ELEGANT SOUVENIR

Rev. Mary Baker Eddy Memorialized By a Christian
24 Science Church

Rev. Mary Baker Eddy, Discoverer of Christian Science,
has received from the members of The First Church of
27 Christ, Scientist, Boston, an invitation formally to accept

the magnificent new edifice of worship which the church 1
has just erected.

The invitation itself is one of the most chastely elegant 3
memorials ever prepared, and is a scroll of solid gold,
suitably engraved, and encased in a handsome plush
casket with white silk linings. Attached to the scroll is a 6
golden key of the church structure.

The inscription reads thus: —

"*Dear Mother:* — During the year eighteen hundred and 9
ninety-four a church edifice was erected at the intersection
of Falmouth and Norway Streets, in the city of Boston,
by the loving hands of four thousand members. This 12
edifice is built as a testimonial to Truth, as revealed by
divine Love through you to this age. You are hereby
most lovingly invited to visit and formally accept this 15
testimonial on the twentieth day of February, eighteen
hundred and ninety-five, at high noon.

"The First Church of Christ, Scientist, at Boston, Mass. 18
"By EDWARD P. BATES,
"CAROLINE S. BATES

"To the Reverend Mary Baker Eddy, 21
"Boston, January 6th, 1895"

———

[*People and Patriot*, Concord, N. H., February 27, 1895]

MAGNIFICENT TESTIMONIAL 24

Members of The First Church of Christ, Scientist, at
Boston, have forwarded to Mrs. Mary Baker Eddy of

1 this city, the Founder of Christian Science, a testimonial which is probably one of the most magnificent examples 3 of the goldsmith's art ever wrought in this country. It is in the form of a gold scroll, twenty-six inches long, nine inches wide, and an eighth of an inch thick.

6   It bears upon its face the following inscription, cut in script letters: —

"Dear Mother: — During the year 1894 a church edi- 9 fice was erected at the intersection of Falmouth and Norway Streets, in the city of Boston, by the loving hands of four thousand members. This edifice is built as a testi- 12 monial to Truth, as revealed by divine Love through you to this age. You are hereby most lovingly invited to visit and formally accept this testimonial on the 20th day of 15 February, 1895, at high noon.

"The First Church of Christ, Scientist, at Boston, Mass.

"By EDWARD P. BATES,

18   "CAROLINE S. BATES

"To the Rev. Mary Baker Eddy,

"Boston, January 6, 1895"

21   Attached by a white ribbon to the scroll is a gold key to the church door.

The testimonial is encased in a white satin-lined box 24 of rich green velvet.

The scroll is on exhibition in the window of J. C. Derby's jewelry store.

[*The Union Signal*, Chicago]   1

[Extract]

THE NEW WOMAN AND THE NEW CHURCH   3

The dedication, in Boston, of a Christian Science temple costing over two hundred thousand dollars, and for which the money was all paid in so that no debt had to be taken 6 care of on dedication day, is a notable event. While we are not, and never have been, devotees of Christian Science, it becomes us as students of public questions not to ignore 9 a movement which, starting fifteen years ago, has already gained to itself adherents in every part of the civilized world, for it is a significant fact that one cannot take up 12 a daily paper in town or village — to say nothing of cities — without seeing notices of Christian Science meetings, and in most instances they are held at "headquarters."   15

We believe there are two reasons for this remarkable development, which has shown a vitality so unexpected. The first is that a revolt was inevitable from the crass 18 materialism of the cruder science that had taken posses- sion of men's minds, for as a wicked but witty writer has said, "If there were no God, we should be obliged to in- 21 vent one." There is something in the constitution of man that requires the religious sentiment as much as his lungs call for breath; indeed, the breath of his soul is a 24 belief in God.

But when Christian Science arose, the thought of the world's scientific leaders had become materialistically 27 "lopsided," and this condition can never long continue.

1 There must be a righting-up of the mind as surely as of a ship when under stress of storm it is ready to capsize. The 3 pendulum that has swung to one extreme will surely find the other. The religious sentiment in women is so strong that the revolt was headed by them; this was inevitable 6 in the nature of the case. It began in the most intellectual city of the freest country in the world — that is to say, it sought the line of least resistance. Boston is emphati- 9 cally the women's paradise, — numerically, socially, indeed every way. Here they have the largest individuality, the most recognition, the widest outlook. Mrs. Eddy we 12 have never seen; her book has many a time been sent us by interested friends, and out of respect to them we have fairly broken our mental teeth over its granitic peb- 15 bles. That we could not understand it might be rather to the credit of the book than otherwise. On this subject we have no opinion to pronounce, but simply state the 18 fact.

We do not, therefore, speak of the system it sets forth, either to praise or blame, but this much is true: the spirit 21 of Christian Science ideas has caused an army of well-meaning people to believe in God and the power of faith, who did not believe in them before. It has made a myriad of 24 women more thoughtful and devout; it has brought a hopeful spirit into the homes of unnumbered invalids. The belief that "thoughts are things," that the invisible 27 is the only real world, that we are here to be trained into harmony with the laws of God, and that what we are here determines where we shall be hereafter — all these ideas 30 are Christian.

The chimes on the Christian Science temple in Boston 1
played "All hail the power of Jesus' name," on the morning of the dedication. We did not attend, but we learn 3
that the name of Christ is nowhere spoken with more
reverence than it was during those services, and that he
is set forth as the power of God for righteousness and the 6
express image of God for love.

———————

[*The New Century*, Boston, February, 1895]

ONE POINT OF VIEW — THE NEW WOMAN   9

We all know her — she is simply the woman of the past
with an added grace — a newer charm. Some of her
dearest ones call her "selfish" because she thinks so much 12
of herself she spends her whole time helping others. She
represents the composite beauty, sweetness, and nobility
of all those who scorn self for the sake of love and her 15
handmaiden duty — of all those who seek the brightness
of truth not as the moth to be destroyed thereby, but as
the lark who soars and sings to the great sun. She is of 18
those who have so much to give they want no time to take,
and their name is legion. She is as full of beautiful possibilities as a perfect harp, and she realizes that all the har- 21
monies of the universe are in herself, while her own soul
plays upon magic strings the unwritten anthems of love.
She is the apostle of the true, the beautiful, the good, com- 24
missioned to complete all that the twelve have left undone.
Hers is the mission of missions — the highest of all — to

1 make the body not the prison, but the palace of the soul, with the brain for its great white throne.

3   When she comes like the south wind into the cold haunts of sin and sorrow, her words are smiles and her smiles are the sunlight which heals the stricken soul. Her hand is

6 tender — but steel tempered with holy resolve, and as one whom her love had glorified once said — she is soft and gentle, but you could no more turn her from her

9 course than winter could stop the coming of spring. She has long learned with patience, and to-day she knows many things dear to the soul far better than her teachers.

12 In olden times the Jews claimed to be the conservators of the world's morals — they treated woman as a chattel, and said that because she was created after man, she was

15 created solely for man. Too many still are Jews who never called Abraham "Father," while the Jews themselves have long acknowledged woman as man's proper

18 helpmeet. In those days women had few lawful claims and no one to urge them. True, there were Miriam and Esther, but they sang and sacrificed for their people, not

21 for their sex.

   To-day there are ten thousand Esthers, and Miriams by the million, who sing best by singing most for their

24 own sex. They are demanding the right to help make the laws, or at least to help enforce the laws upon which depends the welfare of their husbands, their chil-

27 dren, and themselves. Why should our selfish self longer remain deaf to their cry? The date is no longer B. C. Might no longer makes right, and in this fair land at least

30 fear has ceased to kiss the iron heel of wrong. Why then

should we continue to demand woman's love and woman's 1
help while we recklessly promise as lover and candidate
what we never fulfil as husband and office-holder? In 3
our secret heart our better self is shamed and dishonored,
and appeals from Philip drunk to Philip sober, but has
not yet the moral strength and courage to prosecute the 6
appeal. But the east is rosy, and the sunlight cannot long
be delayed. Woman must not and will not be disheartened by a thousand denials or a million of broken pledges. 9
With the assurance of faith she prays, with the certainty
of inspiration she works, and with the patience of genius
she waits. At last she is becoming "as fair as the morn, 12
as bright as the sun, and as terrible as an army with ban-
ners" to those who march under the black flag of oppression and wield the ruthless sword of injustice. 15
   In olden times it was the Amazons who conquered the
invincibles, and we must look now to their daughters to
overcome our own allied armies of evil and to save us from 18
ourselves. She must and will succeed, for as David sang
— "God shall help her, and that right early." When we
try to praise her later works it is as if we would pour 21
incense upon the rose. It is the proudest boast of many
of us that we are "bound to her by bonds dearer than freedom," and that we live in the reflected royalty which 24
shines from her brow. We rejoice with her that at last
we begin to know what John on Patmos meant — "And
there appeared a great wonder in heaven, a woman clothed 27
with the sun, and the moon under her feet, and upon her
head a crown of twelve stars." She brought to warring
men the Prince of Peace, and he, departing, left his scepter 30

1 not in her hand, but in her soul. "The time of times" is near when "the new woman" shall subdue the whole 3 earth with the weapons of peace. Then shall wrong be robbed of her bitterness and ingratitude of her sting, revenge shall clasp hands with pity, and love shall dwell 6 in the tents of hate; while side by side, equal partners in all that is worth living for, shall stand the new man with the new woman.

9   [*The Christian Science Journal*, January, 1895]
[Extract]

THE MOTHER CHURCH

12 The Mother Church edifice — The First Church of Christ, Scientist, in Boston, is erected. The close of the year, Anno Domini 1894, witnessed the completion of 15 "our prayer in stone," all predictions and prognostications to the contrary notwithstanding.

Of the significance of this achievement we shall not 18 undertake to speak in this article. It can be better felt than expressed. All who are awake thereto have some measure of understanding of what it means. But only 21 the future will tell the story of its mighty meaning or unfold it to the comprehension of mankind. It is enough for us now to know that all obstacles to its completion have 24 been met and overcome, and that our temple is completed as God intended it should be.

This achievement is the result of long years of untiring, 27 unselfish, and zealous effort on the part of our beloved teacher and Leader, the Reverend Mary Baker Eddy, the Discoverer and Founder of Christian Science, who

nearly thirty years ago began to lay the foundation of 1
this temple, and whose devotion and consecration to God
and humanity during the intervening years have made 3
its erection possible.

Those who now, in part, understand her mission, turn
their hearts in gratitude to her for her great work, and 6
those who do not understand it will, in the fulness of time,
see and acknowledge it. In the measure in which she has
unfolded and demonstrated divine Love, and built up in 9
human consciousness a better and higher conception of
God as Life, Truth, and Love, — as the divine Principle
of all things which really exist, — and in the degree in 12
which she has demonstrated the system of healing of Jesus
and the apostles, surely she, as the one chosen of God to
this end, is entitled to the gratitude and love of all who 15
desire a better and grander humanity, and who believe
it to be possible to establish the kingdom of heaven upon
earth in accordance with the prayer and teachings of 18
Jesus Christ.

[*Concord Evening Monitor*, March 23, 1895]

TESTIMONIAL AND GIFT   21

To Rev. Mary Baker Eddy, from The First Church of
Christ, Scientist, in Boston

Rev. Mary Baker Eddy received Friday, from the Chris- 24
tian Science Board of Directors, Boston, a beautiful and
unique testimonial of the appreciation of her labors and
loving generosity in the Cause of their common faith. It 27
was a facsimile of the corner-stone of the new church of

1 the Christian Scientists, just completed, being of granite, about six inches in each dimension, and contains a solid
3 gold box, upon the cover of which is this inscription: —

"To our Beloved Teacher, the Reverend Mary Baker Eddy, Discoverer and Founder of Christian Science, from
6 her affectionate Students, the Christian Science Board of Directors."

On the under side of the cover are the facsimile sig-
9 natures of the Directors, — Ira O. Knapp, William B. Johnson, Joseph Armstrong, and Stephen A. Chase, with the date, "1895." The beautiful souvenir is en-
12 cased in an elegant plush box.

Accompanying the stone testimonial was the following address from the Board of Directors: —

15   Boston, March 20, 1895
To the Reverend Mary Baker Eddy, our Beloved Teacher and Leader: — We are happy to announce to you
18 the completion of The First Church of Christ, Scientist, in Boston.

In behalf of your loving students and all contributors
21 wherever they may be, we hereby present this church to you as a testimonial of love and gratitude for your labors and loving sacrifice, as the Discoverer and Founder of
24 Christian Science, and the author of its textbook, "Science and Health with Key to the Scriptures."

We therefore respectfully extend to you the invitation
27 to become the permanent pastor of this church, in connection with the Bible and the book alluded to above, which you have already ordained as our pastor. And we

most cordially invite you to be present and take charge 1
of any services that may be held therein. We especially
desire you to be present on the twenty-fourth day of March, 3
eighteen hundred and ninety-five, to accept this offering,
with our humble benediction.

Lovingly yours, 6

IRA O. KNAPP, JOSEPH ARMSTRONG,
WILLIAM B. JOHNSON, STEPHEN A. CHASE,
The Christian Science Board of Directors 9

Rev. Mrs. Eddy's Reply

Beloved Directors and Brethren: — For your costly offering, and kind call to the pastorate of "The First Church 12
of Christ, Scientist," in Boston — accept my profound
thanks. But permit me, respectfully, to decline their acceptance, while I fully appreciate your kind intentions. 15
If it will comfort you in the least, make me your *Pastor
Emeritus,* nominally. Through my book, your textbook,
I already speak to you each Sunday. You ask too much 18
when asking me to accept your grand church edifice. I
have more of earth now, than I desire, and less of heaven;
so pardon my refusal of that as a material offering. More 21
effectual than the forum are our states of mind, to bless
mankind. This wish stops not with my pen — God give
you grace. As our church's tall tower detains the sun, 24
so may luminous lines from your lives linger, a legacy to
our race.

MARY BAKER EDDY 27

March 25, 1895

1 LIST OF LEADING NEWSPAPERS WHOSE ARTICLES
ARE OMITTED

3 From Canada to New Orleans, and from the Atlantic
to the Pacific ocean, the author has received leading newspapers with uniformly kind and interesting articles on
6 the dedication of The Mother Church. They were, however, too voluminous for these pages. To those which are
copied she can append only a few of the names of other
9 prominent newspapers whose articles are reluctantly
omitted.

EASTERN STATES

12 *Advertiser,* Calais, Me.
Advertiser, Boston, Mass.
Farmer, Bridgeport, Conn.
15 *Independent,* Rockland, Mass.
Kennebec Journal, Augusta, Me.
News, New Haven, Conn.
18 *News,* Newport, R. I.
Post, Boston, Mass.
Post, Hartford, Conn.
21 *Republican,* Springfield, Mass.
Sentinel, Eastport, Me.
Sun, Attleboro, Mass.

24 MIDDLE STATES

Advertiser, New York City.
Bulletin, Auburn, N. Y.
27 *Daily,* York, Pa.
Evening Reporter, Lebanon, Pa.
Farmer, Bridgeport, N. Y.
30 *Herald,* Rochester, N. Y.
Independent, Harrisburg, Pa.
Inquirer, Philadelphia, Pa.

Clippings from Newspapers 89

1   *News-Tribune*, Duluth, Minn.
       Pioneer-Press, St. Paul, Minn.
3   *Post-Intelligencer*, Seattle, Wash.
       Salt Lake Herald, Salt Lake City, Utah.
       Sentinel, Indianapolis, Ind.
6   *Sentinel*, Milwaukee, Wis.
       Star, Kansas City, Mo.
       Telegram, Portland, Ore.
9   *Times*, Chicago, Ill.
       Times, Minneapolis, Minn.
       Tribune, Minneapolis, Minn.
12   *Tribune*, Salt Lake City, Utah.

       Free Press, London, Can.

Rudimental
Divine
Science

Rudimental Divine Science

by MARY BAKER EDDY
*Discoverer and Founder of Christian Science
and Author of Science and Health
with Key to the Scriptures*

Marcas Registradas

Published by The First Church of Christ, Scientist, in Boston, Massachusetts, U.S.A.

The facsimile of the signature of Mary Baker Eddy and the design of the Cross and Crown seal are trademarks of The Christian Science Board of Directors, registered in the United States and other countries.

This little book
is
tenderly and respectfully dedicated
to all
loyal students, working and waiting
for the establishment of the
Science of Mind-healing

MARY BAKER EDDY

Contents

Contents

Rudimental Divine Science

How would you define Christian Science? 1

AS the law of God, the law of good, interpreting and demonstrating the divine Principle and rule of universal harmony. 3

What is the Principle of Christian Science?

It is God, the Supreme Being, infinite and immortal 6 Mind, the Soul of man and the universe. It is our Father which is in heaven. It is substance, Spirit, Life, Truth, and Love, — these are the deific Principle. 9

Do you mean by this that God is a person?

The word *person* affords a large margin for misapprehension, as well as definition. In French the equivalent 12 word is *personne*. In Spanish, Italian, and Latin, it is *persona*. The Latin verb *personare* is compounded of the prefix *per* (through) and *sonare* (to sound). 15

In law, Blackstone applies the word *personal* to *bodily presence*, in distinction from one's appearance (in court, for example) by deputy or proxy. 18

1 Other definitions of *person,* as given by Webster, are "a living soul; a self-conscious being; a moral agent; 3 especially, a living human being, a corporeal man, woman, or child; an individual of the human race." He adds, that among Trinitarian Christians the word stands for one 6 of the three subjects, or agents, constituting the Godhead.

In Christian Science we learn that God is definitely individual, and not a *person,* as that word is used by the best 9 authorities, if our lexicographers are right in defining *person* as especially a finite *human being;* but God is personal, if by *person* is meant infinite Spirit.

12 We do not conceive rightly of God, if we think of Him as less than infinite. The human person is finite; and therefore I prefer to retain the proper sense of Deity by 15 using the phrase *an individual* God, rather than *a personal* God; for there is and can be but one infinite individual Spirit, whom mortals have named God.

18 Science defines the individuality of God as supreme good, Life, Truth, Love. This term enlarges our sense of Deity, takes away the trammels assigned to God by 21 finite thought, and introduces us to higher definitions.

Is healing the sick the whole of Science?

Healing physical sickness is the smallest part of Chris-24 tian Science. It is only the bugle-call to thought and action, in the higher range of infinite goodness. The emphatic purpose of Christian Science is the healing of 27 sin; and this task, sometimes, may be harder than the

cure of disease; because, while mortals love to sin, they 1
do not love to be sick. Hence their comparative acquiescence in your endeavors to heal them of bodily ills, and 3
their obstinate resistance to all efforts to save them from
sin through Christ, spiritual Truth and Love, which
redeem them, and become their Saviour, through the 6
flesh, from the flesh, — the material world and evil.

This Life, Truth, and Love — this trinity of good — was
individualized, to the perception of mortal sense, in the 9
man Jesus. His history is emphatic in our hearts, and it
lives more because of his spiritual than his physical healing.
His example is, to Christian Scientists, what the models 12
of the masters in music and painting are to artists.

Genuine Christian Scientists will no more deviate morally from that divine digest of Science called the Sermon 15
on the Mount, than they will manipulate invalids, prescribe
drugs, or deny God. Jesus' healing was spiritual in its
nature, method, and design. He wrought the cure of 18
disease through the divine Mind, which gives all true
volition, impulse, and action; and destroys the mental
error made manifest physically, and establishes the oppo- 21
site manifestation of Truth upon the body in harmony
and health.

By the individuality of God, do you mean that God has 24
a finite form?

No. I mean the infinite and divine Principle of all
being, the ever-present I AM, filling all space, including 27

1 in itself all Mind, the one Father-Mother God. Life,
Truth, and Love are this trinity in unity, and their uni-
3 verse is spiritual, peopled with perfect beings, harmonious
and eternal, of which our material universe and men are
the counterfeits.

6 *Is God the Principle of all science, or only of Divine or
Christian Science?*

Science is Mind manifested. It is not material; neither
9 is it of human origin.

All true Science represents a moral and spiritual force,
which holds the earth in its orbit. This force is Spirit,
12 that can "bind the sweet influences of the Pleiades," and
"loose the bands of Orion."

There is no material science, if by that term you mean
15 material intelligence. God is infinite Mind, hence there
is no other Mind. Good is Mind, but evil is not Mind.
Good is not in evil, but in God only. Spirit is not in matter,
18 but in Spirit only. Law is not in matter, but in Mind only.

Is there no matter?

All is Mind. According to the Scriptures and Christian
21 Science, all is God, and there is naught beside Him. "God
is Spirit;" and we can only learn and love Him through
His spirit, which brings out the fruits of Spirit and ex-
24 tinguishes forever the works of darkness by His marvellous light.

The five material senses testify to the existence of

matter. The spiritual senses afford no such evidence, 1
but deny the testimony of the material senses. Which
testimony is correct? The Bible says: "Let God be 3
true, and every man a liar." If, as the Scriptures imply,
God is All-in-all, then all must be Mind, since God is
Mind. Therefore in divine Science there is no material 6
mortal man, for man is spiritual and eternal, he being
made in the image of Spirit, or God.

There is no material sense. Matter is inert, inanimate, 9
and sensationless, — considered apart from Mind. Lives
there a man who has ever found Soul in the body or in
matter, who has ever seen spiritual substance with the 12
eye, who has found sight in matter, hearing in the material
ear, or intelligence in non-intelligence? If there is any
such thing as matter, it must be either mind which is 15
called matter, or matter without Mind.

Matter without Mind is a moral impossibility. Mind
in matter is pantheism. Soul is the only real conscious- 18
ness which cognizes being. The body does not see, hear,
smell, or taste. Human belief says that it does; but
destroy this belief of seeing with the eye, and we could 21
not see materially; and so it is with each of the physical
senses.

Accepting the verdict of these material senses, we should 24
believe man and the universe to be the football of chance
and sinking into oblivion. Destroy the five senses as
organized matter, and you must either become non-exist- 27
ent, or exist in Mind only; and this latter conclusion is

1 the simple solution of the problem of being, and leads to
the equal inference that there is no matter.

3   *The sweet sounds and glories of earth and sky, assum-*
ing manifold forms and colors, — are they not tangible and
material?

6   As Mind they are real, but not as matter. All beauty
and goodness are in and of Mind, emanating from God;
but when we change the nature of beauty and goodness
9 from Mind to matter, the beauty is marred, through a
false conception, and, to the material senses, evil takes
the place of good.

12   Has not the truth in Christian Science met a response
from Prof. S. P. Langley, the young American astronomer?
He says that "color is in *us,*" not "in the rose;" and he
15 adds that this is not "any metaphysical subtlety," but a
fact "almost universally accepted, within the *last few*
years, by physicists."

18   *Is not the basis of Mind-healing a destruction of the evi-*
dence of the material senses, and restoration of the true
evidence of spiritual sense?

21   It is, so far as you perceive and understand this predicate and postulate of Mind-healing; but the Science of
Mind-healing is best understood in practical demonstra-
24 tion. The proof of what you apprehend, in the simplest
definite and absolute form of healing, can alone answer
this question of how much you understand of Christian

Science Mind-healing. Not that all healing is Science, 1
by any means; but that the simplest case, healed in Science,
is as demonstrably scientific, in a small degree, as the most 3
difficult case so treated.

The infinite and subtler conceptions and consistencies
of Christian Science are set forth in my work Science and 6
Health.

Is man material or spiritual?

In Science, man is the manifest reflection of God, per- 9
fect and immortal Mind. He is the likeness of God; and
His likeness would be lost if inverted or perverted.

According to the evidence of the so-called physical 12
senses, man is material, fallen, sick, depraved, mortal.
Science and spiritual sense contradict this, and they afford
the only true evidence of the being of God and man, the 15
material evidence being wholly false.

Jesus said of personal evil, that "the truth abode not
in him," because there is no material sense. Matter, as 18
matter, has neither sensation nor personal intelligence.
As a pretension to be Mind, matter is a lie, and "the
father of lies;" Mind is not in matter, and Spirit cannot 21
originate its opposite, named matter.

According to divine Science, Spirit no more changes its
species, by evolving matter from Spirit, than natural 24
science, so-called, or material laws, bring about altera-
tion of species by transforming minerals into vegetables
or plants into animals, — thus confusing and confounding 27

1 the three great kingdoms. No rock brings forth an apple;
no pine-tree produces a mammal or provides breast-milk
3 for babes.

To sense, the lion of to-day is the lion of six thousand
years ago; but in Science, Spirit sends forth its own harm-
6 less likeness.

*How should I undertake to demonstrate Christian Science
in healing the sick?*

9   As I have given you only an epitome of the Principle,
so I can give you here nothing but an outline of the practice. Be honest, be true to thyself, and true to others;
12 then it follows thou wilt be strong in God, the eternal
good. Heal through Truth and Love; there is no other
healer.

15   In all moral revolutions, from a lower to a higher condition of thought and action, Truth is in the minority and
error has the majority. It is not otherwise in the field
18 of Mind-healing. The man who calls himself a Christian
Scientist, yet is false to God and man, is also uttering
falsehood about good. This falsity shuts against him the
21 Truth and the Principle of Science, but opens a way
whereby, through will-power, sense may say the unchristian practitioner can heal; but Science shows that he makes
24 morally worse the invalid whom he is supposed to cure.

By this I mean that mortal mind should not be falsely
impregnated. If by such lower means the health is seem-
27 ingly restored, the restoration is not lasting, and the patient

is liable to a relapse, — "The last state of that man is worse than the first."

The teacher of Mind-healing who is not a Christian, in the highest sense, is constantly sowing the seeds of discord and disease. Even the truth he speaks is more or less blended with error; and this error will spring up in the mind of his pupil. The pupil's imperfect knowledge will lead to weakness in practice, and he will be a poor practitioner, if not a malpractitioner.

The basis of malpractice is in erring human will, and this will is an outcome of what I call *mortal mind*, — a false and temporal sense of Truth, Life, and Love. To heal, in Christian Science, is to base your practice on immortal Mind, the divine Principle of man's being; and this requires a preparation of the heart and an answer of the lips from the Lord.

The Science of healing is the Truth of healing. If one is untruthful, his mental state weighs against his healing power; and similar effects come from pride, envy, lust, and all fleshly vices.

The spiritual power of a scientific, right thought, without a direct effort, an audible or even a mental argument, has oftentimes healed inveterate diseases.

The thoughts of the practitioner should be imbued with a clear conviction of the omnipotence and omnipresence of God; that He is All, and that there can be none beside Him; that God is good, and the producer only of good; and hence, that whatever militates against health, har-

1 mony, or holiness, is an unjust usurper of the throne of
the controller of all mankind. Note this, that if you have
3 power in error, you forfeit the power that Truth bestows,
and its salutary influence on yourself and others.

You must feel and know that God alone governs man;
6 that His government is harmonious; that He is too pure
to behold iniquity, and divides His power with nothing
evil or material; that material laws are only human be-
9 liefs, which govern mortals wrongfully. These beliefs arise
from the subjective states of thought, producing the beliefs of a mortal material universe, — so-called, and of
12 material disease and mortality. Mortal ills are but errors
of thought, — diseases of mortal mind, and not of matter;
for matter cannot feel, see, or report pain or disease.

15   Disease is a thing of thought manifested on the body;
and fear is the procurator of the thought which causes
sickness and suffering. Remove this fear by the true
18 sense that God is Love, — and that Love punishes nothing
but sin, — and the patient can then look up to the loving
God, and know that He afflicteth not willingly the children
21 of men, who are punished because of disobedience to His
spiritual law. His law of Truth, when obeyed, removes
every erroneous physical and mental state. The belief
24 that matter can master Mind, and make you ill, is an
error which Truth will destroy.

You must learn to acknowledge God in all His ways.
27 It is only a lack of understanding of the allness of God,
which leads you to believe in the existence of matter, or

that matter can frame its own conditions, contrary to the 1
law of Spirit.

Sickness is the schoolmaster, leading you to Christ; 3
first to faith in Christ; next to belief in God as omnipotent; and finally to the *understanding* of God and man
in Christian Science, whereby you learn that God is good, 6
and in Science man is His likeness, the forever reflection of
goodness. Therefore good is one and All.

This brings forward the next proposition in Christian 9
Science, — namely, that there are no sickness, sin, and
death in the divine Mind. What seem to be disease, vice,
and mortality are illusions of the physical senses. These 12
illusions are not real, but unreal. Health is the consciousness of the unreality of pain and disease; or, rather, the
absolute consciousness of harmony and of nothing else. 15
In a moment you may awake from a night-dream; just
so you can awake from the dream of sickness; but the
demonstration of the Science of Mind-healing by no means 18
rests on the strength of human belief. This demonstration is based on a true understanding of God and divine
Science, which takes away every human belief, and, 21
through the illumination of spiritual understanding, reveals the all-power and ever-presence of good, whence
emanate health, harmony, and Life eternal.   24

The lecturer, teacher, or healer who is indeed a Christian
Scientist, never introduces the subject of human anatomy;
never depicts the muscular, vascular, or nervous opera- 27
tions of the human frame. He never talks about the

1 structure of the material body. He never lays his hands
on the patient, nor manipulates the parts of the body sup-
3 posed to be ailing. Above all, he keeps unbroken the Ten
Commandments, and practises Christ's Sermon on the
Mount.

6   Wrong thoughts and methods strengthen the sense of
disease, instead of cure it; or else quiet the fear of the
sick on false grounds, encouraging them in the belief of
9 error until they hold stronger than before the belief that
they are first made sick by matter, and then restored
through its agency. This fosters infidelity, and is mental
12 quackery, that denies the Principle of Mind-healing. If
the sick are aided in this mistaken fashion, their ailments
will return, and be more stubborn because the relief is
15 unchristian and unscientific.

Christian Science erases from the minds of invalids
their mistaken belief that they live in or because of matter,
18 or that a so-called material organism controls the health
or existence of mankind, and induces rest in God, divine
Love, as caring for all the conditions requisite for the well-
21 being of man. As power divine is the healer, why should
mortals concern themselves with the chemistry of food?
Jesus said: "Take no thought what ye shall eat."
24   The practitioner should also endeavor to free the minds
of the healthy from any sense of subordination to their
bodies, and teach them that the divine Mind, not material
27 law, maintains human health and life.

A Christian Scientist knows that, in Science, disease

is unreal; that Mind is not in matter; that Life is God, 1
good; hence Life is not functional, and is neither matter
nor mortal mind; knows that pantheism and theosophy 3
are not Science. Whatever saps, with human belief,
this basis of Christian Science, renders it impossible to
demonstrate the Principle of this Science, even in the 6
smallest degree.

A mortal and material body is not the actual individuality
of man made in the divine and spiritual image of God. 9
The material body is not the likeness of Spirit; hence it
is not the truth of being, but the likeness of error — the
human belief which saith there is more than one God, — 12
there is more than one Life and one Mind.

In Deuteronomy (iv. 35) we read: "The Lord, He is
God; there is none else beside Him." In John (iv. 24) 15
we may read: "God is Spirit." These propositions, understood in their Science, elucidate my meaning.

When treating a patient, it is not Science to treat every 18
organ in the body. To aver that harmony is the real and
discord is the unreal, and then give special attention to
what according to their own belief is diseased, is scientific; 21
and if the *healer realizes* the truth, it will free his patient.

*What are the means and methods of trustworthy Christian
Scientists?*   24

These people should not be expected, more than others,
to give all their time to Christian Science work, receiving
no wages in return, but left to be fed, clothed, and sheltered 27

1 by charity. Neither can they serve two masters, giving
only a portion of their time to God, and still be Christian
3 Scientists. They must give Him all their services, and
"owe no man." To do this, they must at present ask a
suitable price for their services, and then *conscientiously*
6 *earn their wages,* strictly practising Divine Science, and
healing the sick.

The author never sought charitable support, but gave
9 fully seven-eighths of her time without remuneration, except the bliss of doing good. The only pay taken for her
labors was from classes, and often those were put off for
12 months, in order to do gratuitous work. She has never
taught a Primary class without several, and sometimes
seventeen, free students in it; and has endeavored to take
15 the full price of tuition only from those who were able to
pay. The student who pays must of necessity do better
than he who does not pay, and yet will expect and require
18 others to pay him. No discount on tuition was made on
higher classes, because their first classes furnished students
with the means of paying for their tuition in the higher
21 instruction, and of doing charity work besides. If the
Primary students are still impecunious, it is their own
fault, and this ill-success of itself leaves them unprepared
24 to enter higher classes.

People are being healed by means of my instructions,
both in and out of class. Many students, who have
27 passed through a regular course of instruction from me,
have been invalids and were healed in the class; but ex-

perience has shown that this defrauds the scholar, though ₁ it heals the sick.

It is seldom that a student, if healed in a class, has left ₃ it understanding sufficiently the Science of healing to immediately enter upon its practice. Why? Because the glad surprise of suddenly regained health is a shock to ₆ the mind; and this holds and satisfies the thought with exuberant joy.

This renders the mind less inquisitive, plastic, and tract- ₉ able; and deep systematic thinking is impracticable until this impulse subsides.

This was the principal reason for advising diseased ₁₂ people not to enter a class. Few were taken besides invalids for students, until there were enough practitioners to fill in the best possible manner the department of healing. ₁₅ Teaching and healing should have separate departments, and these should be fortified on all sides with suitable and thorough guardianship and grace. ₁₈

Only a very limited number of students can advantageously enter a class, grapple with this subject, and well assimilate what has been taught them. It is impossible ₂₁ to teach thorough Christian Science to promiscuous and large assemblies, or to persons who cannot be addressed individually, so that the mind of the pupil may be dissected ₂₄ more critically than the body of a subject laid bare for anatomical examination. Public lectures cannot be such lessons in Christian Science as are required to empty and ₂₇ to fill anew the individual mind.

1   If publicity and material control are the motives for
teaching, then public lectures can take the place of private
3 lessons; but the former can never give a thorough knowledge
of Christian Science, and a Christian Scientist will never
undertake to fit students for practice by such means. Lec-
6 tures in public are needed, but they must be subordinate
to thorough class instruction in any branch of education.

None with an imperfect sense of the spiritual significa-
9 tion of the Bible, and its scientific relation to Mind-
healing, should attempt overmuch in their translation of
the Scriptures into the "new tongue;" but I see that
12 some novices, in the truth of Science, and some impostors
are committing this error.

Is there more than one school of scientific healing?

15   In reality there is, and can be, but one school of the
Science of Mind-healing. Any departure from Science is
an irreparable loss of Science. Whatever is said and
18 written correctly on this Science originates from the Principle and practice laid down in Science and Health, a work
which I published in 1875. This was the first book, re-
21 corded in history, which elucidates a pathological Science
purely mental.

Minor shades of difference in Mind-healing have origi-
24 nated with certain opposing factions, springing up among
unchristian students, who, fusing with a class of aspirants
which snatch at whatever is progressive, call it their first-
27 fruits, or else *post mortem* evidence.

A slight divergence is fatal in Science. Like certain 1
Jews whom St. Paul had hoped to convert from mere
motives of self-aggrandizement to the love of Christ, these 3
so-called schools are clogging the wheels of progress by
blinding the people to the true character of Christian
Science, — its moral power, and its divine efficacy to 6
heal.

The true understanding of Christian Science Mind-
healing never originated in pride, rivalry, or the deification 9
of self. The Discoverer of this Science could tell you of
timidity, of self-distrust, of friendlessness, toil, agonies, and
victories, under which she needed miraculous vision to 12
sustain her, when taking the first footsteps in this
Science.

The ways of Christianity have not changed. Meek- 15
ness, selflessness, and love are the paths of His testimony
and the footsteps of His flock.

No
and
Yes

No
and
Yes

by MARY BAKER EDDY
Discoverer and Founder of Christian Science
and Author of Science and Health
with Key to the Scriptures

Marcas Registradas

Published by The First Church of Christ, Scientist, in Boston, Massachusetts, U.S.A.

The facsimile of the signature of Mary Baker Eddy
and the design of the Cross and Crown seal are
trademarks of The Christian Science Board of Directors,
registered in the United States and other countries.

Preface

IT was the purpose of each edition of this pamphlet to benefit no favored class, but, according to the apostle's admonition, to "reprove, rebuke, exhort," and with the power and self-sacrificing spirit of Love to correct involuntary as well as voluntary error.

By a modification of the language, the import of this edition is, we trust, transparent to the hearts of all conscientious laborers in the realm of Mind-healing. To those who are athirst for the life-giving waters of a true divinity, it saith tenderly, "Come and drink;" and if you are babes in Christ, leave the meat and take the unadulterated milk of the Word, until you grow to apprehend the pure spirituality of Truth.

MARY BAKER EDDY

Contents

Contents

No and Yes

Introduction

TO kindle in all minds a common sentiment of regard 1
for the spiritual idea emanating from the infinite, is
a most needful work; but this must be done gradually, for 3
Truth is as "the still, small voice," which comes to our
recognition only as our natures are changed by its silent
influence. 6

Small streams are noisy and rush precipitately; and
babbling brooks fill the rivers till they rise in floods, de-
molishing bridges and overwhelming cities. So men, when 9
thrilled by a new idea, are sometimes impatient; and,
when public sentiment is aroused, are liable to be borne
on by the current of feeling. They should then turn tem- 12
porarily from the tumult, for the silent cultivation of the
true idea and the quiet practice of its virtues. When
the noise and stir of contending sentiments cease, and 15
the flames die away on the mount of revelation, we can
read more clearly the tablets of Truth.

The theology and medicine of Jesus were one, — in the 18
divine oneness of the trinity, Life, Truth, and Love, which
healed the sick and cleansed the sinful. This trinity in
unity, correcting the individual thought, is the only Mind- 21

1 healing I vindicate; and on its standard have emblazoned
that crystallized expression, CHRISTIAN SCIENCE.

3 A spurious and hydra-headed mind-healing is naturally
glared at by the pulpit, ostracized by the medical faculty,
and scorned by people of common sense. To aver that
6 disease is normal, a God-bestowed and stubborn reality,
but that you can heal it, leaves you to work against that
which is natural and a law of being. It is scientific to rob
9 disease of all reality; and to accomplish this, you cannot
begin by admitting its reality. Our Master taught his
students to deny self, sense, and take up the cross. Men-
12 tal healers who admit that disease is real should be made
to test the feasibility of what they say by healing one case
audibly, through such an admission, — if this is possible.
15 I have healed more disease by the spoken than the unspoken word.

The honest student of Christian Science is modest in his
18 claims and conscientious in duty, waiting and working to
mature what he has been taught. Institutes furnished
with such teachers are becoming beacon-lights along the
21 shores of erudition; and many who are not teachers have
large practices and some marked success in healing the
most defiant forms of disease.

24 Dishonesty destroys one's ability to heal mentally. Conceit cannot avert the effects of deceit. Taking advantage
of the present ignorance in relation to Christian Science
27 Mind-healing, many are flooding our land with conflicting theories and practice. We should not spread abroad

patchwork ideas that in some vital points lack Science. 1
How sad it is that envy will bend its bow and shoot its
arrow at the idea which claims only its inheritance, is nat- 3
urally modest, generous, and sincere! while the trespassing error murders either friend or foe who stands in its
way. Truly it is better to fall into the hands of God, than 6
of man.

When I revised "Science and Health with Key to the
Scriptures," in 1878, some irresponsible people insisted 9
that my manual of the practice of Christian Science Mind-
healing should not be made public; but I obeyed a diviner
rule. People dependent on the rules of this practice for 12
their healing, not having lost the Spirit which sustains the
genuine practice, will put that book in the hands of their
patients, whom it will heal, and recommend it to their 15
students, whom it would enlighten. Every teacher must
pore over it in secret, to keep himself well informed. The
Nemesis of the history of Mind-healing notes this hour. 18

Dishonesty necessarily stultifies the spiritual sense which
Mind-healers specially need; and which they must possess, in order to be safe members of the community. How 21
good and pleasant a thing it is to seek not so much thine
own as another's good, to sow by the wayside for the way-
weary, and trust Love's recompense of love. 24

Plagiarism from my writings is so common it is becoming odious to honest people; and such compilations,
instead of possessing the essentials of Christian Science, 27
are tempting and misleading.

1 Reading Science and Health has restored the sick to
   health; but the task of learning thoroughly the Science
3 of Mind-healing and demonstrating it understandingly
   had better be undertaken in health than sickness.

DISEASE UNREAL

6 Disease is more than *imagination;* it is a human error,
   a constituent part of what comprise the whole of mortal
   existence, — namely, material sensation and mental delu-
9 sion. But an erring sense of existence, or the error of
   belief, named disease, never made sickness a stubborn
   reality. On the ground that harmony is the truth of be-
12 ing, the Science of Mind-healing destroys the feasibility
   of disease; hence error of thought becomes fable instead
   of fact. Science demonstrates the reality of Truth and
15 the unreality of the error. A self-evident proposition, in
   the Science of Mind-healing, is that disease is unreal;
   and the efficacy of my system, beyond other systems of
18 medicine, vouches for the validity of that statement. Sin
   and disease are not scientific, because they embody not
   the idea of divine Principle, and are not the phenomena
21 of the immutable laws of God; and they do not arise
   from the divine consciousness and true constituency of
   being.
24 The unreality of sin, disease, and death, rests on the
   exclusive truth that being, to be eternal, must be harmonious. All disease must be — and can only be — healed

on this basis. All true Christian Scientists are vindicat- 1
ing, fearlessly and honestly, the Principle of this grand
verity of Mind-healing. 3

In erring mortal thought the reality of Truth has an
antipode, — the reality of error; and disease is one of the
severe realities of this error. God has no opposite in 6
Science. To Truth there is no error. As Truth alone is
real, then it follows that to declare error real would be to
make it Truth. Disease arises from a false and material 9
sense, from the belief that matter has sensation. Therefore this material sense, which is untrue, is of necessity
unreal. Moreover, this unreal sense substitutes for Truth 12
an unreal belief, — namely, that life and health are independent of God, and dependent on material conditions.
Material sense also avers that Spirit, or Truth, cannot 15
restore health and perpetuate life, but that material conditions can and do destroy both human health and life.

If disease is as real as health, and is itself a state of 18
being, and yet is arrayed against being, then Mind, or
God, does not meddle with it. Disease becomes indeed a
stubborn reality, and man is mortal. A "kingdom divided 21
against itself is brought to desolation;" therefore the mind
that attacks a normal and real condition of man, is pro-
fanely tampering with the realities of God and His laws. 24
Metaphysical healing is a lost jewel in this misconception
of reality. Any contradictory fusion of Truth with error,
in both theory and practice, prevents one from healing 27
scientifically, and makes the last state of one's patients

1 worse than the first. If disease is real it is not illusive, and it certainly would contradict the Science of Mind-
3 healing to attempt to destroy the realities of Mind in order to heal the sick.

On the theory that God's formations are spiritual, har-
6 monious, and eternal, and that God is the only creator, Christian Science refutes the validity of the testimony of the senses, which take cognizance of their own phenomena,
9 — sickness, disease, and death. This refutation is indispensable to the destruction of false evidence, and the consequent cure of the sick, — as all understand who
12 practise the true Science of Mind-healing. If, as the error indicates, the evidence of disease is not false, then disease cannot be healed by denying its validity; and this
15 is why the mistaken healer is not successful, trying to heal on a material basis.

The evidence that the earth is motionless and the sun
18 revolves around our planet, is as sensible and real as the evidence for disease; but Science determines the evidence in both cases to be unreal. To material sense it is plain
21 also that the error of the revolution of the sun around the earth is more apparent than the adverse but true Science of the stellar universe. Copernicus has shown that what
24 appears real, to material sense and feeling, is absolutely unreal. Astronomy, optics, acoustics, and hydraulics are all at war with the testimony of the physical senses. This
27 fact intimates that the laws of Science are mental, not material; and Christian Science demonstrates this.

SCIENCE OF MIND-HEALING

The rule of divinity is golden; to be wise and true rejoices every heart. But evil influences waver the scales of justice and mercy. No personal considerations should allow any root of bitterness to spring up between Christian Scientists, nor cause any misapprehension as to the motives of others. We must love our enemies, and continue to do so unto the end. By the love of God we can cancel error in our own hearts, and blot it out of others.

Sooner or later the eyes of sinful mortals must be opened to see every error they possess, and the way out of it; and they will "flee as a bird to your mountain," away from the enemy of sinning sense, stubborn will, and every imperfection in the land of Sodom, and find rescue and refuge in Truth and Love.

Every loving sacrifice for the good of others is known to God, and the wrath of man cannot hide it from Him. God has appointed for Christian Scientists high tasks, and will not release them from the strict performance of each one of them. The students must now fight their own battles. I recommend that Scientists draw no lines whatever between one person and another, but think, speak, teach, and write the truth of Christian Science without reference to right or wrong personality in this field of labor. Leave the distinctions of individual character and the discriminations and guidance thereof to

1 the Father, whose wisdom is unerring and whose love is
universal.

3   We should endeavor to be long-suffering, faithful, and
charitable with all.   To this small effort let us add one
more privilege — namely, silence whenever it can substi-
6 tute censure.   Avoid voicing error; but utter the truth of
God and the beauty of holiness, the joy of Love and "the
peace of God, that passeth all understanding," recom-
9 mending to all men fellowship in the bonds of Christ.
Advise students to rebuke each other always in love, as
I have rebuked them.   Having discharged this duty, coun-
12 sel each other to work out his own salvation, without fear
or doubt, knowing that God will make the wrath of man
to praise Him, and that the remainder thereof He will
15 restrain.   We can rejoice that every germ of goodness will
at last struggle into freedom and greatness, and every sin
will so punish itself that it will bow down to the command-
18 ments of Christ, — Truth and Love.

I enjoin it upon my students to hold no controversy or
enmity over doctrines and traditions, or over the miscon-
21 ceptions of Christian Science, but to work, watch, and
pray for the amelioration of sin, sickness, and death.   If
one be found who is too blind for instruction, no longer cast
24 your pearls before this state of mortal mind, lest it turn
and rend you; but quietly, with benediction and hope,
let the unwise pass by, while you walk on in equanimity,
27 and with increased power, patience, and understanding,
gained from your forbearance.   This counsel is not new,

as my Christian students can testify; and if it had been 1
heeded in times past it would have prevented, to a great
extent, the factions which have sprung up among Scientists 3
to the hindrance of the Cause of Truth. It is true that the
mistakes, prejudices, and errors of one class of thinkers
must not be introduced or established among another class 6
who are clearer and more conscientious in their convictions; but this one thing can be done, and should be: let
your opponents alone, and use no influence to prevent 9
their legitimate action from their own standpoint of experience, knowing, as you should, that God will well
regenerate and separate wisely and finally; whereas you 12
may err in effort, and lose your fruition.

Hoping to pacify repeated complaints and murmurings
against too great leniency, on my part, towards some of 15
my students who fall into error, I have opposed occasionally and strongly — especially in the first edition of
this little work — existing wrongs of the nature referred 18
to. But I now point steadfastly to the power of grace to
overcome evil with good. God will "furnish a table in
the wilderness" and show the power of Love. 21

Science is not the shibboleth of a sect or the caba-
listic insignia of philosophy; it excludes all error and
includes all Truth. More mistakes are made in its name 24
than this period comprehends. Divinely defined, Science
is the atmosphere of God; humanly construed, and according to Webster, it is "knowledge, duly arranged and 27
referred to general truths and principles on which it is

1 founded, and from which it is derived." I employ this
awe-filled word in both a divine and human sense; but
3 I insist that Christian Science is demonstrably as true,
relative to the unseen verities of being, as any proof that
can be given of the completeness of Science.

6   The two largest words in the vocabulary of thought are
"Christian" and "Science." The former is the highest
style of man; the latter reveals and interprets God and
9 man; it aggregates, amplifies, unfolds, and expresses the
ALL-God. The life of Christ is the predicate and postulate of all that I teach, and there is but one standard
12 statement, one rule, and one Principle for all scientific
truth.

My hygienic system rests on Mind, the eternal Truth.
15 What is termed matter, or relates to its so-called attributes,
is a self-destroying error. When a so-called material sense
is lost, and Truth restores that lost sense, — on the basis
18 that all consciousness is Mind and eternal, — the former
position, that sense is organic and material, is proven
erroneous.

21   The feasibility and immobility of Christian Science
unveil the true idea, — namely, that earth's discords have
not the reality of Mind in the Science of being; and this
24 idea — dematerializing and spiritualizing mortals — turns
like the needle to the pole all hope and faith to God, based
as it is on His omnipotence and omnipresence.

27   Eternal harmony, perpetuity, and perfection, constitute
the phenomena of being, governed by the immutable and

eternal laws of God; whereas matter and human will, 1
intellect, desire, and fear, are not the creators, controllers,
nor destroyers of life or its harmonies. Man has an im- 3
mortal Soul, a divine Principle, and an eternal being.
Man has perpetual individuality; and God's laws, and
their intelligent and harmonious action, constitute his in- 6
dividuality in the Science of Soul.

In its literary expression, my system of Christian metaphysics is hampered by material terms, which must be 9
used to indicate thoughts that are to be understood metaphysically. As a Science, this system is held back by the
common ignorance of what it is and what it does, and 12
(worse still) by those who come falsely in its name. To
be appreciated, Science must be understood and conscientiously introduced. If the Bible and Science and Health 15
had the place in schools of learning that physiology oc-
cupies, they would revolutionize and reform the world,
through the power of Christ. It is true that it requires 18
more study to understand and demonstrate what these
works teach, than to learn theology, physiology, or physics;
because they teach divine Science, with fixed Principle, 21
given rule, and unmistakable proof.

Ancient and modern human philosophy are inadequate
to grasp the Principle of Christian Science, or to demon- 24
strate it. Revelation shows this Principle, and will rescue
reason from the thrall of error. Revelation must subdue
the sophistry of intellect, and spiritualize consciousness 27
with the dictum and the demonstration of Truth and Love.

1 Christian Science Mind-healing can only be gained by
working from a purely Christian standpoint. Then it
3 heals the sick and exalts the race. The essence of this
Science is right thinking and right acting — leading us to
see spirituality and to be spiritual, to understand and to
6 demonstrate God.

The Massachusetts Metaphysical College and Church
of Christ, Scientist, in Boston, were the outgrowth of the
9 author's religious experience. After a lifetime of ortho-
doxy on the platform of doctrines, rites, and ceremonies,
it became a sacred duty for her to impart to others this
12 new-old knowledge of God.

The same affection, desire, and motives which have stimulated true Christianity in all ages, and given impulse to
15 goodness, in or out of the Church, have nerved her purpose to build on the new-born conception of the Christ, as
Jesus declared himself, — namely, "the way, the truth,
18 and the life." Living a true life, casting out evil, healing
the sick, and preaching the gospel of Truth, — these are
the ends of Christianity. This divine way impels a spirit-
21 ualization of thought and method, beyond doctrine and
ritual; and in nothing else has she departed from the old
landmarks.

24 The unveiled spiritual signification of the Word so enlarges our sense of God that it makes both sense and Soul,
man and Life, immaterial, though still individual. It re-
27 moves all limits from divine power. God must be found
all instead of a part of being, and man the reflection of

His power and goodness. This Science rebukes sin with 1
its own nothingness, and thus destroys sin quickly and
utterly. It makes disease unreal, and this heals it. 3

The demonstration of moral and physical growth, and a
scientific deduction from the Principle of all harmony, declare both the Principle and idea to be divine. If this be 6
true, then death must be swallowed up in Life, and the
prophecy of Jesus fulfilled, "Whosoever liveth and believeth in me shall never die." Though centuries passed 9
after those words were originally uttered, before this reappearing of Truth, and though the hiatus be longer still
before that saying is demonstrated in Life that knows no 12
death, the declaration is nevertheless true, and remains
a clear and profound deduction from Christian Science.

IS CHRISTIAN SCIENCE OF THE SAME LINEAGE AS 15
SPIRITUALISM OR THEOSOPHY?

Science is not susceptible of being held as a mere theory.
It is hoary with time. It takes hold of eternity, voices the 18
infinite, and governs the universe. No greater opposites
can be conceived of, physically, morally, and spiritually,
than Christian Science, spiritualism, and theosophy. 21

Science and Health has effected a revolution in the
minds of thinkers on the subject of mediumship, and given
impulse to reason and revelation, goodness and virtue. A 24
theory may be sound in spots, and sparkle like a diamond,
while other parts of it have no lustre. Christian Science

1 is sound in every part. It is neither warped nor miscon-
ceived, when properly demonstrated. If a spiritualist
3 medium understood the Science of Mind-healing, he
would know that between those who have and those who
have not passed the transition called death, there can be
6 no interchange of consciousness, and that all sensible phenomena are merely subjective states of mortal mind.

Theosophy is a corruption of Judaism. This corruption
9 had a renewal in the Neoplatonic philosophy; but it sprang
from the Oriental philosophy of Brahmanism, and blends
with its magic and enchantments. Theosophy is no more
12 allied to Christian Science than the odor of the upas-tree
is to the sweet breath of springtide, or the brilliant cor-
uscations of the northern sky are to solar heat and
15 light.

IS CHRISTIAN SCIENCE FROM BENEATH, AND NOT FROM ABOVE?

18   Hear the words of our Master: "Go ye into all the
world"! "Heal the sick, cast out devils"! Christian
Scientists, perhaps more than any other religious sect, are
21 obeying these commands; and the injunctions are not
confined to Jesus' students in that age, but they extend
to this age, — to as many as shall believe on him. The
24 demand and example of Jesus were not from beneath.
Are frozen dogmas, persistent persecution, and the doctrine of eternal damnation, from above? Are the dews

of divine Truth, falling on the sick and sinner, to heal 1
them, from beneath? "By their fruits ye shall know
them." 3

Reading my books, without prejudice, would convince
all that their purpose is right. The comprehension of my
teachings would enable any one to prove these books to 6
be filled with blessings for the whole human family. Fa-
tiguing Bible translations and voluminous commentaries
are employed to explain and prop old creeds, and they 9
have the civil and religious arms in their defense; then
why should not these be equally extended to support the
Christianity that heals the sick? The notions of person- 12
ality to be found in creeds are far more mystic than
Mind-healing. It is no easy matter to believe there are
three persons in one person, and that one person is cast 15
out of another person. These conceptions of Deity and
devil presuppose an impotent God and an incredible
Satan. 18

IS CHRISTIAN SCIENCE PANTHEISTIC?

Christian Science refutes pantheism, finds Spirit neither
in matter nor in the modes of mortal mind. It shows 21
that matter and mortal mind have neither origin nor existence in the eternal Mind. Thinking otherwise is what
estranges mortals from divine Life and Love. God is 24
All-in-all. He is Spirit; and in nothing is He unlike Himself. Nothing that "worketh or maketh a lie" is to be

1 found in the divine consciousness. For God to know, is to be; that is, what He knows must truly and eternally 3 exist. If He knows matter, and matter can exist in Mind, then mortality and discord must be eternal. He is Mind; and whatever He knows is made manifest, and must be 6 Truth.

If God knows evil even as a false claim, this knowledge would manifest evil in Him and proceeding from Him. 9 Christian Science shows that matter, evil, sin, sickness, and death are but negations of Spirit, Truth, and Life, which are positives that cannot be gainsaid. The subjective 12 states of evil, called mortal mind or matter, are negatives destitute of time and space; for there is none beside God or Spirit and the idea of Spirit.

15 This infinite logic is the infinite light, — uncomprehended, yet forever giving forth more light, because it has no darkness to emit. Mortals do not understand the 18 All; hence their inference of some other existence beside God and His true likeness, — of something unlike Him. He who is All, understands all. He can have no knowl- 21 edge or inference but His own consciousness, and can take in no more than all.

The mists of matter — sin, sickness, and death — dis- 24 appear in proportion as mortals approach Spirit, which is the reality of being. It is not enough to say that matter is the substratum of evil, and that its highest attenuation is 27 mortal mind; for there is, strictly speaking, *no* mortal mind. Mind is immortal. Death is the consequent of an

antecedent false assumption of the realness of something 1
unreal, material, and mortal.   If God knows the antecedent, He must produce its consequences.   From this logic 3
there is no escape.   Matter, or evil, is the absence of Spirit
or good.   Their nothingness is thus proven; for God is
good, ever-present, and All. 6

"In Him we live, and move, and have our being;" consequently it is impossible for the true man — who is a
spiritual and individual being, created in the eternal 9
Science of being — to be conscious of aught but good.
God's image and likeness can never be less than a good
man; and for man to be more than God's likeness is 12
impossible.   Man is the climax of creation; and God is
not without an ever-present witness, testifying of Himself.
Matter, or any mode of mortal mind, is neither part nor 15
parcel of divine consciousness and God's verity.

In Science there is no fallen state of being; for therein
is no inverted image of God, no escape from the focal 18
radiation of the infinite.   Hence the unreality of error,
and the truth of the Scripture, that there is "none beside
Him."   If mortals could grasp these two words *all* and 21
nothing, this mystery of a God who has no knowledge of
sin would disappear, and the eternal, infinite harmony
would be fathomed.   If God could know a false claim, 24
false knowledge would be a part of His consciousness.
Then evil would be as real as good, sickness as real as
health, death as real as Life; and sickness, sin, and death 27
would be as eternal as God.

1 IS CHRISTIAN SCIENCE BLASPHEMOUS?

Blasphemy has never diminished sin and sickness, nor
3 acknowledged God in all His ways. Blasphemy rebukes
not the godless lie that denies Him as All-in-all, nor does
it ascribe to Him all presence, power, and glory. Chris-
6 tian Science does this. If Science lacked the proof of its
origin in God, it would be self-destructive, for it rests alone
on the demonstration of God's supremacy and omnipo-
9 tence. Right thinking and right acting, physical and
moral harmony, come with Science, and the secret of
its presence lies in the universal need of better health and
12 morals.

Human theories, when weighed in the balance, are
found unequal to the demonstration of divine Life and
15 Love; and their highest endeavors are, to divine Science,
what a child's love of pictures is to art. A child, in his
ignorance, may imagine the face of Dante to be the rapt
18 face of Jesus. Thus falsely may the human conceive of
the Divine. If the schoolmaster is not Christ, the school
gets things wrong, and knows it not; but the teacher is
21 morally responsible.

Good health and a more spiritual religion are the common wants; and these wants have wrought this moral
24 result, — that the so-called mortal mind asks for what
Mind alone can supply. This demand militates against
the so-called demands of matter, and regulates the present

high premium on Mind-healing. If the uniform moral 1
and spiritual, as well as physical, effects of Christian Science were lacking, the premium would go down. That 3
it continues to rise, and the demand to increase, shows its
real value to the race. Even doctors will agree that infidelity, ignorance, and quackery have never met the grow- 6
ing wants of humanity. Christian Science is no "Boston
craze;" it is the sober second thought of advancing
humanity.   9

IS THERE A PERSONAL DEITY?

God is infinite. He is neither a limited mind nor a
limited body. God is Love; and Love is Principle, not 12
person. What the person of the infinite is, we know not;
but we are gratefully and lovingly conscious of the fatherliness of this Supreme Being. God is individual, and man 15
is His individualized idea. While material man and the
physical senses receive no spiritual idea, and feel no sensation of divine Love, spiritual man and his spiritual 18
senses are drinking in the nature and essence of the individual infinite. A sinful sense is incompetent to understand
the realities of being, — that Life is God, and that man 21
is in His image and likeness. A sinner can take no cognizance of the noumenon or the phenomena of Spirit;
but leaving sin, sense rises to the fulness of the stature of 24
man in Christ.

Person is formed after the manner of mortal man, so

1 far as he can conceive of personality. Limitless personality is inconceivable. His person and perfection are
3 neither self-created, nor discerned through imperfection;
and of God as a person, human reason, imagination, and
revelation give us no knowledge. Error would fashion
6 Deity in a manlike mould, while Truth is moulding a
Godlike man.

When the term divine Principle is used to signify Deity
9 it may seem distant or cold, until better apprehended.
This Principle is Mind, substance, Life, Truth, Love.
When understood, Principle is found to be the only term
12 that fully conveys the ideas of God, — one Mind, a perfect
man, and divine Science. As the divine Principle is comprehended, God's omnipotence and omnipresence will
15 dawn on mortals, and the notion of an everywhere-present
body — or of an infinite Mind starting from a finite body,
and returning to it — will disappear.
18   Ever-present Love must seem ever absent to ever-present
selfishness or material sense. Hence this asking amiss
and receiving not, and the common idolatry of man-
21 worship. In divine Science, God is recognized as the
only power, presence, and glory.

Adam's mistiness and Satan's reasoning, ever since the
24 flood, — when specimens of every kind emerged from the
ark, — have run through the veins of all human philosophy. Human reason is a blind guide, a continued series
27 of mortal hypotheses, antagonistic to Revelation and Science. It is continually straying into forbidden by-paths

of sensualism, contrary to the life and teachings of Jesus 1
and Paul, and the vision of the Apocalypse. Human
philosophy has ninety-nine parts of error to the one- 3
hundredth part of Truth, — an unsafe decoction for the
race. The Science that Jesus demonstrated, whose views
of Truth Confucius and Plato but dimly discerned, Science 6
and Health interprets. It was not a search after wisdom;
it was wisdom, and it grasped in spiritual law the universe, — all time, space, immortality, thought, extension. 9
This Science demonstrated the Principle of all phenomena,
identity, individuality, law; and showed man as reflecting God and the divine capacity. Human philosophy 12
would dethrone perfection, and substitute matter and evil
for divine means and ends.

Human philosophy has an undeveloped God, who un- 15
folds Himself through material modes, wherein the human
and divine mingle in the same realm and consciousness.
This is rank infidelity; because by it we lose God's ways 18
and perpetuate the supposed power and reality of evil *ad
infinitum*. Christian Science rends this veil in the pantheon
of many gods, and reproduces the teachings of Jesus, whose 21
philosophy is incontestable, bears the strain of time, and
brings in the glories of eternity; "for other foundation
can no man lay than that is laid, which is Jesus Christ." 24
Divine philosophy is demonstrably the true idea of the
Christ, wherein Principle heals and saves. A philosophy
which cannot heal the sick has little resemblance to Sci- 27
ence, and is, to say the least, like a cloud without rain,

1 "driven about by every wind of doctrine." Such philosophy has certainly not touched the hem of the Christ
3 garment.

Leibnitz, Descartes, Fichte, Hegel, Spinoza, Bishop
Berkeley, were once clothed with a "brief authority;"
6 but Berkeley ended his metaphysical theory with a treatise
on the healing properties of tar-water, and Hegel was an
inveterate snuff-taker. The circumlocution and cold cate-
9 gories of Kant fail to improve the conditions of mortals,
morally, spiritually, or physically. Such miscalled metaphysical systems are reeds shaken by the wind. Com-
12 pared with the inspired wisdom and infinite meaning of
the Word of Truth, they are as moonbeams to the sun, or
as Stygian night to the kindling dawn.

15   IS THERE A PERSONAL DEVIL?

No man hath seen the person of good or of evil. Each
is greater than the corporeality we behold.
18   "He cast out *devils*." This record shows that the term
devil is generic, being used in the plural number. From
this it follows that there is more than one devil. That
21 Jesus cast several persons out of another person, is not
stated, and is impossible. Hence the passage must refer
to the *evils* which were cast out.
24   Jesus defined devil as a mortal who is full of evil. "Have
I not chosen you twelve, and one of you *is a devil?*" His
definition of evil indicated his ability to cast it out. An

incorrect concept of the nature of evil hinders the destruc- 1
tion of evil. To conceive of God as resembling — in personality, or form — the personality that Jesus condemned 3
as devilish, is fraught with spiritual danger. Evil can
neither grasp the prerogative of God nor make evil omnipotent and omnipresent. 6

Jesus said to Peter, "Get thee behind me, Satan;" but
he to whom our Lord gave the keys of the kingdom could
not have been wholly evil, and therefore was not a *devil*, 9
after the accepted definition. Out of the Magdalen, Jesus
cast seven devils; but not one person was named among
them. According to Crabtre, these devils were the dis- 12
eases Jesus cast out.

The most eminent divines, in Europe and America, concede that the Scriptures have both a literal and a moral 15
meaning. Which of the two is the more important to gain,
— the literal or the moral sense of the word *devil*, — in
order to cast out this devil? Evil is a quality, not an 18
individual.

As mortals, we need to discern the claims of evil, and to
fight these claims, not as realities, but as illusions; but 21
Deity can have no such warfare against Himself. Knowledge of a man's physical personality is not sufficient to
inform us as to the amount of good or evil he possesses. 24
Hence we cannot understand God or man, through the
person of either. God is All-in-all; but He is definite and
individual, the omnipresent and omniscient Mind; and 27
man's individuality is God's own image and likeness, —

1 even the immeasurable idea of divine Mind. In the
Science of good, evil loses all place, person, and power.

3   According to Spinoza's philosophy God is amplification.
He is in all things, and therefore He is in evil in human
thought. He is extension, of whatever character. Also,
6 according to Spinoza, man is an animal vegetable, developed through the lower orders of matter and mortal mind.
All these vagaries are at variance with my system of meta-
9 physics, which rests on God as One and All, and denies
the actual existence of both matter and evil. According to
false philosophy and scholastic theology, God is three
12 persons in one person. By the same token, evil is not only
as real as good, but much more real, since evil subordinates good in personality.

15   The claims of evil become both less and more in Christian Science, than in human philosophies or creeds: *more*,
because the evil that is hidden by dogma and human rea-
18 son is uncovered by Science; and *less*, because evil, being
thus uncovered, is found out, and exposure is nine points
of destruction. Then appears the grand verity of Chris-
21 tian Science: namely, that evil has no claims and was
never a claimant; for behold evil (or devil) is, as Jesus
said, "a murderer from the beginning, and the truth abode
24 not in him."

There was never a moment in which evil was real. This
great fact concerning all error brings with it another and
27 more glorious truth, that good is supreme. As there is
none beside Him, and He is all good, there can be no evil.

Simply uttering this great thought is not enough! We 1
must live it, until God becomes the All and Only of our
being. Having won through great tribulation this cardinal 3
point of divine Science, St. Paul said, "But now we are
delivered from the law, that being dead wherein we were
held; that we should serve in newness of spirit, and not 6
in the oldness of the letter."

IS MAN A PERSON?

Man is more than physical personality, or what we cog- 9
nize through the material senses. Mind is more than matter, even as the infinite idea of Truth is beyond a finite
belief. Man outlives finite mortal definitions of himself, 12
according to a law of "the survival of the fittest." Man is
the eternal idea of his divine Principle, or Father. He is
neither matter nor a mode of mortal mind, for he is spir- 15
itual and eternal, an immortal mode of the divine Mind.
Man is the image and likeness of God, coexistent and
coeternal with Him. 18

Man is not absorbed in Deity; for he is forever individual; but what this everlasting individuality is, remains to
be learned. Mortals have not seen it. That which is born 21
of the flesh is not man's eternal identity. Spiritual and
immortal man alone is God's likeness, and that which is
mortal is not man in a spiritually scientific sense. A 24
material, sinful mortal is but the counterfeit of immortal
man.

1 The mind-quacks believe that mortal man is identical with immortal man, and that the immortal is inside the 3 mortal; that good and evil blend; that matter and Spirit are one; and that Soul, or Spirit, is subdivided into spirits, or souls, — *alias* gods. This infantile talk about Mind-6 healing is no more identical with Christian Science than the babe is identical with the adult, or the human belief resembles the divine idea. Hence it is impossible for those 9 holding such material and mortal views to demonstrate my metaphysics. Theirs is the sensuous thought, which brings forth its own sensuous conception. Mine is the 12 spiritual idea which transfigures thought.

All real being represents God, and is in Him. In this Science of being, man can no more relapse or collapse 15 from perfection, than his divine Principle, or Father, can fall out of Himself into something below infinitude. Man's real ego, or selfhood, is goodness. If man's individuality 18 were evil, he would be annihilated, for evil is self-destroying.

Man's individual being must reflect the supreme individual Being, to be His image and likeness; and this 21 individuality never originated in molecule, corpuscle, materiality, or mortality. God holds man in the eternal bonds of Science, — in the immutable harmony of divine 24 law. Man is a celestial; and in the spiritual universe he is forever individual and forever harmonious. "If God so clothe the grass of the field, . . . shall He not 27 much more clothe you, O ye of little faith?"

Sin must be obsolete, — dust returning to dust, noth-

ingness to nothingness. Sin is not Mind; it is but the sup- 1
position that there is more than one Mind. It issues
a false claim; and the claim, being worthless, is in reality 3
no claim whatever. Matter is not Mind, to claim aught;
but Mind is God, and evil finds no place in good. When
we get near enough to God to see this, the springtide 6
of Truth in Christian Science will burst upon us in the
similitude of the Apocalyptic pictures. No night will be
there, and there will be no more sea. There will be no 9
need of the sun, for Spirit will be the light of the city, and
matter will be proved a myth. Until centuries pass, and
this vision of Truth is fully interpreted by divine Science, 12
this prophecy will be scoffed at; but it is just as veritable
now as it can be then. Science, divine Science, presents
the grand and eternal verities of God and man as the 15
divine Mind and that Mind's idea.

Mortal man is the antipode of immortal man, and the
two should not be confounded. Bishop Foster said, in a 18
lecture in Boston, "No man living hath yet seen man."
This material sinful personality, which we misname man,
is what St. Paul terms "the old man and his deeds," to 21
be "put off."

Who can say what the absolute personality of God or
man is? Who living hath seen God or a perfect man? 24
In presence of such thoughts take off thy shoes and
tread lightly, for this is holy ground. Surely the probation
of mortals must go on after the change called death, that 27
they may learn the definition of immortal being; or else

1 their present mistakes would extinguish human existence. How long this false sense remains after the transition called
3 death, no mortal knoweth; but this is sure, that the mists of error, sooner or later, will melt in the fervent heat of suffering, mortality will burst the barriers of sense, and
6 man be found perfect and eternal. Of his intermediate conditions — the purifying processes and terrible revolutions necessary to effect this end — I am ignorant.

9   Inasmuch as these momentous facts in the Science of being must be learned some time, now is the most acceptable time for beginning the lesson. If Science is pointing
12 the way, and is found to bring with it health, holiness, and immortality, then to-day is none too soon for entering this path. The proof that Christian Science is the way of sal-
15 vation given by Christ, I consider well established. The present, as well as the future, reveals the fact that Truth is never understood too soon.

18   Has Truth, as demonstrated by Jesus, reappeared? Study Christian Science and practise it, and you will know that Truth has reappeared. What is demonstrably
21 true cannot be gainsaid; but getting the letter and omitting the spirit of this Science is neither the comprehension of its Principle nor the practice of its Life.

24   HAS MAN A SOUL?

    The Scriptures inform us that "the soul that sinneth, it shall die." Here *soul* means sense and organic life; and

this passage refers to the Jewish law, that a mortal should 1
be put to death for his own sin, but not for another's.
Not Soul, but mortal sense, sins and dies. Immortal man 3
has immortal Soul and a deathless sense of being. Mortal
man has but a false sense of Soul and body. He believes
that Spirit, or Soul, exists in matter. This is pantheism, 6
and is not the Science of Soul. The mind-quacks have
so slight a knowledge of Soul that they believe material
and sinning sense to be soul; and then they doctor this 9
soul as if it were not even a material sense.

In Dr. Gordon's sermon on The Ministry of Healing,
he said, "The forgiven soul in a sick body is not half a 12
man." Is this pantheistic statement sound theology, —
that Soul is in matter, and the immortal part of man a sinner? Is not this a disparagement of the person of man and 15
a denial of God's power? Better far that we impute such
doctrines to mortal opinion than to the divine Word.

To my sense, such a statement is a shocking reflection 18
on the divine power. A mortal pardoned by God is not
sick, he is made whole. He in whom sin, disease, and
death are destroyed, is more than a fraction of himself. 21
Such sermons, though clad in soft raiment, are spiritless waifs, literary driftwood on the ocean of thought;
while Truth walks triumphantly over the waves of sin, 24
sickness, and death.

IS SIN FORGIVEN?

1

The law of Life and Truth is the law of Christ, destroy-
3 ing all sense of sin and death. It does more than forgive
the false sense named sin, for it pursues and punishes it,
and will not let sin go until it is destroyed, — until nothing
6 is left to be forgiven, to suffer, or to be punished. Forgiven thus, sickness and sin have no relapse. God's law
reaches and destroys evil by virtue of the allness of God.

9   He need not know the evil He destroys, any more than
the legislator need know the criminal who is punished by
the law enacted. God's law is in three words, "I am All;"
12 and this perfect law is ever present to rebuke any claim
of another law. God pities our woes with the love of a
Father for His child, — not by becoming human, and
15 knowing sin, or naught, but by removing our knowledge
of what is not. He could not destroy our woes totally
if He possessed any knowledge of them. His sympathy
18 is divine, not human. It is Truth's knowledge of its own
infinitude which forbids the genuine existence of even
a claim to error. This knowledge is light wherein there
21 is no darkness, — not light holding darkness within itself.
The consciousness of light is like the eternal law of God,
revealing Him and nothing else.

24   Sympathy with sin, sorrow, and sickness would dethrone
God as Truth, for Truth has no sympathy for error. In
Science, the cure of the sick demonstrates this grand

verity of Christian Science, that you cannot eradicate dis- 1
ease if you admit that God sends it or sees it. Material
and mortal mind-healing (so-called) has for ages been 3
a pretender, but has not healed mortals; and they are
yet sick and sinful.

Disease and sin appear to-day in subtler forms than 6
they did yesterday. They progress and will multiply into
worse forms, until it is understood that disease and sin are
unreal, *unknown* to Truth, and never actual persons or 9
real facts.

Our phraseology varies. To me *divine pardon* is that
divine presence which is the sure destruction of sin; and 12
I insist on the destruction of sin as the only full proof of
its pardon. "For this purpose the Son of God was manifested, that he might *destroy* the works of the devil" 15
(1 John iii. 8).

Jesus cast out evils, mediating between what is and is
not, until a perfect consciousness is attained. He healed 18
disease as he healed sin; but he treated them both,
not as in or of matter, but as mortal beliefs to be
exterminated. Physical and mental healing were one 21
and the same with this master Metaphysician. If the
evils called sin, sickness, and death had been forgiven
in the generally accepted sense, they would have returned, 24
to be again forgiven; but Jesus said to disease: "Come
out of him, and enter no more into him." He said also:
"If a man keep my saying, he shall never see death;" 27
and "Whatsoever thou shalt bind on earth shall be bound

1 in heaven." The misinterpretation of such passages has retarded the progress of Christianity and the spirituali-
3 zation of the race.

A magistrate's pardon may encourage a criminal to repeat the offense; because *forgiveness,* in the popular
6 sense of the word, can neither extinguish a crime nor the motives leading to it. The belief in sin — its pleasure, pain, or power — must suffer, until it is self-destroyed.
9 "Whatsoever a man soweth, that shall he also reap."

IS THERE ANY SUCH THING AS SIN?

Frequently when I touch this subject my meaning is
12 ignorantly or maliciously misconstrued. Christian Science Mind-healing lifts with a steady arm, and cleaves sin with a broad battle-axe. It gives the lie to sin, in the spirit of
15 Truth; but other theories make sin true. Jesus declared that the devil was "a liar, and the father of it." A lie is negation, — *alias* nothing, or the opposite of something.
18 Good is great and real. Hence its opposite, named *evil,* must be small and unreal. When this sense is attained, we shall no longer be the servants of sin, and shall cease
21 to love it.

The domination of good destroys the sense of evil. To illustrate: It seems a great evil to belie and belittle Chris-
24 tian Science, and persecute a Cause which is healing its thousands and rapidly diminishing the percentage of sin. But reduce this evil to its lowest terms, *nothing,* and slander

loses its power to harm; for even the wrath of man shall 1
praise Him. The reduction of evil, in Science, gives the
dominance to God, and must lead us to bless those who 3
curse, that thus we may overcome evil with good.

If the Bible and my work Science and Health had their
rightful place in schools of learning, they would revolu- 6
tionize the world by advancing the kingdom of Christ.
It requires sacrifice, struggle, prayer, and watchfulness
to understand and demonstrate what these volumes teach, 9
because they involve divine Science, with fixed Principle,
a given rule, and unmistakable proof.

IS THERE NO SACRIFICIAL ATONEMENT? 12

Self-sacrifice is the highway to heaven. The sacrifice of our blessed Lord is undeniable, and it was a million
times greater than the brief agony of the cross; for that 15
would have been insufficient to insure the glory his sacrifice brought and the good it wrought. The spilling of
human blood was inadequate to represent the blood of 18
Christ, the outpouring love that sustains man's at-one-
ment with God; though shedding human blood brought
to light the efficacy of divine Life and Love and its power 21
over death. Jesus' sacrifice stands preeminently amidst
physical suffering and human woe. The glory of human
life is in overcoming sickness, sin, and death. Jesus suf- 24
fered for all mortals to bring in this glory; and his purpose was to show them that the way out of the flesh, out

1 of the delusion of all human error, must be through the
baptism of suffering, leading up to health, harmony, and
3 heaven.

We shall leave the ceremonial law when we gain the
truer sense of following Christ in spirit, and we shall no
6 longer venture to materialize the spiritual and infinite
meaning and efficacy of Truth and Love, and the sacrifice
that Jesus made for us, by commemorating his death
9 with a material rite. Jesus said: "The hour cometh, and
now is, when the true worshippers shall worship the Father
in spirit and in truth." They drink the cup of Christ and
12 are baptized in the purification of persecution who discern
his true merit, — the unseen glory of suffering for others.
Physical torture affords but a slight illustration of the
15 pangs which come to one upon whom the world of sense
falls with its leaden weight in the endeavor to crush out
of a career its divine destiny.

18 The blood of Christ speaketh better things than that
of Abel. The real atonement — so infinitely beyond the
heathen conception that God requires human blood to
21 propitiate His justice and bring His mercy — needs to be
understood. The real blood or Life of Spirit is not yet
discerned. Love bruised and bleeding, yet mounting to
24 the throne of glory in purity and peace, over the steps of
uplifted humanity, — this is the deep significance of the
blood of Christ. Nameless woe, everlasting victories, are
27 the blood, the vital currents of Christ Jesus' life, purchasing the freedom of mortals from sin and death.

This blood of Jesus is everything to human hope and 1
faith. Without it, how poor the precedents of Christianity! What manner of Science were Christian Science 3
without the power to demonstrate the Principle of such
Life; and what hope have mortals but through deep humility and adoration to reach the understanding of this 6
Principle! When human struggles cease, and mortals
yield lovingly to the purpose of divine Love, there will be
no more sickness, sorrow, sin, and death. He who pointed 9
the way of Life conquered also the drear subtlety of death.

It was not to appease the wrath of God, but to show the
allness of Love and the nothingness of hate, sin, and death, 12
that Jesus suffered. He lived that we also might live. He
suffered, to show mortals the awful price paid by sin, and
how to avoid paying it. He atoned for the terrible un- 15
reality of a supposed existence apart from God. He
suffered because of the shocking human idolatry that
presupposes Life, substance, Soul, and intelligence in 18
matter, — which is the antipode of God, and yet governs
mankind. The glorious truth of being — namely, that
God is the only Mind, Life, substance, Soul — needs no 21
reconciliation with God, for it is one with Him now and
forever.

Jesus came announcing Truth, and saying not only "the 24
kingdom of God is at hand," but "the kingdom of God
is within you." Hence there is no sin, for God's kingdom
is everywhere and supreme, and it follows that the human 27
kingdom is nowhere, and must be *unreal*. Jesus taught

1 and demonstrated the infinite as one, and not as two.
He did not teach that there are two deities, — one in-
3 finite and the other finite; for that would be impossible.
He knew God as infinite, and therefore as the All-in-all;
and we shall know this truth when we awake in the divine
6 likeness.   Jesus' true and conscious being never left
heaven for earth.   It abode forever above, even while
mortals believed it was here.   He once spoke of himself
9 (John iii. 13) as "the Son of man which is in heaven," —
remarkable words, as wholly opposed to the popular view
of Jesus' nature.

12   The real Christ was unconscious of matter, of sin,
disease, and death, and was conscious only of God, of
good, of eternal Life, and harmony.   Hence the human
15 Jesus had a resort to his higher self and relation to the
Father, and there could find rest from unreal trials in
the conscious reality and royalty of his being, — holding
18 the mortal as unreal, and the divine as real.   It was this
retreat from material to spiritual selfhood which recuper-
ated him for triumph over sin, sickness, and death.   Had
21 he been as conscious of these evils as he was of God,
wherein there is no consciousness of human error, Jesus
could not have resisted them; nor could he have conquered
24 the malice of his foes, rolled away the stone from the
sepulchre, and risen from human sense to a higher concept than that in which he appeared at his birth.

27   Mankind's concept of Jesus was a babe born in a manger,
even while the divine and ideal Christ was the Son of God,

spiritual and eternal. In human conception God's off- 1
spring had to grow, develop; but in Science his divine
nature and manhood were forever complete, and dwelt 3
forever in the Father. Jesus said, "Ye do err, not knowing the Scriptures, nor the power of God." Mortal thought
gives the eternal God and infinite consciousness the license 6
of a short-lived sinner, to begin and end, to know both
evil and good; when evil is temporal and God is eternal, —
and when, as a sphere of Mind, He cannot know begin- 9
ning or end.

The spiritual interpretation of the vicarious atonement
of Jesus, in Christian Science, unfolds the full-orbed glory 12
of that event; but to regard this wonder of glory, this
most marvellous demonstration, as a personal and material
bloodgiving — or as a proof that sin is known to the 15
divine Mind, and that what is unlike God demands His
continual presence, knowledge, and power, to meet and
master it — would make the atonement to be less than 18
the *at-one-ment,* whereby the work of Jesus would lose
its efficacy and lack the "signs following."

From Genesis to Revelation the Scriptures teach an in- 21
finite God, and none beside Him; and on this basis
Messiah and prophet saved the sinner and raised the dead,
— uplifting the human understanding, buried in a false 24
sense of being. Jesus rendered null and void whatever
is unlike God; but he could not have done this if error
and sin existed in the Mind of God. What God knows, 27
He also predestinates; and it must be fulfilled. Jesus

1 proved to perfection, so far as this could be done in that age, what Christian Science is to-day proving in a small
3 degree, — the falsity of the evidence of the material senses that sin, sickness, and death are sensible claims, and that God substantiates their evidence by knowing their claim.
6 He established the only true idealism on the basis that God is All, and He is good, and good is Spirit; hence there is no intelligent sin, evil *mind* or matter: and this is the only
9 true philosophy and realism. This divine mystery of godliness was the rock of Truth, on which he built his Church of the new-born, against which the gates of hell
12 cannot prevail.

This Truth is the rock which the builders rejected; but "the same is become the head of the corner." This is
15 the chief corner-stone, the basis and support of creation, the interpreter of one God, the infinity and unity of good.

In proportion as mortals approximate the understand-
18 ing of Christian Science, they take hold of harmony, and material incumbrance disappears. Having one God, one Mind, one consciousness, — which includes only His own
21 nature, — and loving your neighbor as yourself, constitute Christian Science, which must demonstrate the nothingness of any other state or stage of being.

24 IS THERE NO INTERCESSORY PRAYER?

All prayer that is desire is intercessory; but kindling desire loses a part of its purest spirituality if the lips try to

express it.   It is a truism that we can think more lucidly 1
and profoundly than we can write or speak.   The silent
intercession and unvoiced imploring is an honest and po- 3
tent prayer to heal and save.   The audible prayer may be
offered to be heard of men, though ostensibly to catch
God's ear, — after the fashion of Baal's prophets, — by 6
speaking loud enough to be heard; but when the heart
prays, and not the lips, no dishonesty or vanity influences
the petition.   9

Prophet and apostle have glorified God in secret prayer,
and He has rewarded them openly.   Prayer can neither
change God, nor bring His designs into mortal modes; but 12
it can and does change our modes and our false sense of
Life, Love, and Truth, uplifting us to Him.   Such prayer
humiliates, purifies, and quickens activity, in the direction 15
that is unerring.

True prayer is not asking God for love; it is learning to
love, and to include all mankind in one affection.   Prayer 18
is the utilization of the love wherewith He loves us.   Prayer
begets an awakened desire to be and do good.   It makes
new and scientific discoveries of God, of His goodness and 21
power.   It shows us more clearly than we saw before,
what we already have and are; and most of all, it shows
us what God is.   Advancing in this light, we reflect it; 24
and this light reveals the pure Mind-pictures, in silent
prayer, even as photography grasps the solar light to portray the face of pleasant thought.   27

What but silent prayer can meet the demand, "Pray

1 without ceasing"? The apostle James said: "Ye ask, and receive not, because ye ask amiss, to consume it on 3 your lusts." Because of vanity and self-righteousness, mortals seek, and expect to receive, a material sense of approval; and they expect also what is impossible, — a 6 material and mortal sense of spiritual and immortal Truth.

It is sometimes wise to hide from dull and base ears the 9 pure pearls of awakened consciousness, lest your pearls be trampled upon. Words may belie desire, and pour forth a hypocrite's prayer; but thoughts are our honest 12 conviction. I have no objection to audible prayer of the right kind; but the inaudible is more effectual.

I instruct my students to pursue their mental ministra- 15 tions very sacredly, and never to touch the human thought save to issues of Truth; never to trespass mentally on in- dividual rights; never to take away the rights, but only 18 the wrongs of mankind. Otherwise they forfeit their ability to heal in Science. Only when sickness, sin, and fear obstruct the harmony of Mind and body, is it right 21 for one mind to meddle with another mind, and control aright the thought struggling for freedom.

It is Truth and Love that cast out fear and heal the sick, 24 and mankind are better because of this. If a change in the religious views of the patient comes with the change to health, our Father has done this; for the human mind 27 and body are made better only by divine influence.

SHOULD CHRISTIANS BEWARE OF CHRISTIAN 1
SCIENCE?

History repeats itself. The Pharisees of old warned 3
the people to beware of Jesus, and contemptuously called
him "this fellow." Jesus said, "For which of these
works do ye stone me?" as much as to ask, Is it the 6
work most derided and envied that is most acceptable to
God? Not that he would cease to do the will of his Father
on account of persecution, but he would repeat his work 9
to the best advantage for mankind and the glory of his
Father.

There are sinners in all societies, and it is vain to look 12
for perfection in churches or associations. The life of
Christ is the perfect example; and to compare mortal
lives with this model is to subject them to severe scrutiny. 15
Without question, the subtlest forms of sin are trying to
force the doors of Science and enter in; but this white
sanctuary will never admit such as come to steal and to 18
rob. Through long ages people have slumbered over
Christ's commands, "Go ye into all the world, and preach
the gospel;" "Heal the sick, cast out devils;" and now 21
the Church seems almost chagrined that by new discoveries
of Truth sin is losing prestige and power.

The Rev. Dr. A. J. Gordon, a Boston Baptist clergyman, 24
said in a sermon: "The prayer of faith shall save the
sick, and it is doing it to-day; and as the faith of the Church

1 increases, and Christians more and more learn their duty
to believe all things written in the Scriptures, will such
3 manifestations of God's power increase among us." Such
sentiments are wholesome avowals of Christian Science.
God is not unable or unwilling to heal, and mortals are not
6 compelled to have other gods before Him, and employ
material forms to meet a mental want. The divine Spirit
supplies all human needs. Jesus said to the sick, "Thy
9 sins are forgiven thee; rise up and walk!" God's pardon
is the destruction of all "the ills that flesh is heir to."

All power belongs to God; and it is not in all the vain
12 power of dogma and philosophy to dispossess the divine
Mind of healing power, or to cast out error with error,
even in the name and for the sake of Christ, and so heal
15 the sick. While Science is engulfing error in bottomless
oblivion, the material senses would enthrone error as omnipotent and omnipresent, with power to determine the
18 fact and fate to being. It is said that the devil is the ape
of God. The lie of evil holds its own by declaring itself
both true and good. The path of Christian Science is be-
21 set with false claimants, aping its virtues, but cleaving to
their own vices. Denial of the authorship of "Science
and Health with Key to the Scriptures" would make a
24 lie the author of Truth, and so make Truth itself a lie.

A distinguished clergyman came to be healed. He said:
"I am suffering from nervous prostration, and have to eat
27 beefsteak and drink strong coffee to support me through
a sermon." Here a skeptic might well ask if the atone-

ment had lost its efficacy for him, and if Christ's power to heal was not equal to the power of daily meat and drink. The power of Truth is not contingent on matter. Our Master said, "Come unto me, all ye that labor and are heavy laden, and I will give you rest." Truth rebukes error; and whether stall-fed or famishing, theology needs Truth to stimulate and sustain a good sermon.

A lady said: "Only He who knows all things can estimate the good your books are doing."

A distinguished Doctor of Divinity said: "Your book leavens my sermons."

The following extract from a letter is a specimen of those received daily: "Your book Science and Health is healing the sick, binding up the broken-hearted, preaching deliverance to the captive, convicting the infidel, alarming the hypocrite, and quickening the Christian."

Christian Science Mind-healing is dishonored by those who take it up from mercenary motives, for wealth and fame, or think to build a baseless fabric of their own on another's foundation. They cannot put the "new wine into old bottles;" they can never engraft Truth into error. Such students come to my College to learn a system which they go away to disgrace. Stealing or garbling my statements of Mind-science will never prevent or reconstruct the wrecks of *"isms"* and help humanity.

Science often suffers blame through the sheer ignorance of people, while envy and hatred bark and bite at its heels. A man's inability to heal, on the Principle of Christian

1 Science, substantiates his ignorance of its Principle and
practice, and incapacitates him for correct comment.
3 This failure should make him modest.

Christian Science involves a new language, and a higher
demonstration of medicine and religion. It is the "new
6 tongue" of Truth, having its best interpretation in the
power of Christianity to heal. My system of Mind-healing swerves not from the highest ethics and from the spirit-
9 ual goal. To climb up by some other way than Truth is
to fall. Error has no hobby, however boldly ridden or
brilliantly caparisoned, that can leap into the sanctum
12 of Christian Science.

In Queen Elizabeth's time Protestantism could sentence
men to the dungeon or stake for their religion, and so
15 abrogate the rights of conscience and choke the channels
of God. Ecclesiastical tyranny muzzled the mouth lisping
God's praise; and instead of healing, it palsied the weak
18 hand outstretched to God. Progress, legitimate to the
human race, pours the healing balm of Truth and Love
into every wound. It reassures us that no Reign of Terror
21 or rule of error will again unite Church and State, or re-
enact, through the civil arm of government, the horrors of
religious persecution.

24   The Rev. S. E. Herrick, a Congregational clergyman of
Boston, says: "Heretics of yesterday are martyrs to-day."
In every age and clime, "On earth peace, good will to-
27 ward men" must be the watchword of Christianity.

Jesus said: "I thank Thee, O Father, Lord of heaven

and earth, that Thou hast hid these things from the wise 1
and prudent, and hast revealed them unto babes."

St. Paul said that without charity we are "as sound- 3
ing brass, or a tinkling cymbal;" and he added: "Charity
suffereth long, and is kind; . . . doth not behave itself
unseemly, . . . thinketh no evil, . . . but rejoiceth in the 6
truth."

To hinder the unfolding truth, to ostracize whatever
uplifts mankind, is of course out of the question. Such an 9
attempt indicates weakness, fear, or malice; and such
efforts arise from a spiritual lack, felt, though unacknowledged.   12

Let it not be heard in Boston that woman, "last at the
cross and first at the sepulchre," has no rights which man
is bound to respect. In natural law and in religion the 15
right of woman to fill the highest measure of enlightened
understanding and the highest places in government, is
inalienable, and these rights are ably vindicated by the 18
noblest of both sexes. This is woman's hour, with all its
sweet amenities and its moral and religious reforms.

Drifting into intellectual wrestlings, we should agree to 21
disagree; and this harmony would anchor the Church in
more spiritual latitudes, and so fulfil her destiny.

Let the Word have free course and be glorified. The 24
people clamor to leave cradle and swaddling-clothes. The
spiritual status is urging its highest demands on mortals,
and material history is drawing to a close. Truth cannot 27
be stereotyped; it unfoldeth forever. "One on God's

1 side is a majority;" and "Lo, I am with you alway," is
the pledge of the Master.

3   The question now at issue is: Shall we have a practical, spiritual Christianity, with its healing power, or
shall we have material medicine and superficial religion?
6 The advancing hope of the race, craving health and holiness, halts for a reply; and the reappearing Christ, whose
life-giving understanding Christian Science imparts, must
9 answer the constant inquiry: "Art thou he that should
come?" Woman should not be ordered to the rear, or
laid on the rack, for joining the overture of angels. Theo-
12 logians descant pleasantly upon free moral agency; but
they should begin by admitting individual rights.

The author's ancestors were among the first settlers of
15 New Hampshire. They reared there the Puritan standard
of undefiled religion. As dutiful descendants of Puritans,
let us lift their standard higher, rejoicing, as Paul did,
18 that we are *free born.*

Man has a noble destiny; and the full-orbed significance
of this destiny has dawned on the sick-bound and sin-
21 enslaved. For the unfolding of this upward tendency to
health, greatness, and goodness, I shall continue to labor
and wait.

Christian
Science
versus
Pantheism

Christian Science versus Pantheism

by MARY BAKER EDDY
*Discoverer and Founder of Christian Science
and Author of Science and Health
with Key to the Scriptures*

Marcas Registradas

Published by The First Church of Christ, Scientist, in Boston, Massachusetts, U.S.A.

*The facsimile of the signature of Mary Baker Eddy
and the design of the Cross and Crown seal are
trademarks of The Christian Science Board of Directors,
registered in the United States and other countries.*

Christian Science versus Pantheism

Pastor's Message to The Mother Church, on the Occasion of the June Communion, 1898

SUBJECT: *Not Pantheism, but Christian Science*

BELOVED brethren, since last you gathered at the feast of our Passover, the winter winds have come and gone; the rushing winds of March have shrieked and hummed their hymns; the frown and smile of April, the laugh of May, have fled; and the roseate blush of joyous June is here and ours.

In unctuous unison with nature, mortals are hoping and working, putting off outgrown, wornout, or soiled garments — the pleasures and pains of sensation and the sackcloth of waiting — for the springtide of Soul. For what a man seeth he hopeth not for, but hopeth for what he hath not seen, and waiteth patiently the appearing thereof. The night is far spent, and day is not distant in the horizon of Truth — even the day when all people shall know and acknowledge one God and one Christianity.

1   CHRISTIAN SCIENCE NOT PANTHEISM

At this period of enlightenment, a declaration from the
3 pulpit that Christian Science is pantheism is anomalous to
those who know whereof they speak — who know that
Christian Science *is* Science, and therefore is neither
6 hypothetical nor dogmatical, but demonstrable, and
looms above the mists of pantheism higher than Mt.
Ararat above the deluge.

9   ANALYSIS OF "PANTHEISM"

According to Webster the word "pantheism" is derived from two Greek words meaning "all" and "god."
12 Webster's *derivation* of the English word "pantheism" is
most suggestive.   His uncapitalized word "god" gives
the meaning of pantheism as a human opinion of "gods
15 many," or mind in matter.   "The doctrine that the universe, conceived of as a whole, is God; that there is no
God but the combined forces and laws which are mani-
18 fested in the existing universe."
The Standard Dictionary has it that pantheism is the
doctrine of the deification of natural causes, conceived as
21 one personified nature, to which the religious sentiment is
directed.
Pan is a Greek prefix, but it might stand, in the term
24 pantheism, for the mythological deity of that name; and
theism for a belief concerning Deity in theology.   However, Pan in imagery is preferable to pantheism in theology.

The mythical deity may please the fancy, while pantheism 1
suits not at all the Christian sense of religion. Pan, as a
deity, is supposed to preside over sylvan solitude, and is a 3
horned and hoofed animal, half goat and half man, that
poorly presents the poetical phase of the genii of forests.[1]

My sense of nature's rich glooms is, that loneness lacks 6
but one charm to make it half divine — a friend, with
whom to whisper, "Solitude is sweet." Certain moods
of mind find an indefinable pleasure in stillness, soft, 9
silent as the storm's sudden hush; for nature's stillness
is voiced with a hum of harmony, the gentle murmur of
early morn, the evening's closing vespers, and lyre of bird 12
and brooklet.

> "O sacred solitude! divine retreat!
> Choice of the prudent! envy of the great! 15
> By thy pure stream, or in thy evening shade,
> We court fair wisdom, that celestial maid."

Theism is the belief in the personality and infinite mind 18
of one supreme, holy, self-existent God, who reveals Himself supernaturally to His creation, and whose laws are
not reckoned as science. In religion, it is a belief in one 21
God, or in many gods. It is opposed to atheism and

---

[1] In Roman mythology (one of my girlhood studies), Pan stood
for "universal nature proceeding from the divine Mind and provi- 24
dence, of which heaven, earth, sea, the eternal fire, are so many members." Pan was the god of shepherds and hunters, leader of the
nymphs, president of the mountains, patron of country life, and guar- 27
dian of flocks and herds. His pipe of seven reeds denotes the celestial
harmony of the seven planets; his shepherd's crook, that care and
providence by which he governs the universe; his spotted skin, the 30
stars; his goat's feet, the solidity of the earth; his man-face, the
celestial world.

1 monotheism, but agrees with certain forms of pantheism
and polytheism. It is the doctrine that the universe owes
3 its origin and continuity to the reason, intellect, and will of
a self-existent divine Being, who possesses all wisdom,
goodness, and power, and is the creator and preserver of
6 man.

A theistic theological belief may agree with physics and
anatomy that reason and will are properly classified as
9 mind, located in the brain; also, that the functions of
these faculties depend on conditions of matter, or brain,
for their proper exercise. But reason and will are human;
12 God is divine. In academics and in religion it is patent
that will is capable of use and of abuse, of right and wrong
action, while God is incapable of evil; that brain is matter,
15 and that there are many so-called minds; that He is the
creator of man, but that man also is a creator, making
two creators; but God is Mind and one.

18 GOD — NOT HUMAN DEVICES — THE PRESERVER
OF MAN

God, Spirit, is indeed the preserver of man. Then, in
21 the words of the Hebrew singer, "Why art thou cast down,
O my soul? and why art thou disquieted within me? hope
thou in God: for I shall yet praise Him, who is the health
24 of my countenance, and my God. . . . Who forgiveth
all thine iniquities; who healeth all thy diseases." This
being the case, what need have we of drugs, hygiene, and
27 medical therapeutics, if these are not man's preservers?
By admitting self-evident affirmations and then contra-

dicting them, monotheism is lost and pantheism is found 1
in scholastic theology.   Can a single quality of God,
Spirit, be discovered in matter?   The Scriptures plainly 3
declare, "The Word was God;"   and "all things were
made by Him," — the Word.   What, then, can matter
create, or how can it exist?   6

JESUS' DEFINITION OF EVIL

Did God create evil? or is evil self-existent, and so
possessed of the nature of God, good?   Since evil is not 9
self-made, who or what hath made evil?   Our Master
gave the proper answer for all time to this hoary query.
He said of evil: "Ye are of your father, the devil, and the 12
lusts of your father ye will do.   He was a murderer from
the beginning, and abode not in the truth [God], because
there is no truth [reality] in him [evil]. When he speaketh 15
a lie, he speaketh of his own: for he is a liar, and the father
of it [a lie]."

Jesus' definition of devil (evil) explains evil.   It shows 18
that evil is both liar and lie, a delusion and illusion.   Therefore we should neither believe the lie, nor believe that it
hath embodiment or power; in other words, we should 21
not believe that a lie, nothing, can be something, but deny
it and prove its falsity.   After this manner our Master cast
out evil, healed the sick, and saved sinners.   Knowing 24
that evil is a lie, and, as the Scripture declares, brought
sin, sickness, and death into the world, Jesus treated the
lie summarily.   He denied it, cast it out of mortal mind, 27
and thus healed sickness and sin.   His treatment of evil

1 and disease, Science will restore and establish, — first,
because it was more effectual than all other means; and,
3 second, because evil and disease will never disappear in
any other way.

Finally, brethren, let us continue to denounce evil as the
6 illusive claim that God is not supreme, and continue to
fight it until it disappears, — but not as one that beateth
the mist, but lifteth his head above it and putteth his foot
9 upon a lie.

EVIL, AS PERSONIFIED BY THE SERPENT

Mosaic theism introduces evil, first, in the form of a
12 talking serpent, contradicting the word of God and thereby
obtaining social prestige, a large following, and changing
the order and harmony of God's creation. But the higher
15 criticism is not satisfied with this theism, and asks, If God
is *infinite* good, what and where is evil? And if Spirit
made all that was made, how can matter be an intelligent
18 creator or coworker with God? Again: Did one Mind,
or two minds, enter into the Scriptural allegory, in the
colloquy between good and evil, God and a serpent? — and
21 if two minds, what becomes of theism in Christianity? For
if God, good, is Mind, and evil also is mind, the Christian
religion has at least two Gods. If Spirit is sovereign, how
24 can matter be force or law; and if God, good, is omnipotent, what power hath evil?

It is plain that elevating evil to the altitude of mind gives
27 it power, and that the belief in more than one spirit, if

Spirit, God, is infinite, breaketh the First Commandment 1
in the Decalogue.

Science shows that a plurality of minds, or intelligent 3
matter, signifies more than one God, and thus prevents the
demonstration that the healing Christ, Truth, gave and
gives in proof of the omnipotence of one divine, infinite 6
Principle.

Does not the theism or belief, that after God, Spirit, had
created all things spiritually, a material creation took 9
place, and God, the preserver of man, declared that man
should die, lose the character and sovereignty of Jehovah,
and hint the gods of paganism?   12

THEISTIC RELIGIONS

We know of but three theistic religions, the Mosaic, the
Christian, and the Mohammedan. Does not each of these 15
religions mystify the absolute oneness and infinity of God,
Spirit?

A close study of the Old and New Testaments in con- 18
nection with the original text indicates, in the third chapter of Genesis, a lapse in the Mosaic religion, wherein
theism seems meaningless, or a vague apology for con- 21
tradictions. It certainly gives to matter and evil reality
and power, intelligence and law, which implies Mind,
Spirit, God; and the logical sequence of this error is idol- 24
atry — other gods.

Again: The hypothesis of mind in matter, or more than
one Mind, lapses into evil dominating good, matter govern- 27
ing Mind, and makes sin, disease, and death inevitable,

1 despite of Mind, or by the consent of Mind! Next, it
follows that the disarrangement of matter causes a man to
3 be mentally deranged; and the Babylonian sun god, moon
god, and sin god find expression in sun worship, lunacy,
sin, and mortality.

6   Does not the belief that Jesus, the man of Galilee, is
God, imply two Gods, one the divine, infinite Person, the
other a human finite personality? Does not the belief
9 that Mary was the mother of God deny the self-existence
of God? And does not the doctrine that Mohammed is
the only prophet of God infringe the sacredness of one
12 Christ Jesus?

SCIENTIFIC CHRISTIANITY MEANS ONE GOD

Christianity, as taught and demonstrated in the first
15 century by our great Master, virtually annulled the so-
called laws of matter, idolatry, pantheism, and polytheism.
Christianity then had one God and one law, namely,
18 divine Science. It said, "Call no man your father upon
the earth, for one is your Father, which is in heaven."
Speaking of himself, Jesus said, "My Father is greater
21 than I." Christianity, as he taught and demonstrated it,
must ever rest on the basis of the First Commandment and
love for man.

24   The doctrines that embrace pantheism, polytheism, and
paganism are admixtures of matter and Spirit, truth and
error, sickness and sin, life and death. They make man
27 the servant of matter, living by reason of it, suffering because of it, and dying in consequence of it. They con-

stantly reiterate the belief of pantheism, that mind "sleeps 1
in the mineral, dreams in the animal, and wakes in man."

"Infinite Spirit" means one God and His creation, and 3
no reality in aught else. The term "spirits" means more
than one Spirit; — in paganism they stand for gods; in
spiritualism they imply men and women; and in Christian- 6
ity they signify a good Spirit and an evil spirit.

Is there a religion under the sun that hath demonstrated
one God and the four first rules pertaining thereto, namely, 9
"Thou shalt have no other gods before me;" "Love thy
neighbor as thyself;" "Be ye therefore perfect, even as
your Father which is in heaven is perfect;" "Whosoever 12
liveth and believeth in me shall never die." (John xi. 26.)

What mortal to-day is wise enough to do himself no
harm, to hinder not the attainment of scientific Chris- 15
tianity? Whoever demonstrates the highest humanity, —
long-suffering, self-surrender, and spiritual endeavor to
bless others, — ought to be aided, not hindered, in his 18
holy mission. I would kiss the feet of such a messenger,
for to help such a one is to help one's self. The demonstration of Christianity blesses all mankind. It loves one's 21
neighbor as one's self; it loves its enemies — and this
love benefits its enemies (though they believe it not), and
rewards its possessor; for, "If ye love them which love you, 24
what reward have ye?"

MAN THE TRUE IMAGE OF GOD

From a material standpoint, the best of people some- 27
times object to the philosophy of Christian Science, on the

1 ground that it takes away man's personality and makes
man less than man. But what saith the apostle? — even
3 this: "If a man think himself to be something, when he is
nothing, he deceiveth himself." The great Nazarene
Prophet said, "By their fruits ye shall know them:" then,
6 if the effects of Christian Science on the lives of men
be thus judged, we are sure the honest verdict of humanity will attest its uplifting power, and prevail over the
9 opposite notion that Christian Science lessens man's individuality.

The students at the Massachusetts Metaphysical Col-
12 lege, generally, were the average man and woman. But
after graduation, the best students in the class averred
that they were stronger and better than before it. With
15 twelve lessons or less, the present and future of those students had wonderfully broadened and brightened before
them, thus proving the utility of what they had been taught.
18 Christian Scientists heal functional, organic, chronic, and
acute diseases that M.D.'s have failed to heal; and,
better still, they reform desperate cases of intemperance,
21 tobacco using, and immorality, which, we regret to say,
other religious teachers are unable to effect. All this is
accomplished by the grace of God, — the effect of God
24 understood. A higher manhood is manifest, and never
lost, in that individual who finds the highest joy, — therefore no pleasure in loathsome habits or in sin, and no
27 necessity for disease and death. Whatever promotes
statuesque being, health, and holiness does not degrade
man's personality. Sin, sickness, appetites, and passions,
30 constitute no part of man, but obscure man. Therefore it

required the divinity of our Master to perceive the real 1
man, and to cast out the unreal or counterfeit. It caused
St. Paul to write, — "Lie not one to another, seeing that 3
ye have put off the old man with his deeds; and have put
on the new man, which is renewed in knowledge after
the image of Him that created him." 6
Was our Master mistaken in judging a cause by its
effects? Shall the opinions, systems, doctrines, and dogmas of men gauge the animus of man? or shall his stature 9
in Christ, Truth, declare him? Governed by the divine
Principle of his being, man is perfect. When will the
schools allow mortals to turn from clay to Soul for the 12
model? The Science of being, understood and obeyed,
will demonstrate man to be superior to the best church-
member or moralist on earth, who understands not this 15
Science. If man is spiritually fallen, it matters not what
he believes; he is not upright, and must regain his native
spiritual stature in order to be in proper shape, as certainly 18
as the man who falls physically needs to rise again.
Mortals, content with something less than perfection —
the original standard of man — may believe that evil de- 21
velops good, and that whatever strips off evil's disguise belittles man's personality. But God enables us to know that
evil is not the medium of good, and that good supreme de- 24
stroys all sense of evil, obliterates the lost image that
mortals are content to call man, and demands man's unfallen spiritual perfectibility. 27
The grand realism that man is the true image of God,
not fallen or inverted, is demonstrated by Christian Science.
And because Christ's dear demand, "Be ye therefore 30

1 perfect," is valid, it will be found possible to fulfil it. Then
also will it be learned that good is not educed from evil,
3 but comes from the rejection of evil and its *modus operandi*.
Our scholarly expositor of the Scriptures, Lyman Abbott,
D.D., writes, "God, Spirit, is ever in universal nature."
6 Then, we naturally ask, how can Spirit be constantly passing out of mankind by death — for the universe includes
man?

9   THE GRANDEUR OF CHRISTIANITY

This closing century, and its successors, will make strong
claims on religion, and demand that the inspired Scriptural
12 commands be fulfilled. The altitude of Christianity openeth, high above the so-called laws of matter, a door that no
man can shut; it showeth to all peoples the way of escape
15 from sin, disease, and death; it lifteth the burden of sharp
experience from off the heart of humanity, and so lighteth
the path that he who entereth it may run and not weary,
18 and walk, not wait by the roadside, — yea, pass gently on
without the alterative agonies whereby the way-seeker
gains and points the path.
21 The Science of Christianity is strictly monotheism, —
it has ONE GOD. And this divine infinite Principle,
noumenon and phenomena, is demonstrably the self-
24 existent Life, Truth, Love, substance, Spirit, Mind, which
includes all that the term implies, and is all that is real and
eternal. Christian Science is irrevocable — unpierced
27 by bold conjecture's sharp point, by bald philosophy, or
by man's inventions. It is divinely true, and every hour

in time and in eternity will witness more steadfastly to its ₁
practical truth. And Science is not pantheism, but Christian Science. ₃

Chief among the questions herein, and nearest my
heart, is this: When shall Christianity be demonstrated
according to Christ, in these words: "Neither shall they ₆
say, Lo, here! or, lo there! for, behold, the kingdom of
God is within you"?

EXHORTATION ₉

Beloved brethren, the love of our loving Lord was never
more manifest than in its stern condemnation of all error,
wherever found. I counsel thee, rebuke and exhort one ₁₂
another. Love all Christian churches for the gospel's
sake; and be exceedingly glad that the churches are united
in purpose, if not in method, to close the war between ₁₅
flesh and Spirit, and to fight the good fight till God's will
be witnessed and done on earth as in heaven.

Sooner or later all shall know Him, recognize the great ₁₈
truth that Spirit is infinite, and find life in Him in whom
we do "live, and move, and have our being" — life in
Life, all in All. Then shall all nations, peoples, and ₂₁
tongues, in the words of St. Paul, have "one God and
Father of all, who is above all, and through all, and in
you all." (Ephesians iv. 6.) ₂₄

Have I wearied you with the mysticism of opposites?
Truly there is no rest in them, and I have only traversed
my subject that you may prove for yourselves the unsub- ₂₇

1 stantial nature of whatever is unlike good, weigh a sigh, and rise into the rest of righteousness with its triumphant 3 train.

Once more I write, Set your affections on things above; love one another; commune at the table of our Lord in one 6 spirit; worship in spirit and in truth; and if daily adoring, imploring, and living the divine Life, Truth, Love, thou shalt partake of the bread that cometh down from heaven, 9 drink of the cup of salvation, and be baptized in Spirit.

PRAYER FOR COUNTRY AND CHURCH

Pray for the prosperity of our country, and for her vic- 12 tory under arms; that justice, mercy, and peace continue to characterize her government, and that they shall rule all nations. Pray that the divine presence may still guide and 15 bless our chief magistrate, those associated with his execu- tive trust, and our national judiciary; give to our congress wisdom, and uphold our nation with the right arm of His 18 righteousness.

In your peaceful homes remember our brave soldiers, whether in camp or in battle.[1] Oh, may their love of coun- 21 try, and their faithful service thereof, be unto them life- preservers! May the divine Love succor and protect them, as at Manila, where brave men, led by the dauntless 24 Dewey, and shielded by the power that saved them, sailed victoriously through the jaws of death and blotted out the Spanish squadron.

27   Great occasion have we to rejoice that our nation, which

---

[1] This refers to the war between United States and Spain for the liberty of Cuba.

fed her starving foe, — already murdering her peaceful 1
seamen and destroying millions of her money, — will be
as formidable in war as she has been compassionate in 3
peace.

May our Father-Mother God, who in times past hath
spread for us a table in the wilderness and "in the midst 6
of our enemies," establish us in the most holy faith, plant
our feet firmly on Truth, the rock of Christ, the "substance
of things hoped for" — and fill us with the life and under- 9
standing of God, and good will towards men.

MARY BAKER EDDY

Message
to
The Mother Church

BOSTON, MASSACHUSETTS
JUNE, 1900

Message
to
The Mother Church

BOSTON, MASSACHUSETTS
JUNE, 1900

by MARY BAKER EDDY

Pastor Emeritus and Author of
Science and Health with Key to the Scriptures

Marcas Registradas

Published by The First Church of Christ, Scientist, in Boston, Massachusetts, U.S.A.

The facsimile of the signature of Mary Baker Eddy and the design of the Cross and Crown seal are trademarks of The Christian Science Board of Directors, registered in the United States and other countries.

Message for 1900

MY beloved brethren, methinks even I am touched 1
with the tone of your happy hearts, and can see
your glad faces, aglow with gratitude, chinked within the 3
storied walls of The Mother Church. If, indeed, we may
be absent from the body and present with the ever-present
Love filling all space, time, and immortality — then I am 6
with thee, heart answering to heart, and mine to thine in
the glow of divine reflection.

I am grateful to say that in the last year of the nine- 9
teenth century this first church of our denomination,
chartered in 1879, is found crowned with unprecedented
prosperity; a membership of over sixteen thousand com- 12
municants in unity, with rapidly increasing numbers, rich
spiritual attainments, and right convictions fast forming
themselves into conduct. 15

Christian Science already has a hearing and following
in the five grand divisions of the globe; in Australia, the
Philippine Islands, Hawaiian Islands; and in most of the 18
principal cities, such as Boston, New York, Philadelphia,
Washington, Baltimore, Charleston, S. C., Atlanta, New
Orleans, Chicago, St. Louis, Denver, Salt Lake City, San 21
Francisco, Montreal, London, Edinburgh, Dublin, Paris,
Berlin, Rome, Pekin. Judging from the number of the
readers of my books and those interested in them, over a 24

1 million of people are already interested in Christian
Science; and this interest increases. Churches of this
3 denomination are springing up in the above-named cities,
and, thanks to God, the people most interested in this
old-new theme of redeeming Love are among the best people
6 on earth and in heaven.

The song of Christian Science is, "Work — work —
work — watch and pray." The close observer reports
9 three types of human nature — the right thinker and
worker, the idler, and the intermediate.

The right thinker works; he gives little time to society
12 manners or matters, and benefits society by his example
and usefulness. He takes no time for amusement, ease,
frivolity; he earns his money and gives it wisely to the
15 world.

The wicked idler earns little and is stingy; he has
plenty of means, but he uses them evilly. Ask how he
18 gets his money, and his satanic majesty is supposed to
answer smilingly: "By cheating, lying, and crime; his
dupes are his capital; his stock in trade, the wages of sin;
21 your idlers are my busiest workers; they will leave a
lucrative business to work for me." Here we add: The
doom of such workers will come, and it will be more sudden,
24 severe, and lasting than the adversary can hope.

The intermediate worker works at times. He says:
"It is my duty to take some time for myself; however, I
27 believe in working when it is convenient." Well, all that
is good. But what of the fruits of your labors? And he
answers: "I am not so successful as I could wish, but I
30 work hard enough to be so."

Now, what saith Christian Science? "When a man is 1
right, his thoughts are right, active, and they are fruitful;
he loses self in love, and cannot hear himself, unless he 3
loses the chord. The right thinker and worker does his
best, and does the thinking for the ages. No hand that
feels not his help, no heart his comfort. He improves 6
moments; to him time is money, and he hoards this capital
to distribute gain."

If the right thinker and worker's servitude is duly valued, 9
he is not thereby worshipped. One's idol is by no means
his servant, but his master. And they who love a good
work or good workers are themselves workers who appre- 12
ciate a life, and labor to awake the slumbering capability
of man. And what the best thinker and worker has said
and done, they are not far from saying and doing. As a 15
rule the Adam-race are not apt to worship the pioneer
of spiritual ideas, — but ofttimes to shun him as their
tormentor. Only the good man loves the right thinker 18
and worker, and cannot worship him, for that would destroy this man's goodness.

To-day it surprises us that during the period of captivity 21
the Israelites in Babylon hesitated not to call the divine
name Yahwah, afterwards transcribed Jehovah; also
that women's names contained this divine appellative and 24
so sanctioned idolatry, — other gods. In the heathen
conception Yahwah, misnamed Jehovah, was a god of
hate and of love, who repented himself, improved on his 27
work of creation, and revenged himself upon his enemies.
However, the animus of heathen religion was not the incentive of the devout Jew — but has it not tainted the reli- 30

1 gious sects? This seedling misnomer couples love and
hate, good and evil, health and sickness, life and death,
3 with man — makes His opposites as real and normal as
the one God, and so unwittingly consents to many minds
and many gods. This precedent that would commingle
6 Christianity, the gospel of the New Testament and the
teaching of the righteous Galilean, Christ Jesus, with the
Babylonian and Neoplatonic religion, is being purged by
9 a purer Judaism and nearer approach to monotheism and
the perfect worship of one God.

To-day people are surprised at the new and forward
12 steps in religion, which indicate a renaissance greater than
in the mediæval period; but ought not this to be an agreeable surprise, inasmuch as these are progressive signs of
15 the times?

It should seem rational that the only perfect religion is
divine Science, Christianity as taught by our great Master;
18 that which leaves the beaten path of human doctrines and
is the truth of God, and of man and the universe. The
divine Principle and rules of this Christianity being de-
21 monstrable, they are undeniable; and they must be found
final, absolute, and eternal. The question as to religion
is: Does it demonstrate its doctrines? Do religionists
24 believe that God is *One* and *All?* Then whatever is real
must proceed from God, from Mind, and is His reflection
and Science. Man and the universe coexist with God in
27 Science, and they reflect God and nothing else. In divine
Science, divine Love includes and reflects all that really
is, all personality and individuality. St. Paul beautifully
30 enunciates this fundamental fact of Deity as the "Father

of all, who is above all, and through all, and in you all." 1
This scientific statement of the origin, nature, and government of all things coincides with the First Commandment 3
of the Decalogue, and leaves no opportunity for idolatry
or aught besides God, good. It gives evil no origin, no
reality. Here note the words of our Master corroborating 6
this as self-evident. Jesus said the opposite of God —
good — named devil — evil — "is a liar, and the father
of it" — that is, its origin is a myth, a lie. 9

Applied to Deity, Father and Mother are synonymous
terms; they signify one God. Father, Son, and Holy
Ghost mean God, man, and divine Science. God is self- 12
existent, the essence and source of the two latter, and their
office is that of eternal, infinite individuality. I see no
other way under heaven and among men whereby to have 15
one God, and man in His image and likeness, loving another as himself. This being the divine Science of divine
Love, it would enable man to escape from idolatry of 18
every kind, to obey the First Commandment of the Decalogue: "Thou shalt have no other gods before me;"
and the command of Christ: "Love thy neighbor as thy- 21
self." On this rock Christian Science is built. It may
be the rock which the builders reject for a season; but
it is the Science of God and His universe, and it will be- 24
come the head of the corner, the foundation of all systems
of religion.

The spiritual sense of the Scriptures understood enables 27
one to utilize the power of divine Love in casting out God's
opposites, called evils, and in healing the sick. Not madness, but might and majesty attend every footstep of 30

1 Christian Science. There is no imperfection, no lack in
the Principle and rules which demonstrate it. Only the
3 demonstrator can mistake or fail in proving its power and
divinity. In the words of St. Paul: "I count not myself
to have apprehended: but this one thing I do, forgetting
6 those things which are behind, and reaching forth to those
things which are before, I press toward the mark for the
prize of the high calling of God in Christ Jesus" — in the
9 true idea of God. Any mystery in Christian Science departs when dawns the spiritual meaning thereof; and the
spiritual sense of the Scriptures is the scientific sense which
12 interprets the healing Christ. A child can measurably
understand Christian Science, for, through his simple faith
and purity, he takes in its spiritual sense that puzzles the
15 man. The child not only accepts Christian Science more
readily than the adult, but he practises it. This notable
fact proves that the so-called fog of this Science obtains
18 not in the Science, but in the material sense which the
adult entertains of it. However, to a man who uses tobacco, is profane, licentious, and breaks God's com-
21 mandments, that which destroys his false appetites and
lifts him from the stubborn thrall of sin to a meek and
loving disciple of Christ, clothed and in his right mind, is
24 not darkness but light.

Again, that Christian Science is the Science of God is
proven when, in the degree that you accept it, understand
27 and practise it, you are made better physically, morally,
and spiritually. Some modern exegesis on the prophetic
Scriptures cites 1875 as the year of the second coming of
30 Christ. In that year the Christian Science textbook,

"Science and Health with Key to the Scriptures," was 1
first published. From that year the United States official
statistics show the annual death-rate to have gradually 3
diminished. Likewise the religious sentiment has increased; creeds and dogmas have been sifted, and a
greater love of the Scriptures manifested. In 1895 it was 6
estimated that during the past three years there had been
more Bibles sold than in all the other 1893 years. Many
of our best and most scholarly men and women, distin- 9
guished members of the bar and bench, press and pulpit,
and those in all the walks of life, will tell you they never
loved the Bible and appreciated its worth as they did after 12
reading "Science and Health with Key to the Scriptures."
This is my great reward for having suffered, lived, and
learned, in a small degree, the Science of perfectibility 15
through Christ, the Way, the Truth, and the Life.

Is there more than one Christ, and hath Christ a second
appearing? There is but one Christ. And from ever- 18
lasting to everlasting this Christ is never absent. In doubt
and darkness we say as did Mary of old: "I know not
where they have laid him." But when we behold the 21
Christ walking the wave of earth's troubled sea, like Peter
we believe in the second coming, and would walk more
closely with Christ; but find ourselves so far from the em- 24
bodiment of Truth that ofttimes this attempt measurably
fails, and we cry, "Save, or I perish!" Then the tender,
loving Christ is found near, affords help, and we are saved 27
from our fears. Thus it is we walk here below, and wait
for the full appearing of Christ till the long night is past
and the morning dawns on eternal day. Then, if sin and 30

1 flesh are put off, we shall know and behold more nearly
  the embodied Christ, and with saints and angels shall be
3 satisfied to go on till we awake in his likeness.

   The good man imparts knowingly and unknowingly
goodness; but the evil man also exhales consciously and
6 unconsciously his evil nature — hence, be careful of your
company. As in the floral kingdom odors emit characteristics of tree and flower, a perfume or a poison, so the hu-
9 man character comes forth a blessing or a bane upon
individuals and society. A wicked man has little real
intelligence; he may steal other people's good thoughts,
12 and wear the purloined garment as his own, till God's
discipline takes it off for his poverty to appear.

   Our Master saith to his followers: "Bring forth things
15 new and old." In this struggle remember that sensitiveness is sometimes selfishness, and that mental idleness or
apathy is always egotism and animality. Usefulness is
18 doing rightly by yourself and others. We lose a percentage
due to our activity when doing the work that belongs to
another. When a man begins to quarrel with himself he
21 stops quarrelling with others. We must exterminate self
before we can successfully war with mankind. Then, at
last, the right will boil over the brim of life and the fire
24 that purifies sense with Soul will be extinguished. It is not
Science for the wicked to wallow or the good to weep.

   Learn to obey; but learn first what obedience is.
27 When God speaks to you through one of His little ones,
and you obey the mandate but retain a desire to follow
your own inclinations, that is not obedience. I some-
30 times advise students not to do certain things which I

know it were best not to do, and they comply with my 1
counsel; but, watching them, I discern that this obedience
is contrary to their inclination. Then I sometimes with- 3
draw that advice and say: "You may do it if you desire." But I say this not because it is the best thing to
do, but because the student is not willing — therefore, 6
not ready — to obey.

The secret of Christian Science in right thinking and
acting is open to mankind, but few, comparatively, see it; 9
or, seeing it, shut their eyes and wait for a more convenient
season; or as of old cry out: "Why art thou come hither
to torment me before the time?" 12

Strong desires bias human judgment and misguide action, else they uplift them. But the reformer continues
his lightning, thunder, and sunshine till the mental at- 15
mosphere is clear. The reformer must be a hero at all
points, and he must have conquered himself before he can
conquer others. Sincerity is more successful than genius 18
or talent.

The twentieth century in the ebb and flow of thought
will challenge the thinkers, speakers, and workers to do 21
their best. Whosoever attempts to ostracize Christian
Science will signally fail; for no one can fight against God,
and win. 24

My loyal students will tell you that for many years I
have desired to step aside and to have some one take my
place as leader of this mighty movement. Also that I 27
strove earnestly to fit others for this great responsibility.
But no one else has seemed equal to "bear the burden and
heat of the day." 30

1 Success in sin is downright defeat. Hatred bites the
heel of love that is treading on its head. All that worketh
3 good is some manifestation of God asserting and developing good. Evil is illusion, that after a fight vanisheth with
the new birth of the greatest and best. Conflict and perse-
6 cution are the truest signs that can be given of the greatness
of a cause or of an individual, provided this warfare is
honest and a world-imposed struggle. Such conflict never
9 ends till unconquerable right is begun anew, and hath
gained fresh energy and final victory.

Certain elements in human nature would undermine
12 the civic, social, and religious rights and laws of nations
and peoples, striking at liberty, human rights, and self-
government — and this, too, in the name of God, justice,
15 and humanity! These elements assail even the new-old
doctrines of the prophets and of Jesus and his disciples.
History shows that error repeats itself until it is extermi-
18 nated. Surely the wisdom of our forefathers is not added
but subtracted from whatever sways the sceptre of self and
pelf over individuals, weak provinces, or peoples. Here
21 our hope anchors in God who reigns, and justice and judgment are the habitation of His throne forever.

Only last week I received a touching token of unselfed
24 manhood from a person I never saw. But since publishing
this page I have learned it was a private soldier who sent
to me, in the name of a first lieutenant of the United States
27 infantry in the Philippine Islands, ten five-dollar gold
pieces snuggled in Pears' soap. Surely it is enough for a
soldier serving his country in that torrid zone to part with
30 his soap, but to send me some of his hard-earned money

cost me a tear! Yes, and it gave me more pleasure than 1
millions of money could have given.

Beloved brethren, have no discord over music. Hold 3
in yourselves the true sense of harmony, and this sense
will harmonize, unify, and unself you. Once I was pas-
sionately fond of material music, but jarring elements 6
among musicians weaned me from this love and wedded
me to spiritual music, the music of Soul. Thus it is with
whatever turns mortals away from earth to heaven; we 9
have the promise that "all things work together for good
to them that love God," — love good. The human sigh
for peace and love is answered and compensated by divine 12
love. Music is more than sound in unison. The deaf
Beethoven besieges you with tones intricate, profound,
commanding. Mozart rests you. To me his composition 15
is the triumph of art, for he measures himself against
deeper grief. I want not only quality, quantity, and variation in tone, but the unction of Love. Music is divine. 18
Mind, not matter, makes music; and if the divine tone be
lacking, the human tone has no melody for me. Adelaide
A. Proctor breathes my thought: — 21

> It flooded the crimson twilight
> Like the close of an angel's psalm,
> And it lay on my fevered spirit 24
> With a touch of infinite calm.

In Revelation St. John refers to what "the Spirit saith
unto the churches." His allegories are the highest criticism 27
on all human action, type, and system. His symbolic
ethics bravely rebuke lawlessness. His types of purity

1 pierce corruption beyond the power of the pen. They are
bursting paraphrases projected from divinity upon human-
3 ity, the spiritual import whereof "holdeth the seven stars
in His right hand and walketh in the midst of the seven
golden candlesticks" — the radiance of glorified Being.

6   In Revelation, second chapter, his messages to the
churches commence with the church of Ephesus. History
records Ephesus as an illustrious city, the capital of Asia
9 Minor. It especially flourished as an emporium in the
time of the Roman Emperor Augustus. St. Paul's life
furnished items concerning this city. Corresponding to
12 its roads, its gates, whence the Ephesian elders travelled to
meet St. Paul, led northward and southward. At the head
of the harbor was the temple of Diana, the tutelary divinity
15 of Ephesus. The earlier temple was burned on the night
that Alexander the Great was born. Magical arts prevailed at Ephesus; hence the Revelator's saying: "I
18 have somewhat against thee, because thou hast left thy
first love . . . and will remove thy candlestick out of his
place, except thou repent." This prophecy has been ful-
21 filled. Under the influence of St. Paul's preaching the
magical books in that city were publicly burned. It were
well if we had a St. Paul to purge our cities of charlatanism.
24 During St. Paul's stay in that city — over two years — he
labored in the synagogue, in the school of Tyrannus, and
also in private houses. The entire city is now in ruins.

27   The Revelation of St. John in the apostolic age is symbolic, rather than personal or historical. It refers to the
Hebrew Balaam as the devourer of the people. Nicolaitan
30 church presents the phase of a great controversy, ready to

destroy the unity and the purity of the church. It is said 1
"a controversy was inevitable when the Gentiles entered
the church of Christ" in that city. The Revelator com- 3
mends the church at Ephesus by saying: "Thou hatest
the deeds of the Nicolaitanes, which I also hate." It is
written of this church that their words were brave and their 6
deeds evil. The orgies of their idolatrous feasts and their
impurities were part of a system supported by their doctrine and their so-called prophetic illumination. Their 9
distinctive feature the apostle justly regards as heathen,
and so he denounces the Nicolaitan church.

Alexander the Great founded the city of Smyrna, and 12
after a series of wars it was taken and sacked. The Revelator writes of this church of Smyrna: "Be thou faithful
unto death, and I will give thee a crown of life." A glad 15
promise to such as wait and weep.

The city of Pergamos was devoted to a sensual worship.
There Æsculapius, the god of medicine, acquired fame; 18
and a serpent was the emblem of Æsculapius. Its medical
practice included charms and incantations. The Revelator refers to the church in this city as dwelling "where 21
Satan's seat is." The Pergamene church consisted of the
school of Balaam and Æsculapius, idolatry and medicine.

The principal deity in the city of Thyatira was Apollo. 24
Smith writes: "In this city the amalgamation of different
pagan religions seems not to have been wholly discoun-
tenanced by the authorities of the Judæo-Christian 27
church."

The Revelator speaks of the angel of the church in
Philadelphia as being bidden to write the approval of this 30

1 church by our Master — he saith: "Thou hast a little strength, and hast kept my word, and hast not denied my 3 name. Behold, I will make them of the synagogue of Satan . . . to know that I have loved thee. . . . Hold that fast which thou hast, that no man take thy crown."

6 He goes on to portray seven churches, the full number of days named in the creation, which signifies a complete time or number of whatever is spoken of in the Scriptures.

9 Beloved, let him that hath an ear (that discerneth spiritually) hear what the Spirit saith unto the churches; and seek thou the divine import of the Revelator's vision — 12 and no other. Note his inspired rebuke to all the churches except the church in Philadelphia — the name whereof signifies "brotherly love." I call your attention to this 15 to remind you of the joy you have had in following the more perfect way, or Golden Rule: "As ye would that men should do to you, do ye." Let no root of bitterness 18 spring up among you, but hold in your full hearts fervently the charity that seeketh not only her own, but another's good. The angel that spake unto the churches cites Jesus 21 as "he that hath the key of David; that openeth and no man shutteth, and shutteth and no man openeth;" in other words, he that toiled for the spiritually indispensable.

24 At all times respect the character and philanthropy of the better class of M.D.'s — and if you are stoned from the pulpit, say in your heart as the devout St. Stephen said: 27 "Lord, lay not this sin to their charge."

When invited to a feast you naturally ask who are to be the guests. And being told they are distinguished indi-30 viduals, you prepare accordingly for the festivity. Putting

aside the old garment, you purchase, at whatever price, a 1
new one that is up to date. To-day you have come to a
sumptuous feast, to one that for many years has been await- 3
ing you. The guests are distinguished above human title
and this feast is a Passover. To sit at this table of their
Lord and partake of what divine Love hath prepared for 6
them, Christian Scientists start forward with true ambition. The Passover, spiritually discerned, is a wonderful
passage over a tear-filled sea of repentance — which of 9
all human experience is the most divine; and after this
Passover cometh victory, faith, and good works.

When a supercilious consciousness that saith "there is 12
no sin," has awakened to see through sin's disguise the
claim of sin, and thence to see that sin has no claim, it
yields to sharp conviction — it sits in sackcloth — it waits 15
in the desert — and fasts in the wilderness. But all this
time divine Love has been preparing a feast for this
awakened consciousness. To-day you have come to Love's 18
feast, and you kneel at its altar. May you have on a wedding garment new and old, and the touch of the hem of
this garment heal the sick and the sinner!   21

In the words of St. John, may the angel of The Mother
Church write of this church: "Thou hast not left thy first
love, I know thy works, and charity, and service, and faith, 24
and thy patience, and thy works; and the last to be more
than the first."

> Watch! till the storms are o'er —   27
>   The cold blasts done,
> The reign of heaven begun,
>   And love, the evermore.   30

Message
to
The Mother Church

BOSTON, MASSACHUSETTS
JUNE, 1901

Message
to
The Mother Church

BOSTON, MASSACHUSETTS
JUNE, 1901

by MARY BAKER EDDY

Pastor Emeritus and Author of
Science and Health with Key to the Scriptures

Marcas Registradas

Published by The First Church of Christ, Scientist, in Boston, Massachusetts, U.S.A.

The facsimile of the signature of Mary Baker Eddy
and the design of the Cross and Crown seal are
trademarks of The Christian Science Board of Directors,
registered in the United States and other countries.

Message for 1901

BELOVED brethren, to-day I extend my heart-and- 1
hand-fellowship to the faithful, to those whose hearts
have been beating through the mental avenues of man- 3
kind for God and humanity; and rest assured you can
never lack God's outstretched arm so long as you are in
His service. Our first communion in the new century 6
finds Christian Science more extended, more rapidly advancing, better appreciated, than ever before, and nearer
the whole world's acceptance. 9

To-day you meet to commemorate in unity the life of
our Lord, and to rise higher and still higher in the individual consciousness most essential to your growth and 12
usefulness; to add to your treasures of thought the great
realities of being, which constitute mental and physical
perfection. The baptism of the Spirit, and the refresh- 15
ment and invigoration of the human in communion with
the Divine, have brought you hither.

All that is true is a sort of necessity, a portion of the 18
primal reality of things. Truth comes from a deep sincerity that must always characterize heroic hearts; it is
the better side of man's nature developing itself. 21

As Christian Scientists you seek to define God to your
own consciousness by feeling and applying the nature and
practical possibilities of divine Love: to gain the absolute 24

1

1 and supreme certainty that Christianity is now what Christ
Jesus taught and demonstrated — health, holiness, im-
3 mortality. The highest spiritual Christianity in individual
lives is indispensable to the acquiring of greater power in
the perfected Science of healing all manner of diseases.

6   We know the healing standard of Christian Science was
and is traduced by trying to put into the *old* garment the
new-old cloth of Christian healing. To attempt to twist
9 the fatal magnetic element of human will into harmony
with divine power, or to substitute good words for good
deeds, a fair seeming for right being, may suit the weak or
12 the worldly who find the standard of Christ's healing too
high for them. Absolute certainty in the practice of divine
metaphysics constitutes its utility, since it has a divine and
15 demonstrable Principle and rule — if some fall short of
Truth, others will attain it, and these are they who will
adhere to it. The feverish pride of sects and systems is
18 the death's-head at the feast of Love, but Christianity is
ever storming sin in its citadels, blessing the poor in spirit
and keeping peace with God.

21   What Jesus' disciples of old experienced, his followers
of to-day will prove, namely, that a departure from the
direct line in Christ costs a return under difficulties; dark-
24 ness, doubt, and unrequited toil will beset all their returning footsteps. Only a firm foundation in Truth can give
a fearless wing and a sure reward.

27   The history of Christian Science explains its rapid
growth. In my church of over twenty-one thousand six
hundred and thirty-one communicants (two thousand four
30 hundred and ninety-six of whom have been added since

last November) there spring spontaneously the higher hope, 1
and increasing virtue, fervor, and fidelity. The special
benediction of our Father-Mother God rests upon this 3
hour: "Blessed are ye when men shall revile you, and persecute you, and shall say all manner of evil against you
falsely, for my sake." 6

GOD IS THE INFINITE PERSON

We hear it said the Christian Scientists have no God
because their God is not a person. Let us examine this. 9
The loyal Christian Scientists absolutely adopt Webster's
definition of God, "A Supreme Being," and the Standard
dictionary's definition of God, "The one Supreme Being, 12
self-existent and eternal." Also, we accept God, emphatically, in the higher definition derived from the Bible, and
this accords with the literal sense of the lexicons: "God is 15
Spirit," "God is Love." Then, to define Love in divine
Science we use this phrase for God — divine Principle.
By this we mean Mind, a permanent, fundamental, intel- 18
ligent, divine Being, called in Scripture, Spirit, Love.

It is sometimes said: "God is Love, but this is no argument that Love is God; for God is light, but light is not 21
God." The first proposition is correct, and is not lost
by the conclusion, for Love expresses the nature of God;
but the last proposition does not illustrate the first, as 24
light, being matter, loses the nature of God, Spirit, deserts
its premise, and expresses God only in metaphor, therefore it is illogical and the conclusion is not properly drawn. 27
It is logical that because God is Love, Love is divine Prin-

1 ciple; then Love as either divine Principle or Person
stands for God — for both have the nature of God.
3 In logic the major premise must be convertible to the
minor.

In mathematics four times three is twelve, and three
6 times four is twelve. To depart from the rule of mathematics destroys the proof of mathematics; just as a departure from the Principle and rule of divine Science
9 destroys the ability to demonstrate Love according to
Christ, healing the sick; and you lose its susceptibility of
scientific proof.

12   God is the author of Science — neither man nor matter
can be. The Science of God must be, is, *divine,* predicated of Principle and demonstrated as divine Love; and
15 Christianity is divine Science, else there is no Science and
no Christianity.

We understand that God is personal in a scientific
18 sense, but is not corporeal nor anthropomorphic. We understand that God is not finite; He is the infinite Person,
but not three persons in one person. Christian Scientists
21 are theists and monotheists. Those who misjudge us because we understand that God is the infinite One instead
of three, should be able to explain God's personality ra-
24 tionally. Christian Scientists consistently conceive of God
as One because He is infinite; and as triune, because He
is Life, Truth, Love, and these three are one in essence
27 and in office.

If in calling God "divine Principle," meaning divine
Love, more frequently than Person, we merit the epithet
30 "godless," we naturally conclude that he breaks faith with

his creed, or has no possible conception of ours, who be- 1
lieves that three persons are defined strictly by the word
Person, or as One; for if Person is God, and he believes 3
three persons constitute the Godhead, does not Person
here lose the nature of one God, lose monotheism, and
become less coherent than the Christian Scientist's sense 6
of Person as one divine infinite triune Principle, named in
the Bible Life, Truth, Love? — for each of these possesses
the nature of all, and God omnipotent, omnipresent, 9
omniscient.

Man is person; therefore divine metaphysics discriminates between God and man, the creator and the created, 12
by calling one the divine Principle of all. This suggests
another query: Do Christian Scientists believe in personality? They do, but their personality is defined spiritually, 15
not materially — by Mind, not by matter. We do not blot
out the material race of Adam, but leave all sin to God's
fiat — self-extinction, and to the final manifestation of the 18
real spiritual man and universe. We believe, according
to the Scriptures, that God is infinite Spirit or Person, and
man is His image and likeness: therefore man reflects 21
Spirit, not matter.

We are not transcendentalists to the extent of extin-
guishing anything that is real, good, or true; for God and 24
man in divine Science, or the logic of Truth, are coexistent
and eternal, and the nature of God must be seen in man,
who is His eternal image and likeness. 27

The theological God as a Person necessitates a creed
to explain both His person and nature, whereas God explains Himself in Christian Science. Is the human person, 30

1 as defined by Christian Science, more transcendental than
theology's three divine persons, that live in the Father and
3 have no separate identity? Who says the God of theology
is a Person, and the God of Christian Science is not a
person, hence no God? Here is the departure. Person is
6 defined differently by theology, which reckons three as
one and the infinite in a finite form, and Christian Science,
which reckons one as one and this one *infinite*.
9   Can the infinite Mind inhabit a finite form? Is the God
of theology a finite or an infinite Person? Is He one
Person, or three persons? Who can conceive either of
12 three persons as one person, or of three infinites? We
hear that God is not God except He be a Person, and this
Person contains three persons: yet God must be One
15 although He is three. Is this pure, specific Christianity?
and is God in Christian Science no God because He is not
after this model of personality?
18   The logic of divine Science being faultless, its consequent
Christianity is consistent with Christ's hillside sermon,
which is set aside to some degree, regarded as impracticable
21 for human use, its theory even seldom named.
    God is Person in the infinite scientific sense of Him, but
He can neither be one nor infinite in the corporeal or an-
24 thropomorphic sense.
    Our departure from theological personality is, that God's
personality must be as infinite as Mind is. We believe in
27 God as the infinite Person; but lose all conceivable idea
of Him as a finite Person with an infinite Mind. That
God is either inconceivable, or is manlike, is not my sense
30 of Him. In divine Science He is "altogether lovely," and

consistently conceivable as the personality of infinite Love, 1
infinite Spirit, than whom there is none other.

Scholastic theology makes God manlike; Christian 3
Science makes man Godlike. The trinity of the Godhead
in Christian Science being Life, Truth, Love, constitutes
the individuality of the infinite Person or divine intelligence 6
called God.

Again, God being infinite Mind, He is the all-wise, all-
knowing, all-loving Father-Mother, for God made man in 9
His own image and likeness, and made them male and
female as the Scriptures declare; then does not our
heavenly Parent — the divine Mind — include within this 12
Mind the thoughts that express the different mentalities
of man and woman, whereby we may consistently say,
"Our Father-Mother God"? And does not this heavenly 15
Parent know and supply the differing needs of the individual mind even as the Scriptures declare He will?

Because Christian Scientists call their God "divine 18
Principle," as well as infinite Person, they have not taken
away their Lord, and know not where they have laid Him.
They do not believe there must be something tangible to 21
the personal material senses in order that belief may attend
their petitions to divine Love. The God whom all Christians now claim to believe in and worship cannot be con- 24
ceived of on that basis; He cannot be apprehended through
the material senses, nor can they gain any evidence of His
presence thereby. Jesus said, "Thomas, because thou 27
hast seen me, thou hast believed: blessed are they that
have not seen, and yet have believed."

1   CHRIST IS ONE AND DIVINE

Again I reiterate this cardinal point: There is but one
3 Christ, and Christ is divine — the Holy Ghost, or spiritual
idea of the divine Principle, Love. Is this scientific statement more transcendental than the belief of our brethren,
6 who regard Jesus as God and the Holy Ghost as the third
person in the Godhead? When Jesus said, "I and my
Father are one," and "my Father is greater than I," this
9 was said in the sense that one ray of light is light, and it
is one with light, but it is not the full-orbed sun. Therefore we have the authority of Jesus for saying Christ is not
12 God, but an impartation of Him.

Again: Is man, according to Christian Science, more
transcendental than God made him? Can he be too spir-
15 itual, since Jesus said, "Be ye therefore perfect, even as
your Father which is in heaven is perfect"? Is God
Spirit? He is. Then is man His image and likeness,
18 according to Holy Writ? He is. Then can man be material, or less than spiritual? As God made man, is he not
wholly spiritual? The reflex image of Spirit is not unlike
21 Spirit. The logic of divine metaphysics makes man none
too transcendental, if we follow the teachings of the
Bible.

24   The Christ was Jesus' spiritual selfhood; therefore
Christ existed prior to Jesus, who said, "Before Abraham
was, I am." Jesus, the only immaculate, was born of a
27 virgin mother, and Christian Science explains that mystic
saying of the Master as to his dual personality, or the spir-

itual and material Christ Jesus, called in Scripture the 1
Son of God and the Son of man — explains it as referring
to his eternal spiritual selfhood and his temporal man- 3
hood. Christian Science shows clearly that God is the
only generating or regenerating power.

The ancient worthies caught glorious glimpses of the 6
Messiah or Christ, and their truer sense of Christ baptized
them in Spirit — submerged them in a sense so pure it
made seers of men, and Christian healers. This is the 9
"Spirit of life in Christ Jesus," spoken of by St. Paul.
It is also the mysticism complained of by the rabbis, who
crucified Jesus and called him a "deceiver." Yea, it is 12
the healing power of Truth that is persecuted to-day, the
spirit of divine Love, and Christ Jesus possessed it, practised it, and taught his followers to do likewise. This 15
spirit of God is made manifest in the flesh, healing and saving men, — it is the Christ, Comforter, "which taketh away
the sin of the world;" and yet Christ is rejected of men! 18

The evil in human nature foams at the touch of good;
it crieth out, "Let us alone; what have we to do with
thee, . . . ? art thou come to destroy us? I know thee who 21
thou art; the Holy One of God." The Holy Spirit takes
of the things of God and showeth them unto the creature;
and these things being spiritual, they disturb the carnal 24
and destroy it; they are revolutionary, reformatory, and —
now, as aforetime — they cast out evils and heal the sick.
He of God's household who loveth and liveth most the 27
things of Spirit, receiveth them most; he speaketh wisely,
for the spirit of his Father speaketh through him; he
worketh well and healeth quickly, for the spirit giveth him 30

1 liberty: "Ye shall know the truth, and the truth shall make you free."

3   Jesus said, "For all these things they will deliver you up to the councils" and "If they have called the master of the house Beelzebub, how much more shall they call 6 them of his household? Fear them not therefore: for there is nothing covered, that shall not be revealed."

Christ being the Son of God, a spiritual, divine emana-9 tion, Christ must be spiritual, not material. Jesus was the son of Mary, therefore the son of man only in the sense that man is the generic term for both male and 12 female. The Christ was not human. Jesus was human, but the Christ Jesus represented both the divine and the human, God and man. The Science of divine metaphysics 15 removes the mysticism that used to enthrall my sense of the Godhead, and of Jesus as the Son of God and the son of man. Christian Science explains the nature of God as 18 both Father and Mother.

Theoretically and practically man's salvation comes through "the riches of His grace" in Christ Jesus. Divine 21 Love spans the dark passage of sin, disease, and death with Christ's righteousness, — the atonement of Christ, whereby good destroys evil, — and the victory over self, sin, disease, 24 and death, is won after the pattern of the mount. This is working out our own salvation, for God worketh with us, until there shall be nothing left to perish or to be pun-27 ished, and we emerge gently into Life everlasting. This is what the Scriptures demand — faith according to works.

30   After Jesus had fulfilled his mission in the flesh as the

Son of man, he rose to the fulness of his stature in Christ, 1
the eternal Son of God, that never suffered and never
died. And because of Jesus' great work on earth, his dem- 3
onstration over sin, disease, and death, the divine nature
of Christ Jesus has risen to human apprehension, and we
see the Son of man in divine Science; and he is no longer 6
a material man, and mind is no longer in matter. Through
this redemptive Christ, Truth, we are healed and saved,
and that not of our selves, it is the gift of God; we are 9
saved from the sins and sufferings of the flesh, and are
the redeemed of the Lord.

THE CHRISTIAN SCIENTISTS' PASTOR   12

    True, I have made the Bible, and "Science and Health
with Key to the Scriptures," the pastor for all the churches
of the Christian Science denomination, but that does not 15
make it impossible for this pastor of ours to preach! To
my sense the Sermon on the Mount, read each Sunday
without comment and obeyed throughout the week, would 18
be enough for Christian practice. The Word of God is a
powerful preacher, and it is not too spiritual to be practical, nor too transcendental to be heard and understood. 21
Whosoever saith there is no sermon without personal
preaching, forgets what Christian Scientists do not, namely,
that God is a Person, and that he should be willing to hear 24
a sermon from his personal God!
    But, my brethren, the Scripture saith, "Answer not a
fool according to his folly, lest thou also be like unto him." 27
St. Paul complains of him whose god is his belly: to

1 such a one our mode of worship may be intangible, for it
is not felt with the fingers; but the spiritual sense drinks
3 it in, and it corrects the material sense and heals the sinning and the sick.   If St. John should tell that man that
Jesus came neither eating nor drinking, and that he bap-
6 tized with the Holy Ghost and with fire, he would naturally reply, "That is too transcendental for me to believe,
or for my worship.   That is Johnism, and only Johnites
9 would be seen in such company." But this is human: even
the word Christian was anciently an opprobrium; —
hence the Scripture, "When the Son of man cometh, shall
12 he find faith on the earth?"

Though a man were begirt with the Urim and Thummim of priestly office, yet should not have charity, or should
15 deny the validity and permanence of Christ's command to
heal in all ages, he would dishonor that office and misinterpret evangelical religion.   Divine Science is not an in-
18 terpolation of the Scriptures, it is redolent with health,
holiness, and love.   It only needs the prism of divine
Science, which scholastic theology has obscured, to divide
21 the rays of Truth, and bring out the entire hues of God.
The lens of Science magnifies the divine power to human
sight; and we then see the allness of Spirit, therefore the
24 nothingness of matter.

NO REALITY IN EVIL OR SIN

Incorporeal evil embodies itself in the so-called corpo-
27 real, and thus is manifest in the flesh.   Evil is neither
quality nor quantity: it is not intelligence, a person or a

principle, a man or a woman, a place or a thing, and God 1
never made it. The outcome of evil, called sin, is another
nonentity that belittles itself until it annihilates its own 3
embodiment: this is the only annihilation. The visible
sin should be invisible: it ought not to be seen, felt, or
acted: and because it ought not, we must know it is not, 6
and that sin is a lie from the beginning, — an illusion,
nothing, and only an assumption that nothing is something.
It is not well to maintain the position that sin is sin and 9
can take possession of us and destroy us, but well that we
take possession of sin with such a sense of its nullity as
destroys it. Sin can have neither entity, verity, nor power 12
thus regarded, and we verify Jesus' words, that evil, *alias*
devil, sin, is a lie — therefore is nothing and the father of
nothingness. Christian Science lays the axe at the root of 15
sin, and destroys it on the very basis of nothingness. When
man makes something of sin it is either because he fears it
or loves it. Now, destroy the conception of sin as some- 18
thing, a reality, and you destroy the fear and the love of
it; and sin disappears. A man's fear, unconquered, conquers him, in whatever direction. 21

   In Christian Science it is plain that God removes the
punishment for sin only as the sin is removed — never
punishes it only as it is destroyed, and never afterwards; 24
hence the hope of universal salvation. It is a sense of sin,
and not a sinful soul, that is lost. Soul is immortal, but
sin is mortal. To lose the sense of sin we must first detect 27
the claim of sin; hold it invalid, give it the lie, and then
we get the victory, sin disappears, and its unreality is
proven. So long as we indulge the presence or believe in 30

1 the power of sin, it sticks to us and has power over us. Again: To assume there is no reality in sin, and yet com-
3 mit sin, is sin itself, that clings fast to iniquity. The Publican's wail won his humble desire, while the Phari-see's self-righteousness crucified Jesus.

6   Do Christian Scientists believe that evil exists? We answer, Yes and No! Yes, inasmuch as we do know that evil, as a false claim, false entity, and utter falsity,
9 does exist in thought; and No, as something that enjoys, suffers, or is *real*. Our only departure from ecclesias-ticism on this subject is, that our faith takes hold of the
12 fact that evil cannot be made so real as to frighten us and so master us, or to make us love it and so hinder our way to holiness. We regard evil as a lie, an illusion,
15 therefore as unreal as a mirage that misleads the traveller on his way home.

It is self-evident that error is not Truth; then it follows
18 that it is untrue; and if untrue, unreal; and if unreal, to conceive of error as either right or real is sin in itself. To be delivered from believing in what is unreal, from fear-
21 ing it, following it, or loving it, one must watch and pray that he enter not into temptation — even as one guards his door against the approach of thieves. Wrong is
24 thought before it is acted; you must control it in the first instance, or it will control you in the second. To over-come all wrong, it must become unreal to us: and it is
27 good to know that wrong has no divine authority; there-fore man is its master. I rejoice in the scientific appre-hension of this grand verity.

30   The evil-doer receives no encouragement from my

declaration that evil is unreal, when I declare that he 1
must awake from his belief in this awful unreality, repent
and forsake it, in order to understand and demonstrate 3
its unreality.　Error uncondemned is not nullified.　We
must condemn the claim of error in every phase in order
to prove it false, therefore unreal.　　　　　　　　6

The Christian Scientist has enlisted to lessen sin, disease, and death, and he overcomes them through Christ,
Truth, teaching him that they cannot overcome us.　The 9
resistance to Christian Science weakens in proportion as
one understands it and demonstrates the Science of
Christianity.　　　　　　　　　　　　　　　　12

A sinner ought not to be at ease, or he would never quit
sinning.　The most deplorable sight is to contemplate the
infinite blessings that divine Love bestows on mortals, and 15
their ingratitude and hate, filling up the measure of
wickedness against all light.　I can conceive of little short
of the old orthodox hell to waken such a one from 18
his deluded sense; for all sin is a deluded sense, and
dis-ease in sin is better than ease.　Some mortals may
even need to hear the following thunderbolt of Jonathan 21
Edwards: —

"It is nothing but God's mere pleasure that keeps you
from being this moment swallowed up in everlasting de- 24
struction.　He is of purer eyes than to bear to have you in
His sight.　There is no other reason to be given why you
have not gone to hell since you have sat here in the house 27
of God, provoking His pure eyes by your sinful, wicked
manner of attending His solemn worship.　Yea, there is
nothing else that is to be given as a reason why you do 30

1 not at this moment drop down into hell, but that God's hand has held you up."

3   FUTURE PUNISHMENT OF SIN

My views of a future and eternal punishment take in a poignant present sense of sin and its suffering, punishing 6 itself here and hereafter till the sin is destroyed. St. John's types of sin scarcely equal the modern nondescripts, whereby the demon of this world, its lusts, falsi-9 ties, envy, and hate, supply sacrilegious gossip with the verbiage of hades. But hatred gone mad becomes imbecile — outdoes itself and commits suicide. Then let the 12 dead bury its dead, and surviving defamers share our pity.

In the Greek *devil* is named *serpent — liar — the god of this world;* and St. Paul defines this world's god as 15 dishonesty, craftiness, handling the word of God deceitfully. The original text defines *devil* as *accuser, calumniator;* therefore, according to Holy Writ these 18 qualities are objectionable, and ought not to proceed from the individual, the pulpit, or the press. The Scriptures once refer to an evil spirit as *dumb,* but in its origin evil 21 was loquacious, and was supposed to outtalk Truth and to carry a most vital point. Alas! if now it is permitted license, under sanction of the gown, to handle with gar-24 rulity age and Christianity! Shall it be said of this century that its greatest discoverer is a woman to whom men go to mock, and go away to pray? Shall the hope for our 27 race commence with one truth told and one hundred falsehoods told about it?

The present self-inflicted sufferings of mortals from sin, 1
disease, and death should suffice so to awaken the sufferer from the mortal sense of sin and mind in matter as 3
to cause him to return to the Father's house penitent and
saved; yea, quickly to return to divine Love, the author
and finisher of our faith, who so loves even the repentant 6
prodigal — departed from his better self and struggling
to return — as to meet the sad sinner on his way and to
welcome him home.   9

MEDICINE

Had not my first demonstrations of Christian Science
or metaphysical healing exceeded that of other methods, 12
they would not have arrested public attention and started
the great Cause that to-day commands the respect of our
best thinkers. It was that I healed the deaf, the blind, the 15
dumb, the lame, the last stages of consumption, pneumonia,
etc., and restored the patients in from one to three interviews, that started the inquiry, What is it? And when the 18
public sentiment would allow it, and I had overcome a
difficult stage of the work, I would put patients into the
hands of my students and retire from the comparative 21
ease of healing to the next more difficult stage of action
for our Cause.

From my medical practice I had learned that the dynam- 24
ics of medicine is Mind. In the highest attenuations of
homœopathy the drug is utterly expelled, hence it must
be mind that controls the effect; and this attenuation in 27
some cases healed where the allopathic doses would not.

1 When the "mother tincture" of one grain of the drug was
attenuated one thousand degrees less than in the beginning,
3 that was my favorite dose.

The weak criticisms and woeful warnings concerning
Christian Science healing are less now than were the
6 sneers forty years ago at the medicine of homœopathy;
and the medicine of Mind is more honored and respected
to-day than the old-time medicine of matter. Those who
9 laugh at or pray against transcendentalism and the Christian Scientist's religion or his medicine, should know the
danger of questioning Christ Jesus' healing, who admin-
12 istered no remedy apart from Mind, and taught his disciples none other. Christian Science seems transcendental
because the substance of Truth transcends the evidence
15 of the five personal senses, and is discerned only through
divine Science.

If God created drugs for medical use, Jesus and his
18 disciples would have used them and named them for that
purpose, for he came to do "the will of the Father." The
doctor who teaches that a human hypothesis is above a
21 demonstration of healing, yea, above the grandeur of our
great master Metaphysician's precept and example, and
that of his followers in the early centuries, should read
24 this Scripture: "The fool hath said in his heart, There is
no God."

The divine Life, Truth, Love — whom men call God —
27 is the Christian Scientists' healer; and if God destroys the
popular triad — sin, sickness, and death — remember it
is He who does it and so proves their nullity.
30   Christians and clergymen pray for sinners; they believe

that God answers their prayers, and that prayer is a divinely 1
appointed means of grace and salvation. They believe
that divine power, besought, is given to them in times of 3
trouble, and that He worketh with them to save sinners.
I love this doctrine, for I know that prayer brings the
seeker into closer proximity with divine Love, and thus 6
he finds what he seeks, the power of God to heal and to
save. Jesus said, "Ask, and ye shall receive;" and if not
immediately, continue to ask, and because of your often 9
coming it shall be given unto you; and he illustrated his
saying by a parable.

The notion that mixing material and spiritual means, 12
either in medicine or in religion, is wise or efficient, is
proven false. That animal natures give force to character
is egregious nonsense — a flat departure from Jesus' 15
practice and proof. Let us remember that the great Metaphysician healed the sick, raised the dead, and commanded even the winds and waves, which obeyed him 18
through spiritual ascendency alone.

MENTAL MALPRACTICE

From ordinary mental practice to Christian Science is a 21
long ascent, but to go from the use of inanimate drugs to
any susceptible misuse of the human mind, such as mesmerism, hypnotism, and the like, is to subject mankind 24
unwarned and undefended to the unbridled individual
human will. The currents of God flow through no such
channels. 27

The whole world needs to know that the milder forms

1 of animal magnetism and hypnotism are yielding to its
aggressive features. We have no moral right and no
3 authority in Christian Science for influencing the thoughts
of others, except it be to serve God and benefit mankind.
Man is properly self-governed, and he should be guided
6 by no other mind than Truth, the divine Mind. Christian
Science gives neither moral right nor might to harm either
man or beast. The Christian Scientist is alone with his
9 own being and with the reality of things. The mental
malpractitioner is not, cannot be, a Christian Scientist; he
is disloyal to God and man; he has every opportunity to
12 mislead the human mind, and he uses it. People may
listen complacently to the suggestion of the inaudible
falsehood, not knowing what is hurting them or that they
15 are hurt. This mental bane could not bewilder, darken, or
misguide consciousness, physically, morally, or spiritually,
if the individual knew what was at work and his power
18 over it.

This unseen evil is the sin of sins; it is never forgiven.
Even the agony and death that it must sooner or later
21 cause the perpetrator, cannot blot out its effects on himself till he suffers up to its extinction and stops practising
it. The crimes committed under this new-old *régime* of
24 necromancy or diabolism are not easily reckoned. At
present its mystery protects it, but its hidden modus and
flagrance will finally be known, and the laws of our land
27 will handle its thefts, adulteries, and murders, and will
pass sentence on the darkest and deepest of human
crimes.

30   Christian Scientists are not hypnotists, they are not

mortal mind-curists, nor faith-curists; they have faith, 1
but they have Science, understanding, and works as well.
They are not the *addenda*, the *et ceteras*, or new editions 3
of old errors; but they are what they are, namely, students of a demonstrable Science leading the ages.

QUESTIONABLE METAPHYSICS   6

In an article published in the *New York Journal*,
Rev. —— writes: "To the famous Bishop Berkeley of the
Church of England may be traced many of the ideas about 9
the spiritual world which are now taught in Christian
Science."

This clergyman gives it as his opinion that Christian 12
Science will be improved in its teaching and authorship
after Mrs. Eddy has gone. I am sorry for my critic, who
reckons hopefully on the death of an individual who loves 15
God and man; such foreseeing is not foreknowing, and
exhibits a startling ignorance of Christian Science, and a
manifest unfitness to criticise it or to compare its literature. 18
He begins his calculation erroneously; for Life is the
Principle of Christian Science and of its results. Death
is neither the predicate nor postulate of Truth, and Christ 21
came not to bring death but life into the world. Does this
critic know of a better way than Christ's whereby to benefit
the race? My faith assures me that God knows more 24
than any man on this subject, for did He not know all
things and results I should not have known Christian
Science, or felt the incipient touch of divine Love which 27
inspired it.

1   That God is good, that Truth is true, and Science is
Science, who can doubt; and whosoever demonstrates the
3 truth of these propositions is to some extent a Christian
Scientist. Is Science material? No! It is the Mind of
God — and God is Spirit. Is Truth material? No!
6 Therefore I do not try to mix matter and Spirit, since
Science does not and they will not mix. I am a spiritual
homœopathist in that I do not believe in such a compound.
9 Truth and Truth is not a compound; Spirit and Spirit is
not: but Truth and error, Spirit and matter, are compounds and opposites; so if one is true, the other is false.
12 If Truth is true, its opposite, error, is not; and if Spirit is
true and infinite, it hath no opposite; therefore matter
cannot be a reality.

15   I begin at the feet of Christ and with the numeration
table of Christian Science. But I do not say that one added
to one is three, or one and a half, nor say this to accom-
18 modate popular opinion as to the Science of Christianity.
I adhere to my text, that one and one are two all the way
up to the infinite calculus of the infinite God. The numer-
21 ation table of Christian Science, its divine Principle and
rules, are before the people, and the different religious
sects and the differing schools of medicine are discussing
24 them as if they understood its Principle and rules before
they have learned its numeration table, and insist that the
public receive their sense of the Science, or that it receive
27 no sense whatever of it.

Again: Even the numeration table of Christian Science
is not taught correctly by those who have departed from
30 its absolute simple statement as to Spirit and matter, and

that one and two are neither more nor less than three; 1
and losing the numeration table and the logic of Christian
Science, they have little left that the sects and faculties 3
can grapple.   If Christian Scientists only would admit
that God is Spirit and infinite, yet that God has an opposite and that the infinite is not all; that God is good and 6
infinite, yet that evil exists and is real, — thence it would
follow that evil must either exist in good, or exist outside
of the *infinite*, — they would be in peace with the 9
schools.

This departure, however, from the scientific statement,
the divine Principle, rule, or demonstration of Christian 12
Science, results as would a change of the denominations
of mathematics; and you cannot demonstrate Christian
Science except on its fixed Principle and given rule, ac- 15
cording to the Master's teaching and proof. He was ultra;
he was a reformer; he laid the axe at the root of all error,
amalgamation, and compounds. He used no material 18
medicine, nor recommended it, and taught his disciples
and followers to do likewise; therefore he demonstrated
his power over matter, sin, disease, and death, as no other 21
person has ever demonstrated it.

Bishop Berkeley published a book in 1710 entitled
"Treatise Concerning the Principle of Human Knowl- 24
edge."   Its object was to deny, on received principles of
philosophy, the reality of an external material world.   In
later publications he declared physical substance to be 27
"only the constant relation between phenomena connected
by association and conjoined by the operations of the
universal mind, nature being nothing more than conscious 30

1 experience. Matter apart from conscious mind is an impossible and unreal concept." He denies the existence of
3 matter, and argues that matter is not *without* the mind, but within it, and that that which is generally called matter is only an impression produced by divine power on
6 the mind by means of invariable rules styled the laws of nature. Here he makes God the cause of all the ills of mortals and the casualties of earth.

9 Again, while descanting on the virtues of tar-water, he writes: "I esteem my having taken this medicine the greatest of all temporal blessings, and am convinced that
12 under Providence I owe my life to it." Making matter more potent than Mind, when the storms of disease beat against Bishop Berkeley's metaphysics and personality he
15 fell, and great was the fall — from divine metaphysics to tar-water!

Christian Science is more than two hundred years old.
18 It dates beyond Socrates, Leibnitz, Berkeley, Darwin, or Huxley. It is as old as God, although its earthly advent is called the Christian era.

21 I had not read one line of Berkeley's writings when I published my work Science and Health, the Christian Science textbook.

24 In contradistinction to his views I found it necessary to follow Jesus' teachings, and none other, in order to demonstrate the divine Science of Christianity — the meta-
27 physics of Christ — healing all manner of diseases. Philosophy, *materia medica,* and scholastic theology were inadequate to prove the doctrine of Jesus, and I relin-
30 quished the form to attain the spirit or mystery of

godliness. Hence the mysticism, so called, of my writings 1
becomes clear to the godly.

Building on the rock of Christ's teachings, we have a 3
superstructure eternal in the heavens, omnipotent on earth,
encompassing time and eternity. The stone which the
builders reject is apt to be the cross, which they reject and 6
whereby is won the crown and the head of the corner.

A knowledge of philosophy and of medicine, the scho-
lasticism of a bishop, and the metaphysics (so called) 9
which mix matter and mind, — certain individuals call
aids to divine metaphysics, and regret their lack in my
books, which because of their more spiritual import heal 12
the sick! No Christly axioms, practices, or parables are
alluded to or required in such metaphysics, and the demonstration of matter minus, and God all, ends in some 15
specious folly.

The great Metaphysician, Christ Jesus, denounced all
such gilded sepulchres of his time and of all time. He 18
never recommended drugs, he never used them. What,
then, is our authority in Christianity for metaphysics based
on materialism? He demonstrated what he taught. Had 21
he taught the power of Spirit, and along with this the
power of matter, he would have been as contradictory
as the blending of good and evil, and the latter superior, 24
which Satan demanded in the beginning, and which has
since been avowed to be as real, and matter as useful, as
the infinite God, — good, — which, if indeed Spirit and 27
infinite, excludes evil and matter. Jesus likened such
self-contradictions to a kingdom divided against itself,
that cannot stand. 30

1   The unity and consistency of Jesus' theory and practice
give my tired sense of false philosophy and material the-
3 ology rest. The great teacher, preacher, and demonstrator
of Christianity is the Master, who founded his system of
metaphysics only on Christ, Truth, and supported it by
6 his words and deeds.

The five personal senses can have only a finite sense
of the infinite: therefore the metaphysician is sensual
9 that combines matter with Spirit. In one sentence he
declaims against matter, in the next he endows it with a
life-giving quality not to be found in God! and turns
12 away from Christ's purely spiritual means to the schools
and matter for help in times of need.

I have passed through deep waters to preserve Christ's
15 vesture unrent; then, when land is reached and the world
aroused, shall the word popularity be pinned to the seamless robe, and they cast lots for it? God forbid! Let
18 it be left to such as see God — to the pure in spirit,
and the meek that inherit the earth; left to them of a
sound faith and charity, the greatest of which is charity
21 — spiritual love. St. Paul said: "Though I speak
with the tongues of men and of angels, and have not
charity, I am become as sounding brass, or a tinkling
24 cymbal."

Before leaving this subject of the old metaphysicians,
allow me to add I have read little of their writings. I was
27 not drawn to them by a native or an acquired taste for
what was problematic and self-contradictory. What I
have given to the world on the subject of metaphysical
30 healing or Christian Science is the result of my own ob-

servation, experience, and final discovery, quite independ- 1
ent of all other authors except the Bible.

My critic also writes: "The best contributions that 3
have been made to the literature of Christian Science have
been by Mrs. Eddy's followers. I look to see some St.
Paul arise among the Christian Scientists who will inter- 6
pret their ideas and principles more clearly, and apply
them more rationally to human needs."

My works are the first ever published on Christian 9
Science, and nothing has since appeared that is correct
on this subject the basis whereof cannot be traced to some
of those works. The application of Christian Science is 12
healing and reforming mankind. If any one as yet has
healed hopeless cases, such as I have in one to three interviews with the patients, I shall rejoice in being informed 15
thereof. Or if a modern St. Paul could start thirty years
ago without a Christian Scientist on earth, and in this
interval number one million, and an equal number of sick 18
healed, also sinners reformed and the habits and appetites of mankind corrected, why was it not done? God is
no respecter of persons. 21

I have put less of my own personality into Christian
Science than others do in proportion, as I have taken out
of its metaphysics all matter and left Christian Science 24
as it is, purely spiritual, Christlike — the Mind of God
and not of man — born of the Spirit and not matter.
Professor Agassiz said: "Every great scientific truth goes 27
through three stages. First, people say it conflicts with
the Bible. Next, they say it has been discovered before.
Lastly, they say they had always believed it." Having 30

1 passed through the first two stages, Christian Science must
be approaching the last stage of the great naturalist's
3 prophecy.

It is only by praying, watching, and working for the
kingdom of heaven within us and upon earth, that we
6 enter the strait and narrow way, whereof our Master said,
"and few there be that find it."

Of the ancient writers since the first century of the
9 Christian era perhaps none lived a more devout Christian
life up to his highest understanding than St. Augustine.
Some of his writings have been translated into almost
12 every Christian tongue, and are classed with the choicest
memorials of devotion both in Catholic and Protestant
oratories.

15 Sacred history shows that those who have followed exclusively Christ's teaching, have been scourged in the
synagogues and persecuted from city to city. But this
18 is no cause for not following it; and my only apology for
trying to follow it is that I love Christ more than all the
world, and my demonstration of Christian Science in
21 healing has proven to me beyond a doubt that Christ,
Truth, is indeed the way of salvation from all that worketh or maketh a lie. As Jesus said: "It is enough for
24 the disciple that he be as his master." It is well to know
that even Christ Jesus, who was not popular among the
worldlings in his age, is not popular with them in this
27 age; hence the inference that he who would be popular
if he could, is not a student of Christ Jesus.

After a hard and successful career reformers usually
30 are handsomely provided for. Has the thought come to

Christian Scientists, Have we housed, fed, clothed, or 1
visited a reformer for that purpose? Have we looked after
or even known of his sore necessities? Gifts he needs not. 3
God has provided the means for him while he was providing ways and means for others. But mortals in the advancing stages of their careers need the watchful and 6
tender care of those who want to help them. The aged
reformer should not be left to the mercy of those who are
not glad to sacrifice for him even as he has sacrificed for 9
others all the best of his earthly years.

I say this not because reformers are not loved, but because well-meaning people sometimes are inapt or selfish 12
in showing their love. They are like children that go out
from the parents who nurtured them, toiled for them, and
enabled them to be grand coworkers for mankind, children 15
who forget their parents' increasing years and needs, and
whenever they return to the old home go not to help
mother but to recruit themselves. Or, if they attempt 18
to help their parents, and adverse winds are blowing, this
is no excuse for waiting till the wind shifts. They should
remember that mother worked and won for them by 21
facing the winds. All honor and success to those who
honor their father and mother. The individual who loves
most, does most, and sacrifices most for the reformer, is 24
the individual who soonest will walk in his footsteps.

To aid my students in starting under a tithe of my own
difficulties, I allowed them for several years fifty cents on 27
every book of mine that they sold. "With this percentage," students wrote me, "quite quickly we have regained
our tuition for the college course." 30

1   Christian Scientists are persecuted even as all other
religious denominations have been, since ever the primi-
3 tive Christians, "of whom the world was not worthy."
We err in thinking the object of vital Christianity is only
the bequeathing of itself to the coming centuries. The
6 successive utterances of reformers are essential to its
propagation. The magnitude of its meaning forbids headlong haste, and the consciousness which is most imbued
9 struggles to articulate itself.

Christian Scientists are practically non-resistants; they
are too occupied with doing good, observing the Golden
12 Rule, to retaliate or to seek redress; they are not quacks,
giving birth to nothing and death to all, — but they are
leaders of a reform in religion and in medicine, and they
15 have no craft that is in danger.

Even religion and therapeutics need regenerating.
Philanthropists, and the higher class of critics in theology
18 and *materia medica,* recognize that Christian Science
kindles the inner genial life of a man, destroying all lower
considerations. No man or woman is roused to the estab-
21 lishment of a new-old religion by the hope of ease, pleasure,
or recompense, or by the stress of the appetites and passions. And no emperor is obeyed like the man "clouting
24 his own cloak" — working alone with God, yea, like the
clear, far-seeing vision, the calm courage, and the great
heart of the unselfed Christian hero.
27   I counsel Christian Scientists under all circumstances
to obey the Golden Rule, and to adopt Pope's axiom:
"An honest, sensible, and well-bred man will not insult
30 me, and no other can." The sensualist and world-wor-

shipper are always stung by a clear elucidation of truth, 1
of right, and of wrong.

The only opposing element that sects or professions 3
can encounter in Christian Science is Truth opposed to
all error, specific or universal. This opposition springs
from the very nature of Truth, being neither personal nor 6
human, but divine. Every true Christian in the near
future will learn and love the truths of Christian Science
that now seem troublesome. Jesus said, "I came not to 9
send peace but a sword."

Has God entrusted me with a message to mankind? —
then I cannot choose but obey. After a long acquaintance 12
with the communicants of my large church, they regard
me with no vague, fruitless, inquiring wonder. I can use
the power that God gives me in no way except in the 15
interest of the individual and the community. To this
verity every member of my church would bear loving
testimony.   18

MY CHILDHOOD'S CHURCH HOME

Among the list of blessings infinite I count these dear:
Devout orthodox parents; my early culture in the Congre- 21
gational Church; the daily Bible reading and family
prayer; my cradle hymn and the Lord's Prayer, repeated
at night; my early association with distinguished Chris- 24
tian clergymen, who held fast to whatever is good, used
faithfully God's Word, and yielded up graciously what
He took away. It was my fair fortune to be often taught 27
by some grand old divines, among whom were the Rev.

1 Abraham Burnham of Pembroke, N. H., Rev. Nathaniel
Bouton, D. D., of Concord, N. H., Congregationalists;
3 Rev. Mr. Boswell, of Bow, N. H., Baptist; Rev. Enoch
Corser, and Rev. Corban Curtice, Congregationalists; and
Father Hinds, Methodist Elder. I became early a child
6 of the Church, an eager lover and student of vital Christianity. Why I loved Christians of the old sort was I
could not help loving them. Full of charity and good
9 works, busy about their Master's business, they had no
time or desire to defame their fellow-men. God seemed
to shield the whole world in their hearts, and they were
12 willing to renounce all for Him. When infidels assailed
them, however, the courage of their convictions was seen.
They were heroes in the strife; they armed quickly, aimed
15 deadly, and spared no denunciation. Their convictions
were honest, and they lived them; and the sermons their
lives preached caused me to love their doctrines.
18　The lives of those old-fashioned leaders of religion explain in a few words a good man. They fill the ecclesiastic measure, that to love God and keep His command-
21 ments is the whole duty of man. Such churchmen and
the Bible, especially the First Commandment of the Decalogue, and Ninety-first Psalm, the Sermon on the Mount,
24 and St. John's Revelation, educated my thought many
years, yea, all the way up to its preparation for and reception of the Science of Christianity. I believe, if those
27 venerable Christians were here to-day, their sanctified
souls would take in the spirit and understanding of Christian Science through the flood-gates of Love; with them
30 Love was the governing impulse of every action; their

piety was the all-important consideration of their being, 1
the original beauty of holiness that to-day seems to be
fading so sensibly from our sight.   3

To plant for eternity, the "accuser" or "calumniator"
must not be admitted to the vineyard of our Lord, and
the hand of love must sow the seed. Carlyle writes: 6
"Quackery and dupery do abound in religion; above all,
in the more advanced decaying stages of religion, they
have fearfully abounded; but quackery was never the 9
originating influence in such things; it was not the health
and life of religion, but their disease, the sure precursor
that they were about to die."   12

Christian Scientists first and last ask not to be judged
on a doctrinal platform, a creed, or a diploma for scientific
guessing. But they do ask to be allowed the rights of con- 15
science and the protection of the constitutional laws of
their land; they ask to be known by their works, to be
judged (if at all) by their works. We admit that they do 18
not kill people with poisonous drugs, with the lance, or
with liquor, in order to heal them. Is it for not killing
them thus, or is it for healing them through the might and 21
majesty of divine power after the manner taught by Jesus,
and which he enjoined his students to teach and practise,
that they are maligned? The richest and most positive 24
proof that a religion in this century is just what it was in
the first centuries is that the same reviling it received
then it receives now, and from the same motives which 27
actuate one sect to persecute another in advance of it.

Christian Scientists are harmless citizens that do not
kill people either by their practice or by preventing the 30

1 early employment of an M.D. Why? Because the effect
of prayer, whereby Christendom saves sinners, is quite
3 as salutary in the healing of all manner of diseases. The
Bible is our authority for asserting this, in both cases.
The interval that detains the patient from the attendance
6 of an M.D., occupied in prayer and in spiritual obedience
to Christ's mode and means of healing, cannot be fatal
to the patient, and is proven to be more pathological than
9 the M.D.'s material prescription. If this be not so, where
shall we look for the standard of Christianity? Have we
misread the evangelical precepts and the canonical writ-
12 ings of the Fathers, or must we have a new Bible and a
new system of Christianity, originating not in God, but
a creation of the schools — a material religion, proscrip-
15 tive, intolerant, wantonly bereft of the Word of God.

Give us, dear God, again on earth the lost chord of
Christ; solace us with the song of angels rejoicing with
18 them that rejoice; that sweet charity which seeketh not
her own but another's good, yea, which *knoweth no evil*.

Finally, brethren, wait patiently on God; return bless-
21 ing for cursing; be not overcome of evil, but overcome
evil with good; be steadfast, abide and abound in faith,
understanding, and good works; study the Bible and the
24 textbook of our denomination; obey strictly the laws that
be, and follow your Leader only so far as she follows
Christ. Godliness or Christianity is a human necessity:
27 man cannot live without it; he has no intelligence, health,
hope, nor happiness without godliness. In the words of
the Hebrew writers: "Trust in the Lord with all thine
30 heart; and lean not unto thine own understanding. In

all thy ways acknowledge Him, and He shall direct thy 1
paths;" "and He shall bring forth thy righteousness as
the light, and thy judgment as the noonday." 3

The question oft presents itself, Are we willing to sacrifice self for the Cause of Christ, willing to bare our bosom
to the blade and lay ourselves upon the altar? Christian 6
Science appeals loudly to those asleep upon the hill-tops
of Zion. It is a clarion call to the reign of righteousness,
to the kingdom of heaven within us and on earth, and 9
Love is the way alway.

> O the Love divine that plucks us
>   From the human agony!   12
> O the Master's glory won thus,
>   Doth it dawn on you and me?
>
> And the bliss of blotted-out sin   15
>   And the working hitherto —
> Shall we share it — do we walk in
>   Patient faith the way thereto?   18

Message
to
The First Church
of Christ, Scientist
or
The Mother Church

BOSTON, JUNE 15, 1902

Message
to
The First Church
of Christ, Scientist
or
The Mother Church

BOSTON, JUNE 15, 1902

by MARY BAKER EDDY

Pastor Emeritus and Author of
Science and Health with Key to the Scriptures

Marcas Registradas

Published by The First Church of Christ, Scientist, in Boston, Massachusetts, U.S.A.

Message for 1902

The Old and the New Commandment

BELOVED brethren, another year of God's loving 1
providence for His people in times of persecution has
marked the history of Christian Science. With no special 3
effort to achieve this result, our church communicants
constantly increase in number, unity, steadfastness. Two
thousand seven hundred and eighty-four members have 6
been added to our church during the year ending June,
1902, making total twenty-four thousand two hundred and
seventy-eight members; while our branch churches are 9
multiplying everywhere and blossoming as the rose. Evil,
though combined in formidable conspiracy, is made to
glorify God. The Scripture declares, "The wrath of man 12
shall praise Thee: the remainder of wrath shalt Thou
restrain."

Whatever seems calculated to displace or discredit the 15
ordinary systems of religious beliefs and opinions wrestling only with material observation, has always met with
opposition and detraction; this ought not so to be, for 18
a system that honors God and benefits mankind should
be welcomed and sustained. While Christian Science,
engaging the attention of philosopher and sage, is circling 21

1

1 the globe, only the earnest, honest investigator sees through the mist of mortal strife this daystar, and whither 3 it guides.

To live and let live, without clamor for distinction or recognition; to wait on divine Love; to write truth first 6 on the tablet of one's own heart, — this is the sanity and perfection of living, and my human ideal. The Science of man and the universe, in contradistinction to all error, 9 is on the way, and Truth makes haste to meet and to welcome it. It is purifying all peoples, religions, ethics, and learning, and making the children our teachers.

12 Within the last decade religion in the United States has passed from stern Protestantism to doubtful liberalism. God speed the right! The wise builders will build on the 15 stone at the head of the corner; and so Christian Science, the little leaven hid in three measures of meal, — ethics, medicine, and religion, — is rapidly fermenting, and en- 18 lightening the world with the glory of untrammelled truth. The present modifications in ecclesiasticism are an outcome of progress; dogmatism, relegated to the past, gives 21 place to a more spiritual manifestation, wherein Christ is Alpha and Omega. It was an inherent characteristic of my nature, a kind of birthmark, to love the Church; 24 and the Church once loved me. Then why not remain friends, or at least agree to disagree, in love, — part fair foes. I never left the Church, either in heart or in doc- 27 trine; I but began where the Church left off. When the churches and I round the gospel of grace, in the circle of love, we shall meet again, never to part. I have always 30 taught the student to overcome evil with good, used no

other means myself; and ten thousand loyal Christian 1
Scientists to one disloyal, bear testimony to this fact.

The loosening cords of non-Christian religions in the 3
Orient are apparent. It is cause for joy that among the
educated classes Buddhism and Shintoism are said to
be regarded now more as a philosophy than as a religion. 6

I rejoice that the President of the United States has put
an end, at Charleston, to any lingering sense of the North's
half-hostility to the South, thus reinstating the old national 9
family pride and joy in the sisterhood of States.

Our nation's forward step was the inauguration of
home rule in Cuba, — our military forces withdrawing, 12
and leaving her in the enjoyment of self-government under
improved laws. It is well that our government, in its brief
occupation of that pearl of the ocean, has so improved her 15
public school system that her dusky children are learning
to read and write.

The world rejoices with our sister nation over the close 18
of the conflict in South Africa; now, British and Boer may
prosper in peace, wiser at the close than the beginning of
war. The dazzling diadem of royalty will sit easier on the 21
brow of good King Edward, — the muffled fear of death
and triumph canker not his coronation, and woman's
thoughts — the joy of the sainted Queen, and the lay of 24
angels — hallow the ring of state.

It does not follow that power must mature into oppression; indeed, right is the only real potency; and the only 27
true ambition is to serve God and to help the race. Envy
is the atmosphere of hell. According to Holy Writ, the
first lie and leap into perdition began with "Believe in 30

1 me." Competition in commerce, deceit in councils, dishonor in nations, dishonesty in trusts, begin with "Who
3 shall be greatest?" I again repeat, Follow your Leader,
only so far as she follows Christ.

I cordially congratulate our Board of Lectureship, and
6 Publication Committee, on their adequacy and correct
analysis of Christian Science. Let us all pray at this
Communion season for more grace, a more fulfilled life
9 and spiritual understanding, bringing music to the ear,
rapture to the heart — a fathomless peace between
Soul and sense — and that our works be as worthy as
12 our words.

My subject to-day embraces the First Commandment
in the Hebrew Decalogue, and the new commandment in
15 the gospel of peace, both ringing like soft vesper chimes
adown the corridors of time, and echoing and reechoing
through the measureless rounds of eternity.

18   GOD AS LOVE

The First Commandment, "Thou shalt have no other
gods before me," is a law never to be abrogated — a divine
21 statute for yesterday, and to-day, and forever. I shall
briefly consider these two commandments in a few of their
infinite meanings, applicable to all periods — past, present,
24 and future.

Alternately transported and alarmed by abstruse
problems of Scripture, we are liable to turn from them as
27 impractical, or beyond the ken of mortals, — and past
finding out. Our thoughts of the Bible utter our lives.

As silent night foretells the dawn and din of morn; as the 1
dulness of to-day prophesies renewed energy for to-morrow,
— so the pagan philosophies and tribal religions of yester- 3
day but foreshadowed the spiritual dawn of the twentieth
century — religion parting with its materiality.

Christian Science stills all distress over doubtful inter- 6
pretations of the Bible; it lights the fires of the Holy
Ghost, and floods the world with the baptism of Jesus.
It is this ethereal flame, this almost unconceived light of 9
divine Love, that heaven husbands in the First Commandment.

For man to be thoroughly subordinated to this com- 12
mandment, God must be intelligently considered and
understood. The ever-recurring human question and
wonder, What is God? can never be answered satisfac- 15
torily by human hypotheses or philosophy. Divine metaphysics and St. John have answered this great question
forever in these words: "God is Love." This absolute 18
definition of Deity is the theme for time and for eternity;
it is iterated in the law of God, reiterated in the gospel of
Christ, voiced in the thunder of Sinai, and breathed in 21
the Sermon on the Mount. Hence our Master's saying,
"Think not that I am come to destroy the law, or the
prophets: I am not come to destroy, but to fulfil." 24

Since God is Love, and infinite, why should mortals
conceive of a law, propound a question, formulate a doctrine, or speculate on the existence of anything which is 27
an antipode of *infinite* Love and the manifestation thereof?
The sacred command, "Thou shalt have no other gods
before me," silences all questions on this subject, and for- 30

1 ever forbids the thought of any other reality, since it is impossible to have aught unlike the infinite.

3   The knowledge of life, substance, or law, apart or other
than God — good — is forbidden. The curse of Love
and Truth was pronounced upon a lie, upon false knowl-
6 edge, the fruits of the flesh not Spirit. Since knowledge
of evil, of something besides God, good, brought death
into the world on the basis of a lie, Love and Truth de-
9 stroy this knowledge, — and Christ, Truth, demonstrated
and continues to demonstrate this grand verity, saving
the sinner and healing the sick. Jesus said a lie fathers
12 itself, thereby showing that God made neither evil nor its
consequences. Here all human woe is seen to obtain in
a false claim, an untrue consciousness, an impossible
15 creation, yea, something that is not of God. The Christianization of mortals, whereby the mortal concept and
all it includes is obliterated, lets in the divine sense of
18 being, fulfils the law in righteousness, and consummates
the First Commandment, "Thou shalt have no other gods
before me." All Christian faith, hope, and prayer, all
21 devout desire, virtually petition, Make me the image and
likeness of divine Love.

   Through Christ, Truth, divine metaphysics points the
24 way, demonstrates heaven here, — the struggle over, and
victory on the side of Truth. In the degree that man becomes spiritually minded he becomes Godlike. St. Paul
27 writes: "For to be carnally minded is death; but to be
spiritually minded is life and peace." Divine Science
fulfils the law and the gospel, wherein God is infinite Love,
30 including nothing unlovely, producing nothing unlike

Himself, the true nature of Love intact and eternal. Divine 1
metaphysics concedes no origin or causation apart from
God. It accords all to God, Spirit, and His infinite mani- 3
festations of love — man and the universe.

In the first chapter of Genesis, matter, sin, disease, and
death enter not into the category of creation or conscious- 6
ness. Minus this spiritual understanding of Scripture, of
God and His creation, neither philosophy, nature, nor
grace can give man the true idea of God — divine Love — 9
sufficiently to fulfil the First Commandment.

The Latin *omni*, which signifies *all*, used as an English
prefix to the words *potence, presence, science,* signifies all- 12
power, all-presence, all-science. Use these words to define
God, and nothing is left to consciousness but Love, without
beginning and without end, even the forever *I AM*, and 15
All, than which there is naught else. Thus we have
Scriptural authority for divine metaphysics — spiritual
man and the universe coexistent with God. No other 18
logical conclusion can be drawn from the premises,
and no other scientific proposition can be Christianly
entertained.   21

LOVE ONE ANOTHER

Here we proceed to another Scriptural passage which
serves to confirm Christian Science. Christ Jesus saith, 24
"A new commandment I give unto you, That ye love one
another; as I have loved you." It is obvious that he
called his disciples' special attention to his *new command-* 27
ment. And wherefore? Because it emphasizes the

1 apostle's declaration, "God is Love," — it elucidates
Christianity, illustrates God, and man as His likeness, and
3 commands man to love as Jesus loved.

The law and the gospel concur, and both will be fulfilled. Is it necessary to say that the likeness of God, Spirit,
6 is spiritual, and the likeness of Love is loving? When
loving, we learn that "God is Love;" mortals hating, or
unloving, are neither Christians nor Scientists. The new
9 commandment of Christ Jesus shows what true spirituality
is, and its harmonious effects on the sick and the sinner.
No person can heal or reform mankind unless he is actuated
12 by love and good will towards men. The coincidence between the law and the gospel, between the old and the new
commandment, confirms the fact that God and Love are
15 *one*. The spiritually minded are inspired with tenderness,
Truth, and Love. The life of Christ Jesus, his words and
his deeds, demonstrate Love. We have no evidence of
18 being Christian Scientists except we possess this inspiration, and its power to heal and to save. The energy that
saves sinners and heals the sick is divine: and Love is the
21 Principle thereof. Scientific Christianity works out the
rule of spiritual love; it makes man *active,* it prompts perpetual goodness, for the ego, or I, goes to the Father,
24 whereby man *is* Godlike. Love, purity, meekness, coexist in divine Science. Lust, hatred, revenge, coincide in
material sense. Christ Jesus reckoned man in Science,
27 having the kingdom of heaven within him. He spake of
man not as the offspring of Adam, a departure from God,
or His lost likeness, but as God's child. Spiritual love
30 makes man conscious that God is his Father, and the con-

sciousness of God as Love gives man power with untold ₁
furtherance. Then God becomes to him the All-presence
— quenching sin; the All-power — giving life, health, ₃
holiness; the All-science — all law and gospel.

Jesus commanded, "Follow me; and let the dead bury
their dead;" in other words, Let the world, popularity, ₆
pride, and ease concern you less, and *love thou.* When
the full significance of this saying is understood, we shall
have better practitioners, and Truth will arise in human ₉
thought with healing in its wings, regenerating mankind
and fulfilling the apostle's saying: "For the law of the
Spirit of life in Christ Jesus hath made me free from the ₁₂
law of sin and death." Loving chords set discords in harmony. Every condition implied by the great Master,
every promise fulfilled, was loving and spiritual, urging ₁₅
a state of consciousness that leaves the minor tones of so-
called material life and abides in Christlikeness.

The unity of God and man is not the dream of a heated ₁₈
brain; it is the spirit of the healing Christ, that dwelt forever in the bosom of the Father, and should abide forever
in man. When first I heard the life-giving sound thereof, ₂₁
and knew not whence it came nor whither it tended, it
was the proof of its divine origin, and healing power, that
opened my closed eyes. ₂₄

Did the age's thinkers laugh long over Morse's discovery of telegraphy? Did they quarrel long with the
inventor of a steam engine? Is it cause for bitter com- ₂₇
ment and personal abuse that an individual has met the
need of mankind with some new-old truth that counteracts
ignorance and superstition? Whatever enlarges man's ₃₀

1 facilities for knowing and doing good, and subjugates
matter, has a fight with the flesh. Utilizing the capacities
3 of the human mind uncovers new ideas, unfolds spiritual
forces, the divine energies, and their power over matter,
molecule, space, time, mortality; and mortals cry out,
6 "Art thou come hither to torment us before the time?"
then dispute the facts, call them false or in advance of the
time, and reiterate, Let me alone. Hence the foot-
9 prints of a reformer are stained with blood. Rev. Hugh
Black writes truly: "The birthplace of civilization is not
Athens, but Calvary."

12   When the human mind is advancing above itself towards
the Divine, it is subjugating the body, subduing matter,
taking steps outward and upwards. This upward ten-
15 dency of humanity will finally gain the scope of Jacob's
vision, and rise from sense to Soul, from earth to heaven.

Religions in general admit that man becomes finally
18 spiritual. If such is man's ultimate, his predicate tending
thereto is correct, and inevitably spiritual. Wherefore,
then, smite the reformer who finds the more spiritual way,
21 shortens the distance, discharges burdensome baggage,
and increases the speed of mortals' transit from matter
to Spirit — yea, from sin to holiness? This is indeed our
24 sole proof that Christ, Truth, is the way. The old and
recurring martyrdom of God's best witnesses is the infirmity of evil, the *modus operandi* of human error,
27 carnality, opposition to God and His power in man.
Persecuting a reformer is like sentencing a man for communicating with foreign nations in other ways than by
30 walking every step over the land route, and swimming the

ocean with a letter in his hand to leave on a foreign shore. 1
Our heavenly Father never destined mortals who seek
for a better country to wander on the shores of time dis- 3
appointed travellers, tossed to and fro by adverse circumstances, inevitably subject to sin, disease, and death.
Divine Love waits and pleads to save mankind — and 6
awaits with warrant and welcome, grace and glory, the
earth-weary and heavy-laden who find and point the path
to heaven.   9

Envy or abuse of him who, having a new idea or a more
spiritual understanding of God, hastens to help on his
fellow-mortals, is neither Christian nor Science.   If a 12
postal service, a steam engine, a submarine cable, a wireless telegraph, each in turn has helped mankind, how
much more is accomplished when the race is helped on- 15
ward by a new-old message from God, even the knowledge of salvation from sin, disease, and death.

The world's wickedness gave our glorified Master a 18
bitter cup — which he drank, giving thanks, then gave
it to his followers to drink.   Therefore it is thine, advancing Christian, and this is thy Lord's benediction upon 21
it: "Blessed are ye, when men shall revile you, and persecute you, and shall say all manner of evil against you
falsely, for my sake.   Rejoice, and be exceeding glad: 24
for great is your reward in heaven: for so persecuted they
the prophets which were before you."

Of old the Jews put to death the Galilean Prophet, the 27
best Christian on earth, for the truths he said and did:
while to-day Jew and Christian can unite in doctrine and in
practice on the very basis of his words and works. The Jew 30

1 believes that the Messiah or the Christ has not yet come;
the Christian believes that Christ is come and is God.
3 Here Christian Science intervenes, explains these doctrinal
points, cancels the disagreement, and settles the whole question on the basis that Christ is the Messiah, the true spir-
6 itual idea, and this ideal of God is *now* and *forever, here* and
everywhere. The Jew who believes in the First Commandment is a monotheist, he has one omnipresent God: thus
9 the Jew unites with the Christian idea that God is come,
and is ever present. The Christian who believes in the
First Commandment is a monotheist: thus he virtually
12 unites with the Jew's belief in one God, and that Jesus
Christ is not God, as he himself declared, but is the Son of
God. This declaration of Christ, understood, conflicts not
15 at all with another of his sayings: "I and my Father are
one," — that is, one in quality, not in quantity. As a drop
of water is one with the ocean, a ray of light one with the
18 sun, even so God and man, Father and son, are one in
being. The Scripture reads: "For in Him we live, and
move, and have our being."
21   Here allow me to interpolate some matters of business
that ordinarily find no place in my Message. It is a privilege to acquaint communicants with the financial transac-
24 tions of this church, so far as I know them, and especially
before making another united effort to purchase more land
and enlarge our church edifice so as to seat the large number
27 who annually favor us with their presence on Communion
Sunday.
    When founding the institutions and early movements of
30 the Cause of Christian Science, I furnished the money from

my own private earnings to meet the expenses involved. 1
In this endeavor self was forgotten, peace sacrificed, Christ
and our Cause my only incentives, and each success in- 3
curred a sharper fire from enmity.

During the last seven years I have transferred to The
Mother Church, of my personal property and funds, to the 6
value of about one hundred and twenty thousand dollars;
and the net profits from the business of The Christian Science Publishing Society (which was a part of this transfer) 9
yield this church a liberal income. I receive no personal
benefit therefrom except the privilege of publishing my
books in their publishing house, and desire none other.   12

The land on which to build The First Church of Christ,
Scientist, in Boston, had been negotiated for, and about one
half the price paid, when a loss of funds occurred, and I 15
came to the rescue, purchased the mortgage on the lot
corner of Falmouth and Caledonia (now Norway) Streets;
paying for it the sum of $4,963.50 and interest, through my 18
legal counsel. After the mortgage had expired and the note
therewith became due, legal proceedings were instituted by
my counsel advertising the property in the Boston news- 21
papers, and giving opportunity for those who had previously
negotiated for the property to redeem the land by paying
the amount due on the mortgage. But no one offering 24
the price I had paid for it, nor to take the property off my
hands, the mortgage was foreclosed, and the land legally
conveyed to me, by my counsel. This land, now valued at 27
twenty thousand dollars, I afterwards gave to my church
through trustees, who were to be known as "The Christian
Science Board of Directors." A copy of this deed is pub- 30

1 lished in our Church Manual. About five thousand dollars
had been paid on the land when I redeemed it. The only
3 interest I retain in this property is to save it for my church.
I can neither rent, mortgage, nor sell this church edifice nor
the land whereon it stands.

6   I suggest as a motto for every Christian Scientist, — a
living and life-giving spiritual shield against the powers of
darkness, —

9   "Great not like Cæsar, stained with blood,
            But only great as I am good."

The only genuine success possible for any Christian — and
12 the only success I have ever achieved — has been accomplished on this solid basis. The remarkable growth and
prosperity of Christian Science are its legitimate fruit. A
15 successful end could never have been compassed on any
other foundation, — with truths so counter to the common
convictions of mankind to present to the world. From the
18 beginning of the great battle every forward step has been
met (not by mankind, but by a kind of men) with mockery,
envy, rivalry, and falsehood—as achievement after achieve-
21 ment has been blazoned on the forefront of the world and
recorded in heaven. The popular philosophies and religions have afforded me neither favor nor protection in the
24 great struggle. Therefore, I ask: What has shielded and
prospered preeminently our great Cause, but the outstretched arm of infinite Love? This pregnant question,
27 answered frankly and honestly, should forever silence all
private criticisms, all unjust public aspersions, and afford
an open field and fair play.

In the eighties, anonymous letters mailed to me con- 1
tained threats to blow up the hall where I preached; yet I
never lost my faith in God, and neither informed the police 3
of these letters nor sought the protection of the laws of my
country. I leaned on God, and was safe.

Healing all manner of diseases without charge, keeping 6
a free institute, rooming and boarding indigent students
that I taught "without money and without price," I struggled on through many years; and while dependent on the 9
income from the sale of Science and Health, my publisher
paid me not one dollar of royalty on its first edition. Those
were days wherein the connection between justice and be- 12
ing approached the mythical. Before entering upon my
great life-work, my income from literary sources was ample,
until, declining dictation as to what I should write, I became 15
poor for Christ's sake. My husband, Colonel Glover, of
Charleston, South Carolina, was considered wealthy, but
much of his property was in slaves, and I declined to sell 18
them at his decease in 1844, for I could never believe that a
human being was my property.

Six weeks I waited on God to suggest a name for the book 21
I had been writing. Its title, Science and Health, came to
me in the silence of night, when the steadfast stars watched
over the world, — when slumber had fled, — and I rose 24
and recorded the hallowed suggestion. The following day
I showed it to my literary friends, who advised me to drop
both the book and the title. To this, however, I gave no 27
heed, feeling sure that God had led me to write that book,
and had whispered that name to my waiting hope and
prayer. It was to me the "still, small voice" that came to 30

1 Elijah after the earthquake and the fire. Six months thereafter Miss Dorcas Rawson of Lynn brought to me Wyclif's
3 translation of the New Testament, and pointed out that
identical phrase, "Science and Health," which is rendered
in the Authorized Version "knowledge of salvation."
6 This was my first inkling of Wyclif's use of that combination of words, or of their rendering. To-day I am the happy
possessor of a copy of Wyclif, the invaluable gift of two
9 Christian Scientists, — Mr. W. Nicholas Miller, K.C., and
Mrs. F. L. Miller, of London, England.

GODLIKENESS

12   St. Paul writes: "Follow peace with all men, and holiness, without which no man shall see the Lord." To attain
peace and holiness is to recognize the divine presence and
15 allness. Jesus said: "I am the way." Kindle the watch-
fires of unselfed love, and they throw a light upon the un-
complaining agony in the life of our Lord; they open the
18 enigmatical seals of the angel, standing in the sun, a glorified spiritual idea of the ever-present God — in whom there
is no darkness, but all is light, and man's immortal being.
21 The meek might, sublime patience, wonderful works, and
opening not his mouth in self-defense against false witnesses, express the life of Godlikeness. Fasting, feasting,
24 or penance, — merely outside forms of religion, — fail to
elucidate Christianity: they reach not the heart nor reno-
vate it; they never destroy one iota of hypocrisy, pride,
27 self-will, envy, or hate. The mere form of godliness,

coupled with selfishness, worldliness, hatred, and lust, are 1
knells tolling the burial of Christ.

Jesus said, "If ye love me, keep my commandments." 3
He knew that obedience is the test of love; that one gladly
obeys when obedience gives him happiness. Selfishly, or
otherwise, all are ready to seek and obey what they love. 6
When mortals learn to love aright; when they learn that
man's highest happiness, that which has most of heaven in
it, is in blessing others, and self-immolation — they will 9
obey both the old and the new commandment, and receive
the reward of obedience.

Many sleep who should keep themselves awake and 12
waken the world. Earth's actors change earth's scenes;
and the curtain of human life should be lifted on reality, on
that which outweighs time; on duty done and life perfected, 15
wherein joy is real and fadeless. Who of the world's lovers
ever found her true? It is wise to be willing to wait on God,
and to be wiser than serpents; to hate no man, to love one's 18
enemies, and to square accounts with each passing hour.
Then thy gain outlives the sun, for the sun shines but to
show man the beauty of holiness and the wealth of love. 21
Happiness consists in being and in doing good; only what
God gives, and what we give ourselves and others through
His tenure, confers happiness: conscious worth satisfies 24
the hungry heart, and nothing else can. Consult thy every-
day life; take its answer as to thy aims, motives, fondest
purposes, and this oracle of years will put to flight all care 27
for the world's soft flattery or its frown. Patience and res-
ignation are the pillars of peace that, like the sun beneath
the horizon, cheer the heart susceptible of light with prom- 30

1 ised joy.   Be faithful at the temple gate of conscience,
wakefully guard it; then thou wilt know when the thief
3 cometh.

The constant spectacle of sin thrust upon the pure sense
of the immaculate Jesus made him a man of sorrows.   He
6 lived when mortals looked ignorantly, as now, on the might
of divine power manifested through man;   only to mock,
wonder, and perish.   Sad to say, the cowardice and self-
9 seeking of his disciples helped crown with thorns the life of
him who broke not the bruised reed and quenched not the
smoking flax, — who caused not the feeble to fall, nor
12 spared through false pity the consuming tares.   Jesus was
compassionate, true, faithful to rebuke, ready to forgive.
He said, "Inasmuch as ye have done it unto one of the
15 least of these my brethren, ye have done it unto me."
"Love one another, as I have loved you."   No estrange-
ment, no emulation, no deceit, enters into the heart that
18 loves as Jesus loved.   It is a false sense of love that, like
the summer brook, soon gets dry.   Jesus laid down his life
for mankind; what more could he do?   Beloved, how much
21 of what he did are we doing?   Yet he said, "The works
that I do shall he do."   When this prophecy of the great
Teacher is fulfilled we shall have more effective healers and
24 less theorizing;   faith without proof loses its life, and it
should be buried.   The ignoble conduct of his disciples
towards their Master, showing their unfitness to follow
27 him, ended in the downfall of genuine Christianity, about
the year 325, and the violent death of all his disciples save
one.

30   The nature of Jesus made him keenly alive to the

injustice, ingratitude, treachery, and brutality that he 1
received. Yet behold his love! So soon as he burst the
bonds of the tomb he hastened to console his unfaithful 3
followers and to disarm their fears. Again: True to his
divine nature, he rebuked them on the eve of his ascension,
called one a "fool" — then, lifting up his hands and bless- 6
ing them, he rose from earth to heaven.

The Christian Scientist cherishes no resentment; he
knows that that would harm him more than all the malice 9
of his foes. Brethren, even as Jesus forgave, forgive thou.
I say it with joy, — no person can commit an offense
against me that I cannot forgive. Meekness is the armor 12
of a Christian, his shield and his buckler. He entertains
angels who listens to the lispings of repentance seen in a
tear — happier than the conqueror of a world. To the 15
burdened and weary, Jesus saith: "Come unto me."
O glorious hope! there remaineth a rest for the righteous,
a rest in Christ, a peace in Love. The thought of it stills 18
complaint; the heaving surf of life's troubled sea foams
itself away, and underneath is a deep-settled calm.

Are earth's pleasures, its ties and its treasures, taken 21
away from you? It is divine Love that doeth it, and
sayeth, "Ye have need of all these things." A danger
besets thy path? — a spiritual behest, in reversion, awaits 24
you.

The great Master triumphed in furnace fires. Then,
Christian Scientists, trust, and trusting, you will find divine 27
Science glorifies the cross and crowns the association with
our Saviour in his life of love. There is no redundant
drop in the cup that our Father permits us. Christ 30

1 walketh over the wave; on the ocean of events, mounting
the billow or going down into the deep, the voice of him
3 who stilled the tempest saith, "It is I; be not afraid."
Thus he bringeth us into the desired haven, the kingdom
of Spirit; and the hues of heaven, tipping the dawn of
6 everlasting day, joyfully whisper, "No drunkards within,
no sorrow, no pain; and the glory of earth's woes is risen
upon you, rewarding, satisfying, glorifying thy unfaltering
9 faith and good works with the fulness of divine Love."

'T was God who gave that word of might
Which swelled creation's lay, —
12   "Let there be light, and there was light," —
That swept the clouds away;
'T was Love whose finger traced aloud
15   A bow of promise on the cloud.

Beloved brethren, are you ready to join me in this proposition, namely, in 1902 to begin omitting our *annual*
18 gathering at Pleasant View, — thus breaking any seeming
connection between the sacrament in our church and a
pilgrimage to Concord? I shall be the loser by this change,
21 for it gives me great joy to look into the faces of my dear
church-members; but in this, as all else, I can bear the
cross, while gratefully appreciating the privilege of meet-
24 ing you all *occasionally* in the metropolis of my native
State, whose good people welcome Christian Scientists.

Christian
Healing
A SERMON DELIVERED
AT BOSTON

Christian Healing

A SERMON DELIVERED AT BOSTON

by MARY BAKER EDDY
*Discoverer and Founder of Christian Science
and Author of Science and Health
with Key to the Scriptures*

Marcas Registradas

Published by The First Church of Christ, Scientist, in Boston, Massachusetts, U.S.A.

Sermon

SUBJECT

Christian Healing

TEXT: *And these signs shall follow them that believe; In my name* 1
shall they cast out devils; they shall speak with new tongues; they
shall take up serpents; and if they drink any deadly thing, it shall 3
not hurt them; they shall lay hands on the sick, and they shall recover.
— MARK XVI. 17, 18

HISTORY repeats itself; to-morrow grows out of to- 6
day. But Heaven's favors are formidable: they are
calls to higher duties, not discharge from care; and whoso
builds on less than an immortal basis, hath built on sand. 9
We have asked, in our selfishness, to wait until the age
advanced to a more practical and spiritual religion before
arguing with the world the great subject of Christian heal- 12
ing; but our answer was, "Then there were no cross to
take up, and less need of publishing the good news." A
classic writes, — 15

> "At thirty, man suspects himself a fool;
> Knows it at forty, and reforms his plan;
> At fifty, chides his infamous delay, 18
> Pushes his prudent purpose to resolve."

The difference between religions is, that one religion has a
more spiritual basis and tendency than the other; and 21

1

1 the religion nearest right is that one. The genius of
Christianity is works more than words; a calm and stead-
3 fast communion with God; a tumult on earth, — religious
factions and prejudices arrayed against it, the synagogues
as of old closed upon it, while it reasons with the storm,
6 hurls the thunderbolt of truth, and stills the tempest of
error; scourged and condemned at every advancing footstep, afterwards pardoned and adopted, but never seen
9 amid the smoke of battle. Said the intrepid reformer,
Martin Luther: "I am weary of the world, and the world
is weary of me; the parting will be easy." Said the more
12 gentle Melanchthon: "Old Adam is too strong for young
Melanchthon."

And still another Christian hero, ere he passed from
15 his execution to a crown, added his testimony: "I have
fought a good fight, . . . I have kept the faith." But
Jesus, the model of infinite patience, said: "Come unto
18 me, all ye that labor and are heavy laden, and I will
give you rest." And he said this when bending beneath
the malice of the world. But why should the world hate
21 Jesus, the loved of the Father, the loved of Love? It was
that his spirituality rebuked their carnality, and gave this
proof of Christianity that religions had not given. Again,
24 they knew it was not in the power of eloquence or a dead
rite to cast out error and heal the sick. Past, present,
future magnifies his name who built, on Truth, eternity's
27 foundation stone, and sprinkled the altar of Love with
perpetual incense.

Such Christianity requires neither hygiene nor drugs 1
wherewith to heal both mind and body; or, lacking these,
to show its helplessness. The primitive privilege of Chris- 3
tianity was to make men better, to cast out error, and heal
the sick. It was a proof, more than a profession thereof;
a demonstration, more than a doctrine. It was the foun- 6
dation of right thinking and right acting, and must be
reestablished on its former basis. The stone which the
builders rejected must again become the head of the 9
corner. In proportion as the personal and material element stole into religion, it lost Christianity and the power
to heal; and the qualities of God as a person, instead of 12
the divine Principle that begets the quality, engrossed the
attention of the ages. In the original text the term *God*
was derived from the word *good*. Christ is the idea 15
of Truth; Jesus is the name of a man born in a remote
province of Judea, — Josephus alludes to several individuals by the name of Jesus. Therefore Christ Jesus was 18
an honorary title; it signified a "good man," which epithet the great goodness and wonderful works of our
Master more than merited. Because God is the Principle of 21
Christian healing, we must understand in part this divine
Principle, or we cannot demonstrate it in part.

The Scriptures declare that "God is Love, Truth, and 24
Life," — a trinity in unity; not three persons in one, but
three statements of one Principle. We cannot tell what is
the person of Truth, the body of the infinite, but we know 27
that the Principle is not the person, that the finite cannot

1 contain the infinite, that unlimited Mind cannot start from
a limited body. The infinite can neither go forth from,
3 return to, nor remain for a moment within limits. We
must give freer breath to thought before calculating the
results of an infinite Principle, — the effects of infinite
6 Love, the compass of infinite Life, the power of infinite
Truth. Clothing Deity with personality, we limit the action of God to the finite senses. We pray for God to re-
9 member us, even as we ask a person with softening of the
brain not to forget his daily cares. We ask infinite wisdom
to possess our finite sense, and forgive what He knows
12 deserves to be punished, and to bless what is unfit to be
blessed. We expect infinite Love to drop divinity long
enough to hate. We expect infinite Truth to mix with
15 error, and become finite for a season; and, after infinite
Spirit is forced in and out of matter for an indefinite period,
to show itself infinite again. We expect infinite Life to
18 become finite, and have an end; but, after a temporary
lapse, to begin anew as infinite Life, without beginning and
without end.

21   Friends, can we ever arrive at a proper conception of the
divine character, and gain a right idea of the Principle of
all that is right, with such self-evident contradictions?
24 God must be our model, or we have none; and if this
model is one thing at one time, and the opposite of it at
another, can we rely on our model? Or, having faith in it,
27 how can we demonstrate a changing Principle? We cannot: we shall be consistent with our inconsistent statement

of Deity, and so bring out our own erring finite sense of 1
God, and of good and evil blending. While admitting
that God is omnipotent, we shall be limiting His power at 3
every point, — shall be saying He is beaten by certain kinds
of food, by changes of temperature, the neglect of a bath,
and so on. Phrenology will be saying the developments of 6
the brain bias a man's character. Physiology will be saying, if a man has taken cold by doing good to his neighbor,
God will punish him now for the cold, but he must wait for 9
the reward of his good deed hereafter. One of our leading clergymen startles us by saying that "between Christianity and spiritualism, the question chiefly is concerning 12
the trustworthiness of the communications, and not the
doubt of their reality." Does any one think the departed
are not departed, but are with us, although we have no 15
evidence of the fact except sleight-of-hand and hallucination?

Such hypotheses ignore Biblical authority, obscure the 18
one grand truth which is constantly covered, in one way
or another, from our sight. This truth is, that we are
to work out our own salvation, and to meet the responsi- 21
bility of our own thoughts and acts; relying not on the
person of God or the person of man to do our work for us,
but on the apostle's rule, "I will show thee my faith by 24
my works." This spiritualism would lead our lives to
higher issues; it would purify, elevate, and consecrate
man; it would teach him that "whatsoever a man soweth, 27
that shall he also reap." The more spiritual we become

1 here, the more are we separated from the world; and
should this rule fail hereafter, and we grow more material,
3 and so come back to the world? When I was told the other
day, "People say you are a medium," pardon me if I
smiled. The pioneer of something new under the sun is
6 never hit: he cannot be; the opinions of people fly too
high or too low. From my earliest investigations of the
mental phenomenon named mediumship, I knew it was
9 misinterpreted, and I said it. The spiritualists abused me
for it then, and have ever since; but they take pleasure in
calling me a medium. I saw the impossibility, in Science,
12 of intercommunion between the so-called dead and the
living. When I learned how mind produces disease on the
body, I learned how it produces the manifestations ig-
15 norantly imputed to spirits. I saw how the mind's ideals
were evolved and made tangible; and it matters not
whether that ideal is a flower or a cancer, if the belief is
18 strong enough to manifest it. Man thinks he is a medium
of disease; that when he is sick, disease controls his body
to whatever manifestation we see. But the fact remains,
21 in metaphysics, that the mind of the individual only can
produce a result upon his body. The belief that produces
this result may be wholly unknown to the individual, be-
24 cause it is lying back in the unconscious thought, a latent
cause producing the effect we see.

"And these signs shall follow them that believe; In
27 my name shall they cast out devils." The word *devil*
comes from the Greek *diabolos;* in Hebrew it is *belial,* and

signifies "that which is good for nothing, lust," etc. The 1
signs referred to are the manifestations of the power of
Truth to cast out error; and, correcting error in thought, 3
it produces the harmonious effect on the body. "Them
that believe" signifies those who understand God's supremacy, — the power of Mind over matter. "The new 6
tongue" is the spiritual meaning as opposed to the material.
It is the language of Soul instead of the senses; it translates
matter into its original language, which is Mind, and gives 9
the spiritual instead of the material signification. It begins
with motive, instead of act, where Jesus formed his estimate; and there correcting the motive, it corrects the act 12
that results from the motive. The Science of Christianity
makes pure the fountain, in order to purify the stream. It
begins in mind to heal the body, the same as it begins in 15
motive to correct the act, and through which to judge of it.
The Master of metaphysics, reading the mind of the poor
woman who dropped her mite into the treasury, said, 18
"She hath cast in more than they all." Again, he charged
home a crime to mind, regardless of any outward act, and
sentenced it as our judges would not have done to-day. 21
Jesus knew that adultery is a crime, and *mind* is the criminal. I wish the age was up to his understanding of these
two facts, so important to progress and Christianity. 24

"They shall take up serpents; and if they drink any
deadly thing, it shall not hurt them." This is an unqualified statement of the duty and ability of Christians to heal 27
the sick; and it contains no argument for a creed or doc-

1 trine, it implies no necessity beyond the understanding of
God, and obedience to His government, that heals both
3 mind and body; God, — not a person to whom we should
pray to heal the sick, but the Life, Love, and Truth that
destroy error and death. Understanding the truth regard-
6 ing mind and body, knowing that Mind can master sickness as well as sin, and carrying out this government over
both and bringing out the results of this higher Chris-
9 tianity, we shall perceive the meaning of the context,
— "They shall lay hands on the sick, and they shall
recover."

12   The world is slow to perceive individual advancement;
but when it reaches the thought that has produced this,
then it is willing to be made whole, and no longer quarrels
15 with the individual. Plato did better; he said, "What
thou seest, that thou beest."

    The mistaken views entertained of Deity becloud the
18 light of revelation, and suffocate reason by materialism.
When we understand that God is what the Scriptures have
declared, — namely, Life, Truth, and Love, — we shall
21 learn to reach heaven through Principle instead of a pardon; and this will make us honest and laborious, knowing
that we shall receive only what we have earned. Jesus
24 illustrated this by the parable of the husbandman. If we
work to become Christians as honestly and as directly
upon a divine Principle, and adhere to the rule of this
27 Principle as directly as we do to the rule of mathematics,
we shall be Christian Scientists, and do more than we are

now doing, and progress faster than we are now pro- 1
gressing. We should have no anxiety about what is or
what is not the person of God, if we understood the 3
Principle better and employed our thoughts more in demonstrating it. We are constantly thinking and talking
on the wrong side of the question. The less said or thought 6
of sin, sickness, or death, the better for mankind, morally
and physically. The greatest sinner and the most hopeless invalid think most of sickness and of sin; but, having 9
learned that this method has not saved them from either,
why do they go on thus, and their moral advisers talk for
them on the very subjects they would gladly discontinue to 12
bring out in their lives? Contending for the reality of
what should disappear is like furnishing fuel for the flames.
Is it a duty for any one to believe that "the curse causeless 15
cannot come"? Then it is a higher duty to know that
God never cursed man, His own image and likeness. God
never made a wicked man; and man made by God had not 18
a faculty or power underived from his Maker wherewith to
make himself wicked.

The only correct answer to the question, "Who is 21
the author of evil?" is the scientific statement that
evil is unreal; that God made all that was made, but
He never made sin or sickness, either an error of mind 24
or of body. Life in matter is a dream: sin, sickness,
and death are this dream. Life is Spirit; and when we
waken from the dream of life in matter, we shall learn this 27
grand truth of being. St. John saw the vision of life in

1 matter; and he saw it pass away, — an illusion. The
dragon that was wroth with the woman, and stood ready
3 "to devour the child as soon as it was born," was the vision
of envy, sensuality, and malice, ready to devour the idea
of Truth. But the beast bowed before the Lamb: it was
6 supposed to have fought the manhood of God, that Jesus
represented; but it fell before the womanhood of God,
that presented the highest ideal of Love. Let us re-
9 member that God — good — is omnipotent; therefore evil
is impotent. There is but one side to good, — it has no
evil side; there is but one side to reality, and that is the
12 good side.

God is All, and in all: that finishes the question of
a good and a bad side to existence. Truth is the real;
15 error is the unreal. You will gather the importance of
this saying, when sorrow seems to come, if you will look
on the bright side; for sorrow endureth but for the night,
18 and joy cometh with the light. Then will your sorrow be
a dream, and your waking the reality, even the triumph
of Soul over sense. If you wish to be happy, argue with
21 yourself on the side of happiness; take the side you wish
to carry, and be careful not to talk on both sides, or to
argue stronger for sorrow than for joy. You are the at-
24 torney for the case, and will win or lose according to your
plea.

As the mountain hart panteth for the water brooks, so
27 panteth my heart for the true fount and Soul's baptism.
Earth's fading dreams are empty streams, her fountains

play in borrowed sunbeams, her plumes are plucked from 1
the wings of vanity. Did we survey the cost of sublunary
joy, we then should gladly waken to see it was unreal. A 3
dream calleth itself a dreamer, but when the dream has
passed, man is seen wholly apart from the dream.

We are in the midst of a revolution; physics are yield- 6
ing slowly to metaphysics; mortal mind rebels at its own
boundaries; weary of matter, it would catch the meaning
of Spirit. The only immortal superstructure is built on 9
Truth; her modest tower rises slowly, but it stands and is
the miracle of the hour, though it may seem to the age like
the great pyramid of Egypt, — a miracle in stone. The 12
fires of ancient proscription burn upon the altars of to-day;
he who has suffered from intolerance is the first to be intolerant. Homœopathy may not recover from the heel of 15
allopathy before lifting its foot against its neighbor, metaphysics, although homœopathy has laid the foundation
stone of mental healing; it has established this axiom, 18
"The less medicine the better," and metaphysics adds,
"until you arrive at no medicine." When you have
reached this high goal you have learned that proportion- 21
ately as matter went out and Mind came in as the remedy,
was its potency. Metaphysics places all cause and cure
as mind; differing in this from homœopathy, where cause 24
and cure are supposed to be both mind and matter. Metaphysics requires mind imbued with Truth to heal the sick;
hence the Christianity of metaphysical healing, and this 27
excellence above other systems. The higher attenuations

1 of homœopathy contain no medicinal properties, and
thus it is found out that Mind instead of matter heals
3 the sick.

While the matter-physician feels the pulse, examines
the tongue, etc., to learn what matter is doing independent
6 of mind, when it is self-evident it can do nothing, the
metaphysician goes to the fount to govern the streams;
he diagnoses disease as mind, the basis of all action, and
9 cures it thus when matter cannot cure it, showing he was
right. Thus it was we discovered that all physical effects
originate in mind before they can become manifest as
12 matter; we learned from the Scripture and Christ's healing
that God, directly or indirectly, through His providence
or His laws, never made a man sick. When studying the
15 two hundred and sixty remedies of the Jahr, the characteristic peculiarities and the general and moral symptoms
requiring the remedy, we saw at once the concentrated
18 power of thought brought to bear on the pharmacy of
homœopathy, which made the infinitesimal dose effectual.
To prepare the medicine requires time and thought; you
21 cannot shake the poor drug without the involuntary
thought, "I am making you more powerful," and the
sequel proves it; the higher attenuations prove that the
24 power was the thought, for when the drug disappears by
your process the power remains, and homœopathists admit the higher attenuations are the most powerful. The
27 only objection to giving the unmedicated sugar is, it would
be dishonest and divide one's faith apparently between

matter and mind, and so weaken both points of action; taking hold of both horns of the dilemma, we should work at opposites and accomplish less on either side.

The pharmacy of homœopathy is reducing the one hundredth part of a grain of medicine two thousand times, shaking the preparation thirty times at every attenuation. There is a moral to this medicine; the higher natures are reached soonest by the higher attenuations, until the fact is found out they have taken no medicine, and then the so-called drug loses its power. We have attenuated a grain of aconite until it was no longer aconite, then dropped into a tumblerful of water a single drop of this harmless solution, and administering one teaspoonful of this water at intervals of half an hour have cured the incipient stage of fever. The highest attenuation we ever attained was to leave the drug out of the question, using only the sugar of milk; and with this original dose we cured an inveterate case of dropsy. After these experiments you cannot be surprised that we resigned the imaginary medicine altogether, and honestly employed Mind as the only curative Principle.

What are the foundations of metaphysical healing? *Mind,* divine Science, the truth of being that casts out error and thus heals the sick. You can readily perceive this mental system of healing is the antipode of mesmerism, Beelzebub. Mesmerism makes one disease while it is supposed to cure another, and that one is worse than the first; mesmerism is one lie getting the better of another,

1 and the bigger lie occupying the field for a period; it is the
fight of beasts, in which the bigger animal beats the lesser;
3 in fine, much ado about nothing. Medicine will not arrive
at the science of treating disease until disease is treated
mentally and man is healed morally and physically. What
6 has physiology, hygiene, or physics done for Christianity
but to obscure the divine Principle of healing and encourage faith in an opposite direction?
9   Great caution should be exercised in the choice of
physicians. If you employ a medical practitioner, be sure
he is a learned man and skilful; never trust yourself in the
12 hands of a quack. In proportion as a physician is enlightened and liberal is he equipped with Truth, and his efforts
are salutary; ignorance and charlatanism are miserable
15 medical aids. Metaphysical healing includes infinitely
more than merely to know that mind governs the body and
the method of a mental practice. The preparation for a
18 metaphysical practitioner is the most arduous task I ever
performed. You must first mentally educate and develop
the spiritual sense or perceptive faculty by which one learns
21 the metaphysical treatment of disease; you must teach
them how to learn, together with what they learn. I
waited many years for a student to reach the ability to
24 teach; it included more than they understood.
    Metaphysical or divine Science reveals the Principle and
method of perfection, — how to attain a mind in harmony
27 with God, in sympathy with all that is right and opposed
to all that is wrong, and a body governed by this mind.

Christian Science repudiates the evidences of the senses 1
and rests upon the supremacy of God. Christian healing,
established upon this Principle, vindicates the omnipo- 3
tence of the Supreme Being by employing no other remedy
than Truth, Life, and Love, understood, to heal all ills
that flesh is heir to. It places no faith in hygiene or drugs; 6
it reposes all faith in mind, in spiritual power divinely
directed. By rightly understanding the power of mind
over matter, it enables mind to govern matter, as it rises 9
to that supreme sense that shall "take up serpents" unharmed, and "if they drink any deadly thing, it shall not
hurt them." Christian Science explains to any one's per- 12
fect satisfaction the so-called miracles recorded in the
Bible. Ah! why should man deny all might to the divine
Mind, and claim another mind perpetually at war with this 15
Mind, when at the same time he calls God almighty and
admits in statement what he denies in proof? You pray
for God to heal you, but should you expect this when you 18
are acting oppositely to your prayer, trying everything else
besides God, and believe that sickness is something He
cannot reach, but medicine can? as if drugs were superior 21
to Deity.

The Scripture says, "Ye ask, and receive not, because
ye ask amiss;" and is it not asking amiss to pray for a 24
proof of divine power, that you have little or no faith in
because you do not understand God, the Principle of
this proof? Prayer will be inaudible, and works more 27
than words, as we understand God better. The Lord's

1 Prayer, understood in its spiritual sense, and given its
spiritual version, can never be repeated too often for the
3 benefit of all who, having ears, hear and understand.
Metaphysical Science teaches us there is no other Life,
substance, and intelligence but God.   How much are you
6 demonstrating of this statement? which to you hath the
most actual substance, — wealth and fame, or Truth and
Love?   See to it, O Christian Scientists, ye who have
9 named the name of Christ with a higher meaning, that you
abide by your statements, and abound in Love and Truth,
for unless you do this you are not demonstrating the
12 Science of metaphysical healing.   The immeasurable
Life and Love will occupy your affections, come nearer
your hearts and into your homes when you touch but the
15 hem of Truth's garment.

A word about the five personal senses, and we will leave
our abstract subjects for this time.   The only evidence we
18 have of sin, sickness, or death is furnished by these senses;
but how can we rely on their testimony when the senses
afford no evidence of Truth ?   They can neither see, hear,
21 feel, taste, nor smell God;   and shall we call that reliable
evidence through which we can gain no understanding of
Truth, Life, and Love?   Again, shall we say that God
24 hath created those senses through which it is impossible to
approach Him?   Friends, it is of the utmost importance
that we look into these subjects, and gain our evidences of
27 Life from the correct source.   Jesus said, "I am the way,
the truth, and the life.   No man cometh unto the Father,

but by me,"—through the footsteps of Truth. Not by the 1
senses — the lusts of the flesh, the pride of life, envy,
hypocrisy, or malice, the pleasures or the pains of the 3
personal senses — does man get nearer his divine nature
and present the image and likeness of God. How, then,
can it be that material man and the personal senses were 6
created by God? Love makes the spiritual man, lust
makes the material so-called man, and God made all that
was made; therefore the so-called material man and these 9
personal senses, with all their evidences of sin, sickness,
and death, are but a dream, — they are not the realities of
life; and we shall all learn this as we awake to behold His 12
likeness.

The allegory of Adam, when spiritually understood,
explains this dream of material life, even the dream of 15
the "deep sleep" that fell upon Adam when the spiritual
senses were hushed by material sense that before had
claimed audience with a serpent. Sin, sickness, and 18
death never proceeded from Truth, Life, and Love. Sin,
sickness, and death are error; they are not Truth, and
therefore are not TRUE. Sin is a supposed mental condi- 21
tion; sickness and death are supposed physical ones, but
all appeared through the false supposition of life and intelligence in matter. Sin was first in the allegory, and 24
sickness and death were produced by sin. Then was not
sin of mental origin, and did not mind originate the delusion? If sickness and death came through mind, so 27
must they go; and are we not right in ruling them out of

1 mind to destroy their effects upon the body, that both
mortal mind and mortal body shall yield to the govern-
3 ment of God, immortal Mind?   In the words of Paul,
that "the old man" shall be "put off," mortality shall
disappear and immortality be brought to light.   People are
6 willing to put new wine into old bottles; but if this be
done, the bottle will break and the wine be spilled.

There is no connection between Spirit and matter.
9 Spirit never entered and it never escaped from matter;
good and evil never dwelt together.   There is in reality
but the good: Truth is the real; error, the unreal.   We
12 cannot put the new wine into old bottles.   If that could be
done, the world would accept our sentiments; it would willingly adopt the new idea, if that idea could be reconciled
15 with the old belief; it would put the new wine into the
old bottle if it could prevent its effervescing and keep it
from popping out until it became popular.

18   The doctrine of atonement never did anything for sickness or claimed to reach that woe; but Jesus' mission
extended to the sick as much as to the sinner: he estab-
21 lished his Messiahship on the basis that Christ, Truth,
heals the sick.   Pride, appetites, passions, envy, and malice
will cease to assert their Cæsar sway when metaphysics is
24 understood; and religion at the sick-bed will be no blind
Samson shorn of his locks.   You must admit that what is
termed death has been produced by a belief alone.   The
27 Oxford students proved this: they killed a man by no other
means than making him believe he was bleeding to death.

A felon was delivered to them for experiment to test the 1
power of mind over body; and they did test it, and proved
it. They proved it not in part, but as a whole; they 3
proved that every organ of the system, every function of
the body, is governed directly and entirely by mind, else
those functions could not have been stopped by mind in- 6
dependently of material conditions. Had they changed
the felon's belief that he was bleeding to death, removed
the bandage from his eyes, and he had seen that a vein had 9
not been opened, he would have resuscitated. The illusive
origin of disease is not an exception to the origin of all
mortal things. Spirit is causation, and the ancient ques- 12
tion, Which is first, the egg or the bird? is answered by
the Scripture, He made "every plant of the field before it
was in the earth." 15

Heaven's signet is Love. We need it to stamp our religions and to spiritualize thought, motive, and endeavor.
Tireless Being, patient of man's procrastination, affords 18
him fresh opportunities every hour; but if Science makes
a more spiritual demand, bidding man go up higher, he is
impatient perhaps, or doubts the feasibility of the demand. 21
But let us work more earnestly in His vineyard, and according to the model on the mount, bearing the cross meekly
along the rugged way, into the wilderness, up the steep 24
ascent, on to heaven, making our words golden rays in the
sunlight of our deeds; and "these signs shall follow them
that believe; . . . they shall lay hands on the sick, and 27
they shall recover."

1   The following hymn was sung at the close: —

"Oh, could we speak the matchless worth,
3   Oh, could we sound the glories forth,
            Which in our Saviour shine,
            We'd soar and touch the heavenly strings,
6   And vie with Gabriel, while he sings,
            In notes almost divine."

The People's Idea of God

Its Effect on Health and Christianity

A SERMON DELIVERED AT BOSTON

The People's Idea of God

Its Effect on Health and Christianity

A SERMON DELIVERED AT BOSTON

by MARY BAKER EDDY
*Discoverer and Founder of Christian Science
and Author of Science and Health
with Key to the Scriptures*

Marcas Registradas

Published by The First Church of Christ, Scientist, in Boston, Massachusetts, U.S.A.

The facsimile of the signature of Mary Baker Eddy
and the design of the Cross and Crown seal are
trademarks of The Christian Science Board of Directors,
registered in the United States and other countries.

Sermon

SUBJECT

The People's Idea of God

Text: *One Lord, one faith, one baptism.* — Ephesians iv. 5   1

EVERY step of progress is a step more spiritual. The
great element of reform is not born of human wis- 3
dom; it draws not its life from human organizations;
rather is it the crumbling away of material elements from
reason, the translation of law back to its original language, 6
— Mind, and the final unity between man and God.
The footsteps of thought, as they pass from the sensual
side of existence to the reality and Soul of all things, are 9
slow, portending a long night to the traveller; but the
guardians of the gloom are the angels of His presence, that
impart grandeur to the intellectual wrestling and colli- 12
sions with old-time faiths, as we drift into more spiritual
latitudes. The beatings of our heart can be heard; but
the ceaseless throbbings and throes of thought are unheard, 15
as it changes from material to spiritual standpoints. Even
the pangs of death disappear, accordingly as the understanding that we are spiritual beings here reappears, and 18

1

1 we learn our capabilities for good, which insures man's
continuance and is the true glory of immortality.

3   The improved theory and practice of religion and of
medicine are mainly due to the people's improved views
of the Supreme Being. As the finite sense of Deity, based
6 on material conceptions of spiritual being, yields its grosser
elements, we shall learn what God is, and what God does.
The Hebrew term that gives another letter to the word
9 *God* and makes it *good,* unites Science and Christianity,
whereby we learn that God, good, is universal, and the
divine Principle, — Life, Truth, Love; and this Principle is
12 learned through goodness, and of Mind instead of matter,
of Soul instead of the senses, and by revelation supporting
reason. It is the false conceptions of Spirit, based on the
15 evidences gained from the material senses, that make a
Christian only in theory, shockingly material in practice,
and form its Deity out of the worst human qualities, else
18 of wood or stone.

   Such a theory has overturned empires in demoniacal con-
tests over religion. Proportionately as the people's belief
21 of God, in every age, has been dematerialized and unfinited
has their Deity become good; no longer a personal tyrant
or a molten image, but the divine Life, Truth, and Love,
24 — Life without beginning or ending, Truth without a
lapse or error, and Love universal, infinite, eternal. This
more perfect idea, held constantly before the people's
27 mind, must have a benign and elevating influence upon
the character of nations as well as individuals, and will

lift man ultimately to the understanding that our ideals 1
form our characters, that as a man "thinketh in his heart,
so is he." The crudest ideals of speculative theology 3
have made monsters of men; and the ideals of *materia
medica* have made helpless invalids and cripples. The
eternal roasting amidst noxious vapors; the election of the 6
minority to be saved and the majority to be eternally punished; the wrath of God, to be appeased by the sacrifice
and torture of His favorite Son, — are some of the false 9
beliefs that have produced sin, sickness, and death; and
then would affirm that these are natural, and that Christianity and Christ-healing are preternatural; yea, that 12
make a mysterious God and a natural devil.

Let us rejoice that the bow of omnipotence already
spans the moral heavens with light, and that the more 15
spiritual idea of good and Truth meets the old material
thought like a promise upon the cloud, while it inscribes
on the thoughts of men at this period a more metaphysical 18
religion founded upon Christian Science. A personal
God is based on finite premises, where thought begins
wrongly to apprehend the infinite, even the quality or the 21
quantity of eternal good. This limited sense of God as
good limits human thought and action in their goodness,
and assigns them mortal fetters in the outset. It has im- 24
planted in our religions certain unspiritual shifts, such as
dependence on personal pardon for salvation, rather than
obedience to our Father's demands, whereby we grow out 27
of sin in the way that our Lord has appointed; namely,

1 by working out our own salvation. It has given to all
systems of *materia medica* nothing but materialism, —
3 more faith in hygiene and drugs than in God. Idolatry
sprang from the belief that God is a form, more than an
infinite and divine Mind; sin, sickness, and death origi-
6 nated in the belief that Spirit materialized into a body,
infinity became finity, or man, and the eternal entered the
temporal. Mythology, or the myth of ologies, said that
9 Life, which is infinite and eternal, could enter finite man
through his nostrils, and matter become intelligent of
good and evil, because a serpent said it. When first good,
12 God, was named a person, and evil another person, the
error that a personal God and a personal devil entered
into partnership and would form a third person, called
15 material man, obtained expression. But these unspiritual and mysterious ideas of God and man are far from
correct.
18   The glorious Godhead is Life, Truth, and Love, and
these three terms for one divine Principle are the three in
one that can be understood, and that find no reflection in
21 sinning, sick, and dying mortals. No miracle of grace can
make a spiritual mind out of beliefs that are as material as
the heathen deities. The pagan priests appointed Apollo
24 and Esculapius the gods of medicine, and they inquired of
these heathen deities what drugs to prescribe. Systems
of religion and of medicine grown out of such false ideals
27 of the Supreme Being cannot heal the sick and cast out
devils, error. Eschewing a materialistic and idolatrous

theory and practice of medicine and religion, the apostle 1
devoutly recommends the more spiritual Christianity, —
"one Lord, one faith, one baptism." The prophets and 3
apostles, whose lives are the embodiment of a living faith,
have not taken away our Lord, that we know not where they
have laid him; they have resurrected a deathless life of 6
love; and into the cold materialisms of dogma and doctrine
we look in vain for their more spiritual ideal, the risen
Christ, whose *materia medica* and theology were one. 9

The ideals of primitive Christianity are nigh, even at
our door. Truth is not lost in the mists of remoteness or
the barbarisms of spiritless codes. The right ideal is not 12
buried, but has risen higher to our mortal sense, and
having overcome death and the grave, wrapped in a pure
winding-sheet, it sitteth beside the sepulchre in angel 15
form, saying unto us, "Life is God; and our ideal of God
has risen above the sod to declare His omnipotence." This
white-robed thought points away from matter and doc- 18
trine, or dogma, to the diviner sense of Life and Love, —
yea, to the Principle that is God, and to the demonstration thereof in healing the sick. Let us then heed this heav- 21
enly visitant, and not entertain the angel unawares.

The ego is not self-existent matter animated by mind,
but in itself is mind; therefore a Truth-filled mind makes 24
a pure Christianity and a healthy mind and body. Oliver
Wendell Holmes said, in a lecture before the Harvard
Medical School: "I firmly believe that if the whole *materia* 27
medica could be sunk to the bottom of the sea, it would be

1 all the better for mankind and all the worse for the fishes."
Dr. Benjamin Waterhouse writes: "I am sick of learned
3 quackery." Dr. Abercrombie, Fellow of the Royal College of Physicians in Edinburgh, writes: "Medicine is the
science of guessing." Dr. James Johnson, Surgeon Ex-
6 traordinary to the King, says: "I declare my conscientious
belief, founded on long observation and reflection, that
if there was not a single physician, surgeon, apothecary,
9 man-midwife, chemist, druggist, or drug on the face of
the earth, there would be less sickness and less mortality
than now obtains." Voltaire says: "The art of medicine
12 consists in amusing the patient while nature cures the
disease."

Believing that man is the victim of his Maker, we natu-
15 rally fear God more than we love Him; whereas "perfect
Love casteth out fear;" but when we learn God aright, we
love Him, because He is found altogether lovely. Thus it
18 is that a more spiritual and true ideal of Deity improves
the race physically and spiritually. God is no longer a
mystery to the Christian Scientist, but a divine Principle,
21 understood in part, because the grand realities of Life and
Truth are found destroying sin, sickness, and death; and
it should no longer be deemed treason to understand God,
24 when the Scriptures enjoin us to "acquaint now thyself
with Him [God], and be at peace;" we should understand
something of that great good for which we are to leave all
27 else.

Periods and peoples are characterized by their highest

or their lowest ideals, by their God and their devil. We are 1
all sculptors, working out our own ideals, and leaving the
impress of mind on the body as well as on history and 3
marble, chiselling to higher excellence, or leaving to rot and
ruin the mind's ideals. Recognizing this as we ought, we
shall turn often from marble to model, from matter to 6
Mind, to beautify and exalt our lives.

"Chisel in hand stood a sculptor-boy,
With his marble block before him; 9
And his face lit up with a smile of joy
As an angel dream passed o'er him.
He carved the dream on that shapeless stone 12
With many a sharp incision.
With heaven's own light the sculptor shone, —
He had caught the angel-vision. 15

"Sculptors of life are we as we stand
With our lives uncarved before us,
Waiting the hour when at God's command 18
Our life dream passes o'er us.
If we carve it then on the yielding stone
With many a sharp incision, 21
Its heavenly beauty shall be our own, —
Our lives that angel-vision."

To remove those objects of sense called sickness and dis- 24
ease, we must appeal to mind to improve its subjects and
objects of thought, and give to the body those better delineations. Scientific discovery and the inspiration of 27
Truth have taught me that the health and character of
man become more or less perfect as his mind-models are
more or less spiritual. Because God is Spirit, our thoughts 30
must spiritualize to approach Him, and our methods grow
more spiritual to accord with our thoughts. Religion and

1 medicine must be dematerialized to present the right idea
of Truth; then will this idea cast out error and heal the
3 sick. If changeableness that repenteth itself; partiality
that elects some to be saved and others to be lost, or that
answers the prayer of one and not of another; if incom-
6 petency that cannot heal the sick, or lack of love that will
not; if unmercifulness, that for the sins of a few tired
years punishes man eternally, — are our conceptions of
9 Deity, we shall bring out these qualities of character in our
own lives and extend their influence to others.

Judaism, enjoining the limited and definite form of a
12 national religion, was not more the antithesis of Christianity than are our finite and material conceptions of
Deity. Life is God; but we say that Life is carried on
15 through principal processes, and speculate concerning
material forces. Mind is supreme; and yet we make more
of matter, and lean upon it for health and life. Mind,
18 that governs the universe, governs every action of the body
as directly as it moves a planet and controls the muscles
of the arm. God grant that the trembling chords of human
21 hope shall again be swept by the divine *Talitha cumi*,
"Damsel, I say unto thee, arise." Then shall Christian
Science again appear, to light our sepulchres with im-
24 mortality. We thank our Father that to-day the uncre-
mated fossils of material systems, already charred, are
fast fading into ashes; and that man will ere long stop
27 trusting where there is no trust, and gorging his faith with
skill proved a million times unskilful.

Christian Science has one faith, one Lord, one baptism; 1
and this faith builds on Spirit, not matter; and this baptism is the purification of mind, — not an ablution of the 3
body, but tears of repentance, an overflowing love, washing away the motives for sin; yea, it is love leaving self
for God. The cool bath may refresh the body, or as com- 6
pliance with a religious rite may declare one's belief; but
it cannot purify his mind, or meet the demands of Love.
It is the baptism of Spirit that washes our robes and makes 9
them white in the blood of the Lamb; that bathes us in the
life of Truth and the truth of Life. Having one Lord, we
shall not be idolaters, dividing our homage and obedience 12
between matter and Spirit; but shall work out our own
salvation, after the model of our Father, who never pardons the sin that deserves to be punished and can be de- 15
stroyed only through suffering.

We ask and receive not, because we "ask amiss;" even
dare to invoke the divine aid of Spirit to heal the sick, and 18
then administer drugs with full confidence in their efficacy,
showing our greater faith in matter, despite the authority
of Jesus that "ye cannot serve two masters."   21

Silent prayer is a desire, fervent, importunate: here
metaphysics is seen to rise above physics, and rest all faith
in Spirit, and remove all evidence of any other power than 24
Mind; whereby we learn the great fact that there is no
omnipotence, unless omnipotence is the *All*-power. This
truth of Deity, understood, destroys discord with the higher 27
and more potent evidences in Christian Science of man's

1 harmony and immortality. Thought is the essence of an
act, and the stronger element of action; even as steam is
3 more powerful than water, simply because it is more
ethereal. Essences are refinements that lose some materiality; and as we struggle through the cold night of physics,
6 matter will become vague, and melt into nothing under the
microscope of Mind.

Massachusetts succored a fugitive slave in 1853, and put
9 her humane foot on a tyrannical prohibitory law regulating
the practice of medicine in 1880. It were well if the sister
States had followed her example and sustained as nobly
12 our constitutional Bill of Rights. Discerning the God-
given rights of man, Paul said, "I was free born." Justice
and truth make man free, injustice and error enslave
15 him. Mental Science alone grasps the standard of liberty,
and battles for man's whole rights, divine as well as human. It assures us, of a verity, that mortal beliefs, and
18 not a law of nature, have made men sinning and sick, —
that they alone have fettered free limbs, and marred in
mind the model of man.

21 We possess our own body, and make it harmonious or
discordant according to the images that thought reflects
upon it. The emancipation of our bodies from sickness
24 will follow the mind's freedom from sin; and, as St. Paul
admonishes, we should be "waiting for the adoption, to
wit, the redemption of our body." The rights of man were
27 vindicated but in a single instance when African slavery
was abolished on this continent, yet that hour was a

prophecy of the full liberty of the sons of God as found in 1
Christian Science. The defenders of the rights of the
colored man were scarcely done with their battles before a 3
new abolitionist struck the keynote of higher claims, in
which it was found that the feeblest mind, enlightened
and spiritualized, can free its body from disease as well as 6
sin; and this victory is achieved, not with bayonet and
blood, not by inhuman warfare, but in divine peace.

Above the platform of human rights let us build another 9
staging for diviner claims, — even the supremacy of Soul
over sense, wherein man cooperates with and is made subject to his Maker. The lame, the blind, the sick, the sen- 12
sual, are slaves, and their fetters are gnawing away life
and hope; their chains are clasped by the false teachings,
false theories, false fears, that enforce new forms of op- 15
pression, and are the modern Pharaohs that hold the children of Israel still in bondage. Mortals, *alias* mortal
minds, make the laws that govern their bodies, as directly 18
as men pass legislative acts and enact penal codes; while
the body, obedient to the legislation of mind, but ignorant
of the law of belief, calls its own enactments "laws of 21
matter." The legislators who are greatly responsible for
all the woes of mankind are those leaders of public thought
who are mistaken in their methods of humanity. 24

The learned quacks of this period "bind heavy burdens," that they themselves will not touch "with one of
their fingers." Scientific guessing conspires unwittingly 27
against the liberty and lives of men. Should we but

1 hearken to the higher law of God, we should think for one
moment of these divine statutes of God: Let them have
3 "dominion over all the earth."   "And if they drink any
deadly thing, it shall not hurt them; they shall lay hands
on the sick, and they shall recover."   The only law of sick-
6 ness or death is a law of mortal belief, an infringement
on the merciful and just government of God.   When this
great fact is understood, the spurious, imaginary laws of
9 matter — when matter is not a lawgiver — will be disputed and trampled under the feet of Truth.   Deal, then,
with this fabulous law as with an inhuman State law; re-
12 peal it in mind, and acknowledge only God in all thy ways,
— "who forgiveth all thine iniquities; who healeth all thy
diseases."   Few there be who know what a power mind is
15 to heal when imbued with the spiritual truth that lifts man
above the demands of matter.

As our ideas of Deity advance to truer conceptions,
18 we shall take in the remaining two thirds of God's plan
of redemption, — namely, man's salvation from sickness
and death.   Our blessed Master demonstrated this great
21 truth of healing the sick and raising the dead as God's
whole plan, and proved the application of its Principle to
human wants.   Having faith in drugs and hygienic drills,
24 we lose faith in omnipotence, and give the healing power
to matter instead of Spirit.   As if Deity would not if He
could, or could not if He would, give health to man; when
27 our Father bestows heaven not more willingly than health;
for without health there could be no heaven.

The worshippers of wood and stone have a more mate- 1
rial deity, hence a lower order of humanity, than those
who believe that God is a personal Spirit. But the wor- 3
shippers of a person have a lower order of Christianity than
he who understands that the Divine Being is more than a
person, and can demonstrate in part this great impersonal 6
Life, Truth, and Love, casting out error and healing the
sick. This all-important understanding is gained in
Christian Science, revealing the one God and His all- 9
power and ever-presence, and the brotherhood of man in
unity of Mind and oneness of Principle.

On the startled ear of humanity rings out the iron tread 12
of merciless invaders, putting man to the rack for his
conscience, or forcing from the lips of manhood shameful
confessions, — Galileo kneeling at the feet of priestcraft, 15
and giving the lie to science. But the lofty faith of the
pious Polycarp proved the triumph of mind over the body,
when they threatened to let loose the wild beasts upon him, 18
and he replied: "Let them come; I cannot change at once
from good to bad." Then they bound him to the stake,
set fire to the fagots, and his pure faith went up through 21
the baptism of fire to a higher sense of Life. The infidel
was blind who said, "Christianity is fit only for women and
weak-minded men." But infidels disagree; for Bonaparte 24
said: "Since ever the history of Christianity was written,
the loftiest intellects have had a practical faith in God;"
and Daniel Webster said: "My heart has assured and re- 27
assured me that Christianity must be a divine reality."

1   As our ideas of Deity become more spiritual, we express
them by objects more beautiful. To-day we clothe our
3 thoughts of death with flowers laid upon the bier, and in
our cemeteries with amaranth blossoms, evergreen leaves,
fragrant recesses, cool grottos, smiling fountains, and
6 white monuments. The dismal gray stones of church-
yards have crumbled into decay, as our ideas of Life have
grown more spiritual; and in place of "bat and owl on the
9 bending stones, are wreaths of immortelles, and white
fingers pointing upward." Thus it is that our ideas of
divinity form our models of humanity. O Christian Scien-
12 tist, thou of the church of the new-born; awake to a
higher and holier love for God and man; put on the whole
armor of Truth; rejoice in hope; be patient in tribulation,
15 — that ye may go to the bed of anguish, and look upon this
dream of life in matter, girt with a higher sense of omnipotence; and behold once again the power of divine Life and
18 Love to heal and reinstate man in God's own image and
likeness, having "one Lord, one faith, one baptism."

The
First Church
of Christ
Scientist
and Miscellany

The
First Church
of Christ
Scientist
and Miscellany

by MARY BAKER EDDY
*Discoverer and Founder of Christian Science
and Author of Science and Health
with Key to the Scriptures*

Marcas Registradas

Published by The First Church of Christ, Scientist, in Boston, Massachusetts, U.S.A.

Foreword

Lord God of Hosts, be with us yet;   1
Lest we forget — lest we forget!

             — Kipling's *Recessional*   3

IN these stirring times of church building, when the attention of the whole world is fixed on Christian Science, when the growth and prosperity of the Cause are 6 matters of general wonderment and frequent comment, when the right hand of fellowship is being extended to this people by other Christian denominations, when pop- 9 ularity threatens to supersede persecution, it is well for earnest and loyal Christian Scientists to fortify themselves against the mesmerism of personal pride and self- 12 adulation by recalling the following historical facts: —

   1. That Mary Baker Eddy discovered Christian Science in 1866, and established the Cause on a sound basis 15 by healing the sick and reforming the sinner quickly and completely, and doing this work "without money and without price." 18

   2. That in 1875, after nine years of arduous preliminary labor, she wrote and published the Christian Science textbook, "Science and Health with Key to the 21 Scriptures;" that over four hundred thousand copies of this book have been sold — an unparalleled record for a work of this description; that it has healed multi- 24 tudes of disease and has revealed God to well-nigh

1 countless numbers — facts which prove, (1) that Science
and Health does not need to be interpreted to those who
3 are earnestly seeking Truth; (2) that it is not possible
to state truth absolutely in a simpler or more pleasing
form.

6   3. That no one on earth to-day, aside from Mrs.
Eddy, knows anything about Christian Science except
as he has learned it from her and from her writings; and
9 Christian Scientists are honest only as they give her full
credit for this extraordinary work.

   4. That Mrs. Eddy organized The First Church of
12 Christ, Scientist, in Boston, Mass., devised its church
government, originated its form of public worship, wrote
its Church Manual and Tenets, and always has been
15 and is now its guide, guardian, Leader, and wise and
unerring counsellor.

   5. That Mrs. Eddy founded *The Christian Science*
18 *Journal* in 1883, was its first editor and for years the
principal contributor to its columns; that she organized
The Christian Science Publishing Society, which in 1898,
21 with its assets valued at forty-five thousand dollars,
she made over to trustees under agreement to pay all
future profits to her church; that at the same time she
24 presented to her church the property at 95 and 97
Falmouth Street, then occupied by the Publishing Society and valued at twenty-five thousand dollars, reserv-
27 ing for herself only a place for the publishing of her
works; that she established the *Christian Science Sentinel*
and authorized *Der Herold der Christian Science,* both of

which, together with *The Christian Science Journal,* are 1
the property of the Publishing Society.

Strive it ever so hard, The Church of Christ, Scientist, 3
can never do for its Leader what its Leader has done
for this church; but its members can so protect their
own thoughts that they are not unwittingly made to de- 6
prive their Leader of her rightful place as the revelator
to this age of the immortal truths testified to by Jesus
and the prophets. 9

Deeds, not words, are the sound test of love; and
the helpfulness of consistent and constant right thinking — intelligent thinking untainted by the emotionalism 12
which is largely self-glorification — is a reasonable service
which all Christian Scientists can render their Leader.

— *The Christian Science Journal,* May, 1906 15

Contents

Part I
The First Church of Christ, Scientist

Contents

Contents

Contents

Part II

Miscellany

Contents

Contents

CHAPTER VIII

Dedicatory Messages to Branch Churches

CHAPTER IX

Letters to Branch Churches

Contents

CHAPTER X
Admonition and Counsel

Contents

Contents

Contents

CHAPTER XVI
Tributes

CHAPTER XVII
Answers to Criticisms

Contents

Contents

PART I

The First Church of Christ Scientist

The First Church of Christ, Scientist

CHAPTER I

"Choose Ye"

MY BELOVED BRETHREN: — The divine might of
Truth demands well-doing in order to demonstrate truth, and this not alone in accord with human 6
desire but with spiritual power. St. John writes: "Blessed
are they that do His commandments, that they may have
right to the tree of life, and may enter in through the gates 9
into the city." The sear leaves of faith without works,
scattered abroad in Zion's waste places, appeal to reformers, "Show me thy faith by thy works." 12
Christian Science is not a dweller apart in royal solitude;
it is not a law of matter, nor a transcendentalism that
heals only the sick. This Science is a law of divine Mind, 15
a persuasive animus, an unerring impetus, an ever-present
help. Its presence is felt, for it acts and acts wisely,
always unfolding the highway of hope, faith, understand- 18
ing. It is the higher criticism, the higher hope; and its
effect on man is mainly this — that the good which has
come into his life, examination compels him to think 21
genuine, whoever did it. A Christian Scientist verifies
his calling. *Choose ye!*

3

1   When, by losing his faith in matter and sin, one finds
the spirit of Truth, then he practises the Golden Rule
3 spontaneously; and obedience to this rule spiritualizes
man, for the world's *nolens volens* cannot enthrall it.
Lust, dishonesty, sin, disable the student; they preclude
6 the practice or efficient teaching of Christian Science, the
truth of man's being. The Scripture reads: "He that
taketh not his cross, and followeth after me, is not worthy
9 of me." On this basis, how many are following the
Way-shower? We follow Truth only as we follow truly,
meekly, patiently, spiritually, blessing saint and sinner
12 with the leaven of divine Love which woman has put
into Christendom and medicine.

A genuine Christian Scientist loves Protestant and
15 Catholic, D.D. and M.D., — loves all who love God,
good; and he loves his enemies. It will be found that,
instead of opposing, such an individual subserves the
18 interests of both medical faculty and Christianity, and
they thrive together, learning that Mind-power is good
will towards men. Thus unfolding the true metal in
21 character, the iron in human nature rusts away; honesty
and justice characterize the seeker and finder of Christian
Science.

24   The pride of place or power is the prince of this world
that hath nothing in Christ. Our great Master said:
"Except ye . . . become as little children, ye shall not
27 enter into the kingdom of heaven," — the reign of righteousness, the glory of good, healing the sick and saving
the sinner. The height of my hope must remain. Glory
30 be to Thee, Thou God most high and nigh.

Whatever is not divinely natural and demonstrably
true, in ethics, philosophy, or religion, is not of God but

originates in the minds of mortals. It is the Adam- 1
dream according to the Scriptural allegory, in which
man is supposed to start from dust and woman to be 3
the outcome of man's rib, — marriage synonymous with
legalized lust, and the offspring of sense the murderers
of their brothers! 6

Wholly apart from this mortal dream, this illusion and
delusion of sense, Christian Science comes to reveal man
as God's image, His idea, coexistent with Him — God 9
giving all and man having all that God gives. Whence,
then, came the creation of matter, sin, and death, mortal
pride and power, prestige or privilege? The First Com- 12
mandment of the Hebrew Decalogue, "Thou shalt have
no other gods before me," and the Golden Rule are the
all-in-all of Christian Science. They are the spiritual 15
idealism and realism which, when realized, constitute a
Christian Scientist, heal the sick, reform the sinner, and
rob the grave of its victory. The spiritual understanding 18
which demonstrates Christian Science, enables the devout
Scientist to worship, not an unknown God, but Him whom,
understanding even in part, he continues to love more and 21
to serve better.

Beloved, I am not with you *in propria persona* at this
memorable dedication and communion season, but I am 24
with you "in spirit and in truth," lovingly thanking your
generosity and fidelity, and saying virtually what the
prophet said: Continue to choose whom ye will serve. 27

Forgetting the Golden Rule and indulging sin, men
cannot serve God; they cannot demonstrate the omnipotence of divine Mind that heals the sick and the sinner. 30
Human will may mesmerize and mislead man; divine
wisdom, never. Indulging deceit is like the defendant

1 arguing for the plaintiff in favor of a decision which the
defendant knows will be turned against himself.

3   We cannot serve two masters. Do we love God
supremely? Are we honest, just, faithful? Are we true
to ourselves? "God is not mocked: for whatsoever a
6 man soweth, that shall he also reap." To abide in our
unselfed better self is to be done forever with the sins
of the flesh, the wrongs of human life, the tempter and
9 temptation, the smile and deceit of damnation. When
we have overcome sin in all its forms, men may revile us
and despitefully use us, and we shall rejoice, "for great
12 is [our] reward in heaven."

You have dexterously and wisely provided for The
Mother Church of Christ, Scientist, a magnificent tem-
15 ple wherein to enter and pray. Greatly impressed and
encouraged thereby, deeply do I thank you for this proof
of your progress, unity, and love. The modest edifice
18 of The Mother Church of Christ, Scientist, began with
the cross; its excelsior extension is the crown. The room
of your Leader remains in the beginning of this edifice,
21 evidencing the praise of babes and the word which proceedeth out of the mouth of God. Its crowning ultimate rises to a mental monument, a superstructure high
24 above the work of men's hands, even the outcome of
their hearts, giving to the material a spiritual significance
— the speed, beauty, and achievements of goodness.
27 Methinks this church is the one edifice on earth which
most prefigures self-abnegation, hope, faith; love catching
a glimpse of glory.

CHAPTER II

The Extension
of The Mother Church
# of Christ, Scientist:
Its Inception, Construction,
and Dedication

MRS. EDDY'S MESSAGE TO THE MOTHER CHURCH,   1
JUNE 15, 1902

[Extract]   3

HERE allow me to interpolate some matters of business that ordinarily find no place in my Message.
It is a privilege to acquaint communicants with the   6
financial transactions of this church, so far as I know
them, and especially before making another united effort
to purchase more land and enlarge our church edifice so   9
as to seat the large number who annually favor us with
their presence on Communion Sunday.

THE ANNUAL MEETING OF THE MOTHER CHURCH, JUNE 12
18, 1902 — TWO MILLION DOLLARS PLEDGED

Edward A. Kimball, C.S.D., offered the following
motion: —   15
"Recognizing the necessity for providing an auditorium
for The Mother Church that will seat four or five thousand persons, and acting in behalf of ourselves and the 18
Christian Scientists of the world, we agree to contribute

7

1 any portion of two million dollars that may be necessary for this purpose."

3 In support of the motion, Mr. Kimball said in part:

"Our denomination is palpably outgrowing the institutional end thereof. We need to keep pace with our own 6 growth and progress. The necessity here indicated is beyond cavil; beyond resistance in your thought."

Judge William G. Ewing, in seconding the motion, said:— 9 "As we have the best church in the world, and as we have the best expression of the religion of Jesus Christ, let us have the best material symbol of both of these, and 12 in the best city in the world.

"Now I am sure that I have but expressed the universal voice of Christian Scientists, that there should be some- 15 thing done, and done immediately, to make reasonable accommodation for the regular business of the Christian Science church, and I believe really, with my faint 18 knowledge of arithmetic and the relationship of figures, that a church of twenty-four thousand members should have a seating capacity of more than nine hundred, if 21 they are all to get in."

The motion was carried unanimously.

Greeting from the Church to Mrs. Eddy

24 "Ten thousand Christian Scientists from throughout the world, convened in annual business meeting in Boston, send our greeting to you, whom we recognize 27 as logically the natural and indispensable Leader of our religious denomination and its activity.

"Since the last report, in 1900, one hundred and five 30 new churches or congregations have been added, and

those previously established have had large accessions 1
to their membership. In recognition of the necessity for
providing an audience-room in The Mother Church which 3
will seat four or five thousand persons, we have agreed to
contribute any portion of two million dollars that may
be needed for that purpose. 6

"The instinctive gratitude which not only impels the
Christian to turn in loving thankfulness to his heavenly
Father, but induces him to glory in every good deed and 9
thought on the part of every man — this would be scant
indeed if it did not continually move us to utter our gratitude to you and declare the depth of our affection and 12
esteem.

"To you, who are standing in the forefront of the effort
for righteous reform, we modestly renew the hope and 15
desire that we may worthily follow with you in the way
of salvation through Christ."

OUR LEADER'S THANKS 18

To the Members of The Mother Church: — I am bankrupt
in thanks to you, my beloved brethren, who at our last
annual meeting pledged yourselves with startling grace 21
to contribute any part of two millions of dollars towards
the purchase of more land for its site, and to enlarge
our church edifice in Boston. I never before felt poor 24
in thanks, but I do now, and will draw on God for
the amount I owe you, till I am satisfied with what my
heart gives to balance accounts. 27

MARY BAKER EDDY

PLEASANT VIEW, CONCORD, N. H.,
July 21, 1902 30

1   [*Christian Science Sentinel*, May 16, 1903]

It is inevitable that the transforming influence of
3 Christian Science should improve the thought, enlarge the
favorable expectation, and augment the achievements of
its followers.   It was inevitable that this mighty impulse
6 for good should have externalized itself, ten years ago,
in an edifice for The Mother Church.   It is inevitable
that this same impulsion should now manifest itself in a
9 beautiful, ample building, embodying the best of design,
material, and situation.

Some money has been paid in towards the fund, and
12 some of the churches and other organizations have taken
steps in this direction, but the time is at hand, now, for
this entire donation to be specifically subscribed as to
15 amount and date of payment.   No appeal has ever been
made in this behalf, and it is probable that none will be
made or ever be needed.   It is doubtful if the Cause of
18 Christian Science could prosper, in any particular, on the
basis of fretful or reluctant sacrifice on the part of its
people.   Christian Scientists are not expected to contrib-
21 ute money against their will or as the result of impor-
tunity or entreaty on the part of some one else.

They will provide the money necessary to this end,
24 because they recognize the importance of The Mother
Church to the Cause.   They realize that there must be
a prosperous parent church, in order to insure the pros-
27 perity of the branch churches; indeed, they know that
it is the prosperous growth of this movement which
now necessitates this onward step.   They know that
30 their own individual welfare is closely interwoven with
the general welfare of the Cause.

Notwithstanding the fact that as Christian Scientists 1
we are as yet but imperfect followers of the perfect Christ,
and although we may falter or stumble or loiter by the 3
way, we know that the Leader of this movement, Mrs.
Eddy, has been constantly at her post during all the
storms that have surged against her for a generation. 6
She has been the one of all the world who has encountered
the full force of antagonism. We know, too, that during
these years she has not tried to guide us by means of 9
forced marches, but has waited for us to grow into readiness for each step, and we know that in all this time she
has never urged upon us a step that did not result in our 12
welfare.

A year ago she quietly alluded to the need of our
Mother Church. She knew that we were ready; the re- 15
sponse was instant, spontaneous. Later on she expressed
much gratification because of prompt and liberal action,
and it needs no special insight to predict that she will be 18
cheered and encouraged to know that, having seized upon
this privilege and opportunity, we have also made good
the pledge. 21

[Editorial in *Christian Science Sentinel*, May 16, 1903]

Our readers have been informed of the purchase of the
land upon which the new building will be erected, and 24
that this land has been paid for. The location is, therefore, determined. The size of the building was decided
last June, but there still remained for definite decision 27
the amount to be expended and the date for commencing building operations. The pledge of the annual
meeting was "any portion of two million dollars that 30

1 may be necessary for this purpose," and this of course
carried the implication that work should be commenced
3 as soon as the money in hand justified the letting of
contracts.

The spontaneous and liberal donations which enabled
6 those having the work in charge to secure the large
parcel of land adjoining The Mother Church, gives
promise of the speedy accumulation of a sum sufficient
9 to justify the decision of these remaining problems.
Each person interested must remember, however, that
his individual desires, both as to the amount to be
12 expended and the date of commencing work, will be best
evidenced by the liberality and promptness of his own
contribution.

15   [Mrs. Eddy in *Christian Science Sentinel*, May 30, 1903]

NOW AND THEN

This was an emphatic rule of St. Paul: "Behold, now
18 is the accepted time." A lost opportunity is the greatest of losses. Whittier mourned it as what "might
have been." We own no past, no future, we pos-
21 sess only *now*. If the reliable *now* is carelessly lost in
speaking or in acting, it comes not back again. Whatever needs to be done which cannot be done now,
24 God prepares the way for doing; while that which can
be done now, but is not, increases our indebtedness to
God. Faith in divine Love supplies the ever-present
27 help and *now*, and gives the power to "act in the living
present."

The dear children's good deeds are gems in the settings
30 of manhood and womanhood. The good they desire to

do, they insist upon doing now. They speculate neither 1
on the past, present, nor future, but, taking no thought
for the morrow, act in God's time.   3

A book by Benjamin Wills Newton, called "Thoughts
on the Apocalypse," published in London, England, in
1853, was presented to me in 1903 by Mr. Marcus 6
Holmes. This was the first that I had even heard of
it. When scanning its interesting pages, my attention
was arrested by the following: "The church at Jerusalem, 9
like a sun in the centre of its system, had other churches,
like so many planets, revolving around it. It was
strictly a *mother* and a ruling church." According to 12
his description, the church of Jerusalem seems to pre-
figure The Mother Church of Christ, Scientist, in
Boston.   15

I understand that the members of The Mother Church,
out of loving hearts, pledged to this church in Boston
any part of two millions of money with which to build 18
an ample temple dedicate to God, to Him "who forgiveth
all thine iniquities; *who healeth all thy diseases;* who
redeemeth thy life from destruction; who crowneth thee 21
with lovingkindness and tender mercies; who satisfieth
thy mouth with good things; so that thy youth is renewed
like the eagle's," — to build a temple the spiritual spire 24
of which will reach the stars with divine overtures, holy
harmony, reverberating through all cycles of systems and
spheres.   27

Because Christian Scientists virtually pledged this
munificent sum not only to my church but to Him who
returns it unto them after many days, their loving giving 30
has been blessed. It has crystallized into a foundation
for our temple, and it will continue to "prosper in the

1 thing whereto [God, Spirit] sent it." In the *now* they
brought their tithes into His storehouse. *Then,* when
3 this bringing is consummated, God will pour them out a
blessing above the song of angels, beyond the ken of
mortals — a blessing that two millions of love currency
6 will bring to be discerned in the near future as a gleam
of reality; not a madness and nothing, but a sanity
and something from the individual, stupendous, Godlike
9 agency of man.

[Editorial in *Christian Science Sentinel*, January 2, 1904]

A few days ago we received a letter from a friend in
12 another city, saying that he had just been informed —
and his informant claimed to have good authority for the
statement — that the entire amount required to complete
15 The Mother Church building fund had been paid in;
consequently further payments or subscriptions were not
desired.

18 Our friend very promptly and emphatically pronounced the story a fabrication of the evil one, and he
was entirely right in doing so. If the devil were really
21 an entity, endowed with genius and inspiration, he could
not have invented a more subtle lie with which to ensnare a generous and loyal people.

24 As a matter of fact, the building fund is not complete,
but it is in such a healthy state that building operations
have been commenced, and they will be carried on without
27 interruption until the church is finished. The rapidity
with which the work will be pushed forward necessitates
large payments of money, and it is desirable that the con-
30 tributions to the building fund keep pace with the dis-
bursements.

[*Christian Science Sentinel*, March 5, 1904]   1

AMENDMENT TO BY-LAW

Section 3 of Article XLI (XXXIV in revised edition) of 3 the Church By-laws has been amended to read as follows: —

THE MOTHER CHURCH BUILDING. — SECTION 3. The edifice erected in 1894 for The First Church of Christ, 6 Scientist, in Boston, Mass., shall neither be demolished nor removed from the site where it was built, without the written consent of the Pastor Emeritus, Mary Baker 9 Eddy.

COMMUNION, 1904

My Beloved Brethren: — My heart goes out to you as 12 ever in daily desire that the Giver of all good transform you into His own image and likeness. Already I have said to you all that you are able to bear now, and thanking 15 you for your gracious reception of it I close with Kate Hankey's excellent hymn, —

> I love to tell the story, 18
>   Of unseen things above,
> Of Jesus and his glory,
>   Of Jesus and his love. 21
> I love to tell the story,
>   Because I know 'tis true;
> It satisfies my longings, 24
>   As nothing else can do.
>
> I love to tell the story;
>   For those who know it best 27
> Seem hungering and thirsting
>   To hear it like the rest.
> And when, in scenes of glory, 30
>   I sing the NEW, NEW SONG,
> 'Twill be the OLD, OLD STORY
>   That I have loved so long. 33

1 EXTRACT FROM THE TREASURER'S REPORT, JUNE 14, 1904

The report of Mr. Stephen A. Chase, treasurer of the
3 building fund of The Mother Church, made to the
annual meeting, showed that a total of $425,893.66 had
been received up to and including May 31, 1904, and that
6 there was a balance of $226,285.73 on hand on that date,
after paying out the sum of $199,607.93, which included
the purchase price of the land for the site of the new
9 building.

THE CORNER-STONE LAID

The corner-stone of the new auditorium for The Mother
12 Church in Boston was laid Saturday, July 16, 1904, at
eight o'clock in the forenoon.   In addition to the members
of the Christian Science Board of Directors, who have
15 the work directly in charge, there were present on this
occasion: Mr. Alfred Farlow, President of The Mother
Church; Prof. Hermann S. Hering, First Reader; Mrs.
18 Ella E. Williams, Second Reader; Mr. Charles Brigham
and Mr. E. Noyes Whitcomb, respectively the architect
and the builder of the new edifice.
21   The order of the services, which were conducted by the
First Reader, was as follows: —
Scripture reading, Isaiah 28 : 16, 17, —

24   "Therefore thus saith the Lord God, Behold, I lay in
Zion for a foundation a stone, a tried stone, a precious
corner stone, a sure foundation: he that believeth shall
27 not make haste.
"Judgment also will I lay to the line, and righteousness to the plummet: and the hail shall sweep away the

refuge of lies, and the waters shall overflow the hiding 1
place."

Also, 1 Peter 2 : 1–6, — 3

"Wherefore laying aside all malice, and all guile, and
hypocrisies, and envies, and all evil speakings,

"As newborn babes, desire the sincere milk of the word, 6
that ye may grow thereby:

"If so be ye have tasted that the Lord is gracious.

"To whom coming, as unto a living stone, disallowed 9
indeed of men, but chosen of God, and precious,

"Ye also, as lively stones, are built up a spiritual house,
an holy priesthood, to offer up spiritual sacrifices, accept- 12
able to God by Jesus Christ.

"Wherefore also it is contained in the scripture,
Behold, I lay in Sion a chief corner stone, elect, precious: 15
and he that believeth on him shall not be confounded."

The reading of selections from "Science and Health
with Key to the Scriptures" by Mary Baker Eddy, — 18

Page 241, lines 13–30
"   136, "   1–5, 9–14
"   137, "   16–5   21
"   583, "   12–19
"   35, "   20–25

This was followed by a few moments of silent prayer 24
and the audible repetition of the Lord's Prayer with its
spiritual interpretation, as given in the Christian Science
textbook, after which the following extracts from Mrs. 27
Eddy's writings were read: —

"Hitherto, I have observed that in proportion as this
church has smiled on His 'little ones,' He has blessed 30
her. Throughout my entire connection with The Mother

1 Church, I have seen, that in the ratio of her love for others, hath His love been bestowed upon her; water-
3 ing her waste places, and enlarging her borders.

"One thing I have greatly desired, and again earnestly request, namely, that Christian Scientists, here and else-
6 where, pray daily for themselves; not verbally, nor on bended knee, but mentally, meekly, and importunately. When a hungry heart petitions the divine Father-Mother
9 God for bread, it is not given a stone, — but more grace, obedience, and love. If this heart, humble and trustful, faithfully asks divine Love to feed it with the bread of
12 heaven, health, holiness, it will be conformed to a fitness to receive the answer to its desire; then will flow into it the 'river of His pleasure,' the tributary of divine Love,
15 and great growth in Christian Science will follow, — even that joy which finds one's own in another's good." (Miscellaneous Writings, p. 127.)
18   "Beloved brethren, the love of our loving Lord was never more manifest than in its stern condemnation of all error, wherever found. I counsel thee, rebuke and exhort
21 one another. Love all Christian churches for the gospel's sake; and be exceedingly glad that the churches are united in purpose, if not in method, to close the war between
24 flesh and Spirit, and to fight the good fight till God's will be witnessed and done on earth as in heaven." (Christian Science versus Pantheism, p. 13.)

27   The corner-stone was then laid by the members of the Christian Science Board of Directors. It contained the following articles: The Holy Bible; "Science and Health
30 with Key to the Scriptures" and all other published writings of the Rev. Mary Baker Eddy, the Discoverer

and Founder of Christian Science; Christian Science 1
Hymnal; "The Mother Church;" the current numbers of
The Christian Science Journal, Christian Science Sentinel, 3
Der Herold der Christian Science, and the *Christian Science
Quarterly.*

The ceremony concluded with the repetition of "the 6
scientific statement of being," from Science and Health
(p. 468), and the benediction, 2 Corinthians 13 : 14:
"The grace of the Lord Jesus Christ, and the love of 9
God, and the communion of the Holy Ghost, be with you
all. Amen."

UNSELFISH LOYALTY 12

To one of the many branch churches which contributed
their local church building funds to The Mother Church
building fund, Mrs. Eddy wrote as follows: — 15

First Church of Christ, Scientist,
  Colorado Springs, Col.

Beloved Brethren: — It is conceded that our shadows 18
follow us in the sunlight wherever we go; but I ask for
more, even this: That this dear church shall be pursued
by her *substance,* the immortal fruition of her unselfed 21
love, and that her charity, which "seeketh not her
own" but another's good, shall reap richly the reward of
goodness. 24

Those words of our holy Way-shower, vibrant through
time and eternity with acknowledgment of exemplary
giving, no doubt fill the memory and swell the hearts of 27
the members of The Mother Church, because of that gift
which you so sacredly bestowed towards its church building fund. These are applicable words: "Verily I say 30
unto you, Wheresoever this gospel shall be preached

1 throughout the whole world, this also that she hath done
shall be spoken of for a memorial of her." (Mark 14 : 9.)
3   Gratefully yours in Christ,
                                    MARY BAKER EDDY
       PLEASANT VIEW, CONCORD, N. H.,
6   September 1, 1904

HOLIDAY GIFTS

Beloved Students: — The holidays are coming, and I
9 trow you are awaiting on behalf of your Leader the
loving liberty of their license. May I relieve you of
selecting, and name your gifts to her, in advance?
12 Send her only what God gives to His church. Bring
all your tithes into His storehouse, and what you would
expend for presents to her, please add to your givings
15 to The Mother Church building fund, and let this
suffice for her rich portion in due season. Send no gifts
to her the ensuing season, but the evidences of glorious
18 growth in Christian Science.
                                    MARY BAKER EDDY
       PLEASANT VIEW, CONCORD, N. H.,
21   October 31, 1904

A WORD FROM THE DIRECTORS, MAY, 1905

In view of the fact that a general attendance of the
24 members of The Mother Church at the communion
and annual meeting in Boston entails the expenditure
of a large amount of money, and the further fact that
27 it is important that the building fund of The Mother
Church should be completed as early as possible, it has
been decided to omit this year the usual large gathering
30 in Boston, and to ask the members to contribute to

the building fund the amount which they would have 1
expended in such an event.

We all know of the loving self-sacrifices which have been 3
made by many of the branch churches in transferring to
this fund the money which had been collected for the
purpose of building church homes of their own, and it will 6
thus be seen that the course suggested will not only
hasten the completion of The Mother Church, but will
also advance the erection of many branch churches. 9
We therefore feel sure that all Christian Scientists will
gladly forego a visit to Boston at this time, in order to
contribute more liberally to the building fund and thereby 12
aid the progress of our Cause throughout the world.

Christian Scientists have learned from experience that
divine Love more than compensates for every seeming 15
trial and deprivation in our loyalty to Truth, and it is
but right to expect that those who are willing to forego
their anticipated visit this year will receive a greater 18
blessing — "good measure, pressed down, and shaken
together, and running over." The local members, who
have always experienced much pleasure in welcoming 21
their brethren from far and near, and who have anticipated much joy in meeting very many of them this year,
will feel that they have been called upon to make no less 24
sacrifice than have others; but we are confident that
they too will be blessed, and that all will rejoice in the
glad reunion upon the completion of the new edifice in 27
Boston.

IRA O. KNAPP,   JOSEPH ARMSTRONG,
WILLIAM B. JOHNSON,   STEPHEN A. CHASE,   30
ARCHIBALD MCLELLAN,
The Christian Science Board of Directors

THE ANNUAL MEETING, JUNE 13, 1905

Extract from the Clerk's Report

In the year 1902 our Leader saw the need of a larger edifice for the home of The Mother Church, one that would accommodate the constantly increasing attendance at all the services, and the large gatherings at the annual meeting; and, at the annual meeting in June, 1902, a sum of money adequate to erect such a building was pledged. Christian Scientists have contributed already for this grand and noble purpose, but let us not be unconsciously blind to the further needs of the building fund, in order to complete this great work, nor wait to be urged or to be shown the absolute necessity of giving.

Since 1866, almost forty years ago, — almost forty years in the wilderness, — our beloved Leader and teacher, Mrs. Eddy, the Founder of Christian Science, has labored for the regeneration of mankind; and time has put its seal of affirmation upon every purpose she has set in motion, and the justification of her labors is the fruit. In these years of work she has shown wisdom, faith, and a spiritual discernment of the needs of the present and of the future that is nothing less than God-bestowed.

In years to come the moral and the physical effects produced by The Mother Church, and by the advanced position taken by our Pastor Emeritus and Leader, will appear in their proper perspective. Is it not therefore the duty of all who have touched the healing hem of Christian Science, to get immediately into the proper perspective of the meaning of the erection of the new edifice of The First Church of Christ, Scientist, in Boston?

It is not necessary for us to delay our contributions in order to find out how much our neighbor has given, or to compute by the total membership of The Mother Church what amount each shall send the Treasurer. The divine Love that prompted the desire, and supplied the means to consummate the erection of the present edifice in 1894, is still with us, and will bless us so long as we follow His commands.

Extract from the Treasurer's Report

Building Fund: — Amount on hand June 1, 1905, $303,189.41; expenditures June 1, 1904 to May 31, 1905, $388,663.15; total receipts June 19, 1902 to June 1, 1905, $891,460.49.

Amount necessary to complete the sum of $2,000,000 pledged at the annual meeting, 1902, $1,108,539.51.

Greeting to Mrs. Eddy from the Annual Meeting

Beloved Teacher and Leader: — The members of your church, The Mother Church, The First Church of Christ, Scientist, in Boston, Mass., in annual business meeting assembled, send their loyal and loving greetings to you, the Discoverer and Founder of Christian Science and author of its textbook.

We rejoice greatly that the walls of our new edifice are rising, not only to faith but also to sight; that this temple, which represents the worship of Spirit, with its inseparable accompaniment, the Christ-healing, is being built in our day; and that we have the privilege of participating in the work of its erection. As the stately structure grows, and stone is laid upon stone, those who pass by are

1 impelled to ask, What means this edifice? and they learn
that the truth which Christ Jesus revealed — the truth
3 which makes free — is to-day being proven and is ready
to heal all who accept its divine ministry. We congratulate you that the building is to express in its ample audi-
6 torium something of the vastness of the truth it represents,
and also to symbolize your unmeasured love for humanity,
which inspires you to welcome all mankind to the privi-
9 leges of this healing and saving gospel. As the walls are
builded by the prayers and offerings of the thousands
who have been healed through Christian Science, we know
12 that you rejoice in the unity of thought and purpose
which is thus expressed, showing that The Mother Church
"fitly framed together groweth unto an holy temple in the
15 Lord."

[Editorial in *Christian Science Sentinel*, November 25, 1905]

We are prompted to state, for the benefit of those who
18 have inquired about the progress of the work on the
extension to The Mother Church, that the erection of the
building is proceeding rapidly; in fact, it is being pushed
21 with the utmost energy, and at the present time there
are no less than fifteen different trades represented. The
beauty of the building, and the substantial and enduring
24 character of its construction, have been remarked by the
many visitors who have recently inspected the work, and
they have gone away with the conviction that the structure
27 is worthy of our Cause and that it will meet the needs of
The Mother Church as well as this can be done by a
building with a seating capacity of five thousand.
30 It therefore occurs to us that there could be no more
appropriate time for completing the building fund than

the present Thanksgiving season; and it is suggested to our 1
readers that there would be great propriety in making a
special effort during the coming week to dispose fully and 3
finally of this feature of the demonstration.

[*Christian Science Sentinel*, March 17, 1906]

GIFTS FROM THE CHILDREN   6

The great interest exhibited by the children who attend
the Sunday School of The Mother Church is shown by
their contributions to the building fund. The following 9
figures are taken from the report of the secretary of the
Sunday School and are most gratifying:

March 1, 1903 to February 29, 1904, $621.10; March 1, 12
1904 to February 28, 1905, $845.96; March 1, 1905 to
February 28, 1906, $1,112.13; total, $2,579.19.

CARD   15

Will one and all of my dear correspondents accept this,
my answer to their fervid question: Owing to the time
consumed in travel, *et cetera*, I cannot be present *in* 18
propria persona at our annual communion and the dedication in June next of The Mother Church of Christ,
Scientist. But I shall be with my blessed church "in 21
spirit and in truth."

I have faith in the givers and in the builders of this
church edifice,—admiration for and faith in the grandeur 24
and sublimity of this superb superstructure, wherein all
vanity of victory disappears and the glory of divinity
appears in all its promise.   27

MARY BAKER EDDY

PLEASANT VIEW, CONCORD, N. H.,
April 8, 1906   30

1   [*Christian Science Sentinel*, April 14, 1906]
       ANNOUNCEMENT OF THE DEDICATION

3   The Christian Science Board of Directors takes pleasure
  in announcing that the extension of The Mother Church
  will be dedicated on the date of the annual communion,
6 Sunday, June 10, 1906.

              [*Christian Science Sentinel*, April 28, 1906]
          TO THE BOARD OF DIRECTORS

9   *My Beloved Students:* — Your generous check of five
  thousand dollars, April 23, 1906, is duly received. You
  can imagine my gratitude and emotion at the touch of
12 memory. Your beneficent gift is the largest sum of money
  that I have ever received from my church, and quite
  unexpected at this juncture, but not the less appreciated.
15 My Message for June 10 is ready for you. It is too
  short to be printed in book form, for I thought it better
  to be brief on this rare occasion. This communion and
18 dedication include enough of their own.

     The enclosed notice I submit to you, and trust that you
  will see, as I foresee, the need of it. Now is the time to
21 *throttle the lie* that students worship me or that I claim
  their homage. This historical dedication should date
  some special reform, and this notice is requisite to give
24 the true animus of our church and denomination.

                          Lovingly yours,
                          MARY BAKER EDDY

27 PLEASANT VIEW, CONCORD, N. H.,
              April 23, 1906

NOTICE

1

To the Beloved Members of my Church, The Mother Church,
The First Church of Christ, Scientist, in Boston: — Divine 3
Love bids me say: Assemble not at the residence of your
Pastor Emeritus at or about the time of our annual
meeting and communion service, for the divine and not 6
the human should engage our attention at this sacred
season of prayer and praise.

MARY BAKER EDDY 9

NOTICE TO CONTRIBUTORS TO THE BUILDING FUND

The contributors to the building fund for the extension
of The Mother Church, The First Church of Christ, 12
Scientist, in Boston, Mass., are hereby notified that
sufficient funds have been received for the completion of
the church building, and the friends are requested to send 15
no more money to this fund.

STEPHEN A. CHASE,
Treasurer of the Building Fund 18

BOSTON, MASS., June 2, 1906

[Editorial in *Christian Science Sentinel*, June 9, 1906]

Christian Scientists will read with much joy and 21
thanksgiving the announcement made by Mr. Chase in
this issue of the *Sentinel* that sufficient funds have been
received by him, as treasurer of the building fund, to 24
pay all bills in connection with the extension of The
Mother Church, and to most of them the fact that he

has been able to make this announcement coincident with the completion of the building will be deeply significant. Our Leader has said in Science and Health (p. 494), "Divine Love always has met and always will meet every human need," and this has been proved true in the experience of many who have contributed to the building fund.

The treasurer's books will show the dollars and cents received by him, but they can give no more than a hint of the unselfish efforts, and in many instances the loving self-sacrifice, of those who have given so generously to the building of this church. Suffice it to say, however, that the giving to this fund has stimulated those gentle qualities which mark the true Christian, and its influence upon the lives of thousands has been of immense value to them.

The significance of this building is not to be found in the material structure, but in the lives of those who, under the consecrated leadership of Mrs. Eddy, and following her example, are doing the works which Jesus said should mark the lives of his followers. It stands as the visible symbol of a religion which heals the sick and reforms the sinful as our Master healed and reformed them. It proclaims to the world that Jesus' gospel was for all time and for all men; that it is as effective to-day as it was when he preached the Word of God to the multitudes of Judea and healed them of their diseases and their sins. It speaks for the successful labors of one divinely guided woman, who has brought to the world the spiritual under-standing of the Scriptures, and whose ministry has revealed the one true Science and changed the whole aspect of medicine and theology.

[*Christian Science Sentinel*, June 16, 1906. Reprinted from   1
Boston Herald]

COMMUNION SERVICE AND DEDICATION   3

Five thousand people kneeling in silent communion;
a stillness profound; and then, rising in unison from the
vast congregation, the words of the Lord's Prayer! Such 6
was the closing incident of the dedicatory services of the
extension of The Mother Church, The First Church of
Christ, Scientist, at the corner of Falmouth and Norway 9
Streets, yesterday morning. And such was the scene
repeated six times during the day.

It was a sight which no one who saw it will ever be able 12
to forget. Many more gorgeous church pageantries have
been seen in this country and in an older civilization;
there have been church ceremonies that appealed more 15
to the eye, but the impressiveness of this lay in its very
simplicity; its grandeur sprang from the complete
unanimity of thought and of purpose. There was some- 18
thing emanating from the thousands who worshipped
under the dome of the great edifice whose formal opening they had gathered to observe, that appealed to and 21
fired the imagination. A comparatively new religion
launching upon a new era, assuming an altogether different status before the world!   24

Even the sun smiled kindly upon the dedication of the
extension of The Mother Church. With a cooling breeze
to temper the heat, the thousands who began to congregate 27
about the church as early as half past five in the morning
were able to wait patiently for the opening of the doors
without suffering the inconveniences of an oppressive day. 30
From that time, until the close of the evening service,

Falmouth and Norway Streets held large crowds of people, either coming from a service or awaiting admission to one. As all the services were precisely the same in every respect, nobody attended more than one, so that there were well over thirty thousand people who witnessed the opening. Not only did these include Scientists from all over the world, and nearly all the local Scientists, but many hundreds of other faiths, drawn to the church from curiosity, and from sympathy, too.

It spoke much for the devotion of the members to their faith, the character of the attendance. In those huge congregations were business men come from far distant points at personal sacrifices of no mean order; professional men, devoted women members, visitors from Australia, from India, from England, from Germany, from Switzerland, from South Africa, from Hawaii, from the coast States.

They gave generously of their means in gratitude for the epoch-making event. The six collections were large, and when the plates were returned after having been through the congregations, they were heaped high with bills, with silver, and with gold. Some of these contributions were one-hundred-dollar bills. Without ostentation and quite voluntarily the Scientists gave a sum surpassing some of the record collections secured by evangelists for the work of Christianity.

Though the church was filled for the service at half past seven, and hundreds had to be turned away, by far the largest crowd of the day applied for admission at the ten o'clock service, and it was representative of the entire body of the Christian Science church.

Before half past seven the chimes of the new church

began to play, first the "Communion Hymn," succeeded 1
by the following hymns throughout the day: "The
morning light is breaking;" "Shepherd, show me how 3
to go;" "Just as I am, without one plea;" "I need
Thee every hour;" "Blest Christmas morn;" "Abide
with me;" "Day by day the manna fell;" "Oh, the 6
clanging bells of time;" "Still, still with Thee;" "O'er
waiting harpstrings of the mind;" Doxology.

Promptly at half past six the numerous doors of the 9
church were thrown open and the public had its first
glimpse of the great structure, the cost of which approximates two millions of dollars, contributed from over the 12
entire world. The first impression was of vastness, then
of light and cheerfulness, and when the vanguard of the
thousands had been seated, expressions of surprise and of 15
admiration were heard on every hand for the beauty and
the grace of the architecture. The new home for worship
that was opened by the Scientists in Boston yesterday 18
can take a place in the front rank of the world's houses
of worship, and it is no wonder that the first sight which
the visitors caught of its interior should have impressed 21
them as one of the events of their lives.

First Reader William D. McCrackan, accompanied by
the Second Reader, Mrs. Laura Carey Conant, and the 24
soloist for the services, Mrs. Hunt, was on the Readers'
platform. Stepping to the front of the platform, when
the congregation had taken their seats, the First Reader 27
announced simply that they would sing Hymn 161,
written by Mrs. Eddy, as the opening of the dedicatory
service. And what singing it was! As though trained 30
carefully under one leader, the great body of Scientists
joined in the song of praise.

1 Spontaneous unanimity and repetition in unison were two of the most striking features of the services. When, 3 after five minutes of silent communion at the end of the service, the congregation began to repeat the Lord's Prayer, they began all together, and their voices rose as 6 one in a heartfelt appeal to the creator.

So good are the acoustic properties of the new structure that Mr. McCrackan and Mrs. Conant could be heard 9 perfectly in every part of it, and they did not have to lift their voices above the usual platform tone.

Following the organ voluntary — Fantasie in E minor, 12 Merkel — the order of service was as follows: —

Hymn 161, from the Hymnal. Words by the Rev. Mary Baker Eddy.[1]
15 Reading from the Scriptures: Deuteronomy 26 : 1, 2, 5–10 (first sentence).

Silent prayer, followed by the audible repetition of the 18 Lord's Prayer with its spiritual interpretation as given in the Christian Science textbook.

Hymn 166, from the Hymnal.[2]
21 Reading of notices.

Reading of Tenets of The Mother Church.

Collection.
24 Solo, "Communion Hymn," words by the Rev. Mary Baker Eddy, music by William Lyman Johnson.

Reading of annual Message from the Pastor Emeritus, 27 the Rev. Mary Baker Eddy.

Reading the specially prepared Lesson-Sermon.

After the reading of the Lesson-Sermon, silent com-30 munion, which concluded with the audible repetition of the Lord's Prayer.

[1] Hymn 306,   [2] Hymn 108, in Revised Hymnal

Singing the Communion Doxology.   1

Reading of a despatch from the members of the church
to Mrs. Eddy.   3

Reading of "the scientific statement of being" (Science and Health, p. 468), and the correlative Scripture,
1 John 3 : 1–3.   6

The benediction.

The subject of the special Lesson-Sermon was "Adam,
Where Art Thou?" the Golden Text: "Search me, O   9
God, and know my heart: try me, and know my
thoughts: and see if there be any wicked way in me,
and lead me in the way everlasting." (Psalms 139 : 23,   12
24.) The responsive reading was from Psalms 15 : 1–5;
24 : 1–6, 9, 10.

  1 Lord, who shall abide in thy tabernacle? who shall   15
dwell in thy holy hill?

  2 He that walketh uprightly, and worketh righteousness, and speaketh the truth in his heart.   18

  3 He that backbiteth not with his tongue, nor doeth
evil to his neighbor, nor taketh up a reproach against his
neighbor.   21

  4 In whose eyes a vile person is contemned; but he
honoreth them that fear the Lord. He that sweareth to
his own hurt, and changeth not.   24

  5 He that putteth not out his money to usury, nor
taketh reward against the innocent. He that doeth these
things shall never be moved.   27

  1 The earth is the Lord's, and the fulness thereof;
the world, and they that dwell therein.

  2 For he hath founded it upon the seas, and established 30
it upon the floods.

1   3 Who shall ascend into the hill of the Lord? or who shall stand in his holy place?

3   4 He that hath clean hands, and a pure heart; who hath not lifted up his soul unto vanity, nor sworn deceitfully.

6   5 He shall receive the blessing from the Lord, and righteousness from the God of his salvation.

6 This is the generation of them that seek him, that 9 seek thy face, O Jacob.

9 Lift up your heads, O ye gates; even lift them up, ye everlasting doors; and the King of glory shall come in.

12   10 Who is this King of glory? The Lord of hosts, he is the King of glory.

The Lesson-Sermon consisted of the following citations 15 from the Bible and "Science and Health with Key to the Scriptures" by the Rev. Mary Baker Eddy, and was read by Mr. McCrackan and Mrs. Conant: —

18   I

The Bible   Science and Health [1]
Genesis 3 : 9–11   224 : 22
21   Proverbs 8 : 1, 4, 7   559 : 8–10, 19
Mark 2 : 15–17   181 : 21–25
                             307 : 31–8

24   II

Psalms 51 : 1–3, 6, 10, 12,   308 : 8, 16–28 *This;*
     13, 17   *Jacob*
27   323 : 19–24, 28–32
                                  When; The effects

    [1] The Science and Health references in this lesson are according 30 to the 1913 edition.

III

1

The Bible	Science and Health	
Hebrews 11 : 1, 3, 6	297 : 20 *Faith*	3
Proverbs 3 : 5, 6	241 : 23–27	
Job 28 : 20, 23, 28	275 : 25	
1 Corinthians 14 : 20	505 : 21–28 *Under-*	6
	standing	
	536 : 8	

IV

9

Psalms 86 : 15, 16	345 : 31	
Matthew 9 : 2–8	337 : 10	
	525 : 4	12
	494 : 30–2 *Our Master*	
	476 : 32–4	
	171 : 4	15

V

Mark 12 : 30, 31	9 : 17–21 *Dost thou*	
John 21 : 1 (first	53 : 8–11	18
clause), 14–17	54 : 29–1	
1 John 4 : 21	560 : 11–19, 22 *The*	
	great; Abuse	21
	565 : 18–22	

VI

John 21 : 4–6, 9, 12, 13	34 : 29–29	24
Revelation 3 : 20		
Revelation 7 : 13, 14, 16, 17		

During the progress of each service, First Reader 27
William D. McCrackan read to the congregation the

1 dedicatory Message from their teacher and Leader, Mrs. Mary Baker Eddy.

3   The telegram from the church to Mrs. Eddy was read by Mr. Edward A. Kimball of Chicago, and the five thousand present rose as one to indicate their approval 6 of it.

REV. MARY BAKER EDDY, *Pastor Emeritus*

Beloved Teacher and Leader: — The members of your 9 church have assembled at this sacred time to commune with our infinite heavenly Father and again to consecrate all that we are or hope to be to a holy Christian service 12 that shall be acceptable unto God.

Most of us are here because we have been delivered from beds of sickness or withheld from open graves or reclaimed 15 from vice or redeemed from obdurate sin. We have exchanged the tears of sorrow for the joy of repentance and the peace of a more righteous living, and now with blessed 18 accord we are come, in humility, to pour out our gratitude to God and to bear witness to the abundance of salvation through His divine Christ.

21   At this altar, dedicated to the only true God, we who have been delivered from the depths increase the measure of our devotion to the daily life and purpose which are in 24 the image and likeness of God.

By these stately walls; by this sheltering dome; by all the beauty of color and design, the Christian Scientists 27 of the world, in tender affection for the cause of human weal, have fulfilled a high resolve and set up this tabernacle, which is to stand as an enduring monument, a sign 30 of your understanding and proof that our Supreme God, through His power and law, is the natural healer

of all our diseases and hath ordained the way of salva- 1
tion of all men from all evil. No vainglorious boast,
no pride of circumstances has place within the sacred 3
confines of this sanctuary. Naught else than the grandeur of humility and the incense of gratitude and compassionate love can acceptably ascend heavenward from 6
this house of God.

It is from the depths of tenderest gratitude, respect,
and affection that we declare again our high appreciation 9
of all that you have done and continue to do for the everlasting advantage of this race. Through you has been
revealed the verity and rule of the Christianity of Christ 12
which has ever healed the sick. By your fidelity and the
constancy of your obedience during forty years you have
demonstrated this Science before the gaze of universal 15
humanity. By reason of your spiritual achievement the
Cause of Christian Science has been organized and maintained, its followers have been prospered, and the philos- 18
ophy of the ages transformed. Recognizing the grand
truth that God is the supreme cause of all the activities of
legitimate existence, we also recognize that He has made 21
known through your spiritual perception the substance
of Christian Science, and that this church owes itself and
its prosperity to the unbroken activity of your labors, 24
which have been and will still be the pretext for our
confident and favorable expectation.

We have read your annual Message to this church. 27
We are deeply touched by its sweet entreaty, its ineffable
loving-kindness, its wise counsel and admonition.

With sacred resolution do we pray that we may give 30
heed and ponder and obey. We would be glad if our
prayers, our rejoicing, and our love could recompense your

1 long sacrifice and bestow upon you the balm of heavenly
joy, but knowing that every perfect gift cometh from
3 above, and that in God is all consolation and comfort,
we rest in this satisfying assurance, while we thank you
and renew the story of our love for you and for all that
6 you are and all that you have done for us.

WILLIAM B. JOHNSON, *Clerk*

By means of a carefully trained corps of ushers, num-
9 bering two hundred, there was no confusion in finding
seats, and when all seating space had been filled no more
were admitted until the next service. The church was
12 filled for each service in about twenty minutes, and was
emptied in twelve, in spite of the fact that many of
the visitors showed a tendency to tarry to examine the
15 church.

It was "children's day" at noon, for the service at half
past twelve was specially reserved for them. They filled
18 all the seats in the body of the church, and when it came
to the singing, the little ones were not a whit behind their
elders, their shrill trebles rising with the roll of the organ
21 in almost perfect time. In every respect their service was
the same as all the others.

There was no more impressive feature of the dedication
24 than the silent communion. Devout Scientists said after
the service that they would ever carry with them the
memory of it.

27   THE ANNUAL MEETING, JUNE 12, 1906

The annual meeting of The First Church of Christ,
Scientist, in Boston, was held in the extension of The
30 Mother Church, Tuesday, June 12, at ten o'clock in the

forenoon, and in order to accommodate those who could 1
not gain admittance at that hour a second session was held
at two o'clock in the afternoon. The meeting was opened 3
by the President, Rev. William P. McKenzie, who read
from the Bible and Science and Health as follows: —

The Bible	Science and Health	
Isaiah 54 : 1–5, 10–15,	571 : 22	6
17	574 : 3–16, 27 *The Revela-*	
Revelation 19 : 1, 6–9	*tor; The very*	9
	577 : 4	

Then followed a short silent prayer and the audible
repetition of the Lord's Prayer, in which all joined. The 12
following list of officers for the ensuing year was read by
the Clerk: —

President, Willis F. Gross, C.S.B.; Treasurer, Stephen 15
A. Chase, C.S.D.; Clerk, William B. Johnson, C.S.D.

In introducing the new President, Mr. McKenzie said: —

When I introduce the incoming President, my modest 18
task will be ended. You will allow me, however, the
privilege of saying a few words of reminder and prophecy.
My thoughts revert to a former occasion, when it was my 21
pleasant duty to preside at an annual meeting when our
Pastor Emeritus, Mrs. Eddy, was present. We remember
her graciousness and dignity. We recall the harmonious 24
tones of her gentle voice. Our hearts were thrilled by her
compassion, and the memory lives with us. But even more
distinctly may we realize her presence with us to-day. 27
Why? Because our own growth in love and unity enables
us to comprehend better the strength and beauty of her
character. 30

1 Moreover, this completed extension of The Mother Church is an evidence to us of her hospitable love. She
3 has desired for years to have her church able to give more adequate reception to those who hunger and thirst after practical righteousness; and we are sure that now
6 the branch churches of The Mother Church will also enlarge their hospitality, so that these seekers everywhere may be satisfied. This will imply the subsidence of criti-
9 cism among workers. It may even imply that some who have been peacebreakers shall willingly enter into the blessedness of peacemakers. Nothing will be lost, how-
12 ever, by those who relinquish their cherished resentments, forsake animosity, and abandon their strongholds of rivalry. Through rivalries among leaders Christendom
15 became divided into warring sects; but the demand of this age is for peacemaking, so that Christianity may more widely reassert its pristine power to bring
18 health and a cure to pain-racked and sorrow-worn humanity. "The wisdom that is from above is first pure, then peaceable, . . . And the fruit of righteous-
21 ness is sown in peace of them that make peace." "Blessed are the peacemakers: for they shall be called the children of God."
24 Our Leader, Mrs. Eddy, has presented to the world the ideal of Christianity, because she is an exact metaphysician. She has illustrated what the poet perceived when he
27 said, "All's love, but all's law." She has obeyed the divine Principle, Love, without regrets and without resistance. Human sense often rebels against law, hence the proverb:
30 *Dura lex, sed lex* (Hard is the law, nevertheless it is the law). But by her own blameless and happy life, as well as by her teachings, our Leader has induced a

multitude — how great no man can number — to be- 1
come gladly obedient to law, so that they think rightly
or righteously. 3

No one can change the law of Christian metaphysics,
the law of right thinking, nor in any wise alter its
effects. It is a forever fact that the meek and lowly in 6
heart are blessed and comforted by divine Love. If the
proud are lonely and uncomforted, it is because they
have thoughts adverse to the law of love. Pride, arro- 9
gance, and self-will are unmerciful, and so receive judgment without mercy; but the law of metaphysics says,
"Blessed are the merciful," and will allow no one to 12
escape that blessedness, howsoever far he may stray,
whatsoever lawlessness of hatred he may practise and
suffer from. 15

So we see that Christian Science makes no compromise
with evil, sin, wrong, or imperfection, but maintains the
perfect standard of truth and righteousness and joy. It 18
teaches us to rise from sentimental affection which ad-
mires friends and hates enemies, into brotherly love which
is just and kind to all and unable to cherish any enmity. 21
It brings into present and hourly application what Paul
termed "the law of the Spirit of life in Christ Jesus," and
shows man that his real estate is one of blessedness. Why 24
should any one postpone his legitimate joy, and disregard
his lawful inheritance, which is "incorruptible and undefiled"? Our Leader and teacher not only discovered 27
Christian Science, but through long years of consecration
has obeyed its every demand, for our sakes as well as
for her own; and we begin to understand how illim- 30
itable is the Love which supports such selfless devotion,
we begin to comprehend the "beauty of holiness," and

1 to be truly grateful to her who has depicted its form
and comeliness. We have found it true that "she
3 openeth her mouth with wisdom; and in her tongue is
the law of kindness."

It is my pleasure to introduce to you a faithful follower
6 of this Leader as the President for the coming year, Willis
F. Gross, C.S.B., one who has for many years "witnessed
a good confession" in the practice of Christian Science.
9 You are no doubt already acquainted with him as one of
the helpful contributors to our periodicals, so that any
further words of mine are unnecessary.

12 Mr. Gross, on assuming office, said: —

Beloved Friends: — Most unexpectedly to me came the
call to serve you in this capacity, and I desire to improve
15 this opportunity to express my thanks for the honor conferred upon me. With a heart filled with gratitude for the
countless blessings which have come into my life through
15 Christian Science, I shall endeavor to perform this service
to the best of my ability.

It affords me great pleasure to welcome you to our first
21 annual meeting held in the extension of The Mother
Church. I shall not attempt to speak of the deep significance of this momentous occasion. I realize that only as
24 infinite good unfolds in each individual consciousness can
we begin to comprehend, even in small degree, how great
is the work that has been inaugurated by our beloved
27 Leader, how faithful is her allegiance to God, how untiring
are her efforts, and how successful she is in the performance
of her daily tasks.

30 "With a mighty hand, and with an outstretched arm"
were the children of Israel delivered from the bondage of

the Egyptians, but this deliverance did not put them in 1
possession of the promised land. An unknown wilderness was before them, and that wilderness must be con- 3
quered. The law was given that they might know what
was required of them, that they might have a definite rule
of action whereby to order aright the affairs of daily life. 6
Obedience to the demands of the law revealed the God
of their fathers, and they learned to know Him. During
their sojourn in the wilderness they suffered defeats and 9
met with disappointments, but they learned from experience and finally became willingly obedient to the voice of
their leader. The crossing of the Jordan brought them 12
into the promised land, and this experience was almost
as marvellous as had been the passage of the Red Sea
forty years before. In obedience to the command of 15
Joshua, twelve stones taken from the midst of the river
were set up on the other side for a memorial. In future
generations when it was asked, "What mean ye by these 18
stones?" it was told them: Israel came over this Jordan
on dry ground.

Forty years ago the Science of Christian healing was 21
revealed to our beloved Leader, the Rev. Mary Baker
Eddy. A few years later she gave us our textbook,
"Science and Health with Key to the Scriptures." Obedi- 24
ence to the teachings of this book has brought us to this
hour. We have learned from experience, and to-day we
rejoice that we have found in Christian Science that 27
which heals and saves.

The world looks with wonder upon this grand achievement,— the completion and dedication of our magnificent 30
temple, — and many are asking, "What mean ye by these
stones?" The answer is, The way out of the wilderness

1 of human beliefs has been revealed. Through the understanding of God as an ever-present help, the sick are being
3 healed, the shackles of sin are being broken, heavy burdens
are being laid down, tears are being wiped away, and
Israel is going up to possess the promised land of eternal,
6 harmonious existence.

Friends, our progress may be fast or it may be slow,
but one thing is certain, it will be sure, if we are obe-
9 dient to the loving counsel of our ever faithful Leader.
The Christ is here, has come to individual consciousness; and the faithful disciple rejoices in prophecy ful-
12 filled, "Lo, I am with you alway, even unto the end of
the world."

Telegram to Mrs. Eddy

15 Judge Septimus J. Hanna then advanced to the
front of the platform, read the following despatch, and
moved that it be forwarded at once to our Leader,
18 Mrs. Eddy. The motion was carried unanimously by a
rising vote.

The despatch was as follows: —

21 To the Rev. Mary Baker Eddy,
      Pleasant View, Concord, N. H.

Beloved Teacher and Leader: — The members of The
24 Mother Church, The First Church of Christ, Scientist,
in Boston, Mass., in annual meeting assembled, hereby
convey to you their sincere greetings and their deep
27 love.

They desire to express their continued loyalty to your
teachings, their unshaken confidence in the unerring wis-
30 dom of your leadership, and their confident assurance

that strict and intelligent recognition of and obedience to 1
the comprehensive means by you provided for the furtherance of our Cause, will result in its perpetuity as well 3
as in the ultimate regeneration of its adherents and of
mankind.

We are witnessing with joy and gratitude the significant 6
events associated with this, one of the greatest and most
important gatherings of Christian Scientists in the annals
of our history. Yet the upwards of thirty thousand who 9
are physically present at the dedication represent only a
small part of the entire body who are of us and with us
in the animus and spirit of our movement. 12

The great temple is finished! That which you have long
prophetically seen has been accomplished. The magnificent edifice stands a fitting monument of your obedience 15
and fidelity to the divine Principle revealed to you in that
momentous hour when purblind mortal sense declared you
to be *in extremis.* You followed unswervingly the guid- 18
ance of Him who went before you by day in a pillar of
cloud to lead you in the way, and by night in a pillar
of fire to give you light, and the results of such following 21
have been marvellous beyond human ken. As clearly
as in retrospect we see the earlier leading, we now discern
the fulfilment of the later prophecy, that "He took not 24
away the pillar of cloud by day, nor the pillar of fire by
night," for each advancing step has logically followed
the preceding one. 27

The great temple is finished! This massive pile of New
Hampshire granite and Bedford stone, rising to a height
of two hundred and twenty-four feet, one foot loftier than 30
the Bunker Hill monument, stands a material type of
Truth's permanence. In solid foundation, in symmetrical

arches, in generous hallways, in commodious foyer and broad stairways, in exquisite and expansive auditorium, and in towering, overshadowing dome, the great structure stands, silently but eloquently beckoning us on towards a higher and more spiritual plane of living, for we know that without this spiritual significance it were but a passing dream.

In the best sense it stands in prophetic verity of the primary declaration of this church in its original organization; namely, "To organize a church designed to commemorate the word and works of our Master, which should reinstate primitive Christianity and its lost element of healing." (Church Manual, p. 17.) To rise to the demands of this early pronouncement is the work of true Christian Scientists.

To preach the gospel and heal the sick on the Christ-basis is the essential requirement of a reinstated Christianity. Only as we pledge ourselves anew to this demand, and then fulfil the pledge in righteous living, are we faithful, obedient, deserving disciples.

On this solemn occasion, and in the presence of this assembled host, we do hereby pledge ourselves to a deeper consecration, a more sincere and Christly love of God and our brother, and a more implicit obedience to the sacred teachings of the Bible and our textbook, as well as to the all-inclusive instructions and admonitions of our Church Manual in its spiritual import, that we may indeed reach "unto the city of the living God, the heavenly Jerusalem, and to an innumerable company of angels, to the general assembly and church of the firstborn."

WILLIAM B. JOHNSON, *Clerk*

BOSTON, MASS., June 12, 1906

Report of the Clerk   1

Beloved Brethren of The First Church of Christ, Scientist, in Boston, Mass.: — It seems meet at this time, when 3 thousands of Christian Scientists have gathered here from all parts of the world, many of whom have not had the means of knowing the steps by which this church has 6 reached its present growth, to present in this report a few of the stages of its progress, as gleaned from the pages of its history.   9

After a work has been established, has grown to great magnitude, and people the world over have been touched by its influence for good, it is with joy that those who have 12 labored unceasingly for the work look back to the picturesque, interesting, and epoch-marking stages of its growth, and recall memories of trials, progress, and victories that 15 are precious each and all. To-day we look back over the years that have passed since the inception of this great Cause, and we cannot help being touched by each land- 18 mark of progress that showed a forward effort into the well-earned joy that is with us now. For a Cause that has rooted itself in so many distant lands, and inspired so 21 many of different races and tongues into the demonstration of the knowledge of God, the years that have passed since Mrs. Eddy founded her first church seem but a short 24 time. And this little church, God's word in the wilderness of dogma and creed, opened an era of Christian worship founded on the commands of Jesus: "Go ye 27 into all the world, and preach the gospel to every creature. . . . And these signs shall follow them that believe; In my name shall they cast out devils; they 30 shall speak with new tongues; they shall take up ser-

1 pents; and if they drink any deadly thing, it shall not hurt them; they shall lay hands on the sick, and they
3 shall recover."

Not until nineteen centuries had passed was there one ready to receive the inspiration, to restore to human con-
6 sciousness the stone that had been rejected, and which Mrs. Eddy made "the head of the corner" of The Church of Christ, Scientist.

9 With the reading of her textbook, "Science and Health with Key to the Scriptures," Mrs. Eddy insisted that her students make, every day, a prayerful study of
12 the Bible, and obtain the spiritual understanding of its promises. Upon this she founded the future growth of her church, and twenty-six years later the following
15 splendid appreciation of her efforts appeared in the *Methodist Review* from the pen of the late Frederick Lawrence Knowles: —

18 "Mrs. Eddy . . . in her insistence upon the constant daily reading of the Bible and her own writings, . . . has given to her disciples a means of spiritual development
21 which . . . will certainly build such truth as they do gain into the marrow of their characters. The scorn of the gross and sensual, and the subordination of merely material
24 to spiritual values, together with the discouragement of care and worry, are all forces that make for righteousness. And they are burned indelibly upon the mind of the
27 neophyte every day through its reading. The intellects of these people are not drugged by scandal, drowned in frivolity, or paralyzed by sentimental fiction. . . . They
30 feed the higher nature through the mind, and I am bound as an observer of them to say, in all fairness, that the result is already manifest in their faces, their conversation,

and their bearing, both in public and private. What
wonder that when these smiling people say, 'Come thou
with us, and we will do thee good,' the hitherto half-
persuaded one is wholly drawn over, as by an irresistible
attraction. The religious body which can direct, and control, in no arbitrary sense, but through sane counsel, the
reading of its membership, stands a great chance of sweep-
ing the world within a generation."

The charter of this little church was obtained August
23, 1879, and in the same month the members extended a
unanimous invitation to Mrs. Eddy to become its pastor.
At a meeting of those who were interested in forming the
church, Mrs. Eddy was appointed on the committee to
formulate the rules and by-laws, also the tenets and church
covenant. The first business meeting of the church was
held August 16, 1879, in Charlestown, Mass., for the purpose of electing officers. August 22 the Clerk, by instructions received at the previous meeting, sent an invitation
to Mrs. Eddy to become pastor of the church. August 27
the church held a meeting, with Mrs. Eddy in the chair.
An interesting record of this meeting reads: "The minutes
of the previous meeting were read and approved. Then
Mrs. Eddy proceeded to instruct those present as to their
duties in the Church of Christ, giving some useful hints as
to the mode of conducting the church."

At a meeting held October 19, 1879, it was unanimously
voted that "Dr. and Mrs. Eddy merited the thanks of the
society for their devoted labors in the cause of Truth,"
and at the annual meeting, December 1 of the same year,
it was voted to instruct the Clerk to call Mrs. Eddy
to the pastorate of the church, and at this meeting Mrs.
Eddy accepted the call. The first meeting of this little

1 church for deliberation before a Communion Sabbath
was held at the home of the pastor, Mrs. Eddy, Jan-
3 uary 2, 1880.

Most of those present had left their former church
homes, in which they had labored faithfully and ardently,
6 and had united themselves into a little band of prayerful
workers. As the Pilgrims felt the strangeness of their
new home, the vast gloom of the mysterious forests, and
9 knew not the trials before them, so this little band of
pioneers, guided by their dauntless Leader and teacher,
starting out on their labors against the currents of dogma,
12 creed, sickness, and sin, must have felt a peculiar sense of
isolation, for their records state, "The tone of this meeting
for deliberation before Communion Sabbath was rather
15 sorrowful;" but as they turned steadfastly from the mortal side, and looked towards the spiritual, as the records
further relate, "yet there was a feeling of trust in the
18 great Father, of Love prevailing over the apparently dis-
couraging outlook of the Church of Christ." The Communion Sunday, however, brought fresh courage to the
21 earnest band, and the records contain these simple but
suggestive words, — "Sunday, January 4, 1880. The
church celebrated her Communion Sabbath as a church,
24 and it was a very inspiring season to us all, and two new
members were added to the church." This was indeed
the little church in the wilderness, and few knew of its
27 teachings, but those few saw the grandeur of its work
and were willing to labor for the Cause.

The record of May 23, 1880, more than twenty-six years
30 ago, states: "Our pastor, Mrs. Eddy, preached her fare-
well sermon to the church. The business committee met
after the services to call a general meeting of the church

to devise means to pay our pastor, so as to keep her with 1
us, as there is no one in the world who could take her place
in teaching us the Science of Life." May 26 of the same 3
year the following resolutions were passed: "That the
members of the Church of Christ, and all others now interested in said church, do most sincerely regret that our 6
pastor, Mrs. Eddy, feels it her duty to tender her resigna-
tion, and while we feel that she has not met with the
support that she should have reason to expect, we venture 9
to hope she will remain with us. That it would be a
serious blow to her Cause to have the public services
discontinued at a time when there is such an interest 12
manifested on the part of the people, and we know of no
one who is so able as she to lead us to the higher understanding of Christianity, whereby to heal the sick and 15
reform the sinner. It was moved to instruct the Clerk to
have our pastor remain with us for a few Sundays if not
permanently." 18

At a meeting of the church, December 15, 1880, an invitation was extended to Mrs. Eddy to accept the pastorate
for the ensuing year; but, as the records state, "she gave 21
no definite answer, believing that it was for the interest
of the Cause, and her duty, to go into new fields to
teach and preach." 24

An interesting record relative to this very early work of
the church, and its appreciation of Mrs. Eddy's tireless
labors, is that of July 20, 1881, which reads, "That we, 27
the members of The Church of Christ, Scientist, tender to
our beloved pastor, Mrs. Eddy, the heartfelt thanks and
gratitude shared by all who have attended the services, in 30
appreciation of her earnest endeavors, her arduous labors,
and successful instructions to heal the sick, and reform

1 the sinner, by metaphysical truth or Christian Science, during the past year. Resolved: That while she had many
3 obstacles to overcome, many mental hardships to endure,
she has borne them bravely, blessing them that curse her,
loving them that despitefully use her, thereby giving in
6 her Christian example, as well as her instructions, the
highest type of womanhood, or the love that heals. And
while we sincerely acknowledge our indebtedness to her,
9 and to God, for these blessings, we, each and all, will make
greater efforts more faithfully to sustain her in her work.
Resolved: That while we realize the rapid growth, and
12 welcome the fact of the spreading world wide of this great
truth, that Mind, Truth, Life, and Love, as taught and
expressed by our pastor, does heal the sick, and, when
15 understood, does bring out the perfection of all things, we
also realize we must use more energy and unselfish labor
to establish these our Master's commands and our pastor's
18 teachings, namely, heal the sick, and preach the gospel,
and love our neighbor as ourselves."

Eighteen years ago, the Rev. James Henry Wiggin, who
21 was not a Christian Scientist, wrote as follows: "Whatever is to be Mrs. Eddy's future reputation, time will
show. Little cares she, if only through her work Truth
24 may be glorified. More than once, in her earnestness, she
has reached her bottom dollar, but the interest of the
world to hear her word has always filled her coffers anew.
27 Within a few months she has made sacrifices from which
most authors would have shrunk, to insure the moral
rightness of her book." This statement "Phare Pleigh"
30 [the *nom de plume* of the Rev. James Henry Wiggin]
makes out of his own peculiar knowledge of the circumstances. "Day after day flew by, and weeks lengthened

into months; from every quarter came important mis- 1
sives of inquiry and mercantile reproach; hundreds of
dollars were sunk into a bottomless sea of corrections; 3
yet not until the authoress was satisfied that her duty
was wholly done, would she allow printer and binder to
send forth her book to the world." This book has now 6
reached its four hundredth edition, each of one thousand
copies.

On September 8, 1882, it was voted that the church 9
hold its meetings of worship in the parlors of Mrs. Eddy's
home, 569 Columbus Avenue, Boston. The services were
held there until November, 1883, and then in the Haw- 12
thorne Rooms, at No. 3 Park Street, the seating capacity
of which place was about two hundred and twenty-
five. At a meeting October 22, 1883, the church voted 15
to wait upon Mrs. Eddy, to ascertain if she would
preach for the society for ten dollars a Sunday, which
invitation she accepted. After establishing itself as a 18
church in the Hawthorne Rooms, the number of attendants steadily increased. The pulpit was supplied by
Mrs. Eddy, when she could give the time to preach, 21
and by her students and by clergymen of different
denominations, among whom was the Rev. A. J. Pea-
body, D.D., of Cambridge, Mass. 24

The annual report of the business committee of the
church, for the year ending December 7, 1885, contains
some very interesting statements, among which is this: 27
"There was a steadily increasing interest in Christian
Science among the people, even though the continuity
of thought must have been very much broken by having 30
so many different ones address them on the subject.
When our pastor preached for us it was found that the

1 Hawthorne Rooms were inadequate for the occasion, hundreds going away who could not obtain entrance;
3 those present enduring the inconvenience that comes from crowding, for the sake of the eternal truth she taught them." The *Boston Traveler* contained the fol-
6 lowing item: "The Church of Christ, Scientist, had their meeting Easter Sunday at Hawthorne Rooms, which were crowded one hour before the service commenced,
9 and half an hour before the arrival of the pastor, the Rev. Mary Baker Eddy, the tide of men and women was turned from the door with the information, 'No
12 more standing-room.'"

On February 8, 1885, communion was held at Odd Fellows Hall, and there were present about eight hundred
15 people. At this time the Hawthorne Rooms, which had been regarded as the church home, were outgrown. During the summer vacation, different places were considered,
18 but no place suitable could be found that was available, and the Sunday services were postponed. There was an expectation that some place would be obtained, but the
21 desire for services was so great that the Hawthorne Rooms were again secured. A record of this period reads, "It should be here stated that from the first of September to
24 our opening, crowds had besieged the doors at the Hawthorne Rooms, Sunday after Sunday." On October 18, 1885, the rooms were opened and a large congregation
27 was present. It was then concluded to engage Chickering Hall on Tremont Street. In the previous consideration of places for meeting it had been decided that this hall
30 was too large, as it seated four hundred and sixty-four. The first Sunday service held in Chickering Hall was on October 25, 1885. Mrs. Eddy preached at this service

and the hall was crowded. This date is memorable as 1
the one upon which the Sunday School was formed.

Meanwhile it was felt that the church needed a place of 3
its own, and efforts were made to obtain by purchase some
building, or church, in a suitable location. Several places
were considered, but were not satisfactory; yet the 6
thought of obtaining a church edifice, although given up
for a time, was not forgotten. In the mean time, not
only was the attendance rapidly growing in this church in 9
Chickering Hall, but the Cause itself was spreading over
the land. September 1, 1892, Mrs. Eddy gave the plot of
ground on which The Mother Church now stands. On 12
the twenty-third day of September, 1892, twelve of the
members of the church met, and, upon Mrs. Eddy's
counsel, reorganized the church, and named it The First 15
Church of Christ, Scientist. This effort of Mrs. Eddy
was an inspiration to Christian Scientists, and plans were
made for a church home. 18

In the mean time Sunday services were held in Chickering Hall, and continued there until March, 1894, and
during the last year the hall was crowded to overflowing. 21
In March, however, the church was obliged to seek other
quarters, as Chickering Hall was to be remodelled. At this
time the church removed to Copley Hall on Clarendon 24
Street, which had a seating capacity of six hundred and
twenty-five, and in that place Sunday services were held
until The Mother Church edifice was ready for occupancy, 27
December 30, 1894. During the months that the congregation worshipped in Copley Hall there was a steady
increase in attendance. 30

Twelve years ago the twenty-first of last month, the
corner-stone of The Mother Church edifice was laid, and

1 at that time it was thought the seating capacity would be adequate for years to come. Attendance at the Sunday
3 service gradually increased, until every seat was filled and many stood in the aisles, and in consequence two services were held, morning and afternoon, the latter a repetition
6 of the morning service. The date of the inauguration of two Sunday services was April 26, 1896. It was soon evident that even this provision was inadequate to meet
9 the need, and it was found necessary to organize branch churches in such suburbs of Boston as would relieve the overcrowded condition of The Mother Church; there-
12 fore three branch churches were organized, one in each of the following named places: Cambridge, Chelsea, and Roxbury.
15   For a while it seemed that there would be ample room for growth of attendance in The Mother Church, but not-withstanding the relief that the organization of branch
18 churches had given, the number of attendants increased faster than ever. From the time that the three foregoing named churches were established, the membership and the
21 attendance at them and at The Mother Church steadily grew, and more branch churches were established in other suburbs, members of which had formerly been attendants
24 at The Mother Church. In the spring of 1905 the over-crowded condition of the morning service showed that still further provision must be made, as many were obliged
27 to leave the church for the reason that there was not even standing-room. Therefore, beginning October 1, 1905, three services were held each Sunday, the second and
30 third being repetitions of the first service.

This continued growth, this continued overcrowding, proved the need of a larger edifice. Our communion ser-

vices and annual meetings were overcrowded in The 1
Mother Church, they were overcrowded in Tremont
Temple, in Symphony Hall, and in the Mechanics Build- 3
ing, and the need was felt of an auditorium that would
be of great seating capacity, and one that would have the
sacred atmosphere of a church home.   6

In Mrs. Eddy's Message to the church in 1902 she suggested the need of a larger church edifice, and at the
annual meeting of the same year the church voted to 9
raise any part of two millions of dollars for the purpose of
building a suitable edifice. The labor of clearing the land
was begun in October, 1903, and the corner-stone was 12
laid July 16, 1904.

The first annual meeting of the church was held in
Chickering Hall, October 3, 1893, and the membership 15
at that date was 1,545. The membership of this
church to-day is 40,011. The number of candidates
admitted June 5 of this year is the largest in the his- 18
tory of the church and numbers 4,889, which is 2,194
more than the hitherto largest admission, that of June,
1903. The total number admitted during the last 21
year is 6,181. The total number of branch churches
advertised in *The Christian Science Journal* of this
June is 682, 614 of which show a membership of 24
41,944. The number of societies advertised in the
Journal is 267.

Shortly before the dedication of The Mother Church in 27
1895, the *Boston Evening Transcript* said: "Wonders will
never cease. Here is a church whose Treasurer has sent
out word that no sums except those already subscribed 30
can be received. The Christian Scientists have a faith
of the mustard-seed variety. What a pity some of our

1 practical Christian folk have not a faith approximate to
that of these impractical Christian Scientists."

3   The fact that a notice was published in the *Christian
Science Sentinel* of last Saturday that no more funds
are needed to complete the extension of The Mother
6 Church, proves the truth of the axiom, "History repeats itself." These are the evidences of the magnificent growth of this Cause, and are sufficient refutation
9 of the statements that have been made that "Christian
Science is dying out."

The majesty and the dignity of this church edifice not
12 only shows the growth of this Cause, but proclaims the
trust, the willingness of those who have contributed to
the erection of these mighty walls.

15   This magnificent structure, this fitting testimonial in
stone, speaks more than words can picture of the love and
gratitude of a great multitude that has been healed and
18 purified through the labor and sacrifice of our revered
Leader and teacher, Mary Baker Eddy, the one through
whom God has revealed a demonstrable way of salvation.
21 May her example inspire us to follow her in preaching,
"The kingdom of heaven is at hand," by healing the
sick and reforming the sinful, and, as she has done, ver-
24 ifying Jesus' words, "Lo, I am with you alway."

LETTERS AND EDITORIAL

Mrs. Mary Baker Eddy,
27   Pleasant View, Concord, N. H.

My Dear Teacher: — Of the many thousands who
attended the dedicatory services at the Christian Science
30 church last Sunday it is doubtful if there was one so deeply

impressed with the grandeur and magnitude of your work 1
as was the writer, whom you will recall as a member of
your *first* class in Lynn, Mass., nearly forty years ago. 3
When you told us that the truth you expounded was
the little leaven that should leaven the whole lump, we
thought this might be true in some far distant day 6
beyond our mortal vision. It was above conception
that in less than forty years a new system of faith and
worship, as well as of healing, should number its adher- 9
ents by the hundreds of thousands and its tenets be
accepted wholly or in part by nearly every religious and
scientific body in the civilized world. 12

Seated in the gallery of that magnificent temple, which
has been reared by you, gazing across that sea of heads,
listening again to your words explaining the Scriptures, 15
my mind was carried back to that first public meeting in
the little hall on Market Street, Lynn, where you preached
to a handful of people that would scarce fill a couple of 18
pews in this grand amphitheatre; and as I heard the sono-
rous tones of the powerful organ and the mighty chorus of
five thousand voices, I thought of the little melodeon on 21
which my wife played, and of my own feeble attempts
to lead the singing.

In years gone by I have been asked, "Did Mrs. Eddy 24
really write Science and Health? Some say she did not."
My answer has invariably been, "Send those who say
she did not to me. I heard her talk it before it was 27
ever written. I read it in manuscript before it was ever
printed." Now my testimony is not needed. No human
being in this generation has accomplished such a work or 30
been so thoroughly endorsed or so completely vindicated.
It is marvellous beyond all imagining to one who knew of

1 your early struggles. I have been solicited by many of
your followers to say something about the early history
3 of Christian Science. I have replied that if Mrs. Eddy
thought it wise to instruct them on the subject she would
doubtless do so.

6   Possibly you may remember the words of my uncle, the
good old deacon of the First Congregational Church of
Lynn, when told that I had studied with you. "My boy,
9 you will be ruined for life; it is the work of the devil."
He only expressed the thought of all the Christian (?)
people at that time. What a change in the Christian
12 world! "The stone which the builders rejected" has
become the corner-stone of this wonderful temple of
"wisdom, Truth, and Love." (Science and Health, p.
15 495.) I have yet the little Bible which you gave me
as a reward for the best paper on the spiritual significance of the first chapter of Genesis. It has this
18 inscription on the fly-leaf in your handwriting, "With
all thy getting get understanding."

Respectfully and faithfully yours,
21   S. P. BANCROFT

CAMBRIDGE, MASS., June 12, 1906

MRS. MARY BAKER EDDY,
24   Pleasant View, Concord, N. H.

Dear Leader and Guide: — Now that the great event,
the dedication of our new church building, is over, may
27 I ask a little of your time to tell you of the interesting
part I had to perform in this wonderful consummation.
On the twenty-fifth of last March I was asked by one
30 of the Directors if I would care to do a little watching

at the church. I gladly answered in the affirmative, and 1
have been in the building part of every night since that
time. To watch the transformation has been very in- 3
teresting indeed, and the lessons I have learned of the
power of divine Mind to remove human obstructions
have been very precious. At first I thought that, since 6
it seemed impossible for the building to be completed
before the end of summer, the communion would likely
be postponed until that time. Then came the announce- 9
ment that the services would be held in the new extension on June 10. I saw at once that somebody had to
wake up. I fought hard with the evidence of mortal 12
sense for a time; but after a while, in the night, as
I was climbing over stones and planks and plaster,
I raised my eyes, and the conviction that the work 15
would be accomplished came to me so clearly, I said
aloud, "Why, there is no fear; this house will be ready
for the service, June 10." I bowed my head before 18
the might of divine Love, and never more did I have
any doubt.

One feature about the work interested me. I noticed 21
that as soon as the workmen began to admit that the work
could be done, everything seemed to move as by magic;
the human mind was giving its consent. This taught me 24
that I should be willing to let God work. I have often
stood under the great dome, in the dark stillness of the
night, and thought, "What cannot God do?" (Science 27
and Health, p. 135.)

As I discovered the many intricate problems which must
necessarily present themselves in such an immense under- 30
taking, I appreciated as never before the faithful, earnest
work of our noble Board of Directors. With unflinching

1 faith and unfailing fidelity they have stood at the breast-
works in the battle, and won the reward, "Well done,
3 good and faithful servant; . . . enter thou into the joy
of thy lord."

But what of this magnificent structure? Whence did it
6 come? To me it is the result of the love that trembled
in one human heart when it whispered: "Dear God, may
I not take this precious truth and give it to my brothers
9 and sisters?" How can we ever thank God enough for
such an one, — ever thank you enough for your unselfed
love. May the glory which crowns the completion of this
12 structure shed its brightest beams on your pathway, and
fill your heart with the joy of Love's victory.

Your sincere follower,

15 JAMES J. ROME

BOSTON, MASS., June 30, 1906

REV. MARY BAKER EDDY,
18   Pleasant View, Concord, N. H.

Beloved Leader and Teacher: — We, the Directors of
your church, send you loving greetings and congratulations
21 upon the completion of the magnificent extension of The
Mother Church of Christ, Scientist, and we again express
our thankful appreciation of your wise counsel, timely
24 instruction, and words of encouragement when they were
so much needed.

We acknowledge with many thanks the valuable services
27 rendered to this Board by the members of the business
committee, who were ever ready to assist us in every way
possible; also the services of other members of the church,
30 who gave freely of their time and efforts when there was
urgent need of both.

We do not forget that it was through you we were en- 1
abled to secure the services of Mr. Whitcomb as builder
in the early days of the construction of the church, and of 3
Mr. Beman in an advisory capacity in the later days; for
this, and for their valuable services, we are grateful.

Lovingly and gratefully your students, 6

THE CHRISTIAN SCIENCE BOARD OF DIRECTORS,

By WILLIAM B. JOHNSON, *Secretary*

BOSTON, MASS., July 10, 1906 9

[Editorial in *Christian Science Sentinel*, June 23, 1906]

Our annual communion and the dedication of the extension of The Mother Church are over, and this happy and 12
holy experience has become a part of our expanding consciousness of Truth, to abide with us and enable us better
to work out the purposes of divine Love. It was scarcely 15
possible to repress a feeling of exultation as friend met
friend at every turn with words of rejoicing; and even the
greetings and congratulations of those not of our faith 18
seemed to say that all the world was in some degree sharing
in our joy. But within our sacred edifice there came a
deeper feeling, a feeling of awe and of reverence beyond 21
words, — a new sense of the magnitude of Christian
Science, this revelation of divinity which has come to the
present age. Grandly does our temple symbolize this 24
revelation, in its purity, stateliness, and vastness; but
even more impressive than this was the presence of the
thousands who had come, as the Master predicted, "from 27
the east, and from the west, and from the north, and
from the south," to tell by their presence that they had
been healed by Christ, Truth, and had found the kingdom 30
of God.

1   As one thought upon the significance of the occasion, the achievements of our beloved Leader and her relation
3 to the experiences of the hour took on a larger and truer meaning. The glories of the realm of infinite Mind, revealed to us through her spiritual attainments and her
6 years of toil, encompassed us, and hearts were thrilled with tender gratitude and love for all that she has done. If to-day we feel a pardonable pride in being known as
9 Christian Scientists, it is because our Leader has made the name an honored one before the world.

In her dedicatory Message to The Mother Church,
12 Mrs. Eddy says, "The First Commandment of the Hebrew Decalogue, 'Thou shalt have no other gods before me,' and the Golden Rule are the all-in-all of Christian Science."
15 In all her writings, through all the years of her leadership, she has been teaching her followers both by precept and example how to obey this commandment and rule, and
18 her success in so doing is what constitutes the high standing of Christian Science before the world. Fearlessly does she warn all her followers against the indulgence of the
21 sins which would prevent the realization of ideal manhood — the reign of the Christ — and now it is ours to address ourselves with renewed faith and love to the high and holy
24 task of overcoming all that is unlike God, and thus prove our worthiness to be "living stones" in the universal temple of Spirit, and worthy members of The Mother
27 Church before men.

APPENDIX TO PART I

As Chronicled
by the Newspapers

[*Boston Journal*, June 19, 1902] 1

AN ASTONISHING MOTION

Assembled in the largest church business meeting ever 3
held in Boston — perhaps the largest ever held in the
United States — the members of The First Church of
Christ, Scientist, Boston, The Mother Church of the de- 6
nomination, voted yesterday afternoon to raise any part
of two million dollars that might be needed to build
in this city a church edifice capable of seating between 9
four and five thousand persons. This astonishing motion
was passed with both unanimity and assurance. It was
not even talked over, beyond two brief explanations why 12
the building was needed. Learning that a big church was
required, the money to provide it was pledged with the
readiness and despatch of an ordinary mortal passing out 15
a nickel for carfare.

[*Boston Globe*, April, 1903]

PROGRESSIVE STEPS   18

The last parcel in the block bounded by Falmouth,
Norway, and St. Paul Streets, in the shape of a triangle,
has passed to the ownership of the Christian Science 21
church, the deed being taken by Ira O. Knapp *et al.*,

65

1 trustees. The purchase of this parcel, which is known as
the Hotel Brookline, a four-story brick building also in the
3 shape of a triangle, gives to the above society the ownership
of the entire block.

During the past two weeks considerable activity has
6 been going on in property on these streets, no less than
ten estates having been conveyed by deed to the Christian
Science church, and now comes the purchase of the last
9 parcel on St. Paul Street by the above society, which
gives them the ownership of the entire block.

Just what use the society will make of the property
12 has not been stated, but it is said that a number of changes
will be made that will enable the church to expand, and
to do so it was necessary to have this property. No block
15 is so well situated for church purposes as this one, being
in a fine part of the city.

[*Boston Post*, June 6, 1906]

18   THE FINISHING TOUCHES

Artisans and artists are working night and day and
craftsmen are hurrying on with their work to make the
21 spacious and elegant edifice complete for the elaborate
observances of Sunday, when six services will be held,
and when the words of Mary Baker Eddy will come from
24 her beautiful home, Pleasant View, in Concord, N. H.,
welcoming her children and giving her blessing to the
structure.

27   The services of Sunday will mark an epoch in the history
of Christian Science. Since the discovery by Mrs. Eddy,
many beautiful houses of worship have been erected, but
30 never before has such a grand church been built as that

which raises its dome above the city at the corner of 1
Falmouth and Norway Streets.

[Boston Post]   3

DESCRIPTION OF THE EXTENSION

Extension of The Mother Church

Cost....................................$2,000,000	6
Shape, triangular........................220x220x236 ft.	
Height.. 224 ft.	
Area of site................................40,000 sq. ft.	9
Seating capacity..............................5,000	
Checking facilities....................3,000 garments	

Notable Dates in Christian Science   12

Christian Science discovered..........................1866	
First church organized................................1879	
First church erected......................................1894	15
Corner-stone of cathedral laid..........................1904	
Cathedral to be dedicated..............................1906	

Two million dollars was set aside for the building of this 18
addition to The First Church of Christ, Scientist, and the
money was used in giving Boston an edifice that is a
marvel of architectural beauty. But one church in the 21
country exceeds it in seating capacity, and, while vaster
sums of money were spent in other instances, never was
a more artistic effect reached.   24

This new temple, begun nearly two years ago, will in
its simple grandeur surpass any church edifice erected
in this city. Notwithstanding its enormous size, it is so 27
proportionately built that its massiveness is unnoticed
in the graceful outlines.

1   Built in the Italian Renaissance style, the interior of
this church is carried out with the end in view of impressing
3 the audiences with the beauty and strength of the design.
The great auditorium, with its high-domed ceiling, supported on four arches springing from the tops of great
6 stone piers, contains about one mile and a half of pews.

The dome surmounting the building is more than twice
the size of the dome on the State House, having a diameter
9 of eighty-two feet and a height of fifty-one feet.

The top of the dome is two hundred and twenty-four feet
above the street, and reaches an altitude twenty-nine feet
12 higher than that of the State House.

The old church at the corner of Falmouth and Norway
Streets, with a seating capacity of twelve hundred, built
15 twelve years ago, will remain as it was, and Mrs. Eddy's
famous room will be undisturbed.

The Readers' platform is of a beautiful foreign marble,
18 and the color scheme for all the auditorium is of a warm
gray, to harmonize with the Bedford stone which enters
so largely into the interior finish.

21   The great organ is placed back of the Readers' platform
and above the Readers' special rooms. It has an architectural stone screen and contributes not a little to the
24 imposing effect of the interior.

Bedford stone and marble form the interior finish, with
elaborate plaster work for the great arches and ceilings.
27 The floors of the first story are of marble.

There are twelve exits and seven broad marble stairways, the latter framed of iron and finished with bronze,
30 marble, and Bedford stone.

Bronze is used in the lighting fixtures, and the pews and
principal woodwork are of mahogany.

The church is unusually well lighted, and one of the extraordinary features is the eight bronze chains, each suspending seventy-two lamps, each lamp of thirty-two candle-power.

Where ceiling or roof and side walls come together no sharp angles are visible, such meetings presenting an oval and dome appearance and forming a gently curved and panelled surface, whereon are placed inscriptions illustrative of the faith of Christian Science.

Two large marble plates with Scripture quotations are also placed on the two sides of the organ.

Everywhere within the building where conditions permitted it pure white marble was used, and the hammer and chisel of the sculptor added magnificent carvings to the rich beauty of the interior.

The auditorium contains seven galleries, two on either side and three at the back, yet not a single pillar or post anywhere in the vast space interrupts the view of the platform from any seat.

Another unusual feature is the foyer, where five thousand people can freely move. Adjoining this foyer are the Sunday School and the administration offices, while in the basement is a cloak-room of the capacity of three thousand wraps.

[*Boston Globe*]
AN IDEA OF THE SIZE

If one would get an idea of the size of this building and the manner in which the dome seems to dominate the entire city, the best point of view is on top of the tower in Mt. Auburn cemetery in Cambridge, some four miles away. From this point the building and dome can be seen

1 in their relation to the city itself, and it certainly looks
imposing.

3   One thing is certain: for a religion which has been
organized only thirty years, and which erected its first
church only twelve years ago, Christian Science has more
6 fine church edifices to its credit in the same time than
any other denomination in the world, and they are all
paid for.

9   [*Boston Evening Transcript*]
                    THE CHIMES

The chimes for the new Christian Science temple are
12 worthy of the dome. The effect on all within earshot is
quite remarkable. They say that workingmen stopped
in the street and stood in silent admiration while the
15 chimes were being tested the other day. Millet's
"Angelus" had living reproductions on every corner in
the neighborhood.

18   [*Boston Post*]
          MAGNIFICENCE OF THE ORGAN

The new church is replete with rare bits of art, chosen
21 from the works of both ancient and modern masters, but
there is nothing more wonderful than the organ which
has been installed. Nowhere in the world is there a more
24 beautiful, more musical, or more capable instrument.
In reality it is a combination of six organs, with four
manuals, seventy-two stops, nineteen couplers, nineteen
27 adjustable combination pistons, three balanced swells,
a grand crescendo pedal, seven combination pedals, and
forty-five hundred and thirty-eight pipes, the largest of
30 which is thirty-two feet long. Attached to the organ is

a set of cathedral chimes, stationed in one of the towers, 1
and some of the most intricate discoveries of organ
builders enable the organist to produce the most beautiful 3
effects by means of the bells. There is also a solo organ
attached.

[Boston Journal] 6

ITS ARCHITECTURE

There is no need of fussing about the underlying spirit
that built the Christian Science cathedral. We can all 9
agree that it is a stunning piece of architecture and a
great adornment to the city.

[Boston Globe] 12

UNIQUE INTERIOR

When these people enter this new cathedral or temple
which has been in process of construction, they will find 15
themselves in one of the most imposing church edifices
in the country — yes, in the world. For in its interior
architecture it is different from any other church in the 18
world. In fact, nearly all the traditions of church interior
architecture have been set aside in this temple, for here
are neither nave, aisles, nor transept — just one vast audi- 21
torium which will seat exactly five thousand and twelve
people on floor and galleries, and seat them comfort-
ably. And what is more, every person seated in the 24
auditorium, either on floor or galleries, can see and hear
the two Readers who conduct the services on the platform
in front of the great organ. 27

This was the aim and object of the architect: to construct an auditorium that would seat five thousand people,
each of whom could see the Readers, and with such nicely 30

1 adjusted acoustic properties that each person could hear
what was said.   To do this it was necessary to set aside
3 the traditions of interior church architecture.

[*Boston Post*]
GATES OF BOSTON OPEN

6   The gates of Boston are open wide in welcome to
nobility.   Never before has the city been more frequented by members of the titled aristocracy of the
9 old world than it is now.   From all the centres of Europe
there are streaming into town lords and ladies who
come to attend the dedication of the new church for
12 Christian Scientists.

[*Boston Globe*]
CHRISTIAN SCIENTISTS HAVE ALL THE MONEY NEEDED

15   "Please do not send us any more money — we have
enough!"

Briefly that is the notice which Stephen A. Chase,
18 treasurer of the building fund of the new Christian Science temple, sent forth to the thirty thousand or more
Christian Scientists who have come to Boston to attend
21 the dedication exercises, and also through the *Christian Science Sentinel* to members of the church all over
the world.

24   This means that nearly two million dollars has
been subscribed for the new building, and that every
cent of it was paid in before the work was actually
27 completed.

That is the way the Christian Scientists began when
they erected the first church in Boston twelve years ago

— The Mother Church. Then it was found necessary 1
to issue a similar notice or order, and even to return
more than ten thousand dollars which had been over- 3
subscribed. They have erected dozens of churches all
over this country and in other countries since that time,
but it is claimed that very few of them owe a cent. 6

If you ask a Christian Scientist how they do it, the
reply will be in the form of a quotation from Science
and Health (p. 494), "Divine Love always has met and 9
always will meet every human need."

[*Boston Globe*]
THE GREAT GATHERING   12

Christian Scientists are flocking from all over the
world to Boston to-day, as they have been for several
days past and will be for several days to come, to attend 15
the June meetings of The Mother Church and the dedication of the new temple.

The headquarters was thrown open to visitors this 18
forenoon in Horticultural Hall, corner of Huntington
and Massachusetts Avenues. It is in charge of G. D.
Robertson, and here the visitors will receive all information 21
concerning rooms and board, hotels, railroads, *etc.* There
is here also a post-office to which all mail may be directed,
and telegraph and telephone service.   24

[*Boston Evening Transcript*]
SPECIAL TRAINS COMING

Special trains and extra sections of trains are due to 27
arrive in Boston to-night, bearing the first instalments of
the crowds of Christian Scientists from the central and

1 western sections of this country. Those from abroad
and from the far West to a large degree are already in
3 Boston. From now until Saturday night the inrush will
be from the sections within two or three days' ride, and
no doubt the night trains of Saturday will bring con-
6 siderable numbers of belated church members from New
York and elsewhere who will arrive in this city just about
in time for the first Sunday service.

9   [*Boston Evening Transcript*]

INTERESTING AND AGREEABLE VISITORS

The Christian Scientists are here in force, and they are
12 very interesting and agreeable visitors, even to those who
are unable to accompany them in their triumph of mind
over matter. Boston is indebted to them for one of the
15 finest architectural achievements in this or any other city,
and other denominations might profit by their example of
paying for their church before dedicating it. It is a monu-
18 ment to the sincerity of their faith; and the pride and
satisfaction that is not only evident from their addresses
but reflected in their faces, is justifiable. They are an
21 intelligent and a happy appearing body, and even if those
outside are unable to believe that they have escaped from
the bondage of the material world, it would be idle to
24 attempt to deny them the satisfaction that springs from
a belief in such emancipation. Our present relations with
them are as the guests of the city, and as such they are
27 welcome.

Within two weeks we have had here the representatives
of the two poles of healing, the material and the mental,
30 and each is interesting, one for its hopefulness and the
other for its novelty. Whatever opinions we may enter-

tain of the value of the latter, we cannot well withhold 1
our respectful acknowledgment of its enthusiasm, its
energy, and its faith in its fundamentals.   Its votaries 3
are certainly holding the centre of the stage this week.

[*Boston Globe*]
READILY ACCOMMODATED   6

Yesterday was a busy day at the headquarters of the
Christian Scientists in Horticultural Hall. They poured
into the city from every direction and most of them 9
headed straight for Horticultural Hall, where they were
assigned rooms in hotels or lodging-houses, if they had
not already been provided for. So perfect have been all 12
the preliminary arrangements for the handling of a great
number of visitors that there has not been the slightest
hitch in the matter of securing accommodations. And 15
if there was it would not make much difference, for these
people would take it all very good-naturedly. They
do not get excited over trifles. They are very patient and 18
good-natured. Crowded as the hall was yesterday, and
warm as the day was, there was not the slightest evidence
of temper, no matter how far they had travelled or what 21
discomforts they might have endured in their travels.

[*Boston Evening Transcript*]
BIG CHURCH IS PAID FOR   24

According to the custom of the Christian Scientists, the
big addition to The Mother Church will be dedicated
to-morrow free from debt. No church has ever yet been 27
dedicated by this denomination with any part of the
expense of its construction remaining unprovided for, and

1 it went without saying that the same practice would be
followed with this new two-million-dollar edifice, the
3 largest of them all. Up to within ten days the notices
that more money was needed had been in circulation,
and new contributions were constantly being received;
6 but on June 2 it became evident to the Board of Directors that enough money was on hand to provide for the
entire cost of the building, and the formal announcement
9 was made that no more contributions to the building fund
were needed. That it was received with rejoicing by the
thousands of church members and their friends only feebly
12 expresses the gratification.

A similar decision was reached and published at the
time of the dedication of The Mother Church in 1895, all
15 of which goes to show the earnestness and loyalty which
Christian Scientists manifest in the support of their
church work, and which enables them to dedicate their
18 churches free of debt without exception. The estimated
cost of the extension of The Mother Church was pledged
by the members assembled in their annual church meeting
21 in Boston, in 1902, and all contributions have been
voluntary.

[*New York Herald*]

24   GIANT TEMPLE FOR SCIENTISTS

There will be dedicated in Boston to-morrow the
first great monument to Christian Science, the new two-
27 million-dollar cathedral erected by the devotees of a
religion which twenty-seven years ago was founded in
Boston by Mrs. Mary Baker Eddy with a membership
30 of twenty-six persons.

The new structure, which is now completed, has for

months been the cynosure of all eyes because of its great 1
size, beautiful architecture, and the novelty of the cult
which it represents. This temple is one of the largest in 3
the world. It has a seating capacity of over five thousand.
In this respect it leads the Auditorium of Chicago. Beside it the dome of the Massachusetts State House, which 6
is the leading landmark of Boston, pales into insignificance,
as its dimensions are only half as great.

From all over the world Christian Scientists are rapidly 9
gathering in this city to participate in the most notable
feature in the life of their cult. From beyond the Rockies,
from Canada, from Great Britain, and practically every 12
civilized country, daily trainloads of pilgrims are pouring
into Boston, and it is estimated that not less than twenty-
five thousand visitors will participate in the dedication. 15

[New York World]
DEDICATION DAY

Over the heads of a multitude which began to gather at 18
daybreak and which filled the streets leading to the magnificent temple of the Christian Science church, there
pealed from the chimes a first hymn of thanksgiving at 21
six o'clock this morning. It was dedication day, and
Christian Scientists from all quarters of the globe were
present to participate in the occasion. 24

It was estimated that nearly forty thousand believers
had gathered in Boston. Word was conveyed to them that
the temple would open its doors absolutely free of debt, 27
every penny of the two million dollars required to build
the imposing edifice in the Back Bay district having
been secured by voluntary subscription. 30

1 The seating capacity of the temple is five thousand, and in order that all might participate in the dedication, 3 six services, identical in character, were held during the morning, afternoon, and evening.

The worshippers saw an imposing structure of gray 6 stone with a massive dome rising to a height of two hundred and twenty-four feet and visible from every quarter of the city. The multitude passed through the 9 twelve entrances beneath a series of arches in the several facades. They looked upon an interior done in soft gray with decorative carvings peculiarly rich and im- 12 pressive. The seating is accomplished in a semi-circular sweep of mahogany pews and in triple galleries.

The offertory taken at the beginning of the services 15 found every basket piled high with bank-notes, everybody contributing, and none proffering small change.

At the close of the Lesson-Sermon, and in accordance 18 with the custom of the Christian Science church, the entire congregation knelt in silent communion, followed by the audible repetition of the Lord's Prayer. One of 21 the remarkable features of the services was the congregation singing in perfect unison. The acoustic properties of the temple, in spite of its vast interior, were found to 24 be perfect.

[*Boston Globe*]
CHILDREN'S SERVICE

27 No mere words can convey the peculiar impressiveness of the half past twelve service; the little children, awed by the grandeur of the great room in which they were seated, 30 drinking in every word of the exercises and apparently understanding all they heard, joining with their shrill

voices in the singing and responsive reading, and then, at 1
the last, kneeling for silent communion before the pews, in
absolute stillness, their eyes closed and their solemn little 3
faces turned upward.

[*Norfolk* (Neb.) *Tribune*]

ON A FAR HIGHER PEDESTAL   6

To those who seem to see no good in Christian Science,
it must stagger their faith not a little to read the account
of the dedication of the vast temple located in the heart 9
of the city of Boston, the supposed fountain of knowledge
and seat of learning of America; the spectacle of thirty
thousand people assembling to gain admission to the 12
temple shows an enthusiasm for Christian Science seldom
witnessed anywhere in the world on any occasion; and
this occurred in staid old Boston, and the fact was heralded 15
in flaming headlines in the leading newspapers of the
world. According to the despatches, that assembly was
not a gathering of "the vulgar throng;" the intelligence 18
and wisdom of the country were there. There certainly
must be something more than a fad in Christian Science,
which was placed upon a far higher pedestal by that 21
demonstration than it ever occupied before.

[*Boston Herald*]

THE WEDNESDAY EVENING MEETINGS   24

Quietly, without a trace of fanaticism, making their
remarkable statements with a simplicity which sprang
from the conviction that they would be believed, scores of 27
Christian Scientists told of cures from diseases, physical
and mental, at the testimony meetings that marked the

1 close of their visit to Boston; cures that carried one back
to the age of miracles. To hear prosperous, contented
3 men and women, people of substance and of standing,
earnestly assure thousands of auditors that they had been
cured of blindness, of consumption in its advanced stages,
6 of heart disease, of cancer; that they had felt no pain
when having broken bones set; that when wasted unto
death they had been made whole, constituted a severe tax
9 upon frail human credulity, yet they were believed.

Meetings were held in the extension of The Mother
Church, in the extension vestry, in the old auditorium
12 of The Mother Church, in The Mother Church vestry,
Horticultural Hall (Exhibition Hall), Horticultural Hall
(Lecture Hall), Jordan Hall, Potter Hall, Howe and
15 Woolson Halls, Chickering Hall.

At each of the meetings the introductory services were
identical, consisting of hymns, an appropriate reading
18 from the Bible, and selections from "Science and Health
with Key to the Scriptures" by Mrs. Mary Baker
Eddy.

21   Fifteen thousand Scientists crowded into the auditorium
of the extension of The Mother Church, into the old
church, into Horticultural Hall, Jordan Hall, Potter Hall,
24 Woolson Hall, and Chickering Hall, and it took ten
meetings to accommodate the great throngs who wanted
to give testimony or who wanted to hear it. And when
27 these places had all been filled, there were many hundreds
waiting vainly in the streets. A few were upon the scene
as early as three o'clock in the afternoon to secure seats
30 in the main body of the church, where the largest meeting
was held, and long before seven the auditorium was com-
fortably filled.

Upon entering The Mother Church one was immediately struck with the air of well-being and of prosperity of the great congregation. The Scientists fairly radiate good nature and healthy satisfaction with life. No pessimistic faces there! So ingrained is this good nature, so complete this self-abnegation, that at the very height of fervor, when bursting with a desire to testify to the benefits and the healing power of the faith, one of them would pause and laughingly give precedence to another who had been the first to catch the Reader's eye.

When Mr. McCrackan announced at the main meeting that they were ready to receive testimony, up leaped half a dozen Scientists. They had been told to name, before beginning, the places where they lived. "Indianapolis!" "Des Moines!" "Glasgow!" "Cuba!" "Dresden!" "Peoria!" they cried. No more cosmopolitan audience ever sat in Boston.

Those who poured out their debts of gratitude for ills cured, for hearts lifted up, spoke simply and gratefully, but occasionally the voices would ring out in a way there was no mistaking. In those people was the depth of sincerity, and, when they sang, the volume of holy song rose tingling to the great dome, swelling as one voice. It was a practical demonstration of the Scientist claims, a fitting close to a memorable week.

If an attempt were made to give any account of the marvellous cures narrated at the meetings of the Scientists, or wherever two or more of them are met together, it would be impossible to convey a conception of the fervor of belief with which each tells his or her experience. These are tales of people of standing and of substance, professional men, hard-headed shrewd busi-

1 ness men.   Yet they all have the same stories of their conversion, either through a cure to themselves or to
3 one near and dear to them.

[*Boston Herald*]
EXODUS BEGINS

6   For a while this morning it looked as though all the Christian Scientists who have been crowding Boston the last week were trying to get away at the same
9 time.   Hotels, boarding-houses, and private houses were disgorging trunks and smaller articles of baggage so fast that it was a matter of wonder where there
12 could be secured express wagons enough to accommodate the demand.

At the dedicatory services of The Mother Church
15 extension on Sunday, and at the sessions of the annual meeting, Tuesday, it was the pride of the Church Directors that the edifice was emptied of its crowds in some-
18 thing like ten minutes.   It would seem that this ability to get away when the entertainment is over is a distinguishing characteristic of Christian Scientists, for at
21 noon to-day [June 14] the indications were that Boston would be emptied of its twenty thousand and more visitors by midnight to-night.

24   Transportation facilities at the two stations were taxed to the utmost from early morning, and trains pulled out of the city in double sections.

27   Although the Scientists came to Boston in such numbers and are departing with such remarkable expedition, their going will not be noticeable to the residents of Boston,
30 except perhaps those living in the streets leading directly

to Horticultural Hall. This fact will be due to the 1
custom Christian Scientists have of never going about
labelled. Ordinarily the holding of a great convention 3
is patent to every one residing in the convention city.
Up at Horticultural Hall the one hundred and fifty
members of the local arrangement committee wore tiny 6
white, unmarked buttons, for their own self-identification,
otherwise there has been no flaunting of badges or
insignia of any kind. Christian Scientists frequently 9
wear a small pin, but this is usually hidden away in
the laces of the women's frocks, and the men go
entirely unadorned. 12

Therefore, with the exception of the street-car men
and policemen, who will doubtless have fewer questions
as to locality to answer, and the hotel and restaurant 15
keepers, who will have time to rest and sleep, the public at large will scarcely realize that the Scientists have
gone. 18

WHAT THE BOSTON EDITORS SAID

[Boston Daily Advertiser]

The meeting of the Christian Scientists in this city 21
naturally takes on a tone of deserved satisfaction, in view
of the announcement, which has just been made, that the
two million dollars needed for the construction of the new 24
temple has been raised even before the building itself has
been completed.

The thirty thousand visitors have other evidences of 27
the strength and growth of their organization, which has
made steady gains in recent years. But of this particular example of the readiness of the members to bear 30
each his or her share of the necessary expense of church

1 work, the facts speak more plainly than mere assertion
could. Nothing is more of a drag on a church than a
3 heavy debt, the interest on which calls for practically all
the resources of the institution. Many a clergyman can
testify from his own experience how a "church debt"
6 cramps and retards and holds back work that would
otherwise be done. It is a rule in some denominations
that a church edifice may not be formally dedicated until
9 it be wholly free from debt. And the experience of many
generations has affirmed its wisdom.

[*Boston Herald*]

12   Boston is the Mecca for Christian Scientists all over the
world. The new temple is something to be proud of. Its
stately cupola is a fitting crown for the other architec-
15 tural efforts in that section of the Back Bay.

[*Boston Evening Record*]

Boston is near to another great demonstration of the
18 growth of the Christian Science idea in numbers, wealth,
vigor, and faithful adherence. It is a remarkable story
which the gathering here tells. Its very magnitude and
21 the cheerful optimism and energy of its followers impress even the man who cannot reconcile himself to
the methods and tenets of the sect. Its hold and
24 development are most notable.

[*Boston Post*]

The gathering of Christian Scientists for the dedication
27 of the beautiful structure on Falmouth Street, which is
to take place on Sunday, is notable in many ways. It

is remarkable in the character of the assembling mem- 1
bership, in its widely international range, and in the
significance of the occasion.   3

The growth of this cult is the marvel of the age. Thirty
years ago it was comparatively unknown; one church
and a mere handful of members measured its vogue. 6
To-day its adherents number probably a million, its
churches have risen by hundreds, and its congregations
meet in Europe and in the antipodes, as from the Atlantic 9
to the Pacific on this continent.

One does not need to accept the doctrines of Mrs.
Eddy to recognize the fact that this wonderful woman 12
is a world power. This is conclusive; it is conspicuously manifest. And here in Boston the zeal and
enthusiasm of the followers of this creed have been 15
manifested in the building of a church structure which
will hold place among the architectural beauties of the
country.   18

[Boston Herald]

Another glory for Boston, another "landmark" set
in the illustrious list for future generations to reverence 21
and admire! The Science church has become the great
centre of attraction, not merely for its thousands of worshippers, but for a multitude of strangers to whom this 24
historic city is the Mecca of their love and duty. Last
Sunday it was entirely credible that the spirit of faith
and brotherhood rested on this structure, which is abso- 27
lutely unique in its symmetrical and appropriate design.
Aside from every other consideration, this church, with
its noble dome of pure gray tint, forming one of the 30
few perfect sky-lines in an American city, is doubly

1 welcomed.   Henceforth the greeting of admiring eyes,
too often unaccustomed to fine architectural effects, will
3 be constant and sincere.

As Boston has ever loved its golden State House
dome, so will it now find pleasure in this new symbol,
6 brooding elevation, guarding as it were, embracing as it
may be, the hosts of a new religion.

[*Boston Globe*]

9   Thousands of Christian Scientists have been pouring
into Boston in the past few days to be present at the
dedication yesterday of their new two-million-dollar
12 church, and to take part in the subsequent ceremonies and
exercises.   Not only was every cent of the estimated cost
contributed before the actual work was completed, but
15 the treasurer of the building fund of the great temple
appealed to his brethren to give no more money, since he
had enough.   This must be regarded as an extraordinary
18 achievement, and one which indicates plainly enough the
generosity of the devotion that the Christian Scientists
maintain towards their church.

21   [*Boston Post*]

The dedication of the edifice of the Christian Scientists
on the Back Bay has proved one of the most interest-
24 ing and in some of its aspects the most notable of such
occasions.

The attendance at the ceremonies yesterday was re-
27 markable, probably unprecedented, as regards numbers.
Not even the great size of the auditorium could accommodate the throng of participants.   At each of the iden-
30 tical services, repeated at intervals from early morning

until the evening, the attendance was greater than the building could contain. And the transportation facilities of the town have been strained to their utmost to care for the multitudes going and coming.

The temporary increase of the population of Boston has been apparent to the most casual observer. And so, we think, must be the characteristics of this crowd of visitors. It is a pleasant, congenial, quietly happy, well-to-do, intellectual, and cheerfully contented multitude that has invaded the town. There are among them visitors of title and distinction, but one does not notice these unless they are pointed out. The impression created is that of a great gathering of people we like to know and like to have here.

We congratulate these comfortable acquaintances upon the fact that they have their costly church fully paid for, and we feel that Boston is to be congratulated upon the acquisition of an edifice so handsome architecturally.

[*Boston Herald*]

I do not think I have ever seen more cheerful looking groups of people than I have met in Boston during the past few days. Their happy faces would make sunshine on the grayest day. If Christian Science gives such serene, beautiful expressions, it would not be a bad thing if all the world turned to the new religion. There is one thing about it: it is certainly imbued with the spirit of unselfishness and helpfulness, and, whatever one's special creed may be, there is nothing antagonistic to it in this doctrine of health, happiness, and in the cheerful doing of good.

GENERAL EDITORIAL OPINION

[Montreal (Can.) *Gazette]*

Twenty thousand Christian Scientists have assembled at Boston to attend the opening of their great new temple. Christian Science, as now before this continent, is the development of a short lifetime. It shows strength in all parts, and among classes above the average in intelligence.

[Concord (N. H.) *Monitor]*

The dedication, Sunday, in Boston, of the new Mother Church of the Christian Science faith was a ceremonial of far more than usual ecclesiastic significance. The edifice itself is so rich in the architectural symbolisms of aspiration and faith, its proportions are so large, and its accommodations are so wide, that its dedication abounds in remarkable external manifestations which must arrest public attention. But externals constitute the smallest feature of the Christian Science faith, and this beautiful temple, striking as are its beauties, is only a slight and material development in evidence of that beauty and serenity of faith, life, and love which finds its temple in the heart of all that increasing host who have found the truths of Christian Science to be a marvellous revelation given to this generation by a noble and devoted woman, to whom they rightfully turn with respect and affection.

[Brooklyn (N. Y.) *Eagle]*

The stoutest enemies of Christian Science will confess at least an æsthetic debt to that great and growing cult, which is implied in the building of a great church in Bos-

ton. This church is one of the largest and seemliest in 1
America, and in its size, if not in its aspect, it may be
held to symbolize that faith which is so much a faith 3
that all facts inhospitable to it are deemed by its professors not to exist at all. The building is of light stone,
with a dome over two hundred and twenty feet high, a 6
chime of bells, and one of the largest organs in the world.
The architect has joined lightness and grace to solidity,
and the edifice needs only an open space about it, such 9
as one finds in the English cathedrals, to achieve its
extreme of beauty. A sect that leaves such a monument
has not lived in vain.   12

A remarkable thing in this building is that, although
it cost two million dollars, it is not blanketed with debts
and mortgages. Everything, even to the flagstones in 15
front of it, is paid for, and subscriptions are not solicited. Here is an occasion for joy that marks it as different from almost all other of the Christian churches, 18
where petitions for money are almost as constant as
petitions for divine mercy.

[Denver (Col.) News]   21

The dedication of the new Mother Church of the
Christian Scientists in Boston is not a matter of interest
to that city alone, but to the nation; not to the nation 24
alone, but to the world; not to this time alone, but to
history.

The growth of this form of religious faith has been one of 27
the marvels of the last quarter century. It is, in some
respects, the greatest religious phenomenon of all history.
That a woman should found a religious movement of 30
international sway; that its followers should number

1 many thousands during her lifetime; that hundreds of great buildings should be filled at every meeting Sun-
3 days or on week-days with devout worshippers, wooed by no eloquence of orator or magnetic ritual, — all these things are new, utterly new, in the history of religious
6 expression.

Unaccountable? Hardly so. Whatever else it is, this faith is real and is given very real tests. Thousands upon
9 thousands believe that it has cured them of diseases many and diverse. All the passionate love for life with which nature endows the children of men, grips hold of their
12 faith and insures fidelity in pain or death for self or dear ones. But, while health-seeking is the door to this gospel for many, it is not the only source of appeal. A faith
15 which teaches that hate is atheism, that discord is poison-ous, that gloom is sin, has a mission that can be readily grasped by sick or well.
18   The world is enormously richer for this reincarnation of the old, old gospel of "on earth peace, good will toward men."

21   [*Terre Haute* (Ind.) *Star*]

The dedication of The Mother Church of Christian Science at Boston, with its paid-up cost of two million
24 dollars and its tremendous outpouring of eager commu-nicants from all over the civilized world, is an event of impressiveness and momentous significance. The historic
27 place of Mrs. Eddy as the Founder of a great denomination can no longer be questioned, and the sources of her power and following can be readily apprehended. Prominent
30 among these is the denomination's peculiar department of healing, the efficacy of which to some extent is established

beyond cavil. The immense membership of the body is 1
proof positive that it supplies these persons, most of
whom were already nominal Christians, something they 3
did not find in other communions. It affords refutation
of the notion that spiritual and mystic mediation has
been drowned out in this so-called commercial age. The 6
Christian Scientists set a good example to other denominations in requiring their church edifices to be fully paid
for before they are dedicated. It is to be said for Chris- 9
tian Science that no person's spiritual aspirations were
ever deadened or his moral standards debased through
its agency. Its communicants are cheerful and shed 12
sunshine about them — no insignificant element in true
Christianity.

[Lafayette (Ind.) *Journal]*   15

The dedication of a Christian Science temple at Boston
serves to call attention to one of the most remarkable
religious movements that this country or any other country 18
has ever known. It has not been very many years since
Christian Science was announced as a discovery of Mary
Baker Eddy of Concord, N. H. The few thousand persons 21
who followed Mrs. Eddy during the first years of her
preaching were the objects of much ridicule, but despite
the obstacles put in the way the church has continued to 24
grow. Its growth in numbers is remarkable, but even
stranger is its increase in wealth. The temple which has
just been dedicated at Boston cost two million dollars, 27
and is one of the finest places of worship in the world,
at least it is the largest in New England. This Mother
Church is absolutely free from debt. After but a few 30
years, Christian Science has congregations in every im-

portant town and city of the United States. Of course the new idea will never have determined its real position in the doctrines of the world until it has stood the test of time. But its beginning has been impressive, and that large numbers of intelligent men and women should be converted to it makes it appear that Science cannot be brushed aside by ridicule alone.

[Springfield (Mass.) *Republican]*

The prodigious convention of Christian Scientists in Boston is a portent worthy of perhaps even more interest than it has evoked in that city, where a new temple to Isis and Osiris would be hardly more than a day's wonder. With the swift growth of the new faith the public has in a general way been familiar; it is but a few years ago that the astonishing revelation was made that since 1890 its following had increased from an insignificant number to hundreds of thousands, a rate at which every other sect in the country would soon be left behind. But mere statistics give a feeble impression in comparison with so huge and concrete a demonstration as the dedication of this vast temple. The statistics have been ridiculed by the hostile as mere guesswork, but one cannot sneer away the two-million-dollar stone edifice or the thirty thousand wor-shippers who entered its portals Sunday.

[Rochester (N. Y.) *Post Express]*

There are two things to be said in favor of Christian Science. Its growth has been wonderfully rapid, and due apparently to nothing save the desire in the human heart for some such comfort as it promises. Christian Scientists,

as a class, so far as the writer knows them, are happy, 1
gentle, and virtuous. They are multiplying without
efforts at proselytizing; they are in no wise at war with 3
society; and they have little of the spirit of bigotry. The
dedication of their great church in Boston is a material
evidence of their prosperity; and it may be said that if 6
their opinions seem visionary, there is nothing in them
to attract any class save the moderately well-to-do, the
intelligent, and the well-behaved. It has been said 9
cynically that a religion prospers according to the pledges
which it holds out to its votaries; and though Christian
Science promises nothing in the way of gratifying the 12
passions or attaining dominion over others, yet it has
rare lures for weary hearts, — physical health and spiritual
peace.   15

[*Topeka* (Kan.) *Daily Capital*]

Those of us who do not accept the doctrine of Christian
Science are possibly too prone to approach it in a spirit 18
of levity, too often disposed to touch upon it with the
tongue of facetiousness. Too often we see only its ridiculous phases, attaching meanwhile no importance to 21
the saneness and common sense which underlie many of
the practices in its name. And many of us have missed
entirely its tremendous growth and the part it has come 24
to play in the economy of our social and religious life.

To those of us who have overlooked these essentials of
its hold upon the public, certain statistics brought to light 27
by the great meeting of the church now being held in
Boston will come in the nature of a revelation. In 1890
the faith had but an insignificant following. To-day its 30
adherents number hundreds of thousands, and if the

1 growth continues in like proportion through another
decade every other sect will be left behind in the race for
3 numerical supremacy. The figures given out by the
church itself have been ridiculed by the hostile as mere
guesswork, but some of the evidence appears in the con-
6 crete and cannot be combated. "One cannot sneer away
the two-million-dollar stone edifice or the thirty thousand
worshippers who entered its portals Sunday," says the
9 *Springfield Republican*. Neither can we overlook the
steady, consistent growth of the sect in every community in which it has found a foothold. In the adherence
12 of its converts to the faith, and in the absence of dissent
among them in the interpretation of its tenets, there is
also much to convince the skeptic.

15   [*Albany* (N. Y.) *Knickerbocker*]

The remarkable growth and the apparent permanency
of Christian Science were noted in the recent dedication in
18 Boston of the magnificent new temple of the cult. When
the doors were opened to the public, the structure was free
from debt. While the dedicatory services were being
21 held at different hours of the day, forty thousand Christian Scientists from every State in the Union and from
many foreign countries were in attendance.
24   Although Mrs. Eddy, the Founder of Christian Science,
was not in attendance, she sent greetings in which she
declared that the "crowning ultimate" of the church
27 "rises to a mental monument, a superstructure high above
the work of men's hands, even the outcome of their
hearts, giving to the material a spiritual significance —
30 the speed, beauty, and achievements of goodness."
But a few years ago, men there were who predicted that

Christian Science would soon be included among the cults 1
which flourish for a time like a green bay-tree, and are
then forgotten. Those predictions have not been verified. 3
The church which has been built upon the tenets first
presented by Mrs. Eddy is being constantly strengthened
by members who represent the intelligence of many 6
communities in different parts of the world.

[*Mexican Herald*, City of Mexico, Mex.]

The dedication of the magnificent Christian Science 9
church in Boston has brought that cheerful and prosperous body of believers before the press gallery of com-
mentators. They have built a huge church, which has 12
cost them about two million dollars, and it has a dome
which rivals that of the famous old Massachusetts State
House. During the great assembly of forty thousand 15
Christian Scientists in Boston they were described in the
newspapers of the Hub as a contented and well-dressed
body of people. 18

The faith of these people is certainly great. They go
about telling of miracles performed in this twentieth century when "advanced" clergymen of other denominations 21
are avowing their disbelief in the miraculous.

The higher critics and the men of science may think
they can banish faith in the supernatural, but no religion 24
of growth and vitality exists without faith in the things
unseen.

[*Sandusky* (Ohio) *Star-Journal*] 27

It is doubtful if, since the days of the primitive Christians, there has been such a wonderful demonstration of
religious faith and enlightened zeal as that exhibited at 30

1 Boston, Sunday, when forty thousand Christian Scientists
from all parts of the world assembled to participate in
3 the dedication of the extension of The Mother Church
of that denomination. These people were of the highest
order of intelligence, many of them prominent figures in
6 the social and business world, and none of them afflicted
with the slightest trace of fanaticism. The gathering
can in no sense, save one, be compared with those of
9 Mecca and the Hindu shrines, where fanaticism dominates everything else. The one point of resemblance is
that the Christian Scientists are thoroughly in earnest
12 and take joy in attesting their faith in the creed of the
church of their choice. It is a faith based upon reason, and reached only through intelligent and unbiased
15 study and comparison with other creeds.

A remarkable feature, perhaps the most remarkable, of
the gathering was the generosity of its adherents towards
18 their church. The building they were in Boston to dedicate cost approximately two million dollars. Members
were invited to contribute what they could to pay for it.
21 The money was sent in such quantities that before the day
set for the dedication arrived the fund was full to overflowing and the members were asked to quit giving.

24   [*Peoria* (Ill.) *Journal*]

It is the custom to sneer at Christian Science, but it is
evident that the cult will soon be beyond the sneering
27 point. The dedication of what is known as The Mother
Church extension in Boston, the other day, was attended
by people from all parts of the United States. And they
30 were people of intelligence.

The fact is that Christian Science just goes a little

beyond what almost every one is inclined to admit. The 1
best physicians now admit the power of mind over matter.
They believe that firm faith on the part of a sick per- 3
son, for instance, will go far towards making the patient
well. These same physicians, however, ridicule the idea
of a patient getting well without the use of medicine. 6
It has yet to be shown that of the sick who abjure
medicine a larger proportion have died than among
those who were medically treated. The *Journal* has 9
kept no books on the subject, and is not a Christian
Scientist, but believes that if the figures could be given
they might show that the Scientists have a little the 12
advantage so far as this goes.

[*Nebraska State Journal*, Lincoln, Neb.]

Zion's Herald, a rather bitter critic of Mrs. Eddy and 15
her cult, speaks of "the audacious, stupendous, inexplicable faith of this well-dressed, good-looking, emi-
nently respectable, evidently wealthy congregation in 18
their teacher and her utterances." The opening of the
new Mother Church of the Christian Science faith
at Boston has opened the eyes of the country anew to 21
the growth of the new church and the zeal of its
membership.

[*Athol* (Mass.) *Transcript*]   24

The Christian Scientists who descended upon Boston
to the number of forty thousand last week to dedicate the
new temple, just built at a cost of two million dollars, have 27
mostly departed, but Boston has not yet recovered from
the effects produced by that stupendous gathering. The
incidents witnessed during the week were calculated to 30

1 impress the most determined skeptic. Forty thousand
people truly make up a mighty host, but these, it is de-
3 clared, are but a twentieth of the Christian Science army
in this country to-day, and this is the wonderful growth
of less than a score of years. Christian Science may be
6 anything that its foes try to prove it to be, but that magnificent church, holding five thousand people, dedicated
free from debt, and the centre of an enthusiasm and rever-
9 ence of worship such as religious annals hardly parallel
in modern times, is a tangible reality, and critics who
seek the light must have done with scoffs and jeers if
12 they would deal with the phenomenon with any effect.

[*Portland* (Ore.) *Telegram*]

The last issue of the *Christian Science Sentinel* contains
15 a rather remarkable announcement to the effect that
friends were requested to send no more money for the
building of the church which was recently dedicated at
18 Boston. This structure cost about two million dollars,
and all of the funds required to build it were raised in a
little less than three years. It was dedicated absolutely
21 free of debt, and no member of the church anywhere,
in this country or elsewhere, was asked to contribute a
dollar. Contributions were entirely voluntary. No re-
24 sort was had to any of the latter-day methods of raising
money. The record is one of which any church might
well be proud.

27   [*Portland* (Me.) *Advertiser*]

The erection in Boston of the two-million-dollar church
of the Christian Scientists and its dedication free from
30 debt has been a wonderful achievement, but as our con-

temporary, the *Boston Times*, comments, it is but one of the marvellous, great, and really good things that this sect is doing. It says: "A faith which is able to raise its believers above the suffering of petty ills; a religion that makes the merry heart that doeth good like a medicine, not a necessity, but a pleasure and an essential; a cult able to promote its faith with so great an aggregation of good and beneficial works, is welcomed within our midst and bidden Godspeed."

[*Denver* (Col.) *Republican*]

Christian Scientists are a remarkably optimistic body of people, and it must be said in their behalf that they are enthusiasts whenever their form of religion is concerned. They have recently built a splendid cathedral in Boston, seating five thousand people, at a cost of two million dollars, and when it was dedicated there was not a cent of indebtedness left. Thirty thousand of the faith, coming from all parts of the world, attended the dedicatory exercises, and the press reports state that the contribution baskets when passed around were literally stuffed and jammed with money.

Less than a generation ago there was not a Christian Science church in the land. To-day there are hundreds of such churches. The denomination has grown with a rapidity that is startling, and the end is not yet.

[*Bridgeport* (Conn.) *Standard*]

Facts and figures are stubborn things, and ignore them as we may their existence points out their meaning and leaves no choice but the acceptance of them at their face value. The recent dedication of a Christian Science

1 temple in Boston has inevitably brought out in connection
with the event some of the facts and figures belonging to
3 it, which are as remarkable in their aggregate as they are
unmistakable in their trend. The temple recently dedicated at Boston cost about two million dollars and is
6 therefore the property of no poverty-stricken sect. On
the Sunday of the dedication, thirty thousand worshippers
were present in the building, coming from all, or nearly
9 all, parts of the country, and representing a vast number
of the followers of the cult.

It is only twenty-five years, or thereabout, since the
12 Christian Science sect made its appearance as a distinctive organization among religious bodies, but its
members are numbered by thousands to-day, and they
15 are very generally of a class who are reputable, intelligent, and who think for themselves.

PART II
Miscellany

Miscellany

CHAPTER I

To the Christian World

IN the midst of the imperfect, perfection is reluctantly 1
seen and acknowledged. Because Science is unim-
peachable, it summons the severest conflicts of the ages 3
and waits on God.

The faith and works demanded of man in our textbooks,
the Bible and "Science and Health with Key to the 6
Scriptures," and the proof of the practicality of this faith
and these works, show conclusively that Christian Science
is indeed Science, — the Science of Christ, the Science of 9
God and man, of the creator and creation. In every age
and at its every appearing, Science, until understood, has
been persecuted and maligned. Infinite perfection is 12
unfolded as man attains the stature of man in Christ
Jesus by means of the Science which Jesus taught and
practised. Alluding to this divine method, the Psalmist 15
said: "Why do the heathen rage, and the people imagine
a vain thing?"

I have set forth Christian Science and its application 18
to the treatment of disease just as I have discovered
them. I have demonstrated through Mind the effects
of Truth on the health, longevity, and morals of men; 21
and I have found nothing in ancient or in modern systems on which to found my own, except the teachings
and demonstrations of our great Master and the lives 24
of prophets and apostles. The Bible has been my only

1 authority. I have had no other guide in the strait and narrow way of Truth.

3   Jewish pagans thought that the learned St. Paul, the Mars' Hill orator, the canonized saint, was a "pestilent fellow," but to-day all sorts of institutions flourish under 6 the name of this "pestilent fellow." That epithet points a moral. Of old the Pharisees said of the great master of metaphysics, "He stirreth up the people." Because 9 they could find no fault in him, they vented their hatred of Jesus in opprobrious terms. But what would be thought to-day of a man that should call St. Paul 12 a "pest," and what will be thought to-morrow of him who shall call a Christian Scientist a "pest"? Again, what shall be said of him who says that the Saviour 15 of men, the healer of men, the Christ, the Truth, "stirreth up the people"?

It is of the utmost concern to the world that men 18 suspend judgment and sentence on the pioneers of Christianity till they know of what and of whom these pioneers speak. A person's ignorance of Christian Sci- 21 ence is a sufficient reason for his silence on the subject, but what can atone for the vulgar denunciation of that of which a man knows absolutely nothing?

24   On November 21, 1898, in my class on Christian Science were many professional men and women of the highest talents, scholarship, and character in this or any other 27 country. What was it that brought together this class to learn of her who, thirty years ago, was met with the anathema spoken of in Scripture: "Blessed are ye, when 30 men shall revile you, and persecute you, and shall say all manner of evil against you falsely, for my sake"? It was the healing of the sick, the saving of sinners, the works

even more than the words of Christ, Truth, which had ₁
of a verity stirred the people to search the Scriptures and
to find in them man's only medicine for mind and body. ₃
This Æsculapius, defined Christianly and demonstrated
scientifically, is the divine Principle whose rules demonstrated prove one's faith by his works.   ₆

After my discovery of Christian Science, I healed consumption in its last stages, a case which the M.D.'s,
by verdict of the stethoscope and the schools, declared ₉
incurable because the lungs were mostly consumed.   I
healed malignant diphtheria and carious bones that could
be dented by the finger, saving the limbs when the sur- ₁₂
geon's instruments were lying on the table ready for their
amputation.   I have healed at one visit a cancer that had
eaten the flesh of the neck and exposed the jugular vein ₁₅
so that it stood out like a cord.   I have physically restored
sight to the blind, hearing to the deaf, speech to the dumb,
and have made the lame walk.   ₁₈

About the year 1869, I was wired to attend the patient
of a distinguished M.D., the late Dr. Davis of Manchester,
N. H.   The patient was pronounced dying of pneumonia, ₂₁
and was breathing at intervals in agony.   Her physician,
who stood by her bedside, declared that she could not live.
On seeing her immediately restored by me without mate- ₂₄
rial aid, he asked earnestly if I had a work describing
my system of healing.   When answered in the negative,
he urged me immediately to write a book which should ₂₇
explain to the world my curative system of metaphysics.
In the ranks of the M.D.'s are noble men and women,
and I love them; but they must refrain from persecuting ₃₀
and misrepresenting a system of medicine which from
personal experience I have proved to be more certain

1 and curative in functional and organic diseases than any
material method. I admonish Christian Scientists either
3 to speak charitably of all mankind or to keep silent, for
love fulfils divine law and without this proof of love
mental practice were profitless.

6　　The list of cases healed by me could be made to include
hopeless organic diseases of almost every kind. I name
those mentioned above simply to show the folly of believ-
9 ing that the immutable laws of omnipotent Mind have not
power over and above matter in every mode and form, and
the folly of the cognate declaration that Christian Science
12 is limited to imaginary diseases! On the contrary, Christian Science has healed cases that I assert it would have
been impossible for the surgeon or *materia medica* to cure.
15 Without Mind, man and the universe would collapse;
the winds would weary, and the world stand still. It is
already proved that Christian Science rests on the basis of
18 fixed Principle, and overcomes the evidence of diseased
sensation. Human mentality, expressed in disease, sin,
and death, in tempest and in flood, the divine Mind calms
21 and limits with a word.

In what sense is the Christian Scientist a "pest"? Is it
because he minds his own business more than does the
24 average man, is not a brawler, an alcohol drinker, a
tobacco user, a profane swearer, an adulterer, a fornicator,
nor a dishonest politician or business man? Or is it
27 because he is the very antipode of all these? In what
sense is the Christian Scientist a charlatan? Is it because
he heals the sick without drugs?
30　　Our great Exemplar, the Nazarene Prophet, healed
through Mind, and commanded his followers to do likewise. The prophets and apostles and the Christians in

the first century healed the sick as a token of their Chris- 1
tianity. Has Christianity improved upon its earlier
records, or has it retrograded? Compare the lives of its 3
professors with those of its followers at the beginning of
the Christian era, and you have the correct answer.

As a pertinent illustration of the general subject under 6
discussion, I will cite a modern phase of medical practice,
namely, the homœopathic system, to which the old school
has become reconciled. Here I speak from experience. 9
In homœopathy, the one thousandth attenuations and
the same triturations of medicine have not an iota of the
drug left in them, and the lower attenuations have so 12
little that a vial full of the pellets can be swallowed without
harm and without appreciable effect. Yet the homœopathist administers half a dozen or less of these same 15
globules, and he tells you, and you believe him, that
with these pellets he heals the sick. The diminishing of
the drug does not disprove the efficiency of the homœo- 18
pathic system. It enhances its efficiency, for it identifies
this system with mind, not matter, and places it nearer the
grooves of omnipotence. O petty scorner of the infinite, 21
wouldst thou mock God's miracles or scatter the shade of
one who "shall abide under the shadow of the Almighty"?
If, as Scripture declares, God made all that was made, 24
then whatever is entitled to a classification as truth
or science must be comprised in a knowledge or understanding of God, for there can be nothing beyond 27
illimitable divinity.

The homœopathist handles in his practice and heals the
most violent stages of organic and inflammatory diseases, 30
stops decomposition, removes enteritis, gastritis, hyper-
æmia, pneumonia, diphtheria, and ossification — the effects

1 of calcareous salts formed by carbonate and sulphate of
lime; and the homœopathic physician succeeds as well in
3 healing his cases without drugs as does the allopath who
depends upon drugs. Then is mind or matter the intelligent cause in pathology? If matter, I challenge matter
6 to act apart from mind; and if mind, I have proved beyond
cavil that the action of the divine Mind is salutary and
potent in proportion as it is seen to act apart from matter.
9 Hence our Master's saying, "The flesh profiteth nothing."
The difference between metaphysics in homœopathy and
metaphysics in Christian Science consists in this forcible
12 fact: the former enlists faith in the pharmacy of the
human mind, and the latter couples faith with spiritual
understanding and is based on the law of divine Mind.
15 Christian Science recognizes that this Mind is the only
lawgiver, omnipotent, infinite, All. Hence the divine
Mind is the sovereign appeal, and there is nothing in
18 the divine Mind to attenuate. The more of this Mind
the better for both physician and patient.

Ignorance, slang, and malice touch not the hem of the
21 garment of Christian Scientists, for if they did once touch
it, they would be destroyed. To be stoned for that which
our Master designated as his best work, saying, "For
24 which of those works do ye stone me," is to make known
the best work of a Christian Scientist.

Finally, beloved brethren in Christ, the words of the
27 New York press — "Mrs. Eddy not shaken" — are valid.
I remain steadfast in St. Paul's faith, and will close with
his own words: "Christ is the head of the church: and he
30 is the saviour of the body."

CHAPTER II

The Christian Science Textbook

MATTER is but the subjective state of mortal mind. 1
Matter has no more substance and reality in our
day-dreams than it has in our night-dreams. All the way 3
mortals are experiencing the Adam-dream of mind in
matter, the dream which is mortal and God-condemned
and which is not the spiritual fact of being. When this 6
scientific classification is understood, we shall have one
Mind, one God, and we shall obey the commandment,
"Love thy neighbor as thyself." 9

If nineteen hundred years ago Christ taught his followers to heal the sick, he is to-day teaching them the
same heavenly lesson. Christ is "the same yesterday, 12
and to-day, and forever." "God is Love," the ever-
operative divine Principle (or Person, if you please) whose
person is not corporeal, not finite. This infinite Person 15
we know not of by the hearing of the ear, yet we may
sometimes say with Job, "But now mine eye [spiritual
sense] seeth Thee." 18

God is one because God is All. Therefore there can
be but one God, one Christ. We are individually but
specks in His universe, the reflex images of this divine 21
Life, Truth, and Love, in whom "we live, and move,
and have our being." Divine metaphysics is not to
be scoffed at; it is Truth with us, God "manifest in the 24
flesh," not alone by miracle and parable, but by proof;

1 it is the divine nature of God, which belongs not to a
dispensation now ended, but is ever present, casting out
3 evils, healing the sick, and raising the dead — resurrecting individuals buried above-ground in material sense.

At the present time this Bethlehem star looks down
6 upon the long night of materialism, — material religion,
material medicine, a material world; and it shines as of
yore, though it "shineth in darkness; and the dark-
9 ness comprehended it not." But the day will dawn and
the daystar will appear, lighting the gloom, guiding the
steps of progress from molecule and mortals outward and
12 upward in the scale of being.

Hidden electrical forces annihilating time and space,
wireless telegraphy, navigation of the air; in fact, all the
15 *et cetera* of mortal mind pressing to the front, remind me
of my early dreams of flying in airy space, buoyant with
liberty and the luxury of thought let loose, rising higher
18 and forever higher in the boundless blue. And what of
reality, if waking to bodily sensation is real and if bodily
sensation makes us captives? The night thought, me-
21 thinks, should unfold in part the facts of day, and open
the prison doors and solve the blind problem of matter.
The night thought should show us that even mortals
24 can mount higher in the altitude of being. Mounting
higher, mortals will cease to be mortal. Christ will have
"led captivity captive," and immortality will have been
27 brought to light.

Robert Ingersoll's attempt to convict the Scriptures of
inconsistency made his life an abject failure. Happily,
30 the misquoting of "Science and Health with Key to the
Scriptures," or quoting sentences or paragraphs torn from
their necessary contexts, may serve to call attention to

that book, and thus reveal truths which otherwise the 1
reader would not have sought. Surely "the wrath of man
shall praise Thee."   3

The nature and truth of Christian Science cannot
be destroyed by false psychics, crude theories or modes
of metaphysics. Our master Metaphysician, the Galilean 6
Prophet, had much the same class of minds to deal with
as we have in our time. They disputed his teachings on
practically the same grounds as are now assumed by many 9
doctors and lawyers, but he swept away their illogical
syllogisms as chaff is separated from the wheat. The
genuine Christian Scientist will tell you that he has found 12
the physical and spiritual status of a perfect life through
his textbook.

The textbook of Christian Science maintains primitive 15
Christianity, shows how to demonstrate it, and throughout is logical in premise and in conclusion. Can Scientists adhere to it, establish their practice of healing on 18
its basis, become successful healers and models of good
morals, and yet the book itself be absurd and unscientific?
Is not the tree known by its fruit? Did Jesus mistake 21
his mission and unwittingly misguide his followers? Were
the apostles absurd and unscientific in adhering to his
premise and proving that his conclusion was logical 24
and divine?

"The scientific statement of being" (Science and Health,
p. 468) may irritate a certain class of professionals 27
who fail to understand it, and they may pronounce it
absurd, ambiguous, unscientific. But that Christian
Science is valid, simple, real, and self-evident, thousands 30
upon thousands attest with their individual demonstrations. They have themselves been healed and have

1 healed others by means of the Principle of Christian
Science. Science has always been first met with denun-
3 ciations. A fiction or a false philosophy flourishes for a
time where Science gains no hearing. The followers of the
Master in the early Christian centuries did just what he
6 enjoined and what Christian Science makes practical to-
day to those who abide in its teachings and build on its
chief corner-stone. Our religious denominations interpret
9 the Scriptures to fit a doctrine, but the doctrines taught
by divine Science are founded squarely and only on the
Scriptures.

12   "Science and Health with Key to the Scriptures" is not
inconsistent in a single instance with its logical premise
and conclusion, and ninety-nine out of every hundred
15 of its readers — honest, intelligent, and scholarly — will
tell you this. The earnest student of this book, understanding it, demonstrates in some degree the truth of its
18 statements, and knows that it contains a Science which
is demonstrable when understood, and which is fully
understood when demonstrated. That Christian Scien-
21 tists, because of their uniformly pure morals and noble
lives, are better representatives of Christian Science
than the textbook itself, is not in accordance with the
24 Scriptures. The tree is known by its fruit. The student
of this book will tell you that his higher life is the result
of his conscientious study of Science and Health in con-
27 nection with the Bible.

A book that through the good it does has won its
way into the palaces of emperors and kings, into the
30 home of the President of the United States, into the chief
cities and the best families in our own and in foreign
lands, a book which lies beside the Bible in hundreds

of pulpits and in thousands of homes, which heals the 1
sick and reclaims sinners in court and in cottage, is
not less the evangel of Christian Science than is he 3
who practises the teachings of this book or he who
studies it and thereby is healed of disease. Can such a
book be ambiguous, self-contradictory, or unprofitable 6
to mankind?

St. Paul was a follower but not an immediate disciple
of our Lord, and Paul declares the truth of the complete 9
system of Christian Science in these brief sentences:
"There is therefore now no condemnation to them which
are in Christ Jesus, who walk not after the flesh, but after 12
the Spirit. For the law of the Spirit of life in Christ Jesus
hath made me free from the law of sin and death." Was
it profane for St. Paul to aspire to this knowledge of Christ 15
and its demonstration, healing sin and sickness, because
he was not a disciple of the personal Jesus? Nay, verily.
Neither is it presumptuous or unscriptural or vain for 18
another, a suckling in the arms of divine Love, to perfect
His praise.

A child will demonstrate Christian Science and have 21
a clear perception of it. Then, is Christian Science a
cold, dull abstraction, or is that unscientific which
all around us is demonstrated on a fixed Principle and 24
a given rule, — when, in proportion as this Principle
and rule are understood, men are found casting out
the evils of mortal thought, healing the sick, and uplift- 27
ing human consciousness to a more spiritual life and
love? The signs of the times emphasize the answer
to this in the rapid and steady advancement of this Sci- 30
ence among the scholarly and titled, the deep thinkers,
the truly great men and women of this age. In the

1 words of the Master, "Can ye not discern the signs of
the times?"

3　Christian Science teaches: Owe no man; be temperate;
abstain from alcohol and tobacco; be honest, just, and
pure; cast out evil and heal the sick; in short, Do unto
6 others as ye would have others do to you.

Has one Christian Scientist yet reached the maximum of these teachings? And if not, why point the
9 people to the lives of Christian Scientists and decry the
book which has moulded their lives? Simply because
the treasures of this textbook are not yet uncovered
12 to the gaze of many men, the beauty of holiness is not
yet won.

My first writings on Christian Science began with notes
15 on the Scriptures. I consulted no other authors and read
no other book but the Bible for about three years. What
I wrote had a strange coincidence or relationship with the
18 light of revelation and solar light. I could not write these
notes after sunset. All thoughts in the line of Scriptural
interpretation would leave me until the rising of the sun.
21 Then the influx of divine interpretation would pour in
upon my spiritual sense as gloriously as the sunlight on the
material senses. It was not myself, but the divine power
24 of Truth and Love, infinitely above me, which dictated
"Science and Health with Key to the Scriptures." I
have been learning the higher meaning of this book since
27 writing it.

Is it too much to say that this book is leavening
the whole lump of human thought? You can trace its
30 teachings in each step of mental and spiritual progress,
from pulpit and press, in religion and ethics, and find
these progressive steps either written or indicated in the

book. It has mounted thought on the swift and mighty 1
chariot of divine Love, which to-day is circling the
whole world.   3

I should blush to write of "Science and Health with
Key to the Scriptures" as I have, were it of human origin,
and were I, apart from God, its author. But, as I was 6
only a scribe echoing the harmonies of heaven in divine
metaphysics, I cannot be super-modest in my estimate of
the Christian Science textbook.   9

CHAPTER III

Personality

PERSONAL CONTAGION

AT a time of contagious disease, Christian Scientists endeavor to rise in consciousness to the true sense of
the omnipotence of Life, Truth, and Love, and this great
fact in Christian Science realized will stop a contagion.

6   In time of religious or scientific prosperity, certain individuals are inclined to cling to the personality of its
leader. This state of mind is sickly; it is a contagion
9 — a mental malady, which must be met and overcome.
Why? Because it would dethrone the First Commandment, Thou shalt have one God.

12   If God is one and God is Person, then Person is infinite;
and there is no personal worship, for God is divine Principle, Love. Hence the sin, the danger and darkness of
15 personal contagion.

Forgetting divine Principle brings on this contagion.
Its symptoms are based upon personal sight or sense.
18 Declaring the truth regarding an individual or leader,
rendering praise to whom praise is due, is not a symp-
tom of this contagious malady, but persistent pursuit
21 of his or her person is.

Every loss in grace and growth spiritual, since time
began, has come from injustice and personal contagion.
24 Had the ages helped their leaders to, and let them alone

in, God's glory, the world would not have lost the Science 1
of Christianity.

"What went ye out for to see?" A person, or a Prin- 3
ciple? Whichever it be, determines the right or the
wrong of this following. A personal motive gratified by
sense will leave one "a reed shaken with the wind," 6
whereas helping a leader in God's direction, and giving
this leader time and retirement to pursue the infinite
ascent, — the comprehending of the divine order and con- 9
sciousness in Science, — will break one's own dream of
personal sense, heal disease, and make one a Christian
Scientist. 12

Is not the old question still rampant? "When saw we
thee a stranger, and took thee in? or naked, and clothed
thee? Or when saw we thee sick, or in prison, and came 15
unto thee?" But when may we see you, to get some good
out of your personality?

"In the beginning was the Word, and the Word was 18
with God, and the Word was God" (St. John). This
great truth of God's impersonality and individuality and
of man in His image and likeness, individual, but not 21
personal, is the foundation of Christian Science. There
was never a religion or philosophy lost to the centuries
except by sinking its divine Principle in personality. 24
May all Christian Scientists ponder this fact, and give
their talents and loving hearts free scope only in the
right direction! 27

I left Boston in the height of prosperity to *retreat* from
the *world,* and to seek the one divine Person, whereby
and wherein to show others the footsteps from sense to 30
Soul. To give me this opportunity is all that I ask of
mankind.

1 My soul thanks the loyal, royal natures of the beloved members of my church who cheerfully obey God and
3 steadily go on promoting the true Principle of Christian Science. Only the disobedient spread personal contagion, and any imaginary benefit they receive is the effect of
6 self-mesmerism, wherein the remedy is worse than the disease.

LETTER TO A CLERGYMAN

9 *My Dear Sir:* — I beg to thank you for your most excellent letter. It is an outpouring of goodness and greatness with which you honor me.
12 In a call upon my person, you would not see me, for spiritual sense demands and commands us; hence I seek to be "absent from the body," and such circumstances
15 embarrass the higher criticism.

The Scripture reads: "Blessed are they that have not seen, and yet have believed." A saving faith comes
18 not of a person, but of Truth's presence and power. Soul, not sense, receives and gives it. One's voluntary withdrawal from society, from furnishing the demands
21 upon the finite to supply the blessings of the infinite, — something impossible in the Science of God and credited only by human belief, by a material and not by the
24 spiritual sense of man, — should come from conscience.

The doctrine of Buddha, which rests on a heathen basis for its Nirvana, represents not the divinity of Christian
27 Science, in which Truth, or Christ, finds its paradise in Spirit, in the consciousness of heaven within us — health, harmony, holiness, entirely apart from limitations, which
30 would dwarf individuality in personality and couple evil

with good. It is convenient for history to record limi- 1
tations and to regard evil as real, but it is impossible
in Science to believe this, or on such a basis to demon- 3
strate the divine Principle of that which is real, harmonious, and eternal — that which is based on one infinite
God, and man, His idea, image, and likeness. 6

In Science, we learn that man is not absorbed in the
divine nature, but is absolved by it. Man is free from
the flesh and is individual in consciousness — in Mind, 9
not in matter. Think not that Christian Science tends
towards Buddhism or any other "ism." *Per contra,*
Christian Science destroys such tendency. Mary of old 12
wept because she *stooped down* and looked into the sepulchre — looked for the person, instead of the Principle that
reveals Christ. The Mary of to-day looks up for Christ, 15
away from the supposedly crucified to the ascended
Christ, to the Truth that "healeth all thy diseases" and
gives dominion over all the earth. The doubting disciple 18
could not identify Christ spiritually, but he could materially. He turned to the person, to the prints of the nails,
to prove Christ, whereas the discharged evidence of mate- 21
rial sense gave the real proof of his Saviour, the veritable
Christ, Truth, which destroys the false sense with the
evidence of Soul, immortality, eternal Life without begin- 24
ning or end of days.

Should I give myself the pleasant pastime of seeing your
personal self, or give you the opportunity of seeing mine, 27
you would not see me thus, for I am not there. I
have risen to look and wait and watch and pray for the
spirit of Truth that leadeth away from person — from 30
body to Soul, even to the true image and likeness of
God. St. John found Christ, Truth, in the Word which

1 *is* God. We look for the sainted Revelator in his writings, and there we find him. Those who look for me in
3 person, or elsewhere than in my writings, lose me instead of find me. I hope and trust that you and I may
meet in truth and know each other there, and know
6 as we are known of God.

Accept my gratitude for the chance you give me to
answer your excellent letter. Forgive, if it needs forgive-
9 ness, my honest position. Bear with me the burden of
discovery and share with me the bliss of seeing the risen
Christ, God's spiritual idea that takes away all sin, disease,
12 and death, and gives to soul its native freedom.

CHAPTER IV

Messages to The Mother Church

COMMUNION, JANUARY 2, 1898   1

M Y BELOVED BRETHREN: — I have suggested a change in the time for holding our semi-annual 3 church meetings, in order to separate these sessions from the excitement and commotion of the season's holidays.   6

In metaphysics we learn that the strength of peace and of suffering is sublime, a true, tried mental conviction that is neither tremulous nor relapsing. This 9 strength is like the ocean, able to carry navies, yet yielding to the touch of a finger. This peace is spiritual; never selfish, stony, nor stormy, but generous, reliable, 12 helpful, and always at hand.

Peace, like plain dealing, is somewhat out of fashion. Yet peace is desirable, and plain dealing is a jewel as beau- 15 tiful as the gems that adorn the Christmas ring presented to me by my students in 1897. Few blemishes can be found in a true character, for it is always a diamond of the 18 first water; but external gentility and good humor may be used to disguise internal vulgarity and villainy. No deformity exists in honesty, and no vulgarity in kindness. 21 Christian Science, however, adds to these graces, and reflects the divine likeness.

Self-denial is practical, and is not only polite to all 24 but is pleasant to those who practise it. If one would

121

1 follow the advice that one gratuitously bestows on
others, this would create for one's self and for the world
3 a destiny more grand than can issue from the brain of
a dreamer.

That glory only is imperishable which is fixed in one's
6 own moral make-up.

Sin is like a dock root. To cut off the top of a plant
does no good; the roots must be eradicated or the plant
9 will continue to grow. Now I am done with homilies
and, you may add, with tedious prosaics.

On the fifth of July last, my church tempted me ten-
12 derly to be proud! The deportment of its dear members
was such as to command respect everywhere. It called
forth flattering comment and created surprise in our good
15 city of Concord.

Beloved brethren, another Christmas has come and gone.
Has it enabled us to know more of the healing Christ that
18 saves from sickness and sin? Are we still searching diligently to find where the young child lies, and are we satisfied to know that our sense of Truth is not demoralized,
21 finitized, cribbed, or cradled, but has risen to grasp the
spiritual idea unenvironed by materiality? Can we say
with the angels to-day: "He is risen; he is not here:
24 behold the place where they laid him"? Yes, the real
Christian Scientist can say his Christ is risen and is not
the material Christ of creeds, but is Truth, even as Jesus
27 declared; and the sense of Truth of the real Christian
Scientist is spiritualized to behold this Christ, Truth,
again healing the sick and saving sinners. The mission
30 of our Master was to all mankind, and included the very
hearts that rejected it — that refused to see the power
of Truth in healing.

Our unity and progress are proverbial, and this church's 1
gifts to me are beyond comparison — they have become
a wonder! To me, however, love is the greater marvel, 3
so I must continue to prize love even more than the gifts
which would express it. The great guerdon of divine
Love, which moves the hearts of men to goodness and 6
greatness, will reward these givers, and this encourages
me to continue to urge the perfect model for your acceptance as the ultimate of Christian Science.   9

To-day in Concord, N. H., we have a modest hall in one
of the finest localities in the city, — a reading-room and
nine other rooms in the same building. "Tell it not in 12
Gath"! I had the property bought by the courtesy of
another person to be rid of the care and responsibility of
purchasing it, and furnished him the money to pay for it. 15
The original cost of the estate was fourteen thousand
dollars. With the repairs and other necessary expenses
the amount is now about twenty thousand dollars. Ere 18
long I will see you in this hall, *Deo volente;* but my outdoor accommodations at Pleasant View are bigger than
the indoor. My little hall, which holds a trifle over two 21
hundred people, is less sufficient to receive a church of ten
thousand members than were the "five loaves and two
fishes" to feed the multitude; but the true Christian 24
Scientist is not frightened at miracles, and ofttimes small
beginnings have large endings.

Seeing that we have to attain to the ministry of right- 27
eousness in all things, we must not overlook small things
in goodness or in badness, for "trifles make perfection,"
and "the little foxes . . . spoil the vines."   30

As a peculiar people whose God is All-in-all, let us say
with St. Paul: "We faint not; but have renounced the

1 hidden things of dishonesty, not walking in craftiness,
nor handling the word of God deceitfully; but by mani-
3 festation of the truth commending ourselves to every
man's conscience."

COMMUNION, JUNE 4, 1899

6   *My Beloved Brethren:* — Looking on this annual assemblage of human consciousness, — health, harmony, growth,
grandeur, and achievement, garlanded with glad faces,
9 willing hands, and warm hearts, — who would say to-day,
"What a fond fool is hope"? The fruition of friendship,
the world's arms outstretched to us, heart meeting heart
12 across continents and oceans, bloodless sieges and tear-
less triumphs, the "well done" already yours, and the
undone waiting only your swift hands, — these are
15 enough to make this hour glad. What more abounds
and abides in the hearts of these hearers and speakers,
pen may not tell.
18   Nature reflects man and art pencils him, but it remains
for Science to reveal man to man; and between these lines
of thought is written in luminous letters, O man, what
21 art thou? Where art thou? Whence and whither? And
what shall the answer be? Expressive silence, or with
finger pointing upward, — Thither! Then produce thy
24 records, time-table, log, traveller's companion, *et cetera,*
and prove fairly the facts relating to the thitherward, —
the rate of speed, the means of travel, and the number
27 *en route.* Now what have you learned? The mystery
of godliness — God made "manifest in the flesh," seen
of men, and spiritually understood; and the mystery of
30 iniquity — how to separate the tares from the wheat,
that they consume in their own fires and no longer

kindle altars for human sacrifice. Have you learned to 1
conquer sin, false affections, motives, and aims, — to be
not only sayers but doers of the law? 3

Brethren, our annual meeting is a grave guardian. It
requires you to report progress, to refresh memory, to
rejuvenate the branches and to vivify the buds, to bend 6
upward the tendrils and to incline the vine towards the
parent trunk. You come from feeding your flocks, big
with promise; and you come with the sling of Israel's 9
chosen one to meet the Goliaths.

I have only to dip my pen in my heart to say, All honor
to the members of our Board of Lectureship connected 12
with The Mother Church. Loyal to the divine Principle
they so ably vindicate, they earn their laurels. History
will record their words, and their works will follow 15
them. When reading their lectures, I have felt the touch
of the spirit of the Mars' Hill orator, which always
thrills the soul. 18

The members of the Board of Education, under the
auspices of the Massachusetts Metaphysical College, have
acquitted themselves nobly. The students in my last 21
class in 1898 are stars in my crown of rejoicing.

We are deeply grateful that the church militant is
looking into the subject of Christian Science, for Zion 24
must put on her beautiful garments — her bridal robes.
The hour is come; the bride (Word) is adorned, and lo,
the bridegroom cometh! Are our lamps trimmed and 27
burning?

The doom of the Babylonish woman, referred to in Revelation, is being fulfilled. This woman, "drunken with the 30
blood of the saints, and with the blood of the martyrs
of Jesus," "drunk with the wine of her fornication,"

1 would enter even the church, — the body of Christ, Truth; and, retaining the heart of the harlot and the purpose 3 of the destroying angel, would pour wormwood into the waters — the disturbed human mind — to drown the strong swimmer struggling for the shore, — aiming for 6 Truth, — and if possible, to poison such as drink of the living water. But the recording angel, standing with "right foot upon the sea, and his left foot on the earth," 9 has in his hand a book open (ready to be read), which uncovers and kills this mystery of iniquity and interprets the mystery of godliness, — how the first is finished and the 12 second is no longer a mystery or a miracle, but a marvel, casting out evil and healing the sick. And a voice was heard, saying, "Come out of her, my people" (hearken 15 not to her lies), "that ye receive not of her plagues. For her sins have reached unto heaven, and God hath remembered her iniquities . . . double unto her double accord- 18 ing to her works: in the cup which she hath filled fill to her double . . . for she saith in her heart, I . . . am no widow, . . . Therefore shall her plagues come in one 21 day, death, and mourning, and famine; . . . for strong is the Lord God who judgeth her." That which the Revelator saw in spiritual vision will be accomplished. The 24 Babylonish woman is fallen, and who should mourn over the widowhood of lust, of her that "is become the habitation of devils, and the hold of every foul spirit, 27 and a cage of every unclean . . . bird"?

One thing is eternally here; it reigns supreme to-day, to-morrow, forever. We need it in our homes, at our fire- 30 sides, on our altars, for with it win we the race of the centuries. We have it only as we live it. This is that needful one thing — divine Science, whereby thought is

spiritualized, reaching outward and upward to Science in 1
Christianity, Science in medicine, in physics, and in
metaphysics.   3

Happy are the people whose God is All-in-all, who ask
only to be judged according to their works, who live to
love. We thank the Giver of all good for the marvellous 6
speed of the chariot-wheels of Truth and for the steadfast,
calm coherence in the ranks of Christian Science.

On comparison, it will be found that Christian Science 9
possesses more of Christ's teachings and example than
all other religions since the first century. Comparing
our scientific system of metaphysical therapeutics with 12
materia medica, we find that divine metaphysics completely overshadows and overwhelms *materia medica,* even
as Aaron's rod swallowed up the rods of the magicians 15
of Egypt. I deliberately declare that when I was in practice, out of one hundred cases I healed ninety-nine to
the ten of *materia medica.*   18

We should thank God for persecution and for prosecu-
tion, if from these ensue a purer Protestantism and monotheism for the latter days of the nineteenth century. A 21
siege of the combined centuries, culminating in fierce attack,
cannot demolish our strongholds. The forts of Christian
Science, garrisoned by God's chosen ones, can never sur- 24
render. Unlike Russia's armament, ours is not costly as
men count cost, but it is rich beyond price, staunch and
indestructible on land or sea; it is not curtailed in peace, 27
surrendered in conquest, nor laid down at the feet of
progress through the hands of omnipotence. And why?
Because it is "on earth peace, good will toward men," — 30
a cover and a defence adapted to all men, all nations,
all times, climes, and races. I cannot quench my

1 desire to say this; and words are not vain when the depth of desire can find no other outlet to liberty.

3 "Therefore . . . let us go on unto perfection; not laying again the foundation of repentance from dead works." (Hebrews 6 : 1.)

6 A coroner's inquest, a board of health, or class legislation is less than the Constitution of the United States, and infinitely less than God's benign government, which is 9 "no respecter of persons." Truth crushed to earth springs spontaneously upward, and whispers to the breeze man's inalienable birthright — *Liberty*. "Where the Spirit of 12 the Lord is, there is liberty." God is everywhere. No crown nor sceptre nor rulers rampant can quench the vital heritage of freedom — man's right to adopt a religion, 15 to employ a physician, to live or to die according to the dictates of his own rational conscience and enlightened understanding. Men cannot punish a man for suicide; 18 God does that.

Christian Scientists abide by the laws of God and the laws of the land; and, following the command of the 21 Master, they go into all the world, preaching the gospel and healing the sick. Therefore be wise and harmless, for without the former the latter were impracticable. A lack 24 of wisdom betrays Truth into the hands of evil as effectually as does a subtle conspirator; the motive is not as wicked, but the result is as injurious. Return not evil for 27 evil, but "overcome evil with good." Then, whatever the shaft aimed at you or your practice may be, it will fall powerless, and God will reward your enemies accord-30 ing to their works. Watch, and pray daily that evil suggestions, in whatever guise, take no root in your thought nor bear fruit. Ofttimes examine yourselves, and

see if there be found anywhere a deterrent of Truth and 1
Love, and "hold fast that which is good."

I reluctantly foresee great danger threatening our na- 3
tion, — imperialism, monopoly, and a lax system of religion. But the spirit of humanity, ethics, and Christianity
sown broadcast — all concomitants of Christian Science 6
— is taking strong hold of the public thought throughout our beloved country and in foreign lands, and is
tending to counteract the trend of mad ambition.   9

There is no night but in God's frown; there is no day
but in His smile. The oracular skies, the verdant earth
— bird, brook, blossom, breeze, and balm — are richly 12
fraught with divine reflection. They come at Love's call.
The nod of Spirit is nature's natal.

And how is man, seen through the lens of Spirit, 15
enlarged, and how counterpoised his origin from dust,
and how he presses to his original, never severed
from Spirit! O ye who leap disdainfully from this rock 18
of ages, return and plant thy steps in Christ, Truth,
"the stone which the builders rejected"! Then will
angels administer grace, do thy errands, and be thy 21
dearest allies. The divine law gives to man health
and life everlasting — gives a soul to Soul, a present
harmony wherein the good man's heart takes hold on 24
heaven, and whose feet can never be moved. These
are His green pastures beside still waters, where faith
mounts upward, expatiates, strengthens, and exults.   27

Lean not too much on your Leader. Trust God to
direct your steps. Accept my counsel and teachings only
as they include the spirit and the letter of the Ten Com- 30
mandments, the Beatitudes, and the teachings and
example of Christ Jesus. Refrain from public contro-

1 versy; correct the false with the true — then leave the
latter to propagate. Watch and guard your own thoughts
3 against evil suggestions and against malicious mental
malpractice, wholly disloyal to the teachings of Christian
Science. This hidden method of committing crime —
6 socially, physically, and morally — will ere long be un-
earthed and punished as it deserves. The effort of
disloyal students to blacken me and to keep my works
9 from public recognition — students seeking only public
notoriety, whom I have assisted pecuniarily and striven to
uplift morally — has been made too many times and has
12 failed too often for me to fear it. The spirit of Truth is
the lever which elevates mankind. I have neither the
time nor the inclination to be continually pursuing a lie
15 — the one evil or the evil one. Therefore I ask the help
of others in this matter, and I ask that according to
the Scriptures my students reprove, rebuke, and exhort.
18 A lie left to itself is not so soon destroyed as it is with
the help of truth-telling. Truth never falters nor fails;
it is our faith that fails.
21 All published quotations from my works must have
the author's name added to them. Quotation-marks are
not sufficient. Borrowing from my copyrighted works,
24 without credit, is inadmissible. But I need not say this
to the loyal Christian Scientist — to him who keeps
the commandments. "Science and Health with Key to
27 the Scriptures" has an enormous strain put upon it,
being used as a companion to the Bible in all your
public ministrations, as teacher and as the embodiment
30 and substance of the truth that is taught; hence
my request, that you borrow little else from it, should
seem reasonable.

Beloved, that which purifies the affections also strength- 1
ens them, removes fear, subdues sin, and endues with
divine power; that which refines character at the same 3
time humbles, exalts, and commands a man, and obedience
gives him courage, devotion, and attainment. For this
hour, for this period, for spiritual sacrament, sacrifice, 6
and ascension, we unite in giving thanks. For the body
of Christ, for the life that we commemorate and would
emulate, for the bread of heaven whereof if a man eat 9
"he shall live forever," for the cup red with loving resti-
tution, redemption, and inspiration, we give thanks. The
signet of the great heart, given to me in a little symbol, 12
seals the covenant of everlasting love. May apostate
praise return to its first love, above the symbol seize the
spirit, speak the "new tongue" — and may thought soar 15
and Soul be.

ADDRESS AT ANNUAL MEETING, JUNE 6, 1899

My Beloved Brethren: — I hope I shall not be found 18
disorderly, but I wish to say briefly that this meeting is
very joyous to me. Where God is we can meet, and where
God is we can never part. There is something suggestive 21
to me in this hour of the latter days of the nineteenth
century, fulfilling much of the divine law and the gospel.
The divine law has said to us: "Bring ye all the tithes into 24
the storehouse, that there may be meat in mine house,
and prove me now herewith, saith the Lord of hosts, if I
will not open you the windows of heaven, and pour you 27
out a blessing, that there shall not be room enough to
receive it."

There is with us at this hour this great, great blessing; 30
and may I say with the consciousness of Mind that the

1 fulfilment of divine Love in our lives is the demand of
this hour — the special demand. We begin with the law
3 as just announced, "Prove me now herewith, . . . if I will
not open you the windows of heaven, and pour you out a
blessing," and we go to the Gospels, and there we hear:
6 "In the world ye shall have tribulation; but be of good
cheer; I have overcome the world."

The Christian Scientist knows that spiritual faith and
9 understanding pass through the waters of Meribah here —
bitter waters; but he also knows they embark for infinity
and anchor in omnipotence.

12   Oh, may this hour be prolific, and at this time and in
every heart may there come this benediction: Thou hast
no longer to appeal to human strength, to strive with
15 agony; I am thy deliverer. "Of His own will begat He us
with the word of truth." Divine Love has strengthened
the hand and encouraged the heart of every member of this
18 large church. Oh, may these rich blessings continue and
be increased! Divine Love hath opened the gate Beautiful to us, where we may see God and live, see good in
21 good, — God all, one, — one Mind and that divine; where
we may love our neighbor as ourselves, and bless our
enemies.

24   Divine Love will also rebuke and destroy disease, and
destroy the belief of life in matter. It will waken the
dreamer — the sinner, dreaming of pleasure in sin; the sick,
27 dreaming of suffering matter; the slothful, satisfied to
sleep and dream. Divine Love is our only physician,
and never loses a case. It binds up the broken-hearted;
30 heals the poor body, whose whole head is sick and whose
whole heart is faint; comforts such as mourn, wipes away
the unavailing, tired tear, brings back the wanderer to

the Father's house in which are many mansions, many 1
welcomes, many pardons for the penitent.

Ofttimes I think of this in the great light of the present, 3
the might and light of the present fulfilment. So shall
all earth's children at last come to acknowledge God, and
be one; inhabit His holy hill, the God-crowned summit 6
of divine Science; the church militant rise to the church
triumphant, and Zion be glorified.

<h2 style="text-align:center">A QUESTION ANSWERED   9</h2>

My beloved church will not receive a Message from
me this summer, for my annual Message is swallowed
up in sundries already given out. These crumbs and 12
monads will feed the hungry, and the fragments gathered
therefrom should waken the sleeper, — "dead in trespasses and sins," — set the captive sense free from self's 15
sordid sequela; and one more round of old Sol give birth
to the sowing of Solomon.

MARY BAKER EDDY   18

PLEASANT VIEW, CONCORD, N. H.,
    May 11, 1903

LETTER OF THE PASTOR EMERITUS, JUNE, 1903   21

My Beloved Brethren: — I have a secret to tell you and
a question to ask. Do you know how much I love you
and the nature of this love? No: then my sacred secret 24
is incommunicable, and we live apart. But, yes: and
this inmost something becomes articulate, and my book
is not all you know of me. But your knowledge with 27
its magnitude of meaning uncovers my life, even as
your heart has discovered it. The spiritual bespeaks

1 our temporal history. Difficulty, abnegation, constant
battle against the world, the flesh, and evil, tell my long-
3 kept secret — evidence a heart wholly in protest and
unutterable in love.

The unprecedented progress of Christian Science is pro-
6 verbial, and we cannot be too grateful nor too humble for
this, inasmuch as our daily lives serve to enhance or to
stay its glory. To triumph in truth, to keep the faith
9 individually and collectively, conflicting elements must
be mastered. Defeat need not follow victory. Joy over
good achievements and work well done should not
12 be eclipsed by some lost opportunity, some imperative
demand not yet met.

Truth, Life, and Love will never lose their claim on us.
15 And here let me add: —

Truth happifies life in the hamlet or town;
Life lessens all pride — its pomp and its frown —
18   Love comes to our tears like a soft summer shower,
To beautify, bless, and inspire man's power.

A LETTER FROM MRS. EDDY

21   At the Wednesday evening meeting of April 3, 1907,
in The First Church of Christ, Scientist, in Boston, the
First Reader, Mr. William D. McCrackan, read the fol-
24 lowing letter from Mrs. Eddy. In announcing this letter,
he said: —

"Permission has been secured from our beloved Leader
27 to read you a letter from her to me. This letter is in
Mrs. Eddy's own handwriting, with which I have been
familiar for several years, and it shows her usual mental
30 and physical vigor."

Mrs. Eddy's Letter   1

Beloved Student: — The wise man has said, "When I
was a child, I spake as a child, I understood as a child, 3
I thought as a child: but when I became a man, I put
away childish things." That this passage of Scripture
and its concluding declaration may be applied to old age, 6
is a solace.

Perhaps you already know that I have heretofore personally attended to my secular affairs, — to my income, 9
investments, deposits, expenditures, and to my employees. But the increasing demands upon my time and
labor, and my yearning for more peace in my advancing 12
years, have caused me to select a Board of Trustees to
take the charge of my property; namely, the Hon. Henry
M. Baker, Mr. Archibald McLellan, and Mr. Josiah E. 15
Fernald.

As you are the First Reader of my church in Boston,
of about forty thousand members, I inform you of this, 18
the aforesaid transaction.

Lovingly yours in Christ,

MARY BAKER EDDY   21

PLEASANT VIEW, CONCORD, N. H.,
    March 22, 1907

LETTER TO THE MOTHER CHURCH   24

THE FIRST CHURCH OF CHRIST, SCIENTIST, BOSTON, MASS.

My Beloved Church: — Your love and fidelity cheer my
advancing years. As Christian Scientists you under- 27
stand the Scripture, "Fret not thyself because of evil-
doers;" also you spiritually and scientifically understand
that God is divine Love, omnipotent, omnipresent, in- 30

1 finite; hence it is enough for you and me to know that our "Redeemer liveth" and intercedeth for us.

3   At this period my demonstration of Christian Science cannot be fully understood, theoretically; therefore it is best explained by its fruits, and by the life of 6 our Lord as depicted in the chapter Atonement and Eucharist, in "Science and Health with Key to the Scriptures."

9   MARY BAKER EDDY
        PLEASANT VIEW, CONCORD, N. H.,
              April 2, 1907

12   CARD

I am pleased to say that the following members constitute the Board of Trustees who own my property: —

15   1. The Hon. Henry M. Baker, who won a suit at law in Washington, D. C., for which it is alleged he was paid the highest fee ever received by a native of 18 New Hampshire.

    2. Archibald McLellan, editor-in-chief of the Christian Science periodicals, circulating in the five grand divisions 21 of our globe; also in Canada, Australia, *etc.*

    3. Josiah E. Fernald, justice of the peace and president of the National State Capital Bank, Concord, N. H.

24   To my aforesaid Trustees I have committed the hard earnings of my pen, — the fruits of honest toil, the labor that is known by its fruits, — benefiting the human race; 27 and I have so done that I may have more peace, and time for spiritual thought and the higher criticism.

                                        MARY BAKER EDDY
30   PLEASANT VIEW, CONCORD, N. H.,
              April 3, 1907

MRS. EDDY'S AFFIDAVIT

The following affidavit, in the form of a letter from Mrs. Eddy to Judge Robert N. Chamberlin of the Superior Court, was filed in the office of the Clerk of the Court, Saturday, May 18. The *Boston Globe,* referring to this document, speaks of it as, "in the main, an example of crisp, clear, plain-speaking English." The entire letter is in Mrs. Eddy's own handwriting and is characteristic in both substance and penmanship: —

HON. JUDGE CHAMBERLIN, CONCORD, N. H.

Respected Sir: — It is over forty years that I have attended personally to my secular affairs, to my income, investments, deposits, expenditures, and to my employees. I have personally selected all my investments, except in one or two instances, and have paid for the same.

The increasing demands upon my time, labors, and thought, and yearning for more peace and to have my property and affairs carefully taken care of for the persons and purposes I have designated by my last will, influenced me to select a Board of Trustees to take charge of my property; namely, the Hon. Henry M. Baker, Mr. Archibald McLellan, Mr. Josiah E. Fernald. I had contemplated doing this before the present proceedings were brought or I knew aught about them, and I had consulted Lawyer Streeter about the method.

I selected said Trustees because I had implicit confidence in each one of them as to honesty and business capacity. No person influenced me to make this selection. I find myself able to select the Trustees I need

1 without the help of others.   I gave them my property to
take care of because I wanted it protected and myself
3 relieved of the burden of doing this.   They have agreed
with me to take care of my property and I consider this
agreement a great benefit to me already.

6   This suit was brought without my knowledge and is
being carried on contrary to my wishes.   I feel that it
is not for my benefit in any way, but for my injury,
9 and I know it was not needed to protect my person or
property.   The present proceedings test my trust in
divine Love.   My personal reputation is assailed and
12 some of my students and trusted personal friends are
cruelly, unjustly, and wrongfully accused.

Mr. Calvin A. Frye and other students often ask me
15 to receive persons whom I desire to see but decline to
receive solely because I find that I cannot "serve two
masters."   I cannot be a Christian Scientist except I
18 leave all for Christ.

Trusting that I have not exceeded the bounds of propriety in the statements herein made by me,
21   I remain most respectfully yours,
                                    MARY BAKER EDDY
PLEASANT VIEW, CONCORD, N. H.,
24   May 16, 1907

STATE OF NEW HAMPSHIRE, Merrimack, ss.

On this sixteenth day of May, 1907, personally appeared
27 Mary Baker Eddy and made oath that the statements
contained in the annexed letter directed to Honorable
Judge Chamberlin and dated May 16, 1907, are true.
30   Before me: ALLEN HOLLIS,
                                    Justice of the Peace

NOTA BENE

Beloved Students: — Rest assured that your Leader is living, loving, acting, enjoying. She is neither dead nor plucked up by the roots, but she is keenly alive to the reality of living, and safely, soulfully founded upon the rock, Christ Jesus, even the spiritual idea of Life, with its abounding, increasing, advancing footsteps of progress, primeval faith, hope, love.

Like the verdure and evergreen that flourish when trampled upon, the Christian Scientist thrives in adversity; his is a life-lease of hope, home, heaven; his idea is nearing the Way, the Truth, and the Life, when misrepresented, belied, and trodden upon. Justice, honesty, cannot be abjured; their vitality involves Life, — calm, irresistible, eternal.

A WORD TO THE WISE

My Beloved Brethren: — When I asked you to dispense with the Executive Members' meeting, the purpose of my request was sacred. It was to turn your sense of worship from the material to the spiritual, the personal to the impersonal, the denominational to the doctrinal, yea, from the human to the divine.

Already you have advanced from the audible to the inaudible prayer; from the material to the spiritual communion; from drugs to Deity; and you have been greatly recompensed. Rejoice and be exceedingly glad, for so doth the divine Love redeem your body from disease; your being from sensuality; your soul from sense; your life from death.

1 Of this abounding and abiding spiritual understanding the prophet Isaiah said, "And I will bring the blind
3 by a way that they knew not; I will lead them in
paths that they have not known: I will make darkness light before them, and crooked things straight.
6 These things will I do unto them, and not forsake
them."

MARY BAKER EDDY

9 CHESTNUT HILL, MASS.

[*Boston Globe*]

ABOLISHING THE COMMUNION

12 In a letter addressed to Christian Scientists the Rev.
Mary Baker Eddy explains that dropping the annual communion service of The First Church of Christ, Scientist,
15 in Boston, need not debar distant members from attending occasionally The Mother Church. The following is
Mrs. Eddy's letter: —

18 *Beloved Christian Scientists:* — Take courage. God is
leading you onward and upward. Relinquishing a material form of communion advances it spiritually.
21 The material form is a "Suffer it to be so now," and
is abandoned so soon as God's Way-shower, Christ,
points the advanced step. This instructs us how to
24 be abased and how to abound.

Dropping the communion of The Mother Church
does not prevent its distant members from occasionally
27 attending this church.

MARY BAKER EDDY

CHESTNUT HILL, MASS.,
30 June 21, 1908

[*Boston Globe*]   1

COMMUNION SEASON IS ABOLISHED

The general communion service of the Christian Science 3
denomination, held annually in The First Church of
Christ, Scientist, in this city, has been abolished by
order of Mrs. Mary Baker Eddy.   The services attended 6
last Sunday [June 14] by ten thousand persons were thus
the last to be held.   Of late years members of the church
outside of Boston have not been encouraged to attend the 9
communion seasons except on the triennial gatherings,
the next of which would have been held next year.

The announcement in regard to the services was made 12
last night [June 21] by Alfred Farlow of the publication
committee as follows: —

The First Church of Christ, Scientist, in Boston, has 15
taken steps to abolish its famous communion seasons.
In former years, the annual communion season of the
Boston church has offered an occasion for the gathering 18
of vast multitudes of Christian Scientists from all parts
of the world. According to the following statement, which
Mrs. Eddy has just given out to the press, these gather- 21
ings will be discontinued: —

"The house of The Mother Church seats only five thousand people, and its membership includes forty-eight 24
thousand communicants, hence the following: —

"The branch churches continue their communion seasons, but there shall be no more communion season in 27
The Mother Church that has blossomed into spiritual
beauty, communion universal and divine.   'For who

1 hath known the mind of the Lord, that he may instruct
  him? But we have the mind of Christ.' (1 Corinthians,
3 2 : 16.)"

  [Mrs. Eddy has only abolished the disappointment of
  communicants who come long distances and then find no
6 seats in The Mother Church. — EDITOR *Sentinel*.]

MRS. EDDY'S REPLY

JUDGE CLIFFORD P. SMITH, LL.B., C.S.B.,
9   First Reader, The Mother Church, Boston, Mass.

Beloved Christian Scientist: — Accept my thanks for
your approval of abolishing the communion season of
12 The Mother Church. I sought God's guidance in doing
it, but the most important events are criticized.

The Mother Church communion season was liter-
15 ally a communion of branch church communicants
which might in time lose its sacredness and merge into
a meeting for greetings. My beloved brethren may
18 some time learn this and rejoice with me, as they so
often have done, over a step higher in their passage
from sense to Soul.
21   Most truly yours,
                                     MARY BAKER EDDY
   BOX G, BROOKLINE, MASS.,
24   June 24, 1908

THE CHRISTIAN SCIENCE BOARD OF DIRECTORS

Beloved Students: — I thank you for your kind invi-
27 tation to be present at the annual meeting of The
Mother Church on June 7, 1909. I will attend the

meeting, but not *in propria persona*. Watch and pray 1
that God directs your meetings and your lives, and your
Leader will then be sure that they are blessed in their 3
results.

Lovingly yours,

BROOKLINE, MASS.,   MARY BAKER EDDY   6
June 5, 1909

MRS. EDDY'S STATEMENTS

To Whom It May Concern: — I have the pleasure to 9
report to one and all of my beloved friends and followers
that I exist in the flesh, and am seen daily by the members of my household and by those with whom I have 12
appointments.

Above all this fustian of either denying or asserting the
personality and presence of Mary Baker Eddy, stands 15
the eternal fact of Christian Science and the honest history
of its Discoverer and Founder. It is self-evident that
the discoverer of an eternal truth cannot be a temporal 18
fraud.

The Cause of Christian Science is prospering throughout the world and stands forever as an eternal and de- 21
monstrable Science, and I do not regard this attack upon
me as a trial, for when these things cease to bless they
will cease to occur.   24

"And we know that all things work together for good
to them that love God, to them who are the called
according to His purpose. . . . What shall we then say 27
to these things? If God be for us, who can be against
us?"

MARY BAKER EDDY   30

CHESTNUT HILL, MASS.,
June 7, 1909

1   Mrs. Eddy also sent the following letter to the members of her church in Concord, N. H.: —

3 FIRST CHURCH OF CHRIST, SCIENTIST, CONCORD, N. H.

My Beloved Brethren: — Give yourselves no fear and spare not a moment's thought to lies afloat that I am sick, 6 helpless, or an invalid. The public report that I am in either of the aforesaid conditions is utterly false.

With love, ever yours,

9   MARY BAKER EDDY

BOX G, BROOKLINE, MASS.,
June 7, 1909

CHAPTER V

Christian Science Hall, Concord, N. H.

IN RETROSPECT

M<small>Y</small> D<small>EAR</small> E<small>DITORS</small>:— You are by this time acquainted with the small item that in October, 1897, I proposed to one of Concord's best builders the plan for Christian Science Hall in Concord, N. H.   He drew the plan, showed it to me, and I accepted it.   From that time, October 29, 1897, until the remodelling of the house was finished, I inspected the work every day, suggested the details outside and inside from the foundations to the tower, and saw them carried out.   One day the carpenters' foreman said to me: "I want to be let off for a few days.   I do not feel able to keep about.   I am feeling an old ailment my mother had."   I healed him on the spot.   He remained at work, and the next morning said to Mr. George H. Moore of Concord, "I am as well as I ever was."

Within the past year and two months, I have worked even harder than usual, but I cannot go upon the platform and still be at home attending to the machinery which keeps the wheels revolving.   This well-known fact makes me the servant of the race — and gladly thus, if in this way I can serve equally my friends and my enemies.

1   In explanation of my dedicatory letter to the Chicago church (see page 177), I will say: It is understood by all
3 Christians that Jesus spoke the truth. He said: "They shall take up serpents; and if they drink any deadly thing, it shall not hurt them." I believe this saying
6 because I understand it, but its verity has not been acknowledged since the third century.

The statement in my letter to the church in Chicago,
9 in substance as follows, has been quoted and criticized: "If wisdom lengthens my sum of years to fourscore, I may then be even younger than now."
12 Few believe this saying. Few believe that Christian Science contains infinitely more than has been demonstrated, or that the altitude of its highest propositions has
15 not yet been reached. The heights of the great Nazarene's sayings are not fully scaled. Yet his immortal words and my poor prophecy, if they are true at all, are
18 as true to-day as they will be to-morrow. I am convinced of the absolute truth of his sayings and of their present application to mankind, and I am equally sure that what
21 I wrote is true, although it has not been demonstrated in this age.

Christian Scientists hold as a vital point that the beliefs
24 of mortals tip the scale of being, morally and physically, either in the right or in the wrong direction. Therefore a Christian Scientist never mentally or audibly takes
27 the side of sin, disease, or death. Others who take the side of error do it ignorantly or maliciously. The Christian Scientist voices the harmonious and eternal, and
30 nothing else. He lays his whole weight of thought, tongue, and pen in the divine scale of being — for health and holiness.

Friends and Brethren:— There are moments when at
the touch of memory the past comes forth like a pageant 3
and the present is prophetic.   Over a half century ago,
between the morning and afternoon services of the First
Congregational Church, the grand old elm on North State 6
Street flung its foliage in kindly shelter over my childhood's Sunday noons.   And now, at this distant day, I
have provided for you a modest hall, in which to assemble 9
as a sort of Christian Science kindergarten for teaching
the "new tongue" of the gospel with "signs following,"
of which St. Mark prophesies. 12

May this little sanctum be preserved sacred to the
memory of this pure purpose, and subserve it.   Let
the Bible and the Christian Science textbook preach the 15
gospel which heals the sick and enlightens the people's
sense of Christian Science.   This ministry, reaching the
physical, moral, and spiritual needs of humanity, will, 18
in the name of Almighty God, speak the truth that
to-day, as in olden time, is found able to heal both sin
and disease. 21

I have purchased a pleasant place for you, and prepared
for your use work-rooms and a little hall, which are already
dedicated to Christ's service, since Christian Scientists 24
never stop ceremoniously to dedicate halls.   I shall be
with you personally very seldom.   I have a work to do
that, in the words of our Master, "ye know not of." 27
From the interior of Africa to the utmost parts of the earth,
the sick and the heavenly homesick or hungry hearts are
calling on me for help, and I am helping them.   You have 30
less need of me than have they, and you must not expect

1 me further to do your pioneer work in this city. Faithfully
and more than ever persistently, you are now, through
3 the providence of God, called to do your part wisely and
to let your faith be known by your works. All that we
ask of any people is to judge our doctrine by its fruits.
6 May the good folk of Concord have this opportunity,
and may the God of all grace, truth, and love be and abide
with you henceforth.

9 ADDRESS TO THE CONCORD CHURCH, FEBRUARY, 1899

My Beloved Brethren: — In the annals of our denomination this church becomes historic, having completed
12 its organization February 22 — Washington's birthday.
Memorable date, all unthought of till the day had passed!
Then we beheld the omen, — religious liberty, — the
15 Father of the universe and the father of our nation in
concurrence.

To-day, with the large membership of seventy-four com-
18 municants, you have met to praise God. I, as usual at
home and alone, am with you in spirit, joining in your
rejoicing, and my heart is asking: What are the angels say-
21 ing or singing of this dear little flock, and what is each
heart in this house repeating, and what is being recorded
of this meeting as with the pen of an angel?

24 Bear in mind always that Christianity is not alone a
gift, but that it is a growth Christward; it is not a creed
or dogma, — a philosophical phantasm, — nor the opinions
27 of a sect struggling to gain power over contending sects
and scourging the sect in advance of it. Christianity is
the summons of divine Love for man to be Christlike —
30 to emulate the words and the works of our great Master.

To attain to these works, men must know somewhat of 1
the divine Principle of Jesus' life-work, and must prove
their knowledge by doing as he bade: "Go, and do thou 3
likewise."

We know Principle only through Science. The Principle of Christ is divine Love, resistless Life and Truth. 6
Then the Science of the Principle must be Christlike,
or Christian Science. More than regal is the majesty
of the meekness of the Christ-principle; and its might is 9
the ever-flowing tides of truth that sweep the universe,
create and govern it; and its radiant stores of knowledge are the mysteries of exhaustless being. Seek ye 12
these till you make their treasures yours.

When a young man vainly boasted, "I am wise, for I
have conversed with many wise men," Epictetus made 15
answer, "And I with many rich men, but I am not rich."
The richest blessings are obtained by labor. A vessel
full must be emptied before it can be refilled. Lawyers 18
may know too much of human law to have a clear perception of divine justice, and divines be too deeply read
in scholastic theology to appreciate or to demonstrate 21
Christian charity. Losing the comprehensive in the
technical, the Principle in its accessories, cause in effect,
and faith in sight, we lose the Science of Christianity, — 24
a predicament quite like that of the man who could not
see London for its houses.

Clouds parsimonious of rain, that swing in the sky with 27
dumb thunderbolts, are seen and forgotten in the same
hour; while those with a mighty rush, which waken the
stagnant waters and solicit every root and every leaf with 30
the treasures of rain, ask no praising. Remember, thou
canst be brought into no condition, be it ever so severe,

1 where Love has not been before thee and where its tender
lesson is not awaiting thee. Therefore despair not nor
3 murmur, for that which seeketh to save, to heal, and to
deliver, will guide thee, if thou seekest this guidance.

Pliny gives the following description of the character of
6 true greatness: "Doing what deserves to be written, and
writing what deserves to be read; and rendering the world
happier and better for having lived in it." Strive thou
9 for the joy and crown of such a pilgrimage — the service
of such a mission.

A heart touched and hallowed by one chord of Christian
12 Science, can accomplish the full scale; but this heart must
be honest and in earnest and never weary of struggling to
be perfect — to reflect the divine Life, Truth, and Love.
15 Stand by the limpid lake, sleeping amid willowy banks
dyed with emerald. See therein the mirrored sky and the
moon ablaze with her mild glory. This will stir your
18 heart. Then, in speechless prayer, ask God to enable you
to reflect God, to become His own image and likeness,
even the calm, clear, radiant reflection of Christ's glory,
21 healing the sick, bringing the sinner to repentance, and
raising the spiritually dead in trespasses and sins to life
in God. Jesus said: "If ye abide in me, and my words
24 abide in you, ye shall ask what ye will, and it shall be
done unto you."

Beloved in Christ, what our Master said unto his
27 disciples, when he sent them forth to heal the sick and
preach the gospel, I say unto you: "Be ye therefore wise
as serpents, and harmless as doves." Then, if the wis-
30 dom you manifest causes Christendom or the disclaimer
against God to call this "a subtle fraud," "let your peace
return to you."

I am patient with the newspaper wares and the 1
present schoolboy epithets and attacks of a portion of
Christendom: 3

(1) Because I sympathize with their ignorance of
Christian Science:

(2) Because I know that no Christian can or does 6
understand this Science and not love it:

(3) Because these attacks afford opportunity for explaining Christian Science: 9

(4) Because it is written: "The wrath of man shall
praise Thee: the remainder of wrath shalt Thou restrain."

Rest assured that the injustice done by press and pulpit 12
to this denomination of Christians will cease, when it no
longer blesses this denomination. "This I know; for God
is for me" (Psalms). And in the words of St. Paul, "If 15
God be for us, who can be against us?"

> "Pass ye the proud fane by,
> The vaulted aisles by flaunting folly trod, 18
> And 'neath the temple of uplifted sky —
> Go forth, and worship God."

MESSAGE, APRIL 19, 1899   21
SUBJECT: "NOT MATTER, BUT SPIRIT"

My Beloved Brethren: — We learn from the Scriptures that the Baalites or sun-worshippers failed to 24
look "through nature up to nature's God," thus missing
the discovery of all cause and effect. They were content
to look no higher than the symbol. This departure from 27
Spirit, this worshipping of matter in the name of nature,
was idolatry then and is idolatry now. When human
thought discerned its idolatrous tendencies, it took a step 30

1 higher; but it immediately turned to another form of
idolatry, and, worshipping person instead of Principle,
3 anchored its faith in troubled waters. At that period,
the touch of Jesus' robe and the handkerchief of St.
Paul were supposed to heal the sick, and our Master
6 declared, "Thy faith hath made thee whole." The
medicine-man, far lower in the scale of thought, said,
"My material tonic has strengthened you." By reposing
9 faith in man and in matter, the human race has not
yet reached the understanding of God, the conception
of Spirit and its all-power.

12   The restoration of pure Christianity rests solely on
spiritual understanding, spiritual worship, spiritual power.
Ask thyself, Do I enter by the door and worship only
15 Spirit and spiritually, or do I climb up some other way?
Do I understand God as Love, the divine Principle of all
that really is, the infinite good, than which there is none
18 else and in whom is all? Unless this be so, the blind is
leading the blind, and both will stumble into doubt and
darkness, even as the ages have shown. To-day, if ye
21 would hear His voice, listen to His Word and serve no
other gods. Then the divine Principle of good, that we
call God, will be found an ever-present help in all things,
24 and Christian Science will be understood. It will also be
seen that this God demands all our faith and love; that
matter, man, or woman can never heal you nor pardon a
27 single sin; while God, the divine Principle of nature and
man, when understood and demonstrated, is found to be
the remote, predisposing, and present cause of all that is
30 rightly done.

I have the sweet satisfaction of sending to you weekly
flowers that my skilful florist has coaxed into loveliness

despite our winter snows. Also I hear that the loving 1
hearts and hands of the Christian Scientists in Concord
send these floral offerings in my name to the sick and 3
suffering. Now, if these kind hearts will only do this in
Christ's name, the power of Truth and Love will fulfil the
law in righteousness. The healing and the gospel ministry 6
of my students in Concord have come to fulfil the whole
law. Unto "the angel of the church in Philadelphia,"
the church of brotherly love, "these things saith He 9
that is holy."

To-day our great Master would say to the aged gentleman healed from the day my flowers visited his bedside: 12
Thy faith hath healed thee. The flowers were imbued
and associated with no intrinsic healing qualities from my
poor personality. The scientific, healing faith is a saving 15
faith; it keeps steadfastly the great and first commandment, "Thou shalt have no other gods before me" — no
other than the spiritual help of divine Love. Faith in 18
aught else misguides the understanding, ignores the power
of God, and, in the words of St. Paul, appeals to an unknown power "whom therefore ye ignorantly worship." 21
This trembling and blind faith, in the past as in the present,
seeks personality for support, unmindful of the divine law
of Love, which can be understood, the Principle of which 24
works intelligently as the divine Mind, not as matter,
casting out evil and healing the sick.

Christian Science healing is "the Spirit and the bride," 27
— the Word and the wedding of this Word to all human
thought and action, — that says: Come, and I will give
thee rest, peace, health, holiness. The sweet flowers 30
should be to us His apostles, pointing away from matter
and man up to the one source, divine Life and Love, in

1 whom is all salvation from sin, disease, and death.   The
Science of all healing is based on Mind — the power of
3 Truth over error.   It is not the person who gives the
drug nor the drug itself that heals, but it is the law of
Life understood by the practitioner as transcending the
6 law of death.

I shall scarcely venture to send flowers to this little hall
if they can be made to infringe the divine law of Love
9 even in thought.   Send flowers and all things fair and
comforting to the dear sick, but remember it is not he
who gives the flowers that confers the blessing, but
12 "my Spirit, saith the Lord;" for "in Him was life," and
that life "was the light of men."

FIRST ANNUAL MEETING, JANUARY 11, 1900

15   *My Beloved Brethren:* — At this, your first annual
meeting, permit me to congratulate this little church in
our city, weaving the new-old vesture in which to appear
18 and to clothe the human race.   Carlyle wrote: "Wouldst
thou plant for eternity, then plant into the deep infinite
faculties of man."   "If the poor . . . toil that we have food,
21 must not the high and glorious toil for him in return, that
he have light, . . . freedom, immortality?"   I agree with
him; and in our era of the world I welcome the means and
24 methods, light and truth, emanating from the pulpit and
press.   Altogether it makes the church militant, embodied
in a visible communion, the foreshadowing of the church
27 triumphant.   Communing heart with heart, mind with
mind, soul with soul, wherein and whereby we are looking
heavenward, is not looking nor gravitating earthward,
30 take it in whatever sense you may.   Such communing

uplifts man's being; it makes healing the sick and reform- 1
ing the sinner a mutual aid society, which is effective here
and now.   3

May this dear little church, nestled so near my heart
and native hills, be steadfast in Christ, always abounding
in love and good works, having unfaltering faith in the 6
prophecies, promises, and proofs of Holy Writ. May this
church have one God, one Christ, and that one the God and
Saviour whom the Scriptures declare. May it catch the 9
early trumpet-call, take step with the twentieth century,
leave behind those things that are behind, lay down the
low laurels of vainglory, and, pressing forward in the on- 12
ward march of Truth, run in joy, health, holiness, the
race set before it, till, home at last, it finds the full fruition of its faith, hope, and prayer.   15

EASTER MESSAGE, 1902

Beloved Brethren: — May this glad Easter morn find
the members of this dear church having a pure peace, a 18
fresh joy, a clear vision of heaven here, — heaven within
us, — and an awakened sense of the risen Christ. May
long lines of light span the horizon of their hope and 21
brighten their faith with a dawn that knows no twilight
and no night. May those who discourse music to-day,
sing as the angels heaven's symphonies that come to 24
earth.

May the dear Sunday School children always be gathering Easter lilies of love with happy hearts and ripening 27
goodness. To-day may they find some sweet scents and
beautiful blossoms in their Leader's love, which she sends
to them this glad morn in the flowers and the cross from 30
Pleasant View, smiling upon them.

1   ANNUAL MEETING, JANUARY 6, 1905

Beloved Brethren: — You will accept my gratitude for
3 your dear letter, and allow me to reply in words of the
Scripture: "I know whom I have believed, and am persuaded that He is able" — "able to do exceeding abun-
6 dantly above all that we ask or think," "able to make
all grace abound toward you; that ye, always having all sufficiency in all things, may abound to every
9 good work," "able to keep that which I have committed unto Him against that day."

When Jesus directed his disciples to prepare for the
12 material passover, which spiritually speaking is the passover from sense to Soul, he bade them say to the goodman of the house: "The Master saith unto thee, Where
15 is the guestchamber, where I shall eat the passover with
my disciples? and he shall show you a large upper room
furnished: there make ready."
18   In obedience to this command may these communicants
come with the upper chambers of thought prepared for the
reception of Truth — with hope, faith, and love ready to
21 partake of the bread that cometh down from heaven, and
to "drink of his blood" — to receive into their affections
and lives the inspiration which giveth victory over sin,
24 disease, and death.

CHAPTER VI

First Church of Christ, Scientist, Concord, N. H.

[*Concord* (N. H.) *Monitor*] 1

MRS. EDDY'S GIFT TO THE CONCORD CHURCH

"BELOVED TEACHER AND LEADER:—The members 3 of the Concord church are filled with profound joy and deep gratitude that your generous gift of one hundred thousand dollars is to be used at once to build a 6 beautiful church edifice for your followers in the capital city of your native State. We rejoice that the prosperity of the Cause in your home city, where, without regard 9 to class or creed, you are so highly esteemed, makes necessary the commodious and beautiful church home you have so freely bestowed. We thank you for this 12 renewed evidence of your unselfish love."

The church will be built of the same beautiful Concord granite of which the National Library Building in Wash- 15 ington is constructed. This is in accord with the expressed wish of Mrs. Eddy, made known in her original deed of trust, first announced in the *Concord Monitor* 18 of March 19, 1898. In response to an inquiry from the editor of that paper, Mrs. Eddy made the following statement: — 21

On January 31, 1898, I gave a deed of trust to three individuals which conveyed to them the sum of one

157

1 hundred thousand dollars to be appropriated in building a granite church edifice for First Church of Christ,
3 Scientist, in this city.

Very truly,

MARY BAKER EDDY

6   CORNER-STONE LAID AT CONCORD

Beloved Brethren: — This day drops down upon the
glories of summer; it is a glad day, in attune with faith's
9 fond trust. We live in an age of Love's divine adven-
ture to be All-in-all. This day is the natal hour of my
lone earth life; and for all mankind to-day hath its gloom
12 and glory: it endureth all things; it points to the new
birth, heaven here, the struggle over; it profits by the
past and joys in the present — to-day lends a new-born
15 beauty to holiness, patience, charity, love.

Having all faith in Christian Science, we must have
faith in whatever manifests love for God and man. The
18 burden of proof that Christian Science is Science rests
on Christian Scientists. The letter without the spirit
is dead: it is the Spirit that heals the sick and the
21 sinner — that makes the heart tender, faithful, true.
Most men and women talk well, and some practise what
they say.

24   God has blessed and will bless this dear band of brethren.
He has laid the chief corner-stone of the temple which
to-day you commemorate, to-morrow complete, and there-
27 after dedicate to Truth and Love. O may your temple
and all who worship therein stand through all time for
God and humanity!

30   MARY BAKER EDDY

MESSAGE ON THE OCCASION OF THE DEDICATION OF
MRS. EDDY'S GIFT, JULY 17, 1904

Beloved Brethren: — Never more sweet than to-day, seem to me, and must seem to thee, those words of our loved Lord, "Lo, I am with you alway, even unto the end." Thus may it ever be that Christ rejoiceth and comforteth us. Sitting at his feet, I send to you the throbbing of every pulse of my desire for the ripening and rich fruit of this branch of his vine, and I thank God who hath sent forth His word to heal and to save.

At this period, the greatest man or woman on earth stands at the vestibule of Christian Science, struggling to enter into the perfect love of God and man. The infinite will not be buried in the finite; the true thought escapes from the inward to the outward, and this is the only right activity, that whereby we reach our higher nature. Material theories tend to check spiritual attraction — the tendency towards God, the infinite and eternal — by an opposite attraction towards the temporary and finite. Truth, life, and love are the only legitimate and eternal demands upon man; they are spiritual laws enforcing obedience and punishing disobedience.

Even Epictetus, a heathen philosopher who held that Zeus, the master of the gods, could not control human will, writes, "What is the essence of God? Mind." The general thought chiefly regards material things, and keeps

1 Mind much out of sight. The Christian, however, strives
for the spiritual; he abides in a right purpose, as in laws
3 which it were impious to transgress, and follows Truth
fearlessly. The heart that beats mostly for self is seldom
alight with love. To live so as to keep human conscious-
6 ness in constant relation with the divine, the spiritual, and
the eternal, is to individualize infinite power; and this is
Christian Science.

9   It is of less importance that we receive from mankind justice, than that we deserve it. Most of us
willingly accept dead truisms which can be buried
12 at will; but a live truth, even though it be a sapling
within rich soil and with blossoms on its branches,
frightens people. The trenchant truth that cuts its
15 way through iron and sod, most men avoid until
compelled to glance at it. Then they open their
hearts to it for actual being, health, holiness, and im-
18 mortality.

I am asked, "Is there a hell?" Yes, there is a hell for
all who persist in breaking the Golden Rule or in dis-
21 obeying the commandments of God. Physical science
has sometimes argued that the internal fires of our earth
will eventually consume this planet. Christian Science
24 shows that hidden unpunished sin is this internal fire, —
even the fire of a guilty conscience, waking to a true sense
of itself, and burning in torture until the sinner is con-
27 sumed, — his sins destroyed. This may take millions of
cycles, but of the time no man knoweth. The advanced
psychist knows that this hell is mental, not material, and
30 that the Christian has no part in it. Only the makers of
hell burn in their fire.

Concealed crimes, the wrongs done to others, are mill-

stones hung around the necks of the wicked. Christ Jesus 1
paid our debt and set us free by enabling us to pay it;
for which we are still his debtors, washing the Way-shower's 3
feet with tears of joy.

The intentional destroyer of others would destroy himself eternally, were it not that his suffering reforms him, 6
thus balancing his account with divine Love, which never
remits the sentence necessary to reclaim the sinner.
Hence these words of Christ Jesus: "Depart from me, all 9
ye workers of iniquity. There shall be weeping and
gnashing of teeth, when ye shall see Abraham, and
Isaac, and Jacob, and all the prophets, in the kingdom of 12
God, and you yourselves thrust out." (Luke 13 : 27, 28.)
He who gains self-knowledge, self-control, and the kingdom of heaven within himself, within his own conscious- 15
ness, is saved through Christ, Truth. Mortals must
drink sufficiently of the cup of their Lord and Master
to unself mortality and to destroy its erroneous claims. 18
Therefore, said Jesus, "Ye shall drink indeed of my
cup, and be baptized with the baptism that I am
baptized with." 21

We cannot boast ourselves of to-morrow; sufficient unto
each day is the duty thereof. Lest human reason becloud
spiritual understanding, say not in thy heart: Sickness is 24
possible because one's thought and conduct do not afford
a sufficient defence against it. Trust in God, and "He
shall direct thy paths." When evil was avenging itself on 27
its destroyer, his preeminent goodness, the Godlike man
said, "My burden is light." Only he who learns through
meekness and love the falsity of supposititious life and 30
intelligence in matter, can triumph over their ultimatum,
sin, suffering, and death.

1   God's mercy for mortal ignorance and need is assured;
then who shall question our want of more faith in His
3 "very present help in trouble"?   Jesus said: "Suffer
it to be so now: for thus it becometh us to fulfil all
righteousness."

6   Strength is in man, not in muscles; unity and power are
not in atom or in dust.   A small group of wise thinkers
is better than a wilderness of dullards and stronger than
9 the might of empires.   Unity is spiritual cooperation,
heart to heart, the bond of blessedness such as my beloved
Christian Scientists all over the field, and the dear Sun-
12 day School children, have demonstrated in gifts to me
of about eighty thousand dollars, to be applied to building, embellishing, and furnishing our church edifice in
15 Concord, N. H.

We read in Holy Writ: "This man began to build, and
was not able to finish."   This was spoken derisively.
18 But the love that rebukes praises also, and methinks the
same wisdom which spake thus in olden time would say
to the builder of the Christian Scientists' church edifice
21 in Concord: "Well done, good and faithful."   Our proper
reason for church edifices is, that in them Christians may
worship God, — not that Christians may worship church
24 edifices!

May the loving Shepherd of this feeble flock lead it
gently into "green pastures . . . beside the still waters."
27 May He increase its members, and may their faith never
falter — their faith in and their understanding of divine
Love.   This church, born in my nativity, may it build
30 upon the rock of ages against which the waves and winds
beat in vain.   May the towering top of its goodly temple
— burdened with beauty, pointing to the heavens, bursting

into the rapture of song — long call the worshipper to 1
seek the haven of hope, the heaven of Soul, the sweet sense
of angelic song chiming chaste challenge to praise him who 3
won the way and taught mankind to win through meekness
to might, goodness to grandeur, — from cross to crown,
from sense to Soul, from gleam to glory, from matter to 6
Spirit.

ANNOUNCEMENT

Not having the time to receive all the beloved ones who 9
have so kindly come to the dedication of this church, I
must not allow myself the pleasure of receiving any of
them. I always try to be just, if not generous; and I 12
cannot show my love for them in social ways without
neglecting the sacred demands on my time and attention
for labors which I think do them more good.   15

A KINDLY GREETING

Dear Editor: — When I removed from Boston in 1889
and came to Concord, N. H., it was that I might find 18
retirement from many years of incessant labor for the
Cause of Christian Science, and the opportunity in Concord's quiet to revise our textbook, "Science and Health 21
with Key to the Scriptures." Here let me add that,
together with the retirement I so much coveted, I have
also received from the leading people of this pleasant city 24
all and more than I anticipated. I love its people —
love their scholarship, friendship, and granite character. I respect their religious beliefs, and thank their 27
ancestors for helping to form mine. The movement of
establishing in this city a church of our faith was far from

1 my purpose, when I came here, knowing that such an
effort would involve a lessening of the retirement I so
3 much desired. But the demand increased, and I consented, hoping thereby to give to many in this city a
church home.

6   ACKNOWLEDGMENT OF GIFTS

To the Chicago Churches

My Beloved Brethren: — I have yearned to express my
9 thanks for your munificent gift to First Church of Christ,
Scientist, in Concord, of ten thousand dollars. What is
gratitude but a powerful *camera obscura,* a thing focus-
12 ing light where love, memory, and all within the human
heart is present to manifest light.

Is it not a joy to compare the beginning of Christian
15 Science in Chicago with its present prosperity? Now
[1904] six dear churches are there, the members of which
not only possess a sound faith, but that faith also possesses
18 them. A great sanity, a mighty something buried in the
depths of the unseen, has wrought a resurrection among
you, and has leaped into living love. What is this
21 something, this phœnix fire, this pillar by day, kindling,
guiding, and guarding your way? It is *unity,* the bond
of perfectness, the thousandfold expansion that will
24 engirdle the world, — unity, which unfolds the thought
most within us into the greater and better, the sum of
all reality and good.
27   This unity is reserved wisdom and strength. It builds
upon the rock, against which envy, enmity, or malice
beat in vain. Man lives, moves, and has his being in God,
30 Love. Then man must live, he cannot die; and Love

must necessarily promote and pervade all his success. 1
Of two things fate cannot rob us; namely, of choos-
ing the best, and of helping others thus to choose. 3
But in doing this the Master became the servant. The
grand must stoop to the menial. There is scarcely an
indignity which I have not endured for the cause of 6
Christ, Truth, and I returned blessing for cursing. The
best help the worst; the righteous suffer for the unright-
eous; and by this spirit man lives and thrives, and by 9
it God governs.

To First Church of Christ, Scientist, New York

Beloved Brethren: — I beg to thank the dear brethren of 12
this church for the sum of ten thousand dollars presented
to me for First Church of Christ, Scientist, in Concord,
N. H. Goodness never fails to receive its reward, for 15
goodness makes life a blessing. As an active portion of
one stupendous whole, goodness identifies man with
universal good. Thus may each member of this church 18
rise above the oft-repeated inquiry, What am I? to the
scientific response: I am able to impart truth, health, and
happiness, and this is my rock of salvation and my reason 21
for existing.

Human reason becomes tired and calls for rest. It has
a relapse into the common hope. Goodness and benevo- 24
lence never tire. They maintain themselves and others
and never stop from exhaustion. He who is afraid of
being too generous has lost the power of being magnani- 27
mous. The best man or woman is the most unselfed.
God grant that this church is rapidly nearing the maximum of might, — the means that build to the heavens, 30
— that it has indeed found and felt the infinite source

1 where is *all,* and from which it can help its neighbor.
Then efforts to be great will never end in anarchy but
3 will continue with divine approbation. It is insincerity
and a half-persuaded faith that fail to succeed and fall
to the earth.

6   Religions may waste away, but the fittest survives;
and so long as we have the right ideal, life is worth living
and God takes care of our life.

9   *To The Mother Church*

My Beloved Brethren: — Your munificent gift of ten
thousand dollars, with which to furnish First Church of
12 Christ, Scientist, of Concord, N. H., with an organ, is
positive proof of your remembrance and love. Days of
shade and shine may come and go, but we will live on and
15 never drift apart. Life's ills are its chief recompense;
they develop hidden strength. Had I never suffered for
The Mother Church, neither she nor I would be practising
18 the virtues that lie concealed in the smooth seasons and
calms of human existence. When we are willing to help
and to be helped, divine aid is near. If all our years were
21 holidays, sport would be more irksome than work. So,
my dear ones, let us together sing the old-new song of
salvation, and let our measure of time and joy be spiritual,
24 not material.

To First Church of Christ, Scientist,
New London, Conn.

27   *Beloved Brethren:* — I am for the first time informed of
your gift to me of a beautiful cabinet, costing one hundred
and seventy-five dollars, for my books, placed in my room
30 at First Church of Christ, Scientist, Concord, N. H.

Accept my deep thanks therefor, and especially for the 1
self-sacrifice it may have cost the dear donors.

The mysticism of good is unknown to the flesh, for 3
goodness is "the fruit of the Spirit." The suppositional
world within us separates us from the spiritual world,
which is apart from matter, and unites us to one another. 6
Spirit teaches us to resign what we are not and to understand what we are in the unity of Spirit — in that
Love which is faithful, an ever-present help in trouble, 9
which never deserts us.

I pray that heaven's messages of "on earth peace, good
will toward men," may fill your hearts and leave their 12
loving benedictions upon your lives.

THANKSGIVING DAY, 1904

Beloved Students: — May this, your first Thanksgiv- 15
ing Day, according to time-tables, in our new church
edifice, be one acceptable in His sight, and full of love,
peace, and good will for yourselves, your flock, and the 18
race. Give to all the dear ones my love, and my
prayer for their health, happiness, and holiness this
and every day. 21

RELIGIOUS FREEDOM

Beloved Brethren: — Allow me to send forth a pæan
of praise for the noble disposal of the legislative question 24
as to the infringement of rights and privileges guaran-
teed to you by the laws of my native State. The constituted religious rights in New Hampshire will, I trust, 27
never be marred by the illegitimate claims of envy,
jealousy, or persecution.

In our country the day of heathenism, illiberal views, 30

1 or of an uncultivated understanding has passed. Freedom to worship God according to the dictates of en-
3 lightened conscience, and practical religion in agreement
with the demand of our common Christ, the Holy One
of Israel, are forever the privileges of the people of my
6 dear old New Hampshire.

Lovingly yours,
MARY BAKER EDDY

9   BOX G, BROOKLINE, MASS.,
          April 12, 1909

CHAPTER VII

Pleasant View and Concord, N. H.

INVITATION TO CONCORD, JULY 4, 1897 ₁

M Y BELOVED CHURCH:— I invite you, one and all, to Pleasant View, Concord, N. H., on July 5, at 3 12.30 P.M., if you would enjoy so long a trip for so small a purpose as simply seeing Mother.

My precious Busy Bees, under twelve years of age, 6 are requested to visit me at a later date, which I hope soon to name to them.

With love, Mother,   9
MARY BAKER EDDY

PLEASANT VIEW, CONCORD, N. H.,
    June 30, 1897   12

[*New York Journal*]

VISIT TO CONCORD, 1901

Please say through the *New York Journal,* to the 15 Christian Scientists of New York City and of the world at large, that I was happy to receive at Concord, N. H., the call of about three thousand believers of my faith, 18 and that I was rejoiced at the appropriate beauty of time and place which greeted them.

1   I am especially desirous that it should be understood that this was no festal occasion, no formal church cere-
3 monial, but simply my acquiescence in the request of my church members that they might see the Leader of Christian Science.

6   The brevity of my remarks was due to a desire on my part that the important sentiments uttered in my annual Message to the church last Sunday should not be confused
9 with other issues, but should be emphasized in the minds of all present here in Concord.

ADDRESS AT PLEASANT VIEW, JUNE, 1903

12   *Beloved Brethren:* — Welcome home! To your home in my heart! Welcome to Pleasant View, but not to varying views. I would present a gift to you
15 to-day, only that this gift is already yours. God hath given it to all mankind. It is His coin, His currency; it has His image and superscription. This gift is a
18 passage of Scripture; it is my sacred motto, and it reads thus: —

"Trust in the Lord, and do good; so shalt thou dwell
21 in the land, and verily thou shalt be fed. Delight thyself also in the Lord; and He shall give thee the desires of thine heart. Commit thy way unto the Lord; trust also in
24 Him; and He shall bring it to pass. And He shall bring forth thy righteousness as the light, and thy judgment as the noonday."

27   Beloved, some of you have come long distances to kneel with us in sacred silence in blest communion — unity of faith, understanding, prayer, and praise — and to return
30 in joy, bearing your sheaves with you. In parting I

repeat to these dear members of my church: *Trust in* 1
Truth, and have no other trusts.

To-day is fulfilled the prophecy of Isaiah: "And the 3
ransomed of the Lord shall return, and come to Zion
with songs and everlasting joy upon their heads: they
shall obtain joy and gladness, and sorrow and sigh- 6
ing shall flee away."

VISIT TO CONCORD, 1904

Beloved Students: — The new Concord church is so 9
nearly completed that I think you would enjoy seeing it.
Therefore I hereby invite all my church communicants
who attend this communion, to come to Concord, and 12
view this beautiful structure, at two o'clock in the afternoon, Monday, June 13, 1904.

Lovingly yours,   15
MARY BAKER EDDY

PLEASANT VIEW, CONCORD, N. H.,
    June 11, 1904   18

The Day in Concord

While on her regular afternoon drive Mrs. Eddy responded graciously to the silent greetings of the people 21
who were assembled on the lawn of the Unitarian church
and of the high school. Her carriage came to a standstill on North State Street, and she was greeted in behalf 24
of the church by the President, Mr. E. P. Bates, to
whom she presented as a love-token for the church a
handsome rosewood casket beautifully bound with bur- 27
nished brass.

The casket contained a gavel for the use of the

1 President of The Mother Church. The wood of the head of the gavel was taken from the old Yale College Athe-3 næum, the first chapel of the college. It was built in 1761, and razed in 1893 to make room for Vanderbilt Hall. The wood in the handle was grown on the farm 6 of Mark Baker, father of the Rev. Mary Baker Eddy, at Bow, N. H.

In presenting this gavel to President Bates, Mrs. Eddy 9 spoke as follows to the members of her church, The First Church of Christ, Scientist, Boston, Mass.: —

"My Beloved Brethren: — Permit me to present to you 12 a little gift that has no intrinsic value save that which it represents — namely, a material symbol of my spiritual call to this my beloved church of over thirty thousand 15 members; and this is that call: In the words of our great Master, 'Go ye into all the world,' 'heal the sick,' cast out evil, disease, and death; 'Freely ye have received, 18 freely give.' You will please accept my thanks for your kind, expert call on me."

In reply Mr. Bates said, —

21 "I accept this gift in behalf of the church, and for myself and my successors in office."

The box containing the gavel was opened the following 24 day in Boston at the annual meeting of The Mother Church of Christ, Scientist, and the enclosed note from Mrs. Eddy was read: —

27 *"My Beloved Brethren:* — You will please accept from me the accompanying gift as a simple token of love."

CARD OF THANKS   1

The following letter appeared in the Concord (N. H.)
newspapers after the visit of the Christian Scientists in 3
1904: —

Dear Mr. Editor: — Allow me through your paper to
thank the citizens of Concord for the generous hospi- 6
tality extended yesterday to the members of my church,
The Mother Church of Christ, Scientist, in Boston.

After the Christian Science periodicals had given notice 9
that no preparations would be made for a large gathering
at this annual meeting of The Mother Church, I scarcely
supposed that a note, sent at the last moment, would bring 12
thousands here yesterday; but as many gifts had come
from Christian Scientists everywhere to help furnish and
beautify our new church building in Concord, it came to 15
me: Why not invite those who attend the communion
in Boston to take a peep at this church edifice on the day
when there are no formal exercises at the denominational 18
headquarters? The number of visitors, about four thousand, exceeded my expectation, and my heart welcomed
each and all. It was a glad day for me — sweet to observe 21
with what unanimity my fellow-citizens vied with each
other to make the Christian Scientists' short stay so
pleasant.   24

Special thanks are due and are hereby tendered to his
Honor, the Mayor, for arranging the details and allowing
the visitors to assemble on the green surrounding the high 27
school; also to Mr. George D. Waldron, chairman of the
prudential committee of the Unitarian church, and to his
colaborers on said committee and to the church itself, 30
for their kindly foresight in granting permission, not only

1 to use the beautiful lawn surrounding their church building, but also for throwing open their doors for the com-
3 fort and convenience of the Christian Scientists during
the day. The wide-spreading elms and soft greensward
proved an ideal meeting place. I greatly appreciate the
6 courtesy extended to my friends by the Wonolancet Club
in again opening their spacious club-house to them on this
occasion; and the courtesy of the efficient city marshal
9 and his staff of police extended to me throughout. And
last but not least, I thank the distinguished editors in my
home city for their reports of the happy occasion.

12   TO FIRST CONGREGATIONAL CHURCH

To the Rev. Franklin D. Ayer, D.D., Pastor Emeritus; the Rev.
George H. Reed, Pastor of the First Congregational Church,
15   Concord, N. H., Edward A. Moulton, John C. Thorne, William P.
Ballard, Henry K. Morrison, Deacons.

Beloved Brethren: — I have the pleasure of thanking
18 you for your kind invitation to attend the one hundred and seventy-fifth anniversary of our time-honored
First Congregational Church in Concord, N. H., where
21 my parents first offered me to Christ in infant baptism.
For nearly forty years and until I had a church of my
own, I was a member of the Congregational Church in
24 Tilton, N. H.

To-day my soul can only sing and soar. An increasing sense of God's love, omnipresence, and omnipotence
27 enfolds me. Each day I know Him nearer, love Him
more, and humbly pray to serve Him better. Thus
seeking and finding (though feebly), finally may we not
30 together rejoice in the church triumphant?

I would love to be with you at this deeply interesting 1
anniversary, but my little church in Boston, Mass., of
thirty-six thousand communicants, together with the 3
organizations connected therewith, requires my constant
attention and time, with the exception of a daily drive.

Please accept the enclosed check for five hundred 6
dollars, to aid in repairing your church building.

PLEASANT VIEW, CONCORD, N. H.,
November 14, 1905   9

GREETINGS

Allow me to say to the good folk of Concord that the
growth and prosperity of our city cheer me. Its dear 12
churches, reliable editors, intelligent medical faculty,
up-to-date academies, humane institutions, provisions for
the army, and well-conducted jail and state prison, — if, 15
indeed, such must remain with us a little longer, — speak
for themselves. Our picturesque city, however, greatly
needs improved streets. May I ask in behalf of the public 18
this favor of our city government; namely, to macadamize a portion of Warren Street and to macadamize North
State Street throughout?   21

Sweeter than the balm of Gilead, richer than the
diamonds of Golconda, dear as the friendship of those
we love, are justice, fraternity, and Christian charity. 24
The song of my soul must remain so long as I remain.
Let brotherly love continue.

I am sure that the counterfeit letters in circulation, 27
purporting to have my signature, must fail to influence the
minds of this dear people to conclusions the very opposite
of my real sentiments.   30

---

1 TO FIRST CHURCH OF CHRIST, SCIENTIST,
WILMINGTON, N. C.

3 IN APPRECIATION OF A GIFT OF FIFTY DOLLARS IN GOLD TOWARDS
THE CONCORD (N. H.) STREET FUND

My Beloved Brethren: — Long ago you of the dear
6 South paved the way to my forever gratitude, and now
illustrate the past by your present love. God grant
that such great goodness, pointing the path to heaven
9 within you, hallow your Palmetto home with palms of
victory and songs of glory.

CHAPTER VIII

Dedicatory Messages to Branch Churches

FIRST CHURCH OF CHRIST, SCIENTIST, CHICAGO, ILL.

1

BELOVED BRETHREN: — Most happily would I com- 3
ply with your cordial invitation and be with you on
so interesting an occasion as the dedication of First
Church of Christ, Scientist, in Chicago. But daily duties 6
require attention elsewhere, and I am glad to say that
there seems to be no special need of my personal presence at your religious jubilee. I am quite able to take 9
the trip to your city, and if wisdom lengthens my sum
of years to fourscore (already imputed to me), I shall
then be even younger and nearer the eternal meridian 12
than now, for the true knowledge and proof of life is in
putting off the limitations and putting on the possibilities
and permanence of Life. 15

In your renowned city, the genesis of Christian Science
was allied to that olden axiom: "The blood of the martyrs
is the seed of the Church;" but succeeding years show in 18
livid lines that the great Shepherd has nurtured and
nourished this church as a fatling of the flock. To-day
the glory of His presence rests upon it, the joy of many 21
generations awaits it, and this prophecy of Isaiah is
fulfilled among you: "I will direct their work in truth,
and I will make an everlasting covenant with them." 24

177

1   Your Bible and your textbook, pastor and ethical
tenets, do not mislead the seeker after Truth.   These
3 unpretentious preachers cloud not the spiritual meaning
of Holy Writ by material interpretations, nor lose the
invincible process and purity of Christianity whereby
6 the sick are healed and sinners saved.   The Science of
Christianity is not generally understood, but it hastens
hourly to this end.   This Science is the essence of religion,
9 distilled in the laboratory of infinite Love and prepared
for all peoples.   And because Science is naturally divine,
is this natural Science less profitable or scientific than
12 "counting the legs of insects"?   The Scripture declares
that God is All.   Then all is Spirit and spiritual.   The
true sense of life is lost to those who regard being
15 as material.   The Scripture pronounces all that God
made "good;"   therefore if evil exists, it exists without
God.   But this is impossible in reality, for He made
18 all "that was made."   Hence the inevitable revelation
of Christian Science — that evil is unreal; and this is
the best of it.
21   On April 15, 1891, the Christian Science textbook lay
on a table in a burning building.   A Christian Scientist
entered the house through a window and snatched this
24 book from the flames.   Instantly the table sank a charred
mass.   The covers of the book were burned up, but not
one word in the book was effaced.   If the world were in
27 ashes, the contents of "Science and Health with Key to
the Scriptures" would remain immortal.
It is said that the nearest approach to the sayings of
30 the great Master is the *Logia* of Papias, written in A.D.
145, and that all else reported as his sayings are translations.   The ancient *Logia,* or imputed sayings of Jesus

by Papias, are undoubtedly the beginning of the gospel 1
writings. The synoptic Scriptures, as set forth in the
first and second chapters of Genesis, were in two dis- 3
tinct manuscripts. The first gave an account of the
spiritual creation, and the second was an opposite story,
or allegory, of a material universe and man made of 6
dust. In this allegorical document the power and prerogative of Spirit are submerged in matter. In other
words, soul enters non-intelligent dust and man becomes 9
both good and evil, both mind and matter, mortal and
immortal, — all of which divine Science shows to be an
impossibility. 12

The Old and the New Testaments contain self-evident
truths that cannot be lost, but being translations, the
Scriptures are criticized. Some dangerous skepticism ex- 15
ists as to the verification of our Master's sayings. But
Christians and Christian Scientists know that if the Old
Testament and gospel narratives had never been written, 18
the nature of Christianity, as depicted in the life of our
Lord, and the truth in the Scriptures, are sufficient to authenticate Christ's Christianity as the perfect ideal. The 21
character of the Nazarene Prophet illustrates the Principle and practice of a true divinity and humanity. The
different renderings or translations of Scripture in no 24
wise affect Christian Science. Christianity and Science,
being contingent on nothing written and based on the
divine Principle of being, must be, are, irrefutable and 27
eternal.

We are indeed privileged in having the untranslated
revelations of Christian Science. They afford such expo- 30
sitions of the therapeutics, ethics, and Christianity of
Christ as make even God demonstrable, the divine Love

1 practical, and so furnish rules whereby man can prove
God's love, healing the sick and the sinner.

3 Whosoever understands Christian Science knows beyond
a doubt that its life-giving truths were preached and
practised in the first century by him who proved their
6 practicality, who uttered Christ's Sermon on the Mount,
who taught his disciples the healing Christianity which
applies to all ages, and who dated time. A spiritual
9 understanding of the Scriptures restores their original tongue in the language of Spirit, that primordial
standard of Truth.

12 Christian Science contains no element whatever of hypnotism or animal magnetism. It appeals alone to God, to
the divine Principle, or Life, Truth, and Love, to whom
15 all things are possible; and this Principle heals sin, sickness, disease, and death. Christian Science meets error
with Truth, death with Life, hate with Love, and thus,
18 and only thus, does it overcome evil and heal disease.
The obstinate sinner, however, refuses to see this grand
verity or to acknowledge it, for he knows not that in justice,
21 as well as in mercy, God is Love.

In our struggles with sin and sinners, when we drop
compliance with their desires, insist on what we know is
24 right, and act accordingly, the disguised or the self-
satisfied mind, not ready to be uplifted, rebels, miscon-
strues our best motives, and calls them unkind. But this
27 is the cross. Take it up, — it wins the crown; and in
the spirit of our great Exemplar pray: "Father, forgive
them; for they know not what they do."

30 No warfare exists between divine theology and Christian
Science, for the latter solves the whence and why of the
cosmos and defines noumenon and phenomena spiritually,

not materially. The specific quest of Christian Science is 1
to settle all points beyond cavil, on the Biblical basis that
God is All-in-all; whereas philosophy and so-called natural 3
science, dealing with human hypotheses, or material cause
and effect, are aided only at long intervals with elementary
truths, and ultimate in unsolved problems and outgrown, 6
proofless positions.

Progress is spiritual. Progress is the maturing conception of divine Love; it demonstrates the scientific, sinless 9
life of man and mortal's painless departure from matter
to Spirit, not through death, but through the true idea of
Life, — and Life not in matter but in Mind. 12

The Puritans possessed the motive of true religion,
which, demonstrated on the Golden Rule, would have
solved ere this the problem of religious liberty and human 15
rights. It is "a consummation devoutly to be wished"
that all nations shall speedily learn and practise the
intermediate line of justice between the classes and masses 18
of mankind, and thus exemplify in all things the universal
equity of Christianity.

Thirty years ago (1866) Christian Science was discovered 21
in America. Within those years it is estimated that
Chicago has gained from a population of 238,000 to the
number of 1,650,000 inhabitants. 24

The statistics of mortality show that thirty years ago
the death-rate was at its maximum. Since that time it
has steadily decreased. It is authentically said that one 27
expositor of Daniel's dates fixed the year 1866 or 1867 for
the return of Christ — the return of the spiritual idea to
the material earth or antipode of heaven. It is a marked 30
coincidence that those dates were the first two years of
my discovery of Christian Science.

1   Thirty years ago Chicago had few Congregational
church.   To-day it is said to have a majority of these
3 churches over any other city in the United States. Thirty
years ago at my request I received from the Congregational Church a letter of dismissal and recommendation
6 to evangelical churches — thenceforth to exemplify my
early love for this church and a membership of thirty
years by establishing a new-old church, the foundations
9 of which are the same, even Christ, Truth, as the chief
corner-stone.

In 1884, I taught a class in Christian Science and
12 formed a Christian Scientist Association in Chicago.
From this small sowing of the seed of Truth, which, when
sown, seemed the least among seeds, sprang immortal
15 fruits through God's blessing and the faithful labor of
loyal students, — the healing of the sick, the reforming
of the sinner, and First Church of Christ, Scientist, with
18 its large membership and majestic cathedral.

Humbly, gratefully, trustingly, I dedicate this beautiful house of worship to the God of Israel, the divine
21 Love that reigns above the shadow, that launched the
earth in its orbit, that created and governs the universe —
guarding, guiding, giving grace, health, and immortality
24 to man.

May the wanderer in the wilderness of mortal beliefs
and fears turn hither with satisfied hope. May the birds
27 of passage rest their weary wings amid the fair foliage of
this vine of His husbanding, find shelter from the storm
and a covert from the tempest. May this beloved
30 church adhere to its tenets, abound in the righteousness
of Love, honor the name of Christian Science, prove the
practicality of perfection, and press on to the infinite

uses of Christ's creed, namely, — "Thou shalt love the 1
Lord thy God with all thy heart, and with all thy soul,
and with all thy strength, and with all thy mind; and 3
thy neighbor as thyself." Thus may First Church of
Christ, Scientist, in this great city of Chicago, verify what
John Robinson wrote in 1620 to our Pilgrim Fathers: 6
"When Christ reigns, and not till then, will the world
have rest."

FIRST CHURCH OF CHRIST, SCIENTIST, 9
LONDON, ENGLAND

Beloved Brethren across the Sea: — To-day a nation is
born. Spiritual apprehension unfolds, transfigures, heals. 12
With you be there no more sea, no ebbing faith, no night.
Love be thy light upon the mountain of Israel. God
will multiply thee. 15

FIRST CHURCH OF CHRIST, SCIENTIST,
BROOKLYN, N. Y.

Beloved Brethren: — I rejoice with you; the day has 18
come when the forest becomes a fruitful field, and the deaf
hear the words of the Book, and the eyes of the blind see
out of obscurity. 21

FIRST CHURCH OF CHRIST, SCIENTIST,
DETROIT, MICH.

Beloved Students and Church: — Thanks for invitation 24
to your dedication. Not afar off I am blending with
thine my prayer and rejoicing. God is with thee. "Arise,
shine; for thy light is come, and the glory of the Lord is 27
risen upon thee."

1　　FIRST CHURCH OF CHRIST, SCIENTIST,
TORONTO, CANADA

3　*My Beloved Brethren:* — Have just received your despatch.　Since the world was, men have not heard with the ear, neither hath the eye seen, what God hath prepared 6 for them that wait upon Him and work righteousness.

WHITE MOUNTAIN CHURCH

My Beloved Brethren: — To-day I am privileged to 9 congratulate the Christian Scientists of my native State upon having built First Church of Christ, Scientist, at the White Mountains.　Your kind card, inviting me to 12 be present at its dedication, came when I was so occupied that I omitted to wire an acknowledgment thereof and to return my cordial thanks at an earlier date.　The 15 beautiful birch bark on which it was written pleased me; it was so characteristic of our Granite State, and I treasure it next to your compliments.　That rustic scroll 18 brought back to me the odor of my childhood, a love which stays the shadows of years.　God grant that this little church shall prove a historic gem on the glowing 21 records of Christianity, and lay upon its altars a sacrifice and service acceptable in God's sight.

　　Your rural chapel is a social success quite sacred in its 24 results.　The prosperity of Zion is very precious in the sight of divine Love, holding unwearied watch over a world.　Isaiah said: "How beautiful upon the mountains 27 are the feet of him that bringeth good tidings, . . . that saith unto Zion, Thy God reigneth!"　Surely, the Word that is God must at some time find utterance and accept-

ance throughout the earth, for he that soweth shall reap. 1
To such as have waited patiently for the appearing of
Truth, the day dawns and the harvest bells are ringing. 3

> "Let us, then, be up and doing,
> With a heart for any fate;
> Still achieving, still pursuing, 6
> Learn to labor and to wait."

The peace of Love is published, and the sword of the
Spirit is drawn; nor will it be sheathed till Truth shall 9
reign triumphant over all the earth. Truth, Life, and
Love are formidable, wherever thought, felt, spoken, or
written, — in the pulpit, in the court-room, by the way- 12
side, or in our homes. They are the victors never to be
vanquished. Love is the generic term for God. Love
formed this trinity, Truth, Life, Love, the trinity no man 15
can sunder. Life is the spontaneity of Love, inseparable
from Love, and Life is the "Lamb slain from the foundation of the world," — even that which "was dead, and 18
is alive again; and was lost, and is found;" for Life is
Christ, and Christ, as aforetime, heals the sick, saves
sinners, and destroys the last enemy, death. 21

In 1888 I visited these mountains and spoke to an
attentive audience collected in the hall at the Fabyan
House. Then and there I foresaw this hour, and spoke 24
of the little church to be in the midst of the mountains,
closing my remarks with the words of Mrs. Hemans: —

> For the strength of the hills, we bless Thee, 27
> Our God, our fathers' God!

The sons and daughters of the Granite State are rich in
signs and symbols, sermons in stones, refuge in mountains, 30

1 and good universal. The rocks, rills, mountains, meadows, fountains, and forests of our native State should be
3 prophetic of the finger divine that writes in living characters their lessons on our lives. May God's little ones cluster around this rock-ribbed church like tender nestlings
6 in the crannies of the rocks, and preen their thoughts for upward flight.

Though neither dome nor turret tells the tale of your
9 little church, its song and sermon will touch the heart, point the path above the valley, up the mountain, and on to the celestial hills, echoing the Word welling up from
12 the infinite and swelling the loud anthem of one Father-Mother God, o'er all victorious! Rest assured that He in whom dwelleth all life, health, and holiness, will supply
15 all your needs according to His riches in glory.

FIRST CHURCH OF CHRIST, SCIENTIST, DULUTH, MINN.

18 *First Church of Christ, Scientist, Duluth, Minn.:* — May our God make this church the fold of flocks, and may those that plant the vineyard eat the fruit thereof. Here
21 let His promise be verified: "Before they call, I will answer; and while they are yet speaking, I will hear."

FIRST CHURCH OF CHRIST, SCIENTIST,
24   SALT LAKE CITY, UTAH

Beloved Brethren: — Accept my thanks for your cordial card inviting me to be with you on the day of your church
27 dedication. It gives me great pleasure to know that you have erected a Church of Christ, Scientist, in your

city. Surely, your fidelity, faith, and Christian zeal 1
fairly indicate that, spiritually as well as literally, the
church in Salt Lake City hath not lost its saltness. I 3
may at some near future visit your city, but am too busy
to think of doing so at present.

May the divine light of Christian Science that lighteth 6
every enlightened thought illumine your faith and understanding, exclude all darkness or doubt, and signal the
perfect path wherein to walk, the perfect Principle whereby 9
to demonstrate the perfect man and the perfect law of
God. In the words of St. Paul: "Now the end of the
commandment is charity out of a pure heart, and of a 12
good conscience, and of faith unfeigned;" and St. John
says: "For this is the message that ye heard from the
beginning, that we should love one another." 15

May the grace and love of God be and abide with
you all.

PLEASANT VIEW, CONCORD, N. H.,   18
    November 16, 1898

FIRST CHURCH OF CHRIST, SCIENTIST,
ATLANTA, GEORGIA   21

My Beloved Brethren: — You have met to consecrate your beautiful temple to the worship of the only
true God. Since the day in which you were brought into 24
the light and liberty of His children, it has been in the
hearts of this people to build a house unto Him whose
name they would glorify in a new commandment — 27
"that ye love one another." In this new recognition of
the riches of His love and the majesty of His might you
have built this house — laid its foundations on the rock 30

1 of Christ, and the stone which the builders rejected you
have made the head of the corner. This house is hallowed
3 by His promise: "I have hallowed this house, which thou
hast built, to put my name there forever; and mine eyes
and mine heart shall be there perpetually." "Now mine
6 eyes shall be open, and mine ears attent unto the prayer
that is made in this place."   Your feast days will not be
in commemoration, but in recognition of His presence;
9 your ark of the covenant will not be brought out of the
city of David, but out of "the secret place of the most
High," whereof the Psalmist sang, even the omniscience
12 of omnipotence; your tabernacle of the congregation will
not be temporary, but a "house not made with hands,
eternal in the heavens;" your oracle, under the wings of
15 the cherubim, is Truth's evangel, enunciating, "God is
Love."

In spirit I enter your inner sanctuary, your heart's
18 heart, breathing a benediction for God's largess. He
surely will not shut me out from your presence, and the
ponderous walls of your grand cathedral cannot prevent
21 me from entering where the heart of a Southron has
welcomed me.

Christian Science has a place in its court, in which, like
24 beds in hospitals, one man's head lies at another's feet.
As you work, the ages win; for the majesty of Christian
Science teaches the majesty of man. When it is learned
27 that spiritual sense and not the material senses convey all
impressions to man, man will naturally seek the Science of
his spiritual nature, and finding it, be God-endowed for
30 discipleship.

When divine Love gains admittance to a humble heart,
that individual ascends the scale of miracles and meets the

warmest wish of men and angels. Clad in invincible 1
armor, grasping the sword of Spirit, you have started in
this sublime ascent, and should reach the mount of revela- 3
tion; for if ye would run, who shall hinder you? So dear,
so due, to God is *obedience*, that it reaches high heaven
in the common walks of life, and it affords even me a 6
perquisite of joy.

You worship no distant deity, nor talk of unknown
love. The silent prayers of our churches, resounding 9
through the dim corridors of time, go forth in waves of
sound, a diapason of heart-beats, vibrating from one
pulpit to another and from one heart to another, till 12
truth and love, commingling in one righteous prayer,
shall encircle and cement the human race.

The government of divine Love derives its omnipotence 15
from the love it creates in the heart of man; for love is
allegiant, and there is no loyalty apart from love. When
the human senses wake from their long slumber to see how 18
soon earth's fables flee and faith grows wearisome, then
that which defies decay and satisfies the immortal cravings
is sought and found. In the twilight of the world's 21
pageantry, in the last-drawn sigh of a glory gone, we are
drawn towards God.

Beloved brethren, I cannot forget that yours is the first 24
church edifice of our denomination erected in the sunny
South — once my home. There my husband died, and
the song and the dirge, surging my being, gave expression 27
to a poem written in 1844, from which I copy this verse: —

> Friends, why throng in pity round me?
> Wherefore, pray, the bell did toll? 30
> Dead is he who loved me dearly:
> Am I not alone in soul?

1   Did that midnight shadow, falling upon the bridal
     wreath, bring the recompense of human woe, which is the
3 merciful design of divine Love, and so help to evolve that
     larger sympathy for suffering humanity which is eman-
     cipating it with the morning beams and noonday glory of
6 Christian Science?

     The age is fast answering this question: Does Christian
     Science equal *materia medica* in healing the worst forms
9 of contagious and organic diseases?   My experience in
     both practices — *materia medica* and the scientific meta-
     physical practice of medicine — shows the latter not only
12 equalling but vastly excelling the former.

     Christians who accept our Master as authority, regard
     his sayings as infallible.   Jesus' students, failing to cure a
15 severe case of lunacy, asked their great Teacher, "Why
     could not we cast him out?"   He answered, "This kind
     goeth not out but by prayer and fasting."   This declara-
18 tion of our Master, as to the relative value, skill, and
     certainty of the divine laws of Mind over the human
     mind and *above matter* in healing disease, remains beyond
21 questioning a divine decision in behalf of Mind.

     Jesus gave his disciples (students) power over all manner
     of diseases; and the Bible was written in order that all
24 peoples, in all ages, should have the same opportunity to
     become students of the Christ, Truth, and thus become
     God-endued with power (knowledge of divine law) and
27 with "signs following."   Jesus declared that his teaching
     and practice would remain, even as it did, "for them also
     which shall believe on me through their word."   Then,
30 in the name of God, wherefore vilify His prophets to-day
     who are fulfilling Jesus' prophecy and verifying his last
     promise, "Lo, I am with you alway"?   It were well for

the world if there survived more of the wisdom of Nico- 1
demus of old, who said, "No man can do these miracles
that thou doest, except God be with him." 3

Be patient towards persecution. Injustice has not a
tithe of the power of justice. Your enemies will advertise
for you. Christian Science is spreading steadily through- 6
out the world. Persecution is the weakness of tyrants
engendered by their fear, and love will cast it out. Continue steadfast in love and good works. Children of 9
light, you are not children of darkness. Let your light
shine. Keep in mind the foundations of Christian
Science — one God and one Christ. Keep personality 12
out of sight, and Christ's "Blessed are ye" will seal your
apostleship.

This glad Easter morning witnesseth a risen Saviour, a 15
higher human sense of Life and Love, which wipes away
all tears. With grave-clothes laid aside, Christ, Truth, has
come forth from the tomb of the past, clad in immortality. 18
The sepulchres give up their dead. Spirit is saying unto
matter: I am not there, am not within you. Behold the
place where they laid me; but human thought has risen! 21

Mortality's thick gloom is pierced. The stone is rolled
away. Death has lost its sting, and the grave its victory.
Immortal courage fills the human breast and lights the 24
living way of Life.

SECOND CHURCH OF CHRIST, SCIENTIST,
CHICAGO, ILL.   27

My Beloved Brethren: — Your card of invitation to this
feast of soul — the dedication of your church — was duly
received. Accept my thanks.   30

1   Ye sit not in the idol's temple.   Ye build not to an unknown God.   Ye worship Him whom ye serve.   Boast 3 not thyself, thou ransomed of divine Love, but press on unto the possession of unburdened bliss.   Heal the sick, make spotless the blemished, raise the living dead, cast 6 out fashionable lunacy.

The ideal robe of Christ is seamless.   Thou hast touched its hem, and thou art being healed.   The risen Christ is 9 thine.   The haunting mystery and gloom of his glory rule not this century.   Thine is the upspringing hope, the conquest over sin and mortality, that lights the living 12 way to Life, not to death.

May the God of our fathers, the infinite Person whom we worship, be and abide with you.   May the blessing of 15 divine Love rest with you.   My heart hovers around your churches in Chicago, for the dove of peace sits smilingly on these branches and sings of our Redeemer.

18   FIRST CHURCH OF CHRIST, SCIENTIST,
              LOS ANGELES, CAL.

Beloved Students: — Your kind letter, inviting me to 21 be present at the dedication of your church, was duly received.   It would indeed give me pleasure to visit you, to witness your prosperity, and "rejoice with them that 24 do rejoice," but the constant recurring demands upon my time and attention pin me to my post.   Of this, however, I can sing: My love can fly on wings of joy to 27 you and leave a leaf of olive;   it can whisper to you of the divine ever-presence, answering your prayers, crowning your endeavors, and building for you a house "eternal 30 in the heavens."

You will dedicate your temple in faith unfeigned, not to 1
the unknown God, but unto Him whom to know aright
is life everlasting. His presence with you will bring to 3
your hearts so much of heaven that you will not feel my
absence. The privilege remains mine to watch and work
for all, from East to West, from the greensward and 6
gorgeous skies of the Orient to your dazzling glory
in the Occident, and to thank God forever "for His
goodness, and for His wonderful works to the children 9
of men."

PLEASANT VIEW, CONCORD, N. H.,
          November 20, 1902   12

SECOND CHURCH OF CHRIST, SCIENTIST,
MINNEAPOLIS, MINN.

Beloved: — The spiritual dominates the temporal. Love 15
gives nothing to take away. Nothing dethrones His
house. You are dedicating yours to Him. Protesting
against error, you unite with all who believe in Truth. 18
God guard and guide you.

FIRST CHURCH OF CHRIST, SCIENTIST,
NEW YORK, N. Y.   21

Beloved Brethren: — Carlyle writes, "Give a thing time;
if it succeeds, it is a right thing." Here I aver that you
have grasped time and labor, taking the first by the fore- 24
lock and the last by love. In this lofty temple, dedicated
to God and humanity, may the prophecy of Isaiah be
fulfilled: "Fear not: . . . I have called thee by thy 27
name; thou art mine." Within its sacred walls may

1 song and sermon generate only that which Christianity
writes in broad facts over great continents — sermons
3 that fell forests and remove mountains, songs of joy
and gladness.

The letter of your work dies, as do all things material,
6 but the spirit of it is immortal. Remember that a temple
but foreshadows the idea of God, the "house not made
with hands, eternal in the heavens," while a silent, grand
9 man or woman, healing sickness and destroying sin,
builds that which reaches heaven. Only those men and
women gain greatness who gain themselves in a complete
12 subordination of self.

The tender memorial engraven on your grand edifice
stands for human self lost in divine light, melted into the
15 radiance of His likeness. It stands for meekness and
might, for Truth as attested by the Founder of your
denomination and emblazoned on the fair escutcheon of
18 your church.

Beloved Students: — Your telegram, in which you present to me the princely gift of your magnificent church
21 edifice in New York City, is an unexpected token of your
gratitude and love. I deeply appreciate it, profoundly
thank you for it, and gratefully accept the spirit of it;
24 but I must decline to receive that for which you have
sacrificed so much and labored so long. May divine
Love abundantly bless you, reward you according to
27 your works, guide and guard you and your church
through the depths; and may you

"Who stood the storm when seas were rough,
30   Ne'er in a sunny hour fall off."

FIRST CHURCH OF CHRIST, SCIENTIST, CLEVELAND, OHIO

Beloved Brethren: — You will pardon my delay in acknowledging your card of invitation to the dedicatory services of your church. Adverse circumstances, loss of help, new problems to be worked out for the field, *etc.*, have hitherto prevented my reply. However, it is never too late to repent, to love more, to work more, to watch and pray; but those privileges I have not had time to express, and so have submitted to necessity, letting the deep love which I cherished for you be hidden under an appearance of indifference.

We must resign with good grace what we are denied, and press on with what we are, for we cannot do more than we are nor understand what is not ripening in us. To do good to all because we love all, and to use in God's service the one talent that we all have, is our only means of adding to that talent and the best way to silence a deep discontent with our shortcomings.

Christian Science is at length learned to be no miserable piece of ideal legerdemain, by which we poor mortals expect to live and die, but a deep-drawn breath fresh from God, by whom and in whom man lives, moves, and has deathless being. The praiseworthy success of this church, and its united efforts to build an edifice in which to worship the infinite, sprang from the temples erected first in the hearts of its members — the unselfed love that builds without hands, eternal in the heaven of Spirit. God grant that this unity remain, and that you continue to build, rebuild, adorn, and fill these spiritual temples with grace, Truth, Life, and Love.

1   FIRST CHURCH OF CHRIST, SCIENTIST,
                    PITTSBURGH, PA.

3   *My Beloved Brethren:* — I congratulate you upon erecting the first edifice of our denomination in the Keystone
State, a State whose metropolis is called the "city of
6 brotherly love." May this dear church militant accept
my tender counsel in these words of the Scripture, to be
engrafted in church and State: —
9   "Let every man be swift to hear, slow to speak, slow to
wrath." "He that is slow to anger is better than the
mighty; and he that ruleth his spirit than he that taketh
12 a city." "If any man offend not in word, the same is
a perfect man, and able also to bridle the whole body."
"By thy words thou shalt be condemned." "Love thy
15 neighbor as thyself."
       "Christ also suffered for us, leaving us an example,
that [we] should follow his steps: . . . who, when he was
18 reviled, reviled not again; when he suffered, he threatened
not; but committed himself to Him that judgeth righteously." "Consider him that endured such contradiction
21 of sinners against himself, lest ye be wearied and faint in
your minds."

           FIRST CHURCH OF CHRIST, SCIENTIST,
24   ST. LOUIS, MO.

    My Beloved Brethren: — The good in being, even the
spiritually indispensable, is your daily bread. Work and
27 pray for it. The poor toil for our bread, and we should
work for their health and holiness. Over the glaciers of
winter the summer glows. The beauty of holiness comes

with the departure of sin. Enjoying good things is not evil, but becoming slaves to pleasure is. That error is most forcible which is least distinct to conscience. Attempt nothing without God's help.

May the beauty of holiness be upon this dear people, and may this beloved church be glorious, without spot or blemish.

FIRST CHURCH OF CHRIST, SCIENTIST, SAN JOSÉ, CAL.

Beloved Students: — Words are inadequate to express my deep appreciation of your labor and success in completing and dedicating your church edifice, and of the great hearts and ready hands of our far Western students, the Christian Scientists.

Comparing such students with those whose words are but the substitutes for works, we learn that the translucent atmosphere of the former must illumine the midnight of the latter, else Christian Science will disappear from among mortals.

I thank divine Love for the hope set before us in the Word and in the doers thereof, "for of such is the kingdom of heaven."

FIRST CHURCH OF CHRIST, SCIENTIST, WILMINGTON, N. C.

My Beloved Brethren: — At this dedicatory season of your church edifice in the home of my heart, I send loving congratulations, join with you in song and sermon. God will bless the work of your hearts and hands.

PLEASANT VIEW, CONCORD, N. H.,
July 27, 1907

1 FIRST CHURCH OF CHRIST, SCIENTIST,
LONDON, ENGLAND

3 *Beloved Students and Brethren:* — Your letters of May 1
and June 19, informing me of the dedication of your
magnificent church edifice, have been received with many
6 thanks to you and great gratitude to our one Father.

May God grant not only the continuance of His favors,
but their abundant and ripened fruit.

9 CHESTNUT HILL, MASS.,
June 26, 1909

CHAPTER IX

Letters to Branch Churches

FIRST CHURCH OF CHRIST, SCIENTIST, 1
PHILADELPHIA, PA.

MY BELOVED STUDENTS AND BRETHREN:— I rejoice 3 with thee. Blessed art thou. In place of darkness, light hath sprung up. The reward of thy hands is given thee to-day. May God say this of the church 6 in Philadelphia: I have naught against thee.

FIRST CHURCH OF CHRIST, SCIENTIST,
WASHINGTON, D. C. 9

Beloved Brethren: — The Board of Directors and Trustees of this church will please accept my grateful acknowledgment of the receipt of their Christian canon 12 pertaining to the hour. The joint resolutions contained therein show explicitly the attitude of this church in our capital towards me and towards the Cause of Christian 15 Science, so dear to our hearts and to all loyal lovers of God and man.

This year, standing on the verge of the twentieth cen- 18 tury, has sounded the tocsin of a higher hope, of strengthened hands, of unveiled hearts, of fourfold unity between the churches of our denomination in this and in other 21

1 lands.   Religious liberty and individual rights under the
Constitution of our nation are rapidly advancing, avow-
3 ing and consolidating the genius of Christian Science.

Heaven be praised for the signs of the times.   Let "the
heathen rage, and the people imagine a vain thing;" our
6 trust is in the Almighty God, who ruleth in heaven and
upon earth, and none can stay His hand or say, "What
doest thou?"

9   FIRST CHURCH OF CHRIST, SCIENTIST,
                    LONDON, ENGLAND

My Beloved Brethren: — The chain of Christian unity,
12 unbroken, stretches across the sea and rises upward to the
realms of incorporeal Life — even to the glorious beatitudes of divine Love.   Striving to be good, to do good, and
15 to love our neighbor as ourself, man's soul is safe;   man
emerges from mortality and receives his rights inalienable
— the love of God and man.   What holds us to the Chris-
18 tian life is the seven-fold shield of honesty, purity, and
unselfed love.   I need not say this to you, for you know
the way in Christian Science.

21   Pale, sinful sense, at work to lift itself on crumbling
thrones of justice by pulling down its benefactors,
will tumble from this scheme into the bottomless
24 abyss of self-damnation, there to relinquish its league
with evil.   Wide yawns the gap between this course
and Christian Science.

27   God spare this plunge, lessen its depths, save sinners and fit their being to recover its connection with
its divine Principle, Love.   For this I shall continue to
30 pray.

God is blessing you, my beloved students and breth- 1
ren. Press on towards the high calling whereunto
divine Love has called us and is fast fulfilling the 3
promises.

Satan is unchained only for a season, as the Revelator
foresaw, and love and good will to man, sweeter than a 6
sceptre, are enthroned now and forever.

FIRST CHURCH OF CHRIST, SCIENTIST, NEW YORK, N. Y.

9

My Beloved Brethren: — Your Soul-full words and song
repeat my legacies in blossom. Such elements of friendship, faith, and hope repossess us of heaven. I thank 12
you out of a full heart. Even the crown of thorns, which
mocked the bleeding brow of our blessed Lord, was over-
crowned with a diadem of duties done. So let us meekly 15
meet, mercifully forgive, wisely ponder, and lovingly
scan the convulsions of mortal mind, that its sudden
sallies may help us, not to a start, but to a tenure of 18
unprecarious joy. Rich hope have I in him who says in
his heart: —

> I will listen for Thy voice,   21
> Lest my footsteps stray;
> I will follow and rejoice
> All the rugged way.   24

SECOND CHURCH OF CHRIST, SCIENTIST, NEW YORK, N. Y.

Beloved Brethren: — Please accept a line from me in lieu 27
of my presence on the auspicious occasion of the opening of your new church edifice. Hope springs exultant

1 on this blest morn. May its white wings overshadow this
white temple and soar above it, pointing the path from
3 earth to heaven — from human ambition, fear, or distrust
to the faith, meekness, and might of him who hallowed
this Easter morn.

6　Now may his salvation draw near, for the night is far
spent and the day is at hand. In the words of St. Paul:
"Render therefore to all their dues: tribute to whom
9 tribute is due; custom to whom custom; . . . honor to
whom honor. Owe no man any thing, but to love one
another: for he that loveth another hath fulfilled the
12 law."

May the benediction of "Well done, good and faithful,"
rest worthily on the builders of this beautiful temple, and
15 the glory of the resurrection morn burst upon the spiritual
sense of this people with renewed vision, infinite meanings, endless hopes, and glad victories in the onward and
18 upward chain of being.

FIRST CHURCH OF CHRIST, SCIENTIST, OAKLAND, CAL.

21　*Beloved Brethren:* — I thank you for the words of cheer
and love in your letter. The taper unseen in sunlight
cheers the darkness. My work is reflected light, — a
24 drop from His ocean of love, from the underived glory,
the divine *Esse.* From the dear tone of your letter,
you must be bringing your sheaves into the store-
27 house. Press on. The way is narrow at first, but it
expands as we walk in it. "Herein is my Father glorified, that ye bear much fruit." God bless this vine of
30 His planting.

FIRST CHURCH OF CHRIST, SCIENTIST, WASHINGTON, D. C.

Beloved Brethren: — I have nothing new to communi- 3
cate; all is in your textbooks. Pray aright and demonstrate your prayer; sing in faith. Know that religion
should be distinct in our consciousness and life, but not 6
clamorous for worldly distinction. Church laws which
are obeyed without mutiny are God's laws. Goodness
and philanthropy begin with work and never stop working. 9
All that is worth reckoning is what we do, and the best of
everything is not too good, but is economy and riches.
Be great not as a grand obelisk, nor by setting up to be 12
great, — only as good. A spiritual hero is a mark for
gamesters, but he is unutterably valiant, the summary of
suffering here and of heaven hereafter. Our thoughts 15
beget our actions; they make us what we are. Dishonesty is a mental malady which kills its possessor; it
is a sure precursor that its possessor is mortal. A deep 18
sincerity is sure of success, for God takes care of it. God
bless this dear church, and I am sure that He will if it is
ready for the blessing. 21

FIRST CHURCH OF CHRIST, SCIENTIST, LONDON, ENGLAND

Beloved Students: — You have laid the corner-stone of 24
your church edifice impressively, and buried immortal
truths in the bosom of earth safe from all chance of being
challenged. 27
You whose labors are doing so much to benefit mankind
will not be impatient if you have not accomplished all you

1 desire, nor will you be long in doing more.   My faith in
God and in His followers rests in the fact that He is infinite
3 good, and that He gives His followers opportunity to use
their hidden virtues, to put into practice the power which
lies concealed in the calm and which storms awaken to
6 vigor and to victory.

It is only by looking heavenward that mutual friendships such as ours can begin and never end.   Over sea
9 and over land, Christian Science unites its true followers
in one Principle, divine Love, that sacred *ave* and essence
of Soul which makes them one in Christ.

12   FIRST CHURCH OF CHRIST, SCIENTIST,
COLUMBUS, OHIO

IN REPLY TO A LETTER ANNOUNCING THE PURPOSE OF THE
15   CHRISTIAN SCIENTISTS TO PRACTISE WITHOUT FEES IN COM-
PLIANCE WITH THE STATE LAWS

Beloved Brethren:— I congratulate you tenderly on the
18 decision you have made as to the present practice of
Christian Science in your State, and thoroughly recommend it under the circumstances.   I practised gratui-
21 tously when starting this great Cause, which was then the
scoff of the age.

The too long treatment of a disease, the charging of
24 the sick whom you have not healed a full fee for treatment, the suing for payment, hypnotism, and the resent-
ing of injuries, are not the fruits of Christian Science,
27 while returning good for evil, loving one's enemies, and
overcoming evil with good, — these are its fruits;
and its therapeutics, based as aforetime on this divine
30 Principle, heals all disease.

We read in the Scriptures: "There is therefore now no 1
condemnation to them which are in Christ Jesus, who walk
not after the flesh, but after the Spirit." "Stand fast 3
therefore in the liberty wherewith Christ hath made us
free." "Be ye therefore wise as serpents, and harmless
as doves." 6

Wisdom is won through faith, prayer, experience; and
God is the giver.

> "God moves in a mysterious way 9
> His wonders to perform;
> He plants His footsteps in the sea
> And rides upon the storm." 12

THIRD CHURCH OF CHRIST, SCIENTIST, LONDON, ENGLAND

Beloved Brethren: — Love and unity are hieroglyphs of 15
goodness, and their philosophical impetus, spiritual
Æsculapius and Hygeia, saith, "As the thought is, so is the
deed; as the thing made is good or bad, so is its maker." 18
This idealism connects itself with spiritual understanding,
and so makes God more supreme in consciousness, man
more His likeness, friends more faithful, and enemies 21
harmless. Scholastic theology at its best touches but the
hem of Christian Science, shorn of all personality, wholly
apart from human hypotheses, matter, creed and dogma, 24
the lust of the flesh and the pride of power. Christian
Science is the full idea of its divine Principle, God; it is
forever based on Love, and it is demonstrated by perfect 27
rules; it is unerring. Hence health, holiness, immortality,
are its natural effects. The practitioner may fail, but the
Science never. 30

1 Philosophical links, which would unite dead matter with animate, Spirit with matter and material
3 means, prayer with power and pride of position, hinder
the divine influx and lose Science, — lose the Principle
of divine metaphysics and the tender grace of spiritual
6 understanding, that love-linked holiness which heals
and saves.

Schisms, imagination, and human beliefs are not
9 parts of Christian Science; they darken the discernment of Science; they divide Truth's garment and cast
lots for it.

12 Seeing a man in the moon, or seeing a person in the
picture of Jesus, or believing that you see an individual
who has passed through the shadow called death, is
15 not seeing the spiritual idea of God; but it is seeing
a human belief, which is far from the fact that portrays
Life, Truth, Love.

18 May these words of the Scriptures comfort you: "The
Lord shall be unto thee an everlasting light, and thy God
thy glory." "The city had no need of the sun, neither
21 of the moon, to shine in it: for the glory of God did
lighten it, and the Lamb is the light thereof." "Ye
are a chosen generation, a royal priesthood, an holy
24 nation, a peculiar people; that ye should show forth the
praises of Him who hath called you out of darkness into
His marvellous light." "Giving thanks unto the Father,
27 which hath made us meet to be partakers of the inheritance of the saints in light: who hath delivered us from
the power of darkness, and hath translated us into the
30 kingdom of His dear Son." "Ye were sometimes darkness, but now are ye light in the Lord: walk as children
of light."

FIRST CHURCH OF CHRIST, SCIENTIST,   1
MILWAUKEE, WIS.

Beloved Brethren: — Your communication is gratefully 3
received. Press on! The wrath of men shall praise God,
and the remainder thereof He will restrain.

A TELEGRAM AND MRS. EDDY'S REPLY   6

Beloved Leader: — The representatives of churches and
societies of Christian Science in Missouri, in annual
conference assembled, unite in loving greetings to you, 9
and pledge themselves to strive more earnestly, day
by day, for the clearer understanding and more perfect
manifestation of the truth which you have unfolded to 12
the world, and by which sin and sickness are destroyed
and life and immortality brought to light.

Yours in loving obedience,   15
CHURCHES AND SOCIETIES OF CHRISTIAN
SCIENCE IN MISSOURI

ST. JOSEPH, MISSOURI,   18
January 5, 1909

Mrs. Eddy's Reply

"Well done, thou good and faithful servant: . . . enter 21
thou into the joy of thy lord" — the satisfaction of
meeting and mastering evil and defending good, thus
predicating man upon divine Science. (See Science 24
and Health, p. 227.)

CHESTNUT HILL, MASS.,
January 6, 1909   27

1   FIRST CHURCH OF CHRIST, SCIENTIST,
SYDNEY, AUSTRALIA

3   *Beloved Brethren:* — Accept my deep thanks for your
highly interesting letter. It would seem as if the whole
import of Christian Science had been mirrored forth by
6 your loving hearts, to reflect its heavenly rays over all the
earth.

Box G, Brookline, Mass.,
9   July 15, 1909

FIRST CHURCH OF CHRIST, SCIENTIST,
EDINBURGH, SCOTLAND

12   *Beloved Christian Scientists:* — Like the gentle dews of
heaven and the refreshing breeze of morn, comes your
dear letter to my waiting heart, — waiting in due expec-
15 tation of just such blessedness, crowning the hope and
hour of divine Science, than which nothing can exceed
its ministrations of God to man.

18   I congratulate you on the prospect of erecting a church
building, wherein to gather in praise and prayer for the
whole human family.

21   Box G, Brookline, Mass.,
November 2, 1909

THE COMMITTEES IN CONFERENCE, CHICAGO, ILL.

24   *The Committees:* — God bless the courageous, far-seeing
committees in conference for their confidence in His
ways and means of reaching the very acme of Christian
27 Science.

COMMENT ON LETTER FROM FIRST CHURCH OF CHRIST, SCIENTIST, OTTAWA, ONTARIO

God will abundantly bless this willing and obedient church with the rich reward of those that seek and serve Him. No greater hope have we than in right thinking and right acting, and faith in the blessing of fidelity, courage, patience, and grace.

CHAPTER X

Admonition and Counsel

1   WHAT OUR LEADER SAYS

BELOVED Christian Scientists, keep your minds so
3 filled with Truth and Love, that sin, disease, and
death cannot enter them. It is plain that nothing can
be added to the mind already full. There is no door
6 through which evil can enter, and no space for evil to fill
in a mind filled with goodness. Good thoughts are an
impervious armor; clad therewith you are completely
9 shielded from the attacks of error of every sort. And not
only yourselves are safe, but all whom your thoughts rest
upon are thereby benefited.
12   The self-seeking pride of the evil thinker injures him
when he would harm others. Goodness involuntarily
resists evil. The evil thinker is the proud talker and
15 doer. The right thinker abides under the shadow of the
Almighty. His thoughts can only reflect peace, good will
towards men, health, and holiness.[1]

18   WAYS THAT ARE VAIN

Certain individuals entertain the notion that Christian Science Mind-healing should be two-sided, and only
21 denounce error in general, — saying nothing, in particu-

[1] Copyright, 1909, by Mary Baker Eddy. Renewed, 1937.

lar, of error that is damning men. They are sticklers 1
for a false, convenient peace, straining at gnats and
swallowing camels. The unseen wrong to individuals 3
and society they are too cowardly, too ignorant, or too
wicked to uncover, and excuse themselves by denying
that this evil exists. This mistaken way, of hiding sin 6
in order to maintain harmony, has licensed evil, allowing
it first to smoulder, and then break out in devouring
flames. All that error asks is to be let alone; even as 9
in Jesus' time the unclean spirits cried out, "Let us
alone; what have we to do with thee?"

Animal magnetism, in its ascending steps of evil, 12
entices its victim by unseen, silent arguments. Reversing the modes of good, in their silent allurements to
health and holiness, it impels mortal mind into error of 15
thought, and tempts into the committal of acts foreign
to the natural inclinations. The victims lose their
individuality, and lend themselves as willing tools to 18
carry out the designs of their worst enemies, even those
who would induce their self-destruction. Animal magnetism fosters suspicious distrust where honor is due, fear 21
where courage should be strongest, reliance where there
should be avoidance, a belief in safety where there is
most danger; and these miserable lies, poured constantly 24
into his mind, fret and confuse it, spoiling that individual's disposition, undermining his health, and sealing
his doom, unless the cause of the mischief is found out 27
and destroyed.

Other minds are made dormant by it, and the victim
is in a state of semi-individuality, with a mental hazi- 30
ness which admits of no intellectual culture or spiritual
growth. The state induced by this secret evil influence

1 is a species of intoxication, in which the victim is led to
believe and do what he would never, otherwise, think
3 or do voluntarily.

This intricate method of animal magnetism is the
essence, or spirit, of evil, which makes mankind drunken.
6 In this era it is taking the place of older and more open
sins, and other forms of intoxication. A harder fight
will be necessary to expose the cause and effects of
9 this evil influence, than has been required to put down
the evil effects of alcohol. The alcoholic habit is the
use of higher forms of matter, wherewith to do evil;
12 whereas animal magnetism is the highest form of mental
evil, wherewith to complete the sum total of sin.

The question is often asked, Why is there so much
15 dissension among mental practitioners? We answer,
Because they do not practise in strict accordance with
the teaching of Christian Science Mind-healing. If they
18 did, there would be unity of action. Being like the
disciples of old, "with one accord in one place," they
would receive a spiritual influx impossible under other
21 conditions, and so would recognize and resist the
animal magnetism by which they are being deceived
and misled.

24 The mental malpractitioner, interfering with the
rights of Mind, destroys the true sense of Science, and
loses his own power to heal. He tries to compensate
27 himself for his own loss by hindering in every way conceivable the success of others. You will find this practitioner saying that animal magnetism never troubles
30 him, but that Mrs. Eddy teaches animal magnetism;
and he says this to cover his crime of mental malpractice, in furtherance of unscrupulous designs.

The natural fruits of Christian Science Mind-healing 1
are harmony, brotherly love, spiritual growth and
activity. The malicious aim of perverted mind-power, 3
or animal magnetism, is to paralyze good and give
activity to evil. It starts factions and engenders envy
and hatred, but as activity is by no means a right of 6
evil and its emissaries, they ought not to be encouraged
in it. Because this age is cursed with one rancorous
and lurking foe to human weal, those who are the 9
truest friends of mankind, and conscientious in their
desire to do right and to live pure and Christian lives,
should be more zealous to do good, more watchful and 12
vigilant. Then they will be proportionately successful
and bring out glorious results.

Unless one's eyes are opened to the modes of mental 15
malpractice, working so subtly that we mistake its suggestions for the impulses of our own thought, the victim
will allow himself to drift in the wrong direction with- 18
out knowing it. Be ever on guard against this enemy.
Watch your thoughts, and see whether they lead you
to God and into harmony with His true followers. 21
Guard and strengthen your own citadel more strongly.
Thus you will grow wiser and better through every
attack of your foe, and the Golden Rule will not rust 24
for lack of use or be misinterpreted by the adverse
influence of animal magnetism.

ONLY ONE QUOTATION   27

The following three quotations from "Science and
Health with Key to the Scriptures" are submitted
to the dear Churches of Christ, Scientist. From these 30

1 they may select one only to place on the walls of their
church. Otherwise, as our churches multiply, promiscu-
3 ous selections would write your textbook on the walls of
your churches.

   Divine Love always has met and always will meet every
6 human need.

MARY BAKER EDDY

   Christianity is again demonstrating the Life that is
9 Truth, and the Truth that is Life.

MARY BAKER EDDY

   Jesus' three days' work in the sepulchre set the seal
12 of eternity on time. He proved Life to be deathless and
Love to be the master of hate.

MARY BAKER EDDY

15   THE LABORER AND HIS HIRE

   In reply to letters questioning the consistency of
Christian Scientists taking pay for their labors, and with
18 the hope of relieving the questioners' perplexity, I will say:
Four years after my discovery of Christian Science, while
taking no remuneration for my labors, and for healing all
21 manner of diseases, I was confronted with the fact that I
had no monetary means left wherewith to hire a hall in
which to speak, or to establish a Christian Science home
24 for indigent students, which I yearned to do, or even to
meet my own current expenses. I therefore halted from
necessity.

27   I had cast my all into the treasury of Truth, but where
were the means with which to carry on a Cause? To
desert the Cause never occurred to me, but nobody

then wanted Christian Science, or gave it a halfpenny. 1
Though sorely oppressed, I was above begging and
knew well the priceless worth of what had been bestowed 3
without money or price. Just then God stretched forth
His hand. He it was that bade me do what I did,
and it prospered at every step. I wrote "Science and 6
Health with Key to the Scriptures," taught students for
a tuition of three hundred dollars each, though I seldom
taught without having charity scholars, sometimes a 9
dozen or upward in one class. Afterwards, with touching tenderness, those very students sent me the full
tuition money. However, I returned this money with 12
love; but it was again mailed to me in letters begging
me to accept it, saying, "Your teachings are worth much
more to me than money can be." 15

It was thus that I earned the means with which to start
a Christian Science home for the poor worthy student, to
establish a Metaphysical College, to plant our first maga- 18
zine, to purchase the site for a church edifice, to give my
church *The Christian Science Journal,* and to keep "the
wolves in sheep's clothing," preying upon my pearls, from 21
clogging the wheels of Christian Science.

When the great Master first sent forth his students, he
bade them take no scrip for their journey, saying, "The 24
laborer is worthy of his hire." Next, on the contrary,
he bade them take scrip. Can we find a better example
for our lives than that of our Master? Why did he send 27
forth his students first without, and then with, provision
for their expenses? Doubtless to test the effect of both
methods on mankind. That he preferred the latter is 30
evident, since we have no hint of his changing this direction; and that his divine wisdom should temper human

1 affairs, is plainly set forth in the Scriptures. Till Christian
Scientists give all their time to spiritual things, live without
3 eating, and obtain their money from a fish's mouth, they
must earn it in order to help mankind with it. All systems of religion stand on this basis.

6 The law and the gospel, — Christian, civil, and educational means, — manufacture, agriculture, tariff, and
revenue subsist on demand and supply, regulated by a
9 government currency, by which each is provided for and
maintained. What, then, can a man do with truth
and without a cent to sustain it? Either his life must
12 be a miracle that frightens people, or his truth not
worth a cent.

THE CHILDREN CONTRIBUTORS

15 *My Beloved Children:* — Tenderly thanking you for
your sweet industry and love on behalf of the room
of the Pastor Emeritus in The First Church of Christ,
18 Scientist, Boston, I say: The purpose of God to you-
ward indicates another field of work which I present to
your thought, work by which you can do much good and
21 which is adapted to your present unfolding capacity. I
request that from this date you disband as a society,
drop the insignia of "Busy Bees," work in your own sev-
24 eral localities, and no longer contribute to The Mother
Church flower fund.

As you grow older, advance in the knowledge of self-
27 support, and see the need of self-culture, it is to be expected
you will feel more than at present that charity begins at
home, and that you will want money for your own uses.
30 Contemplating these important wants, I see that you
should begin now to earn for a purpose even higher, the

money that you expend for flowers. You will want it for
academics, for your own school education, or, if need be,
to help your parents, brothers, or sisters.

Further to encourage your early, generous incentive
for action, and to reward your hitherto unselfish toil, I
have deeded in trust to The Mother Church of Christ,
Scientist, in Boston, the sum of four thousand dollars
to be invested in safe municipal bonds for my dear children contributors to the room of the Pastor Emeritus.
This sum is to remain on interest till it is disbursed in
equal shares to each contributor. This disbursal will
take place when the contributors shall have arrived at
legal age, and each contributor will receive his dividend with interest thereon up to date, provided he has
complied with my request as above named.

A CORRECTION

In the last *Sentinel* [Oct. 12, 1899] was the following
question: "If all matter is unreal, why do we deny the
existence of disease in the material body and not the body
itself?"

We deny *first* the existence of disease, because we can
meet this negation more readily than we can negative all
that the material senses affirm. It is written in "Science
and Health with Key to the Scriptures": "An improved
belief is one step out of error, and aids in taking the
next step and in understanding the situation in Christian
Science" (p. 296).

Thus it is that our great Exemplar, Jesus of Nazareth,
first takes up the subject. He does not require the last
step to be taken first. He came to the world not to
destroy the law of being, but to fulfil it in righteousness.

1 He restored the diseased body to its normal action,
functions, and organization, and in explanation of his
3 deeds he said, "Suffer it to be so now: for thus it becometh us to fulfil all righteousness." Job said, "In
my flesh shall I see God." Neither the Old nor the New
6 Testament furnishes reasons or examples for the destruction of the human body, but for its restoration to life
and health as the scientific proof of "God with us."
9 The power and prerogative of Truth are to destroy all
disease and to raise the dead — even the self-same
Lazarus. The *spiritual* body, the incorporeal idea, came
12 with the *ascension.*

Jesus demonstrated the divine Principle of Christian
Science when he presented his *material* body absolved
15 from death and the grave. The introduction of pure
abstractions into Christian Science, without their correl-
atives, leaves the divine Principle of Christian Science
18 unexplained, tends to confuse the mind of the reader, and
ultimates in what Jesus denounced, namely, straining
at gnats and swallowing camels.

21 QUESTION ANSWERED

A fad of belief is the fool of mesmerism. The belief
that an individual can either teach or heal by proxy is a
24 false faith that will end bitterly. My published works are
teachers and healers. My private life is given to a servitude the fruit of which all mankind may share. Such
27 labor is impartial, meted out to one no more than to
another. Therefore an individual should not enter the
Massachusetts Metaphysical College with the expecta-
30 tion of receiving instruction from me, other than that

which my books afford, unless I am personally present. 1
Nor should patients anticipate being helped by me through
some favored student. Such practice would be erro- 3
neous, and such an anticipation on the part of the sick a
hindrance rather than help.

My good students have all the honor of their success 6
in teaching or in healing. I by no means would pluck
their plumes. Human power is most properly used in
preventing the occasion for its use; otherwise its use 9
is abuse.

CHRISTIAN SCIENCE HEALING

To say that it is sin to ride to church on an electric 12
car, would not be more preposterous than to believe
that man's Maker is not equal to the destruction of disease
germs. Christ, Truth, the ever-present spiritual idea, 15
who raises the dead, is equal to the giving of life and health
to man and to the healing, as aforetime, of all manner of
diseases. I would not charge Christians with doubting 18
the Bible record of our great Master's life of healing, since
Christianity must be predicated of what Christ Jesus
taught and did; but I do say that Christian Science cannot 21
annul nor make void the laws of the land, since Christ,
the great demonstrator of Christian Science, said, "Think
not that I am come to destroy the law, or the prophets: 24
I am not come to destroy, but to fulfil."

I have expressed my opinion publicly as to the pre-
cautions against the spread of so-called infectious and 27
contagious diseases in the following words: —

"Rather than quarrel over vaccination, I recommend, if
the law demand, that an individual submit to this process, 30
that he obey the law, and then appeal to the gospel to

1 save him from bad physical results. Whatever changes
come to this century or to any epoch, we may safely
3 submit to the providence of God, to common justice, to
the maintenance of individual rights, and to govern-
mental usages. This statement should be so interpreted
6 as to apply, on the basis of Christian Science, to the
reporting of a contagious case to the proper authorities
when the law so requires. When Jesus was questioned
9 concerning obedience to human law, he replied: 'Render
to Cæsar the things that are Cæsar's,' even while you
render 'to God the things that are God's.' "

12   I believe in obeying the laws of the land. I practise and
teach this obedience, since justice is the moral signification
of law. Injustice denotes the absence of law. Each day
15 I pray for the pacification of all national difficulties, for
the brotherhood of man, for the end of idolatry and
infidelity, and for the growth and establishment of
18 Christian religion — Christ's Christianity. I also have
faith that my prayer availeth, and that He who is
overturning will overturn until He whose right it is shall
21 reign. Each day I pray: "God bless my enemies; make
them Thy friends; give them to know the joy and the
peace of love."

24   Past, present, or future philosophy or religion, which
departs from the instructions and example of the great
Galilean Prophet, cannot be Christlike. Jesus obeyed
27 human laws and fell a victim to those laws. But nineteen
centuries have greatly improved human nature and
human statutes. That the innocent should suffer for the
30 guilty, seems less divine, and that humanity should share
alike liberty of conscience, seems more divine to-day than
it did yesterday.

The earthly price of spirituality in religion and medicine 1
in a material age is persecution, and the moral distance
between Christianity and materialism precludes Jesus' 3
doctrine, now as then, from finding favor with certain
purely human views. The prophets of old looked for
something higher than the systems and practices of their 6
times. They foresaw the new dispensation of Truth
and the demonstration of God in His more infinite
meanings, — the demonstration which was to destroy sin, 9
disease, and death, establish the definition of omnipotence,
and illustrate the Science of Mind. Earth has not known
another so great and good as Christ Jesus. Then can 12
we find a better moral philosophy, a more complete,
natural, and divine Science of medicine, or a better
religion than his? 15

God is Spirit. Then modes of healing, other than the
spiritual and divine, break the First Commandment of
the Decalogue, "Thou shalt have no other gods before 18
me." There are no other heaven-appointed means than
the spiritual with which to heal sin and disease. Our
Master conformed to this law, and instructed his follow- 21
ers, saying, "He that believeth on me, the works that I
do shall he do also." This is enough.

All issues of morality, of Christianity, of pleasure, or of 24
pain must come through a correct or incorrect state
of thought, since matter is not conscious; then, like a
watchman forsaking his post, shall we have no faith in 27
God, in the divine Mind, thus throwing the door wide
open to the intruding disease, forgetting that the divine
Mind, Truth and Life, can guard the entrance? 30

We earnestly ask: Shall we not believe the Scripture,
"The prayer of faith shall save the sick"? In the seven-

1 teenth chapter of the Gospel according to St. Matthew,
we read that even the disciples of Jesus once failed mentally
3 to cure by their faith and understanding a violent case of
lunacy. And because of this Jesus rebuked them, saying:
"O faithless and perverse generation, how long shall I be
6 with you? how long shall I suffer you? bring him hither to
me." When his disciples asked him why they could not
heal that case, Jesus, the master Metaphysician, answered,
9 "Because of your unbelief" (lack of *faith*); and then
continued: "If ye have faith as a grain of mustard
seed, ye shall say unto this mountain, Remove hence
12 to yonder place; and it shall remove." Also he added:
"This kind goeth not out but by prayer and fasting"
(refraining from admitting the claims of the senses).
15 Even in those dark days Jesus was not arrested and
executed (for "insanity") because of his faith and
his great demands on the faith of his followers, but
18 he was arrested because, as was said, "he stirreth
up the people." Be patient, O Christian Scientist!
It is well that thou canst unloose the sandals of thy
21 Master's feet.

The Constitution of the United States does not provide
that *materia medica* shall make laws to regulate man's
24 religion; rather does it imply that religion shall permeate
our laws. Mankind will be God-governed in proportion
as God's government becomes apparent, the Golden Rule
27 utilized, and the rights of man and the liberty of conscience
held sacred. Meanwhile, they who name the name of
Christian Science will assist in the holding of crime in
30 check, will aid the ejection of error, will maintain law
and order, and will cheerfully await the end — justice and
judgment.

RULES OF CONDUCT

I hereby notify the public that no comers are received at Pleasant View without previous appointment by letter. Also that I neither listen to complaints, read letters, nor dictate replies to letters which pertain to church difficulties outside of The Mother Church of Christ, Scientist, or to any class of individual discords. Letters from the sick are not read by me or by my secretaries. They should be sent to the Christian Science practitioners whose cards are in *The Christian Science Journal*.

Letters and despatches from individuals with whom I have no acquaintance and of whom I have no knowledge, containing questions about secular affairs, I do not answer. First, because I have not sufficient time to waste on them; second, because I do not consider myself capable of instructing persons in regard to that of which I know nothing. All such questions are superinduced by wrong motives or by "evil suggestions," either of which I do not entertain.

All inquiries, coming directly or indirectly from a member of The Mother Church of Christ, Scientist, which relate in any manner to the keeping or the breaking of one of the Church By-laws, should be addressed to the Christian Science Board of Directors and not to the Pastor Emeritus.

A WORD TO THE WISE

The hour is imminent. Upon it lie burdens that time will remove. Just now divine Love and wisdom saith, "Be *still*, and know that I am God." Do all Chris-

1 tian Scientists see or understand the importance of that
demand at the moment, when human wisdom is inade-
3 quate to meet the exigencies of the hour and when they
should wait on the logic of events?

I respectfully call your attention to this demand, know-
6 ing a little, as I ought, the human need, the divine command, the blessing which follows obedience and the bane
which follows disobedience. Hurried conclusions as to
9 the public thought are not apt to be correctly drawn. The
public sentiment is helpful or dangerous only in proportion
to its right or its wrong concept, and the forward footsteps
12 it impels or the prejudice it instils. This prejudice the
future must disclose and dispel. Avoid for the immediate
present public debating clubs. Also be sure that you are
15 not caught in some author's net, or made blind to his
loss of the Golden Rule, of which Christian Science is the
predicate and postulate, when he borrows the thoughts,
18 words, and classification of one author without quotation-
marks, at the same time giving full credit to another more
fashionable but less correct.

21 My books state Christian Science correctly. They may
not be as taking to those ignorant of this Science as
books less correct and therefore less profound. But it is
24 not safe to accept the latter as standards. We would not
deny their authors a hearing, since the Scripture declares,
"He that is not against us is on our part." And we should
27 also speak in loving terms of their efforts, but we cannot
afford to recommend any literature as wholly Christian
Science which is not absolutely genuine.

30 Beloved students, just now let us adopt the classic
saying, "They also serve who only stand and wait."
Our Cause is growing apace under the present persecution

thereof. This is a crucial hour, in which the coward and 1
the hypocrite come to the surface to pass off, while the
loyal at heart and the worker in the spirit of Truth are 3
rising to the zenith of success, — the "Well done, good
and faithful," spoken by our Master.

CAPITALIZATION   6

A correct use of capital letters in composition caps the
climax of the old "new tongue." Christian Science is not
understood by the writer or the reader who does not com- 9
prehend where capital letters should be used in writing
about Christian Science.

In divine Science all belongs to God, for God is All; 12
hence the propriety of giving unto His holy name
due deference, — the capitalization which distinguishes
it from all other names, thus obeying the leading of our 15
Lord's Prayer.

The coming of Christ's kingdom on earth begins in the
minds of men by honoring God and sacredly holding His 18
name apart from the names of that which He creates.
Mankind almost universally gives to the divine Spirit
the name God. Christian Science names God as divine 21
Principle, Love, the infinite Person. In this, as in all
that is right, Christian Scientists are expected to stick
to their text, and by no illogical conclusion, either in 24
speaking or in writing, to forget their prayer, "Hallowed
be Thy name."

In their textbook it is clearly stated that God is divine 27
Principle and that His synonyms are Love, Truth, Life,
Spirit, Mind, Soul, which combine as *one*. The divine
Principle includes them all. The word Principle, when 30
referring to God, should not be written or used as a

1 common noun or in the plural number. To avoid using
this word incorrectly, use it only where you can substi-
3 tute the word God and make sense. This rule strictly
observed will preserve an intelligent usage of the word
and convey its meaning in Christian Science.

6   What are termed in common speech the principle of harmonious vibration, the principle of conservation of number in geometry, the principle of the inclined plane in
9 mechanics, *etc.,* are but an effect of one universal cause, —
an emanation of the one divine intelligent Principle that
holds the earth in its orbit by evolved spiritual power,
12 that commands the waves and the winds, that marks the
sparrow's fall, and that governs all from the infinitesimal
to the infinite, — namely, God. Withdraw God, divine
15 Principle, from man and the universe, and man and the
universe would no longer exist. But annihilate matter,
and man and the universe would remain the forever fact,
18 the spiritual "substance of things hoped for;" and the
evidence of the immortality of man and the cosmos is
sustained by the intelligent divine Principle, Love.
21   Beloved students, in this you learn to hallow His name,
even as you value His all-power, all-presence, all-Science,
and depend on Him for your existence.

24   WHEREFORE?

Our faithful laborers in the field of Science have
been told by the alert editor-in-chief of the *Christian*
27 *Science Sentinel* and *Journal* that "Mrs. Eddy advises,
until the public thought becomes better acquainted with
Christian Science, that Christian Scientists decline to
30 doctor infectious or contagious diseases."

The great Master said, "For which of those works do 1
ye stone me?" He said this to satisfy himself regarding
that which he spake as God's representative — as one who 3
never weakened in his own personal sense of righteousness
because of another's wickedness or because of the minify-
ing of his own goodness by another. Charity is quite as 6
rare as wisdom, but when charity does appear, it is known
by its patience and endurance.

When, under the protection of State or United States 9
laws, good citizens are arrested for manslaughter because
one out of three of their patients, having the same disease
and in the same family, dies while the others recover, we 12
naturally turn to divine justice for support and wait on
God. Christian Scientists should be influenced by their
own judgment in taking a case of malignant disease. 15
They should consider well their ability to cope with the
claim, and they should not overlook the fact that there
are those lying in wait to catch them in their sayings; 18
neither should they forget that in their practice, whether
successful or not, *they are not specially protected by law.*
The above quotation by the editor-in-chief stands for this: 21
Inherent justice, constitutional individual rights, self-
preservation, and the gospel injunction, "Neither cast
ye your pearls before swine, lest they trample them under 24
their feet, and turn again and rend you."

And it stands side by side with Christ's command,
"Whosoever shall smite thee on thy right cheek, turn to 27
him the other also." I abide by this rule and triumph by
it. The sinner may sneer at this beatitude, for "the fool
hath said in his heart, There is no God." Statistics show 30
that Christian Science cures a larger per cent of malignant
diseases than does *materia medica.*

1 I call disease by its name and have cured it thus; so
there is nothing new on this score. My book Science and
3 Health names disease, and thousands are healed by
learning that so-called disease is a sensation of mind, not
of matter. Evil minds signally blunder in divine meta-
6 physics; hence I am always saying the unexpected to
them. The evil mind calls it "skulking," when to me it
is wisdom to "overcome evil with good." I fail to know
9 how one can be a Christian and yet depart from Christ's
teachings.

SIGNIFICANT QUESTIONS

12 Who shall be greatest? Referring to John the Baptist,
of whom he said none greater had been born of women,
our Master declared: "He that is least in the kingdom of
15 heaven is greater than he." That is, he that hath the
kingdom of heaven, the reign of holiness, in the least in his
heart, shall be greatest.

18 Who shall inherit the earth? The meek, who sit at the
feet of Truth, bathing the human understanding with
tears of repentance and washing it clean from the taints of
21 self-righteousness, hypocrisy, envy, — they shall inherit
the earth, for "wisdom is justified of her children."

"Who shall dwell in Thy holy hill? He that walketh
24 uprightly, and worketh righteousness, and speaketh the
truth in his heart."

Who shall be called to Pleasant View? He who strives,
27 and attains; who has the divine presumption to say: "For
I know whom I have believed, and am persuaded that
he is able to keep that which I have committed unto him
30 against that day" (St. Paul). It goes without saying that
such a one was never called to Pleasant View for penance

or for reformation; and I call none but genuine Christian 1
Scientists, unless I mistake their calling. No mesmerist
nor disloyal Christian Scientist is fit to come hither. I 3
have no use for such, and there cannot be found at Pleasant
View one of *this sort*. "For all that do these things are
an abomination unto the Lord: and because of these 6
abominations the Lord thy God doth drive them out from
before thee." (Deuteronomy 18 : 12.)

It is true that loyal Christian Scientists, called to the 9
home of the Discoverer and Founder of Christian Science,
can acquire in one year the Science that otherwise might
cost them a half century. But this should not be the 12
incentive for going thither. Better far that Christian
Scientists go to help their helper, and thus lose all selfishness, as she has lost it, and thereby help themselves and 15
the whole world, as she has done, according to this saying
of Christ Jesus: "And whosoever doth not bear his cross,
and come after me, cannot be my disciple."   18

MENTAL DIGESTION

Will those beloved students, whose growth is taking in
the Ten Commandments and scaling the steep ascent of 21
Christ's Sermon on the Mount, accept profound thanks for
their swift messages of rejoicing over the twentieth century Church Manual? Heaps upon heaps of praise con- 24
front me, and for what? That which I said in my heart
would never be needed, — namely, laws of limitation for a
Christian Scientist. Thy ways are not as ours. Thou 27
knowest best what we need most, — hence my disappointed hope and grateful joy. The redeemed should be
happier than the elect. Truth is strong with destiny; 30
it takes life profoundly; it measures the infinite against

the finite. Notwithstanding the sacrilegious moth of time, eternity awaits our Church Manual, which will maintain its rank as in the past, amid ministries aggressive and active, and will stand when those have passed to rest.

Scientific pathology illustrates the digestion of spiritual nutriment as both sweet and bitter, — sweet in expectancy and bitter in experience or during the senses' assimilation thereof, and digested only when Soul silences the dyspepsia of sense. This church is impartial. Its rules apply not to one member only, but to one and all equally. Of this I am sure, that each Rule and By-law in this Manual will increase the spirituality of him who obeys it, invigorate his capacity to heal the sick, to comfort such as mourn, and to awaken the sinner.

TEACHING IN THE SUNDAY SCHOOL

To the Superintendent and Teachers of The
Mother Church Sunday School

Beloved Students: — I read with pleasure your approval of the amendments to Article XIX, Sections 5 and 6,[1] in our Church Manual. Be assured that fitness and fidelity such as thine in the officials of my church give my solitude sweet surcease. It is a joy to know that they who are faithful over foundational trusts, such as the Christian education of the dear children, will reap the reward of rightness, rise in the scale of being, and realize at last their Master's promise, "And they shall be all taught of God."

Pleasant View, Concord, N. H.,
November 14, 1904

[1] Article XX, Sections 2 and 3 in 89th edition.

CHARITY AND INVALIDS

Mrs. Eddy endeavors to bestow her charities for such purposes only as God indicates. Giving merely in compliance with solicitations or petitions from strangers, incurs the liability of working in wrong directions. As a rule, she has suffered most from those whom she has labored much to benefit — also from the undeserving poor to whom she has given large sums of money, worse than wasted. She has, therefore, finally resolved to spend no more time or money in such uncertain, unfortunate investments. She has qualified students for healing the sick, and has ceased practice herself in order to help God's work in other of its highest and infinite meanings, as God, not man, directs. Hence, letters from invalids demanding her help do not reach her. They are committed to the waste-basket by her secretaries.

"Charity suffereth long and is kind," but wisdom must govern charity, else love's labor is lost and giving is unkind. As it is, Mrs. Eddy is constantly receiving more important demands on her time and attention than one woman is sufficient to supply. It would therefore be as unwise for her to undertake new tasks, as for a landlord who has not an empty apartment in his house, to receive more tenants.

LESSONS IN THE SUNDAY SCHOOL

To the Officers of the Sunday School of Second Church of Christ, Scientist, New York

Beloved Brethren: — You will accept my thanks for your interesting report regarding the By-law, "Subject for Lessons" (Article XX, Section 3 of Church Manual).

232 Miscellany

1 It rejoices me that you are recognizing the proper course,
unfurling your banner to the breeze of God, and sailing
3 over rough seas with the helm in His hands. Steering
thus, the waiting waves will weave for you their winning
webs of life in looms of love that line the sacred shores.
6 The right way wins the right of way, even the way of
Truth and Love whereby all our debts are paid, mankind
blessed, and God glorified.

9 WATCHING *versus* WATCHING OUT

COMMENT ON AN EDITORIAL WHICH APPEARED IN THE CHRISTIAN
SCIENCE SENTINEL, SEPTEMBER 23, 1905

12 Our Lord and Master left to us the following sayings as
living lights in our darkness: "What I say unto you I say
unto all, Watch" (Mark 13 : 37); and, "If the goodman
15 of the house had known what hour the thief would come,
he would have watched, and not have suffered his house
to be broken through." (Luke 12 : 39.)
18 Here we ask: Are Christ's teachings the true authority
for Christian Science? They are. Does the textbook of
Christian Science, "Science and Health with Key to the
21 Scriptures," read on page 252, "A knowledge of error
and of its operations must precede that understanding
of Truth which destroys error, until the entire mortal,
24 material error finally disappears, and the eternal verity,
man created by and of Spirit, is understood and recognized as the true likeness of his Maker"? It does. If
27 so-called watching produces fear or exhaustion and no
good results, does that watch accord with Jesus' saying?
It does not. Can watching as Christ demands harm
30 you? It cannot. Then should not "watching out"
mean, watching against a negative watch, *alias,* no

watch, and gaining the spirit of true watching, even the 1
spirit of our Master's command? It must mean that.

Is there not something to watch in yourself, in your 3
daily life, since "by their fruits ye shall know them,"
which prevents an effective watch? Otherwise, wherefore the Lord's Prayer, "Deliver us from evil"? And 6
if this something, when challenged by Truth, frightens
you, should you not put that out instead of *putting
out your watch?* I surely should. Then are you not 9
made better by watching? I am. Which should we
prefer, ease or dis-ease in sin? Is not discomfort from
sin better adapted to deliver mortals from the effects of 12
belief in sin than ease in sin? and can you demonstrate
over the effects of other people's sins by indifference
thereto? I cannot.   15

The Scriptures say, "They have healed also the hurt
of the daughter of my people slightly, saying, Peace,
peace; when there is no peace" (Jeremiah 6 : 14), thus 18
taking the name of God in vain. Ignorance of self is the
most stubborn belief to overcome, for apathy, dishonesty,
sin, follow in its train. One should watch to know what 21
his errors are; and if this watching destroys his peace in
error, should one watch against such a result? He should
not. Our Master said, "He that taketh not his cross, 24
and followeth after me, is not worthy of me . . . and he
that loseth his life [his false sense of life] for my sake shall
find it." (Matthew 10 : 38, 39.)   27

PRINCIPLE OR PERSON?

Do Christian Scientists love God as much as they love
mankind? Aye, that's the question. Let us examine it 30
for ourselves. Thinking of person implies that one is not

1 thinking of Principle, and fifty telegrams per holiday signalize the thinking of person. Are the holidays blest by
3 absorbing one's time writing or reading congratulations? I cannot watch and pray while reading telegrams; they only cloud the clear sky, and they give the appearance of
6 personal worship which Christian Science annuls. Did the dear students know how much I love them, and how I need every hour wherein to express this love in labor
9 for them, they would gladly give me the holidays for this work and not task themselves with mistaken means. But God will reward their kind motives, and guide them
12 every step of the way from human affection to spiritual understanding, from faith to achievement, from light to Love, from sense to Soul.

15 CHRISTIAN SCIENCE AND CHINA

Beloved Student: — The report of the success of Christian Science in benighted China, when regarded on one side
18 only, is cheering, but to look at both sides of the great question of introducing Christian Science into a heathen nation gives the subject quite another aspect. I believe
21 that all our great Master's sayings are practical and scientific. If the Dowager Empress could hold her nation, there would be no danger in teaching Christian
24 Science in her country. But a war on religion in China would be more fatal than the Boxers' rebellion. Silent prayer in and for a heathen nation is just what
27 is needed. But to teach and to demonstrate Christian Science before the minds of the people are prepared for it, and when the laws are against it, is fraught with
30 danger.

INCONSISTENCY

To teach the truth of life without using the word death, the suppositional opposite of life, were as impossible as to define truth and not name its opposite, error. Straining at gnats, one may swallow camels.

The tender mother, guided by love, faithful to her instincts, and adhering to the imperative rules of Science, asks herself: Can I teach my child the correct numeration of numbers and never name a cipher? Knowing that she cannot do this in mathematics, she should know that it cannot be done in metaphysics, and so she should definitely name the error, uncover it, and teach truth scientifically.

SIGNS OF THE TIMES

Is God infinite? Yes. Did God make man? Yes. Did God make all that was made? He did. Is God Spirit? He is. Did infinite Spirit make that which is not spiritual? No. Who or what made matter? Matter as substance or intelligence never was made. Is mortal man a creator, is he matter or spirit? Neither one. Why? Because Spirit is God and *infinite;* hence there can be no other creator and no other creation. Man is but His image and likeness.

Are you a Christian Scientist? I am. Do you adopt as truth the above statements? I do. Then why this meaningless commemoration of birthdays, since there are none?

Had I known what was being done in time to have prevented it, that which commemorated in deed or in word what is not true, would never have entered into the

1 history of our church buildings. Let us have no more of
echoing dreams. Will the beloved students accept my
3 full heart's love for them and their kind thoughts.

NOTA BENE

My Beloved Christian Scientists: — Because I suggested
6 the name for one central Reading Room, and this name
continues to be multiplied, you will permit me to make
the *amende honorable* — notwithstanding "incompetence"
9 — and to say, please adopt generally for your name,
Christian Science Reading Room. An old axiom says:
Too much of one thing spoils the whole. Too many
12 centres may become equivalent to no centre.

Here I have the joy of knowing that Christian Scientists
will exchange the present name for the one which I sug-
15 gest, with the sweet alacrity and uniformity with which
they accepted the first name.

Merely this appellative seals the question of unity, and
18 opens wide on the amplitude of liberty and love a far-
reaching motive and success, of which we can say, the
more the better.

21 PLEASANT VIEW, CONCORD, N. H.,
July 8, 1907

TAKE NOTICE

24 I request the Christian Scientists universally to read
the paragraph beginning at line 30 of page 442 in the
edition of Science and Health which will be issued Febru-
27 ary 29 [1908]. I consider the information there given to
be of great importance at this stage of the workings of
animal magnetism, and it will greatly aid the students in
30 their individual experiences.

The contemplated reference in Science and Health to the "higher criticism" announced in the *Sentinel* a few weeks ago, I have since decided not to publish.

TAKE NOTICE

What I wrote on Christian Science some twenty-five years ago I do not consider a precedent for a present student of this Science. The best mathematician has not attained the full understanding of the principle thereof, in his earliest studies or discoveries. Hence, it were wise to accept only my teachings that I know to be correct and adapted to the present demand.

TAKE NOTICE

To Christian Scientists: — See Science and Health, page 442, line 30, and give daily attention thereto.

PRACTITIONERS' CHARGES

Christian Science practitioners should make their charges for treatment equal to those of reputable physicians in their respective localities.

Brookline, Mass., December 24, 1909

TAKE NOTICE

The article on the Church Manual by Blanche Hersey Hogue, in the *Sentinel* of September 10 [1910] is practical and scientific, and I recommend its careful study to all Christian Scientists.

CHAPTER XI

Questions Answered

1 ## QUESTIONS AND ANSWERS

Will the Bible, if read and practised, heal as effectually
3 *as your book, "Science and Health with Key to the*
Scriptures"?

THE exact degree of comparison between the effects
6 produced by reading the above-named books can
only be determined by personal proof. Rightly to read
and to practise the Scriptures, their spiritual sense must
9 be discerned, understood, and demonstrated. God being
Spirit, His language and meaning are wholly spiritual.
Uninspired knowledge of the translations of the Scriptures
12 has imparted little power to practise the Word. Hence
the revelation, discovery, and presentation of Christian
Science — the Christ Science, or "new tongue" of which
15 St. Mark prophesied — became requisite in the divine
order. On the swift pinions of spiritual thought man
rises above the letter, law, or *morale* of the inspired Word
18 to the spirit of Truth, whereby the Science is reached
that demonstrates God. When the Bible is thus read
and practised, there is no possibility of misinterpreta-
21 tion. God is understandable, knowable, and applicable
to every human need. In this is the proof that Christian Science is Science, for it demonstrates Life, not

death; health, not disease; Truth, not error; Love, not 1
hate. The Science of the Scriptures coexists with God;
and "Science and Health with Key to the Scriptures" 3
relegates Christianity to its primitive proof, wherein
reason, revelation, the divine Principle, rules, and practice of Christianity acquaint the student with God. In 6
the ratio that Christian Science is studied and understood, mankind will, as aforetime, imbibe the spirit and
prove the practicality, validity, and redemptive power of 9
Christianity by healing all manner of disease, by overcoming sin and death.

Must mankind wait for the ultimate of the millennium — 12
until every man and woman comes into the knowledge of
Christ and all are taught of God and see their apparent
identity as one man and one woman — for God to be 15
represented by His idea or image and likeness?

God is one, and His idea, image, or likeness, man, is one.
But God is *infinite* and so includes *all* in one. Man is the 18
generic term for men and women. Man, as the idea or
image and likeness of the infinite God, is a compound, com-
plex idea or likeness of the infinite *one,* or one infinite, 21
whose image is the reflection of all that is real and eternal
in infinite identity. Gender means a kind. Hence mankind — in other words, a kind of man who is identi- 24
fied by sex — is the material, so-called man born of the
flesh, and is not the spiritual man, created by God,
Spirit, who made all that was made. The millennium 27
is a state and stage of mental advancement, going
on since ever time was. Its impetus, accelerated by
the advent of Christian Science, is marked, and will 30

1 increase till all men shall know Him (divine Love) from
the least to the greatest, and one God and the brother-
3 hood of man shall be known and acknowledged throughout the earth.

THE HIGHER CRITICISM

6   An earnest student writes to me: "Would it be asking
too much of you to explain more fully why you call Christian Science the higher criticism?"
9   I called Christian Science the higher criticism in my
dedicatory Message to The Mother Church, June 10,
1906, when I said, "This Science is a law of divine Mind,
12 . . . an ever-present help.   Its presence is felt, for it
acts and acts wisely, always unfolding the highway of
hope, faith, understanding."
15   I now repeat another proof, namely, that Christian
Science is the higher criticism because it criticizes evil,
disease, and death — all that is unlike God, good — on a
18 Scriptural basis, and approves or disapproves according
to the word of God.   In the next edition of Science and
Health I shall refer to this.
21   MARY BAKER EDDY

CLASS TEACHING

Mrs. Eddy thus replies, through her student, Mr.
24 Adam Dickey, to the question, Does Mrs. Eddy approve
of class teaching: —

Yes!   She most assuredly does, when the teaching is
27 done by those who are duly qualified, who have received certificates from the Massachusetts Metaphysical
College or the Board of Education, and who have the

necessary moral and spiritual qualifications to perform 1
this important work.   Class teaching will not be abolished until it has accomplished that for which it was 3
established; viz., the elucidation of the Principle and
rule of Christian Science through the higher meaning
of the Scriptures.   Students who are ready for this 6
step should beware the net that is craftily laid and cun-
ningly concealed to prevent their advancement in this
direction.   9

INSTRUCTION BY MRS. EDDY

We are glad to have the privilege of publishing an extract from a letter to Mrs. Eddy, from a Christian Scien- 12
tist in the West, and Mrs. Eddy's reply thereto.   The
issue raised is an important one and one upon which
there should be absolute and correct teaching.   Christian 15
Scientists are fortunate to receive instruction from their
Leader on this point.   The question and Mrs. Eddy's
reply follow.   18

"Last evening I was catechized by a Christian Science
practitioner because I referred to myself as an immortal
idea of the one divine Mind.   The practitioner said that 21
my statement was wrong, because I still lived in my
flesh.   I replied that I did not live in my flesh, that
my flesh lived or died according to the beliefs I enter- 24
tained about it; but that, after coming to the light of
Truth, I had found that I lived and moved and had
my being in God, and to obey Christ was not to know 27
as real the beliefs of an earthly mortal.   Please give the
truth in the *Sentinel,* so that all may know it."

1
Mrs. Eddy's Reply

You are scientifically correct in your statement about
3 yourself. You can never demonstrate spirituality until you
declare yourself to be immortal and understand that
you are so. Christian Science is absolute; it is neither
6 behind the point of perfection nor advancing towards
it; it is at this point and must be practised therefrom.
Unless you fully perceive that you are the child
9 of God, hence perfect, you have no Principle to demonstrate and no rule for its demonstration. By this I
do not mean that mortals are the children of God, —
12 far from it. In practising Christian Science you must
state its Principle correctly, or you forfeit your ability
to demonstrate it.

15   TAKE NOTICE

I hereby announce to the Christian Science field that
all inquiries or information relating to Christian Science
18 practice, to publication committee work, reading-room
work, or to Mother Church membership, should be sent
to the Christian Science Board of Directors of The
21 Mother Church; and I have requested my secretary
not to make inquiries on these subjects, nor to reply to
any received, but to leave these duties to the Clerk of
24 The Mother Church, to whom they belong.

MARY BAKER EDDY

September 28, 1910

CHAPTER XII

Readers, Teachers, Lecturers

THE NEW YORK CHURCHES

M Y BELOVED STUDENTS:— According to reports, the belief is springing up among you that the several 3 churches in New York City should come together and form one church. This is a suggestion of error, which should be silenced at its inception. You cannot have lost 6 sight of the rules for branch churches as published in our Church Manual. The Empire City is large, and there should be more than one church in it. 9

The Readers of The Church of Christ, Scientist, hold important, responsible offices, and two individuals would meet meagrely the duties of half a dozen or more of the 12 present incumbents. I have not yet had the privilege of knowing two students who are adequate to take charge of three or more churches. The students in New York 15 and elsewhere will see that it is wise to remain in their own fields of labor and give all possible time and attention to caring for their own flocks. 18

THE NOVEMBER CLASS, 1898

Beloved Christian Scientists: — Your prompt presence in Concord at my unexplained call witnesses your fidelity 21 to Christian Science and your spiritual unity with your

Leader. I have awaited your arrival before informing
you of my purpose in sending for you, in order to avoid
the stir that might be occasioned among those who wish
to share this opportunity and to whom I would gladly
give it at this time if a larger class were advantageous
to the students.

You have been invited hither to receive from me one or
more lessons on Christian Science, prior to conferring on
any or all of you who are ready for it, the degree of C.S.D.,
of the Massachusetts Metaphysical College. This opportunity is designed to impart a fresh impulse to our spiritual
attainments, the great need of which I daily discern.
I have awaited the right hour, and to be called of God
to contribute my part towards this result.

The "secret place," whereof David sang, is unquestionably man's spiritual state in God's own image and likeness, even the inner sanctuary of divine Science, in which
mortals do not enter without a struggle or sharp experience, and in which they put off the human for the divine.
Knowing this, our Master said: "Many are called, but few
are chosen." In the highest sense of a disciple, all loyal
students of my books are indeed my students, and your
wise, faithful teachers have come so to regard them.

What I have to say may not require more than one
lesson. This, however, must depend on results. But
the lessons will certainly not exceed three in number.
No charge will be made for my services.

MASSACHUSETTS METAPHYSICAL COLLEGE

The Massachusetts Metaphysical College of Boston,
Massachusetts, was chartered A.D. 1881. As the people
observed the success of this Christian system of heal-

ing all manner of disease, over and above the approved 1
schools of medicine, they became deeply interested
in it. Now the wide demand for this universal bene- 3
fice is imperative, and it should be met as heretofore,
cautiously, systematically, scientifically. This Christian educational system is established on a broad and 6
liberal basis. Law and order characterize its work
and secure a thorough preparation of the student for
practice.   9

The growth of human inquiry and the increasing popularity of Christian Science, I regret to say, have called
out of their hiding-places those poisonous reptiles and de- 12
vouring beasts, superstition and jealousy. Towards the
animal elements manifested in ignorance, persecution,
and lean glory, and to their Babel of confusion worse 15
confounded, let Christian Scientists be charitable. Let
the voice of Truth and Love be heard above the dire
din of mortal nothingness, and the majestic march of 18
Christian Science go on *ad infinitum,* praising God,
doing the works of primitive Christianity, and enlightening the world.   21

To protect the public, students of the Massachusetts
Metaphysical College have received certificates, and these
credentials are still required of all who claim to teach 24
Christian Science.

Inquiries have been made as to the precise signification of the letters of degrees that follow the names of 27
Christian Scientists. They indicate, respectively, the
degrees of Bachelor and Doctor of Christian Science,
conferred by the President or Vice-President of the 30
Massachusetts Metaphysical College. The first degree
(C.S.B.) is given to students of the Primary class; the

1 second degree (C.S.D.) is given to those who, after
receiving the first degree, continue for three years as
3 practitioners of Christian Science in good and regular
standing.

Students who enter the Massachusetts Metaphys-
6 ical College, or are examined under its auspices by
the Board of Education, must be well educated and
have practised Christian Science three years with good
9 success.

THE BOARD OF EDUCATION

In the year 1889, to gain a higher hope for the race, I
12 closed my College in the midst of unprecedented prosperity, left Boston, and sought in solitude and silence a
higher understanding of the absolute scientific unity which
15 must exist between the teaching and letter of Christianity
and the spirit of Christianity, dwelling forever in the
divine Mind or Principle of man's being and revealed
18 through the human character.

While revising "Science and Health with Key to the
Scriptures," the light and might of the divine concur-
21 rence of the spirit and the Word appeared, and the
result is an auxiliary to the College called the Board of
Education of The Mother Church of Christ, Scientist,
24 in Boston, Mass.

Our Master said: "What I do thou knowest not now;
but thou shalt know hereafter;" and the spirit of his
27 mission, the wisdom of his words, and the immortality of his works are the same to-day as yesterday and
forever.

30　The Magna Charta of Christian Science means much,

multum in parvo, — all-in-one and one-in-all. It stands 1
for the inalienable, universal rights of men. Essentially
democratic, its government is administered by the 3
common consent of the governed, wherein and whereby
man governed by his creator is self-governed. The
church is the mouthpiece of Christian Science, — its 6
law and gospel are according to Christ Jesus; its rules
are health, holiness, and immortality, — equal rights and
privileges, equality of the sexes, rotation in office. 9

TO A FIRST READER

Beloved Student: — Christ is meekness and Truth
enthroned. Put on the robes of Christ, and you will 12
be lifted up and will draw all men unto you. The
little fishes in my fountain must have felt me when I
stood silently beside it, for they came out in orderly 15
line to the rim where I stood. Then I fed these
sweet little thoughts that, not fearing me, sought their
food of me. 18

God has called you to be a fisher of men. It is not a
stern but a loving look which brings forth mankind to
receive your bestowal, — not so much eloquence as *tender* 21
persuasion that takes away their fear, for it is Love alone
that feeds them.

Do you come to your little flock so filled with divine 24
food that you cast your bread upon the waters? Then
be sure that after many or a few days it will return
to you. 27

The little that I have accomplished has all been
done through love, — self-forgetful, patient, unfaltering
tenderness. 30

THE CHRISTIAN SCIENCE BOARD OF LECTURESHIP

Beloved Students: — I am more than satisfied with your
work: its grandeur almost surprises me. Let your watchword always be:

> "Great, not like Caesar, stained with blood,
>   But only great as I am good."

You are not setting up to be great; you are here for the
purpose of grasping and defining the demonstrable, the
eternal. Spiritual heroes and prophets are they whose
new-old birthright is to put an end to falsities in a wise
way and to proclaim Truth so winningly that an honest,
fervid affection for the race is found adequate for the
emancipation of the race.

You are the needed and the inevitable sponsors for the
twentieth century, reaching deep down into the universal and rising above theorems into the transcendental,
the infinite — yea, to the reality of God, man, nature,
the universe. No fatal circumstance of idolatry can fold
or falter your wings. No fetishism with a symbol can
fetter your flight. You soar only as uplifted by God's
power, or you fall for lack of the divine impetus. You
know that to conceive God aright you must be good.

The Christ mode of understanding Life — of extermi-
nating sin and suffering and their penalty, death — I
have largely committed to you, my faithful witnesses.
You go forth to face the foe with loving look and with the
religion and philosophy of labor, duty, liberty, and love,
to challenge universal indifference, chance, and creeds.
Your highest inspiration is found nearest the divine
Principle and nearest the scientific expression of Truth.

You may condemn evil in the abstract without harming 1 any one or your own moral sense, but condemn persons seldom, if ever.   Improve every opportunity to correct 3 sin through your own perfectness.   When error strives to be heard above Truth, let the "still small voice" produce God's phenomena.   Meet dispassionately the raging ele- 6 ment of individual hate and counteract its most gigantic falsities.

The moral abandon of hating even one's enemies ex- 9 cludes goodness.   Hate is a moral idiocy let loose for one's own destruction.   Unless withstood, the heat of hate burns the wheat, spares the tares, and sends forth a 12 mental miasma fatal to health, happiness, and the morals of mankind, — and all this only to satiate its loathing of love and its revenge on the patience, silence, and lives 15 of saints.   The marvel is, that at this enlightened period a respectable newspaper should countenance such evil tendencies.   18

Millions may know that I am the Founder of Christian Science.   I alone know what that means.

READERS IN CHURCH   21

The report that I prefer to have a man, rather than a woman, for First Reader in The Church of Christ, Scientist, I desire to correct.   My preference lies with 24 the individual best fitted to perform this important function.   If both the First and Second Readers are my students, then without reference to sex I should prefer 27 that student who is most spiritually-minded.   What our churches need is that devout, unselfed quality of thought which spiritualizes the congregation.   30

1 WORDS FOR THE WISE

The By-law of The Mother Church of Christ, Scientist,
3 relative to a three years' term for church Readers, was
entitled to and has received profound attention. Rotation
in office promotes wisdom, quiets mad ambition, satisfies
6 justice, and crowns honest endeavors.

The best Christian Scientists will be the first to adopt
this By-law in their churches, and their Readers will
9 retire *ex officio,* after three years of acceptable service as
church Readers, to higher usefulness in this vast vineyard
of our Lord.
12 The churches who adopt this By-law will please send
to the Editor of our periodicals notice of their action.

AFTERGLOW

15 *Beloved Students:* — The By-law of The Mother
Church of Christ, Scientist, stipulating three years as
the term for its Readers, neither binds nor compels the
18 branch churches to follow suit; and the By-law applies
only to Christian Science churches in the United States
and Canada. Doubtless the churches adopting this
21 By-law will discriminate as regards its adaptability to
their conditions. But if now is not the time, the branch
churches can wait for the favored moment to act on this
24 subject.

I rest peacefully in knowing that the impulsion of this
action in The Mother Church was from above. So I have
27 faith that whatever is done in this direction by the branch
churches will be blest. The Readers who have filled this
sacred office many years, have beyond it duties and

attainments beckoning them. What these are I cannot 1
yet say. The great Master saith: "What I do thou
knowest not now; but thou shalt know hereafter."   3

TEACHERS OF CHRISTIAN SCIENCE

I reply to the following question from unknown questioners: 6

"Are the students, whom I have taught, obliged to
take both Primary and Normal class instruction in the
Board of Education in order to become teachers of Pri- 9
mary classes?"

No, not if you and they are loyal Christian Scientists,
and not if, after examination in the Board of Education, 12
your pupils are found eligible to enter the Normal class,
which at present is taught in the Board of Education
only.   15

There is evidently some misapprehension of my meaning
as to the mode of instruction in the Board of Education.
A Primary student of mine can teach pupils the prac- 18
tice of Christian Science, and after three years of good
practice, my Primary student can himself be examined in
the Board of Education, and if found eligible, receive a 21
certificate of the degree C.S.D.

THE GENERAL ASSOCIATION OF TEACHERS, 1903

My Beloved Students: — I call you mine, for all is thine 24
and mine. What God gives, elucidates, armors, and tests
in His service, is ours; and we are His. You have convened only to convince yourselves of this grand verity: 27
namely, the unity in Christian Science. Cherish steadfastly this fact. Adhere to the teachings of the Bible,

1 Science and Health, and our Manual, and you will obey
the law and gospel. Have one God and you will
3 have no devil. Keep yourselves busy with divine Love.
Then you will be toilers like the bee, always distributing
sweet things which, if bitter to sense, will be salutary as
6 Soul; but you will not be like the spider, which weaves
webs that ensnare.

Rest assured that the good you do unto others you do
9 to yourselves as well, and the wrong you may commit
must, will, rebound upon you. The entire purpose of
true education is to make one not only know the truth
12 but live it — to make one enjoy doing right, make one
not work in the sunshine and run away in the storm, but
work midst clouds of wrong, injustice, envy, hate; and
15 wait on God, the strong deliverer, who will reward righteousness and punish iniquity. "As thy days, so shall thy
strength be."

18 THE LONDON TEACHERS' ASSOCIATION, 1903

Beloved Students: — Your letter and dottings are an
oasis in my wilderness. They point to verdant pastures,
21 and are already rich rays from the eternal sunshine of
Love, lighting and leading humanity into paths of peace
and holiness.

24 Your "Thanksgiving Day," instituted in England on
New Year's Day, was a step in advance. It expressed
your thanks, and gave to the "happy New Year" a higher
27 hint. You are not aroused to this action by the allurements of wealth, pride, or power; the impetus comes from
above — it is moral, spiritual, divine. All hail to this
30 higher hope that neither slumbers nor is stilled by the
cold impulse of a lesser gain!

It rejoices me to know that you know that healing 1
the sick, soothing sorrow, brightening this lower sphere
with the ways and means of the higher and everlasting 3
harmony, brings to light the perfect original man and universe. What nobler achievement, what greater glory can
nerve your endeavor? Press on! My heart and hope 6
are with you.

"Thou art not here for ease or pain,
But manhood's glorious crown to gain."   9

THE GENERAL ASSOCIATION OF TEACHERS, 1904

Beloved Brethren: — I thank you. Jesus said: "The
world hath not known Thee: but I have known Thee, 12
and these have known that Thou hast sent me."

THE CANADIAN TEACHERS, 1904

Beloved Brethren: — Accept my love and these words 15
of Jesus: "Holy Father, keep through Thine own name
those whom Thou hast given me, that they may be one,
as we are."   18

STUDENTS IN THE BOARD OF EDUCATION,
DECEMBER, 1904

Beloved Students: — You will accept my profound 21
thanks for your letter and telegram. If wishing is wise,
I send with this a store of wisdom in three words: God
bless you. If faith is fruition, you have His rich blessing 24
already and my joy therewith.

We understand best that which begins in ourselves
and by education brightens into birth. Dare to be 27
faithful to God and man. Let the creature become

1 one with his creator, and mysticism departs, heaven
opens, right reigns, and you have begun to be a Chris-
3 tian Scientist.

THE MAY CLASS, 1905

Beloved: — I am glad you enjoy the dawn of Christian
6 Science; you must reach its meridian. Watch, pray,
demonstrate. Released from materialism, you shall run
and not be weary, walk and not faint.

9 ### THE DECEMBER CLASS, 1905

Beloved Students: — Responding to your kind letter,
let me say: You will reap the sure reward of right think-
12 ing and acting, of watching and praying, and you will
find the ever-present God an ever-present help. I
thank the faithful teacher of this class and its dear
15 members.

"ROTATION IN OFFICE"

Dear Leader: — May we have permission to print, as
18 a part of the preamble to our By-laws, the following
extract from your article "Christian Science Board of
Education" in the June *Journal* of 1904, page 184: —

21 "The Magna Charta of Christian Science means
much, *multum in parvo,* — all-in-one and one-in-all. It
stands for the inalienable, universal rights of men.
24 Essentially democratic, its government is administered
by the common consent of the governed, wherein and
whereby man governed by his creator is self-governed.
27 The church is the mouthpiece of Christian Science,
— its law and gospel are according to Christ Jesus;

its rules are health, holiness, and immortality, — equal 1
rights and privileges, equality of the sexes, rotation
in office." 3

Mrs. Eddy's Reply

Christian Science churches have my consent to publish
the foregoing in their By-laws. By "rotation in office" 6
I do not mean that minor officers who are filling their
positions satisfactorily should be removed every three
years, or be elevated to offices for which they are not 9
qualified.

CHESTNUT HILL, MASS.,
March 6, 1909 12

CHAPTER XIII

Christmas

1   EARLY CHIMES, DECEMBER, 1898

BEFORE the Christmas bells shall ring, allow me
3   to improvise some new notes, not specially musical to be sure, but admirably adapted to the key of my
feeling and emphatically phrasing strict observance or
6 note well.

This year, my beloved Christian Scientists, you must
grant me my request that I be permitted total exemption
9 from Christmas gifts. Also I beg to send to you all a
deep-drawn, heartfelt breath of thanks for those things
of beauty and use forming themselves in your thoughts
12 to send to your Leader. Thus may I close the door of
mind on this subject, and open the volume of Life on
the pure pages of impersonal presents, pleasures, achieve-
15 ments, and *aid*.

CHRISTMAS, 1900

Again loved Christmas is here, full of divine benedic-
18 tions and crowned with the dearest memories in human
history — the earthly advent and nativity of our Lord
and Master. At this happy season the veil of time
21 springs aside at the touch of Love. We count our blessings and see whence they came and whither they tend.
Parents call home their loved ones, the Yule-fires burn,
24 the festive boards are spread, the gifts glow in the dark

green branches of the Christmas-tree. But alas for the 1
broken household band! God give to them more of
His dear love that heals the wounded heart.   3

To-day the watchful shepherd shouts his welcome over
the new cradle of an old truth. This truth has traversed
night, through gloom to glory, from cradle to crown. To 6
the awakened consciousness, the Bethlehem babe has left
his swaddling-clothes (material environments) for the
form and comeliness of the divine ideal, which has passed 9
from a corporeal to the spiritual sense of Christ and is
winning the heart of humanity with ineffable tenderness.
The Christ is speaking for himself and for his mother, 12
Christ's heavenly origin and aim. To-day the Christ is,
more than ever before, "the way, the truth, and the
life," — "which lighteth every man that cometh into the 15
world," healing all sorrow, sickness, and sin. To this
auspicious Christmastide, which hallows the close of the
nineteenth century, our hearts are kneeling humbly. We 18
own his grace, reviving and healing. At this immortal
hour, all human hate, pride, greed, lust should bow and
declare Christ's power, and the reign of Truth and Life 21
divine should make man's being pure and blest.

CHRISTMAS GIFTS

Beloved Students: — For your manifold Christmas memo- 24
rials, too numerous to name, I group you in one benison
and send you my Christmas gift, two words enwrapped,
— *love* and *thanks*.   27

To-day Christian Scientists have their record in the
monarch's palace, the Alpine hamlet, the Christian traveller's resting-place. Wherever the child looks up in 30

1 prayer, or the Book of Life is loved, there the sinner is reformed and the sick are healed. Those are the "signs

3 following." What is it that lifts a system of religion to deserved fame? Nothing is worthy the name of religion save one lowly offering — love.

6   This period, so fraught with opposites, seems illuminated for woman's hope with divine light. It bids her bind the tenderest tendril of the heart to all of holiest

9 worth. To the woman at the sepulchre, bowed in strong affection's anguish, one word, "Mary," broke the gloom with Christ's all-conquering love. Then came her resurrec-

12 tion and task of glory, to know and to do God's will, — in the words of St. Paul: "Looking unto Jesus the author and finisher of our faith; who for the joy that was set be-

15 fore him endured the cross, despising the shame, and is set down at the right hand of the throne of God."

The memory of the Bethlehem babe bears to mortals

18 gifts greater than those of Magian kings, — hopes that cannot deceive, that waken prophecy, gleams of glory, coronals of meekness, diadems of love. Nor should they

21 who drink their Master's cup repine over blossoms that mock their hope and friends that forsake. Divinely beautiful are the Christmas memories of him who sounded

24 all depths of love, grief, death, and humanity.

To the dear children let me say: Your Christmas gifts are hallowed by our Lord's blessing. A transmitted

27 charm rests on them. May this consciousness of God's dear love for you give you the might of love, and may you move onward and upward, lowly in its majesty.

30   To the children who sent me that beautiful statuette in alabaster — a child with finger on her lip reading a book — I write: Fancy yourselves with me; take a peep into

my studio; look again at your gift, and you will see the 1
sweetest sculptured face and form conceivable, mounted
on its pedestal between my bow windows, and on either 3
side lace and flowers. I have named it my *white student*.

From First Church of Christ, Scientist, in London,
Great Britain, I received the following cabled message: — 6

Rev. Mrs. Eddy, Pleasant View,
        Concord, N. H.

Loving, grateful Christmas greetings from members 9
London, England, church.

December 24, 1901

To this church across the sea I return my heart's wire- 12
less love. All our dear churches' Christmas telegrams to
me are refreshing and most pleasing Christmas presents,
for they require less attention than packages and give me 15
more time to think and work for others. I hope that in
1902 the churches will remember me only thus. Do not
forget that an honest, wise zeal, a lowly, triumphant 18
trust, a true heart, and a helping hand constitute man,
and nothing less is man or woman.

[*New York World*]   21

THE SIGNIFICANCE OF CHRISTMAS

Certain occasions, considered either collectively or
individually and observed properly, tend to give the 24
activity of man infinite scope; but mere merry-making
or needless gift-giving is not that in which human capacities find the most appropriate and proper exercise. 27
Christmas respects the Christ too much to submerge
itself in merely temporary means and ends. It represents
the eternal informing Soul recognized only in harmony, 30

1 in the beauty and bounty of Life everlasting, — in the
truth that is Life, the Life that heals and saves man-
3 kind. An eternal Christmas would make matter an alien
save as phenomenon, and matter would reverentially
withdraw itself before Mind. The despotism of material
6 sense or the flesh would flee before such reality, to make
room for substance, and the shadow of frivolity and the
inaccuracy of material sense would disappear.

9 In Christian Science, Christmas stands for the real, the
absolute and eternal, — for the things of Spirit, not of matter. Science is divine; it hath no partnership with human
12 means and ends, no half-way stations. Nothing conditional or material belongs to it. Human reason and philosophy may pursue paths devious, the line of liquids, the
15 lure of gold, the doubtful sense that falls short of substance, the things hoped for and the evidence unseen.

The basis of Christmas is the rock, Christ Jesus; its
18 fruits are inspiration and spiritual understanding of joy
and rejoicing, — not because of tradition, usage, or corporeal pleasures, but because of fundamental and de-
21 monstrable truth, because of the heaven within us. The
basis of Christmas is love loving its enemies, returning
good for evil, love that "suffereth long, and is kind." The
24 true spirit of Christmas elevates medicine to Mind; it
casts out evils, heals the sick, raises the dormant faculties, appeals to all conditions, and supplies every need of
27 man. It leaves hygiene, medicine, ethics, and religion
to God and His Christ, to that which is the Way, in word
and in deed, — the Way, the Truth, and the Life.

30 There is but one Jesus Christ on record. Christ is
incorporeal. Neither the you nor the I in the flesh can
be or is Christ.

CHRISTMAS FOR THE CHILDREN   1

Methinks the loving parents and guardians of youth ofttimes query: How shall we cheer the children's Christ- 3 mas and profit them withal? The wisdom of their elders, who seek wisdom of God, seems to have amply provided for this, according to the custom of the age and to the full 6 supply of juvenile joy. Let it continue thus with one exception: the children should not be taught to believe that Santa Claus has aught to do with this pastime. A 9 deceit or falsehood is never wise. Too much cannot be done towards guarding and guiding well the germinating and inclining thought of childhood. To mould aright 12 the first impressions of innocence, aids in perpetuating purity and in unfolding the immortal model, man in His image and likeness. St. Paul wrote, "When I 15 was a child, I spake as a child, I understood as a child, . . . but when I became a man, I put away childish things." 18

PLEASANT VIEW, CONCORD, N. H.,
        December 28, 1905

[*The Ladies' Home Journal*]   21
WHAT CHRISTMAS MEANS TO ME

To me Christmas involves an open secret, understood by few — or by none — and unutterable except in Chris- 24 tian Science. Christ was not born of the flesh. Christ is the Truth and Life born of God — born of Spirit and not of matter. Jesus, the Galilean Prophet, was born 27 of the Virgin Mary's spiritual thoughts of Life and its manifestation.

1   God creates man perfect and eternal in His own image.
Hence man is the image, idea, or likeness of perfection
3 — an ideal which cannot fall from its inherent unity
with divine Love, from its spotless purity and original
perfection.

6   Observed by material sense, Christmas commemorates
the birth of a human, material, mortal babe — a babe
born in a manger amidst the flocks and herds of a Jewish
9 village.

This homely origin of the babe Jesus falls far short
of my sense of the eternal Christ, Truth, never born and
12 never dying. I celebrate Christmas with my soul, my
spiritual sense, and so commemorate the entrance into
human understanding of the Christ conceived of Spirit,
15 of God and not of a woman — as the birth of Truth, the
dawn of divine Love breaking upon the gloom of matter
and evil with the glory of infinite being.

18   Human doctrines or hypotheses or vague human philosophy afford little divine effulgence, deific presence or
power. Christmas to me is the reminder of God's great
21 gift, — His spiritual idea, man and the universe, —
a gift which so transcends mortal, material, sensual giving that the merriment, mad ambition, rivalry, and
24 ritual of our common Christmas seem a human mockery in mimicry of the real worship in commemoration
of Christ's coming.

27   I love to observe Christmas in quietude, humility,
benevolence, charity, letting good will towards man, eloquent silence, prayer, and praise express my conception
30 of Truth's appearing.

The splendor of this nativity of Christ reveals infinite
meanings and gives manifold blessings. Material gifts

and pastimes tend to obliterate the spiritual idea in con- 1
sciousness, leaving one alone and without His glory.

MRS. EDDY'S CHRISTMAS MESSAGE 3

My Household

Beloved: — A word to the wise is sufficient. Mother
wishes you all a *happy Christmas*, a feast of Soul and a 6
famine of sense.

Lovingly thine,

MARY BAKER EDDY 9

Box G, Brookline, Mass.,
    December 25, 1909

CHAPTER XIV

Contributions to Newspapers and Magazines

1   [*Boston Herald*, May 5, 1900]

A WORD IN DEFENCE

3 I EVEN hope that those who are kind enough to speak well of me may do so honestly and not too earnestly, and this seldom, until mankind learn more of
6 my meaning and can speak justly of my living.

               [*Boston Globe*, November 29, 1900]

CHRISTIAN SCIENCE THANKS

9   On the threshold of the twentieth century, will you please send through the *Globe* to the people of New England, which is the birthplace of Thanksgiving Day, a
12 sentiment on what the last Thanksgiving Day of the nineteenth century should signify to all mankind?

Mrs. Eddy's Response

15   New England's last Thanksgiving Day of this century signifies to the minds of men the Bible better understood and Truth and Love made more practical; the First
18 Commandment of the Decalogue more imperative, and

"Love thy neighbor as thyself" more possible and 1
pleasurable.

It signifies that love, unselfed, knocks more loudly than 3
ever before at the heart of humanity and that it finds
admittance; that revelation, spiritual voice and vision,
are less subordinate to material sight and sound and more 6
apparent to reason; that evil flourishes less, invests less
in trusts, loses capital, and is bought at par value; that
the Christ-spirit will cleanse the earth of human gore; 9
that civilization, peace between nations, and the brotherhood of man should be established, and justice plead not
vainly in behalf of the sacred rights of individuals, peoples, 12
and nations.

It signifies that the Science of Christianity has dawned
upon human thought to appear full-orbed in millennial 15
glory; that scientific religion and scientific therapeutics
are improving the morals and increasing the longevity
of mankind, are mitigating and destroying sin, disease, 18
and death; that religion and *materia medica* should be
no longer tyrannical and proscriptive; that divine Love,
impartial and universal, as understood in divine Sci- 21
ence, forms the coincidence of the human and divine,
which fulfils the saying of our great Master, "The kingdom of God is within you;" that the atmosphere of the 24
human mind, when cleansed of self and permeated with
divine Love, will reflect this purified subjective state in
clearer skies, less thunderbolts, tornadoes, and extremes of 27
heat and cold; that agriculture, manufacture, commerce,
and wealth should be governed by honesty, industry, and justice, reaching out to all classes and peoples. 30
For these signs of the times we thank our Father-
Mother God.

1 [*New York World*, December, 1900]

INSUFFICIENT FREEDOM

3 To my sense, the most imminent dangers confronting the coming century are: the robbing of people of life and liberty under the warrant of the Scriptures; the claims of 6 politics and of human power, industrial slavery, and insufficient freedom of honest competition; and ritual, creed, and trusts in place of the Golden Rule, "Whatsoever ye 9 would that men should do to you, do ye even so to them."

[*Concord* (N. H.) *Monitor*, July, 1902]

CHRISTIAN SCIENCE AND THE TIMES

12 Your article on the decrease of students in the seminaries and the consequent vacancies occurring in the pulpits, points unmistakably to the "signs of the times" 15 of which Jesus spoke. This flux and flow in one direction, so generally apparent, tends in one ultimate — the final spiritualization of all things, of all codes, modes, 18 hypotheses, of man and the universe. How can it be otherwise, since God is Spirit and the origin of all that really is, and since this great fact is to be verified by the 21 spiritualization of all?

Since 1877, these special "signs of the times" have increased year by year. My book, "Science and Health 24 with Key to the Scriptures," was published in 1875. Note, if you please, that many points in theology and *materia medica,* at that date undisturbed, are now agitated, 27 modified, and disappearing, and the more spiritual modes and significations are adopted.

It is undoubtedly true that Christian Science is destined

to become the one and the only religion and therapeutics 1
on this planet. And why not, since Christianity is fully
demonstrated to be divine Science? Nothing can be cor- 3
rect and continue forever which is not divinely scientific,
for Science is the law of the Mind that is God, who is
the originator of all that really is. The Scripture reads: 6
"All things were made by Him; and without Him was
not any thing made that was made." Here let us remember that God is not the Alpha and Omega of man 9
and the universe; He is supreme, infinite, the great forever, the eternal Mind that hath no beginning and no
end, no Alpha and no Omega. 12

[*New York American*, February, 1905]
HEAVEN

Is heaven spiritual? 15
Heaven is spiritual. Heaven is harmony, — infinite,
boundless bliss. The dying or the departed enter heaven
in proportion to their progress, in proportion to their fit- 18
ness to partake of the quality and the quantity of heaven.
One individual may first awaken from his dream of life
in matter with a sense of music; another with that of 21
relief from fear or suffering, and still another with a bitter sense of lost opportunities and remorse. Heaven is
the reign of divine Science. Material thought tends to 24
obscure spiritual understanding, to darken the true conception of man's divine Principle, Love, wherein and
whereby soul is emancipate and environed with ever- 27
lasting Life. Our great Teacher hath said: "Behold, the
kingdom of God is within you" — within man's spiritual
understanding of all the divine modes, means, forms, ex- 30
pression, and manifestation of goodness and happiness.

[*Boston Herald*, March 5, 1905]

PREVENTION AND CURE OF DIVORCE

The nuptial vow should never be annulled so long as the *morale* of marriage is preserved. The frequency of divorce shows that the imperative nature of the marriage relation is losing ground, — hence that some fundamental error is engrafted on it. What is this error? If the motives of human affection are right, the affections are enduring and achieving. What God hath joined together, man cannot sunder.

Divorce and war should be exterminated according to the Principle of law and gospel, — the maintenance of individual rights, the justice of civil codes, and the power of Truth uplifting the motives of men. Two commandments of the Hebrew Decalogue, "Thou shalt not commit adultery" and "Thou shalt not kill," obeyed, will eliminate divorce and war. On what hath not a "Thus saith the Lord," I am as silent as the dumb centuries without a living Divina.

This time-world flutters in my thought as an unreal shadow, and I can only solace the sore ills of mankind by a lively battle with "the world, the flesh and the devil," in which Love is the liberator and gives man the victory over himself. Truth, canonized by life and love, lays the axe at the root of all evil, lifts the curtain on the Science of being, the Science of wedlock, of living and of loving, and harmoniously ascends the scale of life. Look high enough, and you see the heart of humanity warming and winning. Look long enough, and you see male and female one — sex or gender eliminated; you see the designation *man* meaning woman as well, and you see the

whole universe included in one infinite Mind and reflected 1
in the intelligent compound idea, image or likeness, called
man, showing forth the infinite divine Principle, Love, 3
called God, — man wedded to the Lamb, pledged to innocence, purity, perfection. Then shall humanity have
learned that "they which shall be accounted worthy to 6
obtain that world, and the resurrection from the dead,
neither marry, nor are given in marriage: neither can
they die any more: for they are equal unto the angels; 9
and are the children of God." (Luke 20 : 35, 36.) This,
therefore, is Christ's plan of salvation from divorce.

All are but parts of one stupendous whole,   12
Whose body nature is, and God the Soul.
                                        — POPE

[*The Independent*, November, 1906]   15
HARVEST

God hath thrust in the sickle, and He is separating the
tares from the wheat. This hour is molten in the furnace 18
of Soul. Its harvest song is world-wide, world-known,
world-great. The vine is bringing forth its fruit; the
beams of right have healing in their light. The windows 21
of heaven are sending forth their rays of reality — even
Christian Science, pouring out blessing for cursing, and
rehearsing: "I will rebuke the devourer for your sakes, 24
and he shall not destroy the fruits of your ground."
"Prove me now herewith, saith the Lord of hosts, if I
will not open you the windows of heaven, and pour you 27
out a blessing, that there shall not be room enough to
receive it."
The lie and the liar are self-destroyed. Truth is im- 30

1 mortal. "Rejoice, and be exceeding glad: . . . for so
persecuted they the prophets which were before you."
3 The cycle of good obliterates the epicycle of evil.

Because of the magnitude of their spiritual import, we
repeat the signs of these times. In 1905, the First Con-
6 gregational Church, my first religious home in this capital
city of Concord, N. H., kindly invited me to its one hundred and seventy-fifth anniversary; the leading editors
9 and newspapers of my native State congratulate me; the
records of my ancestry attest honesty and valor. Divine
Love, nearer my consciousness than before, saith: I am
12 rewarding your waiting, and "thy people shall be my
people."

Let error rage and imagine a vain thing. Mary Baker
15 Eddy is not dead, and the words of those who say that she
is are the father of their *wish*. Her life is proven under
trial, and evidences "as thy days, so shall thy strength be."
18 Those words of our dear, departing Saviour, breathing
love for his enemies, fill my heart: "Father, forgive them;
for they know not what they do." My writings heal the
21 sick, and I thank God that for the past forty years I
have returned good for evil, and that I can appeal to
Him as my witness to the truth of this statement.
24 What we love determines what we are. I love the
prosperity of Zion, be it promoted by Catholic, by Protestant, or by Christian Science, which anoints with
27 Truth, opening the eyes of the blind and healing the sick.
I would no more quarrel with a man because of his religion
than I would because of his art. The divine Principle of
30 Christian Science will ultimately be seen to control both
religion and art in unity and harmony. God is Spirit,
and "they that worship Him must worship Him in spirit

and in truth." If, as the Scriptures declare, God, Spirit, 1
is infinite, matter and material sense are null, and there
are no vertebrata, mollusca, or radiata. 3

When I wrote "Science and Health with Key to the
Scriptures," I little understood all that I indited; but
when I practised its precepts, healing the sick and reform- 6
ing the sinner, then I learned the truth of what I had
written. It is of comparatively little importance what a
man thinks or believes he knows; the good that a man does 9
is the one thing needful and the sole proof of rightness.

[*The Evening Press*, Grand Rapids, Mich., August, 1907]

MRS. EDDY DESCRIBES HER HUMAN IDEAL 12

In a modest, pleasantly situated home in the city of
Concord, N. H., lives at eighty-six years of age the most
discussed woman in all the world. This lady with sweet 15
smile and snowy hair is Mrs. Mary Baker Eddy, Founder
and Leader of Christian Science, beloved of thousands
of believers and followers of the thought that has made 18
her famous. It was to this aged woman of world-wide
renown that the editor of *The Evening Press* addressed
this question, requesting the courtesy of a reply: — 21

"What is nearest and dearest to your heart to-day?"

Mrs. Eddy's reply will be read with deep interest by all
Americans, who, whatever their religious beliefs, cannot 24
fail to be impressed by the personality of this remarkable
woman.

Mrs. Eddy's Answer 27

Editor of The Evening Press: — To your courtesy and
to your question permit me to say that, insomuch as I
know myself, what is "nearest and dearest" to my heart 30

1 is an honest man or woman — one who steadfastly and
actively strives for perfection, one who leavens the loaf
3 of life with justice, mercy, truth, and love.

Goodness is greatness, and the logic of events pushes
onward the centuries; hence the Scripture, "The law of
6 the Spirit of life in Christ Jesus hath made me [man] free
from the law of sin and death."

This predicate and ultimate of scientific being presents,
9 however, no claim that man is equal to God, for the finite
is not the altitude of the infinite.

The real man was, is, and ever shall be the divine ideal,
12 that is, God's image and likeness; and Christian Science
reveals the divine Principle, the example, the rule, and
the demonstration of this idealism.

15 Sincerely yours,

MARY BAKER EDDY

PLEASANT VIEW, CONCORD, N. H.

18 [*Cosmopolitan*, November, 1907]

YOUTH AND YOUNG MANHOOD

EDITOR'S NOTE. — The *Cosmopolitan* presents this month to its
21 readers a facsimile of an article sent to us by Mrs. Eddy, with the
corrections on the manuscript reproduced in her own handwriting.
Not only Mrs. Eddy's own devoted followers, but the public gen-
24 erally, will be interested in this communication from the extraordinary woman who, nearly eighty-seven years of age, plays so great
a part in the world and leads with such conspicuous success her very
27 great following.

Mrs. Eddy writes very rarely for any publications outside of the
Christian Science periodicals, and our readers will be interested in
30 this presentation of the thought of a mind that has had so much
influence on this generation.

The *Cosmopolitan* gives no editorial indorsement to the teachings

of Christian Science, it has no religious opinions or predilections to 1
put before its readers. This manuscript is presented simply as an
interesting and remarkable proof of Mrs. Eddy's ability in old age 3
to vindicate in her own person the value of her teachings.

Certainly, Christian Scientists, enthusiastic in their belief, are
fortunate in being able to point to a Leader far beyond the allotted 6
years of man, emerging triumphantly from all attacks upon her, and
guiding with remarkable skill, determination, and energy a very
great organization that covers practically the civilized world.   9

King David, the Hebrew bard, sang, "I have been
young, and now am old; yet have I not seen the right-
eous forsaken, nor his seed begging bread."   12

I for one accept his wise deduction, his ultimate or
spiritual sense of thinking, feeling, and acting, and its
reward. This sense of rightness acquired by experience 15
and wisdom, should be early presented to youth and to
manhood in order to forewarn and forearm humanity.

The ultimatum of life here and hereafter is utterly 18
apart from a material or personal sense of pleasure, pain,
joy, sorrow, life, and death. The truth of life, or life in
truth, is a scientific knowledge that is portentous; and 21
is won only by the spiritual understanding of Life as God,
good, ever-present good, and therefore life eternal.

You will agree with me that the material body is mortal, 24
but Soul is immortal; also that the five personal senses
are perishable: they lapse and relapse, come and go, until
at length they are consigned to dust. But say you, 27
"Man awakes from the dream of death in possession of
the five personal senses, does he not?" Yes, because
death alone does not awaken man in God's image 30
and likeness. The divine Science of Life alone gives

1 the true sense of life and of righteousness, and demonstrates the Principle of life eternal; even the Life that
3 is Soul apart from the so-called life of matter or the
material senses.

Death alone does not absolve man from a false material
6 sense of life, but goodness, holiness, and love do this, and
so consummate man's being with the harmony of heaven;
the omnipotence, omnipresence, and omniscience of Life,
9 even its all-power, all-presence, all-Science.

Dear reader, right thinking, right feeling, and right
acting — honesty, purity, unselfishness — in youth tend
12 to success, intellectuality, and happiness in manhood.
To begin rightly enables one to end rightly, and thus it is
that one achieves the Science of Life, demonstrates health,
15 holiness, and immortality.

[*Boston Herald*, April, 1908]

MRS. EDDY SENDS THANKS

18 Mrs. Mary Baker Eddy has sent the following to the
Herald: —

Will the dear Christian Scientists accept my thanks
21 for their magnificent gifts, and allow me to say that I am
not fond of an abundance of material presents; but I
am cheered and blessed when beholding Christian healing,
24 unity among brethren, and love to God and man; this
is my crown of rejoicing, for it demonstrates Christian
Science.

27 The Psalmist sang, "That thy way may be known
upon earth, thy saving health among all nations."

[*Minneapolis* (Minn.) *News*] 1
UNIVERSAL FELLOWSHIP

Christian Science can and does produce universal 3
fellowship. As the sequence of divine Love it explains
love, it lives love, it demonstrates love. The human,
material, so-called senses do not perceive this fact until 6
they are controlled by divine Love; hence the Scripture,
"Be still, and know that I am God."

BROOKLINE, MASS., 9
May 1, 1908

[*New York Herald*]
MRS. EDDY'S OWN DENIAL THAT SHE IS ILL 12

Permit me to say, the report that I am sick (and I
trust the desire thereof) is dead, and should be buried.
Whereas the fact that I am well and keenly alive to the 15
truth of being — the Love that is Life — is sure and steadfast. I go out in my carriage daily, and have omitted
my drive but twice since I came to Massachusetts. 18
Either my work, the demands upon my time at home, or
the weather, is all that prevents my daily drive.

Working and praying for my dear friends' and my dear 21
enemies' health, happiness, and holiness, the true sense
of being goes on.

Doing unto others as we would that they do by us, is 24
immortality's self. Intrepid, self-oblivious love fulfils the
law and is self-sustaining and eternal. With white-winged
charity brooding over all, spiritually understood and de- 27
monstrated, let us unite in one *Te Deum* of praise.

BOX G, BROOKLINE, MASS.,
May 15, 1908 30

[*Christian Science Sentinel*, May 16, 1908]

TO WHOM IT MAY CONCERN

Since Mrs. Eddy is watched, as one watches a criminal or a sick person, she begs to say, in her own behalf, that she is neither; therefore to be criticized or judged by either a daily drive or a dignified stay at home, is superfluous. When accumulating work requires it, or because of a preference to remain within doors she omits her drive, do not strain at gnats or swallow camels over it, but try to be composed and resigned to the shocking fact that she is minding her own business, and recommends this surprising privilege to all her dear friends and enemies.

MARY BAKER EDDY

[*Boston Post*, November, 1908]

POLITICS

Mrs. Mary Baker Eddy has always believed that those who are entitled to vote should do so, and she has also believed that in such matters no one should seek to dictate the actions of others.

In reply to a number of requests for an expression of her political views, she has given out this statement: —

I am asked, "What are your politics?" I have none, in reality, other than to help support a righteous government; to love God supremely, and my neighbor as myself.

CHAPTER XV

Peace and War

[*Boston Herald*, March, 1898] 1

OTHER WAYS THAN BY WAR

IN reply to your question, "Should difficulties between 3 the United States and Spain be settled peacefully by statesmanship and diplomacy, in a way honorable and satisfactory to both nations?" I will say I can see no 6 other way of settling difficulties between individuals and nations than by means of their wholesome tribunals, equitable laws, and sound, well-kept treaties. 9

A bullet in a man's heart never settles the question of his life. The mental animus goes on, and urges that the answer to the sublime question as to man's life shall come 12 from God and that its adjustment shall be according to His laws. The characters and lives of men determine the peace, prosperity, and life of nations. Killing men is 15 not consonant with the higher law whereby wrong and injustice are righted and exterminated.

Whatever weighs in the eternal scale of equity and 18 mercy tips the beam on the right side, where the immortal words and deeds of men alone can settle all questions amicably and satisfactorily. But if our nation's rights or 21 honor were seized, every citizen would be a soldier and woman would be armed with power girt for the hour.

277

1 To coincide with God's government is the proper incentive to the action of all nations. If His purpose for
3 peace is to be subserved by the battle's plan or by the intervention of the United States, so that the Cubans may learn to make war no more, this means and end
6 will be accomplished.

The government of divine Love is supreme. Love rules the universe, and its edict hath gone forth: "Thou shalt
9 have no other gods before me," and "Love thy neighbor as thyself." Let us have the molecule of faith that removes mountains, — faith armed with the understand-
12 ing of Love, as in divine Science, where right reigneth. The revered President and Congress of our favored land are in God's hands.

15   [*Boston Globe*, December, 1904]
            HOW STRIFE MAY BE STILLED

Follow that which is good.
18   A Japanese may believe in a heaven for him who dies in defence of his country, but the steadying, elevating power of civilization destroys such illusions and should
21 overcome evil with good.

Nothing is gained by fighting, but much is lost.

Peace is the promise and reward of rightness. Gov-
24 ernments have no right to engraft into civilization the burlesque of uncivil economics. War is in itself an evil, barbarous, devilish. Victory in error is defeat in Truth.
27 War is not in the domain of good; war weakens power and must finally fall, pierced by its own sword.

The Principle of all power is God, and God is Love.
30 Whatever brings into human thought or action an ele-

ment opposed to Love, is never requisite, never a neces- 1
sity, and is not sanctioned by the law of God, the law
of Love.   The Founder of Christianity said: "My 3
peace I give unto you: not as the world giveth, give
I unto you."

Christian Science reinforces Christ's sayings and doings. 6
The Principle of Christian Science demonstrates peace.
Christianity is the chain of scientific being reappearing in
all ages, maintaining its obvious correspondence with the 9
Scriptures and uniting all periods in the design of God.
The First Commandment in the Hebrew Decalogue —
"Thou shalt have no other gods before me" — obeyed, 12
is sufficient to still all strife.   God is the divine Mind.
Hence the sequence: Had all peoples one Mind, peace
would reign.   15

God is Father, infinite, and this great truth, when
understood in its divine metaphysics, will establish the
brotherhood of man, end wars, and demonstrate "on 18
earth peace, good will toward men."

[*Christian Science Sentinel,* June 17, 1905]
THE PRAYER FOR PEACE   21

Dearly Beloved: — I request that every member of The
Mother Church of Christ, Scientist, in Boston, pray each
day for the amicable settlement of the war between 24
Russia and Japan; and pray that God bless that great
nation and those islands of the sea with peace and
prosperity.   27

MARY BAKER EDDY

PLEASANT VIEW, CONCORD, N. H.,
June 13, 1905   30

a spiritual foresight of the nations' drama presented 1
itself and awakened a wiser want, even to know how
to pray other than the daily prayer of my church, — 3
"Thy kingdom come. Thy will be done in earth, as it
is in heaven."

I cited, as our present need, faith in God's disposal of 6
events. Faith full-fledged, soaring to the Horeb height,
brings blessings infinite, and the spirit of this orison is the
fruit of rightness, — "on earth peace, good will toward 9
men." On this basis the brotherhood of all peoples is
established; namely, one God, one Mind, and "Love thy
neighbor as thyself," the basis on which and by which 12
the infinite God, good, the Father-Mother Love, is ours
and we are His in divine Science.

[*Boston Globe*, August, 1905]   15

PRACTISE THE GOLDEN RULE

[Telegram]

"Official announcement of peace between Russia and 18
Japan seems to offer an appropriate occasion for the expression of congratulations and views by representative
persons. Will you do us the kindness to wire a sentiment 21
on some phase of the subject, on the ending of the war,
the effect on the two parties to the treaty of Portsmouth,
the influence which President Roosevelt has exerted for 24
peace, or the advancement of the cause of arbitration."

Mrs. Eddy's Reply

To the Editor of the *Globe:*   27

War will end when nations are ripe for progress. The
treaty of Portsmouth is not an executive power, although

1 its purpose is good will towards men. The government of
a nation is its peace maker or breaker.

3   I believe strictly in the Monroe doctrine, in our Constitution, and in the laws of God. While I admire the
faith and friendship of our chief executive in and for all
6 nations, my hope must still rest in God, and the Scriptural injunction, — "Look unto me, and be ye saved, all
the ends of the earth."

9   The Douma recently adopted in Russia is no uncertain ray of dawn. Through the wholesome chastisements of Love, nations are helped onward towards
12 justice, righteousness, and peace, which are the landmarks of prosperity. In order to apprehend more,
we must practise what we already know of the Golden
15 Rule, which is to all mankind a light emitting light.

MARY BAKER EDDY

MRS. EDDY AND THE PEACE MOVEMENT

18 MR. HAYNE DAVIS, American Secretary,
International Conciliation Committee,
542 Fifth Avenue, New York City

21   *Dear Mr. Davis:* — Deeply do I thank you for the
interest you manifest in the success of the Association
for International Conciliation. It is of paramount im-
24 portance to every son and daughter of all nations under
the sunlight of the law and gospel.

May God guide and prosper ever this good endeavor.
27   Most truly yours,

MARY BAKER EDDY

PLEASANT VIEW, CONCORD, N. H.,
30   April 3, 1907

MRS. EDDY'S ACKNOWLEDGMENT OF APPOINTMENT 1
AS FONDATEUR OF THE ASSOCIATION FOR
INTERNATIONAL CONCILIATION   3

FIRST CHURCH OF CHRIST, SCIENTIST, NEW YORK CITY,
MR. JOHN D. HIGGINS, *Clerk*

My Beloved Brethren: — Your appointment of me as 6
Fondateur of the Association for International Conciliation is most gracious.

To aid in this holy purpose is the leading impetus of 9
my life. Many years have I prayed and labored for the
consummation of "on earth peace, good will toward
men." May the fruits of said grand Association, preg- 12
nant with peace, find their birthright in divine Science.

Right thoughts and deeds are the sovereign remedies
for all earth's woe. Sin is its own enemy. Right has its 15
recompense, even though it be betrayed. Wrong may be
a man's highest idea of right until his grasp of goodness
grows stronger. It is always safe to be just. 18

When pride, self, and human reason reign, injustice is
rampant.

Individuals, as nations, unite harmoniously on the basis 21
of justice, and this is accomplished when self is lost in
Love — or God's own plan of salvation. "To do justly,
and to love mercy, and to walk humbly" is the stand- 24
ard of Christian Science.

Human law is right only as it patterns the divine.
Consolation and peace are based on the enlightened sense 27
of God's government.

Lured by fame, pride, or gold, success is dangerous, but the choice of folly never fastens on the good 30

1 or the great. Because of my rediscovery of Christian Science, and honest efforts (however meagre)
3 to help human purpose and peoples, you may have accorded me more than is deserved, — but 'tis sweet to be remembered.

6 Lovingly yours,

MARY BAKER EDDY

PLEASANT VIEW, CONCORD, N. H.,
9 April 22, 1907

[*Concord* (N. H.) *Daily Patriot*]

A CORRECTION

12 *Dear Editor:* — In the issue of your good paper, the *Patriot,* May 21, when referring to the Memorial service of the E. E. Sturtevant Post held in my church building,
15 it read, "It is said to be the first time in the history of the church in this country that such an event has occurred." In your next issue please correct this mistake.
18 Since my residence in Concord, 1889, the aforesaid Memorial service has been held annually in some church in Concord, N. H.
21 When the Veterans indicated their desire to assemble in my church building, I consented thereto only as other churches had done. But here let me say that I am
24 absolutely and religiously opposed to war, whereas I do believe implicitly in the full efficacy of divine Love to conciliate by arbitration all quarrels between nations
27 and peoples.

MARY BAKER EDDY

PLEASANT VIEW, CONCORD, N. H.,
30 May 28, 1907

TO A STUDENT 1

Dear Student: — Please accept my thanks for your
kind invitation, on behalf of the Civic League of San 3
Francisco, to attend the Industrial Peace Conference,
and accept my hearty congratulations.

I cannot spare the time requisite to meet with you; 6
but I rejoice with you in all your wise endeavors for
industrial, civic, and national peace. Whatever adorns
Christianity crowns the great purposes of life and demon- 9
strates the Science of being. Bloodshed, war, and oppression belong to the darker ages, and shall be relegated
to oblivion. 12

It is a matter for rejoicing that the best, bravest, most
cultured men and women of this period unite with us in
the grand object embodied in the Association for Inter- 15
national Conciliation.

In Revelation 2 : 26, St. John says: "And he that
overcometh, and keepeth my works unto the end, to 18
him will I give power over the nations." In the words
of St. Paul, I repeat: —

"And they neither found me in the temple disputing 21
with any man, neither raising up the people, neither
in the synagogues, nor in the city: neither can they
prove the things whereof they now accuse me. But 24
this I confess unto thee, that after the way which
they call heresy, so worship I the God of my fathers,
believing all things which are written in the law and in 27
the prophets."

Most sincerely yours,
MARY BAKER EDDY 30

PLEASANT VIEW, CONCORD, N. H.

1   [*The Christian Science Journal*, May, 1908]

WAR

3 For many years I have prayed daily that there be
no more war, no more barbarous slaughtering of our
fellow-beings; prayed that all the peoples on earth and
6 the islands of the sea have one God, one Mind; love
God supremely, and love their neighbor as themselves.

National disagreements can be, and should be, arbi-
9 trated wisely, fairly; and fully settled.

It is unquestionable, however, that at this hour
the armament of navies is necessary, for the purpose
12 of preventing war and preserving peace among nations.

CHAPTER XVI

Tributes

[*New York Mail and Express*] 1
MONUMENT TO BARON AND BARONESS DE HIRSCH

THE movement to erect a monument to the late 3
Baron and Baroness de Hirsch enlists my hearty
sympathy. They were unquestionably used in a remarkable degree as instruments of divine Love. 6

Divine Love reforms, regenerates, giving to human
weakness strength, serving as admonition, instruction, and
governing all that really is. Divine Love is the noumenon 9
and phenomenon, the Principle and practice of divine
metaphysics. Love talked and not lived is a poor shift
for the weak and worldly. Love lived in a court or cot 12
is God exemplified, governing governments, industries,
human rights, liberty, life.

In love for man we gain the only and true sense of love 15
for God, practical good, and so rise and still rise to His
image and likeness, and are made partakers of that Mind
whence springs the universe. 18

Philanthropy is loving, ameliorative, revolutionary; it
wakens lofty desires, new possibilities, achievements, and
energies; it lays the axe at the root of the tree that 21
bringeth not forth good fruit; it touches thought to
spiritual issues, systematizes action, and insures success;

1 it starts the wheels of right reason, revelation, justice, and mercy; it unselfs men and pushes on the ages. Love
3 unfolds marvellous good and uncovers hidden evil. The philanthropist or reformer gives little thought to self-defence; his life's incentive and sacrifice need no apology.
6 The good done and the good to do are his ever-present reward.

Love for mankind is the elevator of the human race;
9 it demonstrates Truth and reflects divine Love. Good is divinely natural. Evil is unnatural; it has no origin in the nature of God, and He is the Father of all.
12 The great Galilean Prophet was, is, the reformer of reformers. His piety partook not of the travesties of human opinions, pagan mysticisms, tribal religion, Greek phi-
15 losophy, creed, dogma, or *materia medica*. The divine Mind was his only instrumentality in religion or medicine. The so-called laws of matter he eschewed; with
18 him matter was not the auxiliary of Spirit. He never appealed to matter to perform the functions of Spirit, divine Love.
21 Jesus cast out evil, disease, death, showing that all suffering is commensurate with sin; therefore, he cast out devils and healed the sick. He showed that every
24 effect or amplification of wrong will revert to the wrong-doer; that sin punishes itself; hence his saying, "Sin no more, lest a worse thing come unto thee." Love
27 atones for sin through love that destroys sin. His rod is love.

We cannot remake ourselves, but we can make the
30 best of what God has made. We can know that all is good because God made all, and that evil is not a fatherly grace.

All education is work. The thing most important is 1
what we do, not what we say. God's open secret is seen
through grace, truth, and love.   3

I enclose a check for five hundred dollars for the
De Hirsch monument fund.

TRIBUTES TO QUEEN VICTORIA   6

Mr. William B. Johnson, C.S.B., *Clerk*

Beloved Student: — I deem it proper that The Mother
Church of Christ, Scientist, in Boston, Massachusetts, the 9
first church of Christian Science known on earth, should
upon this solemn occasion congregate; that a special meeting of its First Members convene for the sacred purpose of 12
expressing our deep sympathy with the bereaved nation,
its loss and the world's loss, in the sudden departure of
the late lamented Victoria, Queen of Great Britain and 15
Empress of India, — long honored, revered, beloved.
"God save the Queen" is heard no more in England, but
this shout of love lives on in the heart of millions.   18

With love,

Mary Baker Eddy

Pleasant View, Concord, N. H.,   21
   January 27, 1901

It being inconvenient for me to attend the memorial
meeting in the South Congregational church on Sunday 24
evening, February 3, I herewith send a few words of con-
dolence, which may be read on that tender occasion.

I am interested in a meeting to be held in the capi- 27
tal of my native State *in memoriam* of the late lamented
Victoria, Queen of Great Britain and Empress of India.

1 It betokens a love and a loss felt by the strong hearts
of New England and the United States. When contem-
3 plating this sudden international bereavement, the near
seems afar, the distant nigh, and the tried and true seem
few. The departed Queen's royal and imperial honors
6 lose their lustre in the tomb, but her personal virtues can
never be lost. Those live on in the affection of nations.

Few sovereigns have been as venerable, revered, and
9 beloved as this noble woman, born in 1819, married in
1840, and deceased the first month of the new century.

LETTER TO MRS. McKINLEY

12 *My Dear Mrs. McKinley:* — My soul reaches out to God
for your support, consolation, and victory. Trust in Him
whose love enfolds thee. "Thou wilt keep him in perfect
15 peace, whose mind is stayed on Thee: because he trusteth
in Thee." "Out of the depths have I cried unto Thee."
Divine Love is never so near as when all earthly joys seem
18 most afar.

Thy tender husband, our nation's chief magistrate, has
passed earth's shadow into Life's substance. Through
21 a momentary mist he beheld the dawn. He awaits to
welcome you where no arrow wounds the eagle soaring,
where no partings are for love, where the high and holy
24 call you again to meet.

"I knew that Thou hearest me always," are the words of
him who suffered and subdued sorrow. Hold this attitude
27 of mind, and it will remove the sackcloth from thy home.

With love,
MARY BAKER EDDY

30 PLEASANT VIEW, CONCORD, N. H.,
September 14, 1901

TRIBUTE TO PRESIDENT McKINLEY   ₁

Imperative, accumulative, holy demands rested on the life and labors of our late beloved President, William McKinley. Presiding over the destinies of a nation meant more to him than a mere rehearsal of aphorisms, a uniting of breaches soon to widen, a quiet assent or dissent. His work began with heavy strokes, measured movements, reaching from the infinitesimal to the infinite. It began by warming the marble of politics into zeal according to wisdom, quenching the volcanoes of partizanship, and uniting the interests of all peoples; and it ended with a universal good overcoming evil.

His home relations enfolded a wealth of affection, — a tenderness not talked but felt and lived. His humanity, weighed in the scales of divinity, was not found wanting. His public intent was uniform, consistent, sympathetic, and so far as it fathomed the abyss of difficulties was wise, brave, unselfed. May his history waken a tone of truth that shall reverberate, renew euphony, emphasize humane power, and bear its banner into the vast forever.

While our nation's ensign of peace and prosperity waves over land and sea, while her reapers are strong, her sheaves garnered, her treasury filled, she is suddenly stricken, — called to mourn the loss of her renowned leader! Tears blend with her triumphs. She stops to think, to mourn, yea, to pray, that the God of harvests send her more laborers, who, while they work for their own country, shall sacredly regard the liberty of other peoples and the rights of man.

1   What cannot love and righteousness achieve for the
race? All that can be accomplished, and more than his-
3 tory has yet recorded. All good that ever was written,
taught, or wrought comes from God and human faith in
the right. Through divine Love the right government is
6 assimilated, the way pointed out, the process shortened,
and the joy of acquiescence consummated. May God
sanctify our nation's sorrow in this wise, and His rod
9 and His staff comfort the living as it did the departing.
O may His love shield, support, and comfort the chief
mourner at the desolate home!

12   POWER OF PRAYER

My answer to the inquiry, "Why did Christians of every
sect in the United States fail in their prayers to save
15 the life of President McKinley," is briefly this: Insufficient faith or spiritual understanding, and a compound of
prayers in which one earnest, tender desire works uncon-
18 sciously against the *modus operandi* of another, would
prevent the result desired. In the June, 1901, Message
to my church in Boston, I refer to the effect of one
21 human desire or belief unwittingly neutralizing another,
though both are equally sincere.

In the practice of *materia medica,* croton oil is not mixed
24 with morphine to remedy dysentery, for those drugs are
supposed to possess opposite qualities and so to produce
opposite effects. The spirit of the prayer of the righteous
27 heals the sick, but this spirit is of God, and the divine
Mind is the same yesterday, to-day, and forever; whereas the human mind is a compound of faith and doubt,
30 of fear and hope, of faith in truth and faith in error.

The knowledge that all things are possible to God ex- 1
cludes doubt, but differing human concepts as to the
divine power and purpose of infinite Mind, and the so- 3
called power of matter, act as the different properties of
drugs are supposed to act — one against the other — and
this compound of mind and matter neutralizes itself.   6

Our lamented President, in his loving acquiescence,
believed that his martyrdom was God's way.   Hundreds, thousands of others believed the same, and hun- 9
dreds of thousands who prayed for him feared that the
bullet would prove fatal.   Even the physicians may have
feared this.   12

These conflicting states of the human mind, of trembling
faith, hope, and of fear, evinced a lack of the absolute
understanding of God's omnipotence, and thus they pre- 15
vented the power of absolute Truth from reassuring the
mind and through the mind resuscitating the body of
the patient.   18

The divine power and poor human sense — yea, the spirit
and the flesh — struggled, and to mortal sense the flesh prevailed.   Had prayer so fervently offered possessed no 21
opposing element, and President McKinley's recovery
been regarded as wholly contingent on the power of God,
— on the power of divine Love to overrule the pur- 24
poses of hate and the law of Spirit to control matter, —
the result would have been scientific, and the patient
would have recovered.   27

St. Paul writes: "For the law of the Spirit of life in
Christ Jesus hath made me free from the law of sin and
death."   And the Saviour of man saith: "What things 30
soever ye desire, when ye pray, believe that ye receive
them, and ye shall have them."   Human governments

1 maintain the right of the majority to rule. Christian
Scientists are yet in a large minority on the subject of
3 divine metaphysics; but they improve the morals and the
lives of men, and they heal the sick on the basis that God
has all power, is omnipotent, omniscient, omnipresent,
6 supreme over *all.*

In a certain city the Master "did not many mighty
works there because of their unbelief," — because of the
9 mental counteracting elements, the startled or the un-
righteous contradicting minds of mortals. And if he were
personally with us to-day, he would rebuke whatever
12 accords not with a full faith and spiritual knowledge of
God. He would mightily rebuke a single doubt of the
ever-present power of divine Spirit to control all the con-
15 ditions of man and the universe.

If the skilful surgeon or the faithful M.D. is not dismayed by a fruitless use of the knife or the drug, has not
18 the Christian Scientist with his conscious understanding
of omnipotence, in spite of the constant stress of the
hindrances previously mentioned, reason for his faith in
21 what is shown him by God's works?

ON THE DEATH OF POPE LEO XIII, JULY 20, 1903

The sad, sudden announcement of the decease of Pope
24 Leo XIII, touches the heart and will move the pen of
millions. The intellectual, moral, and religious energy
of this illustrious pontiff have animated the Church of
27 Rome for one quarter of a century. The august ruler
of two hundred and fifty million human beings has now
passed through the shadow of death into the great forever.
30 The court of the Vatican mourns him; his relatives
shed "the unavailing tear." He is the loved and lost

of many millions. I sympathize with those who mourn, 1
but rejoice in knowing our dear God comforts such with
the blessed assurance that life is not lost; its influence 3
remains in the minds of men, and divine Love holds
its substance safe in the certainty of immortality.
"In Him was life; and the life was the light of men." 6
(John 1 : 4.)

A TRIBUTE TO THE BIBLE

LETTER OF THANKS FOR THE GIFT OF A COPY OF MARTIN LUTHER'S 9
TRANSLATION INTO GERMAN OF THE BIBLE, PRINTED IN NUREM-
BERG IN 1733

Dear Student: — I am in grateful receipt of your time- 12
worn Bible in German. This Book of books is also the
gift of gifts; and kindness in its largest, profoundest
sense is goodness. It was kind of you to give it to me. 15
I thank you for it.

Christian Scientists are fishers of men. The Bible is
our sea-beaten rock. It guides the fishermen. It stands 18
the storm. It engages the attention and enriches the
being of all men.

A BENEDICTION   21
[Copy of Cablegram]

COUNTESS OF DUNMORE AND FAMILY,
    55 Lancaster Gate, West, London, England   24

Divine Love is your ever-present help. You, I, and
mankind have cause to lament the demise of Lord Dunmore; but as the Christian Scientist, the servant of God 27
and man, he still lives, loves, labors.

MARY BAKER EDDY

PLEASANT VIEW, CONCORD, N. H.,   30
    August 31, 1907

1 HON. CLARENCE A. BUSKIRK'S LECTURE

The able discourse of our "learned judge," his flash of
3 flight and insight, lays the axe "unto the root of the
trees," and shatters whatever hinders the Science of
being.
6 MARY BAKER EDDY
PLEASANT VIEW, CONCORD, N. H.,
October 14, 1907

9 "HEAR, O ISRAEL"

The late lamented Christian Scientist brother and the
publisher of my books, Joseph Armstrong, C.S.D., is not
12 dead, neither does he sleep nor rest from his labors in
divine Science; and his works do follow him. Evil has no
power to harm, to hinder, or to destroy the real spiritual
15 man. He is wiser to-day, healthier and happier, than
yesterday. The mortal dream of life, substance, or mind
in matter, has been lessened, and the reward of good
18 and punishment of evil and the waking out of his Adam-
dream of evil will end in harmony, — evil powerless, and
God, good, omnipotent and infinite.
21 MARY BAKER EDDY
PLEASANT VIEW, CONCORD, N. H.,
December 10, 1907

24 MISS CLARA BARTON

In the *New York American,* January 6, 1908, Miss
Clara Barton dipped her pen in my heart, and traced its
27 emotions, motives, and object. Then, lifting the curtains
of mortal mind, she depicted its rooms, guests, standing
and seating capacity, and thereafter gave her discovery

to the press.   Now if Miss Barton were not a venerable 1
soldier, patriot, philanthropist, moralist, and states-
woman, I should shrink from such salient praise.   But 3
in consideration of all that Miss Barton really is,
and knowing that she can bear the blows which may
follow said description of her soul-visit, I will say, Amen, 6
so be it.

MARY BAKER EDDY

PLEASANT VIEW, CONCORD, N. H.,   9
    January 10, 1908

THERE IS NO DEATH

A suppositional gust of evil in this evil world is the 12
dark hour that precedes the dawn.   This gust blows
away the baubles of belief, for there is in reality no evil,
no disease, no death;   and the Christian Scientist who 15
believes that he dies, gains a rich blessing of disbelief in
death, and a higher realization of heaven.

My beloved Edward A. Kimball, whose clear, correct 18
teaching of Christian Science has been and is an inspiration to the whole field, is here now as veritably as when
he visited me a year ago.   If we would awaken to this 21
recognition, we should see him here and realize that he
never died;   thus demonstrating the fundamental truth
of Christian Science.   24

MARY BAKER EDDY

MRS. EDDY'S HISTORY

I have not had sufficient interest in the matter to read 27
or to note from others' reading what the enemies of
Christian Science are said to be circulating regarding my
history, but my friends have read Sibyl Wilbur's book, 30

1 "The Life of Mary Baker Eddy," and request the privilege of buying, circulating, and recommending it to the
3 public. I briefly declare that nothing has occurred in my
life's experience which, if correctly narrated and understood, could injure me; and not a little is already re-
6 ported of the good accomplished therein, the self-sacrifice,
etc., that has distinguished all my working years.

I thank Miss Wilbur and the Concord Publishing Com-
9 pany for their unselfed labors in placing this book before
the public, and hereby say that they have my permission
to publish and circulate this work.

12   MARY BAKER EDDY

CHAPTER XVII

Answers to Criticisms

[Letter to the *New York Commercial Advertiser*] 1

CHRISTIAN SCIENCE AND THE CHURCH

OVER the signature "A Priest of the Church," 3
somebody, kindly referring to my address to First
Church of Christ, Scientist, in Concord, N. H., writes:
"If they [Christian Scientists] have any truth to reveal 6
which has not been revealed by the church or the Bible,
let them make it known to the world, before they claim
the allegiance of mankind." 9

I submit that Christian Science has been widely made
known to the world, and that it contains the entire
truth of the Scriptures, as also whatever portions of truth 12
may be found in creeds. In addition to this, Christian
Science presents the demonstrable divine Principle and
rules of the Bible, hitherto undiscovered in the trans- 15
lations of the Bible and lacking in the creeds.

Therefore I query: Do Christians, who believe in sin,
and especially those who claim to pardon sin, believe 18
that God is good, and that God is *All?* Christian
Scientists firmly subscribe to this statement; yea, they
understand it and the law governing it, namely, that 21
God, the divine Principle of Christian Science, is

299

1 "of purer eyes than to behold evil."   On this basis they
endeavor to cast out the belief in sin or in aught
3 besides God, thus enabling the sinner to overcome
sin according to the Scripture, "Work out your own
salvation with fear and trembling.   For it is God which
6 worketh in you both to will and to do of His good
pleasure."

Does he who believes in sickness know or declare that
9 there is no sickness or disease, and thus heal disease?
Christian Scientists, who do not believe in the reality
of disease, heal disease, for the reason that the divine
12 Principle of Christian Science, demonstrated, heals the
most inveterate diseases.   Does he who believes in
death understand or aver that there is no death, and
15 proceed to overcome "the last enemy" and raise the
dying to health?   Christian Scientists raise the dying to
health in Christ's name, and are striving to reach the
18 summit of Jesus' words, "If a man keep my saying, he
shall never see death."

If, as this kind priest claims, these things, inseparable
21 from Christian Science, are common to his church, we
propose that he make known his doctrine to the world,
that he teach the Christianity which heals, and send out
24 students according to Christ's command, "Go ye into all
the world, and preach the gospel to every creature,"
"Heal the sick, cleanse the lepers, raise the dead, cast
27 out devils."

The tree is known by its fruit.   If, as he implies,
Christian Science is not a departure from the first cen-
30 tury churches, — as surely it is not, — why persecute
it? Are the churches opening fire on their own religious
ranks, or are they attacking a peaceable party quite

their antipode? Christian Science is a reflected glory; 1
it shines with borrowed rays — from Light emitting light.
Christian Science is the new-old Christianity, that which 3
was and is the revelation of divine Love.

The present flux in religious faith may be found to be
a healthy fermentation, by which the lees of religion will 6
be lost, dogma and creed will pass off in scum, leaving a
solid Christianity at the bottom — a foundation for the
builders. I would that all the churches on earth could 9
unite as brethren in one prayer: Father, teach us the
life of Love.

PLEASANT VIEW, CONCORD, N. H.,   12
    March 22, 1899

[Letter to the *New York World*]
FAITH IN METAPHYSICS   15

Is faith in divine metaphysics insanity?
All sin is insanity, but healing the sick is *not* sin.
There is a universal insanity which mistakes fable for 18
fact throughout the entire testimony of the material
senses. Those unfortunate people who are committed to
insane asylums are only so many well-defined instances 21
of the baneful effects of illusion on mortal minds and
bodies. The supposition that we can correct insanity
by the use of drugs is in itself a species of insanity. A 24
drug cannot of itself go to the brain or affect cerebral
conditions in any manner whatever. Drugs cannot
remove inflammation, restore disordered functions, or 27
destroy disease without the aid of mind.

If mind be absent from the body, drugs can produce
no curative effect upon the body. The mind must 30

1 be, is, the vehicle of all modes of healing disease and of producing disease. Through the mandate of mind or
3 according to a man's belief, can he be helped or be killed by a drug; but mind, not matter, produces the result in either case.

6 　Neither life nor death, health nor disease, can be produced on a corpse, whence mind has departed. This self-evident fact is proof that mind is the cause of all
9 effect made manifest through so-called matter. The general craze is that matter masters mind; the specific insanity is that brain, matter, is insane.

12 　　　　　　　[Letter to the *New York Herald*]
　　　　　　　REPLY TO MARK TWAIN

　It is a fact well understood that I begged the students
15 who first gave me the endearing appellative "Mother," not to name me thus. But without my consent, the use of the word spread like wildfire. I still must think the
18 name is not applicable to me. I stand in relation to this century as a Christian Discoverer, Founder, and Leader. I regard self-deification as blasphemous. I may
21 be more loved, but I am less lauded, pampered, provided for, and cheered than others before me — and wherefore? Because Christian Science is not yet popular, and
24 I refuse adulation.

　My first visit to The Mother Church after it was built and dedicated pleased me, and the situation was satisfac-
27 tory. The dear members wanted to greet me with escort and the ringing of bells, but I declined and went alone in my carriage to the church, entered it, and knelt in thanks
30 upon the steps of its altar. There the foresplendor of

the beginnings of truth fell mysteriously upon my spirit. 1
I believe in one Christ, teach one Christ, know of but
one Christ. I believe in but one incarnation, one Mother 3
Mary. I know that I am not that one, and I have never
claimed to be. It suffices me to learn the Science of the
Scriptures relative to this subject.   6

Christian Scientists have no quarrel with Protestants,
Catholics, or any other sect. Christian Scientists need to
be understood as following the divine Principle — God, 9
Love — and not imagined to be unscientific worshippers
of a human being.

In his article, of which I have seen only extracts, Mark 12
Twain's wit was not wasted in certain directions. Christian Science eschews divine rights in human beings.
If the individual governed human consciousness, my 15
statement of Christian Science would be disproved;
but to demonstrate Science and its pure monotheism
— one God, one Christ, no idolatry, no human propa- 18
ganda — it is essential to understand the spiritual idea.
Jesus taught and proved that what feeds a few feeds
all. His life-work subordinated the material to the 21
spiritual, and he left his legacy of truth to mankind. His metaphysics is not the sport of philosophy,
religion, or science; rather is it the pith and finale of 24
them all.

I have not the inspiration nor the aspiration to be
a first or second Virgin-mother — her duplicate, ante- 27
cedent, or subsequent. What I am remains to be proved
by the good I do. We need much humility, wisdom,
and love to perform the functions of foreshadowing and 30
foretasting heaven within us. This glory is molten in
the furnace of affliction.

1   [*Boston Journal*, June 8, 1903]

A MISSTATEMENT CORRECTED

3   I was early a pupil of Miss Sarah J. Bodwell, the
principal of Sanbornton Academy, New Hampshire, and
finished my course of studies under Professor Dyer
6 H. Sanborn, author of Sanborn's Grammar.   Among
my early studies were Comstock's Natural Philosophy,
Chemistry, Blair's Rhetoric, Whateley's Logic, Watt's
9 "On the Mind and Moral Science."   At sixteen years
of age, I began writing for the leading newspapers, and
for many years I wrote for the best magazines in the
12 South and North.   I have lectured in large and crowded
halls in New York City, Chicago, Boston, Portland,
and at Waterville College, and have been invited to
15 lecture in London, England, and Edinburgh, Scotland.
In 1883, I started *The Christian Science Journal,* and
for several years was the proprietor and sole editor of
18 that periodical.   In 1893, Judge S. J. Hanna became
editor of *The Christian Science Journal,* and for ten
subsequent years he knew my ability as an editor.   In
21 a lecture in Chicago, he said: "Mrs. Eddy is from
every point of view a woman of sound education and
liberal culture."
24   Agassiz, the celebrated naturalist and author, wisely
said: "Every great scientific truth goes through three
stages.   First, people say it conflicts with the Bible.
27 Next, they say it has been discovered before.   Lastly,
they say they have always believed it."
       The first attack upon me was: Mrs. Eddy misinterprets
30 the Scriptures; second, she has stolen the contents of her
book, "Science and Health with Key to the Scriptures,"

from one P. P. Quimby (an obscure, uneducated man), 1
and that he is the founder of Christian Science. Failing
in these attempts, the calumniator has resorted to Ralph 3
Waldo Emerson's philosophy as the authority for Christian
Science! Lastly, the defamer will declare as honestly (?),
"I have always known it." 6

In Science and Health, page 68, third paragraph, I
briefly express myself unmistakably on the subject of
"vulgar metaphysics," and the manuscripts and letters 9
in my possession, which "vulgar" defamers have circulated, stand in evidence. People do not know who is
referred to as "an ignorant woman in New Hampshire." 12
Many of the nation's best and most distinguished men
and women were natives of the Granite State.

I am the author of the Christian Science textbook, 15
"Science and Health with Key to the Scriptures;" and
the demand for this book constantly increases. I am
rated in the *National Magazine* (1903) as "standing 18
eighth in a list of twenty-two of the foremost living
authors."

I claim no special merit of any kind. All that I am 21
in reality, God has made me. I still wait at the cross to
learn definitely more from my great Master, but not
of the Greek nor of the Roman schools — simply how to 24
do his works.

A PLEA FOR JUSTICE

My recent reply to the reprint of a scandal in the 27
Literary Digest was not a question of "Who shall be
greatest?" but of "Who shall be just?" Who is or is
not the founder of Christian Science was not the trend 30
of thought, but my purpose was to lift the curtain on

1 wrong, on falsehood which persistently misrepresents
my character, education, and authorship, and attempts
3 to narrow my life into a conflict for fame.

Far be it from me to tread on the ashes of the dead or
to dissever any unity that may exist between Christian
6 Science and the philosophy of a great and good man, for
such was Ralph Waldo Emerson; and I deem it unwise to
enter into a newspaper controversy over a question that
9 is no longer a question. The false should be antagonized
only for the purpose of making the true apparent. I have
quite another purpose in life than to be thought great.
12 Time and goodness determine greatness. The greatest
reform, with almost unutterable truths to translate,
must wait to be transfused into the practical and
15 to be understood in the "new tongue." Age, with
experience-acquired patience and unselfed love, waits
on God. Human merit or demerit will find its proper
18 level. Divinity alone solves the problem of humanity, and that in God's own time. "By their fruits ye
shall know them."

21   REMINISCENCES

In 1862, when I first visited Dr. Quimby of Portland,
Me., his scribblings were descriptions of his patients, and
24 these comprised the manuscripts which in 1887 I advertised that I would pay for having published. Before his
decease, in January, 1866, Dr. Quimby had tried to get
27 them published and had failed.

Quotations have been published, purporting to be Dr.
Quimby's own words, which were written while I was his
30 patient in Portland and holding long conversations with
him on my views of mental therapeutics. Some words in

these quotations certainly read like words that I said to him, and which I, at his request, had added to his copy when I corrected it. In his conversations with me and in his scribblings, the word science was not used at all, till one day I declared to him that back of his magnetic treatment and manipulation of patients, there was a science, and it was the science of mind, which had nothing to do with matter, electricity, or physics.

After this I noticed he used that word, as well as other terms which I employed that seemed at first new to him. He even acknowledged this himself, and startled me by saying what I cannot forget — it was this: "I see now what you mean, and I see that I am John, and that you are Jesus."

At that date I was a staunch orthodox, and my theological belief was offended by his saying and I entered a demurrer which rebuked him. But afterwards I concluded that he only referred to the *coming* anew of Truth, which we both desired; for in some respects he was quite a seer and understood what I said better than some others did. For one so unlearned, he was a remarkable man. Had his remark related to my personality, I should still think that it was profane.

At first my case improved wonderfully under his treatment, but it relapsed. I was gradually emerging from *materia medica,* dogma, and creeds, and drifting whither I knew not. This mental struggle might have caused my illness. The fallacy of *materia medica,* its lack of science, and the want of divinity in scholastic theology, had already dawned on me. My idealism, however, limped, for then it lacked Science. But

1 the divine Love will accomplish what all the powers
of earth combined can never prevent being accom-
3 plished — the advent of divine healing and its divine
Science.

REPLY TO McCLURE'S MAGAZINE

6   It is calumny on Christian Science to say that man is
aroused to thought or action only by ease, pleasure, or
recompense. Something higher, nobler, more imperative
9 impels the impulse of Soul.

It becomes my duty to be just to the departed and to
tread not ruthlessly on their ashes. The attack on me
12 and my late father and his family in *McClure's Magazine,*
January, 1907, compels me as a dutiful child and the
Leader of Christian Science to speak.

15   *McClure's Magazine* refers to my father's "tall, gaunt
frame" and pictures "the old man tramping doggedly
along the highway, regularly beating the ground with a
18 huge walking-stick." My father's person was erect and
robust. He never used a walking-stick. To illustrate:
One time when my father was visiting Governor Pierce,
21 President Franklin Pierce's father, the Governor handed
him a gold-headed walking-stick as they were about to
start for church. My father thanked the Governor,
24 but declined to accept the stick, saying, "I never use
a cane."

Although *McClure's Magazine* attributes to my father
27 language unseemly, his household law, constantly enforced, was no profanity and no slang phrases. *McClure's
Magazine* also declares that the Bible was the only book
30 in his house. On the contrary, my father was a great
reader. The man whom *McClure's Magazine* characterizes

as "ignorant, dominating, passionate, fearless," was 1
uniformly dignified — a well-informed, intellectual man,
cultivated in mind and manners. He was called upon 3
to do much business for his town, making out deeds,
settling quarrels, and even acting as counsel in a lawsuit
involving a question of pauperism between the towns of 6
Loudon and Bow, N. H. Franklin Pierce, afterwards
President of the United States, was the counsel for
Loudon and Mark Baker for Bow. Both entered their 9
pleas, and my father won the suit. After it was decided,
Mr. Pierce bowed to my father and congratulated him.
For several years father was chaplain of the New 12
Hampshire State Militia, and as I recollect it, he was
justice of the peace at one time. My father was a
strong believer in States' rights, but slavery he regarded 15
as a great sin.

Mark Baker was the youngest of his father's family, and
inherited his father's real estate, an extensive farm situ- 18
ated in Bow and Concord, N. H. It is on record that
Mark Baker's father paid the largest tax in the colony.
McClure's Magazine says, describing the Baker home- 21
stead at Bow: "The house itself was a small, square box
building of rudimentary architecture." My father's
house had a sloping roof, after the prevailing style of 24
architecture at that date.

McClure's Magazine states: "Alone of the Bakers, he
[Albert] received a liberal education. . . . Mary Baker 27
passed her first fifteen years at the ancestral home at Bow.
It was a lonely and unstimulating existence. The church
supplied the only social diversions, the district school 30
practically all the intellectual life."

Let us see what were the fruits of this "lonely and

1 unstimulating existence." All my father's daughters were given an academic education, sufficiently advanced so that
3 they all taught school acceptably at various times and places. My brother Albert was a distinguished lawyer. In addition to my academic training, I was privately
6 tutored by him. He was a member of the New Hampshire Legislature, and was nominated for Congress, but died before the election. *McClure's Magazine* calls my
9 youngest brother, George Sullivan Baker, "a workman in a Tilton woolen mill." As a matter of fact, he was joint partner with Alexander Tilton, and together they owned a
12 large manufacturing establishment in Tilton, N. H. His military title of Colonel came from appointment on the staff of the Governor of New Hampshire. My oldest
15 brother, Samuel D. Baker, carried on a large business in Boston, Mass.

Regarding the allegation by *McClure's Magazine* that all
18 the family, "excepting Albert, died of cancer," I will say that there was never a death in my father's family reported by physician or post-mortem examination as
21 caused by cancer.

McClure's Magazine says that "the quarrels between Mary, a child ten years old, and her father, a gray-haired
24 man of fifty, frequently set the house in an uproar," and adds that these "fits" were diagnosed by Dr. Ladd as "hysteria mingled with bad temper." My mother
27 often presented my disposition as exemplary for her other children to imitate, saying, "When do you ever see Mary angry?" When the first edition of Science and
30 Health was published, Dr. Ladd said to Alexander Tilton: "Read it, for it will do you good. It does not surprise me, it so resembles the author."

I will relate the following incident, which occurred later 1
in life, as illustrative of my disposition: —

While I was living with Dr. Patterson at his country 3
home in North Groton, N. H., a girl, totally blind, knocked
at the door and was admitted. She begged to be allowed
to remain with me, and my tenderness and sympathy were 6
such that I could not refuse her. Shortly after, however,
my good housekeeper said to me: "If this blind girl stays
with you, I shall have to leave; she troubles me so much." 9
It was not in my heart to turn the blind girl out, and so
I lost my housekeeper.

My reply to the statement that the clerk's book shows 12
that I joined the Tilton Congregational Church at the age
of seventeen is that my religious experience seemed to
culminate at twelve years of age. Hence a mistake may 15
have occurred as to the exact date of my first church
membership.

The facts regarding the McNeil coat-of-arms are as 18
follows: —

Fanny McNeil, President Pierce's niece, afterwards
Mrs. Judge Potter, presented me my coat-of-arms, say- 21
ing that it was taken in connection with her own family
coat-of-arms. I never doubted the veracity of her gift.
I have another coat-of-arms, which is of my mother's 24
ancestry. When I was last in Washington, D. C., Mrs.
Judge Potter and myself knelt in silent prayer on the
mound of her late father, General John McNeil, the 27
hero of Lundy Lane.

Notwithstanding that *McClure's Magazine* says, "Mary
Baker completed her education when she finished Smith's 30
grammar and reached long division in arithmetic," I was
called by the Rev. R. S. Rust, D.D., Principal of the

1 Methodist Conference Seminary at Sanbornton Bridge, to
supply the place of his leading teacher during her tempo-
3 rary absence.

Regarding my first marriage and the tragic death of my
husband, *McClure's Magazine* says: "He [George Wash-
6 ington Glover] took his bride to Wilmington, South Carolina, and in June, 1844, six months after his marriage, he
died of yellow fever. He left his young wife in a miser-
9 able plight. She was far from home and entirely without
money or friends. Glover, however, was a Free Mason,
and thus received a decent burial. The Masons also paid
12 Mrs. Glover's fare to New York City, where she was
met and taken to her father's home by her brother George.
. . . Her position was an embarrassing one. She was a
15 grown woman, with a child, but entirely without means
of support. . . . Mrs. Glover made only one effort at
self-support. For a brief season she taught school."
18 My first husband, Major George W. Glover, resided in
Charleston, S. C. While on a business trip to Wilmington, N. C., he was suddenly seized with yellow fever and
21 died in about nine days. I was with him on this trip.
He took with him the usual amount of money he would
need on such an excursion. At his decease I was sur-
24 rounded by friends, and their provisions in my behalf were
most tender. The Governor of the State and his staff,
with a long procession, followed the remains of my be-
27 loved one to the cemetery. The Free Masons selected
my escort, who took me to my father's home in Tilton,
N. H. My salary for writing gave me ample support.
30 I did open an infant school, but it was for the purpose of
starting that educational system in New Hampshire.

The rhyme attributed to me by *McClure's Magazine* is

not mine, but is, I understand, a paraphrase of a silly 1
song of years ago. Correctly quoted, it is as follows, so
I have been told: — 3

> Go to Jane Glover,
> Tell her I love her;
> By the light of the moon 6
> I will go to her.

The various stories told by *McClure's Magazine* about
my father spreading the road in front of his house with 9
tan-bark and straw, and about persons being hired to rock
me, I am ignorant of. Nor do I remember any such stuff
as Dr. Patterson driving into Franklin, N. H., with a 12
couch or cradle for me in his wagon. I only know that
my father and mother did everything they could think of
to help me when I was ill. 15
I was never "given to long and lonely wanderings,
especially at night," as stated by *McClure's Magazine*. I
was always accompanied by some responsible individual 18
when I took an evening walk, but I seldom took one. I
have always consistently declared that I was not a medium
for spirits. I never was especially interested in the 21
Shakers, never "dabbled in mesmerism," never was "an
amateur clairvoyant," nor did "the superstitious country folk frequently" seek my advice. I never went 24
into a trance to describe scenes far away, as *McClure's
Magazine* says.
My oldest sister dearly loved me, but I wounded her 27
pride when I adopted Christian Science, and to a Baker
that was a sorry offence. I was obliged to be parted
from my son, because after my father's second marriage 30
my little boy was not welcome in my father's house.

1 *McClure's Magazine* calls Dr. Daniel Patterson, my second husband, "an itinerant dentist." It says that 3 after my marriage we "lived for a short time at Tilton, then moved to Franklin. . . . During the following nine years the Pattersons led a roving existence. The doctor 6 practised in several towns, from Tilton to North Groton and then to Rumney." When I was married to him, Dr. Daniel Patterson was located in Franklin, N. H. He had 9 the degree D.D.S., was a popular man, and considered a rarely skilful dentist. He bought a place in North Groton, which he fancied, for a summer home. At that time he 12 owned a house in Franklin, N. H.

Although, as *McClure's Magazine* claims, the court record may state that my divorce from Dr. Patterson was 15 granted on the ground of desertion, the cause nevertheless was adultery. Individuals are here to-day who were present in court when the decision was given by the judge 18 and who know the following facts: After the evidence had been submitted that a husband was about to have Dr. Patterson arrested for eloping with his wife, the court 21 instructed the clerk to record the divorce in my favor. What prevented Dr. Patterson's arrest was a letter from me to this self-same husband, imploring him not to do it. 24 When this husband recovered his wife, he kept her a prisoner in her home, and I was also the means of reconciling the couple. A Christian Scientist has told me that 27 with tears of gratitude the wife of this husband related these facts to her just as I have stated them. I lived with Dr. Patterson peaceably, and he was kind to me up 30 to the time of the divorce.

The following affidavit by R. D. Rounsevel of Littleton, N. H., proprietor of the White Mountain House, Fabyans,

N. H., the original of which is in my possession, is of 1
interest in this connection: —

About the year 1874, Dr. Patterson, a dentist, boarded 3
with me in Littleton, New Hampshire. During his stay,
at different times, I had conversation with him about his
wife, from whom he was separated. He spoke of her being 6
a pure and Christian woman, and the cause of the separation being wholly on his part; that if he had done as he
ought, he might have had as pleasant and happy home as 9
one could wish for.

At that time I had no knowledge of who his wife was.
Later on I learned that Mary Baker G. Eddy, the Dis- 12
coverer and Founder of Christian Science, was the above-
mentioned woman.

(Signed) R. D. ROUNSEVEL 15

Grafton S. S. Jan'y, 1902. Then personally appeared
R. D. Rounsevel and made oath that the within statement
by him signed is true. 18

Before me,   (Signed) H. M. MORSE,
Justice of the Peace

Who or what is the *McClure* "history," so called, pre- 21
senting? Is it myself, the veritable Mrs. Eddy, whom
the *New York World* declared dying of cancer, or is it
her alleged double or dummy heretofore described? 24

If indeed it be I, allow me to thank the enterprising
historians for the testimony they have thereby given of the
divine power of Christian Science, which they admit has 27
snatched me from the *cradle* and the grave, and made
me the beloved Leader of millions of the good men and
women in our own and in other countries, — and all this 30

1 because the truth I have promulgated has separated the
tares from the wheat, uniting in one body those who love
3 Truth; because Truth divides between sect and Science
and renews the heavenward impulse; because I still hear
the harvest song of the Redeemer awakening the nations,
6 causing man to love his enemies; because "blessed are ye,
when men shall revile you, and persecute you, and shall
say all manner of evil against you falsely, for my sake."

9   [*Christian Science Sentinel,* January 19, 1907]

A CARD

The article in the January number of *The Arena* maga-
12 zine, entitled "The Recent Reckless and Irresponsible
Attacks on Christian Science and its Founder, with a
Survey of the Christian Science Movement," by the
15 scholarly editor, Mr. B. O. Flower, is a grand defence of
our Cause and its Leader. Such a dignified, eloquent
appeal to the press in behalf of common justice and truth
18 demands public attention. It defends human rights and
the freedom of Christian sentiments, and tends to turn
back the foaming torrents of ignorance, envy, and malice.
21 I am pleased to find this "twentieth-century review of
opinion" once more under Mr. Flower's able guardianship
and manifesting its unbiased judgment by such sound
24 appreciation of the rights of Christian Scientists and of
all that is right.

MARY BAKER EDDY

CHAPTER XVIII

Authorship of Science and Health

THE following statement, which was published in 1
the *Sentinel* of December 1, 1906, exactly defining her relations with the Rev. James Henry Wiggin of 3
Boston, was made by Mrs. Eddy in refutation of allega-
tions in the public press to the effect that Mr. Wiggin
had a share in the authorship of "Science and Health 6
with Key to the Scriptures."

MRS. EDDY'S STATEMENT

It is a great mistake to say that I employed the Rev. 9
James Henry Wiggin to correct my diction. It was for
no such purpose. I engaged Mr. Wiggin so as to avail
myself of his criticisms of my statement of Christian 12
Science, which criticisms would enable me to explain
more clearly the points that might seem ambiguous to
the reader. 15

Mr. Calvin A. Frye copied my writings, and he will tell
you that Mr. Wiggin left my diction quite out of the
question, sometimes saying, "I wouldn't express it that 18
way." He often dissented from what I had written,
but I quieted him by quoting corroborative texts of
Scripture. 21

My diction, as used in explaining Christian Science, has
been called original. The liberty that I have taken with

317

1 capitalization, in order to express the "new tongue," has well-nigh constituted a new style of language. In almost
3 every case where Mr. Wiggin added words, I have erased them in my revisions.

Mr. Wiggin was not my proofreader for my book
6 "Miscellaneous Writings," and for only two of my books. I especially employed him on "Science and Health with Key to the Scriptures," because at that date some critics
9 declared that my book was as ungrammatical as it was misleading. I availed myself of the name of the former proofreader for the University Press, Cambridge, to
12 defend my grammatical construction, and confidently awaited the years to declare the moral and spiritual effect upon the age of "Science and Health with Key
15 to the Scriptures."

I invited Mr. Wiggin to visit one of my classes in the Massachusetts Metaphysical College, and he consented
18 on condition that I should not ask him any questions. I agreed not to question him just so long as he refrained from questioning me. He held himself well in check
21 until I began my attack on agnosticism. As I proceeded, Mr. Wiggin manifested more and more agitation, until he could control himself no longer and,
24 addressing me, burst out with:

"How do you know that there ever was such a man as Christ Jesus?"
27 He would have continued with a long argument, framed from his ample fund of historical knowledge, but I stopped him.
30 "Now, Mr. Wiggin," I said, "you have broken our agreement. I do not find my authority for Christian Science in history, but in revelation. If there had never

existed such a person as the Galilean Prophet, it would 1
make no difference to me.   I should still know that
God's spiritual ideal is the only real man in His image 3
and likeness."

My saying touched him, and I heard nothing further
from him in the class, though afterwards he wrote a 6
kind little pamphlet, signed "Phare Pleigh."

I hold the late Mr. Wiggin in loving, grateful memory
for his high-principled character and well-equipped 9
scholarship.

LETTERS FROM STUDENTS

The following letters from students of Mrs. Eddy 12
confirm her statement regarding the work which the
Rev. Mr. Wiggin did for her, and also indicate what he
himself thought of that work and of Mrs. Eddy: — 15

My Dear Teacher: — I am conversant with some facts
which perhaps have not come under the observation of
many of your students, and considering the questions 18
which have recently appeared, it may interest you to be
advised that I have this information. On the tenth day of
January, 1887, I entered your Primary class at Boston. 21
A few days later, in conversation with you about the
preparation of a theme, you suggested that I call on the
late J. Henry Wiggin to assist me in analyzing and arrang- 24
ing the topics, which I did about the twentieth of the
above-named month. These dates are very well fixed in
my memory, as I considered the time an important one 27
in my experience, and do so still. I also recall very
plainly the conversation with you in general as regards
Mr. Wiggin. You told me that he had done some literary 30

1 work for you and that he was a fine literary student and
a good proofreader.

3   Upon calling on Mr. Wiggin, I presented my matter for
a theme to him, and he readily consented to assist me,
which he did.   He also seemed very much pleased to
6 converse about you and your work, and I found that his
statement of what he had done for you exactly agreed
with what you had told me.   He also expressed himself
9 freely as to his high regard for you as a Christian lady,
as an author, and as a student of ability.   Mr. Wiggin
spoke of "Science and Health with Key to the Scrip-
12 tures" as being a very unique book, and seemed quite
proud of his having had something to do with some
editions.   He always spoke of you as the author of this
15 book and the author of all your works.   Mr. Wiggin
did not claim to be a Christian Scientist, but was in
a measure in sympathy with the movement, although
18 he did not endorse all the statements in your textbook;
but his tendency was friendly.

I called on Mr. Wiggin several times while I was in your
21 Primary class at the time above referred to, and several
times subsequent thereto, and he always referred to you as
the author of your works and spoke of your ability without
24 any hesitation or restriction.   Our conversations were at
times somewhat long and went into matters of detail
regarding your work, and I am of the opinion that he
27 was proud of his acquaintance with you.

I saw Mr. Wiggin several times after the class closed,
and the last conversation I had with him was at the
30 time of the dedication of the first Mother Church edifice
in 1895.   I met him in the vestibule of the church
and he spoke in a very animated manner of your

grand demonstration in building this church for your 1
followers. He seemed very proud to think that he had
been in a way connected with your work, but he always 3
referred to you as the one who had accomplished this
great work.

My recollections of Mr. Wiggin place him as one 6
of your devoted and faithful friends, one who knew
who and what you are, also your position as regards
your published works; and he always gave you that 9
position without any restriction. I believe that Mr.
Wiggin was an honest man and that he told the same
story to every one with whom he had occasion to talk, 12
so I cannot believe that he has ever said anything
whatever of you and your relations to your published
works differing from what he talked so freely in my 15
presence.

There is nothing in the circumstances which have
arisen recently, and the manner in which the statements 18
have been made, to change my opinion one iota in this
respect.

It will soon be twenty years since I first saw you and 21
entered your class. During that time, from my connection with the church, the Publishing Society, and my
many conversations with you, my personal knowledge of 24
the authorship of your works is conclusive to me in every
detail, and I am very glad that I was among your early
students and have had this experience and know of my 27
own personal knowledge what has transpired during the
past twenty years.

I am also pleased to have had conversations with 30
people who knew you years before I did, and who have
told me of their knowledge of your work.

1   It is not long since I met a lady who lived in Lynn,
and she told me she knew you when you were writing
3 Science and Health, and that she had seen the manuscript. These are facts which cannot be controverted
and they must stand.

6   Your affectionate student,
                                 EDWARD P. BATES
      BOSTON, MASS., November 21, 1906

9   *My Beloved Teacher:* — I have just read your statement correcting mistakes widely published about the
Rev. James H. Wiggin's work for and attitude towards
12 you; also Mr. Edward P. Bates' letter to you on the
same subject; which reminds me of a conversation I
had with Mr. Wiggin on Thanksgiving Day twenty
15 years ago, when a friend and I were the guests invited
to dine with the Wiggin family.

I had seen you the day before at the Metaphysical
18 College and received your permission to enter the next
Primary class (Jan. 10, 1887). During the evening my
friend spoke of my journeying from the far South, and
21 waiting months in Boston on the bare hope of a few
days' instruction by Mrs. Eddy in Christian Science.
She and Mrs. Wiggin seemed inclined to banter me on
24 such enthusiasm, but Mr. Wiggin kindly helped me by
advancing many good points in the Science, which were
so clearly stated that I was surprised when he told me
27 he was not a Christian Scientist.

Seeing my great interest in the subject, he told me
of his acquaintance with you and spoke earnestly and
30 beautifully of you and your work. The exact words I
do not recall, but the impression he left with me was

entirely in accordance with what Mr. Bates has so well 1
written in the above-mentioned letter. Before we left
that evening, Mr. Wiggin gave me a pamphlet entitled 3
"Christian Science and the Bible," by "Phare Pleigh,"
which he said he had written in answer to an unfair
criticism of you and your book by some minister in the 6
far West. I have his little book yet. How long must it
be before the people find out that you have so identified
yourself with the truth by loving it and living it that you 9
are not going to lie about anything nor willingly leave
any false impression.

In loving gratitude for your living witness to Truth 12
and Love,   FLORENCE WHITESIDE

CHATTANOOGA, TENN.,   15
  December 4, 1906

Beloved Teacher: — My heart has been too full to tell
you in words all that your wonderful life and sacrifice 18
means to me. Neither do I now feel at all equal to expressing the crowding thoughts of gratitude and praise
to God for giving this age such a Leader and teacher to 21
reveal to us His way. Your crowning triumph over error
and sin, which we have so recently witnessed, in blessing
those who would destroy you if God did not hold you up 24
by the right hand of His righteousness, should mean to
your older students much that they may not have been
able to appreciate in times past.   27

I wonder if you will remember that Mr. Snider and
myself boarded in the home of the late Rev. J. Henry
Wiggin during the time of our studying in the second 30
class with you — the Normal class in the fall of 1887?
We were at that time some eight days in Mr. and Mrs.

1 Wiggin's home. He often spoke his thoughts freely about you and your work, especially your book Science 3 and Health. Mr. Wiggin had somewhat of a thought of contempt for the unlearned, and he scorned the suggestion that Mr. Quimby had given you any idea for 6 your book, as he said you and your ideas were too much alike for the book to have come from any one but yourself. He often said you were so original and so 9 very decided that no one could be of much service to you, and he often hinted that he thought he could give a clearer nomenclature for Science and Health. I re-12 member telling you of this, and you explained how long you had waited on the Lord to have those very terms revealed to you.

15 I am very sure that neither Mr. Wiggin nor his estimable wife had any other thought but that you were the author of your book, and were he here to-day he 18 would be too honorable to allow the thought to go out that he had helped you write it. He certainly never gave us the impression that he thought you needed 21 help, for we always thought that Mr. Wiggin regarded you as quite his literary equal, and was gratified and pleased in numbering you among his literary friends. 24 Everything he said conveyed this impression to us — that he regarded you as entirely unique and original. He told us laughingly why he accepted your invitation 27 to sit through your class. He said he wanted to see if there was one woman under the sun who could keep to her text. When we asked him if he found you could do 30 so, he replied "Yes," and said that no man could have done so any better.

Both Mr. and Mrs. Wiggin frequently mentioned

many kindnesses you had shown them, and spoke of 1
one especial day when amidst all your duties you personally called to inquire of his welfare (he had been 3
ill) and to leave luscious hothouse fruit.   One thing
more, that I think will amuse you: Mr. Wiggin was
very much troubled that you had bought your house 6
on Commonwealth Avenue, as he was very sure Back
Bay property would never be worth what you then
paid for it.   He regarded the old part of Boston in 9
which he lived as having a greater future than the new
Back Bay.

New Years ago I offered my services to you in any capacity 12
in which I could serve you, and my desire has never
changed.   Command me at any time, in any way, beloved
Leader. 15

With increasing love and gratitude, ever faithfully your
student,

CARRIE HARVEY SNIDER 18
NEW YORK, N. Y.,
December 7, 1906

CHAPTER XIX

[*The Christian Science Journal*]

A Memorable Coincidence and Historical Facts

1 WE are glad to publish the following interesting letter and enclosures received from our Leader. 3 That legislatures and courts are thus declaring the liberties of Christian Scientists is most gratifying to our people; not because a favor has been extended, but because their 6 inherent rights are recognized in an official and authoritative manner. It is especially gratifying to them that the declaration of this recognition should be coincident 9 in the Southern and Northern States in which Mrs. Eddy has made her home.

MRS. EDDY'S LETTER

12 *Dear Editor:* — I send for publication in our periodicals the following deeply interesting letter from Elizabeth Earl Jones of Asheville, N. C., — the State where my husband, 15 Major George W. Glover, passed on and up, the State that so signally honored his memory, where with wet eyes the Free Masons laid on his bier the emblems of a master 18 Mason, and in long procession with tender dirge bore his remains to their last resting-place. Deeply grateful, I recognize the divine hand in turning the hearts of the noble

326

Southrons of North Carolina legally to protect the practice 1
of Christian Science in that State.

Is it not a memorable coincidence that, in the Court of 3
New Hampshire, my native State, and in the Legislature
of North Carolina, they have the same year, in 1903, made
it legal to practise Christian Science in these States? 6

MARY BAKER EDDY

PLEASANT VIEW, CONCORD, N. H.,
October 16, 1903 9

MISS ELIZABETH EARL JONES' LETTER

Beloved Leader: — I know the enclosed article will make
your heart glad, as it has made glad the hearts of all the 12
Christian Scientists in North Carolina. This is the result
of the work done at last winter's term of our Legislature,
when a medical bill was proposed calculated to limit or 15
stop the practice of Christian Science in our State. An
amendment was obtained by Miss Mary Hatch Harrison
and a few other Scientists who stayed on the field until the 18
last. After the amendment had been passed, an old law,
or rather a section of an act in the Legislature regulating
taxes, was changed as follows, because the representa- 21
tive men of our dear State did not wish to be "discour-
teous to the Christian Scientists." The section formerly
read, "pretended healers," but was changed to read as 24
follows: "All other professionals who practise the art of
healing," *etc.*

We thank our heavenly Father for this dignified 27
legal protection and recognition, and look forward to
the day, not far distant, when the laws of every State
will dignify the ministry of Christ as taught and prac- 30
tised in Christian Science, and as lived by our dear,

1 dear Leader, even as God has dignified, blessed, and
prospered it, and her.

3   With devoted love,

ELIZABETH EARL JONES

105 BAILEY ST., ASHEVILLE, N. C.,
6   October 11, 1903

The following article, copied from the *Raleigh* (N. C.)
News and Observer, is the one referred to in Miss Jones'
9 letter: —

The Christian Science people, greatly pleased at the
law affecting them passed by the last Legislature, are
12 apt also to be pleased with the fact that the law recognizes them as healers, and that it gives them a license
to heal. This license of five dollars annually, required
15 of physicians, has been required of them, and how this
came about in Kinston is told in the *Kinston Free Press*
as follows: —

18 Sheriff Wooten issued licenses yesterday to two
Christian Science healers in this city. This is probably
the first to be issued to the healers of this sect in the
21 State.

Upon the request of a prominent healer of the church,
the section of the machinery act of the Legislature cover-
24 ing it was shown, whereupon application for license was
made and obtained.

The section, after enumerating the different professions
27 for which a license must be obtained to carry them on in
this State, further says, "and all other professionals who
practise the art of healing for pay, shall pay a license fee
30 of five dollars."

This was construed to include the healers of the Chris- 1
tian Science church, and license was accordingly taken
out. 3
The idea prevails that the last General Assembly of
North Carolina relieved the healers of this sect from paying
this fee, but this is not so. The board only excused them 6
from a medical examination before a board of medical
examiners.

Mrs. Eddy's reference to the death of her husband, 9
Major George W. Glover, gives especial interest to the
following letter from Newbern, N. C., which appeared
in the *Wilmington* (N. C.) *Dispatch,* October 24, 1903. 12
Mrs. Eddy has in her possession photographed copies of
the notice of her husband's death and of her brother's
letter, taken from the *Wilmington* (N. C.) *Chronicle* as 15
they appear in that paper in the issues of July 3 and
August 21, 1844, respectively. The photographs are verified by the certificate of a notary public and were pre- 18
sented to Mrs. Eddy by Miss Harrison.

MISS MARY HATCH HARRISON'S LETTER

To the Editor: — At no better time than now, when the 21
whole country is recognizing the steady progress of Christian Science and admitting its interest in the movement,
as shown by the fair attitude of the press everywhere, 24
could we ask you to give your readers the following communication. It will put before them some interesting
facts concerning Mrs. Mary Baker Eddy, and some in- 27
cidents of her life in North and South Carolina which
might not have been known but for a criticism of this

1 good woman which was published in your paper in
August, 1901.

3   I presume we should not be surprised that a noteworthy
follower of our Lord should be maligned, since the great
Master himself was scandalized, and he prophesied that
6 his followers would be so treated. The calumniator who
informed you in this instance locates Mrs. Eddy in Wilmington in 1843, thus contradicting his own statement,
9 since Mrs. Eddy was not then a resident of Wilmington.
A local Christian Scientist of your city, whose womanhood
and Christianity are appreciated by all, assisted by a
12 Mason of good standing there and a Christian Scientist of
Charleston, S. C., carefully investigated the points concerning Major Glover's history which are questioned by
15 this critic, and has found Mrs. Eddy's statements, relating to her husband (who she states was of Charleston,
S. C., not of Wilmington, but who died there while on
18 business in 1844, not in 1843, as claimed in your issue) are
sustained by Masonic records in each place as well as
by Wilmington newspapers of that year. In "Retro-
21 spection and Introspection" (p. 19) Mrs. Eddy says of
this circumstance: —

"My husband was a Free Mason, being a member in St.
24 Andrew's Lodge, No. 10, and of Union Chapter, No. 3, of
Royal Arch Masons. He was highly esteemed and sincerely lamented by a large circle of friends and acquaint-
27 ances, whose kindness and sympathy helped to support me
in this terrible bereavement. A month later I returned to
New Hampshire, where, at the end of four months, my
30 babe was born. Colonel Glover's tender devotion to his
young bride was remarked by all observers. With his
parting breath he gave pathetic directions to his brother

Masons about accompanying her on her sad journey to 1
the North. Here it is but justice to record, they performed their obligations most faithfully." 3
    Such watchful solicitude as Mrs. Eddy received at the
hands of Wilmington's best citizens, among whom she
remembers the Rev. Mr. Reperton, a Baptist clergyman, 6
and the Governor of the State, who accompanied her to
the train on her departure, indicates her irreproachable
standing in your city at that time. 9
    The following letter of thanks, copied from the *Wil-
mington Chronicle* of August 21, 1844, testifies to the love
and respect entertained for Mrs. Eddy by Wilmington's 12
best men, whose Southern chivalry would have scorned
to extend such unrestrained hospitality to an unworthy
woman as quickly as it would have punished the assail- 15
ant of a good woman: —

A CARD

    Through the columns of your paper, will you permit 18
me, in behalf of the relatives and friends of the late
Major George W. Glover of Wilmington and his bereaved lady, to return our thanks and express the feeling 21
of gratitude we owe and cherish towards those friends of
the deceased who so kindly attended him during his last
sickness, and who still extended their care and sympathy 24
to the lone, feeble, and bereaved widow after his decease.
Much has often been said of the high feeling of honor
and the noble generosity of heart which characterized the 27
people of the South, yet when we listen to Mrs. Glover
(my sister) whilst recounting the kind attention paid to
the deceased during his late illness, the sympathy ex- 30
tended to her after his death, and the assistance volun-

1 teered to restore her to her friends at a distance of more
than a thousand miles, the power of language would be
3 but beggared by an attempt at expressing the feelings of
a swelling bosom. The silent gush of grateful tears alone
can tell the emotions of the thankful heart, — words are
6 indeed but a meagre tribute for so noble an effort in behalf of the unfortunate, yet it is all we can award: will our
friends at Wilmington accept it as a tribute of grateful
9 hearts? Many thanks are due Mr. Cooke, who engaged
to accompany her only to New York, but did not desert
her or remit his kind attention until he saw her in the
12 fond embrace of her friends.

Your friend and obedient servant,

(Signed) GEORGE S. BAKER

15   SANBORNTON BRIDGE, N. H.,
August 12, 1844

The paper containing this card is now in the Young
18 Men's Christian Association at Wilmington.

The facts regarding Major Glover's membership in
St. Andrew's Lodge, No. 10, were brought to light in a
21 most interesting way. A Christian Scientist in Charleston was requested to look up the records of this lodge,
as we had full confidence that it would corroborate Mrs.
24 Eddy's claims. After frequent searchings and much in-
terviewing with Masonic authorities, it was learned that
the lodge was no longer in existence, and that during the
27 Civil War many Masonic records were transferred to
Columbia, where they were burned; but on repeated
search a roll of papers recording the death of George
30 Washington Glover in 1844 and giving best praises to
his honorable record and Christian character was found;

and said record, with the seal of the Grand Secretary, is now in the possession of the chairman of the Christian Science publication committee.

In the records of St. John's Lodge, Wilmington, as found by one of your own citizens, a Mason, it is shown that on the twenty-eighth day of June, 1844, a special meeting was convened for the purpose of paying the last tribute of respect to Brother George W. Glover, who died on the night of the twenty-seventh. The minutes record this further proceeding: —

"A procession was formed, which moved to the residence of the deceased, and from thence to the Episcopal burying-ground, where the body was interred with the usual ceremonies. The procession then returned to the lodge, which was closed in due form."

It has never been claimed by Mrs. Eddy nor by any Christian Scientists that Major Glover's remains were carried North.

The *Wilmington Chronicle* of July 3, 1844, records that this good man, then known as Major George W. Glover, died on Thursday night, the twenty-seventh of June. The *Chronicle* states: "His end was calm and peaceful, and to those friends who attended him during his illness he gave the repeated assurance of his willingness to die, and of his full reliance for salvation on the merits of a crucified Redeemer. His remains were interred with Masonic honors. He has left an amiable wife, to whom he had been united but the brief space of six months, to lament this irreparable loss."

From the *Chronicle,* dated September 25, 1844, we copy the following: "We are assured that reports of unusual sickness in Wilmington are in circulation." This periodi-

1 cal then forthwith strives to give the impression that the
rumor is not true. It is reasonable to infer from news-
3 paper reports of that date that some insidious disease
was raging at that time.

The allegation that copies of Mrs. Eddy's book, "Retro-
6 spection and Introspection," are few, and that efforts are
being made to buy them up because she has contradicted
herself, is without foundation. They are advertised in
9 every weekly issue of the *Christian Science Sentinel,* and
still contain the original account of her husband's demise
at Wilmington.

12 May it not be, since this critic places certain circumstances in 1843, which records show really existed in 1844,
that the woman whom he had in mind is some other one?

15 We can state Mrs. Eddy's teaching on the unreality of
evil in no better terms than to quote her own words.
Nothing could be further from her meaning than that evil
18 could be indulged in while being called unreal. She
declares in her Message to The Mother Church [1901]:
"To assume there is no reality in sin, and yet commit
21 sin, is sin itself, that clings fast to iniquity. The Publican's wail won his humble desire, while the Pharisee's
self-righteousness crucified Jesus."

24   MARY HATCH HARRISON

MAJOR GLOVER'S RECORD AS A MASON

Of further interest in this matter is the following ex-
27 tract from an editorial obituary which appeared in 1845 in
the *Freemason's Monthly Magazine,* published by the
late Charles W. Moore, Grand Secretary of the Grand
30 Lodge of Massachusetts: —

Died at Wilmington, N. C., on the 27th June last, Major George W. Glover, formerly of Concord, N. H.

Brother Glover resided in Charleston, S. C., and was made a Mason in "St. Andrew's Lodge, No. 10." He was soon exalted to the degree of a Royal Arch Mason in "Union Chapter, No. 3," and retained his membership in both till his decease. He was devotedly attached to Masonry, faithful as a member and officer of the Lodge and Chapter, and beloved by his brothers and companions, who mourn his early death.

Additional facts regarding Major Glover, his illness and death, are that he was for a number of years a resident of Charleston, S. C., where he erected a fine dwelling-house, the drawings and specifications of which were kept by his widow for many years after his death. While at Wilmington, N. C., in June, 1844, Mr. Glover was attacked with yellow fever of the worst type, and at the end of nine days he passed away. This was the second case of the dread disease in that city, and in the hope of allaying the excitement which was fast arising, the authorities gave the cause of death as bilious fever, but they refused permission to take the remains to Charleston.

On the third day of her husband's illness, Mrs. Glover (now Mrs. Eddy) sent for the distinguished physician who attended cases of this terrible disease as an expert (Dr. McRee we think it was), and was told by him that he could not conceal the fact that the case was one of yellow fever in its worst form, and nothing could save the life of her husband. In these nine days and nights of agony the young wife prayed incessantly for her husband's recovery, and was told by the expert physician that

1 but for her prayers the patient would have died on the seventh day.

3 The disease spread so rapidly that Mrs. Glover (Mrs. Eddy) was afraid to have her brother, George S. Baker, come to her after her husband's death, to take her back to 6 the North. Although he desired to go to her assistance, she declined on this ground, and entrusted herself to the care of her husband's Masonic brethren, who faithfully 9 performed their obligation to her. She makes grateful acknowledgment of this in her book, "Retrospection and Introspection." In this book (p. 20) she also states, 12 "After returning to the paternal roof I lost all my husband's property, except what money I had brought with me; and remained with my parents until after 15 my mother's decease." Mr. Glover had made no will previous to his last illness, and then the seizure of disease was so sudden and so violent that he was unable 18 to make a will.

These letters and extracts are of absorbing interest to Christian Scientists as amplification of the facts given by 21 Mrs. Eddy in "Retrospection and Introspection."

CHAPTER XX

General Miscellany

[*Boston Herald*, Sunday, May 15, 1898]   1

THE UNITED STATES TO GREAT BRITAIN

HAIL, brother! fling thy banner   3
To the billows and the breeze;
We proffer thee warm welcome
    With our hand, though not our knees.   6

Lord of the main and manor!
    Thy palm, in ancient day,
Didst rock the country's cradle   9
    That wakes thy laureate's lay.

The hoar fight is forgotten;
    Our eagle, like the dove,   12
Returns to bless a bridal
    Betokened from above.

List, brother! angels whisper   15
    To Judah's sceptred race, —
"Thou of the self-same spirit,
    Allied by nations' grace,   18

"Wouldst cheer the hosts of heaven;
    For Anglo-Israel, lo!
Is marching under orders;   21
    His hand averts the blow."

337

1   Brave Britain, blest America!
           Unite your battle-plan;
3   Victorious, all who live it, —
          The love for God and man.

TO THE PUBLIC

6   The following views of the Rev. Mary Baker Eddy
upon the subject of the Trinity, are known to us to be
those uniformly held and expressed by her. A reference
9 to her writings will fully corroborate this statement. —
EDITOR *Sentinel.*

The contents of the last lecture of our dear brother,
12 on the subject "The Unknown God Made Known,"
were unknown to me till after the lecture was delivered
in Boston, April 5.
15   The members of the Board of Lectureship are not
allowed to consult me relative to their subjects or the
handling thereof, owing to my busy life, and they seek a
18 higher source for wisdom and guidance. The talented
author of this lecture has a heart full of love towards
God and man. For once he may have overlooked the
21 construction that people unfamiliar with his broad
views and loving nature might put on his comparisons
and ready humor. But all Christian Scientists deeply
24 recognize the oneness of Jesus — that he stands alone
in word and deed, the visible discoverer, founder, demonstrator, and great Teacher of Christianity, whose
27 sandals none may unloose.
The Board of Lectureship is absolutely inclined to
be, and is instructed to be, charitable towards all, and

hating none. The purpose of its members is to sub- 1
serve the interest of mankind, and to cement the bonds
of Christian brotherhood, whose every link leads up- 3
ward in the chain of being. The cardinal points of
Christian Science cannot be lost sight of, namely — one
God, supreme, infinite, and one Christ Jesus.   6

The Board of Lectureship is specially requested to be
wise in discoursing on the great subject of Christian
Science.   9

Mary Baker Eddy

FAST DAY IN NEW HAMPSHIRE, 1899

Along the lines of progressive Christendom, New 12
Hampshire's advancement is marked. Already Massachusetts has exchanged Fast Day, and all that it formerly signified, for Patriots' Day, and the observance 15
of the holiday illustrates the joy, grace, and glory of liberty. We read in Holy Writ that the disciples of St.
John the Baptist said to the great Master, "Why do we 18
and the Pharisees fast oft, but thy disciples fast not?"
And he answered them in substance: My disciples
rejoice in their present Christianity and have no cause 21
to mourn; only those who have not the Christ, Truth,
within them should wear sackcloth.

Jesus said to his disciples, "This kind goeth not out but 24
by prayer and fasting," but he did not appoint a fast.
Merely to abstain from eating was not sufficient to meet
his demand. The animus of his saying was: Silence 27
appetites, passion, and all that wars against Spirit and
spiritual power. The fact that he healed the sick man
without the observance of a material fast confirms this 30

1 conclusion. Jesus attended feasts, but we have no record
of his observing appointed fasts.

3 St. Paul's days for prayer were every day and every
hour. He said, "Pray without ceasing." He classed
the usage of special days and seasons for religious ob-
6 servances and precedents as belonging not to the Christian era, but to traditions, old-wives' fables, and endless
genealogies.

9 The enlightenment, the erudition, the progress of religion and medicine in New Hampshire, are in excess of
other States, as witness her schools, her churches, and
12 her frown on class legislation. In many of the States
in our Union a simple board of health, clad in a little
brief authority, has arrogated to itself the prerogative
15 of making laws for the State on the practice of medicine!
But this attempt is shorn of some of its shamelessness by
the courts immediately annulling such bills and pluck-
18 ing their plumes through constitutional interpretations.
Not the tradition of the elders, nor a paltering, timid,
or dastardly policy, is pursued by the leaders of our rock-
21 ribbed State.

That the Governor of New Hampshire has suggested to
his constituents to recur to a religious observance which
24 virtually belongs to the past, should tend to enhance their
confidence in his intention to rule righteously the affairs
of state. However, Jesus' example in this, as in all else,
27 suffices for the Christian era. The dark days of our forefathers and their implorations for peace and plenty have
passed, and are succeeded by our time of abundance, even
30 the full beneficence of the laws of the universe which
man's diligence has utilized. Institutions of learning and
progressive religion light their fires in every home.

I have one innate joy, and love to breathe it to the 1
breeze as God's courtesy. A native of New Hampshire,
a child of the Republic, a Daughter of the Revolution, I 3
thank God that He has emblazoned on the escutcheon
of this State, engraven on her granite rocks, and lifted
to her giant hills the ensign of religious liberty — "Free- 6
dom to worship God."

SPRING GREETING

Beloved brethren all over our land and in every land, 9
accept your Leader's Spring greeting, while

> The bird of hope is singing
> A lightsome lay, a cooing call, 12
> And in her heart is beating
> A love for all —
> " 'Tis peace not power I seek, 15
> 'Tis meet that man be meek."

[*New York Herald*, May 1, 1901]
[Extract] 18

MRS. EDDY TALKS

Christian Science has been so much to the fore of late
that unusual public interest centres in the personality 21
of Mrs. Mary Baker Eddy, the Founder of the cult.
The granting of interviews is not usual, hence it was
a special favor that Mrs. Eddy received the *Herald* 24
correspondent.

It had been raining all day and was damp without, so
the change from the misty air outside to the pleasant 27

1 warmth within the ample, richly furnished house was
agreeable. Seated in the large parlor, I became aware
3 of a white-haired lady slowly descending the stairs.
She entered with a gracious smile, walking uprightly and
with light step, and after a kindly greeting took a seat
6 on a sofa. It was Mrs. Eddy. There was no mistaking that. Older in years, white-haired and frailer,
but Mrs. Eddy herself. The likeness to the portraits
9 of twenty years ago, so often seen in reproductions, was
unmistakable. There is no mistaking certain lines that
depend upon the osseous structure; there is no mistaking
12 the eyes — those eyes the shade of which is so hard to
catch, whether blue-gray or grayish brown, and which
are always bright. And when I say frail, let it not be
15 understood that I mean weak, for weak she was not.
When we were snugly seated in the other and smaller
parlor across the hall, which serves as a library, Mrs.
18 Eddy sat back to be questioned.

"The continuity of The Church of Christ, Scientist,"
she said, in her clear voice, "is assured. It is growing
21 wonderfully. It will embrace all the churches, one by
one, because in it alone is the simplicity of the oneness
of God; the oneness of Christ and the perfecting of man
24 stated scientifically."

"How will it be governed after all now concerned in
its government shall have passed on?"
27   "It will evolve scientifically. Its essence is evangelical.
Its government will develop as it progresses."

"Will there be a hierarchy, or will it be directed by a
30 single earthly ruler?"

"In time its present rules of service and present rulership will advance nearer perfection."

It was plain that the answers to questions would be 1
in Mrs. Eddy's own spirit. She has a rapt way of talking, looking large-eyed into space, and works around a 3
question in her own way, reaching an answer often
unexpectedly after a prolonged exordium. She explained:
"No present change is contemplated in the rulership. 6
You would ask, perhaps, whether my successor will be a
woman or a man. I can answer that. It will be a man."
"Can you name the man?" 9
"I cannot answer that now."
Here, then, was the definite statement that Mrs. Eddy's
immediate successor would, like herself, be the ruler. 12

Not a Pope or a Christ

"I have been called a pope, but surely I have sought
no such distinction. I have simply taught as I learned 15
while healing the sick. It was in 1866 that the light of
the Science came first to me. In 1875 I wrote my book.
It brought down a shower of abuse upon my head, but 18
it won converts from the first. I followed it up, teaching
and organizing, and trust in me grew. I was the mother,
but of course the term pope is used figuratively. 21
"A position of authority," she went on, "became
necessary. Rules were necessary, and I made a code of
by-laws, but each one was the fruit of experience and the 24
result of prayer. Entrusting their enforcement to others,
I found at one time that they had five churches under
discipline. I intervened. Dissensions are dangerous in 27
an infant church. I wrote to each church in tenderness,
in exhortation, and in rebuke, and so brought all back to
union and love again. If that is to be a pope, then you 30

1 can judge for yourself. I have even been spoken of as a
Christ, but to my understanding of Christ that is impos-
3 sible. If we say that the sun stands for God, then all his
rays collectively stand for Christ, and each separate ray
for men and women. God the Father is greater than
6 Christ, but Christ is 'one with the Father,' and so the
mystery is scientifically explained. There can be but
one Christ."

9   "And the soul of man?"

"It is not the spirit of God, inhabiting clay and then
withdrawn from it, but God preserving individuality and
12 personality to the end. I hold it absurd to say that when
a man dies, the man will be at once better than he was
before death. How can it be? The individuality of him
15 must make gradual approaches to Soul's perfection."

"Do you reject utterly the bacteria theory of the
propagation of disease?"

18   "Oh," with a prolonged inflection, "entirely. If I
harbored that idea about a disease, I should think myself
in danger of catching it."

21   *About Infectious Diseases*

"Then as to the laws — the health laws of the States
on the question of infectious and contagious diseases.
24 How does Christian Science stand as to them?"

"I say, 'Render to Caesar the things that are Caesar's.'
We cannot force perfection on the world. Were vaccina-
27 tion of any avail, I should tremble for mankind; but,
knowing it is not, and that the fear of catching smallpox is more dangerous than any material infection, I
30 say: Where vaccination is compulsory, let your children

be vaccinated, and see that your mind is in such a state 1
that by your prayers vaccination will do the children no
harm.   So long as Christian Scientists obey the laws, I 3
do not suppose their mental reservations will be thought
to matter much.   But every thought tells, and Christian
Science will overthrow false knowledge in the end."   6
    "What is your attitude to science in general?   Do you
oppose it?"
    "Not," with a smile, "if it is really science."   9
    "Well, electricity, engineering, the telephone, the steam
engine — are these too material for Christian Science?"
    "No; only false science — healing by drugs.   I was a 12
sickly child.   I was dosed with drugs until they had no
effect on me.   The doctors said I would live if the drugs
could be made to act on me.   Then homœopathy came 15
like blessed relief to me, but I found that when I prescribed pellets without any medication they acted just
the same and healed the sick.   How could I believe in 18
a science of drugs?"
    "But surgery?"
    "The work done by the surgeon is the last healing that 21
will be vouchsafed to us, or rather attained by us, as we
near a state of spiritual perfection.   At present I am
conservative about advice on surgical cases."   24
    "But the pursuit of modern material inventions?"
    "Oh, we cannot oppose them.   They all tend to newer,
finer, more etherealized ways of living. They seek the finer 27
essences.   They light the way to the Church of Christ.
We use them, we make them our figures of speech.
They are preparing the way for us."   30
    We talked on many subjects, some only of which are
here touched upon, and her views, strictly and always

1 from the standpoint of Christian Science, were continually surprising. She talks as one who has lived with her
3 subject for a lifetime, — an ordinary lifetime; and so
far from being puzzled by any question, welcomes it as
another opportunity for presenting another view of her
6 religion.

Those who have been anticipating nature and declaring
Mrs. Eddy non-existent may learn authoritatively from
9 the *Herald* that she is in the flesh and in health. Soon
after I reached Concord on my return from Pleasant
View, Mrs. Eddy's carriage drove into town and made
12 several turns about the court-house before returning.
She was inside, and as she passed me the same expression of looking forward, thinking, thinking, was on
15 her face.

CONCORD, N. H.,
Tuesday, April 30, 1901

18 MRS. EDDY'S SUCCESSOR

In a recent interview which appeared in the columns
of the *New York Herald*, the Rev. Mary Baker Eddy,
21 Discoverer and Founder of Christian Science, stated that
her successor would be a man. Various conjectures
having arisen as to whether she had in mind any particu-
24 lar person when the statement was made, Mrs. Eddy
gave the following to the Associated Press, May 16,
1901: —

27 "I did say that a man would be my future successor.
By this I did not mean any man to-day on earth.

"Science and Health makes it plain to all Christian
30 Scientists that the manhood and womanhood of God

have already been revealed in a degree through Christ 1
Jesus and Christian Science, His two witnesses. What
remains to lead on the centuries and reveal my successor, 3
is man in the image and likeness of the Father-Mother
God, man the generic term for mankind."

GIFT OF A LOVING-CUP   6

The Executive Members of The Mother Church of
Christ, Scientist, will please accept my heartfelt acknowledgment of their beautiful gift to me, a loving-cup, pre- 9
sented July 16, 1903. The exquisite design of boughs
encircling this cup, illustrated by Keats' touching couplet,

> Ah happy, happy boughs, that cannot shed   12
> Your leaves, nor ever bid the Spring adieu!

would almost suggest that nature had reproduced her
primal presence, bough, bird, and song, to salute me. 15
The twelve beautiful pearls that crown this cup call to
mind the number of our great Master's first disciples, and
the parable of the priceless pearl which purchases our 18
field of labor in exchange for all else.

I shall treasure my loving-cup with all its sweet
associations.   21

[Special contribution to "Bohemia." A symposium.]
FUNDAMENTAL CHRISTIAN SCIENCE

Most thinkers concede that Science is the law of God; 24
that matter is not a law-maker; that man is not the
author of Science, and that a phenomenon is chimerical,
unless it be the manifestation of a fixed Principle whose 27
noumenon is God and whose phenomenon is Science.

1   My discovery that mankind is absolutely healed of so-called disease and injuries by other than drugs, surgery,
3 hygiene, electricity, magnetism, or will-power, induced a deep research, which proved conclusively that all effect must be the offspring of a universal cause. I sought this
6 cause, not within but *ab extra,* and I found it was God made manifest in the flesh, and understood through divine Science. Then I was healed, and the greatest of all ques-
9 tions was solved sufficiently to give a reason for the hope that was within me.

  The religious departure from divine Science sprang from
12 the belief that the man Jesus, rather than his divine Principle, God, saves man, and that *materia medica* heals him. The writer's departure from such a religion was based upon
15 her discovery that neither man nor *materia medica,* but God, heals and saves mankind.

  Here, however, was no stopping-place, since Science
18 demanded a rational proof that the divine Mind heals the sick and saves the sinner. God unfolded the way, the demonstration thereof was made, and the certainty of its
21 value to the race firmly established. I had found unmistakably an actual, unfailing causation, enshrined in the divine Principle and in the laws of man and the universe,
24 which, never producing an opposite effect, demonstrated Christianity and proved itself Science, for it healed the sick and reformed the sinner on a demonstrable Principle
27 and given rule. The human demonstrator of this Science may mistake, but the Science remains the law of God — infallible, eternal. Divine Life, Truth, Love is the basic
30 Principle of all Science, it solves the problem of being; and nothing that worketh ill can enter into the solution of God's problems.

God is Mind, and divine Mind was first chronologi- 1
cally, is first potentially, and is the healer to whom all
things are possible. A scientific state of health is a 3
consciousness of health, holiness, immortality — a consciousness gained through Christ, Truth; while disease
is a mental state or error that Truth destroys. It is self- 6
evident that matter, or the body, cannot cause disease,
since disease is in a sense susceptible of both ease and
dis-ease, and matter is not sensible. Kant, Locke, Berke- 9
ley, Tyndall, and Spencer afford little aid in understanding divine metaphysics or its therapeutics. Christian
Science is a divine largess, a gift of God — understood 12
by and divinely natural to him who sits at the feet of
Jesus clothed in truth, who is putting off the hypothesis
of matter because he is conscious of the allness of God — 15
"looking unto Jesus the author and finisher of our faith."
Thus the great Way-shower, invested with glory, is understood, and his words and works illustrate "the way, the 18
truth, and the life."

Divine modes or manifestations are natural, beyond
the so-called natural sciences and human philosophy, 21
because they are spiritual, and coexist with the God of
nature in absolute Science. The laws of God, or divine
Mind, obtain not in material phenomena, or phenomenal 24
evil, which is lawless and traceable to mortal mind —
human will divorced from Science.

Inductive or deductive reasoning is correct only as it 27
is spiritual, induced by love and deduced from God,
Spirit; only as it makes manifest the infinite nature,
including all law and supplying all the needs of man. 30
Wholly hypothetical, inductive reasoning reckons creation
as its own creator, seeks cause in effect, and from atom

1 and dust draws its conclusions of Deity and man, law and
gospel, leaving science at the beck of material phenomena,
3 or leaving it out of the question. To begin with the
divine noumenon, Mind, and to end with the phenomenon, matter, is minus divine logic and plus human hy-
6 pothesis, with its effects, sin, disease, and death. It was
in this dilemma that revelation, uplifting human reason,
came to the writer's rescue, when calmly and rationally,
9 though faintly, she spiritually discerned the divine idea
of the cosmos and Science of man.

WHITHER?

12 Father, did'st not Thou the dark wave treading
Lift from despair the struggler with the sea?
And heed'st Thou not the scalding tear man's shedding,
15 And know'st Thou not the pathway glad and free?

This weight of anguish which they blindly bind
On earth, this bitter searing to the core of love;
18 This crushing out of health and peace, mankind —
Thou all, Thou infinite — dost doom above.

Oft mortal sense is darkened unto death
21 (The Stygian shadow of a world of glee);
The old foundations of an early faith
Sunk from beneath man, whither shall he flee?

24 To Love divine, whose kindling mighty rays
Brighten the horoscope of crumbling creeds,
Dawn Truth delightful, crowned with endless days,
27 And Science ripe in prayer, in word, and deeds.

A LETTER FROM OUR LEADER

With our Leader's kind permission, the *Sentinel* is privileged to publish her letter of recent date, addressed to Mr. John C. Higdon of St. Louis, Mo. This letter is especially interesting on account of its beautiful tribute to Free Masonry.

Beloved Student: — Your interesting letter was handed to me duly. This is my earliest moment in which to answer it.

"Know Thyself," the title of your gem quoted, is indeed a divine command, for the *morale* of Free Masonry is above ethics — it touches the hem of his garment who spake divinely.

It was truly Masonic, tender, grand in you to remember me as the widow of a Mason. May you and I and all mankind meet in that hour of Soul where are no partings, no pain.

Lovingly yours in Christ,

MARY BAKER EDDY

PLEASANT VIEW, CONCORD, N. H.,
February 9, 1906

TAKE NOTICE

I have not read Gerhardt C. Mars' book, "The Interpretation of Life," therefore I have not endorsed it, and any assertions to the contrary are false. Christian Scientists are not concerned with philosophy; divine Science is all they need, or can have in reality.

MARY BAKER EDDY

BOX G, BROOKLINE, MASS.,
June 24, 1908

1 RECOGNITION OF BLESSINGS

REVEREND MARY BAKER EDDY,
3   Chestnut Hill, Mass.

Beloved Leader: — Informally assembled, we, the ushers
of your church, desire to express our recognition of the
6 blessings that have come to us through the peculiar privileges we enjoy in this church work. We are prompted
to acknowledge our debt of gratitude to you for your
9 life of spirituality, with its years of tender ministry, yet
we know that the real gratitude is what is proved in
better lives.

12   It is our earnest prayer that we may so reflect in our
thoughts and acts the teachings of Christian Science that
our daily living may be a fitting testimony of the efficacy
15 of our Cause in the regeneration of mankind.

THE USHERS OF THE MOTHER CHURCH

BOSTON, MASS., October 9, 1908

18   *Mrs. Eddy's Reply*

*Beloved Ushers of The Mother Church of Christ, Sci-
entist:* — I thank you not only for your tender letter to
21 me, but for ushering into our church the hearers and the
doers of God's Word.

MARY BAKER EDDY

24   Box G, BROOKLINE, MASS.,
         October 12, 1908

MRS. EDDY'S THANKS

27   *Beloved Christian Scientists:* — Accept my thanks for
your successful plans for the first issue of *The Christian
Science Monitor.* My desire is that every Christian

Scientist, and as many others as possible, subscribe for 1
and read our daily newspaper.

MARY BAKER EDDY   3

Box G, BROOKLINE, MASS.,
November 16, 1908

[Extract from the leading Editorial in Vol. 1, No. 1, of *The*   6
Christian Science Monitor, November 25, 1908]

SOMETHING IN A NAME

I have given the name to all the Christian Science 9
periodicals. The first was *The Christian Science Journal,* designed to put on record the divine Science of
Truth; the second I entitled *Sentinel,* intended to hold 12
guard over Truth, Life, and Love; the third, *Der Herold
der Christian Science,* to proclaim the universal activity
and availability of Truth; the next I named *Monitor,* 15
to spread undivided the Science that operates unspent.
The object of the *Monitor* is to injure no man, but to
bless all mankind.   18

MARY BAKER EDDY

ARTICLE XXII, SECTION 17

MRS. EDDY'S ROOM. — SECTION 17. The room in 21
The Mother Church formerly known as "Mother's
Room" shall hereafter be closed to visitors.

There is nothing in this room now of any special in- 24
terest. "Let the dead bury their dead," and the spiritual
have all place and power.

MARY BAKER EDDY   27

354   Miscellany

TO WHOM IT MAY CONCERN

In view of complaints from the field, because of alleged
misrepresentations by persons offering Bibles and other
books for sale which they claim have been endorsed by
me, it is due the field to state that I recommend nothing
but what is published or sold by The Christian Science
Publishing Society. Christian Scientists are under no
obligation to buy books for which my endorsement is
claimed.

MARY BAKER EDDY

Box G, Brookline, Mass.,
            April 28, 1909

EXTEMPORE

JANUARY 1, 1910

I

O blessings infinite!
O glad New Year!
Sweet sign and substance
Of God's presence here.

II

Give us not only angels' songs,
    But Science vast, to which belongs
The tongue of angels
    And the song of songs.

MARY BAKER EDDY

[The above lines were written extemporaneously by
Mrs. Eddy on New Year's morning. The members of her

household were with her at the time, and it was gratifying 1
to them, as it will be to the field, to see in her spiritualized
thought and mental vigor a symbol of the glad New Year 3
on which we have just entered. — EDITOR *Sentinel*]

MEN IN OUR RANKS

A letter from a student in the field says there is a grave 6
need for more men in Christian Science practice.

I have not infrequently hinted at this. However, if
the occasion demands it, I will repeat that men are very 9
important factors in our field of labor for Christian
Science. The male element is a strong supporting arm
to religion as well as to politics, and we need in our ranks 12
of divine energy, the strong, the faithful, the untiring
spiritual armament.

MARY BAKER EDDY   15

CHESTNUT HILL, MASS.,
   February 7, 1910

A PÆAN OF PRAISE   18

"Behind a frowning providence
He hides a shining face."

The Christian Scientists at Mrs. Eddy's home are 21
the happiest group on earth. Their faces shine with
the reflection of light and love; their footsteps are not
weary; their thoughts are upward; their way is onward, 24
and their light shines. The world is better for this
happy group of Christian Scientists; Mrs. Eddy is happier because of them; God is glorified in His reflection 27
of peace, love, joy.

1 When will mankind awake to know their present ownership of all good, and praise and love the spot where God
3 dwells most conspicuously in His reflection of love and
leadership? When will the world waken to the privilege
of knowing God, the liberty and glory of His presence,
6 — where

"He plants His footsteps in the sea
And rides upon the storm."

9   MARY BAKER EDDY
CHESTNUT HILL, MASS.,
April 20, 1910

12   A STATEMENT BY MRS. EDDY

Editor Christian Science Sentinel: — In reply to inquiries, will you please state that within the last five
15 years I have given no assurance, no encouragement nor
consent to have my picture issued, other than the ones
now and heretofore presented in Science and Health.

18   MARY BAKER EDDY
CHESTNUT HILL, MASS.,
July 18, 1910

21   THE WAY OF WISDOM

No man can serve two masters: for either he will hate the one,
and love the other; or else he will hold to the one, and despise the
24 other. Ye cannot serve God and mammon. — MATTHEW 6 : 24.

The infinite is one, and this one is Spirit; Spirit is
God, and this God is infinite good.
27 This simple statement of oneness is the only possible
correct version of Christian Science. God being infinite,

He is the only basis of Science; hence materiality is wholly apart from Christian Science, and is only a "Suffer it to be so now" until we arrive at the spiritual fulness of God, Spirit, even the divine idea of Christian Science, — Christ, born of God, the offspring of Spirit, — wherein matter has neither part nor portion, because matter is the absolute opposite of spiritual means, manifestation, and demonstration. The only incentive of a mistaken sense is malicious animal magnetism, — the name of all evil, — and this must be understood.

I have crowned The Mother Church building with the spiritual modesty of Christian Science, which is its jewel. When my dear brethren in New York desire to build higher, — to enlarge their phylacteries and demonstrate Christian Science to a higher extent, — they must begin on a wholly spiritual foundation, than which there is no other, and proportionably estimate their success and glory of achievement only as they build upon the rock of Christ, the spiritual foundation. This will open the way, widely and impartially, to their never-ending success, — to salvation and eternal Christian Science.

Spirit is infinite; therefore *Spirit is all.* "There is no matter" is not only the axiom of true Christian Science, but it is the only basis upon which this Science can be demonstrated.

A LETTER BY MRS. EDDY

Mrs. Augusta E. Stetson, New York City   27

Beloved Student: — I have just finished reading your interesting letter. I thank you for acknowledging me as your Leader, and I know that every true follower of

1 Christian Science abides by the definite rules which demonstrate the true following of their Leader; therefore,
3 if you are sincere in your protestations and are doing as
you say you are, you will be blessed in your obedience.
The Scriptures say, "Watch and pray, that ye enter
6 not into temptation." You are aware that animal magnetism is the opposite of divine Science, and that this
opponent is the means whereby the conflict against
9 Truth is engendered and developed. Beloved! you need
to watch and pray that the enemy of good cannot separate
you from your Leader and best earthly friend.
12 You have been duly informed by me that, however
much I desire to read all that you send to me, I have not
the time to do so. The Christian Science Publishing
15 Society will settle the question whether or not they shall
publish your poems. It is part of their duties to relieve
me of so much labor.
18 I thank you for the money you send me which was
given you by your students. I shall devote it to a worthy
and charitable purpose.
21 Mr. Adam Dickey is my secretary, through whom all
my business is transacted.
Give my best wishes and love to your dear students
24 and church.
Lovingly your teacher and Leader,
MARY BAKER EDDY
27 Box G, Brookline, Mass.,
July 12, 1909

TAKE NOTICE

30 I approve the By-laws of The Mother Church, and
require the Christian Science Board of Directors to main-

tain them and sustain them. These Directors do not 1
act contrary to the rules of the Church Manual, neither
do they trouble me with their difficulties with individ- 3
uals in their own church or with the members of branch
churches.

My province as a Leader — as the Discoverer and 6
Founder of Christian Science — is not to interfere in
cases of discipline, and I hereby publicly declare that I
am not personally involved in the affairs of the church in 9
any other way than through my written and published
rules, all of which can be read by the individual who
desires to inform himself of the facts. 12

MARY BAKER EDDY

BROOKLINE, MASS.,
October 12, 1909 15

A LETTER FROM MRS. EDDY

In the *Sentinel* of July 31, 1909, there appeared under
the heading "None good but one," a number of quota- 18
tions from a composite letter, dated July 19, which had
been written to Mrs. Augusta E. Stetson by twenty-four
of her students who then occupied offices in the building 21
of First Church of Christ, Scientist, of New York, and
were known as "the practitioners." This letter was forwarded to Mrs. Eddy by Mrs. Stetson with the latter's 24
unqualified approval. Upon receipt of this letter Mrs.
Eddy wrote to Mrs. Stetson as follows: —

My Dear Student: — Awake and arise from this temp- 27
tation produced by animal magnetism upon yourself,
allowing your students to deify you and me. Treat yourself for it and get your students to help you rise out of it. 30

1 It will be your destruction if you do not do this. Answer
this letter immediately.

3   As ever, lovingly your teacher,

MARY BAKER EDDY

BROOKLINE, MASS.,
6   July 23, 1909

A LETTER BY MRS. EDDY [1]

TO THE BOARD OF TRUSTEES, FIRST CHURCH OF CHRIST, SCIENTIST,
9   NEW YORK CITY

Beloved Brethren: — In consideration of the present
momentous question at issue in First Church of Christ,
12 Scientist, New York City, I am constrained to say, if I
can settle this church difficulty amicably by a few words,
as many students think I can, I herewith cheerfully
15 subscribe these words of love: —

My beloved brethren in First Church of Christ, Scientist, New York City, I advise you with all my soul to
18 support the Directors of The Mother Church, and unite
with those in your church who are supporting The Mother
Church Directors. Abide in fellowship with and obedi-
21 ence to The Mother Church, and in this way God will
bless and prosper you. This I know, for He has proved
it to me for forty years in succession.

24   Lovingly yours,

MARY BAKER EDDY

BROOKLINE, MASS.,
27 November 13, 1909

A LETTER BY MRS. EDDY

My Dear Student: — Your favor of the 10th instant is
30 at hand. God is above your teacher, your healer, or any

---

[1] The text here given is that of the original letter as sent by Mrs. Eddy, and
published in the *Christian Science Sentinel* of November 20, 1909. This letter was
republished in the *Sentinel* of December 4, 1909, at Mrs. Eddy's request, with
the words "in Truth" inserted after the word "Abide."

earthly friend. Follow the directions of God as simplified 1
in Christian Science, and though it be through deserts
He will direct you into the paths of peace. 3

I do not presume to give you personal instruction as
to your relations with other students. All I say is stated
in Christian Science to be used as a model. Please find 6
it there, and do not bring your Leader into a personal
conflict.

I have not seen Mrs. Stetson for over a year, and have 9
not written to her since August 30, 1909.

Sincerely yours,

MARY BAKER EDDY 12

BROOKLINE, MASS.,
December 11, 1909

A TELEGRAM AND MRS. EDDY'S REPLY 15

[Telegram]

MRS. MARY BAKER EDDY,
Chestnut Hill, Mass. 18

Beloved Leader: — We rejoice that our church has
promptly made its demonstration by action at its annual
meeting in accordance with your desire for a truly demo- 21
cratic and liberal government.

BOARD OF TRUSTEES,

FIRST CHURCH OF CHRIST, SCIENTIST, 24

NEW YORK, N. Y.,

CHARLES DEAN, *Chairman,*

ARTHUR O. PROBST, *Clerk* 27

NEW YORK, N. Y.,
January 19, 1910

1 *Mrs. Eddy's Reply*

CHARLES A. DEAN, CHAIRMAN BOARD OF TRUSTEES,
3 FIRST CHURCH OF CHRIST, SCIENTIST, NEW YORK CITY

Beloved Brethren: — I rejoice with you in the victory of right over wrong, of Truth over error.

6 MARY BAKER EDDY

CHESTNUT HILL, MASS.,
January 20, 1910

9 A LETTER AND MRS. EDDY'S REPLY

MRS. MARY BAKER EDDY,
Chestnut Hill, Mass.

12 *Revered Leader, Counsellor, and Friend:* — The Trustees and Readers of all the Christian Science churches and societies of Greater New York, for the first time gath-
15 ered in one place with one accord, to confer harmoniously and unitedly in promoting and enlarging the activities of the Cause of Christian Science in this community, as
18 their first act send you their loving greetings.

With hearts filled with gratitude to God, we rejoice in your inspired leadership, in your wise counselling. We
21 revere and cherish your friendship, and assure you that it is our intention to take such action as will unite the churches and societies in this field in the bonds of Chris-
24 tian love and fellowship, thus demonstrating practical Christianity.

Gratefully yours,

27 FIRST CHURCH OF CHRIST, SCIENTIST,
SECOND CHURCH OF CHRIST, SCIENTIST,

THIRD CHURCH OF CHRIST, SCIENTIST,   1
FOURTH CHURCH OF CHRIST, SCIENTIST,
FIFTH CHURCH OF CHRIST, SCIENTIST,   3
SIXTH CHURCH OF CHRIST, SCIENTIST,
FIRST CHURCH OF CHRIST, SCIENTIST, Brooklyn,
FOURTH CHURCH OF CHRIST, SCIENTIST, Brooklyn,   6
FIRST CHURCH OF CHRIST, SCIENTIST, Staten Island,
CHRISTIAN SCIENCE SOCIETY, Bronx,
CHRISTIAN SCIENCE SOCIETY, Flushing, L. I.,   9
By the Committee
NEW YORK, N. Y.,
February 5, 1910   12

Mrs. Eddy's Reply

This proof that sanity and Science govern the Christian
Science churches in Greater New York is soul inspiring.   15
MARY BAKER EDDY

[*The Christian Science Journal*, July, 1895. Reprinted in *Christian
Science Sentinel*, November 13, 1909]   18

TO THE MEMBERS OF THE CHRISTIAN SCIENTIST ASSOCIATION

My address before the Christian Scientist Associa- 21
tion has been misrepresented and evidently misunder-
stood by some students. The gist of the whole subject
was not to malpractise unwittingly. In order to be 24
sure that one is not doing this, he must avoid naming,
in his mental treatment, any other individual but the
patient whom he is treating, and practise only to heal. 27
Any deviation from this direct rule is more or less

1 dangerous. No mortal is infallible, — hence the Scripture, "Judge no man."

3 The rule of mental practice in Christian Science is strictly to handle no other mentality but the mind of your patient, and treat this mind to be Christly. Any
6 departure from this golden rule is inadmissible. This mental practice includes and inculcates the commandment, "Thou shalt have no other gods before me."
9 Animal magnetism, hypnotism, *etc.,* are disarmed by the practitioner who excludes from his own consciousness, and that of his patients, all sense of the realism
12 of any other cause or effect save that which cometh from God. And he should teach his students to defend themselves from all evil, and to heal the sick, by
15 recognizing the supremacy and allness of good. This epitomizes what heals all manner of sickness and dis-
18 ease, moral or physical.   MARY BAKER EDDY

[*Christian Science Sentinel,* February 15, 1908]
CONCORD, N. H., TO MRS. EDDY, AND
21   MRS. EDDY'S REPLY

THE ESTEEM IN WHICH MRS. EDDY IS HELD IN CONCORD HAS
  BEEN OFFICIALLY EXPRESSED IN THE FOLLOWING PREAMBLE
24 AND RESOLUTIONS, WHICH WERE UNANIMOUSLY ADOPTED BY
  THE BOARD OF ALDERMEN AND COMMON COUNCIL OF THAT
  CITY AND THUS HAVE BECOME A PART OF CONCORD'S RECORDS

27   *Concord, New Hampshire, to Rev. Mary Baker G.*
                          Eddy

Whereas, Rev. Mary Baker G. Eddy has decided to
30 make her home in Massachusetts, after a residence of nineteen years in Concord, and

Whereas, her residence here has been the source of so 1
much good to the city, and

Whereas, the most kindly and helpful relations have 3
ever existed between Mrs. Eddy and Concord and Concord people,

Be It Resolved, That the City of Concord, through its 6
Board of Aldermen and Common Council, in joint convention, convey to Mrs. Eddy,

1. Its appreciation of her life in its midst, 9
2. Its regrets over her departure, and
3. The hope that though absent she will always cherish a loving regard for the city, near which she was 12 born, and for its people, among whom she has lived for so many years.

Be It Resolved, That the Mayor and City Clerk be 15
authorized and instructed to sign and attest this testimonial in behalf of the City Council.

Done this tenth day of February, nineteen hundred 18
and eight.

CHARLES R. CORNING, *Mayor*

Attest: HENRY E. CHAMBERLAIN, *City Clerk*   21

Mrs. Eddy's Reply

TO THE HONORABLE MAYOR AND CITY COUNCIL,
CONCORD, N. H.   24

Gentlemen: — I have not only the pleasure, but the honor of replying to the City Council of Concord, in joint convention assembled, and to Alderman Cressy, 27 for the kindly resolutions passed by your honorable body, and for which I thank you deeply. Lest I should acknowledge more than I deserve of praise, I leave their 30 courteous opinions to their good judgment.

1 My early days hold rich recollections of associations
with your churches and institutions, and memory has a
3 distinct model in granite of the good folk in Concord,
which, like the granite of their State, steadfast and
enduring, has hinted this quality to other states and
6 nations all over the world.

My home influence, early education, and church
experience, have unquestionably ripened into the fruits
9 of my present religious experience, and for this I prize
them. May I honor this origin and deserve the continued friendship and esteem of the people in my native
12 State.

Sincerely yours,

MARY BAKER G. EDDY

15 Box G, BROOKLINE, MASS.,
February 13, 1908